Theology and Social Theory

Praise for the first edition of *Theology and Social Theory*

'Milbank's work is a *tour de force* of systematic theology. It would be churlish not to acknowledge its provocation and brilliance.' *Times Higher Education Supplement*

'Its orchestration is stunning in scope as well as in harmonics.' *Modern Theology*

'John Milbank's sprawling, ambitious and intellectually demanding book is in a class of its own.' *Studies in Christian Ethics*

'John Milbank has written a masterful review of the development of modern social thought that at the same time offers a criticism of its dominant paradigms and suggests inherent limits on its accomplishments.' *Journal of Religion*

'It is of a remarkable intensity and intellectual scope, it is a book of the highest importance for the ongoing debate between Christianity and modernity.' **Reinhard Hutter**, *Lutheran School of Theology at Chicago*

Theology and Social Theory

Beyond Secular Reason

John Milbank

Second Edition

Blackwell Publishing

BLACKWELL PUBLISHING
350 Main Street, Malden, MA 02148-5020, USA
9600 Garsington Road, Oxford OX4 2DQ, UK
550 Swanston Street, Carlton, Victoria 3053, Australia

First edition published 1990
Second edition published 2006 by Blackwell Publishing Ltd

3   2008

Library of Congress Cataloging-in-Publication Data

Milbank, John.
    Theology and social theory : beyond secular reason / John Milbank.—2nd ed.
      p. cm.
    Includes bibliographical references and index.
    ISBN 978-1-4051-3683-9 (hardcover : alk. paper)
    ISBN 978-1-4051-3684-6 (pbk. : alk. paper)   1. Christianity and the social
sciences—History of doctrines. 2. Christian sociology. 3. Theology—Methodology.
I. Title.

  BR115 S57M54 2006
  261.5—dc22   2005011799

A catalogue record for this title is available from the British Library.

Set in Palatino 10.5/13pt
by SPI Publisher Services, Pondicherry, India
Printed and bound in Malaysia
by Vivar Printing Sdn Bhd.

For further information on
Blackwell Publishing, visit our website:
www.blackwellpublishing.com

For Alison, and the
surviving members
of the Christendom Trust

Contents

Acknowledgements for the First Edition

My main debts are, first of all, to the Christendom Trust (to whom this book has always been partially dedicated, *not*, as some have mistakenly supposed, to the memory of the Middle Ages!) and the Department of Religious Studies at Lancaster University, whose provision of finance and time, respectively, has made this book possible. Secondly to Fergus Kerr, Ken Surin and Julia Mosse who encouraged me to write it in the first place.

My intellectual debts are manifold: in the long term I am exceptionally grateful to Lindsay Sharp and Richard Tait who first taught me intellectual and cultural history; to Rowan Williams, who taught me theology, and to Leon Pompa, who supervised my doctoral thesis on Vico. I am also indebted to my nurturing within the Anglo-Catholic social tradition in which the Christendom Trust stands, especially the writings of S. T. Coleridge, J. H. Newman, W. G. Ward, F. D. Maurice, Thomas Hancock, Conrad Noel, J. N. Figgis, R. H. Tawney, V. C. Demant and Donald Mackinnon.

More immediately, the present book would not have been conceivable without the writings of Gillian Rose, Alasdair MacIntyre, Stanley Hauerwas, Gilles Deleuze, Michel Foucault and René Girard. Equally important have been the continuously renewed conversations I have enjoyed over the years with Rowan Williams, Ken Surin and Paul Morris. Many others have contributed important insights, or commented on drafts of individual chapters: John Clayton, Sarah Coakley, Adrian Cunningham, Stephen Fowl, Philip Goodchild, Stanley Hauerwas, Paul Heelas, Timothy Jenkins, Gregory Jones, Fergus Kerr, Nicholas Lash, Scott Lash, Ian Mcpherson, Alison Milbank, David Nicholls: I am very grateful to them all.

Thanks are due also to the editors of *New Blackfriars*, for permission to reprint material from my article 'On baseless suspicion: Christianity and the crisis of socialism', in chapter 7.

Finally I would like to thank Pat Fawley, who word-processed the final manuscript, Alison Milbank who criticized and corrected it, and Stephan Chambers, Julian Bell and Andrew McNeillie, its editors.

For both 'civil' and 'fabulous' theologies are alike fabulous and civil.

Augustine, **City of God**

Preface to the Second Edition: Between Liberalism and Positivism

Theology and Social Theory was written in the middle of the Thatcherite era, out of the conviction that a theological vision alone could challenge the emerging hegemony of neo-liberalism. This did not mean, as some have suggested, that I sought to instrumentalize theology and religion. To the contrary, I sought to show why, for reasons quite exceeding the political, a Catholic Christian account of reality might be entertained as the most finally persuasive one. But then, for both theological and historico-philosophical reasons, I sought also to argue that only a new embracing of such an account could free us from our contemporary historical deadlock.

Our current global situation is different, and yet is in essential continuity with the circumstances in which this book was written. Today, neo-liberalism has further extended its sway, but has now begun to mutate into a new mode of political tyranny. (For this reason, in response to the banalities of certain of my politically liberal critics, I simply offer a reading of the current daily newspapers in my defence.)[1] In some ways this makes the essential unity of *Theology and Social Theory* more apparent. For, from the beginning to the end of the book, it is constantly suggested that there is a problematic relationship between the formal openness of liberalism which is designed to mitigate conflict on the one hand, and an arbitrariness of content on the other hand – a 'positivism' which always threatens to overwhelm even the peace of mere suspended hostility which is the best that the *civitas terrena* can ever manage. This positive content can be *either* 'scientific' as in the case of eugenicism and the extermination of the supposedly weak (which happens in far more modes than we usually acknowledge) *or* it can be 'religious' as in the case of recently

---

[1] See, in particular, Christopher J. Insole, *The Politics of Human Frailty: A Theological Defence of Political Liberalism* (London: SCM, 2004). For a more elaborated version of my critique of political liberalism, see John Milbank, 'The gift of ruling: secularisation and political authority', in *New Blackfriars*, vol. 85, no. 996, March 2004, pp. 212–39. This article includes a discussion of Pierre Manent, whose thesis that liberalism assumes the priority of evil is very akin to my thesis about a theoretical assumption of ontological violence. Neither thesis is given any serious consideration by Insole, who falsely presents Hooker as a 'liberal' and judiciously favours those liberals like Burke, Tocqueville and Acton who embraced a more than considerable measure of criticism of liberalism as such (which gives rise of course to the question of whether a still merely partial critique did not leave them with irresolvable quandaries).

emergent 'fundamentalisms' which usually trade off, and theologically confirm, socio-economic liberalism, while also in certain strategic ways surpassing and opposing it.

In many ways the first two treatises of the book on 'liberalism' and 'positivism' respectively, are in consequence the most decisive – because 'dialectics' is seen as but a variant on liberalism in terms of a Christian Gnosticism (a thesis now amply confirmed by the work of Cyril O'Regan)[2] and 'difference' is seen as essentially a radicalization of the positivist vision. (Here the reader needs to be attentive to the fact that I treat 'positivism' in its historical complexity and ambiguity and never mean the term anachronistically – except where appropriate – in the mere sense of scientific or 'logical' positivism.)

These observations accord, I think, with the changed responses that the book is now liable to invoke. At first, there was a certain amount of outraged protest from sociologists, many of whom took it that I was objecting to a supposed 'reduction' of religion to the social, when I was explicitly arguing that 'the social' of sociology was itself an unreal, unhistorical and quasi-theological category.[3] Today, this sort of reaction survives only amongst theologians themselves – who are still so often belated. Within secular social theory by contrast, there is a widespread recognition (only a very little indebted to the impact of my book) that 'sociology' is an exploded paradigm, and in part because of its inbuilt secular bias.[4] The less ideologically-freighted models of ethnography and *histoire totale* are today far more in vogue – in academic practice still more than in academic theory.

There was some protest also from those still committed to the dialectical tradition.[5] Overwhelmingly though, most thinkers of the left have now abandoned the Marxist affirmations of a teleological progressivism or any notion that there must come a necessary 'final' crisis of capitalism. Much more persistent remains the influence of Hegel's philosophy of history. Yet this is increasingly because interpreters confirm the essence of Alexander Kojève's reading of Hegel: the Hegelian metanarrative is plausible because it was *already* akin to a nihilist genealogy and was a kind of anti-metanarrative. For what it traced was the work of negation and redoubled negation in the sense of the dismantling of all bounds against a radically self-grounded freedom. In this sense the story told is of the gradual unleashing of the anarchically positive – even though it took Schelling to be clearer about this,

[2] See, amongst many works on this theme, in particular, Cyril O'Regan, *The Heterodox Hegel* (New York: SUNY, 1994).

[3] See, for example, Kieran Flanagan, 'Sublime policing: sociology and Milbank's city of God', in *New Blackfriars*, vol. 73, no. 861, June 1992, special issue on *Theology and Social Theory*, pp. 333–41.

[4] One could mention here Scott Lash, Neil Turnbull and the circle of leading British social theorists focused round the journal *Theory, Culture and Society* which is edited from Nottingham Trent University.

[5] See Gillian Rose, *The Broken Middle: Out of our Ancient Society* (Oxford: Blackwell, 1992) p. 279ff.

and Hegel himself commendably, but inconsistently, had aspirations to resist such a rule of both the formal and the arbitrary. It is also true that the thesis of an 'end of history', when there emerges a full mutual recognition of autonomy, fails to see that the celebration primarily of freedom has no stable way of securing the value of such mutual recognition over-against the positive affirmation of one particular freedom or set of freedoms as paramount. In consequence it has no surety against history resuming its sinister inventiveness.

Still more markedly, there was a great deal of protest from those influenced by the 'left-Nietzscheanism' stemming from the 1960s, an influence in which *Theology and Social Theory* is itself clearly steeped. This protest almost always took the form of saying that I was wrong to see this discourse as upholding nihilism and 'ontological violence' – rather it supported the diversity of life and held open infinite possibilities of variegated coexistence with others fully acknowledged in their otherness.[6] In retrospect though, one can see yet more strongly how the left-Nietzschean current constantly had to compromise a radical positivism which seeks actively to affirm the ungrounded 'mythical' content of difference beyond mere formal tolerance, with a continued attempt to re-inscribe some mode of stoic or Kantian formal resignation and collective agreement as to abstract procedures. This is as true in the end of Deleuze as it is more evidently true of Foucault, Derrida, Lyotard and even Badiou. These thinkers, therefore, were trapped in the liberal/positivist oscillation.

In this respect it is important to notice that *Theology and Social Theory* more than once suggests that the *soixante-huitarde* thinkers in fact tend to tone down both the critical rigour and the amoralism of Nietzsche and Heidegger. The attempt to bend their diagnoses of the historical sway of arbitrary power to the cause of 'emancipation' was never truly plausible. Moreover, recent research on Nietzsche shows that his entire project *was*, after all, a politically extreme right-wing one (even though not, anachronistically, a 'Nazi' one, nor even in every respect proto-Nazi). His slaves were real not allegorical slaves, his men of power real, wanton, lightly-cruel aristocrats, supposedly the most beloved of women.[7] The crude Nietzsche was also the true one – and yet it was the genuinely critical one, following through on the implications of a realization that 'God' and 'the Good' are but human inventions.

---

[6] See Romand Coles, 'Storied others and the possibility of *caritas*: Milbank and neo-Nietzschean ethics', in *Modern Theology*, vol. 8, no. 4, October 1992, special issue on *Theology and Social Theory*, pp. 331–53. See also, Eve Tabor Bannet, 'Beyond secular theory', Daniel Boyarin, 'A broken olive branch', Shiela Kappler, 'Quid faciemus viri, frater?' and Alan Shandro, 'Politics of postmodern theology', all in 'Symposium: John Milbank's *Theology and Social Theory*', in *Arachne*, vol. 2, no. 1, 1995, pp. 105–45. In addition see Gavin Hyman, *The Predicament of Postmodern Theology: Radical Orthodoxy or Nihilist Textualism* (Louisville: Westminster John Knox Press, 2001).

[7] See the cited nostrum from *Zarathustra* at the beginning of the Third Treatise of the *Genealogy*: Friedrich Nietzsche, *On the Genealogy of Morality*, trans. M. Clark and A. J. Swensen (Indianapolis, Ind: Hackett, 1998) p. 67. For the exposure of the fallacies of the French 'new Nietzsche' see Domenico Losurdo, *Nietzsche, il ribello aristocratico: biografico intelletuale e balancio critico* (Turin: Bollati Boringhieri, 2002); Jan Rehmann, *Postmoderner Links-Nietzscheanismus; Deleuze und Foucault; eine Dekonstruktion* (Hamburg: Argument Verlag, 2004).

Our problem today then, compared with fifteen years ago, is that we are now far more honestly aware that the most incisive thinkers of modernity have belonged to the political right and that some of them were at least semi-complicit with Nazism: Joseph de Maistre (increasingly invoked, even by the critical left), Auguste Comte, Donoso Cortes, Carl Schmitt, Friedrich Nietzsche, Martin Heidegger, even Leo Strauss. For it is these thinkers who have tended most squarely to confront the problematic implication of liberalism with positivism that I have already referred to. Indeed one might very well argue that the most serious essence of the 'postmodern' is best captured by Comte's idea of an inevitable lapse of the 'metaphysical' liberal era of universal laws and abstractions towards the 'positive' era of diverse given facts, reworked myths and rituals and novel or renewed papacies.

It is for this reason that a new and more honest recognition of the far-right character of Nietzsche's politics (as of Heidegger's) does not tend to entail a loss of interest in his thought even on the part of the critical left. To the contrary, this interest rather now takes an altered form: first of all it is noted that Nietzsche is often pushing liberal theses to their logical conclusions in order to subvert them, and also that, in his bitter opposition to socialism (the ultimate real target of his hostility), Nietzsche was driven to conclude that socialism was grounded in the deepest Western legacy of Platonism and Christianity.[8] Most recent thinkers on the left (Badiou, Zizek, Negri amongst others) seem to concur that Nietzsche was right in this realization and that Marx failed fully to realize its importance.

This recent, anti-revisionary attitude towards Nietzsche tends, I think, to make the final treatise of my book on 'difference' now more comprehensible. First of all, the most radical thinker of difference never pretended anything other than that it was grounded in an 'ontology of violence'. Secondly, he directed his philosophy first against socialism and as a consequence against Christianity. This lends a certain crude obviousness to my counter-strategy: defend Christianity and thereby supply again a new ontological and eschatological basis for socialist hope. At the same time though, there is clearly a complication – I appear to embrace certain aspects of the Nietzschean approach: namely the method of genealogy and a version of an ontology of difference.

Here I need to make some more general observations. The careful reader will realize that throughout the book the attitude towards 'secular reason' is never as negative as it appears to be on the surface. For it is viewed not as what it primarily proclaims itself to be, namely the secular; but rather as disguised heterodoxy of various stripes, as a revived paganism and as a religious nihilism. In each case my attitude cannot be simply oppositional, since I regard Catholic Christianity as fulfilling the best pagan impulses, heresy as exaggeration or thinning-down of the truth, and nihilism as a parody both of the Christian view that we are created from nothing and

---

[8] Losurdo, *Nietzsche, il ribello aristocratico.*

that therefore all that is finite is indeterminate, and equally of the likewise Christian view that ordered beauty is paradoxically in-finite. It follows that there remains truth in all these distortions and even that, just as Irenaeus learned much from Valentinus, the distortions develop better certain aspects of orthodoxy which orthodoxy must then later recoup.

Thus despite the fact that I oppose a Catholic ontology to liberalism, positivism, dialectics and nihilism, my attempt to 're-imagine' Christianity in the present (an unfortunately increased imperative for today's theologian, given Christianity's long-term problematic decline and the almost ideologically opposite contemporary forms that it assumes) is newly marked by each one of these four currents. In the case of liberalism, I clearly do affirm some continuing but ideally receding need for a merely 'contractual' peace, as opposed to the real peace of consensus and gift-exchange.[9] Moreover, I present stoicism as proto-liberalism and emphasize that a Christian approach to ethics and society (as can be seen with St Paul) does, indeed, owe something to stoicism. I do not simply line up Christianity with Platonic-Aristotelian virtue and eudemonism, but rather suggest that it offers a kind of *post-liberal* approach stressing ecstatic relationality and gratuity that is at a certain distance both from the cultivation of personal excellence and from 'stoic-modern' other-regarding duty.[10] To a degree, following MacIntyre, I see Plato as having anticipated such a 'post-liberal' perspective in reaction to the sophists.

In the case of 'positivism' I intimate that it is a post-Christian phenomenon which contains many elements of distorted Christianity. These are: an identification of the Good with being, power and positivity; a search for a 'harmonic' non-agonistic social order; an elevation of the particular beyond the general; a realization that reason begins in collective devotion and can never really leave it behind; (sometimes) a non-nominalistic recognition that there are surd 'general facts' and irreducible relations and a refusal to pretend that we can see with certainty beyond the givenness of appearances. (Via Brentano, phenomenology is a child of positivism.) Insofar as these traits are found within the sociological tradition, then I clearly learn from it. Purged of the secular metaphysics which I disinter, sociology has contributed to the writing of history an indispensable insistence upon the synchronic and the geographical and to social ethics a refusal of a merely contractualist notion of the ideal society.

In the case of 'dialectics' I acknowledge in Hegel a correct post-Renaissance attempt to integrate theology and philosophy around an account of history and the creative development of the human spirit: indeed, *Theology and Social Theory* is a kind of initial attempt to re-do Hegel in a non-gnostic fashion that

---

[9] This seems to be completely lost on Insole whose ascription to me of a kind of blithe wilful Maytime optimism entirely ignores my Pauline insistence on the utter fallenness and demonic captivity of the current world. Only with strenuous difficulty, only indeed as a form of Christian *gnosis* – which Paul yet dared to proclaim in the public forum – are we able to discern the hidden realm of real peaceful being that cosmic evil obscures from our view.

[10] There is some resemblance here between my position and that of Robert Spaemann in *Happiness and Benevolence*, trans. Jeremiah Alberg, SJ (Notre Dame, Ind: Notre Dame UP, 2000).

refuses a Hegelian transparency of reason and identification of Creation with Fall. And although I argue that the ultimate logic of history is not dialectical and that dialectical processes are never entirely necessitated, I acknowledge that certain historical developments can be understood in dialectical terms – such that aspects of my own metanarrative are, indeed, as Rowan Williams pointed out, transparently dialectical.[11]

Finally, to return to the question of 'difference', I embrace its accentuation of positivism which dispenses with much of the nominalist, rationalist and ahistorical residue in the latter: what is 'positive', is now the various unfounded regimes and fictions of power. But I suggest that only Catholic Christianity can be completely 'positivist', since it understands all evil and violence in their negativity to be privation. This opens the possibility of *the most radical imaginable modern pluralism*: namely that positive differences, insofar as they are all instances of the Good (a condition which of course will never be perfectly fulfilled in fallen time), must for that reason analogically concur in a fashion that exceeds mere liberal agreement to disagree. If that is the case, then a counter-genealogy to that of Nietzsche (such as already envisaged by Augustine and Vico) becomes feasible: one narrates not simply the military tale of the devices and victories of arbitrary power, but also the continuous and sometimes decisive interruption of this story by instances of the reflecting of perfect infinite peaceful power which is the Good in finite acts of goodness and their necessary compossibility.

But how to choose between these two alternative genealogical strategies? My book seemed to suggest that there are no grounds for such a choice. But in that case, as Gavin Hyman and others have astutely pointed out, is there not a meta-discourse of anarchic and so nihilistic non-reason that lies beyond even my metanarrative of the two cities and my ontology of peaceful difference? They are right to demand clarification.[12]

This would take two forms. First of all, from the point of view of my ontology, the 'choice' for peaceful analogy and the Augustinian metanarrative is *not* really an ungrounded decision, but a 'seeing' by a truly-desiring reason of the truly desirable. The second form of clarification, however, offers a certain limited mode of apologetic (a mode which I have never refused). Just as I can appeal to a certain inchoate current human preference for peace over violence that is both innate (from my metaphysical point of view) and a post-Christian residue, so also I can appeal to a certain bias towards reason rather than unreason (present for similar reasons). This is because the nihilistic vision concludes – from a cold reason that disallows to the 'moods' of eros, anxiety, boredom, trust, poetic response, faith, hope, charity and so forth an ontologically disclosive status – that, in the end, there is an incomprehensible springing of all from nothing and that further-

---

[11] Rowan Williams, 'Saving time: thoughts on practice, patience and vision', in *New Blackfriars* special issue, pp. 319–26.
[12] Hyman, *The Predicament of Postmodern Theology*.

more the real ultimate nothing only 'is' through the unwarranted diversity of the all, which in turn constantly reveals its own secondary and illusory character as a papering-over of the void. Nihilism has then to take the form of a mystical monism. And the same is true of nihilism as a univocal ontology of difference: difference here, as 'original', must spring from a continuous auto-differentiation, in which, just *because* the One is never its unified self, it is *all the more dominant* even in its fated lapse. It is possible to read this meta-physics as the completion of Hegel's gnostic dialectics just as, inversely, it is possible to read Hegel's metaphysics as already a nihilism (as he himself sometimes describes it) in which final identity is only actual (as Slavoj Zizek has pointed out) as the infinite production of an *un*mediated residue of meaningless difference.[13]

But however it is presented, nihilism is the conclusion of 'pure reason' (reason in the mood of cold regard), not just to the void or to ontological violence, but also to the ontological reign of non-sense or unreason. This indeed was Nietzsche's central tragic crux: fully honest Western reason real-izes that reason itself is but a pathetic human projection.

So, by contrast, it becomes possible to argue that a Catholic perspective saves not just the human bias towards peace and order, but also the human bias towards reason. Reason, for Catholic tradition, 'goes all the way down' – it is consistent with the infinite and it leaves behind no residue of chaos. For this reason a full 'rationalism' is linked with a Biblical *mythos* alone. It then follows that to 'choose' the Augustinian metanarrative and an Augustinian ontology of peace is also to 'elect reason', to fulfil the ineradicable bias of the human mind towards meaning (which *might* be just an accident of our animality) in the sense that this choice alone allows one to say that reason is ontologically ultimate – that there is, indeed, a final reason for things, a reason for being as such. And yet, to save the appearances of reason in this fashion requires the supplementation of reason by true desire and by faith – including the desire for and faith in, infinite reason. By contrast, to remain with reason alone turns out to mean (as Nietzsche correctly saw) the election of unreason. Apologetically one can suggest that in some profound sense to elect unreason is irrational... And yet if one does make this election, there is no neutral, uninflected reason that can gainsay such a fatal preference.[14]

I hope that the above detour helps to clarify my embracing of genealogy against Nietzsche himself. In a similar fashion, my relationship to the Nietz-schean celebration of power is a complex one. On the one hand I am pitting a Dostoyevskyan notion of strength in weakness against this celebration (a theoretical tussle that was best expressed in dramatic form by John Cowper Powys in his great novel *Wolf Solent*). Since we are created, we are received, even as ourselves, before ourselves. Likewise, in order to exercise strength we

---

[13] Slavoj Zizek, *The Sublime Object of Ideology* (London: Verso, 1989) pp. 201–33.

[14] For a much more extended version of arguments about reason and mood, see my response to the *Arachne* symposium, 'On theological transgression', *Arachne*, vol. 2, no. 1, 1995, Sympo-sium, pp. 145–76.

must first be sensitive and attentive, which always involves a vulnerable exposure to risk, failure and the tragic misinterpretation by others of our own ventures (as Rowan Williams has so repeatedly stressed in his theology). Negation is not inevitable, yet it is always going to be involved in a fallen Creation. And this situation reveals that power itself has a precondition in relational receptiveness which can indeed mean, as the Bible teaches, that it is the 'weak' who will turn out to be strong, for mostly unNietzschean reasons.

On the other hand, just because receptivity is for us ontologically primordial, it cannot begin as a passivity in the ordinary sense: as I am *entirely* received, even as an I, there is no original 'I' that could be the subject of a passivity. Reception is therefore from the outset active and affirmative and this ontological circumstance is reflected ontically in our best attention towards others. Since we cannot be in their position save by falsely feigning an absolute sympathy which secretly seeks to displace them, our true attention weaves further the interval of a 'between', such that we most accurately sympathize by creatively responding with our own perspective. In this way the work of solidarity in its essence promotes, in their shared compossibility, both the power of others and our own. This Spinozistic and Leibnizian – ultimately Scotist-derived – perspective (which nonetheless I believe requires the ontological ground of Creation *ex nihilo*, and Thomistic real relationality together with a created primacy of analogy) points more in the direction of an agreement with the Nietzschean affirmation of power – a side of my position developed further in writings since *Theology and Social Theory*.[15] For if, as for Catholic truth, the Good is entirely positive, then power as power is indeed the Good itself in its original inexhaustible plenitude: insofar as it is evil, it is weakness in a final, ontological sense of false unnecessary limitation, rather than the sense of receptivity, or suffering of evil undergone in order to overcome it. (In a fallen world this suffering of limits, and sacrificial foregoing in the face of evil scarcity, is indeed our only way to reinvoke true joy and original peace and plenitude. Nevertheless, I tend to insist on the ambivalence of suffering and the ever-lurking danger for Christianity of preferring suffering to cure: to give and to suffer for others 'charitably' means, as St Paul intimates, not simply to meet a need, but in meeting this need to re-invoke and restore a hedonistic gratuity and mutuality prior to all need.)

Because he conceived of a new sort of 'giving' virtue that acted non-reactively out of the plenitude of power, St Paul, as Alain Badiou has pointed out, was already more Nietzschean than Nietzsche.[16] He refused the idea that goodness begins in a weak 'resistance' to evil (this is why, for him, *nomos* cannot redeem), whereas Nietzsche failed to see that even the affirmation of the strong over the hordes of the weak was a mode of 'weak' resistance to weakness. St Paul also realized that a true metaphysics of power must entail a

---

[15] See, in particular, 'Can morality be Christian?', in John Milbank, *The Word Made Strange: Theology, Language and Culture* (Oxford: Blackwell, 1997), pp. 219–33. I am indebted to past discussions with Regina Schwartz on plenitude and scarcity.

[16] Alain Badiou, *Saint Paul: la fondation de l'universalisme* (Paris: PUF, 1997).

primacy of *unthreatened* peace, and of the collective over the individual, since only a reciprocal 'weak' receptivity will build a real, shared strength.

The relation of the book to Nietzsche and his developers is therefore pivotal, not so much because they represent something altogether new and 'postmodern', as rather because the three post-Christian strands of liberalism, positivism and dialectics are here brought to a decisive head (including the inevitable residue of double negation that is the persistence of dialectics within nihilism) and pitted against Christianity itself, as well as its modern child, socialism.

The latter is read by me as, in its best mode, legitimately seeking further to realize latent dimensions in the medieval Christian tradition, yet in an idiom free of the dominant modern philosophy rooted in univocity, representation, soul/body dualism, ontotheology, univocal partitioning between divine and created causality and transcendentalism. The latencies concern the proper place of the laity, of the collective, of labour, of sexuality, of the arts, of language, of the material realm and of history. I would now see (following the historical insights of the Christian socialists Sergius Bulgakov and Stanislas Breton)[17] the beginnings of traces with such concerns not just in Augustine, but also in the pagan neo-Platonist Proclus, whereas I would now regard Plotinus, via Avicenna (whose influence then runs through Scotus, Henry of Ghent etc. and so ultimately to Kant), as the ultimate grandfather of the 'main report' of modernity.[18] Thus to my mind 'an alternative modernity' (which is much *more* modern than the essentially frightened Cartesian/Kantian dogmatic and domineering defence of the inner subjective citadel against historicist scepticism) would develop the theurgic side of neo-Platonism Christianized by Dionysius and Maximus.[19] This side was more attentive to time, matter, artistic making and ritual rather than to an 'inward' turn that was ultimately born from Plotinus's relative abandonment of Platonic recollection of the Forms, which requires temporal 'triggers', in favour of a retreat to always latent psychic understanding. This retreat was linked to his non-Platonic supposition that there is a dimension of the human soul that is 'undescended' into time and space.[20] (For all Augustine's talk of a turning within, I see him as having made parallel moves in his doctrine of illumination to those of Proclus in relation to Plotinus, not as essentially Plotinian.)[21] A version of Thomism and aspects of Pico della Mirandola and Nicholas of

---

[17] See Sergius Bulgakov, *Philosophy of Economy: The World as Household*, trans. Catherine Evtuhov (New Haven, Conn: Yale UP, 2000) and Stanislas Breton, *The Word and the Cross*, trans. Jacquelyn Porter (New York: Fordham UP, 2002) esp. 'Translator's introduction', pp. vii–xvii.

[18] See Conor Cunningham, *Genealogy of Nihilism* (London: Routledge, 2002).

[19] See for example Gregory Shaw, *Theurgy and the Soul: The Neoplatonism of Iamblichus* (University Park, Penn: Penn State UP, 1995) and Ysabel de Andia, *Henosis: L'Union à Dieu chez Denys l'Aréopagite* (Leiden: Brill, 1996).

[20] See Jean Trouillard, *La Mystagogie de Proclos* (Paris: Les Belles Lettres, 1982).

[21] For a summary and fine extension of this sort of interpretation, see Michael Hanby, *Augustine and Modernity* (London: Routledge, 2003).

Cusa's blending of Dominican and more emphatically theurgic (including Hermetic and Cabbalistic) perspectives can be newly harvested within this *schema*.[22] Indeed, it is tempting (though of course vastly over-simplifying in relation to the inwardly diverse theological inclinations of the religious orders) to describe our actual, 'Plotinian' intellectual modernity as also 'Franciscan', and the shadow, 'Proclean' modernity as also 'Dominican' (if one insists that Dominican neo-scholasticism was essentially contaminated with Scotism).

This contrast also permits me an improved genealogy for my consistent distinguishing of a modern-yet-conservative 'internal' and 'idealist'constructivism – of appearances by thought – from a 'shadow-modern' yet more radical external and more 'realist' constructivism – of culture and to a degree nature by the human psychic-corporeal unity. The former is 'Plotinian', the latter 'Proclean' in their ultimate derivation, even though the contrast between these two thinkers is in reality far more complex than this would indicate.

The understanding that socialism must be grounded in a Platonic, theurgic and Christian vision (one can also think of Thomas More, Tommaso Campanella and Jan Amos Comenius in this regard) is increasingly shared by the secular left – this was already intimated by the late Gillian Rose in her final phase, and more recently it has been emphasized, though in a problematic, atheist form, by Alain Badiou and, to a degree, Slavoj Zizek and Giorgio Agamben. In a certain fashion there is much more concurrence in tone between all these thinkers and the theses of *Theology and Social Theory* than is the case with those of the thinkers of transcendental difference. The latter, and especially their Christian *epigones*, tended to protest that postmodernity makes any notion of a 'metanarrative' impossible.[23] Much more perceptively, the theologian Gavin Hyman accepted my assertion that there is still a nihilist metanarrative (for example, the *Genealogy of Morals*) but then argued to an *aporia*: there has to be/cannot be a single metanarrative.[24] The upshot of this is to suggest an endless competition between metanarratives. Yet this is unthinkable: it would of course be agonistic, and no proponent of a single metanarrative would really accept the validity of the others. There would, indeed, have to be a 'playful' (but the game is played with money and guns) wandering between these grand stories, implying once more that there is really one single nihilist metanarrative and ontology of violence.

[22] Catherine Pickstock's 'liturgical consummation of philosophy' offers exactly the same innovative theurgic emphasis. See Catherine Pickstock, *After Writing: On the Liturgical Consummation of Philosophy* (Oxford: Blackwell, 1998). See also Geoffrey Hill, *Scenes from Comus* (London: Penguin, 2005) p. 19: 'I say imagine them I mean create them –/ another remnant of alchemical twaddle/that ceases to be twaddle in some cases.'

[23] See the respondents cited in note 6 above. Important (though I think in the end unsuccessful) attempts to find some balance between my position and that of the French postmodernists are those of Graham Ward in 'John Milbank's Divina Commedia', in *New Blackfriars* special issue, pp. 311–19 and Gerard Loughlin, 'Christianity at the end of the story, or the return of the master narrative', in *Modern Theology* special issue, pp. 365–85.

[24] Hyman, *The Predicament of Postmodern Theology*.

As against this, one can point out, first of all, that the Augustinian and the Nietzschean metanarratives are *not* entirely distinct. Their mirroring disagreement implies agreement about many, even most, of the facts, even if a disagreement of interpretation certainly involves some factual dispute also. Gavin Hyman's citations of passages where Nietzsche insists on the subjectivity of his viewpoint really apply more to the interpretation of the genealogy than the latter as such (more to Book 3 of the *Genealogy of Morals*).[25] And I would want to insist that my own version of an Augustinian metanarrative, while being a seamless weave of fact and interpretation, is still presented as a debatable account of actual real history – in relation to which one could urge facts, reasons, probabilities and persuasions both for and against. It is only a 'fiction' in the sense that it is a reflexive doubling of the 'lived fiction' (human makings; makings of humanity) which composes enacted history itself.[26]

But the more recent ponderings of the secular left (as chiefly represented by Badiou, but also by Peter Hallward) suggest a general acceptance of the argument that the philosophy of difference grounds only a social *agon* and therefore is complict with late capitalism.[27] Likewise its nihilism and immanentism is always at once both monistic and dualistic. For if difference is original and univocal, then it is the non-relational expressive *glissando* of a problematic transcendental *Unum* which engenders a series of necessary but bad failures-to-attain pure continuous variation (which would be impossible). It thereby gives rise to the universes of 'presence' and 'representation' over-against the good but unattainable or always postponed, since 'non-actual' world of absolute difference, pure gift, the wholly other or whatever.[28] This severe, even incipiently Manichean dualism can undergird a liberal politics of self-satisfied gesture, but not one that attempts to build a new form of just community around an accepted common good: such an enterprise requires instead, as Peter Hallward says, an ontology of relation and mediation, of *metaxu* (*not* really there in Hegel, as William Desmond has brilliantly argued) 'between' the one and the many.[29] Precisely a Platonic, neo-Platonic and Catholic 'analogical ontology', as my book contended. But the full argument

[25] Ibid., p. 109. And see Friedrich Nietzsche, *On the Genealogy*, Preface 8, pp. 6–7 and Third Treatise: What do Ascetic Ideals Mean?, pp. 67–111; *The Gay Science*, trans. Walter Kaufmann (New York: Vintage, 1974) sections 373–4, pp. 334–7.

[26] For a much more extended consideration of my historical method and notions of metanarrative and ontology, see John Milbank, 'The invocation of Clio', in *Journal of Religious Ethics*, vol. 33, no. 1, March 2005, pp. 3–45. This was in response to the summer 2004 special issue on my ethical thought with contributions by James Wetzel (Augustine) Gordon Michalson (Kant and modernity) Jennifer Herdt (charity and sympathy) and David Craig (Ruskin).

[27] See, especially, Peter Hallward, 'The one or the other: French philosophy today', in *Angelaki*, vol. 8, no. 2, August 2003, pp. 1–33.

[28] See Alain Badiou, *Deleuze: The Clamor of Being*, trans. Louise Burchill (Minneapolis: Minnesota UP, 2000) and Catherine Pickstock, '*Quasi una Sonata*: music, postmodernism and theology', in Jeremy Begbie (ed.), *Theology through Music* (Cambridge: CUP, 2006).

[29] William Desmond, *Being and the Between* (New York: SUNY, 1995); *Hegel's God: A Counterfeit Double?* (London: Ashgate, 2003).

for a genuinely theological and realist version of these claims and intimations lies ahead of us and cannot be made here.

It remains the case, nevertheless, that there is a new recognition of a need for a universal discourse if we are to sustain any political hope. At the same time, those who remain critical of liberalism have still absorbed Nietzsche's lesson that the urge towards universalism as such is contingently and historically rooted in Platonism, the Hebrew Bible and Christianity. It is this insight which prevents any sort of return simply to 'enlightenment' rational universality as if this had just been dangerously forgotten by the fancy footwork of the postmodernists. Instead, there is a newly serious post-secular, rather than neo-modern, investigation under way into the paradoxical specificity of the European commitment to the universal.[30]

I hope that *Theology and Social Theory* can still make a contribution to this urgent task. However, critics have rightly demanded clarification of precisely what I mean by an analogical ontology of peace which is also an ontology of the participation of the Creation in divine creativity.

For it seems that here I face in two directions at once: towards a call for a return to the pre-modern prior to 1300 on the one hand, but towards an invocation of modern romantic expressivism and 'postmodern' ultra-constructivism on the other. It is perhaps mainly for this reason that reactions to my work have, in turn, tended to take two opposite forms. One reaction tends to see my own position as too 'positivist', while the other tends to see it as far too 'liberal'.

So on the one hand I am perceived as nostalgic, as appealing back to a static organic community and also as fideistic: as arbitrarily and violently asserting the hegemonic claims of one particular 'positive' cultural formation, namely Christianity, against the claims of all others. It is argued that I wish to subsume all philosophy within a positive theological discourse and that I favour politically a new theocratic order.[31]

On the other hand, I am perceived by other commentators as all too modern: as calling for an ultimate unleashing of all human expressive freedoms in terms of a dangerously utopian (still Rousseauian and Marxist) faith in their compossibility. In this case I am also perceived as far too rationalistic: as reducing the notion of revelation to an immanent historical and rational event, and as formally evacuating the concrete content of Christology and ecclesiology in a recognizably 'liberal' idiom.[32]

---

[30] See also Remi Brague, *Eccentric Culture: A Theory of Western Civilisation*, trans. Samuel Lester (South Bend Ind: St Augustine's Press, 2002).

[31] See the essays by Bannet, Boyarin, Kappler and Shandro in the *Arachne* symposium. Also the contribution by Jennifer Herdt in the *Journal of Religious Ethics* special issue.

[32] See Rusty Reno, 'The Radical Orthodoxy project', in *First Things*, 100 (2000) pp. 37–44 and Lewis Ayres (who is nonetheless generally very favourable towards my views) in his magisterial and fascinating *Nicaea and its Legacy: An Approach to Fourth-Century Trinitarian Theology* (Oxford: OUP, 2004) p. 403.

Sometimes it is suggested that I incoherently or else inevitably tend in both these directions at once. It should be said here that I regard the second 'liberal' charge as more subtle and plausible than the first 'positive' charge, even though I deny both of them. For while 'positively' I recommend Catholic Christianity as the one final and universal truth, I quite clearly envisage Catholicism in 'liberal' terms, if by 'liberal' one conotes the generous, open-ended and all-inclusive.

Nevertheless, both sets of critics are right to detect some haziness as to how the 'pre-modern' and the 'postmodern' elements in this book and my work in general belong together. There is no space here to give a fully satisfactory account of this, but I can at least offer some indicators.

First of all, in the wake of the *nouvelle théologie*, but still more strongly, I contend that there really were not two different discourses of philosophy and theology for the Church Fathers and that this was not a failure of conceptual clarification later cleared up in the Middle Ages. For Augustine it is not that 'faith seeks understanding', but rather that all knowledge, by faith, seeks wisdom.[33] He takes over the temporal dimension of knowledge that Platonism *already* recognized in the mode of the Meno problematic: how is it that we must search to find what we must in some sense already know, else we would not know to search for it in the first place? In Augustine's hands, the 'metahistorical' dimension of this metaphysics is accentuated: a far greater place is now given both to a mysterious protology and a mysterious eschatology. And because the question of an 'ontological forgetting' is now doubled by the affirmation of a contingent sinful forgetting that distorted finite being as such, the temporal dimension of understanding is newly projected onto an entire historical plane, with the Incarnation and birth of the *ecclesia* at its centre.

This means that, already in Augustine, theology is in some sense the third term that links the philosophical elaboration of a general ontology with the historical interpretation of particular events. Moreover, as J.-L. Chrétien has argued, Augustine was perhaps the first thinker decisively to suggest that human art was in some measure 'like' divine creation. Chrétien's very fine essay on this topic is in fact critical of Augustine's innovation, but his own contention that divine creation in the Bible is always a matter of 'speaking', and not artisanal 'making', does not seem to take account of numerous passages.[34] Likewise, Chrétien's view that assimilation of human art to creation downgrades an older Greek craft-like attention to the thing-to-be-made in favour of expression of the artistic subject, ignores the fact that in ancient Greece making tended to be envisaged as simply material approximation to a pre-given form (albeit not idiosyncratic subjectivity), while, by contrast, the Augustinian notion of *verbum* and *ars* involves a participation in the Paternal

[33] Here I am indebted to recent discussions with Ellen Charry who has independently arrived at similar conclusions and is developing her own detailed scholarly elaboration of them.

[34] Jean-Louis Chrétien, 'From God the artist to man the creator', in *Hand to Hand: Listening to the Work of Art*, trans. Stephen E. Lewis (New York: Fordham, 2002) pp. 94–130. For an appreciation and critique of this essay and several others by Chrétien, see Catherine Pickstock, 'Platonism and phenomenology in the work of Jean-Louis Chrétien', in *Nunc*, Autumn 2005.

uttering of the *Logos* who, as the divine Son, is more than simply a formal blueprint.[35] Hence this entire conception tends to have the opposite implication to that claimed by Chrétien, in that it reduces the difference between 'art' as prior process on the one hand, and 'art' as product on the other. It thereby encourages *both* a new stress on the expressive originality of human art *and* an attention to a newness that can only result with the emergence of the product itself. In this perspective the relatively 'expressive' reworking of this theme by a romantic such as Joseph Joubert on the one hand, and a relatively 'artisanal' and objective reworking of it by a modernist such as David Jones on the other, can be seen as two variants within one now very ancient paradigm.[36]

Thus on my reading, from Augustine – and also, in a different idiom, from the Christian Procleanism of Dionysius – there is inherited first an integration of philosophy and theology and secondly a latent and linked concern both with historicity and with human *poesis* (see my remarks on Dionysius in this book). Aquinas, again on my (to some controversial) reading, synthesizes Augustine with Dionysius as well as with Aristotle, and at the deepest level essentially sustains this integration, even though he bequeaths a certain conceptual apparatus, which, misread, later permit a drastically dualistic conception of the relation of faith to reason to emerge.[37]

As to what happened after Aquinas, a classically conservative, anti-modern reading of the later Middle Ages was provided by Hans Urs von Balthasar.[38] Theology goes in two opposite directions, which are both, for Balthasar, distortions. The first direction is consummated by Duns Scotus: finite and infinite being are seen as equally and univocally 'in being' – hence *esse* threatens to become greater than God and God to be idolatrously reduced to the status of a partner with his Creation in causal processes (and there is indeed ample evidence that this second tendency is already under way in Scotus himself).[39] The second direction is supremely represented by Meister Eckhart: God is *identified* with *esse* such that the true being of the Creation and especially of created spirit is to be located only within the Trinity itself. A kind of acosmic pantheism thereby threatens, which is the counterpart to the more cosmic, Spinozistic pantheism threatened by Scotism. In the wake of Eckhart, Pico and Cusanus also come under Balthasar's partial condemnation.

It now appears to me though, that Henri de Lubac did not clearly go along with this genealogy and that this accords with a tendency in his thought to hold a problematic balance, prior to beatitude, between the natural and the

---

[35] See J.-P. Vernant, 'Remarques sur les formes et les limites de la pensée technique des Grecs', in *Mythe et Pensée chez les Grecs*, vol. 2 (Paris: Maspero, 1978) pp. 44–64

[36] See *The Notebooks of Joseph Joubert: A Selection*, ed. and trans. by Paul Auster (San Francisco: North Point Press, 1983).

[37] See John Milbank and Catherine Pickstock, *Truth in Aquinas* (London: Routledge, 2001).

[38] Hans Urs von Balthasar, *The Glory of the Lord: A Theological Aesthetics V: The Realm of Metaphysics in the Modern Age*, trans. O. Davies et al. (Edinburgh: T. and T. Clark, 1991) B. 1: 'The parting of the ways', pp. 9–48.

[39] See Jacob Schmutz, 'La doctrine médiévale des causes et la théologie de la nature pure (xiiiᵉ–xviiᵉ siècles)', in *Revue Thomiste*, Jan–June 2001, pp. 217–64.

supernatural, reason and faith, philosophy and theology, despite the fact that the first sets of terms enjoy for him no pure neo-scholastic autonomy. By contrast, Balthasar much more emphatically insisted upon the 'reason of faith' as such (likewise the aesthetics and ethics of faith), but given this more Barthian fideistic drift, he was also always more likely to allow a relatively more autonomous realm of reason. In retrospect, it seems to me that my own intentions are far more like those of de Lubac than they are like those of Balthasar.[40] Even though I see philosophy, in its very nature as philosophy, as only completed by theology, I also see the latter, short of the final intuition of God, as always inevitably blending its intuitions of the advents of presence with a philosophical and abstracting discursiveness (which a narrative mode already implicitly assumes), as well as an empirical appeal to lived history and geographical situatedness.

In keeping with this revised conception (but not alteration) of my stance, I do not altogether accept Balthasar's conservative account of the late Middle Ages and the Renaissance – and this difference is implicitly present in my original book. But it is now clearer to me that this involves a certain *recognition* of the rational power of the arguments of Duns Scotus and later of the terminists.

This new acknowledgement can be briefly summed up:[41]

---

[40] For a much fuller account of this, see John Milbank, *The Suspended Middle: Henri de Lubac and the Debate Concerning the Supernatural* (Grand Rapids, III: Eerdmans, 2005).

[41] See Catherine Pickstock, 'Modernity and scholasticism: a critique of recent invocations of univocity', in *Antonianum*, 77, pp. 3–56; another version: 'Duns Scotus: his historical and contemporary significance', in *Modern Theology*, October 2005. This article is a comprehensive reply to the critics of the 'Radical Orthodoxy' account of Scotus. See also for a much longer elaboration of some of the historico-philosophical points made in this preface, John Milbank, 'Vérité et identité: le telescope Thomiste', in *Revue Thomiste, Veritas* special issue, Jan–June 2004, pp. 318–52. In general the idea that there is 'a controversial RO, reading of Scotus' is a chimera. The new insistence that Scotus is perhaps the central figure (amongst many others including Avicenna, Gilbert Porreta, Abelard, Roger Bacon, Henry of Ghent, etc.) in *the* crucial shift within Western thought *within which* Kant is still located is not original to RO, but has been elaborated by L. Honnefelder, J.-F. Courtine, O. Boulnois, J.-L. Marion and J. Schmutz, amongst many others, ultimately in the wake of Etienne Gilson, whose views they have nonetheless heavily qualified. (See, in particular, L. Honnefelder, *Scientia Transcendens: Die Formale Bestimmung der Seiendheit et Realität in der Metaphysik der Mittelalters und der Neuzeit (Duns Scotus – Suarez – Wolff – Kant – Peirce)* (Hamburg: Fleix Meiner, 1990)). The real controversy concerns the *assessment* of this shift and, regrettably, this point has been obfuscated by certain critics in a way that seems tactically dubious. As regards the assessment, one needs to note the following: first, the more 'analytic' and 'Anglo-Saxon' historians of medieval thought naturally favour the Scotist shift because it establishes the ultimate presuppositions of analytic philosophy itself. Second, the more phenomenological historians of medieval thought tend to be ambivalent because of their residual Heideggereanism: attribution of the invention of 'onto-theology' to Scotus (or the Scotist moment) now sets the date for this much later than it was set by Heidegger himself and exculpates the grand tradition of Christian theology from this charge. However, a sense remains that onto-theology somehow *needed* by fate to emerge so that it could also be exceeded. (By implication the 'grand tradition' is confusingly seen as *not* entirely free of onto-theology or metaphysics in a bad sense.) This exceeding is seen as emerging already in Scotus himself, in his focus on love and the will. RO by comparison tends to see Scotus's primacy of will and love over intellect and truth as still *in keeping with* or as colluding with his new onto-theology founded on the univocity of being (for the reasons why, see the Pickstock and Milbank articles); hence it tends to prefer Eckhart's intellectualist radicalization of the grand tradition, and to defend the

1 Scotus implicitly and cogently asks how, if created being simply shares in Being, it can really, integrally be.

2 Scotus and Ockham rightly question whether analogy of attribution does not violate the principle of non-contradiction, since there *is* no third term between the univocal and the equivocal.[42]

3 Ockham likewise tends to suggest that certain realist conceptions of universals and real relations tend to violate the principle of identity. (How can a particular form *as* this form – which might, for example, in the case of the form of a man, be white *or* black – also be, or be able to become, the same form as universal – which, as denoting nominally a *genus* like 'humanity', might be determined as *either* white or black? How, likewise, can a thing be by necessary relation also what it is not?)[43]

4 According to Ockham, every supposed grasp of a universal has clearly been arrived at through a process of linguistic naming.

5 Since Being is now univocal, it becomes less clear than it was for Aquinas that *ens commune* can only be the effect of an infinite cause. Already Ockham suggests, following the implications of univocity of Being (and well before the 'Renaissance') that while creatures cannot cause totally, they can still bring about finite being as such, in collaboration with God, on the same ontological level. And although we have no *experience* of this, even a human productive action presupposing no pre-given substrate, cannot be logically ruled out.[44]

Now I depart from Balthasar's conservatism in contending that thinkers like Eckhart, Dietrich of Freibourg, Nicholas of Cusa and Pico della Mirandola, as well as, rather later, Pierre Bérulle and Ralph Cudworth, all in various ways defended the analogical-participatory world-view, but realized that Aquinas could not at every point simply be repeated, because the new Scotistic and terminist insights had to be responded to. (It has to be said here that whether these are intentional responses cannot always be shown; yet it seems striking that these thinkers seem to offer what are in effect responses.) In each case (to grossly summarize) their diverse responses tend to go as follows:

(1) For Eckhart, to ensure that God is not trumped by *esse*, one must indeed face up more radically to the *aporias* of the doctrine of creation *ex nihilo*: if this doctrine insists that God is the plenitude of being and that all created being derives from God, then in some sense the ground of created being must be

---

idea that there can be a non onto-theological theological 'ontology' or 'metaphysics' (for want perhaps of better terms).

[42] Duns Scotus, *Ordinatio* I d.3 Q.2 a2. 26;I d.8 Q 3.121; *Collatio* 24.24. William of Ockham, *Quodlibetal Questions*, 4.12

[43] William of Ockham, *Quodlibetal Questions*, 5.11; 5.12; 6.9; 6.10; 6.12; 6.13; 6.14.

[44] William of Ockham, *Quodlibetal Questions*, 1.1; 2.1: 2.9; *Reportatio*, 2.6.

uncreated.[45] But on the other hand, Trinitarian doctrine suggests that God within himself includes the 'impossible' creative going beyond himself. Thus while Eckhart maintained the orthodox distinction between divine generation/ procession (of Son and Spirit) and divine creation, he not only connected these two motions (as did Aquinas) but also (like Eriugena much earlier) problematized their distinction by validly arguing that they must also be in one aspect identical in order to be distinguished: God's creating, since he is omnipotent, can 'only' be in one aspect his going forth within himself and returning to himself in responding to this going forth, while our created derivation from God and returning to God can 'only' be, again because of this omnipotence, entirely one with the event of divine generation and procession. The latter then is in some eminent sense identical with the inexhaustible kenosis of the uncreated indefinite into the created definite in which it ceaselessly and indefinitely defines itself. (The God who freely creates *is* the God who is internally expressive. Yet he does not 'become' in creating, nor in the history of the Creation undergo a process of alienation and its overcoming in Hegelian fashion.)

Eckhart therefore claims that, while the relation of creature to Creator remains always analogical, that nonetheless the relation of the soul to God in its ground is univocal, since there is a horizontal 'univocity' between the persons of the Trinity who are equal in being (a univocity that nonetheless exceeds the terms of any conceivable finite 'unity' that is defined over-against diversity, and which also lies beyond any finitely univocal contrast of opposites) within whose dynamic the soul is ultimately included.

It might be possible to qualify Eckhart here by saying that the perfect likeness of Son to Father which nonetheless alone constitutes the Father as 'original' is a kind of 'absolute analogue' that exceeds the analogy/univocity contrast – yet his basic point is correct. Perhaps, also, a threatened acosmism opened up by Eckhart's perspective needs balancing by a sophiological sense that God is in his own 'feminine' dynamic essence 'more than God'. This does further justice to the *aporia* of creation *ex nihilo*, in an opposite but complementary direction to that which was primarily taken by the German Dominican – and salves the Scotist anxiety about the integral actuality of the created order, without lapsing into Scotist ontotheology. Such a sophiological approach is naturally linked with a stronger stress on Trinitarian theurgic descent of God to humans in the liturgical community, beginning with ancient Israel. Maximus the Confessor's idea that the infinite points back to the finite as well as vice versa already indicated such considerations.[46]

---

[45] See Burkhard Mojsisch, *Meister Eckhart: Analogy, Univocity, Unity*, trans. Orrin F. Summerell (Amsterdam/Philadelphia: B.R. Grüner, 2001). This book represents the consummation of a new, much more precise reading of Eckhart. Nonetheless, one may wonder whether Mojsisch interprets Eckhart too much backwards through Fichte. See also, for the view that Eckhart is writing in opposition to Franciscan univocity, Alain de Libera, *Le Problème de l'être chez Maitre Eckhart: Logique et Métaphysique de l'Analogie* (Geneva: Cahiers de la Revue de Théologie et de Philosophie, 1980).

[46] Maximus the Confessor, *Mystagogy*, chapter 2. The modern Russian tradition of sophiology has also fundamentally to do with the problematic that I am indicating here.

Eckhart therefore radicalized analogy (perhaps against Scotus) by insisting on the full implications of Aquinas's view that the primary term (here God) in an analogical comparison 'gives all' to the secondary terms, which are but problematic approximations – at once, and in the same respects of finite perfection, like and unlike the primary term, else one could sift such approximation between the univocal and the equivocal. But as we have just seen, this meant that he also newly insisted on a different sort of univocity (compared to that of Scotus) within the relational and productive (Trinitarian) co-ordinations of the infinite itself. As with Scotus, he now declares that being is primarily univocal even in its inner dispersal, but unlike Scotus he locates this in infinite actuality and not in the logical (and by extension for Scotus – in a new, formal and proto-transcendentalist sense – the ontological) basis of 'vertical' infinite/finite relations.

He then concludes that every being and especially every spiritual being is grounded in, is in a mysterious way ultimately identical-with, this infinitude as its 'image', and so is finally drawn into a univocal ambience (albeit one beyond the contrast of identity and difference in a way that one should regard as supra-analogical) – yet this conclusion is required in part precisely by the logic of analogy of attribution.

(2) Eckhart and then Cusa, with a sophistication that is only now being fully explored, daringly decided to save analogy by abandoning non-contradiction at the ultimate level of being, because they were able to demonstrate that this cannot possibly apply to the *aporias* generated by notions of the infinite and the indefinite and their relation to the finite and definite. (For example the divine indefinite for Eckhart both must be and cannot be definitely defined over against the finite definite: this reasoning expresses the principle of Eriugena and later Cusa's *non aliud*.)[47]

(3) In a similar fashion, Cusa, especially through mathematical examples, tends to treat universals and real relations in a way that advertises their irreducibly paradoxical character.

(4) Eckhart and Cusa (followed by several Renaissance and Baroque thinkers, including the neo-scholastic John of St Thomas) develop further the Augustinian and Thomist view that all thinking is speaking, and Cusa newly emphasizes external modes of expression. This tends in the direction of countering the nominalist reduction of universals to names by showing that a grasp of particulars is *also* a matter of constructive naming.

(5) Nicholas of Cusa accepts in the wake of the terminists that human art is now a mode of creation and that the finite is a scene of real originality, but tries to see this in analogical and not univocalist terms as a participation of human artistic arriving at 'new things' in the solely divine act of absolute creative positing of being.[48]

[47] See Mojsisch, *Meister Eckhart*, pp. 102–9.
[48] Nicholas of Cusa, *Idiota de Mente*, chapters 1 and 2.

In terms of these five new shifts, one can notice something broader and still more decisive. In effect, the neo-Platonizing Dominicans (in whom there is a complex mix of my 'Plotinian' and 'Proclean' tendencies, seeds of both a Vico/Jacobi/Hamann/Coleridge type 'external' constructivism and an inner Fichtean constructivism)[49] and the orthodoxly Christian Renaissance thinkers are conceding that Aquinas relied too much upon abstract reason (even if there is a latent poetics in his thought).[50] This means that in strictly rationalist terms of graspable logic, his theology can indeed be called into question, in the ways envisaged by Scotus and Ockham. If analogy must instead be conceptually seen in the conceptually impossible terms of *coincidentia oppositorum*, then the expressible reality of this re-conceived analogy will in fact be the more consciously necessary deployment of metaphor. Likewise, if universals are constructed, but are not thereby to be regarded as mere human fictions, then fictioning as such must participate in the Paternal fictioning of the filial *ars*. The two human modes of linguistic fashioning – history and literature, in their complex inter-entanglement both as enacted and as recited history (and there is, furthermore, no historical act that is not also a new addition to historiography) – are now seen as essential to the disclosing of truth.

In this way the latent humanism of Augustine's thought is much more brought to the fore and it becomes far more evident that philosophy as well as theology cannot be prised apart from event and image. This tends to mean that – in sharp contradistinction to neo-scholasticism – philosophy and theology are yet more radically fused into one discourse. Thus for Eckhart, the Bible is the profoundest of all works of metaphysics (as his Biblical commentaries reveal) while, inversely, spiritual intelligence as such is orientated by grace.[51] For both Eckhart and Cusa the Creation itself must be primarily a finite reflection of the divine intelligence, such that God creates primarily 'through' created/uncreated spirit (humans, angels – and, for some in this sort of tradition, the *anima mundi*) in keeping with the Biblical doctrine that

---

[49] For example, Dietrich of Freibourg rejected Aquinas's view that the reflexivity of human intelligence must be mediated by the initial understanding of external objects. This sounds 'Plotinian'. On the other hand (whatever his position may have been on that issue), more 'Proclean', as well as Trinitarian, sounds Eckhart's insistence that the human intelligence in its radical inward 'spark' or 'divine image' lies in the divine simplicity beyond the doubling of reflection. (The intelligence of the divine 'henads' or gods lies similarly beyond for Proclus.) See Ruedi Imbach, 'Le Prétendue primauté de l'être sur le connaître: perspectives cavalières sur Thomas d'Aquin et l'école dominicain allemande', in J. Jolivet et al. (eds.) *Lectiones Varietates: Hommage a Paul Vignaux (1904–1987)* (Paris: J. Vrin, 1991) pp. 121–32; F.-X. Putallaz, *Les Sens de la Refléxion chez Thomas d'Aquin* (Paris: J. Vrin, 1991); Alain de Libera, *La Mystique rhénane d'Albert le Grand à Maître Eckhart* (Paris: Editions du Seuil, 1994). p. 243.

[50] See the multi-volume work of Olivier-Thomas Venard, *Thomas d'Aquin, Poète Théologian*. So far published, Volume 1, *Littérature et Théologie: une Saison en Enfer*; Volume 2, *La Langue de l'Ineffable: Essai sur le fondement théologique de la métaphysique* (Geneva: Ad Solem, 2002–4). The second volume generously takes up and extends certain of my theses about language and creativity, but with a greater rigour and explication.

[51] Alain de Libera, *La Mystique rhénane: D'Albert le Grand à Maître Eckhart*, pp. 231–317.

hypostasized wisdom is the first of God's works. (For Cusa, as later for Bérulle, to exist as created gift must mean to exist by giving oneself to oneself and this is first of all shown in the reflexive structure of the created intelligences – even if this reflection is mediated by a knowledge of other things besides oneself.)[52] But this does *not* subsume theology into gnostic speculation, precisely in the measure that philosophy itself is now seen as bound to the modes of art, history and liturgy – thus for Cusa, as already arguably for Aquinas, there can only be for us truth *tout court* because the Truth has redemptively become incarnate in time.[53]

There is one final but crucial point to be made about Eckhart in particular. His project (in this respect like that of Dante) involved the communication to the laity in the vernacular of the speculative and mystical Catholic tradition that centred on analogical participation. His condemnation in some measure interrupted this process, which one can think of as constituting the heart of my 'shadow modernity'. Instead one got the neo-scholastic (Protestant as well as Catholic) reservation to the clergy of a positivized theological discourse on the one hand and the emergence within the new theological space of 'pure nature' of a sheerly secular discourse – dangerously poised between liberalism and positivism – on the other.

I hope that this newly extended genealogy helps better to explain why I see myself as *radically* traditional in Catholic terms, rather than as conservatively orthodox or conventionally liberal. Crucial for me now is the idea of two alternative 'modern' traditions that reach back into neo-Platonism itself, plus the thesis that a post-nominalist realism has to be both a more drastically mystical and a more humanistic realism.

In terms of mysticism this may mean something like Eckhart's radical mysticism of identity, required by a deeper exploration of the idea of divine creation. But this is balanced (in accordance with the other, 'sophiological' side of the *aporia* of creation *ex nihilo*) by a humanism which gives initial and co-equally final primacy to the descent of God in the Incarnation. In this event, according to Pierre Bérulle (the French seventeenth-century Oratorian General who lies firmly within the lineages which I have just been discussing), God creates 'more than God' since he here makes up for the necessary divine lack of the worship of himself as an experience of grateful dependence. (This consideration need not necessarily imply an ontological necessity for incarnation.) Thus if, for Eckhart, the human soul in its ground creates itself (though in terms of Trinitarian relationality), Bérulle balances this notion with the thought that God himself has from eternity contingently received himself as something created.

---

[52] Nicholas of Cusa, *De Visione Dei* 7; *De Dato Patris Luminum* 2; Pierre Bérulle, *Oeuvres de la Piété* xxxii–xxxiii (Paris: Cerf, 1995–6) pp. 32, 33. See also Mojsisch, *Meister Eckhart*, p. 131, Henri de Lubac, *Pic de la Mirandole* (Paris; Aubier-Montaigne, 1974) pp. 334–5 and Claude Bruaire, *L'être et l'esprit* (Paris: PUF, 1983) esp. pp. 9–88.

[53] See Nicholas of Cusa, *De Docta Ignorantia*, III 3; Milbank and Pickstock, *Truth in Aquinas*, pp. 60–88; S.-T. Bonino, 'La théologie de la vérité dans *La Lectura super Ioannem* de Saint Thomas d'Aquin', in *Revue Thomist, Veritas* special issue, Jan–June 2004, pp. 141–66.

So in the Incarnation, God as God was able perfectly to fulfil the worship of God which is nevertheless, as worship, only possible for the creature.[54] This descent is repeated and perpetuated in the eucharist which gives rise to the *ecclesia*, that always 'other-governed' rather than autonomous human community, which yet is the beginning of universal community as such, since it is nothing other than the lived project of universal reconciliation. *Not* reducible to its institutional failures and yet not to be seen as a utopia *either*, since the reality of reconciliation, of restored unity-in-disparity, must presuppose itself if it is to be realizable (always in some very small degree) in time and so must be always already begun. The Incarnation was the 'impossible' arrival of that always-already and for that reason involved the coincidence of a finite personality with an infinite *hypostasis*. The concrete social realization of this always-already must run, as Rowan Williams frequently emphasizes, only through and despite the mess of constant institutional wranglings and re-negotiations, as well as inter-personal tribulations (since we must not forget that 'Church' may most be there when two or three idly or perplexedly wander besides a river). *Although* ontologically non-reactive, it is always temporally present *despite* temporal false deprivations.

Therefore I hope that my integrated discourse in this book which is at once that of reason and of faith and also – both fortunately and lamentably – of neither, successfully points beyond both liberalism and positivism in every sense. It was not intended as offering either simply the formal nor simply the chosen, but rather as aspiring to echo, however remotely, the sounding shapes of shared celestial glory.

The text of this second edition has been in places slightly modified (especially in Part Four) to ensure that it is more in keeping with my original intentions, as well as substantially in line with my current thinking. In particular, I have adjusted my presentation of the thought of Deleuze; slightly modified my account of de Lubac;[55] rendered the account of Plato and Socratic dialectics still more positive; and removed exaggerations of the differences between Augustine and Aquinas. At several points in the text certain claims have been somewhat qualified or re-configured.

I have also corrected factual mistakes, grammatical solecisms, diacritical superfluities and some of the grosser stylistic infelicities. I hope that all these changes will render the book now more useful to the reader, and I have in addition provided several cross-references to my own more recent writings and to those within, or sympathetic to, the 'Radically Orthodox' perspective. Here again I hope that this will assist readers to make connections between some older and some newer thoughts. The alterations do not, however, amount to a complete revision. I felt that this would be inappropriate, first

---

[54] Pierre Bérulle, *Oeuvres de la Piété* XIII. And see Jean-Louis Chrétien's wonderful essay, 'The offering of the world', in *The Ark of Speech*, trans. Andrew Brown (London: Routledge, 2004) pp. 111–49.

[55] This needs to be supplemented by my new book *The Suspended Middle*.

of all because the book belongs to a specific time and place of composition and secondly because adequate modifications would have made an already very long book impossibly long. Ideally I feel that the book should say more about the Middle Ages, more about the history of rights theory, more about certain intersections of theory with practice (for example in relation to 'charity') and more about the social, narrative and ontological ideas of the Bible itself, particularly St Paul. However, to some extent I or else others have tried to make good these deficiencies elsewhere.[56] Yet others, quite independently, have done work that also tends in these directions.[57]

I would like to thank everyone who took the time to read the first edition of this book, and still more all those who have done me the honour of writing about it, whether positively, negatively or critically. Their responses have already rendered it a different book from the one that I wrote and all have contributed to the making of this new edition.

Thanks are due also to Andrew Humphries and other editors at Blackwell who saw this second edition through to production.

Finally I should like to express my gratitude to Rebecca Harkin, Publisher for Blackwell's religion and theology list, who suggested that I prepare this revised version in the first place and managed to overcome my considerable reluctance to do so.

Southwell, Nottinghamshire, May 2005

---

[56] See in particular, for a brief treatment of Pauline political theology and a response to critical discussions of my ecclesiology by Rowan Williams, Fergus Kerr and others, John Milbank, 'Enclaves, or, where is the Church' in *New Blackfriars*, special issue, pp. 341–52. See also, John Milbank, 'The invocation of Clio', in *Journal of Religious Ethics*, March 2005, pp. 3–45 for an extensive response to the *Journal of Religious Ethics* special issue (summer 2004) (see nn. 6, 26 above). The various sections of my response on historical method, Augustine and fallenness, Kant and Swedenborg, charity and sympathy and John Ruskin, all supply in effect crucial footnotes to different sections of *Theology and Social Theory*. There was no space to include a further section on Brian Tierney's important treatment of the history of rights theory, but I hope to publish this material in some form in the future. Briefly, I accept Tierney's contention against Richard Tuck (whom I substantially follow in chapter 1 of this book) that something like 'claim rights' are well-rooted in medieval corporate law independently of nominalism-voluntarism. However, I contend that the presence of a notion of a right to claim an objective *ius* to the possession of something, or relatively free disposal of it, does not amount to a liberal grounding of right in self-ownership or absolute ownership, since it is still granted by equitable distribution in the first place, nor imply that a free and rightful disposing of something need not be always primarily attentive to considerations of the common good. Where Tierney locates a genuine shift towards liberalism in Bonaventure and Godfrey of Fontaines and rightly notes that these are independent of nominalism, he does not fully take cognizance of the fact that they are still linked to tendencies that stress the priority of will over intellect (with a linked tendency to follow Abelard in shifting the moral focus from act to intention and motivation) and lean towards a univocal conception of perfection terms as well as of the interaction of divine and human causality. For logical reasons it was within this broad current that nominalism and a more extreme voluntarism later arose.

[57] See in particular, on the Bible, Oliver O'Donovan, *The Desire of the Nations: Rediscovering the Roots of Political Theology* (Cambridge: CUP, 1996).

Introduction

This book is addressed both to social theorists and to theologians. To social theorists I shall attempt to disclose the possibility of a sceptical demolition of modern, secular social theory from a perspective with which it is at variance: in this case, that of Christianity. I will try to demonstrate that all the most important governing assumptions of such theory are bound up with the modification or the rejection of orthodox Christian positions. These fundamental intellectual shifts are, I shall argue, no more rationally 'justifiable' than the Christian positions themselves.

The book can, therefore, be read as an exercise in sceptical relativism. If my Christian perspective is persuasive, then this should be a persuasion intrinsic to the Christian *logos* itself, not the apologetic mediation of a supposedly neutral human reason. However, to theologians, I offer my perspectival reading for positive appropriation. What follows is intended to overcome the pathos of modern theology, and to restore in postmodern terms, the possibility of theology as a metadiscourse.

The pathos of modern theology is its false humility. For theology, this must be a fatal disease, because once theology surrenders its claim to be a metadiscourse, it cannot any longer articulate the word of the creator God, but is bound to turn into the oracular voice of some finite idol, such as historical scholarship, humanist psychology, or transcendental philosophy. If theology no longer seeks to position, qualify or criticize other discourses, then it is inevitable that these discourses will position theology: for the necessity of an ultimate organizing logic (as I shall argue in Part Four) cannot be wished away. A theology 'positioned' by secular reason suffers two characteristic forms of confinement. Either it idolatrously connects knowledge of God with some particular immanent field of knowledge – 'ultimate' cosmological causes, or 'ultimate' psychological and subjective needs. Or else it is confined to intimations of a sublimity beyond representation, so functioning to confirm negatively the questionable idea of an autonomous secular realm, completely transparent to rational understanding.

I have chosen to contest this secular positioning of theology within one particular field: that of social theory. This is the most obvious site of struggle, because theology has rightly become aware of the (absolute) degree to which it is a contingent historical construct emerging from, and reacting back upon, particular social practices conjoined with particular semiotic and figural codings. It is important to realize that my entire case is constructed from a complete *concession* as to this state of affairs, and that the book offers no proposed restoration of a pre-modern Christian position. However, there is a very common perception amongst theologians that once this concession is made, most of what is to be known about social processes in general and the socio-historical 'aspects' (an unwarranted qualification) of Christianity in particular, must be learned from social scientists. Contemporary 'political theologians' tend to fasten upon a particular social theory, or else put together their own eclectic theoretical mix, and then work out what residual place is left for Christianity and theology within the reality that is supposed to be authoritatively described by such a theory. Curiously enough, theologians appear specially eager to affirm both the 'scientific' and the 'humanist' discourses of modernity, although one can, perhaps, suggest reasons for this. First, the faith of humanism has become a substitute for a transcendent faith now only half-subscribed to. Second, there is a perceived need to discover precisely how to fulfil Christian precepts about charity and freedom in contemporary society in an uncontroversial manner, involving cooperation with the majority of non-Christian fellow citizens. Purportedly scientific diagnoses and recommendations fulfil precisely this role.

Yet the alliance of theology with the modernist legacy of social theory from the nineteenth century, which is at once 'scientific' and 'humanist', appears all the more curious in the light of recent developments within social theory itself. First of all, those 'postmodernist' thinkers broadly influenced by Nietzsche have tended to dismantle the claims both of sociology and the Marxist-Hegelian tradition to uncover the governing factors of human association and to tell naturalistic, evolutionary stories about the whole of human history. While the Nietzschean tracing of cultural formations to the will-to-power still results in a 'suspicion' of religion, it also tends to assert the inevitably religious or mythic-ritual shape that these formations must take. In this mode of suspicion, therefore, there ceases to be any social or economic reality that is permanently more 'basic' than the religious.

Secondly, the question has now arisen for social theory as to whether Nietzschean suspicion is the final and truly non-metaphysical mode of secular reason, or else itself embodies an ontology of power and conflict which is simply another *mythos*, a kind of re-invented paganism. To pass critically beyond Nietzsche is to pass into a recognition of the necessity and yet the ungrounded character of some sort of metanarrative, some privileged transcendent factor, even when it comes disguised as the constant element in an immanent process. At this new critical juncture, which is postmodern, yet also post-Nietzschean, one recognizes that suppositions about transcendence are ungrounded and mutually incommensurable, although necessary for the slightest cultural decision. This idea of the critical non-avoidability of the theological and metaphysical is canvassed in very diverse yet not wholly disconnected ways by Alasdair MacIntyre, Gillian Rose (despite the fact that her project cannot be strictly classified as either postmodern or post-Nietzschean), René Girard and Guy Lardreau with Christian Jambet.

An extraordinary contrast therefore emerges between political theology on the one hand, and postmodern and post-Nietzschean social theory on the other. Theology accepts secularization and the autonomy of secular reason; social theory increasingly finds secularization paradoxical, and implies that the mythic-religious can never be left behind. Political theology is intellectually atheistic; post-Nietzschean social theory suggests the practical inescapability of worship.

The present book attempts to take cognizance of this strange situation, and to persuade theologians to acknowledge theoretical developments which they have woefully ignored. I wish to challenge both the idea that there is a significant sociological 'reading' of religion and Christianity, which theology must 'take account of', and the idea that theology must borrow its diagnoses of social ills and recommendations of social solutions entirely from Marxist (or usually sub-Marxist) analysis, with some sociological admixture. Two of the central chapters of this book, chapter 5, 'Policing the Sublime' and chapter 7, 'Founding the Supernatural' are devoted to these respective purposes.

However, these attempts can only carry conviction if I succeed in demonstrating the questionability of the assumptions upon which secular social theory rests. To this end I have adopted an 'archaeological' approach and traced the genesis of the main forms of secular reason, in such a fashion as to unearth the arbitrary moments in the construction of their logic. This object could have been partially achieved by a deconstructive analysis of the present manifestations of these discourses, but the archaeological approach has at least two inestimable advantages. First of all, it enables me to show how the genesis of discourse is intertwined with the genesis of a new practice; in particular this allows me to demonstrate that secular social theory *only applies* to secular society, which it helps to sustain. Secondly, it permits me to show just how elusive 'the secular' really is. For, on my reading, secular discourse does not just borrow inherently inappropriate modes of expression from religion as the only discourse to hand (this is Hans Blumenberg's interpretation)[1], but is actually *constituted* in its secularity by 'heresy' in relation to orthodox Christianity, or else a rejection of Christianity that is more 'neopagan' than simply anti-religious.

By taking the reader through this genetic account, I hope to make it apparent that 'scientific' social theories are themselves theologies or antitheologies in disguise. Contemporary theologies which forge alliances with such theories are often unwittingly rediscovering concealed affinities between positions that partake of the same historical origins.

---

[1] Hans Blumenberg, *The Legitimacy of the Modern Age*, trans. Robert M. Wallace (Cambridge, Mass: MIT Press, 1986) pp. 3–120.

The book is divided into four sub-treatises, corresponding to four distinct variants of secular reason. The first treatise, 'Theology and Liberalism' is a prolegomenon to the next three, because it is in the discourses of liberalism – 'scientific politics' and political economy – that the secular is first constructed. Here I show that from the outset the secular is complicit with an 'ontology of violence', a reading of the world which assumes the priority of force and tells how this force is best managed and confined by counter-force. Secular reason has continued to make this ontology seem coterminous with the discovery of the human construction of the cultural world; I seek to demonstrate that the latter is a distinct thesis and that human construction does not *necessarily* mark out an autonomous human space. It was made to do so by Hobbes, but other early modern thinkers construe human making as an opening to transcendence, so inaugurating a kind of 'counter-modernity' which later, through the writings of Vico, Hamann, Herder, Coleridge, Kierkegaard and Blondel, continues to shadow actual, secular modernity.

The theme of the human construction of culture is, however, aporetically crossed in secular reason by the idea of the cultural construction of humanity. Where this moment is privileged, secular reason produces a discourse about providence, which, unlike medieval theology, violates the distinction between primary and secondary causes, and invokes a final cause – 'God' or 'nature' – to plug some supposed gap in immanent understanding. This kind of fusion of theological and scientific discourse has been identified by Amos Funkenstein.[2] However, he sees it as terminating with Kant. I see it as an element in political economy, and even as reinforced in the intellectual moves which generate 'sociology'.

The second part of the book, 'Theology and Positivism', traces this genesis. It stresses in particular how there is a very complex, and by no means merely oppositional, relationship between theology and positivism; the latter term in fact indicates a wider field of affinities than is commonly supposed. In this expanded sense, *all* sociology, including Weberian sociology, turns out to be positivist, and this has implications for how theology should relate to sociological theses. In effect, theology encounters in sociology only a theology, and indeed a church in disguise, but a theology and a church dedicated to promoting a certain secular consensus. The final chapter of Part Two seeks to 'end' the dialogue between theology and sociology.

The third part of the book, 'Theology and Dialectics', shows how the most radical and critical elements in Hegelian-Marxist tradition are precisely those which come nearest to deconstructing the secular, and, in the case of Hegel, to promoting a *thinking* which embodies a specifically Christian *logos*, 'beyond secular reason'. However they allow these moments to be entirely re-recruited by scientific politics and political economy, conjoining these to Christianity (Hegel) or Utopia (Marx) by the thread of a 'gnostic' plot about a historically

---

[2] Amos Funkenstein, *Theology and the Scientific Imagination from the Middle Ages to the Seventeenth Century* (Princeton, NJ: Princeton University Press, 1986).

necessary fall and reconstruction of being, with a gain achieved through violence undergone. The final chapter of this section seeks to show how theology which is over-enthusiastic about Marxism (and sociology), and underrates an earlier tradition of specifically Christian socialism, is itself a theology which has surrendered to liberalism in the form of transcendental philosophy.

In all three of these treatises, the reader will discern two often confused and yet different voices speaking. The first is that of the classical and medieval inheritance: a 'MacIntyrean voice' that is Platonic-Aristotelian-Augustinian-Thomist, opposing the modern 'management of power' in the name of ancient virtue, or common consensus round metaphysically secured values. The second is a 'nihilistic voice' which offers a historicizing critique, seeking to show that every supposedly objective reasoning simply promotes its own difference, and disguises the power which is its sole support.

The final treatise of the book, 'Theology and Difference', makes explicit the character of this nihilism, disentangles the two voices, and pits them against each other. The real perspective of the book then turns out to be that of virtue rather than nihilistic difference. However, there are two further twists which partially separate my work from that of MacIntyre. First, I reject MacIntyre's merely *philosophic* realism in favour of 'linguistic idealism' and a variant of pragmatism – even though this assumes a realist cast within my final *theological* perspective. Secondly, my perspective is that of *Christian virtue*, and I contend that this is more critical of antique virtue than MacIntyre allows; that it is, in fact, a kind of synthesis of virtue with difference, and stands over against both antiquity and modernity.

Indeed, I argue that, from the perspective of Christian virtue, there emerges to view a hidden thread of continuity between antique reason and modern, secular reason. This thread of continuity is the theme of 'original violence'. Antique thought and politics assumes some naturally given element of chaotic conflict which must be tamed by the stability and self-identity of reason. Modern thought and politics (most clearly articulated by Nietzsche) assumes that there is *only* this chaos, which cannot be tamed by an opposing transcendent principle, but can be immanently controlled by subjecting it to rules and giving irresistible power to those rules in the form of market economies and sovereign politics. If one tries, like MacIntyre, to oppose antique thought to modern thought, then the attempt will fail because antique thought – as Plato already saw in *The Sophist* – is deconstructible into 'modern' thought: a cosmos including both chaos and reason implies an ultimate principle, the 'difference' between the two, which is *more* than reason, and enshrines a permanent conflict.

Christianity, however, recognizes no original violence. It construes the infinite not as chaos, but as a harmonic peace which is yet beyond the circumscribing power of any totalizing reason. Peace no longer depends upon the reduction to the self-identical, but is the *sociality* of harmonious difference. Violence, by contrast, is always a secondary willed intrusion upon this possible infinite order (which is actual for God). Such a Christian logic is *not* deconstructible by modern secular reason; rather, it is Christianity which exposes the non-necessity of supposing, like the Nietzscheans, that difference, non-totalization and indeterminancy of meaning *necessarily* imply arbitrariness and violence. To suppose that they do is merely to subscribe to a particular encoding of reality. Christianity, by contrast, is the coding of transcendental difference as peace.

This vital argument is made in my last chapter, where I briefly try to sketch out a theology aware of itself as culturally constructed, yet able to elaborate its own self-understanding in terms of a substantive and critical theory of society in general. The emergent 'third voice' of this final chapter, beyond both antique virtue and nihilistic difference, picks up the shadowy hints of a 'counter-modern' position – historicist and pragmatist, yet *theologically* realist – as suggested in particular by Maurice Blondel. In such a position, no claim is made simplistically to 'represent' an objective social reality; instead, the social knowledge advocated is but the continuation of ecclesial practice, the imagination in action of a peaceful, reconciled social order, beyond even the violence of legality. It is this lived narrative which itself both projects and 'represents' the triune God, who is transcendental peace through differential relation. And the same narrative is also a continuous reading and positioning of other social realities. If truth is social, it can only be through a claim to offer the ultimate 'social science' that theology can establish itself and give any content to the notion of 'God'. And in practice, providing such a content means making an historical difference in the world.

As I shall finally argue, the difference that Christianity has made includes a tragic dimension, because its failure to sustain a 'peace beyond the law' enabled a transition from the antique containing of a given violence by reason, to the modern regulation of violence through greater violence. Yet the capacity of nihilism to deconstruct antiquity shows that there can be no going back; only Christian theology now offers a discourse able to position and overcome nihilism itself. This is why it is so important to reassert theology as a master discourse; theology, alone, remains the discourse of non-mastery.

Part I

Theology and Liberalism

1

Political Theology and the New Science of Politics

The New Object of Political Science

Once, there was no 'secular'. And the secular was not latent, waiting to fill more space with the steam of the 'purely human', when the pressure of the sacred was relaxed. Instead there was the single community of Christendom, with its dual aspects of *sacerdotium* and *regnum* The *saeculum*, in the medieval era, was not a space, a domain, but a time – the interval between fall and *eschaton* where coercive justice, private property and impaired natural reason must make shift to cope with the unredeemed effects of sinful humanity.

The secular as a domain had to be instituted or *imagined*, both in theory and in practice. This institution is not correctly grasped in merely negative terms as a desacralization. It belongs to the received wisdom of sociology to interpret Christianity as itself an agent of secularization, yet this thesis is totally bound up with the one-sided negativity of the notion of desacralizing; a metaphor of the removal of the superfluous and additional to leave a residue of the human, the natural and the self-sufficient. For this negative conception it is convenient that there should always have been some perception of the pure remainder, and the hybrid 'Judeo-Christianity' is cast in this role: from its inception, it supposedly removes sacral allure from the cosmos and then, inevitably, from the political, the social, the economic, the artistic – the human 'itself'.[1]

Received sociology altogether misses the positive institution of the secular, because it fully embraces the notion of humanism as the perennial destiny of the West and of human autonomous freedom as always gestating in the womb of 'Judeo-Christianity'. However, in this respect it is doomed to repeat the self-understanding of Christianity arrived at in late-medieval nominalism, the Protestant reformation and seventeenth-century Augustinianism, which completely privatized, spiritualized and transcendentalized the sacred, and concurrently reimagined nature, human action and society as a sphere of autonomous, sheerly formal power. Sociology projects this specific mutation

---

[1] See chapters 4 and 5 below.

in Christianity back to its origins and even to the Bible. It interprets the theological transformation at the inception of modernity as a genuine 'reformation' which fulfils the destiny of Christianity to let the spiritual be the spiritual, without public interference, and the public be the secular, without private prejudice. Yet this interpretation preposterously supposes that the new theology simply brought Christianity to its true essence by lifting some irksome and misplaced sacred ecclesial restrictions on the free market of the secular, whereas, in fact, it instituted an entirely different economy of power and knowledge and had to invent 'the political' and 'the State', just as much as it had to invent 'private religion'.

This consideration should govern how we view the first social theory that claimed to be a 'science', namely 'political science'. With the writings of Grotius, Hobbes and Spinoza, political theory achieved a certain highly ambiguous 'autonomy' with regard to theology. However, autonomization was not achieved in the sphere of knowledge alone; it was only possible because the new science of politics both assumed and constructed for itself a new autonomous object – the political – defined as a field of pure power. Secular 'scientific' understanding of society was, from the outset, only the self-knowledge of the self-construction of the secular as power. What theology has forgotten is that it cannot either contest or learn from this understanding as such, but has either to accept or deny its object.

This autonomous object was, first of all, 'natural'. According to Grotius, the natural laws governing property and sovereignty could be known *etsi Deus non daretur*.[2] For Aquinas, natural law had meant transcendental equity and therefore precisely that which conjoined the particular instance of justice to the divine and eternal in the surpassing of all mere regularity of convention.[3] But now, for modernity, natural law transcribes the sealed-off totality of nature, where eternal justice consists in the most invariable rules. These are not derived (as for Aquinas) from the inner tendencies of the Aristotelian practical reason towards the *telos* of the good, but rather from purely theoretical reflections on the necessity for every creature to ensure its own self-preservation. Because nature, since the Renaissance, was regarded as an 'open book' which might be almost exhaustively read, Grotius, Hobbes and Spinoza can be confident that the self-preserving *conatus* provides the universal hermeneutic key for both nature and society.[4] And the *etsi* is entirely a ruse, because the finite totality presupposes that nature is a legally governed domain, obeying completely regular laws of the operation of power and passion, which yet are wilfully laid down by the retired deity. The bond between 'natural' and 'social' science is here perfect, and present even as far

[2] Hugo Grotius, *The Law of War and Peace*, trans. Francis W. Kelsey et al., *Prolegomena*, XI (Indianapolis: Bobbs-Merrill, 1925) pp. 9–30.

[3] Thomas Aquinas, *Summa Theologiae* II.I.Q.94.

[4] Robert D. Cumming, *Human Nature and History: A Study of the Development of Liberal Political Thought*, vol. 2 (Chicago: Chicago University Press, 1969). Benedict de Spinoza, *A Theological-Political Treatise*, trans. R. H. M. Elwes, ch. 12 (New York: Dover, 1951) p. 200.

back as Pierre d'Ailly, for whom an exclusively positive character of legal obligation reflects a natural causality which is the merely accidental regularity of divine, legally imposed connections between entirely discrete particulars.[5]

The autonomous object, although natural, was *also* artificial. The new political knowledge could rest on the material foundations of *conatus*, but from then on, the knowledge of power was simply a retracing of the paths of human construction, an analysis of *factum* (the made). Here again, social science did not lag behind natural science, but rather, in both cases, the specificity of modern 'scientific' knowledge is to do with an 'artificial' method and an infallible knowledge of artifice, as the seventeenth century was universally aware (although there were divergent sceptical, rationalist and 'experimentalist' versions of this specificity).[6] Already, as far back as the *trecento*, Coluccio Salutati declared legal knowledge to be more certain than medical knowledge because it lay more within the command and insight of the human will.[7] Later, for Hobbes, Wilkins and Locke, ethical understanding is more susceptible to geometrization or probabilization than physics because here alone technical control can be coextensive with the object of understanding.[8]

The conception of society as a human product and therefore 'historical' remains one of the basic assumptions of secular social science, although it has always been aporetically crossed, as we shall see in the next chapter, by the accompanying reflection that human beings are the product of society. Not only to social scientists, but also to theologians like Harvey Cox, it has consequently seemed obvious that the sphere of the artificial, of *factum*, marks out the space of secularity. For Harvey Cox it is precisely this area of the free play of human constructive choice which formed the 'dominion' granted to Adam in Eden, as the counterpart to the individual and secret submission of the soul to God.[9]

However, the 'obvious' connection of the *factum* and the secular can and must be called into question. It is not enough just to point out, like Hannah Arendt or Jurgen Habermas, that the concentration of post-Hobbesian political science on instrumental reason tended to obscure another dimension of human action, namely Aristotelian *praxis*, where one seeks not to control with precision, but with a necessary approximation to persuade, exhort and

---

[5] Francis Oakley, *The Political Thought of Pierre d'Ailly* (New Haven and London: Yale University Press, 1964) pp. 17ff, 71–89.

[6] Amos Funkenstein, *Theology and the Scientific Imagination* (Princeton, NJ: Princeton University Press, 1986) pp. 327–345. Steven Shapin and Simon Schaffer, *Leviathan and the Air-Pump* (Princeton, NJ: Princeton University Press, 1985).

[7] Coluccio Salutati, *De Nobilitate Legum et Medicinae* (Florence: Vallechi, 1947) pp. 40–55, 95.

[8] W. Molesworth (ed.), *The English Works of Thomas Hobbes*, vol. 1 'Elements of Philosophy: the First Section Concerning Body' (London, 1845). *De Corpore Politico*, IV, p. 126, pp. 73–4, 87. John Wilkins, *Of the Principle and Duties of Natural Religion*, ch. 2 (London, 1680) pp. 12–19. John Locke, *Essay Concerning Human Understanding* (Oxford: Oxford University Press, 1975) pp. 515–18, 548, 552, 643.

[9] Harvey Cox, *The Secular City* (London: SCM, 1967) pp. 21–4.

encourage a growth in the virtues as ends in themselves.[10] This displacement of classical politics by a new political 'science' is of course very important, yet what these thinkers ignore is the fact that the sphere of the 'artificial' is not necessarily identical with that of the instrumental, any more than poetry is merely technology.

To make it appear that the scope of *factum* is necessarily identical with the rights of the secular, thinkers like Hobbes had to construct a *factum* whose essence was its formality and predictability. One can begin to grasp the contingency and the questionability of this procedure, if one considers as a contemporary counter-example the new 'conceptist' notion of the Idea in mannerist art-theory and Baroque rhetoric.[11] Here, precisely the same new recognition of the humanly artificial arises, such that the artistic or poetic 'Idea' is no longer what 'precedes' the work in the artist's mind as a reflection of the ideas of God, but instead becomes that which is conveyed as meaning to the receiver from the peculiar constitution of *the work itself*. Yet this is not a Hobbesian, nominalist move, because the Idea, though now inseparable from its own 'image', still conserves for the mannerists the full Platonic value of a participation in divine understanding. Behind this 'pragmatist' reconception of the idea one can trace, not a secularizing impulse, but rather influences of Trinitarian theology, where the Father has eternal understanding only in the 'image' of the Son. The conceptist 'Idea' is already anticipated by Nicholas of Cusa's view that *factibilitas* is the condition of possibility for human knowing and belongs to a human conjectural *explicatio* of the divine intellectual 'comprehension' in the second person of the Trinity.[12]

The mannerist counter-example shows that far from the *factum* (the made) self-evidently staking out an area of secular autonomy, it could, on the contrary, for the heirs of a Christian-humanist sensibility be seen as the gateway to transcendence. Hence just as 'obvious' as the Hobbesian move was an effortless Baroque integration of the 'modern' discovery of human making into a traditional Platonic, participatory framework. It would therefore be legitimate to look for an alternative 'Baroque' politics that was equally 'modern' yet remained both humanist and metaphysical – later one catches traces of such a thing in the writings of Giambattista Vico.[13]

[10] Jurgen Habermas, 'The classical doctrine of politics in relation to social philosophy', in *Theory and Practice*, trans. John Viertel (London: Heinemann, 1974) pp. 41–82.

[11] Sforza Pallavicino, *Trattato dello stile e del dialogo*, ch. 10 (Rome: Masardi, 1662) pp. 112–18. Jean-Marie Wagner, 'Théorie de l'image et pratique iconologique', in *Baroque*, 9–10 (1980) p. 71. Guido Morpurgo Tagliabue, 'Aristotelismo e Barocco', in E. Castelli (ed.) *Retorica e Barocco* (Rome: Bocca, 1955) pp. 119–95.

[12] Sforza Pallavicino, *Trattato dello stile*, ch. 1 (1662). Nicholas of Cusa, 'On actualised possibility' ('De Possest'), in Jasper Hopkins (ed.) *A Concise Introduction to the Philosophy of Nicholas of Cusa* (1941) pp. 95–7; *De Docta Ignorantia*, III, 3; III, 2; *The Idiot*, introduced by W. R. Dennes (Los Angeles: California State Library, 1942) p. 11. John Milbank, 'Man as creative and historical being in the theology of Nicholas of Cusa', *Downside Review*, vol. 97, no. 329, October 1979.

[13] Giambattista Vico, *On the Most Ancient Wisdom of the Italians*, trans. L. M. Palmer, I i, VII (New York: Cornell University Press, 1988) pp. 45, 97–104. 'Orazioni Inaugurali', in Paolo Cristofolini (ed.) *Opere Filosofiche* (Florence: Sansoni, 1971). 'Institutioni Oratorie', in G. Ferrari

Both insofar as it was deemed natural and insofar as it was deemed artificial, the new autonomous object of political science was not, therefore, simply 'uncovered'. The space of the secular had to be invented as the space of 'pure power'. However, this invention was itself, as we shall now see, a theological achievement, just as only a particular sort of theology could pronounce the *etsi Deus non daretur*.

The Theological Construction of Secular Politics

For the *factum* (the made) to become identified with the secular, it was necessary that Adam's *dominium* be redefined as power, property, active right, and absolute sovereignty, and that Adam's personhood be collapsed into this redefined mastery that is uniquely 'his own'.

Dominium over oneself, 'self-government', was traditionally a matter of the rational mastery of the passions and this was also the basis for one's legitimate control and possession of external objects. One's self-identity, what was 'proper' to one and what belonged to 'propriety', was very clearly bound up with the rational and ethical management of one's 'property'.[14] Yet at the margins of this classical and medieval theme there persists the trace of a more brutal and original *dominium*, the unrestricted lordship over what lies within one's power – oneself, one's children, land or slaves – in Roman private law.

In the later Middle Ages and in the seventeenth century this original Roman sense not only returns, but for the first time advances from the margins into the centre. Originally this 'sheer power' was before and outside the city, belonging to the sphere of the household, but now, for the developers of the Roman law tradition, legal *ius*, which forms the bonds of justice within the political community, is identified with *dominium*.[15] This puts an end to Aquinas's attempt to tame Roman *dominium* by understanding Adam's *dominium* as *dominium utile*, a property right of free 'procuration and disposal' whose final justification was still *usus* by society in general.[16] Instead, *dominium* is traced by Jean Gerson to the *facultas* which possesses the power to do as it likes with its own, such that a property right is as much 'the right to exchange' as the 'right to make use of'.[17] However, this *facultas* is also for Gerson the whole root of natural law, such that a *ius* is no longer what is 'right' or just, or a 'claim right' to justice, but active right over property. As the traditional link

---

(ed.) *Opere Complete* (Milan: Società Tipografica, 1852–4). Andrea Sorrentino, *La Retorica e la Poetica di Vico ossia la Prima Concezione Estetica del Linguaggio* (Turin: Bocca, 1927).

[14] Cumming, *Human Nature and History*, pp. 129–136. Grotius *The Law of War and Peace*, Bk. I, V, p. 35. Thomas Hobbes, *Leviathan*, Part II, ch. 18 (Harmondsworth: Penguin, 1968) p. 234.

[15] Richard Tuck, *Natural Rights Theories: Their Origin and Development* (Cambridge: Cambridge University Press, 1979) pp. 3–20.

[16] Aquinas, *ST* II.II.Q.66.a1, a2.

[17] Jean Gerson, 'De Vita Spirituali Animae', in P. Glorieuse (ed.) *Oeuvres Complètes – Lectio Tertia*. (Pierre d'Ailly collaborated on this work). (Paris: Desclée et Cie, 1962) pp. 141–5.

between person and ownership remains, this means that self-identity, the *suum*, is no longer essentially related to divine rational illumination, or ethics, but is a sheer 'self-occupation' or 'self-possession'. 'Every man has a property in his own person', as Locke will later say.[18]

Dominium or 'the private', which for Roman law was at first the natural and 'chaotic', to be restrained by the laws of justice, has now so far moved into the *forum* as to abolish the antique public space altogether. Thus Sir Robert Filmer, who traced all political sovereignty back to Adam's private and paternal power, achieved thereby a hierocratic genealogy of an entirely *modern* sort. A fundamentally common origin for both private property and state sovereignty was also affirmed (though in a different manner) by Grotius and Hobbes.[19] The political state, for the nominalist Hobbes, is only conceivable as an 'Artificial Man' (Leviathan) whose identity and reality are secured by an unrestricted right to preserve and control his own artificial body.[20] The contradiction of Hobbes's State, however, resides in the fact that, while it is artificially generated through the wills of many private persons, these persons can only be public persons capable of mutual recognition as bearers of private rights, once the 'nominal' being is really and truly enacted through the sheerly physical mechanisms of sovereign power. It is here, precisely, that one perceives the antinomic strain in the formal, instrumental and secular account of *factum*. Because it is rooted in an individualistic account of the will, oblivious to questions of its providential purpose in the hands of God, it has difficulty in understanding any 'collective making', or genuinely social process. To keep notions of the State free from any suggestions of a collective essence or generally recognized *telos*, it must be constructed on the individualist model of *dominium*.

It is in this inescapable imperative of nominalism-voluntarism that one discovers the kinship at root of modern absolutism with modern liberalism. The same notion of *dominium* promotes both Hobbes's dictum that the sovereign power can never bind itself, *and* his view that the greatest liberty of subjects depends on the silence of the law.[21] It is precisely the formal character of state power as guaranteeing personal security and non-interference in 'private' pursuits (selling, contracts, education, choice of abode) which demands that this power be otherwise unlimited and absolutely alone. Hobbes was simply more clear-sighted than later apparently more 'liberal' thinkers like Locke in realizing that a liberal peace requires a single undisputed power, but not necessarily a continued majority consensus, which may not be forthcoming.

One can conclude that 'unrestricted' private property, 'absolute sovereignty' and 'active rights', which compose the 'pure-power' object of the

---

[18] John Locke, *Two Treatises on Government*, Book II, ch. 5 (Cambridge: Cambridge University Press, 1967) p. 27.

[19] James Tully, *A Discourse on Property* (Cambridge: Cambridge University Press, 1980) p. 58.

[20] Hobbes, *Leviathan*, the Introduction pp. 81–3.

[21] Ibid., Part II, ch. 21, p. 271 (marginal summary).

new politics, are all the emanations of a new anthropology which begins with human persons as individuals and yet defines their individuality essentialistically, as 'will' or 'capacity' or 'impulse to self-preservation'.

The question then becomes, how did this anthropology ever secure legitimacy in a theological and metaphysical era? The answer is that it was theologically promoted. *Dominium*, as power, could only become the human essence, because it was seen as reflecting the divine essence, a radical divine simplicity without even formal differentiation, in which, most commonly, a proposing 'will' is taken to stand for the substantial identity of will, essence and understanding. (Although the voluntarists rejected 'participation' in favour of a theology of will, it is precisely in their treatment of will that a shadow of participation seems to lurk).[22] The later Middle Ages retrieved in a new and more drastic guise the antique connection between monotheism and monarchic unity which was affirmed in Christian tradition by the semi-Arian Eusebius and then became part of both imperial and papal ideology. For this tradition, political substance is grounded in the unity and self-identity of the rational subject, whereas the orthodox Cappadocian Father, Gregory of Nazianzus, had pointed out that it is possible for a single person to be at variance with himself and affirmed that the 'Monarchy' implied by the Christian Trinity was more 'a union of mind, and an identity of motion, and a convergence of the elements to unity'.[23] In the thought of the nominalists, following Duns Scotus, the Trinity loses its significance as a prime location for discussing will and understanding in God and the relationship of God to the world.[24] No longer is the world participatorily enfolded within the divine expressive *Logos*, but instead a bare divine unity starkly confronts the other distinct unities which he has ordained.

It is possible to dispute the precise tenor of the more extreme voluntarist statements – to the effect, for example, that God might will us to hate himself.[25] This dispute, however, is not all important; what matters is the overwhelming nominalist stress on the gulf between God's *potentia ordinata*, his declared will, which is factually, precisely known and serves as the basis for legal covenants with humanity, and his *potentia absoluta*, the infinite power of God which is absolutely unknowable for theology and knowable only formally, for *logic*.[26] No doubt thinkers like Ockham and d'Ailly understood the divine concessions in his revealed will as always in fact expressions of his *misericordia*, but this cannot disguise the point that they derive the *force* of these concessions, our obligation with respect to them (for example, our obligation to keep the natural law, if we wish to merit grace, which God is

[22] S. E. Ozment, *Homo Spiritualis* (Leiden: E. J. Brill, 1969) pp. 25–26, 54–57, 83. H. A. Oberman, *The Harvest of Mediaeval Theology* (Cambridge, Mass.: Harvard University Press, 1963) p. 83.

[23] Gregory of Nazianzus, *Theological Orations*, III, 2. E. Peterson, 'Der Monotheismus als politisches Problem', in *Theologische Traktate* (Munich: Hochland, 1951).

[24] Etienne Gilson, *Jean Duns Scot* (Paris: Vrin, 1952) pp. 216–306.

[25] Oberman, *The Harvest of Mediaeval Theology*, pp. 92–8.

[26] Ibid., p. 51ff.

not *absolutely* bound to grant) from the formalism of a logic about power and rights.[27] Hence already for Gerson, Adam's *dominium* is in no way morally charged, but merely the consequence of Adam's *facultas*, a power greater in scope than other natural powers.[28] Yet because of the radical contingency which d'Ailly and Gerson attributed to the actual *according* of rights and obligations in natural law (as opposed to its formal truth, which holds even for God's absolute power) it is also the case for them that *dominium* is a grant of grace – but a mere *gratia gratis data* not *gratia gratis faciens*.[29] This dominance of logic and of the *potentia absoluta* is finally brought to a peak by Hobbes: 'The right of Nature, whereby God reigneth over men, and punisheth those that break his Lawes, is to be derived, not from his creating them, as if he required obedience as of gratitude for his benefits; but from his *Irresistible Power*'.[30]

In two ways, therefore, theology helped to determine the new anthropology and the new 'science' of politics. First of all, it ensured that men (*sic*), when enjoying unrestricted, unimpeded property rights and even more when exercising the rights of a sovereignty that 'cannot bind itself', come closest to the *imago dei*. Secondly, by abandoning participation in divine Being and Unity for a 'covenantal bond' between God and men, it provided a model for human interrelationships as 'contractual' ones.[31] It is not an accident that in Molina, the sixteenth-century Spanish Jesuit theologian, an identification of *dominium* with *ius* goes along with the idea that there is an area of 'sheer' human freedom in response to grace, whereas for Thomism even our freedom is mysteriously determined by God, without ceasing to be freedom.[32] Hence it can be seen how theology stakes out *factum* as an area of human autonomy, by making *dominium* into a matter of absolute sovereignty and absolute ownership. *This* is the space in which there *can be* a 'secular', or secular knowledge of the secular – and it is just as fictional as all other human topographies.

For this reason, it would be inadequate to suppose that late medieval and seventeeth-century voluntarism are 'ideological' legitimations of modern absolutism/liberalism regarded as 'really' secular and material processes. On the contrary, theology enters into the very construction of the new realities 'property' and 'sovereignty', helping to create a new space for human manoeuvre. For while it is true that there is a certain recuperation of the Roman patriarchalist notion of possession (though this shows that the *mythos* of the *law* is also constitutively necessary) *dominium* could only have achieved

[27] Oberman, *The Harvest of Mediaeval Theology*, p. 44.

A. S. McGrade, 'Ockham and individual rights', in Brian Tierney and Peter Lineham (eds.) *Authority and Power* (Cambridge: Cambridge University Press, 1980) pp. 149–65. Graham White, 'Pelagianisms' in *Viator*, vol. 20, 1989, pp. 233–54.

[28] Gerson, *De Vita Spirituali Animae*, p. 145. Tuck, *Natural Rights Theories*, p. 25ff.

[29] Oakley, *The Political Thought of Pierre d'Ailly*, pp. 66–92.

[30] Hobbes, *Leviathan*, Part II, ch. 31, p. 397. Carl Schmitt, *Politische Theologie: Vier Kapitel zur Lehre von der Souveranität* (Munich: Duncker und Humboldt, 1935) pp. 71, 49–66.

[31] Oberman, *The Harvest of Mediaeval Theology*, p. 93.

[32] Tuck, *Natural Rights Theories*, pp. 50–53. Jacques Maritain, *Integral Humanism*, trans. Joseph W. Evans (Notre Dame University Press, Notre Dame Ind., 1968) pp. 17–21.

universal sway in the context of a theology of creation *ex nihilo*, reinterpreted in terms of infinite, uninhibited power.

Yet this is not to say that what mattered was theory and not practice. On the contrary, the new theory was very much a mode of action. By laying claim to a 'plenitude' of quasi-imperial power early in the Middle Ages, the Papacy embarked on a course of adjudication which more and more forced it to decide issues in terms of formal rights. Here, as Max Weber realized, 'modern' rationalization and bureaucratization were already under way.[33] Moreover, this formalization, theologically grounded in the theory of the Papacy, served as an indispensable practical and theoretical resource in a period of increasing inner-ecclesiastical disputes amongst religious orders, between religious orders and the hierarchy and finally between Pope and Pope. Hence one discovers the beginning of modern 'contractual' arrangements in canon law regulations governing the dealings between different ecclesiastical bodies and the start of entrepreneurial practices in the external transactions of certain Cistercian monasteries.[34] Perhaps in reaction against the new, power-seeking reality of monastic ownership, the mendicant Franciscans sought to redefine apostolic poverty with the concept of a *simplex usus facti* in relation to possessions that was in no way a *dominium*.[35] The ultimate response to the radical threat inherent in this notion was not to reassert the Thomist *dominium utile* possessed by Adam even in paradise (a concept perhaps no less radical and also saner than the Franciscan one) but rather to press *dominium* back into the very construction of the subject, by founding the *ius* to anything in a natural or contractual *facultas*.[36] Modern natural rights theory had, as its 'practical' occasion, the need to declare traditional apostolic poverty and paradisal community to be, as it were, 'ontologically impossible'.

In retrospect, it appears that the *simplex usus facti* was itself also the start of a spiritualizing retreat whereby the need to disassociate the Church from formal coercive power turns into a wish also to depublicize it and separate it from any kind of rule whatsoever. The sort of poverty which is not 'a way of owning' but rather a simple 'not owning', is bound to become, in time, just 'poverty of the heart'. This retreat leaves vacant a formal, autonomous space where the Pope 'owns' the Franciscan possessions in the sense that he has the power to dispose of them.[37] Likewise, in the thought of a Franciscan conciliarist like Ockham, the Church as a collectivity has ceased to be a 'mystical' matter in the sacred sense, a corporeity focused on the eucharist, and 'mystical body' is now so nominalized that Gerson can apply the term to the

[33] See chapter 4 below.

[34] Randall Collins, *Weberian Sociological Theory* (Cambridge: Cambridge University Press, 1986) pp. 45–76. Oakley, *The Political Thought of Pierre d'Ailly*, p. 109.

[35] M. D. Lambert, *Franciscan Poverty* (London: SPCK, 1961) pp. 231–2.

[36] William of Ockham, *Opera Politica*, Vol. 3 (Manchester: Manchester University Press, 1940) pp. 466–7. Tuck, *Natural Rights Theories*, pp. 22–4.

[37] Lambert, *Franciscan Poverty*, pp. 243–4.

nation, France.[38] One should note here that conciliarists are on common ground with the papalists in arguing about church rule in terms of purely legal *dominium*, and the difference between a 'hierocratic absolutism' and a 'conciliar contractualism' is really an oscillation within a single *episteme*. Thus in the contrast between Aegidius Romanus's view that *dominium* is first granted by grace to the Pope, and Robert Fitzralph's view that there is a direct grant to each individual, one could say that there is already foreshadowed the contrast within a basic agreement between a Hobbes and a Locke.[39] Furthermore, the unrestricted scope of conciliar authority, especially as allowed and summoned by the Emperor, is no less a harbinger of absolutism than the canonical *plenitudo potestas* of the Pope, later invoked by Bodin in his invention of secular sovereignty.[40]

That it was first of all the Church, the *sacerdotium*, rather than the *regnum*, which assumed traits of modern secularity – legal formalization, rational instrumentalization, sovereign rule, economic contractualism – ought to give us pause for thought. In a way, it was the increasing failure of the Church to be the Church, to preserve the 'rule of the Gospel' in the monasteries, and somehow to extend this to the laity (a failure of which the Christian humanist movement was often profoundly aware), which created a moral vacuum which the *regnum* could not easily fill, because ideals of a *purely political* virtue had been half-obliterated by Christianity. In such a vacuum, it seems likely that formal instrumentalism must increasingly reign, and this becomes still more likely after the further ecclesiastical failure which led to a divided Christendom. However, this is a retrospectively interpolated likelihood; one much too easily assumes that this formalism would be inevitably forthcoming. On the contrary, one must suppose that it could only fill the gaps because it was elaborated in theological terms, and by an ecclesiastical practice increasingly ready to redraw the bounds of *regnum* and *sacerdotium* as that between public, coercive power (the hierocratic state) and private faith (the Church as consequently mere 'aggregate'). Hence it may be that the voluntarist theological legacy allowed Europe to survive the Reformation by helping to engender the extraordinary seventeenth-century discovery of a politics that might persist and grow altogether 'without virtue' and without any substantive consensus.

Modern Politics as Biblical Hermeneutics

So far, we have seen how 'the secular' became an artificial *space* which was sheer *dominium*, or the sphere of the arbitrary. However, modern political science had also to cope with the secular which remained an interval of *time* (the *saeculum*) and with that ecclesial time with which it was concurrent. The

---

[38] Oakley, *The Political Thought of Pierre d'Ailly*, p. 55ff.
[39] Ibid., pp. 71–2. Tuck, *Natural Rights Theories*, pp. 22–4.
[40] Jean Bodin, *Six Books of the Commonwealth*, trans. M. J. Todey (Oxford: Blackwell, 1964) p. 29.

new, secular *dominium* could not, according to the totalizing logic of wilful occupation which now mediated transcendence in the public realm, really tolerate a 'political' Church as a cohabitant. Hence it was first necessary, with Marsiglio and Luther, to produce the paradox of a purely 'suasive' Church which must yet involve external state coercion for its self-government.[41] It was then further necessary, with Hobbes, to exclude all 'private' inspiration from politics, by declaring the temporal 'interval' to be for the present 'the all', because the time of inspiration was over, bound and canonized, and its promises now exclusively referred to an eschatological, though literal and material, future.[42] Nevertheless, the surviving presence of the authoritative text of the Scriptures within the new space of sovereign power could not be denied. It was even essentially *required* by this power, as the source of a positive divine reconfirmation of the covenantal principle, and for the truth that God stood behind the positive authority of nature. However, one use of the Bible had to be prohibited. This was its truly Catholic use, which accorded interpretative authority to a *tradition* of reading, to readers whose power proceeded not from arms, property or contract, but rather from their socially made available time for reading. It was therefore necessary for the new political science to 'capture' from Catholic Christianity the text of the Bible: to produce a new Biblical hermeneutic.

This is the reason why both Hobbes's *Leviathan* and Spinoza's *Tractatus Theologico-Politicus* comprise a political science and a Biblical hermeneutics bound together in one volume. The hermeneutics, just like the politics, possesses both liberal and absolutist aspects which turn out to be really identical.

Just as the absolute State guarantees a measure of private economic freedom and of freedom of choice in things publicly 'indifferent', so, also, for Hobbes and Spinoza, its peace and security ensures some freedom of private opinion. There remains for Hobbes the possibility that the Bible speaks directly to the 'inward man' about the inward man, and he is more than happy that like-minded 'souls' should form 'independent' congregations.[43] However, it is Spinoza who discovers that the State based on negative freedom and founded by science is also the State which permits the kind of 'free time' where science can flourish. It is not an accident that Spinoza lived for a time within a quasi-monastic community of male intellectuals; the point of freedom of opinion for Spinoza is that uncoerced people will be found to acknowledge the 'geometric' truths about *deus sive natura* and so achieve blessedness.[44]

---

[41] Marsilius of Padua, *The Defender of the Peace*, trans. Alan Gewirth, vol. 2 ch. 6 (New York: Columbia University Press, 1956) pp. 24, xix, 274ff.

[42] Hobbes, *Leviathan*, Part III, ch. 35, p. 447; Part IV, ch. 44, pp. 629–30. J. G. A. Pocock, 'Time, history and eschatology in the thought of Thomas Hobbes', in *Politics, Language and Time* (London: Methuen, 1972).

[43] Hobbes, *Leviathan*, Part IV, ch. 47, pp. 710–11.

[44] Spinoza, *A Theologico-Political Treatise*, ch. 7, p. 118; ch. 20, pp. 259–60.

However, in Spinoza's text, we can unmask this liberal 'freedom of enquiry' which grounds both natural and human science (including Biblical criticism) at its very inception. For the promotion of the free time of quasi-monastic science is also the cancellation of the free time of monastic *lectio*. The trouble with Christianity, according to Spinoza, is that it is founded on a private and 'subtle' reading of the Scriptures whose characteristic is a false admixture of theology with philosophy, which takes time to prepare.[45] Spinoza wishes to contrast a 'total' freedom of *opinion* with an absolute unfreedom of public *action*, yet this distinction breaks down, because the traditional Catholic reading is always potentially seditious, always involves an interpretative writing which is an act of denial that all and every decree of the sovereign must be seen to be obeyed. For decrees which negated the authority of traditional Catholic interpretation could not be obeyed by genuine Catholics, yet a mere 'opinion' against *sovereignty* counts as the action of violating the civic contract.[46] Hobbes, more logically, allows for a public censor who will deal with writings as the precise moment where opinions become actions. Opinion is free so long as it is silent, for Hobbes, but professions of faith may be commanded by Leviathan.[47]

If, for Spinoza, the free time of science is to replace the free time of Catholic *lectio*, then it must have as one of its central objects the 'scientific' reading of the Bible, and the possibility of Biblical criticism comes close to providing the very definition of genuine 'freedom'. For the presence of a 'scientific' reading of the Bible is publicly checkable in terms of its correspondence to rational method. As Spinoza describes it, this method is universally available and accords hermeneutic priority to the most general, most accessible, most clear and most (supposedly) 'rational' meanings of Scripture. Although each free individual confronts the Biblical text without traditional mediation, this confrontation paradoxically *irons out* all idiosyncrasy, because the Bible, like nature, is a self-interpreting totality, a world articulated by its own widest and most unambiguous meanings, as is nature by the most general motions.[48] Yet Spinoza's rationalist hermeneutics promoted two principles – both the priority for interpretation of what is 'clear' and in accordance with philosophy, *and* the priority of what is most general (in the text) which may have some 'meaning' and yet, for us, no truth.[49] To make such meanings without truth only secondary, he must 'relativize' them, confine their significance to a past time and place. Hence only the 'irrational' compels a quest for context, whereas those meanings which accord with 'geometric' truths require no more historical elucidation than do Euclid's theorems.[50] And the 'scientific' content of the Bible is very restricted and precise. As it is not philosophy, it

[45] Spinoza, *A Theologico-Political Treatise*, ch. 19, pp. 254–6.
[46] Ibid., ch. 16, pp. 205, 212; ch. 19, pp. 247–8, 250, 254; ch. 20, p. 259.
[47] Hobbes, *Leviathan*, Part II, ch. 18, p. 233; ch. 26, pp. 332–5.
[48] Spinoza, *A Theologico-Political Treatise*, ch. 7, pp. 99, 100–03.
[49] Ibid., ch. 7, p. 101.
[50] Ibid., ch. 7, pp. 103, 112–13.

fails to uncover *deus sive natura*, but at least it inculcates obedience to a supreme power, which philosophy knows as the 'one substance'. This, for Spinoza, is the 'different' truth of the Bible, the truth of submission to sovereign will, or the revelation that one can be saved solely through obedience.[51] However, to obey God is to obey sovereign political power, for even in the case of the positive Mosaic dispensation this must have remained private (to Moses) and unknown, had not Moses been established as ruler.[52]

Hence, for Spinoza, 'free scientific enquiry' into the Bible is constituted in two ways. First, through its banishing of the other freedom of *tradition* with its metaphors, idiosyncrasies and unclarities. Secondly, through its always having as *object* of meaning, liberal freedom and absolute power – which are the only things that can be *rationally* acknowledged as *different* to reason. This second, 'absolutist' aspect of Hobbes's and Spinoza's hermeneutics is really rooted in the Lutheran *sola scriptura* which lies behind Spinoza's rule of interpreting Scripture 'only through Scripture'. Given the problems, as pointed out by the Catholic sceptic, François Veron, of how the Bible is to authorize itself, or to provide an exhaustive guide to its own reading,[53] one is bound, in the end, to arrive at either voluntarist-formalist or rationalist solutions, or else a mixture of both. Thus for Spinoza and Hobbes, the Bible provides a kind of rational foundation which 'mirrors' the self-percipience of subjective reason ('read thyself' says Hobbes, and the ruler must 'read in himself', in the regular operations of his passions, 'Man-Kind' in general),[54] and at the same time the Bible can only legitimate itself if it is found to contain within itself the formal principle of submission to established power. It is the destiny of the *sola scriptura* to be so deconstructed as to come to mean that we must believe the Scriptures because they are politically authorized.

To derive the modern doctrine of sovereignty and the 'science' of this construct, it was necessary for the new 'single' power to lay claim to the 'right' to interpret the Bible in all publicly significant respects and to neutralize all other acts of interpretation. This could only be done by promoting a positivistic concept of revelation, according to which revelation is a 'present' and 'direct' occurrence interrupting the normal self-sufficiency of reason. In consequence, revelation is usually 'private' and its authority is entirely incommunicable *unless* mediated through the contractual artifice of human power: inheritances or actual transfers were equivalent to 'suppositions' of God's will according to d'Ailly.[55] Or else it is public and 'miraculous' – but miracles are at an end. What must not be allowed is for any charisma to attach to *transmission*, other than the formal circumstance of continuity. Above all, it is *allegory* that must be banished, because this traditional mode of

---

[51] Ibid., ch. 15, pp. 194–8.
[52] Ibid., ch. 18, pp. 237–9; ch. 19, p. 247–8.
[53] P. K. Feyerabend, *Realism, Rationalism and Scientific Method: Philosophical Papers*, vol. 1 (Cambridge: Cambridge University Press, 1981) pp. 35–6.
[54] Hobbes, *Leviathan*, the Introduction, pp. 82–3.
[55] Oakley, *The Political Thought of Pierre d'Ailly*, p. 81ff.

interpretation located transcendent significance in the historical-textual syn-
copes between old and new covenant, and in turn between these, ecclesial
time and the *eschaton*.

The traditional 'fourfold', 'spiritual' or 'allegorical' interpretation assumed
and demanded a literal, historical meaning: every Biblical *signum* referred to a
res. However, it conceived the *res*, as a divine, 'natural' sign, to have a
plenitude of meaning which allowed the allegorical edifice to be erected.
The literal, historical 'violence' of the *res* in the old covenant effaced itself,
not just vertically towards 'eternal' meanings, but horizontally in the direction
of the new reality of Christ-*ecclesia* with its charity, mercy and peace.[56] This
allowed the fullness of divine authority to devolve on Christ and then on the
tropological interpretations of present Christians in the community of the
Church. As Henri de Lubac showed, there is a link from the Antiochenes
onwards between those who will admit allegory only as very precise, 'literal'
fulfilment of prophecy and those who see the more 'political'-sounding
promises of the Old Testament as devolving squarely upon temporal
power.[57] Thus William of Ockham's objections to applying promises of universal rule in allegorical fashion to Christ served to preserve a 'literal' and
'historical' picture of Christ's kingly sway as not only non-coercive but also
not of this present world at all.[58] Both allegory and 'scholastic' interpolations
were banished by Hobbes and Spinoza because they implied an uncontrollable proliferation of Christocentric meaning which inserted divine communication into the process of human historical becoming and must forever
escape from sovereign mastery.

This 'capturing of the Biblical text' may not seem quite so constitutive for
modern politics as voluntarist theology. Nevertheless, it remains latent, and
the banishing of traditional ecclesial time served to reinforce a commitment to
the illusion of spatial immediacy and to the exorcism of the metaphorically
ambiguous. Hobbes's 'Leviathan' remained truly haunted by the 'Kingdom
of the Fairies' who 'inhabit Darknesse, Solitudes and Graves',[59] because
the latter's nominality echoes the nominality of Leviathan itself, and both
'engines of meaning' are equally arbitrary, although Hobbes's alone claims
natural, subjective and even Biblical foundations.

Polybian Cycles versus Ecclesial Time

The abstraction of 'politics', the turning of it into a new sort of deductive
science based on accident not substance and on 'artificial' and arbitrary causal

---

[56] Henri de Lubac, *Exégèse Mediévale: Les Quatres Sens de L'Ecriture* (4 vols.) (Paris: Auber,
1964). Gerard E. Caspary, *Politics and Exegesis: Origen and the Two Swords* (Berkeley: California
University Press, 1979) pp. 131–2.

[57] Henri de Lubac, *Exégèse Mediévale*, II, II pp. 198–207, 317–28, 249–352.

[58] Ockham, *Opera Politica*, I., pp. 16–18, 41–5, 49–52.

[59] Hobbes, *Leviathan*, Part IV, ch. 47, p. 713.

connections, was the achievement of a voluntarist political theology. Here the 'secular' as an area of human autonomy is actually promoted by a theological anthropology for which human wilfulness, in certain circumstances, guarantees divine origin. This politics is a spatial abstraction out of 'matters of fact' whose 'register', according to Hobbes, is 'civil history', not 'Books of Philosophy' like *Leviathan*.[60] Yet from the Renaissance onwards, another root of a more 'scientific' politics was historicism, which tended to the conclusion that political practice must be adapted to customs, manners, religions and times.

It is false to see in the gradual emergence of a historicist perspective a wholly sudden break with traditional modes of thought. It was not, for example, necessarily incompatible with the allegorical mode of ecclesial time; a humanist like Erasmus could easily contain his sense of historical 'distance' within allegory, because the very tension involved in typological figuration between the overarching unity of divine revelation and the difference between its successive phases can actually promote such an awareness.[61] Equally, the traditional perspectives of a 'civic' politics, inherited from Aristotle and the Romans, encouraged a reflection upon the given historical circumstances in which a civic, participatory virtue (rendered redundant by Hobbes) could best flourish.

If there is a break, then it is not rightfully located (as, for example, by J. G. A. Pocock) between a timeless, Christian, hierocratic politics and a 'purely human' temporal and activist politics.[62] This is to fail to see that doing and making remained 'sacralized' for Christian humanists from Salutati onwards, and to forget, also, that monastic institutions were regarded as humanly-instituted *politeiai*.[63] Rather, one must understand what Pocock calls 'the Machiavellian Moment' as the astonishing re-emergence of pagan political and philosophical time no longer as a makeshift, nor a Thomist preparation for grace, but rather as something with its own integrity, its own goals and values, which might even contradict those of Christianity. It is, as Grabmann recognized, a parallel phenomenon to 'Averroism', where philosophical truths may be in contradiction with the truths of the faith.[64]

Here then is another and completely different root of the secular. Yet the Machiavellian secular was not an area of pure neutrality with respect to faith. On the contrary, it only came to exist as the discovery of a new sort of *virtù* which could not be reconciled with the Christian virtues. If the Hobbesian

[60] Ibid., Part I, ch. 9, pp. 147–8. Tito Magri, *De Cive* (Introduction) (Rome: Riuniti, 1981) pp. 12–13.

[61] Henri de Lubac, *Exégèse Mediévale*, II, II, pp. 317–28, 249–352.

[62] J. G. A. Pocock, *The Machiavellian Moment: Florentine Political Thought and the Atlantic Republican Tradition*, pp. 31–80 (Princeton N.J.: Princeton UP, 1975).

[63] Salutati, *De Nobilitate*, ch. 31, pp. 218–220. J. H. Hexter, *The Vision of Politics on the Eve of the Reformation* (New York: Basic Books, 1973).

[64] A. S. McGrade, *The Political Thought of William of Ockham* (Cambridge: Cambridge University Press, 1974) pp. 197–206.

Alan Gewirth, 'Philosophy and political thought in the fourteenth century', in *The Forward Movement of the Fourteenth Century* (Columbus: Ohio State University Press, 1981) p. 183ff.

field of power seems to be constructed by a perverse theology, then the Machiavellian field of power is constructed by a partial rejection of Christianity and appeal to an alternative *mythos*.

The humanist and historicist legacy was no less important for the emergence of modern social theory than the natural rights legacy of liberalism/absolutism. As we shall see in the next chapter, the eighteenth-century enlightenment was much preoccupied with an attempt to find a new version of antique virtue. Yet for all this, there is an important point of convergence between the two currents, which ensures that even the 'civic humanist' tradition is infected by individualism and instrumentalism. This point of convergence is the Roman stoic legacy, which directs attention to a pre-social human being which seeks sociation through an impulse belonging to its own *conatus*, or drive to self-preservation, and which also tends to redefine virtue as knowledge of, agreement with, action within or indifference to, historical *fate*.

In its Machiavellian version, civic humanism sheers off an Aristotelianism compatible with Christianity in favour of a notion of political *prudentia* as instrumental manipulation.[65] At the same time, it subscribes to a *mythos* of fate which takes it outside Christian theological bounds. Whereas, for natural rights theory, conflict is endemic to fallen human nature and this original conflict must be suppressed by a hierocratic counter-violence imposing a fearful peace, for Machiavellianism there is a simultaneous 'heroic' promotion of both internal civic solidarity and external enmity, a mixture which is most gloriously human and yet also most fatefully doomed.[66]

The Machiavellian republic emerges not gradually, through the ironic disciplines of linear time, but suddenly and sporadically in a favourable moment, against the background of an unpredictable *fortuna*.[67] For medieval Christianity, the uncontrollable reverses of fortune represented the deep-seatedness of original sin within an overall providential design, but for Machiavelli *fortuna* is again an antique and impersonal compound of chaos and fatality. The aim of political *virtù* is to 'use' and surmount, for a time, this fortune. Machiavelli makes historicist, relativizing observations about the chances of different republics, observing that a relatively democratic republic like Venice should not make war, because the capture of foreigners will lead to the introduction of class divisions, whereas a class-divided republic like ancient Rome is well-equipped to make war and expand its population.[68] However, it is not really this relativism which makes Machiavelli a forebear of a modern and non-Christian politics. Rather, it is his explicit *preference* for the Roman option and his return to the etymological root of virtue as 'heroic manliness', to be cultivated supremely in war. This preference encompasses

---

[65] Niccolò Machiavelli, *The Prince*, trans. Henry C. Mansfield, jun., XXV (Chicago: Chicago University Press, 1985) pp. 98–9.

[66] Niccolò Machiavelli, *The Discourses*, trans. Leshe S. Watter (London: Penguin, 1970) pp. 15, 16, 118–26. Pocock, *The Machiavellian Moment*, pp. 49–80, 156–218.

[67] Ibid.

[68] Machiavelli, *The Discourses*, 5; 6 (1970) pp. 118–26.

also the view that continued class conflict within the republic is functionally useful in preserving political 'liberty' – the habit of independence.[69] While Machiavelli by no means wishes to deny the validity of 'more moral' social virtues within their proper sphere, it is this option for internal conflict which ensures that a manipulative bias must be dominant among those who rule.

As the republic emerges 'suddenly', so its course is contained within a cyclical time. Machiavelli is heavily dependent upon the late-antique Greek-born writer Polybius, who, standing outside and at the end of Rome, interpreted its history as a progression from the rule of the few through the rule of the one to the rule of the many, culminating, through innumerable private conflicts, in an ultimate loss of aristocratic virtue.[70] Whereas the theological natural rights tradition discovered a 'self-sustaining' world of pure power without virtue, the non-Christian Machiavellian tradition derived from Polybius insisted that human power was a form of virtue, and hence just as historically precarious as the rarity of true virtue. The latter tradition ultimately lies behind the later dialectical and historicist theses of Hegel and Marx, but the eschatological 'resolutions' which these thinkers project depend, as we shall see, on the overlay of another theological programme, that of *theodicy*. For the pure Machiavellian tradition, by contrast, human meaning is 'present' and temporarily glorious – besides this there is only a lapsing back into the unmeaning fatality of history without the republic. The stance of this tradition towards Christianity is ambiguous. On the one hand it often supports a 'civil religion' – Christian or otherwise – which will 'functionally' promote civic solidarity. On the other hand, it attempts to revive, against Christianity, an antique sacrality, producing a new *mythos* of heroes without gods (though still, for Machiavelli, to be rewarded for the exercise of civic virtue by a single God) which is the second aspect of the modern 'secular'.[71]

Both the natural rights and the Machiavellian traditions in 'scientific politics' are heavily presupposed by all later social science. Yet from both a Christian *and* a metacritical perspective (meaning the historicist questioning of 'rational' foundations) it might seem that we have here only to do with heterodoxy on the one hand and the half-return of paganism on the other. For just as the first makes a perfect analysis only of its own artefact, so the second traces correctly the historical fate only of 'heroic man', which is precisely the ethical ontology which Christianity calls into question. In either case, it seems that, from the outset, the 'science of conflict' is not merely one branch of social science but rather that the 'scientific' approach seeks 'to know' power and conflict as ontologically fundamental. It follows that if Christianity seeks to 'find a place for' secular reason, it may be perversely compromising with what, on its own terms, is either deviancy or falsehood.

---

[69] Ibid., 4; 4, pp. 113–15.
[70] Pocock, *The Machiavellian Moment*, pp. 49–80.
[71] Machiavelli, *The Prince*, XXVI, p. 103.

2

Political Economy as
Theodicy and Agonistics

Introduction

The 'New Science of Politics' was concerned with *creation*, or the institution of a new, secular space. Hobbesian politics dealt in absolute beginnings, the original will of consciously contracting parties and of the sovereign ruler; Machiavellian politics dealt with the short-lived and tragic fate of a military and political *virtù*, sporadically surmounting the tide of fortune. By contrast, political economy was interested in *providence* or a process of prudent conservation. It was the heir of both the natural rights and the humanist traditions, but it investigated much more closely just how a non-ethical regulation of passion and desire might be possible. Although it continued to think of this regulation as ultimately supervised by the State, in the interests of political strength, it was more interested in the formal consistency, or the 'regularity' of power, rather than power as occasional intervention.

Moreover, it also discovered a regularity in human affairs not humanly planned, nor humanly intended: the operations of 'the market'. Here political economy filled up a *lacuna* in the new political theory which tried to deduce conclusions from the demiurgic wills of human individuals. As we saw, the 'natural rights' perspective was unable to solve the problem of apparently spontaneous human collaboration, suspended between the isolated individual on the one hand and the sovereign power on the other. At this point, it had to resort to theories of original contract. Political economy, on the other hand, took a much more realist and historicist view of human collaboration because it was concerned with the problem of an unintended harmonious effect. It is precisely the space of reflection opened up by this problem which ensured that 'the new science of politics' could not of itself give a full knowledge of the secular. This inherent and constitutive *lack* had to be supplemented in the eighteenth century by 'political economy' and 'speculative history', and in the following century by 'economics', 'sociology' and 'anthropology'.

Only in certain respects, as we shall see, does political economy extend and complete a Hobbesian or a Machiavellian politics. The main purpose of this chapter will be to argue that the emergence of political economy represents not only a perfecting of secular order but also secular order's first coming up against an antinomy. The new science of politics presupposed *homo faber*, the human making of human institutions, and it treated this making technically and instrumentally – so banishing both antique *praxis* and modern Baroque *poesis*. Yet the problem of spontaneous collaboration reveals the difficulty of grounding the social in human will; thus 'humanity's self-formation' gets gradually displaced by the 'historical formation of humanity'. This tendency, right from the start, meant that providence, or a greater than human ordering, was brought back into the picture. Whereas Hobbes and Spinoza concentrated on that part of the stoic natural law tradition which tried to deduce norms from self-preserving *conatus*, another aspect of the same tradition – namely conformity to the processes of nature – now became equally important. Moreover, whereas these earlier rationalists proposed politics as a deductive science, concerned with the logic of manipulation of material forces within a universe that was a material *plenum*, political economy emerged from a discourse which sought truth from *observation* of reality and claimed to 'demonstrate' the presence of a spiritual power filling the vacuous 'gap' between human intentions and social outcomes.[1]

As there is discontinuity as well as continuity between the new politics and political economy, modern secular social theory stands in a double (and doubly paradoxical) relationship to theology. In the first place, there is what has already been traced, namely science as knowledge of 'how to make', which, in its Hobbesian version, presupposed the myth of the self-present and self-sufficiently initiating 'person' who echoes the pure will of a creator God. Here I am not saying that the same substantive concept – namely 'voluntarist sovereignty' – is transferred from God and the sacred to the human and secular. This would be the facile theme of 'secularization'. On the contrary, I am suggesting that *only* the theological model permits one to construct the *mythos* of the sovereign power, or sovereign person, so that it is not a case of 'essentially' secular and pragmatic realities being temporarily described in antique theological guise. In the midst of the crisis posed by religious conflict, Bodin and Hobbes contrived solutions at once sacred and pragmatic, founded upon a new metaphysics of political power. Only *within* the terms of their new theology is divine sanction pushed into the remote background, and this sanction is nonetheless still required to legitimate the human power which authenticates itself in the foreground, as the purely arbitrary. It is when theology finally *drops out of* modern theories of sovereignty that the real moment of mystification occurs, because here the 'mythical' character of sovereignty is forgotten.

More or less in accordance with this reflection, it is now often recognized that Hobbes and Locke remain within theological and iusnaturalist modes of understanding.[2] But there remains a tendency to think of eighteenth-century

---

[1] Shapin and Schaffer, *Leviathan and the Air-Pump*. pp. 80–110.
[2] Tuck, *Natural Rights Theories*. Tully, *A Discourse on Property*.

French and Scots writers as the first truly secular, or 'sociological' theorists.[3] This, however, altogether ignores the intellectual genesis of political economy, which began among thinkers concerned that the Hobbesian politics neglected and insulted divine providence. Here arises the second strand in the relation of secular social theory to theology. Political economy actually *turns away* from the seemingly ultra-modern themes of anarchy and autonomy mooted in the seventeenth century by Hobbes and others, and seeks to supplement science as making with a science of providence, or a social theodicy.[4] There is a concern to display history as the natural process of the self-emergence of an immanent reason, *within which* 'man' or 'humanity' arises.

Thus, I shall argue, the further articulation of the space of the secular by political economy coincides with a different and somewhat contrariwise theological insertion. No longer is God the ultimate arbitrary power behind human arbitrary power; instead he is a God regularly and immediately present to human society, holding it together, just like the Newtonian God among the planetary bodies in Newtonian space. This does not, however, amount to the reintroduction of the traditional providence of Catholic ortho- doxy. Such a providence was ultimately unknown and could only be dimly apprehended. This providence can be *exactly* known about, and it is invoked at the level of finite causality.

Moreover, the appeal to a more 'immediate' God does not reverse the 'de- ethicization' of political theory already set in train. On the contrary, it con- firms and extends it, because in political economy the field of social relations between individuals falls under a 'providential' discourse about how bad or self-interested actions can have good long-term outcomes, rather than under traditional 'ethical' discourse. Hence the de-ethicization of the eco- nomic domain does not, as one might suppose, coincide in any straightfor- ward way with 'secularization'. Here again, the institution of the 'secular' is paradoxically related to a shift *within* theology and not an emancipation *from* theology.

Political Economy and Moral Economy

It has recently become common to argue that the Scots political economists were not responsible for the separation of economics from morality. Instead they are seen as standing within a 'civic humanist' tradition that is centrally concerned with questions of character and virtue. Their humanism, it is suggested, has become invisible to us because it is a genuinely secular

---

[3] John Dunn, 'From applied theology to social analysis: the break between John Locke and the Scottish Enlightenment', in Istvan Hunt and Michael Ignatieff (eds.) *Wealth and Virtue* (Cam- bridge: Cambridge University Press, 1983) pp. 119–35.

[4] Milton L. Myers, *The Soul of Modern Economic Man: Ideas of Self-Interest from Thomas Hobbes to Adam Smith* (Chicago: Chicago University Press, 1983). Jacob Viner, *The Role of Providence in the Social Order* (Philadelphia: American Philosophical Society, 1972).

humanism, which does not, like Christian Aristotelianism, advert to any sort of transcendence.[5]

For this view, there is no essential continuity between iusnaturalists like Hobbes and Locke, who built their theories upon the rights of *personae* over *res* and other *personae*, and the Scots economists who subordinate questions of right to the pursuit of public virtue, or political collaboration. However, this contention must be considered an exaggerated one. The Roman law concentration of the new politics on questions of property, right and power remains one important root of political economy and lends to it a somewhat de-ethicized colouring.

It is true that the Scots tradition did not follow the Hobbesian line of attempting to build social theory solely upon the rational calculation of self-interest. Instead, it developed, in the wake of the Cambridge Platonists, Shaftesbury and Hutcheson, stoic ideas about natural impulses of 'benevolence' and 'sympathy'.[6] At the same time, the theory of moral sympathy as expounded, for example, by David Hume, has to be distinguished from Aristotelian humanism insofar as the theme of 'sympathy' actually supplants the irreducible primacy of an inherently ethical end or *telos*. Instead of referring the moral to a hierarchy of true goals for genuine human fulfilment, Hume grounds the moral in something specifically pre-moral, natural and sub-rational, namely our common animal inclinations and aversions, and our ability to place ourselves imaginatively in the position of others.[7] This moral philosophy will not permit public laws and institutions to be considered under the heading of common goals of virtue, but construes them only in terms of their usual empirically observable effects upon individuals, once they are in place. It is seen that laws and institutions have the capacity to overawe and intimidate the individual imagination, so that its reaction to them acquires the force of the true natural impulses. Only on the basis of this force of habit are the 'virtues' of justice, which are to do with respect for persons' lives and property, and the keeping of promises, able to arise. We come to experience, almost 'physically', our own security as bound up with the regular exercise of property and contractual laws, so that we perceive that we have an 'interest' in justice. Next, we instinctively sympathize with the victims of those who violate these laws and in consequence attach notions of

[5] J. G. A. Pocock, 'The myth of John Locke and the obsession with liberalism', in J. G. A. Pocock and Richard Ashcraft (eds.) *John Locke* (Los Angeles: William Andrews Memorial Library, 1980) pp. 3–21; 'Cambridge paradigms and Scotch philosophers: a study of the relations between the civic humanist and the civil jurisprudential interpretation of eighteenth century social thought', in Istvan Hunt and Michael Ignatieff (eds.) *Wealth and Virtue*, pp. 235–52. Albert O. Hirschman, *The Passions and the Interests* (Princeton, NJ: Princeton University Press, 1977).

[6] Adam Smith, *The Theory of Moral Sentiments* (New York: Augustus N. Kelley, 1966) Part VII, ch. 3, pp. 440–8.

Myers, *The Soul of Modern Economic Man*, p. 33ff.

[7] David Hume, *A Treatise of Human Nature* (Darmstadt: Scientia Verlag Aalen, 1964) vol. 2, Book III, Part I, Section I, p. 233ff, and Part II, Section I, p. 253.

'virtue' and 'vice' to the conventions of justice and injustice, although there can be nothing 'naturally' moral or immoral about them.[8]

Adam Smith exhibits (without using the terms) a similar distinction to that of Hume between the 'natural' virtues grounded in imaginative sympathy, which promote benevolence, especially towards relations and friends, and the 'artificial' virtues, founded upon our experience of property and contract, which lead to the exercise of justice. However, neither Smith nor Hume makes the contractualist mistake of supposing that the individual subject assents to justice in general because of a deliberate utilitarian calculation that this will be for his best *self*-interest in the long run.[9] Instead, for Smith, justice in general is only the accidental sum of justice in particular, which is founded in an individual's sympathetic sense of outrage at any crime which goes unpunished.[10] Smith adds to this that 'simply as a matter of contingent fact' and at the level of passion rather than reason, 'nature' has made stronger our resentment at a failure of justice than at a failure of benevolence and 'has not thought it necessary to guard and enforce the practice of it [benevolence] by the terrors of merited punishment'.[11] If there is a utilitarian design at work here, then it is on the part of 'nature', not man, because nature realizes that whereas a 'malevolent' society where all are ready to injure is non-sustainable, yet even without benevolence, society 'can be upheld by a mercenary exchange of good offices according to an agreed valuation'.[12] While it is true that the institutions of justice *once in place* induce an exercise of virtue and sympathy, the initial coming to be of these institutions is neither a matter of original contract nor of 'public virtue', but rather of the gradual historical limiting of self-interest by self-interest.

Thus there is, despite the differences, a fundamental continuity between the iusnaturalism of the new science of politics and the iusnaturalism of political economy. 'By nature', for Adam Smith, every man is 'principally recommended to his own care',[13] although this is now exemplified, not in a contract, but in a 'natural course' which develops either through the violent negotiations of war, or the 'peaceful' negotiations of trade. Yet it remains the case, as for Hobbes and Locke, that 'public interest' is mostly confined to the securing of the private interests of life, property and contract. Thus it is assumed by both Hume and Smith that justice has only a negative concern with violations of these instances of possession, and that the feeling that only such violations, and not failures of beneficence, deserve punishment, is a manifestation of the natural disposition of human passion.

---

[8] Hume, *Treatise*, Book III, Part II, Section I, p. 252ff.
[9] Adam Smith, *The Theory of Moral Sentiments*, Part II, Section II, chs. 1–3, pp. 112–32 (1966).
[10] Hume, *Treatise*, Part II, Section II, pp. 268–71. Adam Smith, *The Theory of Moral Sentiments*, Part II, Section II, chs. 1–3, pp. 113–15, 129–32 (1966).
[11] Ibid., ch. 1, p. 125.
[12] Ibid., ch. 3, p. 124.
[13] Ibid., Part II, Section II, p. 119.

This realm of justice, or of 'artificial virtue', rather than the whole scope of virtue, is clearly delineated by Smith as the area to which political economy is confined. There is no 'problem' about squaring *The Theory of Moral Sentiments* with *The Wealth of Nations*, because Smith makes it clear that political economy is founded specifically upon that area of morality which is to do with self-interest.[14] 'Pure benevolence' he avers, is suited only to a non-dependent being, namely God, whereas human beings must take account of the more self-interested virtues of 'propriety', which entail habits of economy, industry and discretion, the judicious spending of our own resources.[15] The justice founded upon this propriety is clearly not the 'distributive justice' of classical political theory, nor a justice first and foremost concerned with the common good. For Aquinas it had appeared that liberality and magnanimity were naturally more self-interested than justice, as they concerned especially the virtue of the donor, whereas justice was uniquely concerned with the well-being of the other person.[16] Yet for Smith the position is reversed: as 'self-interest' is to do with 'self-preservation', not 'being virtuous', justice which secures private self-interest is the most 'interested' virtue and benevolence the most 'disinterested'. (Note, however, that Aquinas is here discussing 'natural' virtue and perhaps reflects too Greek a view-point.[17] Does not charity, which is equally 'interested' and 'disinterested', really subsume magnanimity for Christianity?) Benevolence and charity, moreover, are confined to a private and familial world. Here alone one can in some measure depend upon selfless actions which are inherently unpredictable, but for society at large benevolence is merely ornamental or compensatory. Political economy therefore defines itself at the outset by obliterating the Christian sphere of public charity. Thus Sir James Stewart, appropriately the great theorist of 'primary accumulation', scorns the Catholic practice of Spain where the surplus of public wealth is given to the needy. This, he says, is like the miracle of manna from heaven, whereas political economy advocates a more regular and invariable providence: 'the regulation of need', and not charity, is a more reliable means of social control and increasing the population.[18] By not distributing the surplus in an act of charity, but instead concentrating it and investing it in future industry, the element of need among workers is constantly preserved and thereby the stimulus to work with the possibility of a continuous, organized discipline.

One can conclude, then, that the theme of 'possessive individualism' does remain central for political economy. For Hume, Stewart and Smith, as for Hobbes and Locke, property and contract are seen as 'artificial' matters.

---

[14] Ibid., Part IV, Section I, pp. 445–6.
An Inquiry into the Nature and Causes of the Wealth of Nations (Oxford: Oxford University Press, 1976) vol. I, I.ii, pp. 26–7.
[15] Adam Smith, *The Theory of Moral Sentiments*, Part VII, Section II, pp. 429, 440–8 (1966).
[16] Aquinas, *ST* II.II.Q.58.a.12.
[17] See chapter 12 below.
[18] James Stewart, *The Works: Political, Metaphysical and Chronological* (New York: Augustus M. Kelley, 1967) vol. 1, p. 118.

However, the Scots understand this as a continuous, historical and factual artifice, not the 'fiction' of a primal contract. In addition, the Scots see self-possession, along with various 'passions' and 'sympathies', as an instinctual matter rather than the subject of a rational calculus. This opens up a space where 'the general interest' cannot be readily grasped in contractualist terms. At this point the solutions offered are either 'Machiavellian' or 'natural theological' or else a mixture of both.

The Machiavellian Dimension

Where a humanist element is recognizable among the thinkers of the Scottish Enlightenment, it tends to assume a Machiavellian colouring. The idea of the sovereign ruler able to manipulate internal conflicts in the interests of an outward-facing political strength is connected with the possibility of a polit-ical-economic surrogate for political *virtu*.[19] Montesquieu, whose influence on the Scots through Stewart was very important, had already noted how mod-ern absolute monarchies which undermined the power of the old, landed, military aristocracy, also substitute a false 'honour' for old-fashioned virtue.[20] Whereas aristocratic honour traditionally included a fixed code of behaviour involving moral virtues of courage and magnanimity, the new 'bizarre' hon-our was concerned only with fashion, reputation and appearances. It evolved constantly new rules, so that the 'honourable' man was now the successful 'speculator' in the signs of esteem. No longer did political strength emerge from the collective adherence to certain noble ideals; instead the modern monarch must manipulate the rivalries of honour, like a system of checks and balances.[21]

Montesquieu records here a level of change in the social imagination which later historians tended to overlook. Equally important as any rise of a middle-class is the changing definition of 'nobility', allowing the possibility of a 'specu-lative' aristocracy where fortune is a matter of a gamble on one's reputation, just as economic fortune was now no longer so firmly tied to landed property, but could be built on successful investment in the future success of trade, or strength of government. As Montesquieu noted, the power of England was founded on aristocratic whiggery – the nobility and gentry had financially gambled on England's success and the very strength of this 'confidence' had become translated into a new sort of mercantile power. As a 'free nation' England could 'bring to bear against its enemies immense sums of imaginary riches which the credit and nature of its government might turn into reality'.[22]

---

[19] Pocock, *The Machiavellian Moment*, pp. 462–506. Hirschman, *The Passions and the Interests*.
[20] Montesquieu, *The Spirit of the Laws*, in *The Political Theory of Montesquieu* (Cambridge: Cambridge University Press, 1977) p. 193.
[21] Montesquieu, *The Spirit of the Laws*, pp. 190, 211–12, 218, 228.
[22] Ibid., p. 285.

Montesquieu's observations suggest that, for the beginnings of a capitalist economy, it was not sufficient that the old guild and corporation restrictions on production, trade and usury be lifted. This merely negative picture assumes that the 'desire for wealth' is natural and unproblematic. Instead, the capitalist take-off presupposed a shift in the very economy of desire. Previously, modes of public style and behaviour were regarded as desirable or otherwise because they were ultimately related to accepted standards of the common good. Now, by contrast, public style and behaviour becomes the subject of fashion and of an endless 'diversion'. What now matters, as thinkers like Montesquieu and Helvetius noted, is not the 'proper' object of desire but rather the promotion of desire itself, and the manipulation and control of this process.[23] Only this reversal of the order of priority between desire and goal permitted a new code of social practice where people could start to see themselves as primarily 'producers' and 'consumers'. For to 'abstract desire' corresponded a new 'abstract wealth', meaning the maximum diversification and increase of production, and the maximum circulation of products and their representative species through exchange.[24]

The attitude of eighteenth-century social thinkers towards this shift (which they helped to promote) was highly ambiguous; often, like Montesquieu and Ferguson, they lamented the loss of true political virtue, founded on political participation of those with a 'genuine', not a 'speculative' interest in the country, grounded in landed property.[25] Yet it was a Machiavellian interpretation of the old political virtue which allowed them to come to terms with its new bureaucratic and economic surrogate. Antique political virtue had never been quite detached from the primacy of 'honour' and 'glory' – thus Aristotle sees the strong, wealthy aristocrat who is able to exercise 'magnanimity' as the very type of civic excellence.[26] However, in Machiavelli the supremacy of virtues of heroic strength related to the 'glory' of the republic becomes much more marked. Along the lines of Machiavellian logic, it was possible to conceive of an individual pursuit of civic virtue transformed into a 'passion for glory' which is no longer even an aspiration to the heroic substance of nobility, but merely the quest for a public repute.[27] Adam Smith contends that the desire for gain is as much to do with 'vanity' as security or comfort-seeking, and he develops a new fundamental image of 'man' as *homo mercans*, a figure engaged in a constant struggle to match persuasively his own desire to the desires of others in the most advantageous manner possible.[28]

[23] Ibid., pp. 190, 199. Eric Voegelin, 'Helvetius and the genealogy of passions', in *From Enlightenment to Revolution* (Durham, NC: Duke University Press, 1975) pp. 35–52.

[24] Michel Foucault, *The Order of Things* (London: Tavistock, 1970) pp. 166–214.

[25] Montesquieu, *The Spirit of the Laws*, p. 190.
Adam Ferguson, *An Essay on the History of Civil Society* (Edinburgh: Edinburgh University Press, 1966) p. 261ff.

[26] See chapter 11 below.

[27] Eric Voegelin, 'Helvetius and the genealogy of passions', p. 52.

[28] Smith, *The Theory of Moral Sentiments*, Part I, Section III, pp. 70–83; *The Wealth of Nations*, I.ii, pp. 25–7; *Lectures on Justice, Police, Revenue and Arms* (New York: Augustus M. Kelley, 1964) Part II, Division II, p. 171.

Moreover, Smith envisages the inequalities of the competitive economy as a kind of solution. We are charmed, he says, by 'the beauty of that accommodation which reigns in the palaces of the great' and 'the machine or the economy by which it is produced'.[29] A fascination with the formal mechanisms of Montesquieu's 'bizarre honour' holds in thrall even the losers in the game of wealth. Thus a new secular aesthetic, detached from its transcendental link with the True and the Good, is as essential here to the new 'economic' regime as the abstract conception of wealth. The economy, or the endless 'balancing' of human passions according to 'the laws of supply and demand', can become an object of desire, because a new 'classical' beauty has been identified, which consists in the inner consistency and 'harmony' of the operations of utility.

Nevertheless, this beauty is also strength. At the centre of sovereignty the goal of a genuine Machiavellian *virtù* is still all-important. Throughout the history of political economy, from the 'proto-economist' William Petty to the nineteenth century, the primary context for economic reflection remained the interest of the State's strength abroad and the possibility of a 'regular', predictable control of events at home.[30] It is in this context that one has to interpret the Scots theorists' critical remarks about the new capitalist order. James Stewart and Adam Ferguson were mainly worried that the trading society would ultimately sap the resources of noble strength required for warfare and political devotion.[31] On the other hand, an economic order could appear as the very perfecting of the Homeric *agon*, of a 'playful' warfare, within limits, according to rules and permitting the testing and exercise of a constant ingenuity. According to Ferguson, conflict is essentially motiveless, just as for Helvetius desire engenders new objects. It arises because 'we are fond of distinctions', the 'gates of Janus', and hence warfare is coeval with language and reason.[32] In Ferguson's agonistic vision, 'to overawe, to intimidate' is the greatest human triumph; 'fractures and death are often made to terminate the pastimes of idleness and festivity' and 'love of amusement' opens 'the path that leads to the grave'.[33]

Ceaseless economic conflict appeared to Stewart and to others as a more than acceptable substitute for this Homeric functioning of warfare. It could, in fact, solve the Machiavellian conundrum. This conundrum required the promotion of 'rational' warfare between nations rather than (supposedly) 'irrational' religious or ideological warfare within the nation, and yet the simultaneous provision of some sort of heroic testing ground within domestic society itself. The conundrum appears solved, because a fully 'economic' society provided in an ideal way a ceaseless rivalry in the developing of

---

[29] Smith, *The Theory of Moral Sentiments*, Part IV, ch. 1, pp. 263–5.

[30] Michael Perelman, *Classical Political Economy: Positive Accumulation and the Social Division of Labour* (Totowa, NJ: Rowman and Allenheld, 1984).

[31] Stewart, *The Works*, vol. 1, p. 82. Ferguson, *An Essay on the History of Civil Society*, pp. 154–5, 285ff.

[32] Ferguson, *An Essay*, pp. 20–5. See chapters 11 and 12 below.

[33] Ferguson, *An Essay*, p. 24.

minutely discriminating 'taste' and inventive 'ingenuity', without the danger of distinction and competition spilling over into civil warfare. The economic society, as it emerges from the key texts of Montesquieu and Stewart, is at once a sort of substitute or token for the heroic or military society, and at the same time, a more perfect fulfilment of the agonistic ideal of a 'lawful conflict'.

Moreover, economic or 'civil' society is also a promissory note to the effect that when it becomes necessary, at the limits of self-preservation and political expansion, payment will be in military kind. Hence, while the mercantile ideal is seen as a 'peaceful' one, it is also true that Adam Smith prefers economic growth and high wages because this favours a growing population and the increase in strength of the nation state.[34] However, the connection between economic and politico-military interests is seen more clearly in the earlier writings of James Stewart, whose theory corresponds more closely to the actual process of emergence of the capitalist mode of production.[35]

Stewart focuses his political economy on the question of how it is possible to produce a surplus and to increase the population. His mode of posing this question reveals the way in which political economy breaks with the norms of Christendom and assumes the paradigm of the classical *polis*. For the 'surplus' in Stewart is something produced in the realm of the *oikos* (the household) which makes possible the civilized addition of a political and military life. The goal of a large population is also a political and military, rather than an economic one. The preference for 'accumulating' the surplus, and not distributing it as charity, marks the refusal of the idea that the boundaries of 'the household' are, as in Christian familial conceptions of the social whole ('the household of faith'), coterminous with the boundaries of the *polis*.[36] Stewart's antique ideal (as so often in the eighteenth century) is the slave society of Sparta, where society was divided between a disciplined and fully controlled class of producers and another class of frugal politician-warriors.[37] He regards a society based on wage-labour as the next best thing to Spartan slavery, although this surrogate also has its own advantages in terms of an 'automatic' regulation through self-interest.

Nonetheless, the accent here is clearly on wage-labour as a mode of *discipline*, not as a mode of freedom (as in Smith). Stewart argues that manufacturing industries should model themselves on the organization of hospitals and workhouses. The 'poor' are to be dealt with by various modes of disciplinary surveillance and confinement (Stewart calls for 'great lists of births, deaths and marriages'), 'the poor' meaning all those who have no means of subsistence and are forced to labour for others.[38] A wise government will *make* as many people poor as possible, because political authority (which Stewart traces to paternal

---

[34] Smith, *The Wealth of Nations*, IV, vii. 6, p. 566.
[35] Perelman, *Classical Political Economy*, pp. 76–99. Hirschman, *The Passions and the Interests*, pp. 67–115.
[36] Stewart, *The Works*, vol. 1, pp. 77–8, 324. See chapters 11 and 12 below.
[37] Stewart, *The Works*, vol. 1, pp. 332–41.
[38] Ibid., pp. 94–8.

origins) arises out of economic dependency.[39] Whereas Adam Smith later presents the social division of labour (in which different components of a final product are exchanged in the marketplace) as arising naturally out of the historical development of human skills, Stewart insists on the need for 'primary accumulation', an initial forcible appropriation of land from subsistence farmers by government and landowners.[40] Agriculture as subsistence he considers to be useless to the State, in contrast to agriculture as trade. Yet the maximum of trade and surplus will only be possible if subsistence is kept to a minimum. This requires not only an initial violent extrusion of people into the marketplace, but also a constant vigilance on the part of government to ensure that no goods of production in excess of market demand are retained by the producers, for this would tend to destroy the stimulus of need which allows for a constantly shifting competitive balance between the supply of labour and the demand for it. This balance involves 'alternate risings and sinkings', but time necessarily destroys the balance altogether, and government must constantly intervene to ensure the right level of supply of labour.[41]

In Stewart's vision, the marketplace is a self-regulating *agon*, but its bounds are initially marked out and constantly redrawn by arbitrary political violence. The 'regularity' of economic competition promotes, in the last analysis, the strength of this constitutional force. This vision reveals, whereas Smith's conceals, the actual increase of dependency and of 'disciplinary' procedures which was presupposed by the growth of capitalist freedom. The historical importance of the 'carceral' society has been noted in recent years by Michel Foucault but he appears at times (though not always) to understand this in terms of the essentially non-political growth of 'local' practices.[42] By contrast, the work of Stewart and others, in a line stretching back to William Petty, suggests just how *consciously* incarceration could be pursued, and its essential *link* (apparently denied by Foucault) to the emergence of modern (but *theological*) notions of sovereignty. For the most perfected theories of absolutism (in the Hobbesian and Filmerian line) relied not simply upon iusprudential notions of original contract, but instead seamlessly integrated ideas of *de facto* property right and legally enforceable contractual obligation with 'positive' notions of power as ordering and placement.[43]

The Machiavellian dimension in political economy, which emerges most clearly in Stewart, is important because of its startling candour. Already it anticipates Marx, because it presents capitalism, not as founded upon the spontaneous activity of supposedly free subjects, but rather as depending upon class struggle and an initial 'confinement' of the majority of the popu-

---

[39] Stewart, *The Works*, vol. 1, pp. 2, 77, 319.

[40] Ibid., pp. 77, 110, 304. Perelman, *Classical Political Economy*, pp. 76–99.

[41] Stewart, *The Works*, vol. 1, pp. 299–307.

[42] Michel Foucault, *Discipline and Punish*, trans. Alan Sheridan (Harmondsworth: Penguin, 1977) pp. 293–308. *Power/Knowledge*, trans. Colin Gordon et al. (Brighton: Harvester, 1986) pp. 92–108, 146–65. See also 'The political technology of individuals', in Luther H. Martin et al. (eds.) *Technologies of the Self* (Massachusetts: Massachusetts University Press, 1988) pp. 143–62.

[43] Perelman, *Classical Political Economy*, pp. 100–01.

lation: a removal of their freedom and resources and a destruction of their talents. However, unlike Marxism, the Scots often intimate in an ominous fashion just why a system of 'lawful conflict' can exert its fascination over even its victims, in a manner that has nothing to do with 'false consciousness'.[44] In the case of Stewart, the arbitrary and evident opening of this conflict is openly recognized and openly advocated, because (like Ferguson) he regards a 'playful conflict' as a fundamental aspect of human ontology. He deliberately (and *not* ideologically) opts for capitalism, though he does not regard it as historically inevitable and is not blind to many of its arbitrary and even (from a certain point of view) irrational features.

By detailing the Machiavellian dimension, one completes the picture of the alteration in the 'moral economy' presupposed by capitalism. This alteration occurred in the text of social reality – often at its upper, aristocratic levels – but this text is abridged, condensed, concentrated and assisted in the bound volumes of the economic theorists where the essential movements are abstracted and most clearly set forth. The alteration itself involved a re-imagining of desirable social character and possible social control. It was a contingent event and yet without it a capitalist society would not have been possible. The 'moral' and the Machiavellian elements in political economy open out for us a dimension of the imagination of *homo economicus* not really appreciated by Marx, for whom capitalism was, in the last analysis, the outcome of technical developments and of contradictions in the feudal mode of production. In this respect, as we shall see, Marx still located capitalism, like Smith, within a narrative of rational development. By contrast, one finds in Stewart and his later followers a clearer view of capitalism as a system contingently inaugurated – a new 'Spartan republic' resisting, with new subtlety, the vagaries of *fortuna*. As will be seen in the third part of this book, it is difficult to refute such an unblinkered endorsement of capitalism merely on the grounds that it is irrational, ideological, or self-deluding.[45]

What matters here, from a historical point of view, is not rationality or irrationality, but rather the 'neo-pagan' character of this clear-sighted vision of political economy and its outright celebration of what Christian theology rejected, namely the *libido dominandi*.[46] Here again, the 'autonomy' of secular reason involves as a condition of its very independence, the endorsement of a viewpoint which Christianity earlier presumed to call into question.

Providence and Unintended Outcomes

Political economy, in its open, candid and scarcely ideological version, is to be described as an 'agonistics' and accounted 'pagan' rather than 'heretical'. However, in its more ideological versions, which tend to conceal

[44] See chapter 7 below.
[45] Ibid.
[46] see chapter 12 below.

historical contingency and violence, it should be characterized as a heterodox 'theodicy'.

The crucial difference lies in the mode of connecting 'private' with 'general' interests, once contractualist solutions are eschewed. For the 'agonistic' version, there is a heterogenesis of ends (separate individual actions resulting in a non-intended harmony) within the market system, but this system itself is deliberately or quasi-deliberately set up through a series of violent appropriations on the part of inherited, military power, which therefore retains its antique primacy in the background. For the 'theodicist' version, by contrast, the economic heterogenesis of ends, or 'the hidden hand' of the marketplace, holds the initiative throughout history. God, or 'providence' or 'nature', is the Machiavellian sovereign who weaves long-term benefits out of short-term interests and individual discomfitures. While this version gave scope for ideological occlusions, especially of the process of 'primary accumulation', it also paid more serious attention to the problem of 'spontaneous' harmony in situations where social order cannot be attributed to deliberate imposition.

One should not, however, exaggerate the difference between 'agonistics' and theodicy. At a deep level, the vision of the designing God and the Machiavellian sovereign reinforced each other. Thus the theodicies made room for a certain participation in providence, or economic 'fine-tuning' on the part of governments, while the Machiavellians embedded their vision of a lawful conflict within a Christian stoic account of a providence distilling continuous or final order from the tensional play of warring forces.[47]

It is certainly important that Scottish political economy can be traced to a line of thought ill at ease with Hobbes's Epicurean politics. *Leviathan* placed human making against a background of anarchic conflict of self-interest. Thinkers like Cumberland, Shaftesbury and Hutcheson tried to refute this imputation against the state of nature by insisting both on an inborn 'benevolence' and on the idea that even selfish passions were providentially directed by God towards the general social good.[48] A whole important chapter of 'natural theology', constantly rewritten all the way from Derham in the seventeenth century to Sumner in the nineteenth, concerned the demonstration of design not just in the natural world but also in the social order.[49] This reinsertion of 'providence' into scientific discourse means that one cannot tell the story of the development of 'social science' simply under the rubric of the

---

[47] Stewart, *The Works*, vol. 6, pp. 83–90. Hirschman, *The Passions and the Interests*, pp. 7–67.

[48] Myers, *The Soul of Modern Economic Man*, pp. 33ff, 68–71.

[49] John Derham, *Physico-Theology* (Dublin: Fairbrother, 1727) vol. 2, pp. 143–4, 164. *Civil Polity: A Treatise Concerning the Nature of Government (1705)*. Soame Jemyns, *A Free Inquiry into the Nature and Origin of Evil* (London, 1757). Abraham Tucker, *The Light of Nature Pursued* (Cambridge: Hilliard and Brown, 1831). William Paley, *The Principles of Moral and Political Philosophy* (London: R. Foulder, 1796). Thomas Chalmers, *On Political Economy in Connection with the Moral State and Moral Prospects of Society* (Glasgow: W. Collins, 1832). Richard Whately, *Introductory Lectures on Political Economy* (London: John W. Parker, 1835). John Bird Sumner, *Records of the Creation* (London: J. Hatchard, 1825).

substitution of human for divine agency. Indeed, divine agency is invoked much more *directly* as an explanatory cause in the eighteenth century (both in natural and social science) than in the Middle Ages.

Within the *schema* of natural theology, the division of labour was thought of as a natural and providential process, which ensured social connection and cohesion without any human plan. At the same time, the endless subdividing of tasks was regarded as a necessary instrument for an equivalent subdividing or *analysis* of nature. Nature was characteristically thought of an an infinite *series*, without gaps, part of a plenitudinous realization of all rational possibilities. Knowledge, therefore, was a more or less accurate measurement or *mathesis* and aspired to an exact 'representation' of the order of occurrence and the teleological adaptation of reality.[50] The division of labour provided a mode of access to plenitude, and market exchanges measured (insofar as they were 'free') the variety of things according to a one-dimensional scale of their usefulness or rarity. Thus the processes of production and exchange not only exhibited a divinely executed social design, they also brought further and further to light the design of nature.

If there was a social variant of the 'argument from design', there was also a social variant of theodicy. Attempts were made, by Joseph Butler and others, to show that self-interest was frequently not anti-social.[51] Even where it appeared on the face of things to be so, it was argued that it could contribute indirectly to the public good. Soame Jemyns became the first thinker to argue that crime had an important social function, and saw in this circumstance exquisite evidence of the divine care.[52] More commonly it was contended that the various manifestations of self-love cancelled themselves out in such a way as to channel self-interest into public benefit. This 'economy' could also operate at the cultural level (thus Shaftesbury declared that 'wit is its own remedy')[53] and within the individual (thus Pascal, Nicole and Donat already thought that passion could be tempered by passion, affection by affection).[54] In this way an 'economic' discourse originally belonged to a theodicy, an attempt to 'justify the ways of God to men'.

This fact has been very well delineated by Milton L. Myers, among others. However, Myers attempts to distinguish a tendency, culminating with Adam Smith, to conceive the heterogenesis of ends in gradually more 'natural' and 'realist' terms and so finally to dispense with the theological fiction which had nonetheless heuristically assisted the final scientific 'discovery'.[55] Yet in truth there was *no* point at which a theological or metaphysical thesis got translated

[50] Richard Cumberland, *A Treatise on the Laws of Nature*, trans. John Maxwell (London, 1727) p. 108. Myers, *The Soul of Modern Economic Man*, pp. 45–6. Foucault, *The Order of Things*, pp. 63–5.

[51] Joseph Butler, 'Sermons', in L. A. Selby-Bigge (ed.) *British Moralists* (New York: Dover, 1965) p. 201.

[52] Myers, *The Soul of Modern Economic Man*, p. 71.

[53] Shaftesbury, Earl of, *Characteristics of Men, Manners, Opinions, Times* (Indianapolis: Bobbs-Merrill, 1964).

[54] Hirschman, *The Passions and the Interests*, pp. 7–67.

[55] Myers, *The Soul of Modern Economic Man*, pp. 93–125.

into a scientific and empirical one, no Bachelardian 'epistemological break'. The only change was a relatively trivial one, from ascribing design to a transcendent God, to ascribing it to an immanent 'nature'. The 'scientific discovery' of the division of labour as a means of reconciling individual and public interest had *already* been made by the natural theologians and Smith only elaborated the idea with more technical precision.

In Smith's discussion of justice in *The Theory of Moral Sentiments* (already alluded to), he makes it clear just how he conceives of the role of 'nature'. As people are primarily motivated by passion and sentiment and not reason, one cannot imagine that they are really making a utilitarian calculation when they demand punishment for acts of injustice. On the contrary, it is at one level just a positive fact that the passion of 'resentment' against injury to person or property is an especially strong one. Yet on another level, when one reflects how vital this passion is to the very constitution of society, one must suppose here a design on the part of nature, which is the utilitarian calculator. Thus it 'seems the darling care of nature' to support the 'immense fabric of human society'.[56]

According to Smith, the great mistake is to attribute to reason what belongs to sentiment and so 'to imagine that to be the wisdom of man, which is in reality the wisdom of God'.[57] The disciplinary division of intellectual labour implied by this remark is a subtle one. For Smith sees attention to 'sympathy', rather than to reason, as equivalent to a concentration on efficient rather than final causes in natural science. Social science, like natural science, is to rid itself of metaphysical illusion by no longer ascribing to things or persons an inherent 'striving' towards their appointed goals; efficient mechanism is substituted for immanent teleology.[58] Consequently, in society, as in nature, final causes belong to God alone. However, this is *not* just to deliver questions of 'finality' over to an extrascientific and ineffable realm; on the contrary, in nature there *is* design and in human affairs there *is* 'social utility'. This undeniable and visible fact cannot any longer, as in Aristotelian science, be ascribed to immanent formality and finality. Instead, it must be attributed to the extrinsic work of a designing agent – either 'God' or 'Nature'. Hence God-Nature is not merely invoked as a primary or creative cause operating 'through' secondary causes, as for traditional Christian thought. On the contrary, natural theology is invoked as a 'scientific' complement to science because it *also* traces a level of primary and immediate causality operating 'alongside' efficient causation. However, by ascribing all finality and purpose to a single agent – God-Nature – it leaves empirical science free to confine itself to traceable and provable efficient operations.

On this model, Smith's social science includes a 'finitized' providence, thought of univocally as a single and especially powerful and consistent

---

[56] Smith, *The Theory of Moral Sentiments*, p. 125.
[57] Ibid., Part II, Section II, p. 127.
[58] Ibid., pp. 126–7.

agency, whether conscious or not. The 'hidden hand' of the marketplace is somewhat more than a metaphor, because God-Nature has placed self-interest and the 'trucking dispensation' in individuals in such a way that their operation will result in an overall harmony. The 'direct' causation of God-Nature does not, however, in any way imply a constantly intervening and 'particular' providence. *Neither* in Smith *nor* in the earlier natural theologians is providential intervention required to ensure each particular heterogeneous outcome. Rather, the constant providential causality consists in the setting up and perpetuation of the heterogeneously-derived market systems.

As he ascribes the division of labour and 'free' market exchange to a system belonging to the design of nature, Smith tends to suppress the reality of primary accumulation.[59] Instead, basic social history, progressing from the hunter-gatherer stage to 'commercial society', is a peaceful and 'economic' process, coincident with the growth of knowledge and skill, and with nature's gradual self-representation to humanity.[60] In this way, the 'theological' (though 'heretical') version of political economy tends to mystify the description of capitalism, producing in Smith what Marx called 'the trinity formula', or the idea that there are three 'original', pre-given sources of wealth, namely land, labour and capital, each deserving a certain recompense for their contribution.[61] The reality of a purposive, or semi-purposive human violence at the origins is transcribed by Smith as a perpetual providential manipulation of peaceful origins always already in place.

Smith's version of the heterogenesis of ends does not then escape the implication of a certain sort of providentialism. This is linked with the idea of a *mathesis*: at bottom human history is the measure of an incremental growth of reason, a gradual display of the full range of talents and resources. Formal economic complexity is in itself a guarantee of beauty and quality, and it is a 'natural' rather than a human product. This providentialism should lead us to be more suspicious of the whole discourse about 'heterogeneity' which constitutes such a large proportion of all later social science.

Critique of Heterogenesis

Social explanations in terms of design, or of theodicy, appear as an alternative to contractualist interpretations of the social whole. Yet they *remain* basically individualist. Human subjects are thought of as primarily moved by *conatus*, and as only able to take account of others insofar as they are proximate, next to them in the social series. The reverse side of Adam Smith's notion of non-planned collaboration is a fiction of unrelated individual starting points – persons and properties sprung from nowhere.

---

[59] Perelman, *Classical Political Economy*, pp. 644, 127–72.
[60] Smith, *The Wealth of Nations*, I.ii, p. 25ff, iii, pp. 31–6, v.i., p. 783.
[61] Simon Clarke, *Marx, Marginalism and Modern Sociology from Adam Smith to Max Weber* (London: Macmillan, 1982) pp. 20–43.

Likewise, Smith's heterogenesis supposes an individualist view of knowledge, purpose and responsibility. One is able to erect an absolute contrast between these and final social outcomes *because* it is held possible to define precisely and isolate 'individual' reasons and purposes, leaving room for the 'demonstration' of a spiritual causal power directly present to human history, binding human actions together and not acting through them, like a 'final cause' in medieval thought. However, such private reasons and purposes are only possible because individuals are already socially situated within language and, as we shall see, one of the roots of 'sociology' is precisely the deepening of the problematic about the social whole with the realization that social outcomes are 'always already there'. If individual reasons and purposes always have to make social sense to begin with, then they already appeal to certain collective (although indeterminate) norms and modes of social interaction.

Moreover, one cannot answer questions about an individual's 'real' purpose by imagining an access to her inner consciousness. The individual herself cannot know what she 'really' thinks or intends in this way, but only by conjecturing as to where her thoughts and opinions may lead. In another Scottish discussion of the heterogenesis of ends, namely that of Adam Ferguson, the non-planned character of social outcomes is seen as paralleled by the non-planned character of *individual* works and actions.[62] Whereas Smith works with a duality of 'blind' instincts over against a designing nature, Ferguson suggests that all reason consists of 'projects', in which action precedes a knowledge that is always a coming to know what exactly it is we have done. The social outcome is the upshot of various competing and collaborating projects, but social heterogenesis merely extends a heterogenesis proper to individual reason. With Giambattista Vico also, there may be a continuity between his view that knowledge is 'of the made' and his account of unplanned social outcomes. In both these cases, social theory seems to take account of Baroque *poesis*, or a making where motive, will and plan are not prior to execution, and ideality and teleological direction emerge with the shaping of the action or product.[63] If one thinks, in this way, of individual intention as only arising with the gradual taking shape of a project, then it becomes less easy to distinguish 'deliberate' intention from the implicit 'tendency' of an action. So, for example, the capitalist who seeks self-gain within a rule-governed system is constantly articulating his desire for such a system and for characters like himself within it.

The heterogenesis of ends can only appear as a fundamental mode of social description because one thinks of an imaginary intending agent standing 'behind' her projects, whereas the agent really becomes an agent through her projects. Choice, in its most basic options, is not discovered at

---

[62] Ferguson, *An Essay*, pp. 1–16.

[63] Vico, *On the Most Ancient Wisdom of the Italians*, ch. 1, pp. 45–7. *The New Science*, paras. 341–2. See chapter 1 above.

the individual level, but within social discourse. Only by forgetting this can one establish an economic 'science' which divides and rules in terms of private sentiments and 'natural' design. Once this is recognized, there can be no more discovery of a fundamental 'economic' dimension to all human history, and no alienation of human purpose (which is not primarily 'conscious') to the side of nature, reason, or providence. There is no gap to be bridged between commencement and conclusion by any natural legal process because destinations are by definition 'other' than starting points, even though starting points can only be narrated as the way to destinations.

Theological Malthusianism

In the 'neo-pagan' version of political economy there takes place not so much a de-ethicization, as an identification of virtue with Machiavellian *virtù*. In the theologically 'heterodox' version, by contrast, there is *more* of a de-ethicization, because the transcendent is not invoked in order to secure the metaphysical objectivity of social choice, nor an immanent teleology, but rather to account for the social whole and to 'justify' the prevalence of individual social ills. Instead of these ills being accounted for in the terms of traditional dogmatic theology, as the result of human free-will and human fallenness, they now belong with 'natural ills' among the given data of natural order and must be accounted for in terms of a theodicy.

The political economy which develops after Malthus has been correctly perceived as completely removed from the humanist concerns of the Scots and as much more indifferent to questions of immediate neighbourly responsibility towards the poor than Adam Smith.[64] However, this post-Malthusian political economy continues to form an alliance with theodicy, and its ethical indifference proceeds apace with yet greater justificatory contortions. Furthermore, the new post-Malthusian theodicy permits an ideological conjuncture between natural theology and specifically 'evangelical' virtues applying more to self-development than to social concern.

Post-Malthusian political economy differs from that of the eighteenth century in two specific ways. First of all, whereas eighteenth-century economics concentrated on exchange, and taught the mutual, circular determination of all the various factors of price, rent, profits, capital and wages, post-Malthusian economics was 'unidirectional' because it assigned primary causal efficacy either to the fertility of land (as with Malthus) or else to both fertility and the productivity of labour (as with Ricardo).[65] Thus, for these theorists, the

---

[64] Gertrude Himmelfarb, *England in the Early Industrial Age* (London: Faber and Faber, 1984) pp. 23–41, 100–32.

[65] David Ricardo, 'On the principles of political economy and taxation', in P. Sraffa (ed.) *Works and Correspondence*, vol. 1, pp. 49–51, 126–7. Foucault, *The Order of Things*, pp. 253–63. Alessandro Roncaglia, 'Hollander's Ricardo', in Giovanni A. Caravale (ed.) *The Legacy of Ricardo* (Oxford: Blackwell, 1985).

ultimate determination of wealth lay in the ratio of food to population and (for Ricardo) the possibility of reproducing labour power. The second difference lay in the denial of eighteenth-century optimism. Whereas Smith and others held forth a prospect of unlimited growth, Malthus and Ricardo identified absolute limits to growth in terms of falling demand, decreasing fertility and over-population.[66]

It is actually not easy to account for this change, which has something of the character of 'an epistemic switch'. Certainly no more 'evidence' had accrued to lead Malthus to his arbitrary assertion that whereas population increased geometrically, food stocks increased only arithmetically. The new political economy indeed justified further restrictions on poor-relief, held merely to encourage 'surplus mouths', but other ideological reasons for restriction were available from earlier theories, like those of Stewart. It is also true that the new ideas fitted with the philosophy of the 'liberal Tories' who sought to give priority to agrarian capitalism, but again, earlier ideas in the physiocratic tradition, favouring a concentration on rural development, were in theory available.[67]

Michel Foucault suggested that one should interpret the change in terms of a broader intellectual transformation.[68] Whereas, in the 'classical' *episteme* of the eighteenth century, linguistic signs and economic exchange 'represent', in an infinite approximation, the order of nature, now there is a *hiatus*, as for Kant, between human knowledge and an ultimately inaccessible realm of 'things'. For Malthus and Ricardo, human engagement with nature lies not in the sphere of representation and classification, but in the direct participation in processes of growth and physical transformation. Although 'representation' takes time to complete, and so wealth and knowledge were associated for that classification with historical progress and also (one should add to Foucault) with production, this was really thought of as an infinite analysis, a gradual traversing of natural 'space'. However, where knowledge is instead seen as something which 'develops' by means of labour providing the 'necessities' of life, then this temporal focus can tend (not, I think *must* tend, as Foucault implies) to give primacy to finitude, to death as the end of growth and infertility as the limit on production. Likewise, fundamental 'value' comes to be seen (by Ricardo) not as the labour that the price of a product can command in the marketplace, but as the labour directly 'embodied' in the product.[69] Value has become more fixed, finite and determining of other economic components.

According to Foucault, 'representation' survives, no longer as representation of nature, but now of the fundamental characteristics of human subjectivity. For Ricardo there is a representation of 'man' as a labouring animal, and

---

[66] Ricardo, *On the Principles of Political Economy and Taxation*, pp. 67ff, 106–7.

[67] Foucault, *The Order of Things*, pp. 256–7. Himmelfarb, *England in the Early Industrial Age*, p. 131.

[68] Foucault, *The Order of Things*, p. 217ff.

[69] Clarke, *Marx, Marginalism, and Modern Economics*, p. 39ff.

for Malthus as a creature engaged in a hopeless fending-off of death, which nonetheless permits him to emerge as a 'spiritual' being.

Malthus expounds his anthropology in the final part of the first edition of *The Principle of Population*, where he seeks to justify the God who has made increase of wealth ultimately incompatible with human survival.[70] It would seem to be obvious that Malthus's 'scientific' theory poses a problem for Christian belief in a benevolent God, which the theodicy of the final part seeks to overcome. Here Malthus suggests that only the perpetual spur of fear for our survival prompts the gradual distillation of a 'spiritual' being out of inherently sluggish matter. To be merely sunk in matter is, he suggests (very dualistically), a literal 'hell', but only the constant though hopeless struggle against matter and finitude permits 'soul' and spiritual resilience to arise. No genuine virtue could exist if there were not the need to overcome difficulties, 'evils' and temptations.[71]

In the second edition and the shorter *Summary View*, the section on theodicy was omitted and a new stress on sexual continence and household economy as a means to stave off demographic disaster was added.[72] It appears to commentators like Gertrude Himmelfarb that these two changes are correlated and that the greater practical optimism rendered the theodicy redundant.[73] However, the idea that the 'natural law' of population is beneficial in its encouragement of effort does *not* disappear from the later works. Instead, the new optimism adds a new theme to the theodicy: sexual self-control is also providentially encouraged, and *this* virtue is more directly rewarded in this earthly life.[74] It is notable that Malthus's follower, the Scots divine Thomas Chalmers, takes over the modified theodicy *along with* the new relative optimism.[75] Both Malthus and Chalmers not only see sexual and economic 'saving' as socially functional, but also value frugality as an aspect of self-restraint and planned regulation, which they deem to be of the essence of virtue.[76]

In view of this, it is more than tempting to read Malthusianism 'back to front'. Secretly, it is the appeal of the new theodicy which encourages the pessimistic science and *not*, as appears on the surface, the theodicy which 'compensates' for this pessimism. For *why* is Malthus opposed to the optimism of Adam Smith? The answer appears to be that Smithian theodicy all too clearly tended in a direction which legitimated an endless hedonism and

[70] Thomas Malthus, *An Essay on the Principles of Population* (Harmondsworth: Penguin, 1978) pp. 200–17.

[71] Ibid., pp. 209, 214.

[72] Malthus, 'A summary view of the principles of population', in *The Principles of Population*, pp. 212–72.

[73] Himmelfarb, *England in the Early Industrial Age*, p. 118.

[74] Malthus, 'A summary view of the principles of population', in *The Principles of Population*, pp. 271–2.

[75] Chalmers, *On Political Economy*, pp. 551–66. *The Application of Christianity to the Commercial and Ordinary Affairs of Life* (Glasgow: Chalmers and Collins, 1820) pp. 67–102, 248–78.

[76] Malthus, 'A summary view of the principles of population', in *The Principles of Population*, p. 271. Chalmers, *The Application of Christianity*, pp. 9–67.

luxury and envisaged the long-term 'good outcome' of progress as the *only* human destiny. Thus one of Malthus's main targets was Godwin, who held out the prospect of a kind of finite immortality.[77] However, the Malthusian theodicy, which sees nature as ultimately futile and even chaotic, makes the 'long-term outcome' coincide with the preparation of individual souls for heaven.[78] His thought is much more distinctly 'bourgeois' than that of the eighteenth century, and he says that the whole point of 'upper' and 'lower' in nature and society is to ensure that there is a middle region of balance: in social terms this means a class that is neither totally discouraged, nor too complacent.[79] This detail shows that even in the first edition Malthus associates 'soul formation' with a certain degree of temporal stability and worldly success.

By reading Malthusianism 'backwards' and according priority to the theodicy, one gets a more plausible picture of the early nineteenth-century epistemic shift. This new ideology allows political economy to be more widely disseminated because it is no longer primarily focused upon 'high policy' for the general well-being of the State or the universe. For the latter perspective neither poverty, nor hard work, nor consumption, were in themselves especially commendable or otherwise. However, for Malthusianism, the hard-working and frugal are the desirable products of the system, and to a certain extent and for a certain time, they are responsible for their own betterment. Within an *overall* functional and theodicist framework, the new political economy permitted a new relevance for the 'direct' exercise of certain virtues. (Thus Malthusianism could be readily popularized by evangelical clergymen like John Bird Sumner and Thomas Chalmers.) In consequence, wealth was no longer to do with an infinite and Promethean extension of knowledge; instead it promoted only a 'practical reason', linked nonetheless (as with Kant) to the transcendent. It is a certain kind of moralizing and pietistic theology which wants to define 'man' in terms of strict and knowable limits, although it *appears* that theodicy is only reckoning with a new 'scientific' discovery of finitude.

Thus at the heart of the epistemic switch (at least in Britain and the United States) lies a new *rapprochement* between natural theology and the Calvinist or evangelical work ethic. The 'this worldly asceticism' uncovered by Weber could never have been sufficient for the deliberate promotion of a market economy and wage-earning dependence, because Calvinism either was not interested in the functioning of the whole system, or when it was, as among the seventeenth-century puritans, it tended to give the 'relief of man's estate' an eschatological value which was still in line with traditional notions of 'the common good', the duty to relieve poverty and the direct encouragement of the talents and virtue of all.[80] Yet, following Malthus, Thomas Chalmers is able to combine the themes of theodicy with the idea of a spiritual training of

---

[77] Malthus, *The Principles of Population*, pp. 132–82.
[78] Ibid., pp. 200–8.
[79] Ibid., pp. 206–7.
[80] Charles Webster, *The Great Instauration* (London: Duckworth, 1975) pp. 324–484.

the elect. Like all the natural theologians, Chalmers still observes that God erects a 'beauteous order' on the foundations of human selfishness, but he is in any case rather dismissive of charity and forgiveness which are 'general virtues' found in every religion and culture.[81] By contrast, self-interest is more obviously compatible with the greater development of what Chalmers considers to be the *specifically Christian* virtues of sexual continence, sobriety, punctiliousness, discipline and Sabbath observance(!) This combination of theodicy with the Calvinist work ethic already allows Chalmers to be a 'Weberian sociologist' – for he observes that while such virtues are not practised for worldly reasons, they still produce worldly effects.[82] They non-intentionally maintain a market system whose providential goal is, in turn, the reproduction of such virtues. In this way the apparent 'frivolity' of expanding wealth and exchange is no longer located as the providential end, but merely as a means to a final puritan seriousness.

Once one has seen how unfounded Malthusian pessimism and finitism was, and how governed by theodicy, then Chalmers' social theory appears not as a Christian adaptation to contemporary science, but simply as a heretical redefinition of Christian virtue and a heretical endorsement of the manipulation of means by ends. Economic theodicy is conjoined with an evangelicalism focused on a narrow, individualist practical reason which excludes the generous theoretical contemplation of God and the world (this is thinned down to a simple acceptance of positive revealed data which ensures salvation). However, this strange conjuncture goes on providing a background legitimation for capitalism which long survives its specifically Malthusian form. Indeed, such a mean little heresy today increasingly defines 'Christianity', and once again helps to shape Anglo-Saxon social reality.

Political economy was not, we can conclude, an emancipated secular science which explored the formal aspects of economic relations in abstraction from moral considerations. Rather, it imagined and helped to construct an amoral formal mechanism which allows not merely the institution but also the preservation and the regulation of the secular. This 'new science' can be unmasked as agonistics, as theodicy and as a redefinition of Christian virtue.

[81] Chalmers, *The Application of Christianity*, pp. 37–102.
[82] Ibid., pp. 102–43.

Part II

Theology and Positivism

3
Sociology I:
From Malebranche to Durkheim

Introduction

Liberal discourse presupposed only the isolated, self-conserving individual. From the interrelationships of such individuals, the political and the economic had to be deduced as an artificial construct, or else as the 'cunning' operation of providence. In either case, the collective order was related to the individual in a negative and indirect fashion.

In the nineteenth century, initially in France, a different, 'positive' discourse arose. This presupposed, as an irreducible 'fact', not only the individual but also the 'social whole' or the 'social organism'. Unlike the political and the economic, the 'social' did not have to be deduced; instead it was merely given, in all its unfathomable finitude. New scientific approaches focused upon the new object, 'society', were not, therefore, trying to explain social phenomena as liberalism had sought to explain political and economic phenomena: instead they sought to identify and describe the social as a 'positive' *datum* and to explain *other* human phenomena in relation to this general facticity. In opposition to liberalism, the moral relationship of the individual to the collective order was also declared to be a positive one: from the given 'social' order, with its implied collective purposes, he derives his own goals and values.

'Sociology' emerged within the ambit of positivism. However, within the same ambit and with a historical priority, there emerged also a new kind of social theology. In the wake of the French Revolution, various Catholic thinkers denied the possibility of a secular politics on the grounds that politics had its basis in a 'social' order directly revealed or created by God. This conclusion was not at all an obscurantist and temporary interruption of the forward march of liberal enlightenment. On the contrary, it represented a new attempt to resolve the great antinomy encountered by secular social science – do humans construct society, or does society construct humanity? The first, 'economic' solution to this antinomy, was to reintroduce providence to supplement a scientific politics predicated upon a human making of political reality. However, a new solution was proferred by the new 'social' theology. If, for this theology, it is true that the individual is always already situated within society, then it appears to make sense to think of society neither as an *artificium*, nor as an unintended outcome governed by providential design, but instead as an aspect of the original divine creation.

Positivist discourse goes further than political economy in invoking God as an 'immediate' cause of social reality. Yet, paradoxically, it is within this same discourse that the first markedly secular and post-theological ideology arises – that is, Comtean and later Durkheimian sociology. In this chapter I shall show that, despite the secularist reversal, there is a fundamental continuity in terms of both method and metaphysical assumptions between 'social theology' and 'sociology'. The 'social', which for the Catholic counter-revolutionaries was directly created or revealed by God, becomes for Comte and Durkheim something in the gift and control of nature. Yet sociology will use this category of the social to explain, reduce or redefine all religious phenomena. Here lies the further paradox: sociology is only able to explain, or even illuminate religion, to the extent that it conceals its own theological borrowings and its own quasi-religious status. 'Society is God' can always be deconstructed to read 'society is God's presence', and between a naturalistic and a theological positivism, there must persist a fundamental indecidability. My own view, of course, is that neither form of positivism need be entertained at all.

Sociology after Enlightenment

In recent years there has been considerable discussion as to whether sociology, especially in its French guise, is to be considered a child of Counter-Enlightenment, or a grandchild of Enlightenment.[1] Both Anthony Giddens and Steven Seidman have argued for its essential continuity with Enlightenment aims and liberal values.[2] They point to Durkheim's indebtedness to Kant and the neo-Kantians, to the concern of Montesquieu, Turgot and the Scots with historical contextuality and relativity, and even to elements of pessimism about certain trends of human 'progress' in their writings.

All of these points are true, but they need to be considered in context. Throughout the nineteenth century, there was a gradual integration of positivism with elements of liberalism amongst *both* Catholic *and* secular thinkers. However, the specifically 'sociological' element in Durkheim, as we shall see, remains connected to the positivist tradition. In the case of the eighteenth-century writers, to understand the admitted historicist elements in their thought as 'foreshadowing' sociology amounts to an anachronistic begging

---

[1] Robert Nisbet, *The Sociological Tradition* (London: Heinemann, 1966). Alan Swingewood, *A Short History of Sociological Thought* (London: Macmillan, 1984).

[2] Anthony Giddens, 'Four myths in the history of social thought' in *Studies in Social and Political Theory* (New York: Basic Books, 1977). Steven Seidman, *Liberalism and the Origins of European Social Theory* (Oxford: Blackwell, 1983) pp. 21–77.

of the question about sociology's identity. Thinkers like Montesquieu, Vico and Ferguson were certainly interested in the way in which there are hidden connections between the character of laws, language, customs and social divisions at any one period within a nation's history. Yet this extension of humanist jurisprudence tried to uncover these connections genetically; it did not, like sociology, pursue the method of observing a 'constant concomitance' between certain cultural phenomena and then seek to 'explain' this concomitance by reference to their function with a social whole more fundamental than the phenomena themselves. If there was an element in their thought of elaborating 'social laws', then this was to do with an adherence to the classical political typology which distinguished between societies governed by the few, the many, or the one. The genetic connections were fitted into this typological framework, and a measure of social prediction became possible if one took the Polybian view that the republic of the many which succeeds the aristocracy of the few is always threatened by loss of *virtue*, or anarchic dissolution. The remedy for this crisis (as with Vico) could be a monarchic one, and in Montesquieu's case (as we have seen) that solution was elaborated as absolutist rule without virtue, employing an 'economy' of honour and self-interest.[3] St Simon was therefore able to classify Montesquieu as merely an 'industrial' or 'economic' philosopher and not, like the Catholic counter-revolutionaries, a philosopher of *système*.[4]

For positivism was not a philosophy concerned with an upholding of the collective sense through an individual exercise of virtue, nor with the possibility of replacement of the political republic by a despotic or economic regime. Instead, it sought to identify a social *système* which preceded any politics and any *prise de conscience* on the part of individuals; a set of social facts and laws *prior* to virtue and prior to the setting of goals for action. Unlike the republic, the prior collectivity of 'society' could not really disappear, or be displaced. Thus it was supposed by the counter-revolutionaries that when the French Revolution, in a frenzy of liberal negativity, sought to deny altogether the positive basis of society in family hierarchy and absolute sovereignty, the social nonetheless made itself felt in an ever-increasing shedding of blood which could only be brought to a halt by a renewed recognition of the positive *système*.[5] The 'social', for sociology, begins as and remains a fundamentally ahistorical category – hence the irrelevance of appealing to Enlightenment historicism as evidence of precursorship.

---

[3] See chapter 2 above. For a reliable account of Vico, see Robert Miner, *Vico: Genealogist of Modernity* (Notre Dame: Notre Dame UP, 2002) and *Truth in the Making: Creative Knowledge in Theology and Philosophy* (London: Routledge, 2004). Also John Milbank, *The Religious Dimension in the Thought of Giambattista Vico*, 2 vols. (Lewiston, NY: Edwin Mellen, 1991–2).

[4] Henri Gouhier, *La Jeunesse d'Auguste Comte et la Formation du Positivisme* (Paris: J. Vrin, 1964) vol. 3, pp. 149, 156.

[5] Joseph de Maistre, *Considerations on France*, trans. G. Lebrun (Montreal: McGill, 1974) pp. 59–61. *Essai sur le Principe Générateur des Constitutions Politiques* (Lyon: Pélagaud, 1851) p. 84. Henri Gouhier, *La Jeunesse d'Auguste Comte* (Paris: J. Vrin, 1964) vol. 3/pp. 404, 156.

Just as irrelevant is the question of whether sociological 'pessimism' – its recognition of the disintegrating, alienating, anomic tendencies of modern society – was anticipated by the *philosophes*. In a way, their humanism permitted a much more genuine pessimism: only substitutes for *virtù* can now be found, and progress entails also some element of loss. Yet for positivism nothing essential can *ever* be lost and its pessimism is only temporary: the negative era of liberalism is soon to give way to a stage where the social will be transparently grasped and organic community will flourish as never before.[6]

A key contrast in attitudes is shown by St Simon and Comte's transformation of themes from political economy. Both thinkers accept Adam Smith's identification of the division of labour as a 'natural' process of differentiation which is the basic determinant of human history.[7] However, they reject the belief that differentiation is necessarily associated with individualism, competition and the untrammelled marketplace; these 'antagonistic' phenomena only belong to an intermediate, metaphysical era dominated by negative notions of natural right. At bottom, differentiation is a self-elaboration of the social organism, which, through the division of labour, increases mutual dependency and the sway of human sympathy.[8] In coming to recognize this, positive philosophy supposedly inaugurates a positivist era in which all industry will be organized for collective ends. The complex, differentiated society is a society where reason must rule, and reason pursues simply the goals of positive science, where there can be no real disagreement. The positive polity is thus 'harmonistic' and the only remaining struggle is the struggle to control nature. It is also a 'social', post-political order, because its organization is simply the 'givenness' of an elaborated organic complexity.

Social Facts as Revealed Truths

Robert Nisbet has argued that sociology shared a common ideological ethos with conservative Catholic thought in the nineteenth century: a stress on the need for common belief, the irreplaceable function of religion in maintaining social order, the political primacy of education, the need for a hierarchical 'spiritual power' to maintain cultural continuity, the importance of 'intermediary associations' like corporations and guilds.[9] The connection of Comte with such an ethos is undeniable, but against Nisbet, Giddens has claimed that Durkheim takes over from Comte not so much an ideology, as merely certain elements of scientific method.[10] This response is basically

---

[6] Auguste Comte, *The Crisis of Industrial Civilization: The Early Essays of Auguste Comte*, pp. 221–41. Henri Gouhier, *La Jeunesse d'Auguste Comte* (Paris: J. Vrin, 1964) vol. 3/pp. 280, 326ff.

[7] Ibid, pp. 323–4. Comte, *The Crisis of Industrial Civilization*, p. 231.

[8] Ibid, pp. 38, 232, 238–9. *Cours de Philosophie Positive* (Paris: Bachelier, 1839) vol. 4/p. 629ff. Gouhier, *La Jeunesse d'Auguste Comte*, vol. 3/p. 326ff.

[9] Nisbet, *The Sociological Tradition*.

[10] Giddens, 'Four myths in the history of social thought'.

correct; however, it is sufficient only because Nisbet failed to make the 'strong case' for the conservative origins of sociology.

The strong case argues for a basic continuity from de Bonald and de Maistre through Comte to Durkheim, not in terms of ideology, nor only in terms of method, but in terms of both method and metaphysical assumptions. Nisbet and others tend to suggest that St Simon and Comte took over from the two great Counter-Enlightenment thinkers certain 'attitudes' which they then conjoined with a new, scientific analysis. However both de Maistre and (more especially) de Bonald *already* understood their social theories as strictly scientific, although they also regarded them as theological. One has to approach these writers as still working in the tradition of what Funkenstein calls 'secular theology', namely a discourse which collapses together empirical discussion of finite realities and invocation of the transcendent. As Funkenstein says, such a discourse is an heir to the Scotist doctrine of univocity of meaning between finite and infinite being.[11] It becomes possible within this perspective to apply terms like 'cause' and 'power' without equivocation to both human and divine agents, and so to discover 'evidence' for God and to invoke the divine presence as an immediate explanatory cause.

It is also misleading simply to dub these thinkers as 'Counter-Enlightenment'. In a way, they belong more to a 'hyper' or 'post' Enlightenment, which even anticipates elements in the thought of Nietzsche. De Maistre at least (who had Masonic connections) can scarcely be considered an orthodox Catholic, and his thought exhibits a 'mystical materialism' which feeds into secular positivism in a more direct manner than has often been supposed.[12] Like the materialist Thomas Hobbes, de Bonald and de Maistre associate God with the operation of arbitrary and material power. Where they differ from Hobbes (or perhaps place a different emphasis) and from liberal discourse in general, is in focusing on the arbitrary itself, rather than on the formalistic manipulations of the arbitrary which is liberalism's very essence. The post-Enlightenment case, in a nutshell, is that while, from a formal point of view, any old *mythos* of power will do, in practice what holds societies together is not a formal ordering of the arbitrary, but rather the *content* of the arbitrary, or devotion to a particular *mythos*.[13] Hence de Maistre's famous denial that one can legislate for public festivals; confronted with the revolutionary religion of reason, the people remain eccentrically attached to the commemoration of the

---

[11] Funkenstein, *Theology and the Scientific Imagination*, pp. 57–9, 89–90. Sheldon S. Wolin, *Politics and Vision* (Boston: Little Brown, 1960) pp. 359–61.

[12] Joseph de Maistre, 'Éclaircissements sur les sacrifices', in *Les soirées de St. Petersbourg* (London/Paris: Dent/Mignon, 1912) pp. 206–7. Jean-Yves le Borgne, *Joseph de Maistre et La Révolution* (Brest: Université de Bretagne Occidentale, 1976). Robert Triomphe, *Joseph de Maistre* (Geneva: Ambilly-Annermasse, 1968).

[13] De Maistre, *Considerations on France*, pp. 80, 92, 94, 99, 103. *Essai sur le Principe Générateur*, pp. 79, 82. R. A. LeBrun, *Throne and Altar* (Ottowa: Ottowa University Press, 1965) pp. 67–8, 90–1. *Essai Analytique sur les Lois Naturelles de l'Ordre Sociale, ou du Pouvoir, du Ministre et du Subject dans la Société* (Paris, 1800) pp. 82–3.

half-forgotten deeds of local saints.[14] No longer then, is it possible, as for liberalism, to found and legitimate arbitrary power in terms of the formal property deeds of prior ownership and self-possession; instead, all power in its real, factual occurrence is entirely self-founded – it has no legitimation whatsoever outside its own self-establishment through mythical inscription.

Whereas liberalism prevaricated about the arbitrary, and so was able to claim a universal, secular rights-theory based on 'reason' which could eventually emancipate itself from religion, the post-Enlightenment thinkers elaborate a much more naked power-theory, which declares that *mythos* or religion is indispensable, because it is the all-essential *content* of the arbitrary. Hence, at times, de Maistre just sounds Machiavellian: 'if you wish to conserve everything, dedicate everything'; 'religion . . . true or false . . . is the basis of all durable institutions'.[15] Violent seizure of power must be concealed, and cities endure in proportion to the hiddenness and mysteriousness of their origins.[16] However, because the formal considerations about power point to the primacy of a mystifying content, Machiavellianism passes over into a kind of self-negation, such that one chooses to believe that at different stages of history a divine power really *has* willed a certain positive content for religion, which is the true foundation for any possible social order.[17]

According to de Bonald, this attention to the unfounded difference of content marks the contrast between a possible *société positive* and an impossible *société negative*.[18] He establishes this primacy, nevertheless, through a strictly formalistic, iusnaturalist argument.[19] In stoic fashion, everything in the universe seeks to use its power to conserve itself; this applies to societies as well as individuals, although societies can only be societies if there is paternal or monarchic sovereignty. For there is no real unity outside the unity of the individual will – thus far de Bonald is in the line of Bodin, Hobbes and Filmer. But beyond the narrow range of its own organism, the individual will is powerless, and it requires supplementation by a mediating power or powers, if it is to dominate other wills or entities. Thus throughout the cosmic and the political order runs a universal triadic logic of *faits sociales* which are 'general', 'external' and 'visible'.[20] The universal ratio *pouvoir/ministre/sujet* is found expressed as I/you/he, father/mother/child, sovereign/executive/subject and God/priest/faithful.[21] As the divine *Logos* is said to be also the *ministre* of God, it is clear that a certain Eusebian semi-Arianism

---

[14] De Maistre, *Considerations on France*, pp. 83–4.
[15] Cited in LeBrun, *Throne and Altar*, pp. 90–1.
[16] De Maistre, *Essai sur le Principe Générateur*, pp. 43–4.
[17] Louis de Bonald, *Théorie du Pouvoir, Politique et Religieux* (Paris: Le Derc, 1843) tome III. p. 188. LeBrun, *Throne and Altar*, p. 64.
[18] De Bonald, *Essai Analytique*, p. 11.
[19] Ibid., pp. 1–82.
[20] Ibid., pp. 85, 108, 215–16.
[21] Ibid., p. 1ff. Paul Bourget and Michel Solomon (eds.), *De Bonald* (extracts) (Paris: Bloud, 1903) p. 9ff.

is present here; the 'ordering' of the *Logos* is reduced to a mere executive function.[22] De Bonald argues that secondary representation can only be executive in character because, while one can act for another, one cannot will on his behalf.

If any society wishes to conserve itself, then, according to de Bonald, it must conform to the hierarchic power-logic of this triadic relationship. Prior to any political institution is the given social order which this logic embodies. It is then clear that de Bonald understands the primacy of the social over the political in terms of the primacy of natural over civic law, but it is also true that he already 'sociologizes' the very idea of natural law. This happens in the following way.

The natural law of the triadic relationship is not, for de Bonald, known to us through rational introspection. Instead, the *rapports*, as he calls them, are embodied externally in social and linguistic relationships, and only later reflected upon by individuals.[23] It is for this reason that the formal order of power can only be known about, even in its formality, because there is a particular positive order. De Bonald and all the French 'traditionalist' thinkers of the early nineteenth century reason from the fact that thought as a reflection on social relationship is made possible through public language, to an esoteric theory of both language and society. Finite reason and activity, he argues, never extends beyond *conservation*; all origination which effects something genuinely unprecedented, like language, belongs to the order of creation, and lies within the power of God alone.[24] Thus for de Bonald, de Maistre and their followers, language, writing, the family and political sovereignty are all *revealed* institutions, and every human culture represents a post-Babel fragment of God's original self-presence to humankind.[25] This attempt to understand revelation as a universal category shows that it would be a mistake to think of these thinkers as simply 'natural theologians'; instead, the turn to the 'positive' moment within formalistic natural law theory corresponds to an attempt to integrate seamlessly the history of revelation with a strictly 'scientific' theory. So while de Maistre and de Bonald distinguish between a universal natural religion and particular Christian revelation, they insist that natural religion was also revealed and that the Christian revelation was also 'natural'. The difference between the two arises from the necessity for a complete sacrificial atonement which de Bonald thinks can be logically demonstrated within his new natural law of society.[26]

The traditionalists derive their effort to integrate natural and revealed theology from the Malebranchian tradition, mediated by thinkers like Charles

[22] Ibid., pp. 33–8, 41. Bonald, *Essai Analytique*, p. 74. See chapter 1 above, note 23. De Bonald, *Théorie du Pouvoir*, tome II, p. 187. *Essai Analytique*, pp. 36ff, 71, 75.

[23] Ibid., pp. 17–18, 52. *Du Pouvoir*, pp. 25–9, 190.

[24] Ibid., pp. 187–90. De Bonald, *Essai Analytique*, pp. 48–52, 117, 130. Bourget, *De Bonald*, pp. 16ff, 26.

[25] De Maistre, *Essai sur le Principe Générateur*, pp. 30ff, 68.

[26] De Bonald, *Essai Analytique*, p. 79ff. *Du Pouvoir*, tome II, p. 38. Bourget, *De Bonald*, pp. 33–8.

Bonnet.[27] It is in Malebranche that one first finds the claim that if ideas and forms are not to be causally reduced to a material substructure, then their novelty must be ascribed to a creation *ex nihilo*. As it is hubristic blasphemy to attribute such a creation to human beings, we must suppose that all our thought really belongs to the 'vision in God'; we do not create our ideas but we are granted direct univocal access to a portion of the divine mind.[28] God also causes this mental vision to harmonize exactly with our sensory vision, so that our thought of a tree coincides with our vision of a tree, although the vision is not finitely connected with the thought. Human beings are nonetheless granted a general insight into the coordination between the order of facts and the order of ideas; this is part of the *rapports de perfection* which include also the general principles of harmony internal to the realms of both material and ideal 'extension'.[29]

De Bonald takes over from Malebranche, through Bonnet, the notion that *idées générales* are the widest possible 'relations' within intellectually extended being. Positivist discourse is thus, from the start, imbued with the peculiarly Malebranchian version of nominalism, which conceives the universal as the very 'general' particularity of interrelationship and coordination of *function*. However, de Bonald argues that the true metaphysics, or *science de réalités*, realizes that the only access to the *rapports* is through language and society.[30] The idea of the 'vision in God' is retained by de Bonald, but its site is displaced from the individual to the collective. It is only human beings in relationship who have access to the realm of 'general ideas', which like gravity in the Newtonian universe, is to be regarded as the direct conserving presence of God – so that, indeed, society is literally a 'part of' God, just as ideas were 'part of' God for Malebranche.[31] This, however, entails two further differences from Malebranche's philosophy. First of all, 'general ideas' are not occasionally coordinated with general facts: they are, equally and immediately, general 'social facts'. Secondly, for de Bonald, it seems to be only general ideas – only the *rapports de perfection* – and not every particular idea which belongs to the vision in God. This means that de Bonald erects a strict dualism between *faits sociales* which have a categorical function, and other, particular facts and ideas which are explained and comprehended through their positioning within a categoric framework. As for Kant, the categoric framework is inscrutably fixed and not subject to historical change; unlike

[27] Charles Bonnet, *La Palingénésie Philosophique* (Geneva: Philibert, 1769). *Philosophical and Critical Inquiries Concerning Christianity*, trans. John Lewis Boissier (Philadelphia: Woodward, 1803) pp. 22, 30, 33, 34, 56. De Bonald, *Essai Analytique*, pp. 17–18, 94–5. Gouhier, *La Jeunesse d'Auguste Comte*, vol. 2, pp. 13–14. LeBrun, *Throne and Altar*, p. 34ff.

[28] Nicolas Malebranche, 'De la recherche de la vérité', in G. Rodis-Lewis (ed.) *Oeuvres Complétes* (Paris: J. Vrin, 1962) vol. 1, p. 422.

[29] Desmond Connell, *The Vision in God* (Paris: Louvain, 1967) pp. 203–4.

[30] De Bonald, *Essai Analytique*, pp. 14, 17–18, 47. Bourget, *Du Pouvoir*, vol. 2, pp. 28–9. Bourget, *De Bonald*, pp. 38, 50.

[31] De Bonald, *Essai Analytique*, pp. 17–18, 51. Jack Lively (ed.), *The Works of Joseph de Maistre* (London: Allen and Unwin, 1965) p. 277.

Kant, it is given externally and socially. Indeed, de Bonald claims that only historical experience *demonstrates* Malebranche's theory that *idées générales* are seen in God.[32]

It is thus a transformed ontologism-occasionalism which establishes the positivist principle that *il n'y a de général que ça qui est extérieur ou publique*.[33] The same metaphysics ensures that efficient causality and temporal genesis have only a very limited explanatory power. What matters is the observation of constant concomitance between different particular items, this method being saved from scepticism (as with Kant) precisely at the point where those items can be located by virtue of their function within a synchronic whole: the realm of the *faits sociales*. It follows from this that all genuine scientific generalizations, including those about nature, have their foundation in more basic *observations*, which transcribe the 'general facts' about society. John Stuart Mill saw this as the very 'back-bone' of positivism and it is already firmly in place in de Bonald.[34] Only for God, considers the latter, is knowledge truly creative; but finite knowledge is nonetheless practical, as it is entirely to do with conserving bodies. Physical sciences have their *rationale* in the conservation of the physical body, human sciences in the conservation of the social body. Just as arts are the means of science, so other sciences are the means of the *science de la société*. For the conservation of society provides not only the ultimate good of all sciences, but also their ultimate principles.[35]

Two other constants of positivist science are also articulated within de Bonald's metaphysics. The first is the identification of the social order with the positive legal order. For Montesquieu, law and social structure had a reciprocal effect upon each other, and de Bonald's belief that political legislation should remember the bounds of social and customary constraint appears to echo this tradition of civic reflection. However, de Bonald foregrounds the stoic element within this tradition, which stressed the institutive role of law, and the priority of the fixed legal norms over ethical practice. Perfect laws, he believes, *precede* perfect morals, and only in imperfect, pre-Christian societies, do morals tend to alter laws, rather than the other way around.[36] The absolute prohibitions of divorce, prostitution, infanticide and slavery by Christianity remain constantly in advance of actual behaviour, although they progressively transform it. Thus, although the social and the natural is prior to the political and variable, paternal authority and political sovereignty together with the most fixed and most *positive* aspects of law, belong on the side of the social and natural, which is also the most grace-given. They are the 'ideal' aspects of 'social facts'.

The second is the idea that love or social affection should be regarded as equally primordial with individual self-interest. Only God acts entirely out of

[32] Ibid., p. 11ff.
[33] De Bonald, *Du Pouvoir*, vol. 2, p. 38.
[34] Cited in Bourget, *De Bonald*, p. 29.
[35] Ibid., pp. 9ff, 26.
[36] De Bonald, *Essai Analytique*, pp. 88–90.

an interest in *self*-conservation because he alone is not externally dependent. Original creation proceeds purely from self-love, but the merely conserving action of finite beings has to include also a love of the similar. Religious and political societies are therefore *réunions d'êtres semblables* and all conservation has to be mutual.[37] Unlike the Scots economists, the positivists, beginning with de Bonald, moved sympathy fully into the public and economic sphere. If individual identity is only available through the exercise of a public role in a given social whole, then self-sacrifice must be considered a primordial social phenomenon. However, this love is thought of as a kind of social gravity; it takes its moral authority from the absolute right of the sovereign social will. Where persuasion fails, then love may always act by force, and in fact will always automatically do so. Thus the presence of power and the operation of draconian laws are taken by de Bonald and de Maistre as evidence of the secret strength of the *fait sociale*, of the reactive potential of thwarted love. Crime and punishment are not to be considered from the point of view of equity, but factually and objectively as the upsetting of a social balance in the one case and as a natural mechanism of readjustment on the other, whose operation can never be 'excessive', while its mercy should merely surprise us.[38]

Under the light of de Bonald's claim that society is directly created and revealed, there first spring to view the terms *positive* and *fait sociale*. It has been shown that these terms already indicate the primacy of the synchronic over the diachronic, the distinction of science from pragmatic and creative 'art', the primacy of social over natural science, the priority of functional causation, the identification of law with society, and an affirmation of the primordial character of social affection. Not only do these themes persist through Comte's positivism to Durkheim's 'refounding' of sociology, but some of them, as we shall see, are articulated more forcefully by Durkheim than by Comte.

Mutations of the *Fait Sociale* (1)

There is no doubt whatsoever about the importance of de Maistre and de Bonald's influence on Comte. His other mentor was St Simon, but the influence of the Counter-Enlightenment is important in that case also. One can go further and say that just as Marx stood Hegel on his head, so Comte did the same to de Bonald.[39] Here also, the reversal leaves intact the metaphysical framework within which the reversal occurs.

St Simon identified God with gravity, and wanted a 'new Christendom' founded upon a religion of science.[40] However, as we have seen, de Bonald's

---

[37] De Bonald, *Du Pouvoir*, tome II, pp. 23–9, 33–4.

[38] Ibid., p. 188. LeBrun, *Throne and Altar*, p. 34ff, 110–12.

[39] Gouhier, *La Jeunesse d'Auguste Comte*, vol. 3, p. 156. Robert Spaemann, *Der Ursprung der Soziologie aus dem Geist der Restauration* (Munich: Kosel, 1959) pp. 199–201.

[40] Henri de St Simon, *Le Nouveau Christianisme* (Paris: Editions du Seuil, 1969) pp. 59–85, 141–85.

example already made the identification of science with religion a natural one. Even Auguste Comte's 'overcoming' of metaphysics involved, paradoxically, a naturalistic mutation of de Bonald's social ontologism. Whereas de Bonald claimed to make it 'evident' that society was revealed, Comte claimed to make it 'evident' that all religious beliefs were more or less imperfect approximations to 'sociology', or to the truth of the ultimate determining power of the social whole.[41] While de Bonald and de Maistre bolstered their social theology with organicist metaphors, for Comte the metaphors became self-sufficient: the whole is more than the sum of its parts, and social outcomes can never be adequately described, much less accounted for, in terms of their causal genesis.

Apart from the naturalistic reversal, much else remains unchanged. Comte claims that where political economy studies the antagonistic forces which tend to dissolution, his 'social physics' deals with the 'life of the spirit' and the *rapports de dépendance* among human activities.[42] These concern the *necessary* hierarchies of family, education and social organization which are proper to every age. The most fundamental division of labour, ignored by the economists, is that between the spiritual and temporal powers, already realized in European history during the Middle Ages.[43] According to the principles of sociological science, the spiritual power should always enjoy hierarchical supremacy, in the same way that theory naturally precedes practice, and law precedes obedience to the law. However, just as for de Bonald, law, theory and spiritual power enjoy this supremacy for Comte not in the mind of the individual but in the givenness of social institutions.[44] For this reason, Comte does not regard the papal power merely as an anachronism; a reading of de Maistre's *Du Pape* has enabled him to understand this institution as a theological precursor of a positive order, when society will be guided by scientific theory and by a new secular spiritual power directing both education and the division of labour. He regards this third, positive era as in certain aspects a *ricorso* to the first theological times, after the period of 'metaphysics', with its reductions of gods to conceptual abstractions and its 'negative' theories of natural rights. Primitive religion involved, according to Comte, a fetishistic attachment to the immediate natural and social environment, and to this extent it reveals the 'essence' of all religion, whose true function is more to do with nurturing a feeling of social union than with holding the threat of divine vengeance over people's heads.[45] The positive religion is, therefore, a kind of demystified fetishism, because it involves the worship of humanity in 'social' reality. Only with the disappearance of promises of heavenly rewards

[41] Comte, *The Crisis of Industrial Civilization*, pp. 24–7, 187–8. *A General View of Positivism*, trans. J. H. Bridge (London: Trubner, 1865) p. 39.
[42] Ibid., pp. 39, 231. Gouhier, *La Jeunesse d'Auguste Comte*, vol. 3, p. 326.
[43] Comte, *The Crisis of Industrial Civilization*, pp. 217ff, 233ff.
[44] Ibid., pp. 135, 187.
[45] Gertrude Lenzer (ed.) *Auguste Comte and Positivism: the Essential Writings* (New York: Harper and Row, 1975) pp. 152, 159, 168.

does the self-sacrifice and social sympathy so stressed by the Counter-Enlightenment really come into its own: in the positive era, 'altruism' will finally be realized as an ultimate human and social truth.[46]

It is clear, then, that Comte retains both a dualism of irreducible social whole over against particular constituent parts, and the association of the former totality with religion. According to Comte, religion regulates a sphere which religion institutes, and there is 'a great analogy between language and religion' because both embody a particular concrete order of attachments in which alone social unity consists. 'Property', he declares, provides the object of religion, because it gives 'free action' to energies which it has to discipline. Likewise, language grows from individual material needs, but in its fundamental aspect it exists to 'regulate' these needs as the symbolic 'expression' of religion, which gains its 'moral power' from familial affection and the more intense emotion of women.[47] Thus, from the start, the two components of a 'normal' or 'industrial' order are present – both the positivity of individual property and wealth creation, and the positivity of the regulating, affective and supra-rational spiritual totality. In this conception one sees the emergence of a complex attitude towards religion which survives intact in Durkheim: while supernatural religion disguises the fact that it is really to do with the maintaining of society, religion cannot simply be reduced to the social, because the social includes an ideal or theoretical component which, even in its evolved state as 'science', remains in a certain sense 'religion'. This is because each particular organic whole is ultimately incomparable, and therefore its order is (in terms of its particular substantive content rather than its formality) 'arbitrary', and devotion to it more than material. Unlike the Enlightenment, Comte takes heteronomy to be a *datum* and gives to it an authoritarian form: every human being has a need for a superior power to which it can submit. Positive science is not a pragmatic enterprise which finds its conclusion in showing how a particular result may be attained. Instead, it finds its terminus in the identification of a prior and external influence at the widest possible circumference of individual existence. As 'society' is this circumference, it must have been always already present in human history.

Mutations of the *Fait Sociale* (2)

The relationship of sociology to de Bonald is not as frequently recognized as the relationship of Marxism to Hegel, in part because the work of Durkheim has occluded the work of Comte, and Durkheim did not refer back to the Catholic reactionaries in the way that Hegel was reinvoked by Lukács. It has, in fact, seemed plausible to present Durkheim as sorting out the hybrid confusion in Comte between positive science and reactionary politics.[48] Yet,

---

[46] Comte, *A General View*, p. 426.

[47] Lenzer, *Auguste Comte and Positivism*, pp. 393–9, 415–19.

[48] Seidman, *Liberalism and the Origins*, pp. 145–200.

as we have seen, it is positivist purity itself which tends to encourage a 'post-liberal' political outlook. Thus it was not surprising that Comteanism was later re-Catholicized, nor that it gave rise to the 'atheist Catholicism' of the *Action Française*. To see these things as peculiar and transitional 'hybrids' may be to make onself the victim of a certain 'whiggish' progressivism in relation to intellectual history.

Durkheim imbibed through Comte the metaphysics of the *fait sociale* which had its origins in de Bonald. It is certainly true that his own ideological affinities were not with conservatism, but with neo-Kantian liberalism and republican socialism.[49] But in the latter case one should not ignore the fact that many of the associationist and corporatist elements in a thinker like Durkheim belong to a movement by which these Catholic and romantic themes migrated from right to left (often within Catholic thought itself) during the 1830s.[50] The earlier, more secular, proto-communist thinkers of the eighteenth century tended, by comparison, not to stress a mystical collect-ivism, but to deduce equal or common property rights from a liberal natural law foundation.[51] Durkheim's radical republicanism does not necessarily provide him with an unambiguous Enlightenment pedigree.

On the other hand, there is no doubt that neo-Kantianism altered, one might well say diluted, the positivist heritage. Durkheim's version of society's self-worship combines the liberal value of absolute respect for individual self-determination with religious devotion to the nation. Obviously, he is able to integrate liberalism into positivism by appealing back to Rousseau's defence of the absolute sovereignty of the general will as grounded in a particular legal framework which guaranteed a freedom for the individual subject so long as it did not interfere with the freedom of others. But Durkheim also incorporates elements of Kant's transcendentalist reworking of Rousseau's civic morality.[52] For Kant, the 'general will' became the impersonal and absolute imperative of the categorical norm in ethics. Just as, for Rousseau, obedience to the general will does not contradict our autonomy, because we are thereby willing a freedom greater than the freedom of the state of nature, so, for Kant, obedience to a categorical imperative which is 'over against us', still follows from the logic of maintaining our nature as free, not totally-determined beings. It is, confusingly, for reasons both of formal, logical consistency, and of sacred respect for the general *idea* of freedom (that we never quite live up to) that in upholding our own freedom we must respect the freedom of other spiritual beings. Durkheim exploits this Kantian

[49] Ibid. Anthony Giddens, *Durkheim* (Glasgow: Fontana, 1978) p. 13ff.

[50] Buchez, P. J. B. *Traité de Politique et Science Sociale* (Paris: Amyot, 1866) tome I, pp. 2–23, 55–68, 99–119; tome II, pp. 69–89, 486.

[51] Jean Meslier, *Oeuvres* (Paris: Editions Anthropologiques, 1970). Morelly, *Code de la Nature* (Paris, 1950) pp. 205–7. Ernest A. Whitfield, *Gabriel Bonnot de Mably* (London: Routledge, 1930) p. 86. Walter Bernardi, *Morelly e Dom Deschamps* (Florence: Olshki, 1979) pp. 69–113.

[52] Emile Durkheim, 'Individualism and the intellectuals in Durkheim', in *On Morality and Society* (ed.) Robert N. Bellah (Chicago: Chicago University Press, 1973) pp. 46–7, 54.

'antinomy of law', whereby autonomy becomes paradoxically a matter of obedience, to co-ordinate liberalism with the positivist notion of sacred respect for the social whole.[53] In a sense, he returns Kant back to Rousseau, by grounding the imperative in the civic order; but by denying the contractual origin of this order, he holds onto the transcendental element in Kant. Ethical norms are at once social and transcendental. By making this move, Durkheim considered that he had been able to show that transcendental philosophy belongs to science itself, and is not something in addition to science. For Kant, so Durkheim argues, was never able to demonstrate his *a priori* categories, but by indicating their social origin one is able to establish their objectivity.[54]

It is obvious that the element in Durkheim which goes beyond Kant and Rousseau and combines them, namely the socializing of the transcendental, is exactly parallel to de Bonald's socializing of Malebranche's *visio in Dei*. Just as de Bonald thought he had provided historical 'proof' for Malebranche's ontologism, so Durkheim thought he had provided 'evidence' for Kant's transcendentalism. By comparison, the neo-Kantian philosophers who influenced Durkheim, Renouvier and Hamelin, never approved of this sociologization, and the 'personalist' stress in their writings on social interrelationship is not at all the same as the kind of appeal to a social totality that one finds in Durkheim.[55] It is true, nevertheless, that the neo-Kantian element in Durkheim sometimes appears to modify his positivist insistence on externality, as when public religious symbols are seen as merely the 'objectivization' of emotions which exist purely in the minds of individual subjects.[56] Here Durkheim seems close to seeing the social object as merely the objectified projection of the universal moral law.

However, this countervailing influence only makes it all the clearer that it is the positivist-derived conflation of the social with the ideal, and not neo-Kantianism, which induces Durkheim to see the categorical imperative as virtually immanent within every human social structure. Thus Durkheim tends to see belief in 'the soul' as a universal component of religion, because belief in a super-finite and super-material element in the individual foreshadows the paradoxically *social* creed of the *personne humaine* as an ineffable and contentless freedom which transcends any given social role.[57] Moreover, at the other end of the evolutionary scale, in characterizing the emergent, scientific society, Durkheim adds to a liberal tolerance of differences a positivist belief in the collaboration of citizens to produce public harmony

[53] Emile Durkheim, 'Individualism and the intellectuals in Durkheim', in *On Morality and Society* (ed.) Robert N. Bellah (Chicago: Chicago University Press, 1973) pp. 46–56.

[54] Emile Durkheim, *The Elementary Forms of the Religious Life*, trans. J. W. Swain (London: Allen and Unwin, 1968) p. 445. Giddens, *Durkheim*, pp. 88, 98.

[55] Charles Renouvier, *Le Personnalisme* (Paris, 1903). Octave Hamelin, *Le Systéme de Renouvier* (Paris: Mouy, 1927). Steven Lukes, *Emile Durkheim* (Harmondsworth: Penguin, 1977) p. 57.

[56] Durkheim, *Elementary Forms*, p. 419.

[57] Emile Durkheim, 'The dualism of human nature and its social conditions', in *On Morality and Society*, p. 159.

round a particular, arbitrary, symbolic representation of the sacrality of the human individual.[58]

In another respect, however, Durkheim's Kantianism was actually in harmony with the positivist inheritance. It has been seen how de Bonald contrasted the general *rapports* and particular facts in a way which approximated to Kant's scheme/content dualism. In Durkheim, the two traditions blend to produce an intensified dualism which governs all aspects of human existence. The essence of religion, according to Durkheim, lies in the distinction between sacred and profane, and he thinks that this divide receives its true decoding in the Kantian separation of categorical universal from empirical intuition, and of categorical imperative from the empirical subject.[59] In the case of both theoretical schematization and political obedience, the individual surrenders to the force of something impersonal and unchanging, detached from the circumstances of history. This is why law, in its condensation and detachment, is a more basic site of the *fait sociale* than actual social behaviour, however habitual.[60] Durkheim, like Comte, is a declared 'Platonist' here: the individual confronts the general categories provided by society, rather as Plato's *nous* confronted the region of ideas.[61] Concepts are by their nature unalterable and this is why science is possible. If any change in concepts becomes necessary, it is because the apprehension of them has so far been imperfect.

Kantianism not only supplemented positivist dualism, it also had a direct relation to the secularization of the positivist tradition. Already, according to Comte, Kant anticipated his idea that all knowledge was 'relative', to do with one's environmental setting, and he also realized that this principle made transcendent metaphysics impossible.[62] The relativity of knowledge, however, was more firmly established by biology and sociology, and Comte took this as a deepening of the Kantian critique of metaphysics, so that he was able to salute his new discipline as that on which now depended the complete elimination of a transcendent absolute.[63] This assumption that sociology is a continuing critique of both theology and metaphysics is entirely taken over by Durkheim.

But it is in fact fraudulent: for if, as Johann Georg Hamann realized, one advances against Kant a 'metacritique', according to which the categories of knowledge are linguistically and historically determined (which is in part what Comte does also), then the very grounds of a clear distinction between a

[58] Durkheim, *Elementary Forms*, pp. 424–8. 'Organic solidarity and contractual solidarity', in *On Morality and Society*, pp. 86–113.

[59] Ibid., pp. 432–5. Durkheim, 'Individualism and the intellectuals'; 'The dualism of human nature and its social conditions', p. 159. *The Rules of Sociological Method*, trans. Sarah A. Solovay and John H. Mueller (New York: The Free Press, 1938) p. 23.

[60] Durkheim, *Rules*, p. 45.

[61] Durkheim, *Elementary Forms*, pp. 435–6.

[62] Kenneth Thompson, *Auguste Comte: The Founder of Sociology* (Selections) (London: Nelson, 1976) pp. 68–9.

[63] Comte, *The Crisis of Industrial Civilization*, pp. 193–201.

'necessary' finite knowledge and a superfluous and pretended transcendent knowledge are undermined.[64] This distinction depended on our being able to 'round upon finitude', to list once and for all the general *a priori* categories, both conceptual and sensory, into which the finite is organized. Yet if this cannot be done, if local and particular experiences always enter into our general conception of epistemological categories, making them endlessly revisable, and justifiable neither *de facto* and *a posteriori*, nor *de jure* and *a priori*, then these culturally particular categories can only justify themselves as a kind of 'conjecture' about the transcendent, and the relation of this transcendence to finitude. Comte and Durkheim have succeeded in instilling in us the illusion that sociological critique further 'finitizes' and humanizes religion, only because they endow the social and linguistic source of categorization with a transcendental colouring. They suppose, wrongly, that one can 'round upon' society as a finite object, and give an exhaustive inventory, valid for all time, of the essential categorical determinants for human social existence.

Kantian transcendentalism thus actually compounds the illusions which have their real root in a positivist theology. While de Maistre and de Bonald hypostasized society, they at least showed glimmerings of the postmodern insight that no social explanations can be sought beyond the unfounded *mythos* which a particular society projects and enacts for itself. Comte and Durkheim, by comparison, tend much more to lapse back into a formalism which refers all particular mythical or religious content to the constant exigencies of 'social' relations.

The secularization of positivism, which makes sociology a 'scientific' translation of Kantian critique, tends inevitably to modify positivism in a formalist direction which is in harmony with a liberal and 'negative' ethos. Durkheim carries this reintegration of liberalism further forwards than Comte. However, at certain moments Durkheim presents himself as a much purer positivist than his forebear. This is when he accuses Comte (rightly or wrongly) of subordinating social explanation to pre-given psychological needs for affection and knowledge.[65] The sentiment of sympathy, Durkheim insists, is not psychologically ingrained, but secondary to the social existence of family, state and so forth. One could almost talk of 'a return to de Bonald' here, as also in the case of Durkheim's fear that Comte regards his 'law of three stages' as more than simply empirical. Durkheim re-emphasizes that efficient causality is not to be thought of as the operation of any immanent force or tendency. There is no law of progress, and change must be explained in terms of observed modifications in the social whole rather than of ideological development from what went before.[66] However, for Durkheim, the social whole remains fundamentally the same for all societies, and the modifications

---

[64] J. G. Hamann, 'Metacritique of the purism of reason', in Ronald Gregor Smith, *J. G. Hamann: A Study in Christian Existence* (London: Collins, 1960) pp. 213–21.

[65] Durkheim, *Rules*, p. 29.

[66] Ibid., pp. 98ff, 117–18.

involve a change in self-apprehension of this social whole which *does* progress towards a clearer, more scientific grasp of its essential structures. Whereas, for Comte, the ultimate motor of social change appears to be alterations in the conceptualization of the natural order, Durkheim, like the traditionalists, gives priority to the self-apprehension of society. It is true that he does manage to preserve also the Comtean idea that religious notions are in part primitive explanations for natural phenomena.[67] But this is because, following the neo-Kantians, he grounds theoretical in practical reason, and voices a metaphysical faith that general concepts which are of service in social science always prove to have a secondary application in natural science, because of the general (pre-established?) harmony and economy of nature, of which human society forms a part.[68]

Although Durkheim abandons Comte's conservative ideology, he reaffirms, ostensibly against Comte, de Bonald's *fait sociale*, and in doing so endorses not simply a 'method', but also an ontology which constitutes the object to which the method is to apply. In keeping with this, the content and the method of Durkheim's thought constantly reaffirm each other, in a manner which sustains the illusion of 'objective' rationality. All knowledge is supposedly grounded in practical reason, but this grounding is confirmed within the object of study itself, in such a way that Durkheim, like Comte, claims to deduce the 'ought' from the 'is'.[69] Likewise knowledge, though practical, is a conserving 'science' rather than a creative art (unlike economics, which according to Durkheim deals only in ideal models).[70] But this 'Platonic' priority of theory is confirmed by an empiricism which discovers society to be the most general and most given 'thing'. Ultimately, Durkheim's method has as its foundation simply his conception of society itself, for society is inwardly constituted by a religious classification of reality, which later, through more rigorous usage, evolves into the very science by which it is studied.

For this reason, Durkheim does not consistently see social structure as prior to religion, but sometimes insists that society only exists through its symbolic self-representation.[71] The reductive element in Durkheim's sociology of religion consists rather in the notion that all religion, when clear about itself, would turn out to be the Comtean-Kantian religion of humanity. Here the choice of Australian totemic religion as an object of study, and the claim that this is the most primitive kind of religion, turns out to be a vital ruse by which to maintain both methodical and substantive presuppositions.[72] For the impersonality of *mana*, and the contagious non-localizability of the sacred, which is even supposed to render particular rites and symbols of 'secondary' importance, exactly corresponds to the theory that devotion to the impersonal

---

[67] Durkheim, *Elementary Forms*, pp. 203–4.
[68] Ibid., p. 440ff.
[69] Durkheim, *Rules*, pp. 23, 47ff.
[70] Ibid., pp. 23–7.
[71] Durkheim, *Elementary Forms*, p. 422.
[72] Ibid., especially pp. 23–102.

and spiritual law of the social is the true content of all religion. Durkheim claims to be 'testing' this theory empirically, and yet he can only define his very idea of the social by appealing in a circular fashion to the always 'primitive' notion of a given and categorical sacrality over against a profane and particular content. His experimental proof of the social character of religion in the Australian case only applies to all cases because he uses fetishist religion as an optical 'frame' for the classification of other societies and other religious practices. Both the subject and object, and the historical beginning and end of science, are locked in a mutually self-confirming circle, just as religion is really science and society, because science and society are really religion.

Another heir of Comte, the Catholic reactionary Donoso Cortes, declared that 'universal facts' and Catholic dogmas (being earlier and later editions of revelation) were mutually explanatory. Durkheim, one could say, thought much the same thing about social facts and social science.[73]

The 'truth' of Durkheimian sociology is spelled out in his political programme: since only the Nation State embodies and guarantees the new totemism, which is the cult of the sacrality of individual freedom and choice, there can be no opting out of state institutions, including its secular education, where 'sociology' will be found on the curriculum. As Charles Péguy well understood, this was still the voice of the positivist new papacy, the secular transformation-through-disguise of a new and perverse theology.[74]

Clarifications Concerning Sacrifice

The identification of the *fait sociale* with the 'sacred' suggests that sociology has always been, by definition, primarily sociology of religion, and that it is constituted, as a discipline, by a theory of secularization, or of 'normal religion'. This conclusion, however, is reinforced and clarified if one realizes that it is also constituted as a discourse about *sacrifice*.

Having cast unreason into shadow, the Enlightenment had to explain why this darkness had dominated human history hitherto. Unreason was either described as the occasional aberration of madness, or, in its more consistent occurrence, it was narrated as a gradual approximation towards reason. But at the heart of the Counter-Enlightenment lies the claim that throughout human history, and persisting today, occur fundamental phenomena which can neither be dismissed as aberrations, nor be seen as primitive gropings towards knowledge. For Joseph de Maistre, the most striking of these phenomena is that of sacrifice. In all cultures, he claims, we discover the notion and practice of sacrificial substitution. Reason can in no way make

---

[73] John Donoso Cortes, *Essay on Catholicism, Liberalism and Socialism Considered in their Fundamental Principles*, trans. William McDonald (Dublin: William M. Kelly, 1874) p. 240.

[74] Romain Rolland, *Péguy* (Paris: Albin Michel, 1944) tome I, pp. 137–9, 309.

sense of this substitution, so it must be regarded as a given fact, as primary as reason itself.[75] Without reason, it happens that people, animals or institutions that are sanctified, are also actual or potential offerings.[76] Furthermore, another surd but universal factor in human life, namely the occurrence of war and violence, also frequently without reason, must, according to de Maistre, be linked with this phenomenon.[77] He considers that both war and sacrifice reflect the fact that 'there is nothing but violence in the universe, everything is in the wrong place'.[78] Christian religion reveals that this state of affairs is the result of the Fall, and for this reason all pain is to be regarded as both punishment and expiation.[79] De Maistre claims that a rationalist like David Hume was able to understand sacrifice as an 'offering' to placate or influence the gods, but not to see it as an atoning 'substitute' for a committed offence.[80] The law of *salut par le sang* is just an arbitrary given fact, and the death of the innocent in war belongs to a cosmic ritual which is objectively efficacious. No punitive justice can be called into question, because it enacts a divinely ordained and necessary compensation for human sin.[81]

De Bonald also understood his thought to be 'a philosophy of sacrifice', and both thinkers thought that they had demonstrated that 'the power of the Cross' was the hidden reality of the social and political order.[82] According to de Bonald, there has been a gradual diminution of the need for war and bloody sacrifice, because an infinite and all-sufficient sacrifice has been offered to the Father by the Son. The universality and finality of the Catholic religion is bound up with its focus upon completely external and public events which are also sacrifices: Golgotha and the repeated immolations of the Mass. Just as, says de Maistre, the word passes to the ear by 'circular undulations', yet is heard 'with integrity', so also *le sang théandrique* passes by the circular route of constant substitution into *entrailles coupables*[83] (in both cases because of the coordinating intervention of a Malebranchian God).

The logic of sacrificial substitution provides the key confirmation of positivism, because it affirms that arbitrary power responds to rebellion against itself with a further arbitrary demand. As the offence is not against reason, but against power, mere repentance and belated fulfilling of the injunction will not do; the failure to obey in one particular instance must be compensated for. Violated power demands ceaseless blood to replenish its absolute sway. Thus de Maistre notes that an offering, *anathema*, is also the casting out and rejection of something, and the term expiation suggests not an ethical resanctification

---

[75] Lively, *The Works of Joseph de Maistre*, p. 294. De Maistre, *Considerations on France*, p. 62. See also John Milbank, 'Stories of sacrifices', in *Modern Theology*, vol. 12, no. 1 (Jan 1996), pp. 27–56.
[76] De Maistre, *Eclaircissements sur les sacrifices*, pp. 193–4.
[77] Ibid. Lively, *The Works*, p. 296. De Maistre, *Considerations on France*, pp. 59–61.
[78] Ibid., p. 62.
[79] Ibid., pp. 59–61. LeBrun, *Throne and Altar*, pp. 31–2.
[80] Lively, *Works*, p. 209.
[81] LeBrun, *Throne and Altar*, pp. 110–11.
[82] De Maistre, *Considerations on France*, p. 80. De Maistre, *Eclaircissements*, p. 212.
[83] Ibid.

of the individual, but an expulsion of a sacred thing or person.[84] The *sacer* is both holy and profane, and the sacrality of the social *rapports* is only maintained through a ceaseless economy of expiatory terror. Consecration for preservation involves, also, rejection and termination.

From de Maistre to Durkheim, only the source of legitimacy changes. Like de Maistre, Durkheim refuses to rationalize sacrifices, after the fashion of Robertson Smith, who saw them as primitively involving 'participation' in the sacred and not as in any way expiatory.[85] Durkheim does, indeed, agree with the Scotsman that primitive religion is to do with social solidarity. But he adds his own Comtean/transcendentalist gloss to this: sacrifice is offering, as well as communion, because the sacred is sustained by the projected emotions of individuals, although these emotions only arise in the context of the social whole. Therefore there *must* be a break: what is given must really belong to the divine receiver, and sacrifice represents the moment of constant reaffirmation of the sacred. Not only is sacrifice interpreted formalistically, as society's confirmation of itself, it is also discovered to be a surd element of human culture, because its innermost meaning is the categorical imperative, where the personal will discovers that it is subject to its own law, named 'society'.

But sacrifice is closely linked to piacular 'rites of mourning', and the pure/impure character of *sacer* (to which Durkheim alludes) is an ambiguity opened up by the fracture of self-immolation.[86] With offering, there is also a shedding of blood, shown most notably in the frenzy of mutual anger and wounding which occurs in the event of a death. The native Australians ascribe this to the anger of the soul of the dead person, but, according to Durkheim, this myth has been superimposed upon a more primary ritual. Any death is a threat to the community, and the 'social' must register this fact by making its presence felt in a negative fashion. The mere manifest expression of negative emotions serves the purposes of 'society', and so the rites of mourning automatically bear in their train an expiatory effect. This, for Durkheim, explains why the mourning is an entirely tribal duty, not necessarily associated with any 'personal' feeling.

Yet Durkheim has here substituted his own mythical account for that of the natives. For a start, nothing warrants his according to ritual a pre-narrative primacy. Durkheim discovers a gap for the intrusion of sociology in the fact that the dead souls are unaccountably angry for a time, but then benign. Yet if 'the social' can be angry for a time, but then be appeased, why not also souls? This is, in fact, as Durkheim himself records, what the myths supposed, and in that case the relation of mythical explanation to ritual performance is completely seamless, with no room for the 'extra' contribution of science. It seems entirely plausible that the natives should conceive of the souls as angry at being cut off from their previous relationships, and the usual attentions

---

[84] De Maistre, *Considerations on France*, p. 80. De Maistre, *Eclaircissements*, p. 193.
[85] Durkheim, *Elementary Forms*, pp. 326–50.
[86] Ibid., pp. 351–69, 409–14.

these entail, yet Durkheim tries to deny this. In this manner he makes ritual surplus to myth, and having thus disconnected behaviour from beliefs, he is forced to posit the behaviour as natural, given, universal, and to claim, like de Maistre, that expiatory sacrifice is constitutive of the social as such. For Durkheim also, there is a kind of law of the social circulation of blood, such that every time 'society' is threatened, its 'contagious' power is released, mere sorrow proves insufficient, and to this must always be added the shedding of compensatory blood.

Like de Maistre, also, Durkheim believes that crime and punishment should be looked at objectively and naturalistically. In Durkheim this takes the form of the view than in any given society there is a 'normal' level for crime, because crime is an inevitable by-product of creative freedom. In addition, crime usefully 'legitimizes' less venial offences, and provides an occasion for the negative demonstration of social presence.[87] In this respect its functionality and universality belongs to the same circulation of blood as the sacrificial and piacular rites of primitive religion.

So here we have a new confirmation of the paradox of secular positivism. Durkheim rejects as 'theological' or 'metaphysical', the usual religious or ethical accounts of sacrifice or crime, yet he can only do so by substituting a 'scientific' account which itself embodies a naturalized version of the myth of a universal expiatory law traceable back to *theological* positivism. Three orientations to other thinkers help us to 'place' Durkheim here.

In the first instance one can call into question Durkheim's 'sociological' reversal of his teacher Fustel de Coulanges's more strictly historical conclusion that Roman legal, familial property institutions could only be accounted for in terms of their informing religious *mythos*.[88] Secondly, one can note that Robertson Smith, Durkheim's *exemplar* for his ethnographic *excursus*, already qualifies Fustel, for highly confession-orientated reasons. Following the seventeenth-century work of John Spencer, who saw the 'primitive' elements of sacrifice and taboo in the Old Testament as divine concessions to primitive understanding, Robertson Smith tried to comprehend these things as belonging naturally to primitive attempts to categorize merely natural phenomena, and so as quite separate from true, revealed religion, although they later provided a mythical vehicle for an initial revelation of essentially 'ethical' and 'rational' religious goals.[89] Through Durkheim, this forgotten apologetics has an ironic legacy – it will issue in Lévi-Strauss's attempt to deny that totemic phenomena be accounted 'religious' at all.[90] In Durkheim himself, Robertson Smith's apparently 'expert' voice reinforced an inclination to see

[87] Durkheim, *Rules*, pp. 71–5.
[88] Numa Denis Fustel de Coulanges, *The Ancient City* (New York: Doubleday, 1955) esp. pp. 15–42, 120–22, 389–96.
[89] W. Robertson Smith, *Lectures on the Religion of the Semites* (1st Series) (Edinburgh: A. and C. Black, 1889) pp. 196–421. Franz Steiner, *Taboo* (Harmondsworth: Penguin, 1956) pp. 55–58.
[90] Claude Lévi-Strauss, *The Savage Mind* (London: Weidenfeld and Nicolson, 1966) esp. p. 220ff.

primitive religion as a religion without gods, which foreshadows a post-metaphysical religion of society.

A third comparison is more remote, but the most important. This is with the thought of another Catholic traditionalist, writing in the 1830s, Pierre Simon Ballanche, who moved this theology in a politically leftwards direction and drastically modified de Maistre's ideas about sacrifice.

In contrast to de Bonald and de Maistre, Ballanche distinguishes much more sharply between a universal primitive revelation and the new revelation given with Christ. De Maistre expected a third, post-Christian revelation which would close the age of revolutionary catastrophe, and this actually anticipates Comte's notion of a positive era to succeed the age of metaphysical 'enlightenment'.[91] By contrast, and influenced here by the more orthodox de Bonald, Ballanche stresses the unbloody nature of Christian sacrifice and the possibility of a 'harmonistic' progress in the Christian age.[92] Adapting both Augustine and Vico, he seeks to show that de Maistre's law of sacrifice merely transcribes the founding *mythos* of pagan religion. In Roman and Greek antiquity, the sacrificial degradation of some for the benefit of the rest was indeed regarded as inevitable in a society where, primitively, only some human animals were accorded full 'humanity': full knowledge of language, the rights of legal, sacred marriage and ownership of the domestic hearth. Like Fustel later, but with much more mystical interest, Ballanche interprets Roman class struggle as an attempt by the plebs to secure full access both to language and to religious rites. This antique history, according to Ballanche (like other traditionalists he was a freemason as well as a Catholic), was entirely a history of 'initiation', but initiation won through struggle, or 'antagonism'.[93]

According to Ballanche, Augustine's 'two cities' should be reinterpreted not as two races (pagans and Jews) but as the initiated and the uninitiated who comprised every ancient society.[94] Yet Christianity implicitly (if not in practice) puts an end to this division, because in the life of Christ a new *mythos* is established which replaced and resituated the *mythos* of antiquity. Christianity is now the *lien logique du mythe et de l'histoire* in the following way:[95] Christ is the founder of a new city, which, uniquely, does not refer to a story of primal murder, primal sacrifice and expulsion (like the story of Romulus and Remus) but traces its descent from a sacrificial victim who had no material issue. The story of Cain and Abel in the book of Genesis suggests, for Ballanche, that Cain's civic destiny at once perpetuates and 'contains' the economy of sacral violence which he has inaugurated.[96] Cain's sin was to despair of divine justice, and so it was, in a sense, already the law of the

---

[91] Pierre-Simon Ballanche, 'Essais de Palingénésie Sociale', in *Oeuvres* (Paris/Geneva: 1830) tome III, p. 203.

[92] Pierre-Simon Ballanche, *La Ville des Expiations* (Lyon: Presses Universitaires de Lyon, 1981) pp. 15, 172.

[93] Ibid., pp. 29, 101, 172.

[94] Ibid., p. 101.

[95] Ibid., p. 17.

[96] Ibid., pp. 24, 37.

earthly city. By contrast, the 'city of expiations', founded by Christ, rejects the idea that sacrificial pain and punishment are constantly required to compensate for human guilt. The real meaning of original sin is the limitless sway of co-responsibility, such that expiatory initiative is now always from the innocent on behalf of the guilty and no longer an induction of the innocent into the realm of sacrificial violence. As there is no limit to human responsibility, no instance of wrong where one cannot say that it is ultimately the duty of all of us to put it right, one can also say that without the idea of co-responsibility there can be no notion of justice. In the Christian era, justice should mean not punishment, but voluntary expiation, and social participation in the process of atonement, of which the 'agent and type' is Christ himself. Charity and co-responsibility redefine expiation and make a society without sacrifice possible: Ballanche spells out his social programme in terms of the wider distribution of property, 'houses of refuge' for prostitutes (whose profession, like sacrifice, is not an inevitable necessity), and the housing of criminals and mendicants with families rather than in carceral institutions.[97] In this way a new 'harmonistic' progress proceeds forwards, and a new 'mutual' initiation occurs, which is always from the innocent and excluded to the guilty and included – a total reversal of antique norms.[98]

Whereas Comte and Durkheim see 'harmony' as properly belonging to a future era of human history, after the necessary phase of antagonism where rational insight is incomplete, Ballanche more critically saw harmony as posited by a *different* myth/history which decodes the history of antagonism in (what one might call) a 'counter-historical' fashion. Likewise, Durkheim is still confined by the myth of a symbolic substitutionary pain which is at once arbitrary and naturally necessary, whereas Ballanche reinterpreted expiation as the voluntary 'bearing' of the baleful consequences of sin (whether one's own or another person's). His radical Christian vision (very much linked to Augustine's) goes some way to fulfil what is interesting in the traditionalist project: namely to make the central content of Christian doctrine relevant to social thought. By comparison, Durkheim is still confined by the sub-Christian element in the thought of de Maistre and de Bonald. And to accept what Durkheim has to say about sacrifice, expiation, crime and contagion is not to take seriously the deliverances of science, but rather to see as less than ultimately true the teachings of the gospel and the acts of Jesus. By comparison, Ballanche makes us see how a certain 'reading' of the historical text is inseparable from the very content of Christian belief. For theology to accept or to adapt Durkheim's ideas is, in fact, to displace the primacy of this reading.

Positivist discourse solved the antinomy of social creation by invoking a direct divine/natural presence which is benign organicism and harmony, but also the necessary violence of sacrifice. This had the effect of prising

---

[97] Ibid., pp. 27, 182–3.

[98] Ibid., p. 29. Pierre Emmanuel, 'Avec Ballanche dans la Ville des Expiations', in *L'Homme est Intérieur* (Paris: Le Seuil, 1962) pp. 206–25.

both harmony and conflict out of the contingent, narrative context to which they both belong (and to which Ballanche's theology to some extent restores them). Against this discourse, one should insist that the antinomy itself is fundamental, because it arises in the inspection of even the most minute social action. Every action of an individual presupposes a cultural-linguistic context, and every action (as a 'project' in Adam Ferguson's sense) has always already passed over into further, more general consequences, which escape the individual's reach, yet which the individual decisively helps to form. One cannot, therefore, commence a 'science' with either the social whole, nor the individual act – there can be neither a positive, not a liberal science. But *nor* can there be some mixture of the two, because both the social and the individual contribution are entirely contingent, and constantly being modified, the one by the other. One never *sees* the social, except in the instance of its manifestation in 'individual' (bodily and linguistic) action, and one can never read the intention of this action except in terms of its objectively 'tensional' situation within a more general process which it assumes and modifies. The relation society/individual is not that of scheme to content, nor of whole to atomic parts. Thus the antinomy can only be mediated by narration; an adequate 'transcendental' reflection on the conditions of possibility for social action discovers the inevitability of historiography, but finds no room whatsoever for 'social science'.

4

Sociology II: From Kant to Weber

Introduction

Modern sociology derives from two sources. Besides the French tradition, which has just been retraced, there is also the German intervention. It is usually stressed that the German contributors sought to overcome positivism in sociology, which was mediated to them not only through Comte, but also English writers like Mill and Spencer. However, while it is true that the more scientific aspect of positivism – the attempt to confine genuine social explanation to the subsumption of particulars under universal laws of constant concomitance – was apparently abandoned, several features of the positivist mentality were quite evidently maintained. One can mention, at the outset, the association of 'the social' with given, permanent categories; a dualistic conception of humanity as caught between 'real' nature and 'spiritual' values; an identification of 'the religious' with irrational and arbitrary forces which are irreducible and unexplainable; the importance still given to functional causality; an empiricistic attitude to 'facts', and a historical narrative which compares the postreligious stage to the stage of primitive religion. And like Durkheim, Weber, Simmel and Troeltsch seek in their political outlook to combine liberal freedom with a positivist attitude to law and sovereignty. Like Durkheim also, they modify the sociological tradition with an infusion of Kantian and neo-Kantian philosophy.

In the German case, however, the modification is more drastic. Here, the social organism is not itself identified with the *a priori* in the manner borrowed from 'social occasionalism'. Instead, the German thinkers employ neo-Kantian conceptions to describe supposed *a priori* possibilities of relationship between the individual social actor and other individuals. In an apparently contradictory reversal, specifically sociological explanation is conceived of as an appeal to the motives and intentions of individual actors, to the degree that these can be comprehended under the *a priori* forms of social relationship. This 'interpretative sociology', by according primacy to the acting subject, is supposed to allow room for the influence of values and meaning in history, alongside the congealed intransigence of economic and political structures which remain a fatally inescapable phenomenon.

In fact, as I shall argue, the methodology of the German sociologists ensures that their substantive accounts of history conform to the questionable assumptions of Kantian and neo-Kantian philosophy. Their version of sociological explanation perpetuates the Kantian programme with regard to theology and metaphysics, namely the denial that the categories used to understand the finite world (here, society) can be speculatively extended to apply to the ultimate and transcendent 'in itself'. For this reason, religion is presented as more properly concerned with the supra-social, with a world of universal 'personal' value. This is a new version of Kant's identification of true religion with true morality, where we have a practical, though not speculative access, to the realm of 'transcendental objects' or 'things in themselves'. Whereas, with Durkheim, the problem with his 'social' explanation of religion turned out to be that 'religion' and 'the social' were really identical, here the problem is precisely the opposite: the 'religious' and the 'social' are conceived of as always and forever categorically separate realms. Thus history can be narrated as the story of interaction between personal religious charisma and substantive value on the one hand, and the various public processes of routinization and instrumental reason on the other. It may indeed seem overwhelmingly reasonable to say that the ideological and the social-economic mutually interact, without reduction of the one to the other. Yet this seductive presentation of things is not at all commonsensical, but deeply metaphysical and illusory, not allowing us to look at the content of either religion, nor socio-economic processes. It turns out to be a device for leaving the true content of the one and the desirability of the other quite unquestioned.

In the first three parts of this chapter I shall argue that German sociology extends the Kantian programme in its most dubious aspect; namely, in its claims to provide an exhaustive inventory of the essential aspects of our (social) finitude in such a manner as to make theological or metaphysical explanation of the content of this finitude impossible and redundant. At the same time, it repeats the Kantian identification of religion with the private, the subjective and the evaluative, in contradistinction to a public, natural or social realm of objective, but humanly meaningless fact.

In the fourth part of the chapter I shall specify the 'metanarrative' of German sociology, or its would-be rational account of universal history. Here it will be seen that the neo-Kantian methodological approach itself preempts all the important issues of empirical substance with regard to human culture. At the same time, and at a deeper level, it will be realized that it is not so much that the story is dictated by the method, as rather that the method itself both enshrines and conceals a particular history, namely the emergence of protestantism, liberal protestantism, and the Enlightenment, and together with these the rise of the bureaucratic state and capitalist economics. Thus the retracing of this history acquires the status of a metanarrative because, first, the whole of the rest of human history is emplotted with reference to it, and second, its main synchronic and diachronic structures cease to be regarded as items of a particular temporal sequence, but are elevated to the status of an eternal logic of social possibility.

Neo-Kantian Method in Rickert and Simmel

Both Georg Simmel and Max Weber, though more especially the former, were closely associated with the South-West German school of neo-Kantianism, and influenced by its leading thinkers, in particular Wilhelm Windelband and Heinrich Rickert.[1] Neo-Kantianism in general is best approached if one thinks of it in the context of a reaction against Hegel's claims to identify the ontologically real with a reason graspable by the human mind.[2] This reaction did not, however, call into question the identification of reason with the humanly graspable, nor the confinement of the rational to a logically determinate process (subordinating, for example, the cognitive claims of aesthetic reason). Instead, a gulf grew between the realm of the factually given, regarded as infinite, indeterminate and even finally irrational in character, and the realm of the meaningful, or of human valuation.[3] Following Fichte, who deduced even the empirical contents of theoretical reason from the practical exigency of freedom, and the 'self-positing' of the ego, the neo-Kantians made the logic of 'valuation' (*Geltungslogik*) the ground for judgements of empirical truth. But unlike Fichte, they were not necessarily or only concerned with the subordination of theoretical understanding to ethics; instead, they wanted to regard truth and beauty as in themselves modes of 'valuation'. Unlike Fichte again, they did not try to ground objective knowledge in transcendental subjectivity – instead, they thought of the realm of values in a 'quasi-Platonic' fashion, as a set of pseudo-objects 'objectively present' to the mind of the subject.

It is this conception that marks neo-Kantianism off from Kant and his original idealist progeny. For 'values' are *not* really conditions of possibility for the knowing of objects or the realization of freedom. They are not 'categories' in this Kantian sense, but nor, on the other hand (as the neo-Kantians more strongly insisted as time went on), do they belong to the realm of 'the real'. (It was only Husserl's phenomenology which turned 'values' into the real, essential objects of our intentional cognition.) Values are described as 'irreal', and the term 'good' for moral value is avoided, precisely because of the traditional metaphysical implication of convertibility with *ens*. And yet this does not at all mean that values have only an instrumental, heuristic function; on the contrary, as Hermann Lotze had put it, one is to seek the basis of what *is*, in what *should be* – though for his successors who are 'critical' and

[1] Gillian Rose, *Hegel Contra Sociology* (London: Athlone, 1981) pp. 1–47. Swingewood. *A Short History of Sociological Thought*, p. 129ff.

[2] Herbert Schnädelbach, *Philosophy in Germany*, 1831–1933 (Cambridge: Cambridge University Press, 1984) p. 41.

[3] Ibid., pp. 161–92.

Kantian (in contrast to Lotze's own neo-Leibnizian predilections) there can never be any perfect coincidence between value and reality.[4]

For neo-Kantian epistemology, to claim that a statement is true is not to claim a 'correspondence' between a mental idea and a state of affairs, nor is it to claim (in Kantian fashion) that a particular sense-datum can be brought under the schematic organization of the categories of the understanding. Instead, it is equivalent to saying that the statement 'holds validly', or that some factual, empirical content can be meaningfully grasped as constituted by the logic of valuation. So, for example, in natural science, any particular phenomenon can be correctly understood if it occurs regularly in a law-like fashion, according to the 'value' of scientific truth. It will be noted that the normative specifications of this value were, in fact, entirely positivistic.

The South-West German Kantians, in particular, were concerned with the problem of the mode of truthful valuation in the study of history, and with whether it could really qualify as scientific. This concern with the specificity of historical science is the source for the later sociological methodologies of Simmel and Weber. Wilhelm Windelband made a famous distinction between 'nomothetic' science, on the one hand, and 'idiographic' science on the other.[5] Nomothetic science is concerned with discovery of laws; idiographic science with the specification of the particular. History cannot be adequately brought under the model of nomothetic science, because often what is of decisive importance in history is the unique and non-repeated.

Windelband's distinction shows some kinship with Wilhelm Dilthey's separation of the *Geistwissenschaften* from the *Naturwissenschaften*, which also had some influence on the sociologists.[6] Dilthey had sought to extend Friedrich Schleiermacher's general hermeneutics into a methodology for the human sciences in general. He took over from Schleiermacher the idea partly derived from Hamann (and ultimately ignored by Hegel), that all reason begins as a process of interpretation, or 'divinatory' understanding of meaning. For Schleiermacher this meant that we must try to comprehend the parts of a text or a spoken utterance in terms of the whole and vice versa – a process which in principle can never be complete.[7] Unfortunately, neither Schleiermacher nor Dilthey grasped Hamann's related point, that the primacy of linguistic interpretation makes a Kantian-type self-critique of reason (in which a categorizing reason arbitrarily extracted from discursive processes is seen as making its 'own' contribution to discourse) simply impossible.[8] Instead of philosophical hermeneutics commencing as simultaneously a

---

[4] Herbert Schnädelbach, *Philosophy in Germany, 1831–1933* (Cambridge: Cambridge University Press, 1984) pp. 169–89.

[5] Wilhelm Windelband, 'History and natural science', trans. Guy Oakes, in *History and Theory*, XIX, pp. 175–82 (1980).

[6] Wilhelm Dilthey, *Einleitung in die Gesammelte Schriften*, vol. 1, *Geistwissenschaften* (Stuttgart/Göttingen: Tuebner/Vandenhoeck and Ruprecht, 1959); *Der Aufbau der Geschichtlichen Welt in den Geisteswissenschaften* (Frankfurt: Suhrkamp, 1970) esp. p. 177ff.

[7] Friedrich Schleiermacher, *Hermeneutics: The Handwritten Manuscripts*, trans. James Duke and Jack Forstman (Missoula, Montana: Scholars Press, 1977) pp. 45, 74–7.

[8] J. G. Hamann, *Metacritique of the Purism of Reason*, pp. 213–21.

'metacritique' of transcendentalism, Schleiermacher made hermeneutics into a new sort of transcendental philosophy. In consequence, however distant his notion of interpretation was from any crude notions of empathetic intuition, it remains the case that he saw a need to ground the possibility of interpretation in a possible identity between the mind of the author and the mind of the interpreter, who is able to retrace the 'spiritual' course of the original composition.[9] The same conception persists in Dilthey and it means that, despite his grasp of the primacy of interpretation and the beginnings of a sense of the temporality of all understanding, his hermeneutic methodology remains focused on capturing with precision the original moment of spiritual action or construction. It is this focus, indeed, which permits the claim that history has a 'scientific' objectivity. In fact, the concern to isolate and exactly describe a historical moment is, in one sense, a form of positivism. In the case of hermeneutics, this positivism is finally traceable to the exigencies of the Protestant *sola scriptura*, which, instead of a traditional accumulation of meanings, requires methodological guarantees that it can reproduce 'the original' and untrammelled word of God.

Windelband's nomothetic science was similarly positivist, in this sense of having as its goal the isolation and description of a particular fact or cultural complex.[10] But in several important respects, his notion was quite unlike that of Dilthey. First of all, Windelband could not remain content with the irreducibility of the hermeneutic circle; interpretative reconstruction of the past must be referred to *a priori* conditions of truthfulness if it is to acquire validity. Secondly, Dilthey, following a long tradition, both theological and humanistic, founds the difference of the *Geistwissenschaften* in the fact that cultural processes, unlike natural ones, are humanly made and therefore, in principle, humanly comprehensible. This is basically an ontological point, although Dilthey (in contrast to earlier thinkers like Vico) obfuscates this by locating cultural 'repeatability' (of the known by the knower) not simply in signifying structures, but in an *a priori* identity of subjective with objective *geist*. Windelband, however, refuses an ontological basis for the distinction of nomothetic and idiographic science, in accordance with the Kantian inheritance which focuses less on the (real, historical) contrast between linguistic-cultural processes and pre-given nature but on a (wholly imaginary) contrast between 'internal' processes of the individual faculties of understanding, feeling and desiring on the one hand and the 'external' world – which includes society as much as nature – on the other. Hence, as Rickert and Weber emphasize, the division between nomothetic and idiographic does not wholly coincide with that between nature and culture; 'natural history' is partly idiographic, and there are elements of law-like regularity in history – especially in the case of economic processes.[11]

---

[9] Schleiermacher, *Hermeneutics*, pp. 42, 62–4. Hans Georg Gadamer, *Truth and Method*, trans. William Glen-Doepel (London: Sheed and Ward, 1975) pp. 162–214.

[10] Windelband, *History and Natural Science*, p. 182.

[11] Guy Oakes, 'Introduction: Rickert's theory of historical knowledge', in Heinrich Rickert, *The Limits of Concept Formation in Natural Science*, trans. Guy Oakes (Cambridge: Cambridge University Press, 1986) pp. vii–xxxi.

For the neo-Kantians, history, just as much as nature, confronts the mind of the subject in the shape of an uncontrollable mass of irrational 'life'. For this reason, it is not enough to say that history concerns knowledge of the particulars, for there are in history an infinite number of particulars, and every given particular can never be exhaustively analysed.[12] There arises in consequence a double problem for the historian concerning which particulars or 'individuals' should be selected, and which features of these selected individuals are historically relevant. In this context, Heinrich Rickert develops his concepts of 'the historical centre' and the 'in-dividual' to designate historical particulars which are accorded an orientating value for entire cultures.[13] For Rickert, history is only objective to the extent that it seeks to identify the 'historical centre' of any particular culture, which means picking out empirical individuals who are in-dividuals by virtue of the fact that unconditional values attach to, or are associated with them. The historian need not himself subcribe to any particular values, and yet history itself must have 'value relevance' (*wertbeziehung*).

This might appear unexceptionable insofar as 'the historical centres' are thrown up by the historical process itself. However, what is problematic about Rickert's conception is the idea that one must be able to locate a *single* historical centre or a series of unequivocal foci.[14] For Rickert is not simply saying that the values of the historical culture under examination are all-important, although the historian's values must be bracketed out. Rather, he is saying that one must try to uncover the unique value-perspective that is constitutive of a particular culture, and which derives from the non-historical, *a priori* realm of valuation. So it is not enough merely to show what norms are customarily held to; one must rather be able to point to something that holds unconditionally, universally, for the culture in question. This means that one applies to the society under study the Kantian test for a genuine categorical imperative – can what I am willing in this particular situation be elevated into a universal maxim?[15] The trouble, however, with this methodological approach is that it may be that certain cultures have no conceptions of value, or of 'the good', whose substantive content can be prised apart from the varied obligations specific to definite roles and situations. For such cultures, 'value considerations' are not separable from their conception of the true 'nature' of social reality, nor the factual position of human beings within the natural order. Yet Rickert assumes that all cultures have at their heart a value-allegiance which can be pressed into the mould of the Kantian categorical imperative.

Furthermore, while Rickert's historian is neutral with respect to the content of universal value, he remains committed to the premise that there is *some* unknown value which holds unconditionally.[16] The South-West German

[12] Rickert, *The Limits of Concept Formation*, pp. 50–1, 57–8, 66ff.
[13] Ibid., pp. 78–81.
[14] Ibid., pp. 123–9, 135–47, 173–4.
[15] Ibid., pp. 78ff.
[16] Ibid., pp. 205, 234–5.

neo-Kantians (unlike the Marburg neo-Kantians who adopted a reverse schema) held that all truthful *validity* is ultimately grounded in moral or quasi-moral value – this being guaranteed by the value which evey substantive ethic must supposedly accord to the valuing will itself.

In the case of Rickert, one has the attempt to link empirically crucial historical complexes with an *a priori* value concept which is ultimately akin to Kant's notion of a categorical imperative. But the *a priori* content involved here seems rather thin. By contrast, the sociological version of neo-Kantianism was much more specific about the *a priori* element, and it is here, precisely, that it was able to locate a difference (which this book rejects as false) between 'history' and 'sociology'. First of all, Georg Simmel elaborated a theory of 'pure forms' of human interrelationship. The specific sphere of sociology opens up, according to Simmel, because there are aspects of human relationship which display formal similarities whatever the concrete circumstances.[17] Hence the dynamics of groups of twos and threes and of the division of labour apply just as much in a family, a factory, or a primitive tribe. The sphere of sociology can also be distinguished from psychology by the same token; the only motivations it deals with are those objectively consequent upon such universal structures.

Simmel is a complex theorist to understand, because alongside his neo-Kantianism there remain residues from an earlier phase of a more purely positivist sociology. Thus, like Comte, he says that there are factual, 'energetic' aspects specific to the organic social whole, not derivable from its particular parts (this whole he also associates with religion). Likewise he stresses that the functional operation of society is not derivable from individual intentions. And at times he seems to suggest a kind of 'pre-established harmony' between the *a priori* conditions for the self-realization of the individual and the total set of interactions of the social organism.[18] This represents a kind of Leibnizian alternative to the occasionalism of French sociology.

Nature, including social nature, is for Simmel perfectly adapted, by way of this pre-established harmony, to the operations of the *a priori Geltungslogik*, which works in the interest of individual freedom. Natural objects, other people, and society in general, stand over against the individual, as barriers to his wishes and desires.[19] On the other hand, he only is an individual in relation to objects and other persons, and requires other individuals for the full realization of his desires and the establishment of his freedom – as one can see, supremely, in the case of the division of labour.[20] According to Simmel, understanding is coterminous with self-possession of one's own will and desires, such that perfect sympathy with the other is always

[17] Georg Simmel, 'The problem of sociology', in *On Individuality and Social Forms* (Chicago: Chicago University Press, 1971) pp. 23–40. *Sociology of Religion*, trans. Curt Rosenthal (New York: Philosophical Library, 1959) pp. 67, 72.
[18] Simmel, 'How is society possible', in *On Individuality*, pp. 6–22, 31.
[19] Ibid.
[20] Ibid. 'Exchange', in *On Individuality*, pp. 43–69.

impossible.[21] The only possibility of social harmony for Simmel (in the stoic natural law tradition) arises at the level of a coordination of the ultimate interests of the 'private' core of the striving will with the ultimate unity of the natural or social whole.[22]

Simmel illustrates once again the way in which secular social science tends to promote 'an ontology of conflict' in radical antithesis to Christianity. Thus he assumes that the most authentic, 'fully present' knowledge is derived from direct access to the promptings of our own will, and insofar as this is initially mediated to us by the resistances of others, the heterogeneous remains an irreducibly alien, less accessible and so 'oppositional' element. Simmel himself knows the spiritual implications of this, when he tells us that the Dantean vision of the saints in harmony in the rose of paradise is 'empirically impossible', whereas Raphael's picture of the apostolic *Disputata* presents the only possible unity, a unity in conflict.[23] Likewise, both Simmel and Weber deny the possibility of any sort of erotic, desiring love which is non-coercive.[24] Even if there is complicity in desire, desire means that one compels the other by various blandishments to be an objective means for the fulfilment of one's own wants. But this thesis assumes a duality between a controlling and directing will and an instrumental body; it disallows the idea that desire might be precisely for a particular expressed, embodied will which can only be 'objectively' enjoyed (with genuineness) as the freedom of the other, as a will *desiring us* in turn. In a similar fashion, it is not true that the other is inevitably 'alien' to us if we think of the other as fully given in his or her external presentation (exhaustively, an offering to, openness to, the other) rather than as a secret chamber of essential will to which we are forever forbidden access.

For Simmel, the specifically sociological concerns an *a priori* constitution of the self, and the other in relation to the self, which is in pre-established harmony with the 'natural' organism of social relationships. There are formal circumstances involved in both the face-to-face relationship – the 'next to each other' – and the more complex relationships of three persons or more – the 'with each other' – which are universal and irreducible.[25] It turns out that these circumstances are especially to do with the non-avoidability of violence. Hence, for Simmel, it is an *a priori* condition of all 'valuation', and so of all social constitution, that it involves an arbitrary loss, or *sacrifice*. He combines

---

[21] Simmel, 'How is society possible'.

[22] Simmel, *Sociology of Religion*, p. 1ff.

[23] Simmel, 'Conflict', in *On Individuality*, p. 72.

[24] Ibid., pp. 70–95. Max Weber, 'Intermediate reflections', in *From Max Weber: Essays in Sociology*, trans. H. H. Gerth and C. Wright Mills (London: RKP, 1948) pp. 323–59. Roslyn Wallach Bologh, 'Max Weber on erotic love: a feminist inquiry', in Scott Lash and Sam Whimster (eds.) *Max Weber: Rationality and Modernity* (London: Allen and Unwin, 1987) pp. 242–59.

[25] Simmel, *Sociology of Religion*, p. 72. 'The nature of historical understanding', in *Essays on Interpretation in Social Science*, trans. Guy Oakes (Manchester: Manchester University Press, 1980).

this theme (which as we have already seen is constitutive of sociology in general) with the derivation of value from processes of exchange – which is another way of conceiving the *a priori* as also 'social'.[26]

Right from the outset, the neo-Kantians connected their notion of an 'irreal' value with economic value that is not intrinsic to things in themselves, but attributed to them in connection with processes of exchange and production. Simmel says that it is only when things are compared that they are seen to have value, but in addition, this exchange must involve some loss and some gain for value to be ascribed.[27] Therefore it is not that the 'sacrifice' involved in loss constitutes an external barrier to the goal of establishing value, but rather that sacrifice is an inner condition for there being this goal at all. There can only be joy in heaven because of the conquest of sin, says Simmel, thereby connecting the idea of value through loss in exchange with the Kantian view that the only genuine moral virtue is an overcoming of resistant natural desires.[28] One 'proves' value where there is some denial, something foregone.

Such a view runs counter to the traditional, Catholic opinion that value, or rather goodness, attaches to Being as such, insofar as it exists and is 'rightly ordered'. Likewise, it takes the conditions for the establishment of value in capitalist society – the formal possibility of economic advantage – and projects them back upon all earlier cultures. But for many historical cultures, comparison through exchange involves valuation not primarily *because of* the possible loss and gain, but rather with reference to the relative importance of the exchanged objects within the life of the community.

In a similar fashion, Simmel's 'pure forms of sociation' also turn out to be hypostasizations of particular historical conditions. For he claims that the money economy, and the domination of society by the intellect, stand in the closest possible relationship to each other. Only now, in the modern 'Metropolis', does social understanding cease to rest upon mutual sympathy and empathy, and this is no contingent circumstance, because such sentiments were always somewhat illusory, tending to obfuscate the reality of individual will. In the Metropolis it is as if the permanent *a priori* conditions of sociation are now empirically presented. Thus the characteristic figure of the modern city – the 'stranger' – who is neither a mere traveller, nor yet a person truly 'at home', is not merely a phenomenon of modernity. On the contrary, he is the 'real' social person, whose ultimate non-assimilability and permanent suspension between the boundaries of belonging and not-belonging expresses a universally valid axiology.[29]

[26] Simmel, 'Exchange' and 'Conflict', in *On Interpretation*, pp. 43–69, 70–95.
[27] Simmel, 'Exchange'.
[28] Ibid., p. 48.
[29] Simmel, 'The stranger' and 'The metropolis and mental life', in *On Interpretation*, pp. 324–39.

Neo-Kantian Method in Max Weber

In the work of Max Weber, 'social forms' mutate into 'ideal types'.[30] At times in his methodological essays, Weber sounds as if he is just elaborating a historical method, and here the ideal types seem close to Rickert's 'individuals'. Hence, like Rickert, Weber rejects the notion that historical science can be adequately comprised under the nomothetic model.[31] Instead, he stresses the importance for history of what can be dubbed 'narrative causality': one 'imputes' causality by referring a particular, unique, historical 'constellation' to a foregoing constellation without reference to a general law – although law-like generalizations have a vital role in telling us what is likely and unlikely in history.[32] As for Rickert, the historian faces a problem of selection, and here 'ideal types' have an indispensable heuristic use. One can identify historical specificity by seeing how historical actors are orientated towards 'ideal typical values', with which their own actions and motivations never perfectly coincide.[33] As for Simmel with his social forms, history itself throws up ideal types, and the elaboration of their number is an 'endless task'.

But Weber is a 'sociologist', precisely because he defines the methodological use of ideal types much more narrowly than this. Unlike Nietzsche, Weber fails to expose the metaphysical nature of the category of 'cause' (and more especially, efficient causality). Thus he does not see that one can never fully 'account for' what comes after in terms of what precedes, without a reduction of the specificity of the later event: preceding conditions are only causally adequate at the point where they have already been superseded by the new circumstances. Hence Paul Veyne is quite right to radicalize Weber's theory of history by making narrative relation more fundamental than causal explanation.[34] But as Veyne argues, this shift makes 'sociology' redundant. For Weber, explanation only remains more basic than narrative relation, because he clings to the notion of an 'interior' subject, whose ideals and motivations can be 'compared with' the external course of events. Adequate historical explanation, which is achieved by sociology, consists for Weber in reaching back towards the consciousness of individual social actors.

In consequence Weber thinks, like Dilthey, that empathy with historical actors really adds something to the reading of the visible, historical 'text'. At the same time, like the neo-Kantians, he regards this as a chancy business, and thinks that, for the requirements of objectivity, something additional is needed. Therefore he argues (and this is the crucial point in his methodology) that diagnoses of personal intentions and motivations have to be 'checked'

---

[30] Swingewood, *A Short History of Sociological Thought*, p. 146.

[31] Max Weber, 'Objectivity in social science', in *The Methodology of the Social Sciences*, trans. Edward A. Shils and Henry A. Finch (New York: Free Press, 1949), p. 75.

[32] Weber, 'Objectivity in social science', pp. 78–9.

[33] Ibid., pp. 76–81, 86–94.

[34] Paul Veyne, *Writing History: Essay on Epistemology*, trans. Nina Moore-Rinvolucri (Middletown, Conn.: Wesleyan University Press, 1984) p. 270ff.

against the course of external events. It is very important to be clear about this; Weber is *not* saying that one only has access to intentions in terms of the reasons implicit in what people say and do (in other words 'practice' in its totality). If this were the case, it would be impossible to compare 'outcomes' with 'intentions', except as stages within a single inter-subjective process. On the contrary, Weber really does want to 'test' something that belongs to a supposed 'inner realm' of the subject. But how, given this internal/external dualism, can outcomes possibly tell us anything about 'original' intentions? This is where the *Geltungslogik* aspect of the 'ideal types' comes into play.

Like Rickert, Weber is opposed to scientific philosophies of history which explain everything that happens, or at least all important occurrences, with reference to 'laws of nature'. In such philosophies, the real motor of history turns out to be the operation of means-end rationality in technical or economic processes (Comte and Marx are obviously in mind). Weber's focus on individual motive is tied to a desire to show that while individuals may often be motivated by such *Zweckrational* goals, they can be motivated by substantive *Wertrational* goals also. And yet, at the same time, Weber is much closer to positivism (and so to sociology) than Rickert, because he deems processes of formal, means-end rationality to be the only thing that can be *directly* understood by the scientific historian with full objectivity. One can have fully objective, but indirect knowledge of *Wertrational* motivations only to the extent that one registers deviations from the 'ideal type' of means-end rationality.[35] Thus one can counterfactually project what would have happened according to this ideal type – if, for example all the actors had simply sought to maximize their own advantage within the given conditions – and so measure the deviation from this type in actuality. One then knows that other, not purely rational factors, have been at work.

But note the very great peculiarity of all this. Weber is really saying that fully objective history (sociology) is *primarily* about economic rationality, formal bureaucracy, and Machiavellian politics. What lies outside these categories cannot be read as a certain distinctive pattern of symbolic action, but only negatively registered. For the things outside – religion, art, traditional organic communities – do not for this view really belong to the realm of the factual at all; instead they belong to the 'irreal' realm of valuation, and they exist primarily as hidden, subjective forces.

This is why Weber gives such prominence to the category of 'charisma' in his theory of religion. It is certainly not empirical investigation, but rather Weber's *a priori* assumptions, which make him trace all religion back to an initial 'inspired' figure, able to attract others by his powers of fascination. Exactly the same thing applies to Weber's celebrated categories of 'routinization' and 'traditional authority'. Any religious pattern of valuation which semi-permanently distorts the operations of pure means-end rationality

[35] Max Weber, *Economy and Society: An Outline of Interpretative Sociology*, vol. 1 (Berkeley: California University Press, 1978) p. 6.

cannot be acknowledged as a factual presence in terms of its symbolic ordering of the world; instead it can only be registered as an inertia, as a mechanical
persistence of the effect of response to charisma, after the original charisma
has passed away. No doubt, of course, religions do undergo something like a
'routinization of charisma' (it did not take sociology to observe this) but it is
not metaphysically inevitable in the way that Weber makes it. Neither does it
make sense to reduce all tradition to *stasis*, and even less to suppose a primal
charisma arising before and apart from regular symbolic patternings.

The above considerations indicate that Weber's ideal types are not innocent
heuristic devices. But this is for two main underlying reasons. In the first
place, as Adorno and others have pointed out, Weber takes his 'ideal types'
of normative social rationality from the ideas of marginalist economics.[36]
The marginalists confined economics to the formal logic of the individual
maximization of 'marginal utility' in circumstances of relative scarcity. They
occluded from view the fact that people's positions within the market are
established through power-relationships which occur inside modes of appropriation and production, as well as exchange. All economic activity in history,
in all three categories, is in fact constituted through the organization of social
relationships. It is *these* which establish relative values and so forth, and
therefore there is no element of historical economic activity which is 'essentially' economic rather than 'social'. This first merely appears to be the case in
capitalist society, where the maximization of self-interest within certain fixed
rules of 'possession' is turned into a prime mode of social regulation. However, this regulation only works because of the acceptance of a not self-
evidently 'rational' (though not necessarily irrational) circumstance, namely
the dominance of the principle of abstract equivalence, which measures all
commodities on a single scale, and makes their 'value' equal merely their
formal substitutability.

While Weber is to be commended for his discovery that rationalization
processes are at work not merely and 'fundamentally' in the economy, as
Marx thought, but also in the production of politics, religion and law, he fails
to develop equivalents in these fields to Marx's analysis of the fetishistic and
'non-rational' character of the capitalist economy, just as he fails to acknowledge this in the case of the economy itself. Hence he is unable to describe all
forms of 'rationalization' in terms of their symbolic specificity and parallel
disjunctive codings which generate symbolic power. (For example there is
'lay language' in law, for jurors and the accused, and 'expert' language, for
lawyers. The latter involves, in modern times, a greater ability of manipulation, but no deeper insight into justice.)

It is often argued, by Marxists, that because Weber accepts the marginalist
confinement of economics to formal models, he makes it appear that econom-

---

[36] Theodore W. Adorno et al., *The Positivist Dispute in German Sociology*, trans. Glyn Adey and
David Frisby (London: Heinemann, 1976) pp. 61–3. Clark, *Marx, Marginalism and Modern
Sociology*, pp. 145–85, 205–38.

ics require supplementation by sociology. And it is true that Weber wrongly excludes specific historic and social arrangements from the realm of the economic. But he then does *the same thing* with the operations of government and with legal processes – and it is this general occlusion of power, not just of the social relations of production, which permits the sociological illusion. In all these cases, he only discusses power as an act of initially visible violence – the appropriation of land, conquest in war, monarchic suppression of feudal authority. After the initial act of violence, power operates merely with formal regularity, and Weber makes no attempt to see how the 'fictions' of power are constantly reconstituted and upheld. In this respect, it is significant that there is a strong parallel in Weber between the operation of sheer physical violence 'at the outset', and the commencement of religion with 'charisma'. In either case, a neat division is effected between a quite arbitrary foundation, and an area of self-contained rationality which it henceforth permits. Thus Weber (like Comte) sees the two first divisions of labour as being that between the religious expert and the layperson on the one hand, and the warrior and the civilian on the other.[37] And in the charismatic exhortation of the primitive warrior band, religion and founding violence are originally inseparable. This parallelism of religion and military powers shows that arguments about whether Weber's view of history is 'idealist' or 'materialist' are really beside the point.

This leads us to the second main reason why Weber's ideal types are more than heuristic devices. Weber, very much in the Comtean positivist tradition, erects a homology between his commitment to scientific *method* on the one hand, and his recognition of 'rational' processes as the central, recognizable social *object* on the other. Admittedly, Weber is teasingly ambiguous here: at times the norm of *Zweckrationalität* is a mere matter of methodological convenience, at other times it is the dark business of our Western fate – the ungrounded value of scientific validity which we are yet inexorably committed to.[38] Yet all that matters in practice is that Weber defines his other ideal types only negatively, with reference to the formally measurable disturbance of ends-mean rationality. Thus besides perfectly 'rational' authority, there can only be authority *before* all process, ineffable in its origins: 'charismatic' authority, which causes the rational course to deviate. If it continues to persist, then the name for this perverse inertia is 'traditional' authority.[39]

Given this fundamental situation, there can be no real argument as to whether Weber privileges the specifically Western form of rationality. Much has been made recently of the fact that Weber sees Hinduism as having the most rational theodicy, and as informing the most 'rational' variant of social order.[40] It is argued that these forms of 'substantive rationality' are

[37] Weber, *Economy and Society*, vol. 1, pp. 54–5, 401; vol. 2, pp. 1150ff, 1350ff.
[38] Weber, 'Politics as a vocation', in *From Max Weber*, pp. 77–128.
[39] Weber, *Economy and Society*, vol. 1, pp. 226–54.
[40] Wolfgang Schluchter, 'Weber's sociology of rationalism and typology of religious rejections of the world', trans. Ralph Schroeder, in *Max Weber, Rationality and Modernity*, pp. 92–115.

methodologically on a level with the West's most extreme development of 'formal rationality'. However, this fails to realize that Weber's category of 'substantive rationality' should get re-labelled 'quasi-substantive'. For all he means is a rationality that makes substantive *assumptions*, but then develops these with formal consistency (as opposed to Western legal rationality which is not substantive even in its assumptions). To apply this category to Hinduism is orientalism *in extremis*, because it assumes that Hindu religion is rather like a post-Spinozan philosophy in which one begins with a set of axioms and then proceeds to make regular deductions. A real category of substantive rationality would have to recognize that a particular symbolic patterning enters into the developmental logic of a system and its manner of self-propagation.

Weber's Sociology of Religion

As we have seen, there are three basic components to Weber's sociology: the normative measure of formal-instrumental rationality; arbitrary physical violence; and the arbitrariness of religious charisma. Weber repeats in an altered form the positivist connection of religion with the arbitrary and of both with a post-liberal politics. The problem with his whole sociology is that he makes religion, in its essence, to be an extra-social affair, and only provides 'social explanations' (of a more or less functionalist sort) for religious organization, and religious doctrine – both being seen as 'secondary' phenomena. Insofar as the effect of religion (i.e. charisma) persists, it has to conform to the conditions of social persistence as defined universally and *a priori* by Weber; that is to say, it must persist either as inertia or through legal formalization. The terms of religious persistence can then be wholly explained through the application of sociological categories. To disseminate itself, a religion requires narratives, doctrines, consistent norms – but one should note, against Weber, that it is quite impossible to define the supposedly initial, 'charismatic' assumptions in abstraction from these categories. A religion commences in its dissemination.

The 'social' conditions in which a religion can be disseminated are, for Weber, partly given by the economic and political circumstances in which it finds itself, and partly newly created in the form of a 'church' (meaning just the self-organization of the religion). In either case, the necessity for 'social factors' in religion indicates that an organization can only survive in the public sphere through appeal to self-interest, whether material or spiritual (religious prestige, promise of salvation and so forth).[41] Yet this is an unwarranted *a priori* assumption, grounded in Weber's definition of the public realm as essentially, and for all time, the formal organization of 'rational' self-interest, whether or not it pursues, at the margins, any substantive goals. Thus Weber's *methodology* already rules out the idea that there might be societies where conduct regularly presumed a more nuanced and less egotis-

---

[41] Weber, *Economy and Society*, vol. 1, pp. 246–54, 464–8.

tic notion of 'self-interest'. Like Rickert and Simmel, Weber makes the Kantian assumption that genuine value must be absolutely indifferent to any ideas of self-interest and happiness; in consequence, value can only be intermittently and strenuously upheld by figures of 'prophetic' stature, whereas the usual hypothetical imperatives of public society necessarily obey (as for Kant) a Machiavellian logic of *raison d'état* or *raison des affaires*. It follows that the Machiavellian assumptions of modern political theory and modern economics are intrinsic to the constitution of Weberian sociology.

The methodological value assumptions in Weber rework the Machiavellianism which helps constitute the 'imaginary' of secular reality. And it is only these assumptions which allow the specific idiom of sociological suspicion of religious organization and systematization (as opposed to the ineffability of founding charisma). This is something quite different from an *ad hoc* questioning of the individual motivations of religious adherents or the unconscious hypocrisies of particular religious structures. It proposes a *general* thesis and the thesis must hold generally, or not at all (and in this proposal of a constant concomitance, Weber still offers us a positivist law, after all). Hence he puts forward a theory of correlation between social class position and religious affiliation: salvation-religions, for example, are generally most promoted by lower-middle-class strata in towns and cities.[42] This correlation suggests, for Weber, that the continuing attractiveness of salvation-religions, with their strong ethical stress, must be connected with an individualistic, enterprising and socially aspiring way of life, to which rational predictability, the matching of promise to conduct, and strong eschatological expectation make a great appeal. Now to some extent, Weber (and Troeltsch perhaps more strongly) is making an important and original point here. This is that the moral universe of, for example, Christianity, has an affinity with certain modes of social action and not with others. It *is* clearly easier for an artisan to be a Christian than a warrior noble or a wealthy merchant. This may always have been known, but Weber and Troeltsch establish the point much more systematically. Yet in this form the point is an historical or even a theological one, not a sociological one. Troeltsch clearly recognizes this when he says that the 'societies' consequent upon religious beliefs themselves are not a 'sociological' matter in the full sense; what is properly sociological is social relationship connected to *economic* organization.[43]

For to say that, typically, lower-middle-class artisans are attracted to Christianity is not in itself a mode of sociological suspicion. This fact may very easily follow from the *ethos* that Christianity itself recommends for internal ethical reasons: how can peasants, or military overlords, or merchants, so easily fulfil a way of life which values strict honesty, brotherly sharing, and a certain independent integrity regarding one's dealings with others? This is a

---

[42] Ibid., pp. 481–4.
[43] Ernst Troeltsch, *The Social Teaching of the Christian Churches*, trans. Olive Wyon, vol. 1 (New York and London: G. Allen and Unwin/Macmillan, 1911) p. 23ff.

point brilliantly made by Troeltsch when he says that perhaps the medieval town, dominated by guilds of self-regulating producers, an economics of frugality, and relatively free from aristocratic and kinship dominations, was uniquely able to instil a Christian ethos.[44] This kind of observation only becomes 'sociological' when a 'social factor' is identified as being universally the prime determinant of the religious ethos itself. But both Troeltsch and Weber do in fact make this kind of claim.

Against such claims one can point out that in the case of a social entity like a medieval town, or still more a medieval monastery, it often makes little sense to argue about the relative primacy of 'ideal' or 'social' factors. For a start, there is nothing identifiably 'social' that can be separated from political, economic or religious arrangements. And the political and economic practices are themselves more or less infused by religious norms – such that one would look for religious 'belief' as much in the practices of guilds as in the writings of monks. The very existence of a large number of independent corporations, associated with the medieval town yet not identical with the town's political unity, is an effect of the spread of the idea of non-political, free, religious association made possible by Christianity. While, of course, the impact of Christianity on economic life was always very imperfect, it nonetheless remains the case that here (just as in the case of medieval Islam) one finds an economic practice that cannot be fully separated from religious practice (this would be most of all true in the case of a monastery where one could see the 'economy' as virtually a part of liturgical life itself). If one were to ask, what is ultimately 'determinative' here? then one would have to refer not to 'ideas' or to 'economics', but to a certain 'deep' level of practice, to a certain 'form of life'.

The more it is the case – as for example, with Islamic society – that the social order is totally 'inside' a religion, then the more the idea of a 'social factor' dissolves away into nothingness, or else into tautology. (Indeed, Ernst Troeltsch admits that there can be no proper sociology of 'prehistorical' times, before differentiation has occurred.)[45] Thus, precisely to the degree that the society of the medieval town coincided with the Christian ethos, and was informed by it, it is impossible to give explanatory 'priority' to social causation over religious organization, as Weber and Troeltsch seek to do. They only attempt this because their *Geltungslogik* establishes an *a priori* separation of the economic and political spheres from the religious. This ensures that economic and political influences are by definition 'extra-religious' and on this boundary one can stake out the realm of 'sociology'. 'Social factors' in Weber actually hover uneasily between instrumental (politico-economic) and evaluative ('religious') reason; they concern an instrumental pursuit of 'interest' which yet exceeds merely instrumental norms because this is the interest of a particular sectional grouping, best promoted by pre-

---

[44] Troeltsch, *Social Teaching*, pp. 254ff, 318.
[45] Troeltsch 'Religion, Wirtschaft und Gesellschaft' in Hans Baron (ed.) *Aufsatze zur Geistegeschichte und Religionsoziologie*, vol. 4, pp. 21–33 (1966).

senting itself in 'evaluative' garb. There is also a diachronic factor involved here which I shall revert to presently; for Troeltsch, the medieval town economy, partly influenced by substantive ethical norms (the *pretium justum* and so forth) is an improper economy – an economy that has not fully defined itself as an economy, and so as a sphere separated from absolute morality.[46] The supposed latent tension in the medieval town is caused precisely by the gradual bringing to consciousness of the *a priori* separation of value spheres.

Thus Weberian sociology betrays and subverts history. It takes as an *a priori* principle of sociological investigation what should be the *subject* of a genuine historical enquiry: namely the emergence of a secular polity, the modern *imagining* of incommensurable value spheres and the possibility of a formal regulation of society. But this eventuality, like earlier imaginings, can only be *narrated*, and is not traceable to 'fundamental' influences. Social differentiation is a contingent historical event (albeit both immensely widespread and persistent) in Western history, and not the outworking of rationality itself.

It is only *after* the modern event of differentiation that one can talk, in a more or less 'general' way, about economic influences on religion and vice versa. In the Middle Ages, political economy and sociology could not have been discovered, because their ontological objects were not yet present. But with the privatization of religion it does become more and more true that religious organization falls under the general patternings of all public institutions. So, in the modern world, 'sociology' does seem to apply. But mostly this discipline is content with a repeating of truisms about the present, with the surface level of our differentiated history, instead of conducting an enquiry into the deep level of the continued imagining of this differentiation. This is what is really inadequate about Weber's treatment of Protestantism and capitalism. He confines himself to the vague, unhistorical level of 'elective affinity' between religious belief and economic practice, and sees Protestantism's uniqueness as lying in its transference of asceticism to a totally 'this-worldly' sphere of activity.[47] However, the 'this-worldly' is a category assumed by Weber *a priori*, as the boundary of finitude traced by the 'natural' character of economic, political or erotic activity. By contrast, the point about theological influence on modern economic practice was not the transference of asceticism to 'this world', but rather (as I tried to show in Part One) the theological *invention* of 'this world', of the secular as a realm handed over by God to human instrumental manipulation. It is this invention which establishes the possibility of a new kind of asceticism, one no longer concerned with the relative ordering of 'goods' towards our 'final end' as in all previous Christian tradition, but rather only interested in the formal exercise of self-control, treating the realm of 'discipline' as a field for the 'testing' of grace and election – ultimate truths to which the ascetic practice is now only extrinsically

---

[46] Troeltsch, *Social Teaching*, pp. 257, 295.

[47] Max Weber, *The Protestant Ethic and the Spirit of Capitalism*, trans. Talcott Parsons (London: Allen and Unwin, 1985) pp. 95–154. 'The Protestant sects and the spirit of capitalism', in *From Max Weber*, pp. 302–22.

related. Weber only half-grasps this change, concentrating on the different field for the modern exercise of *ascesis*, rather than on the sundering of *ascesis* from genuine teleology. He too much makes it sound as if Protestant asceticism realized more precisely the 'essential' Christian approach, just as he sees the differentiation of spheres as always imminent within the historical process.

In view of these considerations, the general theses of Weberian sociology about class and religion are open to question, not so much empirically, as in terms of their conceptual import. When, for example, Weber says that military-aristocrats are not attracted to salvation-religions, is this not really a subtle tautology?[48] For it is true that the heroic celebration of one's own capacity, and the ultimacy of codes of honour, do not sit easily with, for example, the ethos of the Old Testament. But the heroic ethos is not, as Weber (following Nietzsche) tends to present it, the more 'natural' one; rather the military-aristocratic life is itself sustained by a particular ideological code, itself a kind of religion. Thus Weber's observation is true, but true only in the sense that one 'religion' may be by definition quite incompatible with another. Such a reduction is not intended to belittle Weber; on the contrary his observations about religion and society often do break new ground, precisely to the degree that they call attention to the fact that religions are practices as much as beliefs, and therefore require the right kind of 'social breathing space'. However, his *a priori* assumptions precisely *contradict* the very notion of a 'religious practice' and it is at *this point* (strange as it seems) that Weber becomes 'sociological'. This can be seen when he considers the case of Islam.[49]

Here we have a military society following a salvation religion. For Weber, this is a sociological anomaly, only to be accounted for by Muhammad's Machiavellian ensuring of a routinization of his own charisma by adjoining a specific content of promise of military conquest to his own prophetic utterances. This is clearly a travesty, which glosses over the fact that Islam produced a *different kind* of military society, contradicting some of Weber's claims about the universal features of the military-aristocratic ethos.

It would, however, be false to give the impression that Weberian sociology only concerns the point of intersection between charismatic forces and formal-instrumental rationality. It has, also, a secondary interest in internal religious arrangements – the phenomena of routinization, tradition, and 'substantive rationality'. Here, as modern commentators like Pierre Bourdieu observe, there is more room for realizing that class and power-structures themselves embody ideology in their patterns of symbolic interaction.[50] In this case, the sociological reduction takes the form, not of referring dogmas and ecclesiastical structures to 'outside' forces, but to an internal functionality of religious self-maintenance. But here again, sociology must be deconstructed. To explain beliefs and practices in terms of power relationships *universally*,

---

[48] Weber, *Economy and Society*, vol. 1, pp. 472–6.
[49] Ibid.
[50] Pierre Bourdieu, 'Legitimation and structural interests in Weber's sociology of religion', in *Max Weber, Rationality and Modernity*, pp. 119–37.

demands that one hypostasize 'power' by thinking of it in isolation from beliefs and practices. Yet the always specific forms of power are 'fictions' elaborated precisely by beliefs and practices, so that trying to see 'power' as more fundamental than these things is a hopeless task.

Bourdieu points to Weber's treatment of 'priestly' and 'prophetic' religion as being the site of his 'internal' religious sociology. He usefully suggests that one must reconceive charismatic authority more socially than Weber, in terms of the intense invoking and reformation through words and deeds of existing symbolic structures by particular individuals who then become 'representative'. This, however, is really to relativize the distinction between 'routine' and 'charisma', and once this is done, then it is no longer possible, as Bourdieu thinks, to see the contrast of the 'priestly' and the 'prophetic' as a universal sociological determinant of religious practice. For how can dogmas, canonical texts and fixed liturgies be seen as primarily devices for maintaining the 'routine' and 'traditional' power of priests over against charismatic eruptions, if it is admitted that there can be no charisma without a certain symbolic closure being always already present? Individuals who set their 'personal' authority over against established texts, norms, and customs, have always already begun to 'perpetuate' themselves in the form of a re-textualization, a re-normalization. Routine and charisma are complexly involved phases within a single religious tradition, while 'charismatic sects' are machines for the constant reproduction of the conventional 'signs' of inspiration – this circumstance makes such sects alone the real example (paradoxically) of tradition as mere 'inertia'. There is then absolutely no warrant for reading religious history in terms of a fundamental and structurally determined power struggle between 'prophetic' and 'mystical' types on the one hand, and 'priestly' types on the other. This is only possible if one maintains Weber's *a priori* dualism of charisma over against tradition. In the following section it will be seen how Weber is here rehearsing the historical prejudices of liberal Protestantism.

Weber's sociology of religion has been arguably more influential than Durkheim's in more recent times. Yet his approach has been taken up without reference to its inextricable connection to the methodological foundations of Weber's sociology as a whole. When these are unscrambled, the whole notion of a 'social' explanation of religion simply disintegrates. It is not that religion should not be *reduced* to social influences – Weber agrees about this, all too strongly. It is rather than there is nothing 'social' which it could be reduced to. For 'the social' for Weber means first of all the idea that there is a fixed, *a priori* boundary between the religious/substantively-evaluative and the economic, and secondly, that there is another *a priori* division between forms of 'asocial' authority based on pure violence/charisma and social authority which is the mere inertia of repetition. As these boundaries are not ahistorical absolutes, there is nowhere in reality that Weberian 'society' can truly find a home. It follows *a fortiori*, that religion never rests, not even to a degree, on any 'social' basis.

The Liberal Protestant Metanarrative

Besides the synchronic elements already detailed, Weber's sociology of religion has a strong diachronic component. This diachronic element is in fact vital to his substantive sociology, which has as its main theme the emergence of formal-instrumental rationality.[51]

For if this is the norm for human knowledge and association, then sociology must come up with a plausible account of the long concealment and gradual emancipation of this norm. The emancipation is not, indeed, inevitable, and Weber therefore presents us with no philosophy of history in the Hegelian sense. He does, however, advance a substantive philosophy of history of a Kantian variety, because by taking the norm of reason for granted, he does not have to describe the contingent construction of 'reason', but only its liberation from other constricting influences. But just as for Comte, the major problem for Weber is the role, in the emergence of reason, of the irrational, and primarily of religion. Like Comte also, Weber responds by erecting a three-phase theory of historical becoming: there is a first, 'magical' phase; a second phase of the great salvation-religions; and a third, modern, secular phase.[52] Weber regards the second phase in the way that Kant regarded pre-critical metaphysics: other-worldly speculation helped to train the powers of reason, preparing the way for an eventual distinction between arational valuations and strivings of the will which 'overcome' the supposedly perceptible boundaries of the finite, and the finite 'disenchanted' realm itself, where alone, critical reason can operate. To this Weber adds a Nietzschean thematic: the salvation-religions also, through their ascetic bent, train the will in the exercise of power, which can then be visited back upon 'this world'.[53]

The problem about this metanarrative is that the third stage is really only exemplified in the case of the West. One has to make two moves to avoid the obvious conclusion that 'rationalization' is just one event in Western history that happens to have swamped the world, rather than an always latent phenomenon. The first move is an orientalist one. The questions are constantly posed: *why* no capitalism, bureaucratic rationalization, formal law, harmonic music, in the East? The East is defined as a lack, a *stasis* and a set of factors of retardation.[54] The second move is to acclaim Christianity as the 'most religious religion'. If only the West has arrived at the universal goal, then Christianity must be in some sense the universal religion. What Christianity is supposed uniquely to achieve is the separating out of the religious value-sphere as a purely private matter to do with the will rather than the

[51] Ralph Schroeder, 'Nietzsche and Weber: two prophets of the modern world', in *Max Weber, Rationality and Modernity*, pp. 207–21.

[52] Ibid. Weber, *Economy and Society*, vol. 1, pp. 399–634.

[53] Weber, *The Protestant Ethic*, pp. 95–183. 'Intermediate reflections', in *From Max Weber*, pp. 323–59.

[54] Weber, *Economy and Society*, vol. 1, pp. 259–62, 551–6; vol. 2, pp. 816–23. Troeltsch, *Social Teachings*, p. 213.

intellect. It is able to develop a unique asceticism of work, because it finally realizes that the 'other-worldly' is sublimely inaccessible, a matter of faith, and that all concrete behaviour takes place in a world of 'works' which are religiously indifferent. Absolute, religious morality is an essentially private affair.

There is a kind of hidden, diachronic functionalism at work here. If Christianity ushers in the modern world, then, right from the start, Christianity must be understood in these terms. Thus Troeltsch and Weber fail to see individualism, voluntarism, fideism, and Kantian ethicization as contingent *changes* in Christian doctrine and ethos, but project these things back into the beginnings of Christianity and even the Old Testament. The history of the West is turned into the always-coming-to-be of liberal Protestantism or its secular aftermath, and this means precisely the always-coming-to-be of Weber's and Troeltsch's methodology, their instrument of investigation. It is at the diachronic level therefore that method and ontological content are most seen to be locked in a mutually self-confirming circle.

The liberal-Protestant metanarrative is still powerfully present in recent thought, so it will be useful to detail its main elements as they already appear in both Troeltsch and Weber:

1   Polytheism and magic

Like Comte, Weber thinks of primitive 'man' as a rationalist. Pre-religious magic was strictly linked to natural and technological purposes.[55] Thus the primitive age was 'proto-scientific', and in other respects also it foreshadowed modernity: plurality of gods meant plurality of purposes and values. Needless to say, this reductive view of magic, sharp separation of magic from religion, and ascription of 'pluralism' to all primitive societies are all highly questionable.

2   The importance of Roman law

Alongside the universal role which Weber accords to Christianity, one should not overlook the similar function which he accords to Roman law.[56] But Weber traces the beginnings of cautelary jurisprudence (formal dealings with contracts, promises and so forth) to Roman *sacred* law and connects this with the fact that the Romans craved *dii certi*, and sought to multiply gods to match things, occasions and functions. The 'nominalism' that confined one god to one role permitted a 'rational' systematization of religious duties and an easy system of commutational equivalences for arduous ritual performance. There is no doubt that Weber is right to see this as momentously significant, but instead of stressing the first beginnings of a universal rationality, he should

---

[55] Weber, *Economy and Society*, vol. 1, pp. 422–39.
[56] Ibid., vol. 2, pp. 796–808, 839–59.

rather have pointed out (as Vico had already done) that the univocal prejudices of the formal, abstract language of Roman law are just as 'fictional' as the mythical system from which Weber admits their derivation.[57]

3   Ancient Judaism

Weber sees ancient Judaism, along with Rome, as the true source of peculiarly Western 'rationality' because of its monotheistic and ethical stress. However, the dualisms of Weber's religious categorizations (mystical/ascetic; priestly/prophetic) really derive from a crudified version of the liberal Protestant 'higher-critical' reading of the Old Testament, which is now seen to be a serious distortion.[58] Following a common misreading of Wellhausen, Weber considers that 'the prophetic element' in Judaic religion was alone responsible for a rigorous monotheism, and for a stress on 'ethics' rather than on magic. Yet in point of fact the Deuteronomic reforms which codified ritual observance, and insisted on its connection with ethical behaviour, were made by a priestly party. There was no total cleavage between priestly and prophetic functions, nor was Israelite religious experience ignorant of mystical 'unity with God', as Weber claims. Within the body of the Torah no qualitative distinction seems to have been made between 'ethical' norms, and ritual observances which have a certain 'magical' character to them.[59] Hence Weber was simply wrong to discover in ancient Judaism the germs of a 'Protestant' religion which is prophetic, anti-ritualistic, anti-mystical, ethical and 'this-worldly'.

4   Christian origins

According to Troeltsch, Christianity was originally, with Jesus, an individualistic ethical creed. Only with Paul did elements of an 'organicist' ethic intrude (the 'body of Christ') and this is to be explained sociologically, in terms of the need for a strong ecclesiastical organization to preserve the original message.[60] However, there is no reason to suppose any identifiable Christianity before the emergence of strong ecclesial themes, which are indeed in continuity with Jesus's own preaching about 'the kingdom'. Christian teaching about the significance of 'the person' cannot really be abstracted from the stress that true personhood is realized 'in Christ' and that the Christic form is mediated through the Church. Troeltsch, in point of fact, seems to have had a secret hankering after organicism, and he explains very well (following Otto von Gierke) the model of Christian medieval corporate ecclesiology for which, while each person was of unique value, this value remained connected to his place within the whole, which was more than a

[57] Weber, *Economy and Society*, vol. 1, p. 408. Vico, *The New Science*, para. 1037 (1952).

[58] Weber, *Ancient Judaism*, trans. H. Gerth and Don Martindale. I am indebted to Paul Morris for discussion of this point. Irving M. Zeitlin, *Ancient Judaism* (Cambridge: Polity, 1984).

[59] Steiner, *Taboo*, pp. 78–93.

[60] Troeltsch, *Social Teachings*, pp. 51–4, 69ff.

nominal fiction, and so could be 'personally' represented by a bishop.[61] But for Troeltsch (unlike Gierke) this model remains inconsistent, because it supposedly confuses a *sittlich* morality (where different value spheres can be made the subject of sociological study) with the 'morality of conscience' which concerns the direct relation of the individual to the absolute. This was what Christianity (which Troeltsch considers to be virtually identical with stoicism in this regard) was supposedly all about in the beginning, and it is the identification of a 'pure' sphere of morality, focused on the sanctity of the will, which allows Christianity to become the agent of social differentiation – releasing the autonomy of the aesthetic, the economic and the political.[62]

5   The Christian Middle Ages

Weber's thesis about Protestantism and capitalism is really a thesis about Christianity and capitalism. He notes very well that the independence of the medieval city is vastly increased compared to antique times, because the primacy of confessional association finally removes the form of an aristo-cratic, clan-based nexus which subordinated the 'non-initiated', religiously-excluded functionaries, responsible for economic activity.[63] He notes also how the Church was a prime vehicle for 'rationalization', because lack of a religious law (as in Judaism and Islam) and the growth of inner-ecclesial conflicts meant that, increasingly, these had to be formally adjudicated. Elab-orators of Weber have stressed how later monasticism, especially the Cister-cian order, assumed a more hierarchical division of labour within the monastic walls, and adopted a more profit-orientated approach to its external economic dealings.[64]

All these developments are empirically verifiable, but this does not mean that they somehow belong to the 'essence' of Christianity. On the contrary, they seem more connected to the management of a failure of the Christian ethos. And what is especially wrong-headed about recent developments of the metanarrative is to see all monasticism, in its character of voluntary association, as a prototype for a society of contracting individuals.[65] This is really to suggest, like Troeltsch, that the corporate element in monastic society is inconsistent with its founding basis in a moment of individual 'decision'. However, decision to enter a monastery means a further affiliation to a tradition in which one is already 'placed'; such a tradition can only be thought of as inherently 'individualist', compared to 'family inheritance',

---

[61] Ibid., pp. 97–8.
[62] Ibid., p. 98; 'Religion, Wirtschaft und Gesellschaft'.
[63] Weber, *Economy and Society*, vol. 2, pp. 1241ff, 1343–8.
[64] Ibid., pp. 828–31. Randall Collins, *Weberian Sociological Theory* (Cambridge: Cambridge University Press, 1986) pp. 45–76. Steven Collins, 'Monasticism, utopias, and comparative social theory' in *Religion*, vol. 18, April 1988, pp. 101–39.
[65] Collins, 'Monasticism, utopias and comparative social theory'.

if one supposes that the cultural aspects of the latter are as 'natural' as the biological ones.

Likewise, there is no case for supposing, just because medieval canon law gravitated towards a formal, contractual construal of economic relationships, that the Church was always destined to be the prototype of the modern State. This is a version of 'diachronic functionalism' in which one supposes that the idea of a 'society of individuals' was first of all elaborated as a heavenly society and then transferred to 'this world'. There are two things wrong with this idea. First of all, the Christian stress on the *persona* cannot be seen as having an elective affinity with the *persona* of Roman law, which from denoting a mere 'mask' evolved into the notion of an abstract, possessing and self-possessed will. Sociology sees in this transition something universal – the emergence of the modern 'individual' from the earlier cultural determination of person as mere 'role'.[66] But from a Christian viewpoint both mythical mask *and* abstract will reduce the *persona* to a form of equivalence. In Augustine, for example, the background to the anthropological *persona* is Christological and Trinitarian rather than jurisprudential, so that what he stresses is the concrete, specific unity of the person, including both soul and body, a situated unity like the unity of God and man which occurs in the specific divine personhood of Christ – inseparable from its relationship to the Father and the Holy Spirit.[67]

Secondly, it is not true that before the Pope's assumption of imperial powers, the Church was an essentially 'spiritual' body of individuals. Louis Dumont, who, following Troeltsch and Weber, takes this view, sees this event as the beginning of the socialization of the Church and its transformation into the modern, liberal State.[68] But even before this event, in the period of a looser Church-Empire alliance, all true *auctoritas* was ascribed to the Church, and while functions of natural justice were left to the State *potestas*, it was axiomatic that there could be no true justice without the influence of grace.[69] The externality of the imperial *potestas* with regard to the Church (whereby only the ruler, not the empire as such, was wholly *within* the Church) was maintained to register the imperfectly Christian character of the empire, and the realm of *res divinae* over which the Church was sovereign was certainly not confined to matters of 'private' salvation as the modern age might conceive them.

[66] Marcel Mauss, 'A category of the human mind: the notion of person, the notion of self', in Michael Carruthers et al. (eds.), *The Category of the Person* (Cambridge: Cambridge University Press, 1985) pp. 1–26.

[67] Hubertus R. Drobner, *Person-Exegese und Christologie bei Augustinus* (Leiden: E. J. Brill, 1986) esp. pp. 114–26.

[68] Louis Dumont, 'A modified view of our origins: the Christian beginnings of modern individualism', in *The Category of the Person*, pp. 93–122; *Essays on Individualism: Modern Ideology in Anthropological Perspective* (Chicago: Chicago University Press) p. 43ff.

[69] R. W. and A. J. Carlyle, *A History of Mediaeval Political Thought in the West*, vol. 1 (Edinburgh: Blackwood, 1862) pp. 175–93. Walter Ullmann, *A History of Political Thought: The Middle Ages* (London: Penguin, 1965) pp. 18, 38. Yves Congar, *L'Ecclésiologie du Haut Moyen-Age* (Paris: Editions du Cerf, 1968) pp. 253–9. Lactantius, *Divine Institutions*, V. 14, 11.

The 'liberal protestant metanarrative' is then questionable at all its specific points. It has the merit of recognizing the unmistakable uniqueness of both the Jewish presence in history (as a kind of 'counter-State') and the Christian ecclesial presence as a new sort of universal society quite distinct from tribe, empire or *polis*. But it tries to read this uniqueness as the always implicit presence in the West of a private realm of value, a presence which makes Western history, in turn, the key to the history of the whole world.

The metanarrative has also its modern and 'prophetic' culmination. Weber was of the decided opinion that the Old Testament prophets were more concerned with foreign policy than with social justice, and he maintains the emphasis.[70] The modern world is for Weber basically a fusion of monotheism turned into this-worldly formal rationality with a resurgent polytheism which applies to the realm of private values. In a curious way, a Kantian respect for universal absolute values – the categorical imperative – now operates at a more distant meta-level, so that Weber shows respect for many different imperatives, albeit seeing them as arbitrarily held to (and so objectively *hypothetic*).[71]

For the monotheism of formal rationality, being a pure formalism, must, 'at its margins', have some arbitrary, substantive purpose, just as, for Troeltsch, Kantian ethics must be supplemented in the social sphere by a *sittlich* one.[72] What Weber really fears (and this is normally misunderstood) is the 'orientalization' of formal rationality, which means its capturing by a substantive purpose at the hands of a 'patriarchal' regime.[73] Weber considers that socialism (*especially* non-Marxist socialism) represents a threat to Western destiny, because it reintroduces into law and politics substantive values which can never be perfectly verifiable according to formal, positive criteria. A bureaucratic regime of a socialist, or other kind, will suppress polytheistic variety, and with this the impulse of the liberative will which is the legacy of Western monotheism.[74] Like Nietzsche, Weber seeks for new sources of 'charisma' after the decline of religion, which will guard against such Oriental dangers. But it is in the political realm that the crucial question arises: what supraformal element can there be that does not lead to a substantive subversion of legal positivism? How can there be politicians who are more than bureaucrats (for bureaucrats would not be alert to the possible subversion of bureaucracy by substantive goals) and yet not mere demagogues?[75] Weber's answer is that the modern leader must link his charisma to the internal and external unity in power of the State, and must guard against party-political demagoguery by

[70] Weber, *Economy and Society*, vol. 1, p. 443.
[71] Weber, 'Science as a vocation', in *From Max Weber*, p. 149. 'Politics as a Vocation', 'Intermediate Reflections'.
[72] Troeltsch, *Christian Thought*, pp. 62–7, 71–99.
[73] Weber, *Economy and Society*, vol. 2, pp. 1192–3, 1402.
[74] Ibid., pp. 873–5.
[75] Ibid., pp. 1381–1410.

appealing directly for his authority to all the people. After Weber, Carl Schmitt connected this idea with the Catholic positivist Donoso Cortes' theory of 'elective dictatorship', and thereby contributed to the ideology of both fascism and national socialism.[76]

Troeltsch has his own, once again theological version of this classically positivist politics. *Die Weltgeschichte ist ungeheuer aristokratische*, he declares, and tells us that from time to time there have arisen 'elect', grace-infused individuals who have won the struggle of will against the background of irrational nature – an unchanging realm of passions that must be ceaselessly 'overcome'.[77] This declaration underlines the fact that both Troeltsch and Weber create a 'sociology' which is nothing but a spurious promotion of what they study – namely the secular culture of modernity. What is ultimately crucial in their accounts is their political and ethical stance: on the one hand there is only the integrity of the private will respecting the freedom of others (whether in a Kantian 'monotheist' or Nietzschean 'polytheist' fashion) and on the other hand, the Machiavellian sphere of political 'rationality'. What is squeezed out in between is, not accidentally, Christianity, and by this I mean a sphere for the operation of charity. Such a sphere requires substantive norms for society and indeed (dare it be said) a continuous exercise of 'pastoral' oversight. Only in the light of such norms can one do more than limit or merely regulate the operations of power and public discipline. From the perspective of charity, one aspires to discriminate between just and unjust power, ultimately coercive and ultimately non-coercive rule. Weberian sociology is a mode of the denial of this possibility.

[76] Schmitt, *Politische Theologie*, I, pp. 69–84, 70–1.

[77] Troeltsch, *Der Historismus und seine Probleme, Gesammelte Schriften*, Band III (Aalen: Scientia Verlag, 1961) pp. 100–02. Hans Bosse, *Marx-Weber-Troeltsch: Religionssoziologie und Marxistische Ideologiekritik*, pp. 51–3.

5

Policing the Sublime: A Critique of the Sociology of Religion

Convergence on Sublimity

Peter Berger, a modern American sociologist, has claimed that 'sociology' is now the name of the scientific and humanist critique of religion, the fiery brook through which contemporary theology must pass.[1] And, to a large extent, theologians themselves have accepted the idea that it is possible to give a 'social' explanation for at least some of the features of religious belief. Their response to this situation has been an exercise in damage limitation; although they admit the validity of a reductive suspicion of religion in sociological terms, they seek to limit the scope of this suspicion by staking out a dimension to religion or theology which must remain irreducible. A sensibly critical faith is supposed to admit fully the critical claims of sociology (as indeed of Marxism and Freudianism) as a propaedeutic to the explication of a more genuine religious remainder.

At this point, it is salutary to pay attention to the perplexity of more rigorous sociologists in the Durkheimian tradition, such as Mary Douglas, about the status of this remainder.[2] If it concerns some realm of 'private experience', then we have every reason to believe that this does not really escape social mediation, and we should remain open to the possibility that even the most apparently personal religious outlook reflects a 'social' situation. These kinds of admission have been possible, not for liberal theology, which tends to ground itself in 'authentic experience', but rather for certain styles of neo-orthodoxy that insist on the absolute contrast between the revealed word of God and human 'religion', which as a mere historical product can safely be handed over to any reductive analyses whatsoever. However, this sort of neo-orthodoxy is itself but a variant of liberal Protestantism: a revealed word of God which speaks only of itself, which does not really penetrate the realm of human symbolic constructions without getting tainted and distorted, must continue to be without impact upon the world, and therefore remains locked in a category of

---

[1] Peter L. Berger, *A Rumour of Angels* (Harmondsworth: Penguin, 1969) pp. 44–5.
[2] Mary Douglas, 'The effects of modernization on religious change', in *Daedalus*, Winter, 1982.

the specifically religious, just as much as the liberal Protestant notion of 'religious experience'.

If one admits the claims of sociology, then the liberal Protestant hermeneutic *via media* between trust and suspicion is likely to appear unsatisfactory, and the neo-orthodox *bravura* about reductive claims may be seen as merely a relocation of the same middle path at the far bounds of possible human experience, such that the claimed 'beyond' is characterized by an ineffability without issue and without effect.

The preceding two chapters, however, have suggested an entirely different course: instead of a partial admission of 'suspicion', one should develop a 'meta-suspicion' which casts doubt on the possibility of suspicion itself. By this, of course, I do not mean the sort of 'commonsense' suspicion which has always been with us (and of which sociology has very usefully extended the range), as when we say 'Alfred's Methodism has always seemed a matter of time-keeping to me' (and do *not* add, 'this kind of functional purpose is constitutive of Methodism in general') or 'Papal practice is often more about power than grace.' I mean rather a 'foundational suspicion' which seeks to show that, universally, something 'questionable' is reducible to something else which is 'unquestionable'. Hence in retracing the genesis of sociology I have opened the way, not to denying 'reduction to the social', but rather to casting doubt on the very idea of there being something 'social' (in a specific, technical sense) to which religious behaviour *could be* in any sense referred.

By retracing this genesis, we have come to see just how the terms 'social' and 'society' have so insinuated themselves that we never question the assumption that while 'religions' are problematic, the 'social' is obvious. The idea that the former should be referred to the latter appears like an innocent, genial inspiration. However, we can now see that the emergence of the concept of the social must be located within the history of 'the secular', its attempt to legitimate itself, and to 'cope' with the phenomenon of religion. Already, in Hobbes and Spinoza (and before them in Bodin), the emergence of a critical, non-theological metadiscourse about *certain aspects* of religion – its local variations, its particular traditions, its public rituals – was of one birth with the concept of political sovereignty.[3] It sprang up alongside 'the State' which was a new perspective upon things, a perspective of power and a power operating by perspective, through watchful presence in every part of the social 'body' (to use Hobbes's metaphor) with which it is one. From 'the new science of politics' onwards, through political economy and positivism, there persists a double element in the practical and intellectual approach to religion: its particular, historical manifestations must fall under the superior glance (the 'higher perspective') of a critical discourse, but at the same time the 'higher perspective' which is that of the State, the whole body, and so of

---

[3] J. Samuel Preuss, *Explaining Religion* (New Haven, Conn.: Yale University Press, 1987) pp. 3–23.

'humanity', often identifies itself with a universal religion, a distilled essence of religiousness, which is a construction for the sake of the secular peace.

In the French positivist tradition, the redescription of the political whole as 'society' permits a more thoroughgoing organicism and the imbuing of secular order with a religious quality. After Durkheim's neo-Kantian reworking of this tradition, the social becomes a name for the finite presence to us of the Kantian 'kingdom of ends': it sanctifies and embodies the sublime freedom of every individual within the State. It is also the *a priori* schema which supplies the categorical universals under which are to be comprehended all empirical contents. Traditional and particular religions are thought to encode in a non-perspicuous fashion this priority of the social, and only insofar as this is recognized is religion itself universalized and brought to perfection. Max Weber, by contrast, is at a further distance from Comtean positivism; for him the social is not the site of the *a priori*, rather the social itself is to be known *a priori* in terms of the primacy of instrumental reason and economic relationship. Nevertheless, this still universalizes religion in a different fashion: religion has its source in 'charisma' which interrupts instrumental reason in many ways, registered by sociology as negative deviation. Universalization is here a way of 'managing' the many particular religions, and of confining them to the private sphere, but charisma also appears in the public realm as the supra-rational purpose of the political whole which instrumental reason is unable to specify or adjudicate. (Because publicly-acknowledged political charisma is an arbitrary force, Weber is here *more* positivist, and less Kantian, than Durkheim.)

Both Durkheim and Weber categorize societies in terms of the relation of the individual to something social and universal, and this reflects the perspective of modern Western politics, whose prime concern is the 'bodily' mediation between the unlimited sovereignty of the State and the self-will of the individual. As a grid, or frame through which to view all societies, this perspective tends to occlude the fact that for many non-Western, or pre-modern societies, what matters is not the binary individual/society contrast, but the hierarchical ordering of different status groupings, and the distribution of roles according to a complex sense of common value.[4] Sociology, of course, registers this difference, but it does so *negatively*, in terms of the observation that organic and hierarchical societies exercise strong 'control' over the individual, as if the member of this traditional society were secretly shadowed by the presence of the modern, self-determining subject. In consequence, the relation of the individual to the whole – which defines only *modern* politics – is seen as the universal site of the social, and it follows that all the complex rituals, hierarchies, and religious views which go to make up a stratified, organic society can be 'explained' in terms of their functional maintaining of strong control of the whole over the individual parts. Such 'explanation' is only regarded as more than tautology because

---

[4] Serge Tcherkezoff, *Dual Classification Reconsidered*, trans. Martin Thorn (Cambridge/Paris: Cambridge University Press, 1983).

the normative perspective of modernity allows one to think that there is always a dimension of pure 'social action', pure 'social power', occurring between the individual and the social, and separable from its ritual, symbolic or linguistic embodiment. But 'a social whole' apart from the interactions of the various norms and strata is a reifying abstraction, and there is no 'social action' definable or comprehensible apart from its peculiar linguistic manifestation, the inexplicability of a particular symbolic system.

Religions, characteristically, involve 'eccentric' customs, attachments to particular times and places, constant repetition of the singular. It is the spurious claim of sociology to be able to master, through a superior metadiscourse, this eccentricity, singularity and repetition. And it makes this claim because of the perspectival bias I have outlined above. For if a traditional society is registered only negatively, then the particularity of its religion, the *kind* of organic whole which it is, the *content* of its hierarchy of values, will be subordinated and even ascribed to the mere general fact of its being strongly cohesive. This reduction, however, only applies to the particularity of religion – it must be emphasized, once again, that sociology, like liberal theology, usually wants to identify and protect a 'real' essence of religion. This real essence is not to do with the power-dimension of society, its relationships of action, but rather with a sphere of 'value' which justifies and legitimates social action and power. Now in reality, and this is especially clear from traditional societies, legitimation is inseparably interwoven with power in all its distributed complexity. Sociology refers this complexity to one general fact – the social whole, or the core of instrumental action – and similarly abstracts from the symbolic embodiment of values, situating them at the inner or outer edge of society. Thus, for Durkheim, values are the constants which preserve social *stasis* at the level of the organic whole; for Weber, they are things which are arbitrarily wished by the isolated individual.

Normative value, including religion, is consequently relocated by sociology 'at the margins' – either at the point where the individual is supposed to stand outside and over-against the social, meaning the realm of verifiable facts (Weber), or else as the mysterious ether which mediates between one ineffable individual and the other and yet goes to make up the social substance of practical reason (Durkheim and Simmel). Thus religion is regarded by sociology as belonging to the Kantian sublime: a realm of ineffable majesty beyond the bounds of the possibility of theoretical knowledge, a domain which cannot be imaginatively represented, and yet whose overwhelming presence can be acknowledged by our frustrated imaginative powers.[5] For this presence of religion is also the presence of freedom, of the soul, the transcendental 'apperceived' self, and therefore, of irreducible humanity. The sublime is to be protected and treasured, although it causes no positively definable effects within the objective factual world – insofar as this *appears* to

[5] Immanuel Kant, *The Critique of Judgement*, trans. Werner S. Pluhar (Indianapolis: Hackett, 1987) pp. 97–141.

be the case (as religions so often believe) then it can be shown by sociology that the conditions for the representation of the sublime are in fact entirely given by the social, whether as factual *a priori* or as *a priori* norm.

As a 'science of the sublime', sociology is locked into the paradox of the Kantian critique of metaphysics and of any claims to the representation of the absolute. To make the critical claim that categories applicable to the finite apply to the finite alone and are extended only illegitimately to the infinite, one has to make two assumptions. First of all, one must assent to a division between *a priori* concept and empirical 'intuition', and the view that one cannot really conceive of the one without the other: for example, the concept of cause, although *a priori*, only has application to our 'understanding' of the appearances of things in space and time. Because it is denied that concepts like cause themselves arise from the series of empirical appearances, it appears that two different series, of conceptual analyses on the one hand, and spatio-temporal instances on the other, were pre-arranged (for our subjective apprehension) to exist only for each other. In consequence, to make an extrapolation of a category to an infinite, constitutive application, is to break the bounds of the natural circle within which it applies and where every bringing of intuitions under categories *prevents* precisely an infinite regress in either series, which would result in irresolvable antinomies preventing any certain, determinate knowledge.

If, however, as is the case, it is impossible to isolate the pre-given, categorical element (which for sociology is schematized as 'society' – as fact or norm) from the flux of becoming, then one cannot be so sure of the range of applications of a particular concept, nor does it appear as necessarily enclosed within the circumscription of finitude.

The second assumption follows closely from the first. It is that one is able to make an exhaustive list of the *a priori* categories of possible finite knowledge. It is here that the paradox arises: one can only define, once for all, the limits of human understanding, and so 'exclude metaphysics', if one is standing, as it were, on the boundary, with one eye on the other side, giving a glimpse of the sublime.[6] Hence, for example, one grasps causality as a closed, determinate chain, precisely in contrast with freedom which one can actualize, although certainly not comprehend. One can only deny the possibility that causality, or necessity, or particular finite perfections belong pre-eminently (though we cannot 'see' this) to the infinite 'in itself', because one falsely supposes that in 'freedom' one has access to something standing outside the spatio-temporal series, which constitutes the transcendence of 'things in themselves' over against material subsistence, causality, relation and so forth. (This is why Kant only allows analogous talk of God as a 'regulative' discourse concerning his relationship to the world; he does not, like Aquinas, analogously 'attribute' notions like necessity to God 'in himself' – insofar as created effects resemble their formal-final causes – although our practical insight into

---

[6] Kant, *Critique of Judgement*, pp. 106–17.

freedom gives us, for Kant, a univocal grasp of the essence of transcendence, which Aquinas could not have allowed.) Wittgenstein put it very well: 'in so far as people think they can see "the limits of human understanding", they believe of course that they can see beyond these'.[7]

The 'critique of metaphysics' which sociology, as Berger says, claims to carry forwards, thus turns out to be a new metaphysics which lays claim to a totalizing and once-for-all representation of finitude, and also a humanism which safeguards a free and ineffable subject that only 'has an apparent effect' within this finitude, yet always, in essence, transcends it. For sociology, religion is a component of the protected 'human' sphere, although this sphere is sometimes (for Durkheim) made to coincide with the schematic possibility of theoretic understanding. But although religion is recognized and protected, it is also 'policed', or kept rigorously behind the bounds of the possibility of empirical understanding. Hence sociology is inevitably at variance with the perspectives of many traditional religions, which make no separation between 'religious' and 'empirical' reality, and who do not distinguish their sense of value from the stratified arrangement of times, persons and places in their own society. Sociology's 'policing of the sublime' exactly coincides with the actual operations of secular society which excludes religion from its modes of discipline and control, while protecting it as a 'private' value, and sometimes invoking it at the public level to overcome the antimony of a purely instrumental and goalless rationality, which is yet made to bear the burden of ultimate political purpose.

In the three following sections I am going to show how all twentieth-century sociology of religion can be exposed as a secular policing of the sublime. Deconstructed in this fashion, the entire subject evaporates into the pure ether of the secular will-to-power. Concentrating mainly on the most influential, American tradition, I shall first explicate American sublimity, which embraces the Durkheimian sublime of the whole, the Weberian sublime of the marginal subject, and works up a third sublime of sacrificial 'transition', which mediates the other two. In the next section, I shall proceed to show how all three variants of the sublime permit a secular policing or 'encompassing' of religion within the flattened dimension of modern public space. Then, in the penultimate section of this chapter, I shall show how evolutionary accounts consolidate this 'discipline' by tracing the gradual discovery in time of the 'proper' sublime sites of religion. In the fifth and final section I shall deal with the sociological contention that religions have interfered with our awareness of cultural temporality by transgressing the bounds of negative sublimity and painting an 'ideological' tincture over past facts, so disguising their true character.

---

[7] Ludwig Wittgenstein, *Culture and Value*, 15e. Immanuel Kant, *Critique of Pure Reason*, trans. Norman Kemp Smith (London: Macmillan, 1978) pp. 517–18.

Parsons and the American Sublime

Twentieth-century developments in the sociology of religion have tended, through the writings of Geertz, Berger, Luckmann, Bellah, and Luhmann, to follow in the wake of the American sociologist Talcott Parsons, even where this connection is denied. As is well known, Parsons sought to achieve a synthesis of Durkheim and Weber, and his critics have often claimed to offer a better path to the same goal. Three things are striking about Parsons' attempt: first of all, he claims that Durkheim and Weber, along with Freud, respect the limits of the rational, and the place of the non-rational.[8] He makes a connection here between Durkheim's 'effervescence' and Weber's 'charisma'. Secondly, while religion is deemed to be concerned with 'non-empirical' beliefs, Parsons increasingly acknowledges that religion refers to some 'real' realm beyond the factual, that sounds somewhat like the neo-Kantian 'irreal'.[9] In this respect he is usually outdone by his American successors, like Berger and Bellah, who effectively re-theologize sociology, making explicit its buried affinity with both old voluntarist and new liberal Protestant tendencies. In the third place, the desire to hold on to both the Durkheimian and the Weberian 'protection' of religion can be seen to coincide with the exigencies of the American situation. Of course Weber's pluralism finds an echo in a country of multiple sects and religious groupings, but so too does Durkheim's Rousseauian-Comtean theme of 'civil religion', in a country where the State has always been associated with some 'common' element of belief in God, and where devotion to the constitution can be equivalent to a religion of individual freedom.

Because Talcott Parsons' attempt to mediate between Weber and Durkheim has proved in many ways exemplary for the sociology of religion (as for sociology in general), the most relevant features of this attempt must be briefly described. Quite correctly, Parsons realized that the third term between Weberian action and Durkheimian structure had to be the genesis of language. Hence he sought to incorporate into sociology the American pragmatist G. H. Mead's theory of 'symbolic interaction'. According to this theory, communication, and hence society, becomes possible when a repeated action is isolated by a particular subject and the assumption is made that another subject is making the same isolation.[10] After this, imitation and patterns of expectation permitting the use of signs can arise. Moreover,

---

[8] Talcott Parsons, 'Belief, unbelief and disbelief', in *Action Theory and the Human Condition* (New York: The Free Press, 1978) pp. 233–63. Robert N. Bellah, 'The sociology of religion', in *Beyond Belief: Essays on Religion in a Post-Traditional World* (New York: Harper and Row, 1970).

[9] Talcott Parsons, 'Durkheim on religion revisited: another look at *The Elementary Forms of the Religious Life*', in *Action Theory*, pp. 213–30.

[10] Talcott Parsons, *The Social System* (London: RKP, 1951) p. 19. Jackson Toby, 'Parsons' theory of societal evolution', in Talcott Parsons, (ed.) *The Evolution of Societies* (Englewood Cliffs, NJ: Prentice-Hall, 1977). G. H. Mead, 'A behavioristic account of the significant symbol', in Andrew J. Beck (ed.) *Selected Writings* (Indianapolis: Bobbs-Merrill, 1964).

it is only through imitation, and the use of signs, that a sense of self-identity emerges. Because other people first recognize and respond to our repeated actions, we are able to arrive at a self-response, but only insofar as we initially take the part of the 'generalized other', performing actions with a fixed and regular meaning. For Parsons, this model allows one to say, with Weber, that voluntary action has causal priority, but also to rescue the valid intuition in the Durkheimian 'social fact' by recognizing that meaning is first of all public and universal in character.[11] The priority given in Mead's theory to absolute consistency and regularity, as the first possibility of there being any meaning at all, becomes for Parsons the equivalent of Durkheim's idea of static social universals which provide the categories of possible understanding.

The trouble with this mediating sociology is that it does not really resolve the *aporia* of action and structure, but instead manages to incorporate, at different moments of its model of social genesis, the contradictions inherent in privileging either one or the other. For on the side of 'action', it is not really possible to think of a pre-social individual 'isolating' certain gestures – to do so he would already have to have selective criteria, would already be communicating with himself and so be self-reflective. Already then, he would be playing a private language game, although this should not be possible if self-reflection and identity are given only socially. Conversely, on the side of structure, Parsons makes an unwarranted assumption that the 'first' social interaction will be democratic and equal, because each actor will be able to assume an identical interpretation of a univocal sign on the part of the other. But it may be that as soon as one action is significantly connected with another, superior value and more central significance will be accorded to one of the actions, and it may be also that this asymmetry will be reflected in the role-identifications made by the particular actors. Not the resemblance of signs and actions, but their difference as generating a first order and meaning is in fact the more likely starting point, because 'communication' is merely a secondary phenomenon within a language that has first 'positioned' both things and people.

Moreover, as soon as reflective association has come into play, the creative contribution of individual action *does* become possible, and one has no guarantee that different readings of common public signs (which are ultimately just the intersection of all these different readings/writings) will coincide, nor, in consequence, that the allocation of roles and values will remain static. One has then to recognize the 'always already' of both action and structure, and one must refuse not only the prioritization of one over the other, but also the Parsonian mental picture which presents the two as 'external' to each other. And without this picture there is no 'sociology', but only historiography (including historical geography) in all its variation and endless revisability.

---

[11] Parsons, *The Social System*, pp. 3–23. Toby, 'Parson's theory of societal evolution'.

If Parsons had adopted a 'stronger' pragmatist thesis, then he might have arrived at this conclusion. For then he would have recognized that one cannot imagine a genesis beginning with the individual and proceeding to inter-action, and neither can one take a univocal meaning of the sign to be socially fundamental. But his watered-down pragmatism merely permits him to syn-thesize the two sociologies as a double illusion. This has great consequence for his conceptualization of religion. Insofar as he thinks of individual action as having a genetic priority, he tends also to think of religion in substantive terms, as designating a certain area of experience, which only later gets symbolically 'expressed'. Insofar, however, as he thinks of action as strictly bound by fixed norms of categorical meaning, he tends to think of religion in functionalist terms as legitimating and sacralizing the common conventions and social unity. Religion, therefore, for Parsons (as later Bellah, Berger, Luckmann and Geertz) is at once 'charismatic', belonging to a private 'exist-ential' sphere, and also 'integrative' – providing a necessary ideology for the public realm.[12]

The Parsonian picture, however, is really a little more complicated than this contrast of expressive action and categorical structure will allow. Through the process of evolution, society becomes differentiated into a series of sub-systems, each providing relatively self-contained 'action frames of reference' with their own norms and their own relative autonomy.[13] These sub-systems remain perfectly discrete from each other, because their symbolic norms operate univocally, as categories defining once and for all fields of possible knowledge and action. So, for example, the economy operates according to 'purely economic' criteria of scarcity, supply and demand, without reference to morality, truth, beauty, or political power and consent. There are also relatively independent cultural systems to which religion belongs, which value and preserve expressive originality. Hence, as Robert Bellah empha-sizes, there can be no 'science' of the entire social system in its every aspect.[14] Nevertheless, science *can* comprehend the points at which all the sub-systems function in relation to each other, the supposed level of 'society' itself. And here, in fact, economic metaphors predominate: a society has limited energetic 'resources' which it has to 'conserve' and preserve in 'equilibrium'. Religion is useful for imagining and representing this invisible 'whole', and also for temporarily 'storing up' energies in an 'ideal' realm, which can later be put to 'real' social use.[15]

Given this more complex picture, one has also to revise the presentation of the way in which 'religion' intervenes in 'society' for American sociology. At the level of private experience, the content of religion is universal, and

[12] Parsons, *The Social System*, pp. 367–79. 'Durkheim on religion revisited'.
[13] Parsons, *The Social System*, pp. 3–23.
[14] Robert N. Bellah, 'Between religion and social science', in *Beyond Belief*, pp. 237–87.
[15] Talcott Parsons, 'Christianity and modern industrial society', in *Sociological Theory and Modern Society* (New York: Free Press, 1967) pp. 385–422. 'Durkheim on religion revisited'.

concerns a permanent dimension of human being. At the level of the cultural sub-systems it is plural and diverse, reflecting various arbitrary symbolic conventions. But at the level of 'society' as a whole, of civil religion, it is once again universal, because *at this level only*, symbolic arbitrariness is a cipher for something real, namely, an organic whole, a self-contained system able to conserve its energies in a self-adjusting equilibrium.

For American sociology then, there is both the sublime of ineffable private experience, situated before and outside linguistic expression, and the sublime of the whole system, the ultimate frontier which can only be conceived in formal, economic terms. But there is also a third sublime, a point where the two universalities of religion merge into one. This is the point of transition – the point of *sacrifice*, where the civic law of the whole is freely surrendered to by each individual will, and the point of *rites de passage* where one must traverse the limbo between different symbol systems which mark out our lives both in time and in space.

American sociology therefore reveals that, as a secular policing, its secret purpose is to ensure that religion is kept, conceptually, at the margins – both denied influence, and yet acclaimed for its transcendent purity. Hence it must be shown to 'really' exist, for all societies, either at the level of ineffable experience, or at the level of the functioning whole, or, again, at the level of 'liminal' transitions, where ambiguities and indeterminations must be negotiated. What is refused here is the idea that religion might enter into the most basic level of the symbolic organization of society, and the most basic level of its operations of discipline and persuasion, such that one would be unable to abstract a 'society' behind and beneath 'religion'. If this were the case, then it would become impossible to 'account for' religions in terms of 'other' social phenomena. One would only be able to narrate religions, with varying degrees of favour of disfavour, and any thoroughgoing suspicion of religion would have to take the form also of suspicion of a whole society, and its version of humanity, as not being anything other than a particular configuration of the intersecting contentions of the will-to-power.

In the following three sections, this policing will be catalogued. At the end of this catalogue, it will become apparent that sociology of religion cannot claim to be a true metadiscourse about religion, in contrast to theologies which merely represent world views. Such a claim only appears sustainable because sociology creates the illusion of a 'social fact', which can be contrasted with religion defined in such a way as to confine it and yet preserve it, in an irreal sublimity. The confinement is achieved in the dimension of space, where religion is subordinated to the social and deemed to be functional in relation to it; in the dimension of an open time, where religion is described as evolving to a true self-recognition of its own marginality; and in the dimension of a concealed time where religion is described as a later, 'ideological' legitimation of an earlier, purely social arrangement.

Religion and Functionality

1   *Functions of integration*

Supposing a sociologist were to say, 'A function of the eucharist is to bind together the disparate elements of the Christian community.' The main problem with this statement is that it seems to explain a phenomenon (the eucharist) in terms of what it is and does, and so verges on tautology. For this reason it could equally well be a *theological* statement. It is only regarded as more than tautology because one mentally splits what is only one item into three: so that, rather like a bad theologian, one thinks of the eucharist as a reified 'something in itself' apart from what it does; then one refers what it does, its function, to an ecclesial community thought of in abstraction from all the sets of collective actions, including the eucharist, which alone give it any reality. Thus the claim to decode an internal ecclesiological understanding in objective sociological terms actually imports epistemological illusions to which *ecclesiology* is not necessarily prey.

This example can be seen as typical for functional explanation as a whole: it claims to add to the narrative description of a thing an explanation of its occurrence in some sort of 'universal' terms – yet on inspection this explanation is itself reducible to the narrative form, or else is shown to imagine illusory 'essences' of things which 'cause' things to happen, and illusory teleological wholes which anticipate their own composition.

The situation does not alter if one gives a much less 'obvious' example of functioning: for example 'a function of Christianity is to shore up patriarchal domination'. Even if this is a hidden and disguised function of Christianity, it can only be demonstrated if one gives particular narrations of exactly how it works, revealing a hitherto unnoticed sequence of connections. In other words, one is only here explaining Christianity to the degree that one redescribes it, though this is not to say that such redescription is 'merely subjective'. The limit of such redescription will be reached when one asks: why, in *this* society, has patriarchal power, which is more or less universal, exercised itself in *this* way, disguised itself using *these* symbols?

Functional explanation, which appears to provide new explanations, is therefore really a mode of narrative redescription. It is not a matter of experimentally establishing correlations, nor of establishing a general law that given society of type *a* one will discover function *b*, as sociology tends to assume. For example, it might be that a sociologist would try to show that all hierarchic societies, with a strongly centralized source of power, must have monotheistic religions. To this end he would solemnly 'test' his hypothesis by collecting all the known examples of such societies, and finding out whether or not they were monotheist. But if it turns out that they are, he will not want to stop at this point, but rather to show in some detail, in each particular case, just how monotheism functions to support kingship and hierarchy. This means that the detailed demonstration of the correlation is the work of narrative historiography ('plots' can concern structures, symbols and institutions just as much as they can individuals). However, in a society where kingship is understood in thoroughly sacral terms, where the king is only king because he is a 'son of God', and where, inversely, God is conceived of as a heavenly monarch, the historiographical narrative will be unable to establish any causal priority as between the religiously validated social structure on the one hand, and the socially-pictured religion on the other. Thus the more strongly the narrative describes and explains the universally observed correlation, the more the notion of 'correlation' is dissolved, along with the need for any empirical law. For social structures are just as much an aspect of monotheistic religions as are its beliefs, while monarchic hierarchy is in itself a religious institution. Hence the only warranted general conclusion is not the 'scientific' one that centralized hierarchical societies 'require' monotheism, but simply that there is a class of societies which roughly resemble each other.

This is not to say that beliefs and practices can never diverge, but where they do, this is always the result of a narratable historical outcome; the creation of a separate realm of practice to do with beliefs that is in part permitted to 'go its own way'. Thus the claim that given society of type *a*, one will discover *b*, always reduces to a simple explication of the character of this type of society.

My argument, therefore, is that functionalist sociology adds nothing that is not metaphysical to historiography. To substantiate this claim I shall now take, as an extended example, recent attempts by Biblical scholars to supplement their historical criticism with attempts at functionalist explanation.

2 Functionalism in Biblical criticism and the historiography of Christian origins

Sociology employing functional explanation is supposed to transcend historiographical narration of deeds, purposes and uses; as the New Testament critic John Gager puts it, 'history describes, sociology explains'.[16] This claim can only mean that sociology gives us atemporal knowledge of a finite range of social possibilities, such that, given an example of a particular kind of society, one can predict the sorts of function it will require; history, as Paul Veyne says, would then become 'applied sociology'.[17] We have, however, just looked at some of the reasons why this sort of typology may be impossible – in which case functional explanation lapses back into tautology, and sociological explanation into narrative description.

If this is true, then why should it be so widely thought, by theologians and Biblical critics, that sociology is able to illuminate Biblical and Christian history? Is one mistaken in thinking that critics who employ sociological

---

[16] John G. Gager, 'Social description and sociological explanation in the study of early Christianity: a review essay', in Norman K. Gottwald (ed.) *The Bible and Liberation: Political and Social Hermeneutics* (New York: Orbis Maryknoll, 1983) p. 429.

[17] Veyne, *Writing History*, p. 270.

tools, like Norman Gottwald, Gerd Thiessen, Wayne Meeks and Peter Brown, have produced works which give new illumination on familiar themes?

The answer to this question must be certainly not. However, it is possible to admire these works, and *still* to argue that they tend to mislead, precisely at the point where they are most 'sociological'. In the case of Gottwald's *The Tribes of Yahweh*, one finds the passionate insistence that Israel was not unique only for her religion, but also for the singular attempt, in the context of the ancient Near-East, to set up social mechanisms which would prevent economic inequality and the concentration of political power.[18] This is a salutary correction to many of the usual Christian critical readings of the Old Testament, which are far too 'spiritualizing', but just to the degree that Gottwald assumes that his insights are 'sociological', he is in fact still negatively conditioned by precisely such readings. For Jews have always insisted on the connection between their religious and social distinctiveness: this is what the centrality of *torah* implies. What Gottwald does is to perpetuate the assumption of a certain sort of Christianity that the religious and the social are essentially separate concerns, but then go on to argue that Yahwism was primarily a 'social' movement, to which its religious aspects stood in a 'functional' relation. A true historical assessment, which would say that the sense of Yahweh was indissociable from a concern for justice and the sacred commonality of the land, gets displaced onto the sociological plane.

Gottwald's mode of reasoning nicely illustrates the problems about the notion of social primacy. The basic question that arises is why, if Yahwism was first of all a social and political idea, were religious functions necessary at all? Gottwald argues that Yahweh, as the one true owner of the land, underwrote the mechanisms which guarded against the over-accumulation of property and the slavery of debt, and that, as a God above nature, he guaranteed the primacy of people, and their non-subordination to nature as power or fate.[19] But as the best anthropologists, like Franz Steiner or Mary Douglas would argue, this implausibly suggests a set of privately-intuited moral principles which later shore themselves up with religious and ritual reinforcement.[20]

If one does not fall into the trap of seeing egalitarian social arrangements as 'natural', then it should be obvious that the religious sanctions are by no means secondary, but rather *constitutive* of such notions as responsibility to the community and the evil consequences of holding debtors in subjection. The name 'Yahweh' actually introduces such a new level of 'conscience', and without this name, without this belief, only the idolatrous cults of power and blood would remain. To think otherwise is to suppose that our modern notions of duty and guilt represent natural intuitions, not dependent upon a

[18] Norman K. Gottwald, *The Tribes of Yahweh: A Sociology of the Religion of Liberated Israel, 1250–1050 BCE* (New York/London: Orbis/SCM, Maryknoll, 1979) p. 592ff.

[19] Gottwald, *The Tribes of Yahweh*, pp. 608–21, 703.

[20] Steiner, *Taboo*. Mary Douglas, *Purity and Danger: An Analysis of the Concepts of Pollution and Taboo* (London: RKP, 1976).

symbolic code which institutes certain exclusions and imagines certain 'forces' of moral conscience. It is, in fact, this highly abstract and secular mythology which leads us to think, in Kantian terms, of religion as an *additional* level of sanction 'on top of' the level of mere morality. Gottwald actually projects these assumptions back onto ancient Israel, ignoring the historical genesis of our separation between morality and religion.

The more one says that religion was necessary for the functioning of Israel's egalitarianism because it provided the necessary symbolic means for conceiving equality, then the more it becomes impossible to make Gottwald's distinction between society and religion. This distinction certainly does not appear at the level of the Old Testament texts, and Gottwald is forced to give an entirely imaginary genesis for Yahwism, inventing a stage at which there was only a revolutionary *praxis*, which later adopted for itself a religion suitable to its own social project.[21] With still greater historical implausibility, it appears that, according to the logic of Gottwald's account, there must have been a brief historical moment at which Israelites entertained Yahwism as a kind of 'conscious projection' of a 'primitive religious consciousness' focused (in pure positivist fashion) on the immanent spirit of group identity.[22] By contrast, the development of Yahwism into a mere system of beliefs coincided with the monarchical corruption of Israel's initial social arrangements.[23] This singular suggestion is the ultimate upshot of Gottwald's unhappy attempt to blend functionalism with Marxism; he has then to reconcile his contradictory desires both to defend Israel's religion as functional for a liberated society, and to insist that such a society has no requirement for any mythological or transcendent beliefs.

One can conclude that, as a *historian*, Gottwald rightly draws our attention to those dimensions of the Old Testament text which suggest the strong connection of religion with social arrangement in ancient Israel. But as a *sociologist* (or a sociologist/Marxist) he makes the incredible discovery that for a certain brief moment, not traceable in the texts, the ancient Israelites arrived at Kantian insights: they distinguished morality from custom, ritual, and religion, and already realized that theological representations, while not 'operationable' like empirical concepts, still had a regulative function, giving a certain 'onlook towards *praxis*'. And Gottwald is *never more* sociological than when he defends the relative autonomy of theology within this sphere of non-objective, symbolic 'representation'.

The example of Gottwald begins to suggest just how cautious one needs to be in assessing the topic of 'Biblical sociology'. On the one hand, it is very much to be welcomed, because it treats dimensions of the texts-as-given too often overlooked by commentators only interested in 'religious' themes, or else in reconstructing the history of textual sources. Biblical sociology usually

---

[21] Gottwald, *The Tribes of Yahweh*, pp. 617–20, 693–4.
[22] Ibid., pp. 632–7.
[23] Ibid., p. 704.

returns us to the level of the final text, which must, one can plausibly assume, tell us something about the community in which it was written. However, there is also the tendency to suppose that, by invoking 'sociology' we are given a magical access to a pre-textual level. Quite often this can seem to compensate for the absence of supporting historical evidence about, for example, the early New Testament communities and their circumstances. Wayne Meeks claims that sociology allows us to make inferences 'on the basis of presumed regularities in human behaviour'.[24] If these inferences are not permitted, he contends, then this is tantamount to suggesting that one can have mere retailing of facts without interpretation. But such identifying of sociology with necessary hermeneutics is a sleight of hand: the reader must, indeed, 'divinate' by synthesizing his material into a whole, but such wholes may transcend the constraints of any universal topology. Indeed, such an encounter belongs to the very essence of good reading. And a truly sufficient explanation would be more like a divination which led to 'a good narration', than any bringing of particulars under universal norms.

What Biblical sociology tends to forget is that, were more historical 'evidence' available, it would only consist of more texts. These other texts might or might not confirm the account of, for example, Christian genesis that is given in the Gospels, but they would not reveal to us a level of 'social genesis' unmediated by a series of interpretative perspectives. The point here is not that one never has 'unbiased' access to the social genesis, but rather that there *is* no pre-textual genesis: social genesis itself is an 'enacted' process of reading and writing. Curiously enough, it is much easier to talk about 'the social background' of a text when it stands relatively alone; in the mesh of intertextuality provided by a situation of rich evidence, the supposed purely social object much more evidently disappears. Thus, it can be contended, Biblical sociology is at its best when it appeals to extra-Biblical historical archives, although this work least of all permits it to arrive at sociological conclusions.

This can be seen in the case of the debate about the social allegiances of the early Christians. Some variants of sociological explanation would want to see religion as functional for the articulation of the grievances and aspirations of certain social groups. For example, Engels saw Christianity as the religion of the oppressed lower orders in the Roman Empire; Nietzsche saw it as an expression of the resentment of the powerless and excluded; Weber, on the other hand, saw Christianity as a 'salvation-religion' of the urban middle classes, displaced and individualist, in contrast to the merely magical religion of peasants and aristocratic cults of honour.[25] However, the historical evidence does not support any of these claims (though Weber is far nearer the mark than the others). Nor, on the other hand, does it support an

---

[24] Wayne A. Meeks, *The First Urban Christians: The Social World of the Apostle Paul* (New Haven, Conn.: Yale University Press, 1983) p. 5.

[25] Weber, *Economy and Society*, vol. 1, pp. 481–4.

'anti-sociological' claim that social class was simply irrelevant to Christian allegiance. The real picture is much more complex.

In the first place it seems likely, from the New Testament, that there is a contrast between the initial setting of Jesus's teaching in Galilee, an area of considerable social deprivation characterized by a 'sub-Asiatic mode of production', absentee landlordship, client kingship, theocratic legal control of day-to-day life, and the later urban setting which was also the main site for the first church communities.[26] Here one finds a slave economy, many socially intermediate groups, and some extension of Roman legal rule. What is involved here is an immense transition from a provincial context where Jesus seems to be the leader of a temporally displaced, almost archaic movement, harking back to the prophets and the Deuteronomic reforms, to a global context where the message of a dead and resurrected Jesus is to be universally proclaimed. One might say that the books of the New Testament have a foundational status for Christianity because they claim to give an account of this transition. To imagine that sociology can 'encompass' this transition from a perspective more fundamental than the theological one, is therefore a serious matter for a religion basing itself upon this historical narrative. To be able to do so, however, sociology must deconstruct the thematic continuity of this transition, such as to make it appear that 'original' Christianity corresponded to the circumstances of radical marginalization of outcast groups in Galilee, while later ecclesial Christianity corresponded to the circumstances found in the towns. At the same time, the discontinuity must not become so great as to leave the transition as, once again, an unsolvable mystery.

One attempt to achieve such an encompassing, that of Fernando Belo, makes similar mistakes in the case of Christian origins to those made by Gottwald for the origins of Israel. The suggestion is made that Jesus, as the leader of a peaceful, but revolutionary movement, proffers 'real' communistic solutions for economic and social problems, whereas later Christianity proffers only 'ideological' solutions.[27] However, Jesus's 'real' solution quite evidently involved the re-imagination of Israel as a symbolic entity, and the linking of this re-imagination to apocalyptic expectations which one cannot plausibly characterize as 'materialist' in the Marxist sense. And his violations of the purity code cannot be presented, as they are by Belo, as a denial of the 'sacral' theme of purity in favour of the 'secular' theme of debt; instead Jesus *redefines* purity in terms of the holiness of all created being, even where it suffers the contagion of sin and disease, and redefines impurity as sheer 'intrusion' or as a 'coming from within' ('what comes out of a man'), from a negative or demonic source.[28] And just as he moves from the containment

---

[26] John Pairman Brown, 'Techniques of imperial control: the background of gospel events', in Gottwald (ed.), *The Bible and Liberation*, pp. 357–77.

Fernando Belo, *A Materialistic Reading of the Gospel of Mark* (New York: Orbis, Maryknoll, 1981) pp. 60–86.

[27] Ibid., pp. 16–19, 235, 241–97.

[28] Mark 7:14–23.

and regulation of impurity to a radical dualism which excludes as impurity only that which *negates Being*, so, also, Jesus moves from the mere restriction of debt-obligation to the universal requirement of forgiveness – or the cancellation of debt altogether. And this radicalizing of Israel's vision is nothing other than the reconceiving of the creative, self-giving God as before and ahead of the requirements of the law. Against Belo, therefore, one can show that Jesus's social revisions kept exact pace with his religious and symbolic ones.

Furthermore, because there is no reason to doubt that Jesus made a connection between his own mission and the present or future coming of an apocalyptic figure, there is also every reason to see continuity between his own self-understanding and the later rethinking of that message and the 'exodus to the Gentiles' which took place after his violent death. Just as Jesus, in his life, provided various bodily signs which defined and so made possible a new sort of practice, so there was an attempt made after his violence-refusing death to continue this practice under the one great sign of the cross which had apparently spelled the premature end for that practice altogether. There is no textual warrant whatsoever to suggest the switch from a 'real and horizontal' to a 'symbolic and vertical' plane. It is a different matter entirely to argue that theologies of the atonement quite quickly began to abstract the vertical dimension from the horizontal: so turning Jesus's life and works into a mere prelude for a fore-ordained drama of necessary sacrifice. One can admit that this began to happen, yet one should realize also that Christological reflection continued and in fact radicalized Jesus's reconception of Israel and of God. There is a continuity between Jesus's refusal of any seizure of power and the early churches' refusal to overthrow existing structures, in favour of the attempt to create alternative ones, as 'local' areas of relative peace, charity and justice. Thus social setting was palpably *not* in charge: the archaic and agrarian seeds of the Gospel took root in the cities and cracked the pavements of the ancient world apart.

The foregoing analysis suggests that there can be no genuine sociological comprehension of an inherently 'inexplicable' historical event (of which there could be many other examples – my account of Jesus is not meant as apologetic) such as the adoption of an originally rural and peasant vision by a motley assortment of town-dwellers. The fact just tends to over-whelm causality.

To continue with this example of the social make-up of early Christianity, it can be shown that sociology is also unable to provide an explanation of the social structure of urban Christianity once in place. Obviously, there are many respects in which the early churches resembled already-existing institutions in the Roman Empire. Writers like Peter Brown and Wayne Meeks are illuminating, not because they locate Christianity within some Weberian typology (they admirably avoid this) but because they show how Christianity operated within the very specific structures of patronage and *amicitia* characteristic of Mediterranean society and of late antiquity.[29] Thanks to the researches of these scholars and others, we now know, first, that individuals who were at least in some respect high-ranking within society also occupied prominent positions within the churches as protectors and over-seers.[30] Secondly, we know that the churches took over the pre-existing structure of the *oikos*, which often included hired workers and trade partners as well as family and slaves as its first basic unit of association. The Church was also merely one example of the many voluntary associations which flourished in the late antique *polis*, including, for example, the *collegia tenuorum*, or burial clubs.[31].

As Meeks emphasizes, however, none of the other voluntary associations envisaged themselves as encompassing the totality of a person's true life and concerns; none, moreover, took the *oikos* as its basic unit; none had an inter-civic network of associations and none described itself as *ecclesia* – a name hitherto reserved for civic voting assemblies.[32] So here one can say that the 'social factors' (although this is a misnomer) only tell us about the features of the Church that are relatively unsurprising, whereas its surprising, unique features are precisely the reason why it made a historical difference, why we are still interested in it at all. There is something, then, almost contradictory about trying to level it down to a 'social' level. In reality, one is not measuring 'social' as against 'religious' influences, but rather the influences of surround-ing pre-constituted and themselves contingently historical modes of social organization as against the new socio-religious element, in a new social grouping, the Church. So the most *significant* social element in the new situation escapes 'sociology' altogether, and can only be referred to its own textual self-genesis. Suspicion of this self-narration is possible, but can never be 'scientific'. (And again I am not making an apologetic point here, but only an historical one.)

Despite his demonstration of the complexity of social constitution of early Christianity, Wayne Meeks nevertheless puts forward a sociological thesis, at least with respect to the Pauline churches. A large number of people within those churches, he suggests (on the basis of the descriptions in the Pauline epistles) suffered from 'status inconsistency', meaning that their economic, political or ritual standing were not in harmony; he mentions independent women with moderate means, wealthy Jews in Roman cities, skilled freemen and freed slaves.[33] Such people, he suggests, would be attracted to a religion which proclaimed that the world was living 'between times', and was shortly to end altogether in its present form, ushering in a new divine order in which all worldly powers would be displaced. Apocalyptic symbolism then serves

---

[29] Meeks, *The First Urban Christians*. Peter Brown, *Society and the Holy in Late Antiquity* (London: Faber and Faber, 1982).
[30] Meeks, *The First Urban Christians*, pp. 64–79.
[31] Ibid., p. 77.
[32] Ibid., pp. 78–84.
[33] Ibid., pp. 53–75.

to dramatize both the original social condition of marginalization and the total social break experienced with conversion.

There is much in this suggestion which may be historically (and theologically) valuable, and it seems probable that Christianity appealed more to those badly integrated within civic society. However, the sociological term 'status inconsistency' can cause us to overlook the fact that the prevalence of such a condition within late antiquity was itself the result of a break-up of the institutions of the *polis*, and the liberation of economic forces from social control through the devaluation of citizenship with the extension of empire. This disintegration involved also the collapse of a certain mode of religious organization (where *pietas* was to the gods of the city) and it is therefore fair to say that 'status inconsistency' reflected a moral and a religious as much as a social condition. All that Meeks really does therefore, is describe a situation in which one religious/political unity has vanished, and people are desperately searching for new religious/social solutions which often have a new, 'apolitical' character.

Diverse solutions were in fact on offer: stoicism itself, a very well-disseminated creed, could be regarded as providing, through its teaching of indifference, a solution for the marginalized person. If one argues that Christianity was somehow the uniquely right, the *most* functional solution, then it has to be suspected that this is just a baptizing with necessity of what we now know to have occurred. Christianity was not uniquely well-adapted to those suffering from status inconsistency, and the problem which sociology cannot answer is why *this* solution? – although again, this is the only interesting question. Meeks suggests that, in the first place, use of apocalyptic reflected the social experience of converts and of conversion, while in the second place it may have reinforced this experience. Yet the real problem here is that apocalyptic only reflects the experience of status inconsistency to the extent that it redefines it: the homology only exists once the occupier of a social state has already transformed herself and is able to 'regard' her former self. Thus to be able to say that apocalyptic is a very appropriate and functional response to status inconsistency, the sociologist must continue to occupy the standpoint of the apocalyptician, although this is precisely what he most tries to avoid.

In point of fact, stoic resignation seems more like a pure reflection and dramatization of individual isolation. Christians, by contrast, made the experience bearable only by imagining its end, both in apocalyptic, and in the ecclesial anticipation of the kingdom. It is this imaginary element which did not simply reflect a foregoing social or religious experience, and yet provided the Church with its unprecedented effectiveness.

Another example of insupportable functionalist claims in the treatment of the social composition of the early Church is given by Peter Brown's analysis of the role of the holy man in the later, patristic period.[34] Brown decisively

---

[34] Peter Brown, 'The rise and function of the holy man in late antiquity', in *Society and the Holy*, pp. 103–52.

gets rid of Weberian assumptions which would tend to see the mediating role of the holy man, with his miracles, his exorcisms and his intercessions on behalf of the community, as aspects of 'popular religion' or even as 'pagan survivals'. Instead, he places the holy man in the context of *amicitia*, and the increased resort to the direct rule of 'person over person' rather than government by statute (precisely the 'oriental', substantive justice which Weber, of course, so despised). However, while it is unexceptionable to say that the 'function' of the holy man was to embody certain values generally held to but loosely adhered to, and to provide a 'measured penance' (the sense of function is weak), it may not be quite fair to say that the holy man 'compensated for a remote God'. This tends to imply that his mediatory role had no connection at all with the representation of Christ, whereas the still greater fragility of 'the rule of person over person', and the culture of mediation, in Islam, might tend to suggest otherwise.[35] Brown allows that an iconic element in Christianity may have been connected with nostalgia for the 'face to face', and resistance to the growing abstraction and centralization of mediatory power, yet in insisting that icons were first of all of 'holy men', rather than Christ, he overlooks the fact that the notion of 'transmission of holiness' already plants the idea of the holy man in the realm of the iconic, and so the explicitly Christological and ecclesial right from the outset. In fact one of the very earliest icons that has come down to us, of St Maenus, from the sixth century, depicts the saint as a squat figure, standing at the right side of a similarly squat Christ, the original 'holy man', who has his arm around the saint's shoulder.[36]

In this way Brown tends perhaps to downplay the degree to which only Christianity could make stable and 'traditional' the very provisionality and intermittently local character of 'face to face' rule. So once again, a social element that is only *given* with Christianity – the Church – tends to be suppressed by sociological approaches.

The second criticism of Brown concerns the way in which he suggests that mediation by the holy man was somehow uniquely appropriate – uniquely 'functional' – for the circumstances of the second century. He argues that in the new social situation where *amicitia* was coming to dominate, the impersonality and indirectness of the oracle became less well adapted to the times.[37] However, Robin Lane Fox has shown that private resort to oracles was also increasing during this period, along with visions of gods as purely 'imaginary' protectors.[38] (It is here significant that Brown, who views iconicity as 'secondary', thinks that the move to 'imaginary protectors' in Christianity comes only after the decline of the holy man, whereas perhaps it was always simultaneous with this institution.) So it seems that one cannot claim that the Christian 'holy man' was uniquely functional for this period: it was just one of

---

[35] Peter Brown, 'The rise and function of the holy man in late antiquity' p. 148.
[36] David Talbot Rice, *Art of the Byzantine Era* (London: Thames and Hudson, 1970) p. 29. I am very grateful to Sarah Coakley for pointing this out to me.
[37] Ibid., pp. 134–5.
[38] Robin Lane Fox, *Pagans and Christians* (London: Viking, 1987) pp. 283–4, 677–8.

various different religious and social responses made to the same crisis in centralized authority and civic *pietas*.

It can be seen then, from the above discussions, that the more effective theses of the sociologists of Christian origins are historical, not sociological. This is by no means intended as a denial that there can be 'elective affinities' between social position and religious allegiance. However, one should not ignore the fact that 'social position' may itself be constituted by moral, ritual and religious convention, or else the decayed ruins of these things; the affinity may be often one of 'religion for religion' or 'practice for practice' – not just 'practice for religion'. Nor is it possible to erect some universal or exhaustive typology. At the same time, I do not want to deny the place of what one might call *ad hoc* reductive suspicion, nor that sociology (and Marxism), as error not without benefit, have vastly extended our awareness of how mere self-interest can persist and disguise itself over long periods, and across wide collective spaces. The errors and delusions exposed, however, by such an *ad hoc* divinatory suspicion, are themselves historical eruptions: their persistence must not be attributed to something ontologically or epistemologically fundamental.

Yet Biblical sociologists consistently fall into this trap. Besides the appeals to extra-Biblical evidence to illuminate the social structure of the early Church, as just discussed, they have also, more questionably, tried to reconstruct inner-ecclesial transitions on the basis of universal sociological speculations about group behaviour. So, for example, John Gager suggests that the followers of Jesus after the crucifixion can be considered as an example of a group suffering from 'cognitive dissonance', meaning that they could not reconcile their previous expectations with what was now happening to them.[39] 'Research' apparently suggests that groups in such situations may paradoxically seek to proselytize, to reduce the effects of dissonance, by at least ensuring that all participate in it. The problem with this view, another attempt to 'comprehend', sociologically, the transition from Jesus's life and teachings to the Church, is that it is so condescending about the kinds of groups it describes. Many movements or ideas in such situations just fizzle out, and one can suggest that those that do not, usually make some sort of attempt to bring order into their beliefs, and that proselytization may itself be an aspect of such attempts. In the case of the early Church, Gager's view seems to imply that the Church was left at first *only* with a continuity of beliefs now rendered discordant, whereas one might want to suggest that one reason for the survival of 'dissonance' was the unbroken continuity of action, the carrying forwards of fellowship, teaching and healing. Indeed, there is every reason to suppose that 'exodus to the Gentiles' had always been envisaged, although Jesus's death may well have redoubled the sense that this must be the meaning of an otherwise 'failed' mission.

---

[39] John S. Gager, *Kingdom and Community: The Social World of Early Christianity* (Englewood Cliffs, NJ: Prentice-Hall, 1975) pp. 37–57.

With much greater subtlety, Wayne Meeks has tried to show that differences between Johannine and Pauline theology correspond to early-emergent differences in social attitude between different ecclesial groupings. His speculative reconstruction of the homology between belief and society is well done, although the idea that there is a conveniently simple 'reflection' of a particular community in a particular Gospel text remains merely a speculation. But what is incomprehensible is the implication that the 'social' aspects of Church life have some degree of causal determinacy over beliefs. The problem here is: how is one even to think of the being of *this* society in abstraction from its beliefs? Thus Meeks admirably shows that the centre of Paul's theology is not justification by faith, but rather participation in the body of Christ, and the reconciliation of Jew and Gentile.[40] But to see this as a demonstration of the primacy of the 'social' situation for Paul, is to rewrite the neglected Catholic truth of Paul's *ecclesiology* as *sociology*. If one takes justification by faith as meaning that one can only live a truly good life through incorporation in the social body dedicated to Christ's memory – out of the resources which this provides – then it is only a residual Lutheranism which will lead one to think that 'social' elements are here displacing the 'theological' ones.

Similar considerations apply to Meeks's treatment of John's Gospel.[41] He claims to discover in John strange 'gaps', 'discontinuities', and 'irrational metaphors', which cannot be dealt with in terms of the history of ideas, and so are supposed to betray the presence of 'the social'. But why should one assume that behind a logic which appears to us irrational and alien, must be concealed a reality of action which we will more readily comprehend? The only clue one would have to go on would be the text's opacity (for us), and sure enough Meeks declares that the self-referentiality of John's Gospel, its constant revolving round 'a secret', or 'a name' which is never imparted, suggests a self-enclosed, fearful, but expectant community, guarding a *gnosis* that is yet to be fully imparted. Without necessarily doubting the relatively enclosed character of the Johannine community, one can still suggest that Meeks ignores a level of *explicit* linking of the name with social unity in John's Gospel. The name is given 'that they may be one, even as we are one'.[42] Thus the secret is not altogether without content; it is at least the fact of a continued presence of personal self-giving and resultant social unity. Such a close unity is not pre-given before the text, but rather is promoted by the text as an ethical and religious goal. In appealing to a 'society' before the text (why is it there? why is it enclosed? etc.) Meeks in fact ignores a level of social inscription in the text itself. All his 'sociological' reading ends up doing is substituting a different ecclesiology (an esoteric grouping round an unknown name) for the one actually promoted by the Gospel.

[40] Meeks, *The First Urban Christians*, pp. 154ff, 168.
[41] Wayne A. Meeks, 'The man from heaven in Johannine secretarianism', in *Journal of Biblical Literature*, 91 (1972) pp. 44–72.
[42] John 17:6–12.

The foregoing critique of functional explanation in Biblical criticism and the historiography of Christian origins, tends to suggest that sociology cannot explain, and that the finding of causes in human affairs can only be a matter of redefinition and redescription. This particular area of scholarship confirms Paul Veyne's general view that only the absence of a 'total history', and a history which reclaims from mystification the dimension of synchronic structure, permits the continued prestige of sociology.[43]

But if one admits this, one will go on to become aware of the fact that the historical narratives which appear *to us* to be realistic are those where one treats as 'most real', 'most basic', 'most probably causal', those things which we permit to be most significant in our own history, our own lived narrative. In this case our desire to substitute for narratives like those of the New Testament 'more historical' narratives, embodying things like 'social' and 'economic' factors, may merely reflect our desire to reassure ourselves that the past was really like the present, and fail to recognize that the plot it was enacting was not the 'human', 'social' plot which we consciously live out today. Perhaps we have to take more seriously the Biblical narratives, which often chronicle rather than causally diagnose, and which presumably tell how things happened in the very idiom adopted by the historical characters of the chronicles for the making-of-things-to-happen.

3   *Functions of transition*

In the previous two sections it has been shown why it is impossible to comprehend religion by relating it to the level of society as a whole. However, one can identify a different categorical set of functions of religion: namely those which are supposed to cope with the exceptional or the problematic. Talcott Parsons and Clifford Geertz (following Weber) have both suggested that while religion is not reducible to theodicy, or coping with anxiety, nonetheless its point of intersection with society can be primarily understood in these terms.[44] Thus we have another way of 'encompassing': religion is to be understood as a late entrant upon social discourse, and its function is to deal with the inevitable *lacunae* thrown up by a social or ideological system.

One can detect three variants on this theme: liminality, sacrifice, and theodicy. In the first case, the influence of Victor Turner (following the works of Arnold von Gennep) has encouraged a certain tendency to see *rites de passage*, and all phenomena of journey and transition, as the fundamental clue to the essence of religion.[45] All cultures institute life-stages, and this means that

---

[43] Veyne, *Writing History*, pp. 73–6.

[44] Talcott Parsons, *The Social System*, pp. 163–7. *Action Theory*, pp. 371–2. Clifford Geertz, 'Religion as a cultural system', in *The Interpretation of Cultures* (London: Hutchinson, 1975) pp. 87–126.

[45] Arnold van Gennep, *The Rites of Passage*, trans. Monika B. Vizedon and Gabrielle L. Coffee, (Chicago: Chicago University Press, 1960) esp. pp. 189–94. Victor Turner, *Dramas, Fields and Metaphors: Symbolic Action in Human Society* (Ithaca and London: Cornell University Press, 1974).

there will be times and moments of ambiguity when an individual has shorn off an old role, and not yet quite assumed a new one. In a similar fashion, all cultures attempt a classification of things into types, and as no such classification is ever exhaustive, there always remain certain things of ambiguous status. It can be argued that, in either case, the threats to social identity are defused by sacralizing the uncertain times and places, by rendering them taboo, and hedging them about with ritual and ceremonies. That which is ambiguous may be either carefully excluded or carefully included, or even both at once – what matters is that it be held at a mediated distance.

For Victor Turner, the character of 'sacredness' derives from its situation at the margins, the realm of indefinability. Normally, the liminal is held safely at a distance, but a drastic entry into the liminal sphere can also be the source of radical social renewal. Turner thus treats liminality as an equivalent of Weber's charisma or Durkheim's effervescence, and makes it the site of the most intense religious experience of unstructured, unbounded *communitas*, which stands over-against the bounds and restrictions of everyday social life.[46]

While, however, intense collective experiences of *communitas* are rare, a constant dropping in and out of the liminal sphere is unavoidable, and must be socially regulated. This means that for Turner the sublime is no longer outside the social, at the margin of individuality, and nor is it the social whole; instead it is situated within society in the constant negotiation of dangerous passages. Paradoxically, it is empty, marginal sublimity which enters into the most fundamental social transits.

But this interpretation, once again, superimposes on all history a modern perspective for which religion concerns a suprarational, existential sphere. It is simply not the case that in most societies it is the elusive moment of transition that is the prime site of the sacred. On the contrary, there are only transitions *because* there are stages and distinctions, and these have a hierarchic, value-laden quality such that they are themselves imbued with sacrality. Most transitions are usually initiations, like baptism, in which the journey is not a dropping in and out of the everyday, but rather a once-for-all passage from the realm of the profane to the realm of the sacred. Likewise with most cases of taboo: it is not the case that sacrality is invoked to manage the unclassifiable. On the contrary, a prime interest in classification is to separate the relatively pure and sacred from what is impure. So, for example, in the case of the Levitical code, things 'mixed', or not in their proper 'place', or too much 'the same' are shunned, but only in relation to norms which place a positive sacred value on preserving a balance between sameness and difference, and which select the 'proper places' as being in particular earth, land and sea.[47]

Victor Turner and Edith Turner, *Image and Pilgrimage in Christian Culture: Anthropological Perspectives* (New York: Columbia University Press, 1978) pp. 1–39, 231–55.

[46] Ibid., pp. 1–39, 232, 243–55. Victor Turner, *Dramas, Fields and Metaphors*, p. 255.

[47] Steiner, *Taboo*. Douglas, *Purity and Danger*, pp. 41–58.

Religion, then, can neither be protected within, nor contained within, a realm of the liminal. There is no such domain, because transition is entirely created by the structural ordering of times and places.

Rites de passage can be seen as belonging together with the other major categories of social movement used by anthropologists and sociologists: the others are exchange, reversal and sacrifice. In every case, the attempt to identify the 'essence' of religion with one of these categories betokens another variation on the single Durkheimian theme: only the formal characteristics of social movement are attended to – that is to say the consequences of a general custom for the individual (rather than the substantive content of the custom), and this fundamental social relation is identified with 'religion'. Here there is only space to deal with sacrifice, my second example of a function of coping with *lacunae*.

Hubert, Mauss and Durkheim's views on sacrifice – namely that it really concerns the constant re-creation of the individual's affirmation of the social whole – have continued to find wide acceptance. Concentration on the theme of sacrifice does, in fact, allow one to give Durkheimian sociology a slightly more nominalist and Kantian individualist twist: *only* the sacrificial surrender creates the sense of a social whole.[48] What matters here is not so much the treatment of sacrifice as a particular cultural phenomenon, but rather the way in which a sacrificial thematic can organize an entire sociology.

In her formulation of her general views during the 1980s (they have since then shifted), the British anthropologist Mary Douglas (who stands in a Durkheimian, not a Parsonian tradition) posited a correlation between religious cosmology and ethical system, or 'the realm of interaction'. Given this definite Kantianization of her Durkheimian sociology, Douglas could then announce that all religions are fundamentally to do with ethical behaviour, although the latter can be observed independently of cosmological beliefs.[49] She had a single device both for dealing with cosmological views apparently unconnected with ethics, and for keeping ethical and cosmological beliefs apart. This was the definition of 'serious' belief as that which is actionable, subject to penalty and judgement: beliefs for which one individual can make another individual accountable.[50] Such a criterion, however, seems to render otiose the endeavour to search for correspondences between cosmology and the realm of interaction, for the only 'serious' correspondences are those which interaction already acknowledges and enforces. The criterion of 'actionability' does not really serve to distinguish belief that is 'seriously' held and socially relevant, from lightly-entertained belief; instead it refuses to recognize any seriousness other than violence. That is to say, serious value is only acknowledged in the case where the individual is constrained to give

---

[48] Henri Hubert and Marcel Mauss, *Sacrifice: Its Nature and Function*, trans. W. P. Halls (Chicago: Chicago University Press, 1964) esp. pp. 95–103. See also John Milbank, 'Stories of sacrifice', in *Modern Theology*, vol. 12, no. 1 (Jan 1996), pp. 27–56.

[49] Douglas, 'Cultural bias', in *In the Active Voice* (London: RKP, 1982) pp. 183–247.

[50] Ibid., pp. 247. Talcott Parsons, *The Social System*, pp. 367–79.

something up, to make a sacrifice, or where a penalty is imposed. Again, the substantive content of sacrifice – *what* is purged away, *what* is retained and purified – is not made the focus of interest. Rather, it is unjustifiably maintained that all serious value involves sacrifice, and that sacrifice is primarily the submission of the individual to the whole, or the giving of something from one individual to another, according to fixed, universal procedures. Only the approximately 'contractual' and 'modern' features of all societies are to be deemed significant.

Similar considerations apply to the earliest strata of Douglas's work: the reflections on purity codes and bodily symbolism. Just as the mere formalism of the individual/society relation is focused upon, so too, bodily symbolism gets reduced to the scale of rejection/promotion of the body.[51] This bequeaths to the middle-period work the apparent paradox that societies exercising strong social and cultural control both 'spiritualize' and suppress the individual body, and yet are forced to appeal to organic metaphors to express their own constitution.[52] Between the polarity of collective/individual body, the whole variety of selective ordering and hierarchization of the body is, in consequence, simply denied its true significance. So, for example, Douglas ignores that asceticism is as much a different ordering of the body as it is 'rejection' of the body. Nor, as she suggests, is tabooing of excreta a sign of 'body rejection' – it is merely a preference for the front of the body to the back.[53] The thing which gets excluded, or socially tabooed, is not a *natural* reality, but rather what is culturally and symbolically defined as impure and evil. There should thus be no room for Freudian-type reflections like those which Douglas at first entertained, according to which there are somehow 'natural' limits to the exclusion of death, dirt, danger, eroticism and violence, such that a certain level of such individual 'bodily' expression must be integrated into any balanced society. This is yet another variant of 'sacrificial positivism': to counterbalance the tribute which the individual must be coerced to pay to society, there is also the economy of loss to be sustained by a functioning society with respect to individual energy and will.[54]

Besides *rites de passage* and sacrifice, the sociology of coping with imaginary 'gaps' also concentrates on 'theodicy', although the 'gap' involved here is something more like a supposedly universal psychological 'need', and not a social gulf. From Weber and Parsons it takes up the suggestion that the most primary function of religion is to cope with the chances and changes of this life, by providing us with a reflection on the problem of misfortune, suffering and evil.

However, there are reasons to be suspicious of the idea that religion is basically theodicy. The notion is itself derived from the intellectual history of

---

[51] Douglas, *Purity and Danger*.
[52] Douglas, *Natural Symbols: Explorations in Cosmology* (London: Barrie and Jenkins, 1973) pp. 74, 93–100, 103, 193.
[53] Douglas, *Purity and Danger*, pp. 159–79.
[54] Ibid.

the West, where, from the late seventeenth century onwards, the word 'God' came to denote merely an ultimate causal hypothesis, rather than the eminent origin and pre-containment of all created perfection. A first cause conceived on the model of efficient causality, or the instantiation of logical possibility (Leibniz), was not, like the medieval God, good by definition. Instead, his goodness had to be 'demonstrated' in terms of the necessity of local imperfections for the most perfect harmony of the whole. In the Middle Ages, by comparison, although there were indeed many intimations of such an approach, there was not, on the whole, any dominantly recognized 'problem of evil'. This was because, as Kenneth Surin has shown, suffering and evil were not defined in such a way as to make them a *theoretical* problem.[55] On the contrary, they were regarded as negative or predatory in relation to Being and therefore as a problem only 'solvable' in practice. Where evil was seen as the manifest upshot of a perverse will (it being presumed that without free assent there could be no perfect goodness in creatures) and suffering as the sign of the deep-seated effect of such perversity, there *was* no real problem of evil, and so no science of 'theodicy'. In the seventeenth century, by contrast, attributions of evil to the effects of the fall of demonic powers and of humanity went into decline, and thus evil was approximated to the theoretically observable fact of imperfection, to be rationally accounted for.

Sociology, as heir of post-Leibnizian theodicy, tends also to assume that evil and misfortune are given observable facts within a society, and that religion's prime social role is to make fortune conform to the expectations of justice. However, perception of misfortune is itself culturally defined: Philippe Ariès, for example, has shown that up to the fourteenth century and the Black Death, death itself was perceived as another natural transition, rather than as a 'problem', or an ever-menacing danger.[56] Yet if this is conceded, one must go on to say that religion is not just a belated mode of coping with the *lacunae* of social existence; rather, its explanation of evil and suffering are part and parcel of its description of the world, where the definition of evil and the location of really serious misfortune enters into cultural constitution at an initial, primary level. Only in our society has the inculcation of such descriptions become thoroughly secularized.

Because sociology is really projecting back the assumptions of post-Leibnizian theodicy on all cultures and religions, it only accepts as fundamental 'types' of theodicy those systems which can be presented as offering a rationally consistent explanation for the occurrence of sheerly positive and 'obvious' phenomena of misfortune and evil. Thus Weber declares (and he is precisely followed by Berger) that the only three fundamental types of the-

[55] Kenneth Surin, *Theology and the Problem of Evil* (Oxford: Blackwell, 1986) pp. 1–58. Alasdair MacIntyre, 'Is understanding religion compatible with believing?', in Bryan R. Wilson (ed.) *Rationality* (Oxford: Blackwell, 1974) p. 73. G. W. Leibniz, *Theodicy*, trans. E. M. Huggard (La Salle, Ill: Open Court, 1985) pp. 123–373, esp. pp. 340–1. See chapter 2 above.

[56] Philippe Ariès, *The Hour of our Death*, trans. Helen Weaver (Harmondsworth: Penguin, 1983).

odicy are a dualism of the Zoroastrian variety, Hindu doctrines of Karma and theories of predestination.[57] In the first case, evil is seen as a primordial 'fact' to rival the fact of God; in the second misfortune is attributed to a cause-and-effect process always within our control; in the third the appearance of evil is subordinated to the inscrutable will of God. Yet in none of these cases is it asked how these theodicies belong within the context of particular symbolisms and philosophies of evil: is evil seen as positive or negative, a *sui generis* phenomenon or a secondary upshot of temporality, desire or finitude, a predatory intrusion or a power within its own right? The most significant fact about the sociological typology of theodicies is its *omission* of the orthodox Christian (Augustinian-Thomist) account of evil, which ascribes evil to a misdirection of the will, and so refuses to reify it, or ascribe to it a positivity which would require compensatory, consoling, or apologetic 'explanation'. For precisely *this* example tends to show, not merely that religion is not primarily theodicy, but also that it can dispense with such 'problem-management' altogether.

Religion and Evolution

Religion cannot be encompassed in space as the social whole, the social margin or as social transition: so here the discourse of sociology collapses. Equally, it cannot be encompassed in time as origin, stage or final goal.

Parsonian sociology attempts to conjoin the 'liberal Protestant meta-narrative' as articulated by Weber and Troeltsch, and described in the previous chapter, with the evolutionism of Herbert Spencer which was part of his English adaptation of Comtean positivism. In the Parsonian view, society evolves through a process of gradual differentiation into separate social subsystems: gradually art is distinguished from religion, religion from politics, economics from private ethical behaviour and so forth.[58] The upshot of this process is (as for Weber) that it is now possible for something to be beautiful without being good or true, and possible for there to be a valid exercise of power without it having a bearing on either goodness or truth. At the same time, a realm of 'pure' science emerges which (as in Spinoza's ideal of intellectual freedom) can pursue truth independently of coercive pressure, or of practical consequences. These ideas stand squarely within the Cartesian-Kantian tradition because they both deny the traditional Christian and metaphysical affirmation of 'the convertibility of the transcendentals' (Being as such is true, good and beautiful, so what is true is also good and so forth) and also seek to evade the modern and post-Baconian problematic which reveals the indissoluble connection between truth and power.

[57] Max Weber, *Economy and Society*, vol. 1, pp. 518–22. Peter L. Berger, *The Social Reality of Religion* (London: Faber, 1969) pp. 71–82.
[58] Parsons, *The Evolution of Societies*, pp. 48–9, 71–98.

The Kantian ruse is to deny the convertibility of the transcendentals with objective being, and yet try to establish the objectivity of knowledge, aesthetic judgement and ethical will in terms of the necessary *a priori* modes of operation of these three faculties. (For Kant himself they were, indeed, interconnected through judgement, but the secret of this connection is but dimly felt, in the sphere of art alone.) This thesis transcribes the modern Western separation of spheres of value which legitimates the operation of a power politics, because it is held to preserve the sanctity and purity of the scientific, aesthetic and private-ethical domains. In this vision of things, the division of labour, and more precisely the particular form taken by the division of labour in modern Western history, is regarded as an objective instrument of classification, the bringing to social awareness of an objective separation of spheres. Thus, for Parsons, sociology is the discipline which tells the story of how history culminates in American democracy, with its protection of private choice of separate values, and its synthesis of coercion and consent through the voting system and the formal operation of law.[59]

Evolutionary views of this sort are 'historicist' merely in the sense of advocating a historical determinism or a single possible direction for 'advance'. For it is only possible to describe history as consistent change in one essential dimension if one assumes that there is some truth about society or human knowledge which remains, ahistorically, 'the same'. What remains the same, for Parsons and his followers, are the transcendental conditions for the different value-sphere of the various social sub-systems, even though these are only 'emergent' from the symbolic interaction which sets these systems in motion. (Parsons talks of 'the action frame of reference' as providing a 'phenomenology' of the conditions of action as such.)[60] At the synchronic level, this emergence of value-spheres appears to be a purely contingent upshot, but at the diachronic level it seems that the distinction of values is objective, at least in the sense that this is functional for the increased adaptability of the human race, and for making society strong and flexible. Because the distinction of sub-systems is accorded the status of an establishment and/or revelation of *a priori* conditions of possibility, a particular Western history is universalized, and the boundaries between the sub-systems are declared to be inviolable.

Within the theory of evolutionary differentiation, religion is supposedly 'encompassed'. This is not a true historicization of religion, because the encompassing is only possible if religion, also, is assigned to a category which remains essentially 'the same'. Thus, for Robert Bellah, 'religious meaning' does not itself evolve, only the institutionalization of this meaning, and its intersection with other social elements.[61] For Clifford Geertz, religion can be eternally distinguished from 'science', because it 'suspends the

[59] Ibid., pp. 168–73, 198–9. Toby, 'Parsons' theory of societal evolution, pp. 15–18.

[60] Parsons, *The Social System*, pp. 3–23.

[61] Robert N. Bellah, 'The sociology of religion', 'Between religion and social science', in *Beyond Belief*, pp. 3–19, 20–50, 237–87.

pragmatic mode'; from art, because religious imaginings are not treated as fictions but are ritually enacted and believed in; and finally from the realm of everyday 'common sense'.[62] But just as it is impossible to specify with sufficient precision a residually universal 'everydayness', so too it is not universally clear that practices and beliefs considered 'religious' are separate from socially fundamental techniques of prediction and control over things and persons, nor that one can draw an easy line in every society between inventions truly believed in, and imaginings merely 'entertained'.

For Bellah and Geertz, as for Parsons, religion is grounded in ineffable private experience; at the same time, although distinct from science, art, and ethics, it partakes of the three modes of knowledge, imagination, and moral imperative, in its public and symbolic instantiation. As religion becomes more differentiated, it is also more properly apprehended, and gets confined to the sphere of experience which is supposedly the true starting point for theology. The problem with this view, is, of course, that if religion is essentially to do with private experience, it becomes ineffable and non-identifiable, and if non-identifiable, then it cannot be shown to be a universal constant.

Yet equally, for Bellah, religion retains its unique capacity for reflection on the social whole, and ability to integrate the diverse realms of value without negating their autonomy. This means, in essence, the public recognition of freedom, and the sacralization of the formal mechanisms of power. Thus Bellah celebrates the continuing need for 'civil religion', but also identifies the 'evolving' factor in religious awareness as the gradual 'discovery of the self': first of all, there is the private confessing self in direct relation to God (Christianity), then an 'ambiguous' religious self distinguished from the ethical self (Luther), and finally a discovery of the 'laws' of this ambiguity which yet acknowledges its necessity (Freud).[63]

Bellah therefore reproduces and hypostasizes a particular Western history in which it is increasingly announced that 'the real self' lies behind public action in the hidden recesses of the will or the subconscious, and yet, at the same time, objective techniques for the public deciphering or control of this hidden private self are gradually articulated and refined in the confessional manual or protocols of psychoanalysis.[64] But he fails to reflect that this 'invention of the soul', which makes 'religious' matters more and more private and discrete, and yet also subject to impersonal management, may be but a particular ruse of public power. The more 'matters of the soul' concern a private realm which is always the same, then the more public discourse concerning such things can detach itself from tradition, and declare itself to be both universal and scientific. Thus Parsons and Bellah link the civic religion theme with the idea that Weber, Durkheim and Freud have laid the

[62] Geertz, 'Religion as a cultural system'. Talil Asad, 'Anthropological conceptions of religion: reflections on Geertz', in *Man*, 18, pp. 237–59.

[63] Bellah, 'The sociology of religion', 'Religious evolution', 'Between religion and social science', 'Civil religion in America', in *Beyond Belief*, pp. 168–9.

[64] Michel Foucault, *A History of Sexuality*, vol. 1 See chapter 10 below.

foundations for a scientific yet non-reductive discourse about religion – our 'permanent' need for charisma, sacrifice, sublimation, and so forth. Far from transcending positivism, as they claim, this just reinstates positivism's latent religious dimension.

Religion can be diachronically comprehended, according to Bellah, because what has happened, historically, is the gradual differentiation of religion as such. In the interim, however, the 'confusion' of religion with other spheres has not been without its uses, because religion can function like a kind of storehouse of latent energy, developing and holding in suspense resources and purposes which come to their true fruition in their own proper time.[65] Thus religion encourages the imagination, invents 'spiritual' equality before the coming of social and political equality, and gives an imaginary sense and meaning to nature, or magical control over it, before the arrival of science and technology. It is at this point that the Comtean inheritance arrives at its greatest resemblance to the dialectical, Hegelian one: we are asked to believe that history embodies a logic in which, first of all, knowledge must be developed, powers stored up in an 'alien' fashion, in an illusory but temporarily necessary mode. But a 'higher positivism', truly emancipated from dialectics, might rather want to suggest that all that we have here is modern technological science and modern formalized politics legitimating their claims to universal power and validity in a necessarily narrative mode. According to this narrative, previously recognized human goals must now be clarified to reveal their true essence, and the previously seamless unity of imagination, ethics, and relation to nature, as once comprised under religion, must be shown to be a socially-instituted category mistake. At the same time, the wide prevalence of earlier illusion must be accounted for as the necessary but fruitful error of immaturity.

This legitimating narrative has to present the modern West as the culmination of a 'universal' history. Thus non-Western societies with relatively simple technologies are all classified as 'primitive', and positioned in various 'stages'. At the lowest level of non-differentiation, religion is supposed to be identical with the 'everyday', so that only societies with religions containing no gods and apparently little sense of transcendence, like those of aboriginal Australia, are allowed to be 'truly primitive'.

Against this kind of classification can be placed evidence, not only that 'primitive' religion varies unpredictably, but also that primitive societies can be markedly 'secular' in character, sometimes including a separate economic practice unhedged about by ritual and taboo, and a corresponding exaltation of individual entrepreneurship and socially destructive aggrandizement.[66] On the other hand, it is equally true that in societies dominated by 'gift

[65] Bellah, 'The sociology of religion', 'Religious evolution'.
[66] Roy A. Rappaport, *Pigs for the Ancestors: Ritual in the Ecology of a New Guinea People* (New Haven, Conn.: Yale University Press, 1968). Leonard Pospisil, *Kapauku Papuan Economy* (New Haven, Conn.: Human Relations Area Files Press, 1972) pp. 85–119, 400. Marcel Mauss, *The Gift*, trans. W. D. Halls (London: Routledge,1990).

exchanges', where goods circulate through the constant practice of an expected generosity (which does, however, usually take the form of rivalry in generosity and power through generosity), it is not really possible to distinguish, even vestigially, or latently, a distinctive 'economic' sphere: exchange of material goods happens only through exchange of symbolic meanings, and the motive of pure 'material gain' is not operative. An anthropologist like Mary Douglas is right to insist that differentiation and non-differentiation, 'religiosity' and 'secularity', do not occur in a uni-directional diachronic sequence.[67]

This legitimating narrative is still 'the liberal protestant metanarrative' that 'encompasses' the specificity of the Christian religion (which lets religion be truly religious) and releases the other cultural spheres to their own autonomy. Weber and Troeltsch's misreadings of ancient Judaism as 'desacralizing' nature and human society, and of Christianity as by-passing the social to concentrate on the immediate relation between God and the individual, are endlessly repeated by American sociology. There is therefore little point in restating here the critique set forth in the previous chapter.

What must be dealt with, however, is the twist given to this metanarrative by the German sociologist, Niklas Luhmann. In Luhmann's hands the 'liberal protestant' label no longer applies so securely: in certain ways he now gives to this a 'neo-orthodox' turn, although the fact that he is able to do so is, in my interpretation, a sign that neo-orthodoxy itself is in some respects but another variant on Protestant liberalism.

Common to the entire post-Parsons approach, is the idea that modern secularity does not really mark a decline of religion – only its proper differentiation. What has declined is merely the improper influence of religion in the public sphere, and the institutional and ritual 'trappings' of religion. But true religion, the 'religion of the self' and of experience, may flourish as never before.

For Luhmann also, true religion has been gradually differentiated in the history of the West. Like Parsons, and unlike Durkheim, he does not simply identify religion with society as a whole, but rather accords to religion a function which relates to this level, while itself occupying its own sub-system and its own relatively autonomous cultural sphere.[68] However, for Luhmann, this sphere is *not* characterized by personal experience: mere abstraction of the state of salvation, as (supposedly) found in Buddhism, belongs to a lower stage of differentiation from that achieved in the West, where Christianity abstracts the *conditions* of salvation.[69] 'True religion', in Luhmann's view, turns out, curiously enough, to coincide with the neo-orthodox understanding of Christianity as 'not a religion', but rather the word of God, purely

---

[67] Douglas, 'The effects of modernization on religious change'.

[68] Niklas Luhmann, *Funktion der Religion* (Frankfurt-am-Main: Suhrkamp, 1982) pp. 191–8, 223.

[69] Niklas Luhmann, *Religious Dogmatics and the Evolution of Societies*, trans. Peter Beyer, from chapter 2 of *Funktion der Religion* (New York and Toronto: Edwin Mellen, 1984) p. 76.

grounded in a self-confirming divine revelation.[70] What is fundamental for truly differentiated religion is not experience, but faith in the revealed word. It is only theology which knows this, and therefore dogma, not practice, discloses to sociology the essence of religion, just as (one could note) for Durkheim it is law which discloses the essence of society.

In the Parsonian view, as variously refracted by Bellah, Geertz, Berger et al., the legitimately integrating function of religion is finally connected to the public securing of the sanctity of private freedom and private religious experience. For Luhmann, by contrast, the replacement of experience with faith corresponds to the replacement of the function of integration with the function of 'contingency management'. Just as the word of God is arbitrarily given, so, too, the order of society is as it is, though it might equally be otherwise, and it is the function of religion as faith to sacralize this contingent order as perfect by virtue of divine appointment, or better still as the unquestionable 'gift' of the divinity.

By this switch of emphasis, Luhmann effectively 're-positivizes' sociology: he starts to reintroduce the original emphasis of de Bonald and Comte. For he declares that the real problem of the conditions of the possibility of the social does not concern only the Hobbesian 'problem of order', or the belonging of the individual to the social whole. Durkheim and Parsons diluted positivism by suggesting that the truly evolved society is legitimate, in liberal Kantian terms, because it embodies rationally universalizable norms of behaviour. Luhmann repudiates this Kantian admixture, and returns to the view that the institutions and conventions of any particular society always represent a mere possibility which cannot be preferred to any other possibility by purely rational criteria.[71] The ultimate social function is then no longer that of securing integration, something to be realized by religion as society itself, but rather of a slightly distanced reflection on the sheer contingent givenness of the social whole.

In Luhmann's terminology, society, or the whole social system, reduces the 'indeterminate complexity' of the *Umwelt* (its environment) to 'determinate complexity', while in establishing such fixed determinations it also constitutes, through 'appresentation', a particular shadowy horizon of unrealized possibility or barely suggested counterfactual indeterminacy. Although Luhmann dispenses with human 'subjects' in favour of 'communicative acts', he still treats the social system as a kind of Husserlian quasi-subject which is 'self-reflective', 'appresenting' and 'constitutive of a horizon'. This is the point where he reifies social interaction and still preserves, in phenomenological jargon, the positivist myth of a social whole which categorically organizes its constituents and transcends their factual being.[72]

---

[70] Ibid., pp. 53–61, 92.
[71] Ibid., pp. 7–13. *Funktion der Religion*, pp. 182–225.
[72] Ibid., p. 200.

According to Luhmann, societies gradually evolve to self-consciousness of the need for contingency-management, and this is precisely like Comte's evolution to 'the positive state'. In primitive societies, ritual is scarcely differentiated from 'daily life', but it is a prime function of ritual to disguise and gloss over indeterminate complexity and social contingency by rendering taboo all transitions, anomalies and hybrids.[73] We have, however, already seen that taboo and *rites de passage* do not cover up 'gaps' in primitive logic, but are themselves necessary constituents of that logic: in any system of hierarchized value-preference the negative and the transitional are the counterparts to the positive and the final goal. Nor is there any reason to think of theocratic legitimation as something super-added to a merely arbitrary empirical order: on the contrary, this order only exists and ceaselessly re-establishes itself insofar as it makes its arbitrary selection of possibility in terms of a mythical justification of this solution. In Luhmann's own terms, the determinate reduction of indeterminancy within the system can *only* be made as a definite speculation about the *Umwelt*.

Luhmann argues that doctrine gradually comes to replace ritual. The more societies undergo change and differentiation, the less can contingency be disguised by taboo and *rites de passage*; instead, contingency must be thematized and 'managed' by a doctrine of revelation.[74] Here the development from the Old Testament, through Christianity to the Reformation, is presented as 'prototypical', and other religious traditions are regarded as immature and abortive by comparison. Luhmann has therefore to evade the fact of Israel's singularity by presenting its religion as a national, 'social' development. Initially, Israel worshipped a tribal, 'federation God'. Then, in a precarious situation, God was reconceived as a providence encompassing both Israel and her environment. Prolonged crisis gave rise to an 'expanding awareness of time' which allowed further separation of 'God' from 'Israel' and finally the idea of a transcendent God who chooses Israel, in a contingent act, as subject of his promise.[75] This genetic reconstruction, however, is a purely speculative one; the Old Testament texts themselves perhaps suggest a widening grasp of divine providence, but they do not divulge to us any stage at which the idea of transcendence was not already present, nor at which God was not already associated with certain unique acts in time. The granting of significance to time and to non-repetition is part of the 'grammar' of Israel's monotheism, and even if this grammar was first articulated as a response to threat or crisis, such a response was by no means inevitable, and it effectively created a new social identity, without which 'Israel' might have simply ceased to be.

Like Troeltsch and Weber, Luhmann sees contingent 'election' and contractual covenant as the key features of Israel's religion, and so plays down all elements of immanence and symbolic or participatory reflection of the inner

---

[73] Luhmann, *Religious Dogmatics*, p. 40.
[74] Ibid., pp. 49ff.
[75] Ibid., pp. 51–3.

divine reality. In the case of Christianity, the evolution of religion is supposedly taken further when Duns Scotus grasps contingency as a *modus positivus entis* and Luther grounds theology in faith and revelation, so distinguishing religion from ethics or reflection on natural reality, the 'creation'.[76] Even Christological doctrine can be integrated into this scheme, because the inevitable abstractness of a pure concentration on contingency, and the concept of God as an empty 'will' needs to be balanced by a doctrine of the 'second person', which gives a concrete focus for devotion, and substance to the affirmation that the absolute divine will is also a 'good' will.[77] The more it bases itself on a series of clear and particular revealed facts, the more theology is able to distinguish doctrine from reason, and yet remain a universal and rule-governed discourse.

Luhmann believes that, although religion is eventually differentiated as 'contingency management', it is never able to arrive at a perfect self-consciousness of its own function, as this would tend to be self-defeating.[78] Thus, while later Christian theology was able to focus on contingency, it still had to show that the way things are is a mode of perfection. Here faith achieves what reason cannot, by claiming such perfection in terms of the derivation of things from a perfect being, however inscrutable.

Thus the Leibnizian problematic, which seeks to show that what is given is at the same time 'the best', is also regarded by Luhmann as a further refinement of the Judeo-Christian reflection on religion.[79] In the modern age, however, even this conception breaks down, because cultural differentiation produces different and incompatible 'perfections', and evolutionary consciousness denies the notion of a 'completed' perfection by positing instead the possibility of infinite progress.[80] In such a situation, faith is yet further differentiated as pure acceptance of the given, but there can be a still stronger concentration on 'the second person'. Luhmann provides an interpretation very akin to that of the neo-orthodox theologian Eberhard Jüngel: God's 'perfection' is only seen in his self-negation in Christ, in his free taking upon himself of human life and death, which can now be reinterpreted as 'pure givenness'. In the acceptance of what is, there is no further need for a happy ending, but the 'resurrection' means that 'possibility' is no longer conditioned by what has occurred so far (here Jüngel is explicitly cited).[81] Luhmann tentatively envisages a theology fully aware of itself as enshrining the *proprium* of religion – namely contingency management, and it seems that something like Jüngel's theology, interpreted in Luhmann's fashion, might fit this role.[82]

Such a theology (thinks Luhmann) would self-consciously operate in harmony with sociology: it would come to a mature acceptance of the fact that, because its not-essentially-religious social functions are now catered for

[76] Ibid., pp. 53ff.
[77] Ibid., pp. 98–9. *Funktion der Religion*, pp. 200, 205ff.
[78] Luhmann, *Religious Dogmatics*, pp. 97–8.
[79] Luhmann, *Funktion der Religion*, pp. 218–24.
[80] Luhmann, *Religious Dogmatics*, p. 87.
[81] Ibid., pp. 88–9, 92. Luhmann, *Funktion der Religion*, pp. 199, 206, 209ff.
[82] Luhmann, *Religious Dogmatics*, pp. 134, n. 210.

elsewhere, ecclesial practice is likely to be reduced to a minimum.[83] Likewise, Christianity can have nothing to say about the content of contemporary *mores*; Karel Dobbelaere, applying Luhmann's theories, suggests that once one acknowledges that the family today has mainly a 'companionship' function, one will realize the hopelessness of trying to implement traditional Catholic views on sexual practice.[84] To do so is to try to deny evolution, and make religion once again more than a 'sub-system'. But to this it might be countered that if one is unable to question 'what has happened', however persistently, and seemingly irreversibly, then only the most vestigial moral critique is possible. One could never, for example, pose the question: what sort of companionship is it that cannot even conceive of the notion of betrayal?

It is possible to see how a theology reduced to its 'true specificity', the problem of contingency, could still be an orthodox Protestant theology, at least in its formal appearance. But all its concepts would be empty ones: nothing would be said of divine *preference* – the way in which God loves, the content of his giving.

What Luhmann's work shows is that, through its complete de-sacralization of the world and refusal of analogy and participation, neo-orthodoxy renders itself liable to be supplemented by positivism, and so to appear on the rational level as subordinate to a sociological metadiscourse, which itself embodies a new version of the 'liberal protestant meta-narrative'. Luhmann gives us a 'sociological' view of the development of doctrine; but this can be deconstructed as the self-narration of sociology in terms of a Protestant view of doctrinal development.

It is certainly true that voluntarist theology and Leibnizian theodicy are closely related to modern political and social structures. But it is not the case that contingency first showed up in the social sphere and was later reflected on by theology. On the contrary, a particular theological concentration on the will, anxious to distance Christianity from the Platonic and Aristotelian inheritance, served to encourage the idea that social reality could be seized only under the aspect of its positive occurrence. All evolutionary sociology does is to pretend that this contingent development represents the essence of the Western tradition and the true outcome of human history.

Religion as Ideology

1   *Ideology and alienation: Peter Berger*

Sociology fails to encompass religion in space as the whole, the outside, or the transitional. It also fails to encompass religion in open time as the growth of knowledge, or as a necessary transitional phase. Its third device is to

---

[83] Luhmann, *Funktion der Religion*, pp. 222–4.
[84] Karel Dobbelaere, 'Secularization theories and sociological paradigms: convergences and divergences', in *Social Compass*, XXI/2–3, 1984, pp. 199–219.

encompass religion as the concealed temporal process of social self-occlusion, or as 'ideology'.

The notion of ideology is taken over from Marxism, but modified. For sociology, ideology relates not primarily to the ruses and self-disguisings of asymmetrical power *within* society, but rather to the problem of the contingency of the social whole, which we have just been examining. The key issue at stake here is whether, and to what extent, sociology is correct to see all societies as 'occluding' their own contingency through ideological strategies which constitute religions.

The work of Peter Berger provides a good example of a theory of general occlusion of contingent and rationally non-justifiable features. Together with Thomas Luckmann, Berger develops his theory of ideology on the basis of the sociological version of symbolic interactionism that has already been considered. According to Berger and Luckmann's theory of social genesis, the very first social arrangements do not require 'a sacred canopy', but exist only as conventions which have accidentally grown up through the symbolic interaction between individuals which establish simultaneously the first social rules, and the first sense of personal identity.[85] These arrangements are then passed on to the 'second generation', and only at the point of transmission to the 'third generation' do questions start to arise about their *rationale*. Questions arise, simply because the circumstances of the genesis of the arrangements have now been forgotten, and instead of the true, forgotten history, a mythical one is substituted, which relates existing social facts to some imagined eternal or natural order. Only at *this* stage does society come to require a 'sacred canopy', and this secondary and ideological character of religion distances Berger's ideas from those of Durkheim. When he wants to establish an 'irreducible' religious sphere, he refers to private experience, not to religion as social bonding.

One can, however, question this notion of an originally innocent and positive social practice, which religion later conceals. In the first place, Berger does not claim textual evidence from any culture for such a process – this is not available, precisely because (in Berger's terms) societies must do a thorough job of self-forgetting and self-obscuration. But in that case, the genetic reconstruction is doomed to remain conjectural, and can only appeal to criteria of probability. And, in the second place, the proposed genesis does not seem probable in the least: the main question here is why an 'innocent' origin should ever require ideological supplementation. For one thing, the Meadian model of 'the generalized other' suggests reciprocal and egalitarian norms, without asymmetries of power which might require further justification. For another, why should not the memory of the purely pragmatic and arbitrarily conventional genesis of the social norms continue beyond the second generation, just as myths can be persistently transmitted with little

---

[85] Peter L. Berger and Thomas Luckmann, *The Social Construction of Reality* (Harmondsworth: Penguin, 1969) pp. 29, 43ff. Peter L. Berger, *The Social Reality of Religion*, p. 39.

alteration. Berger fails to consider this possibility because, together with Luckmann, he assumes that the I-thou experience of dyadic 'face to face' relations provides the ultimate phenomenological conditions for social knowledge (there is a similarity to Simmel here). At a distance from such direct encounter with truth, knowledge grows weaker. It is, however, much easier to suppose that ideology is 'always already there'. In that case, social institutions get established simultaneously with the mythical and ritual frameworks which legitimate them. For example, Berger and Luckmann suggest that an institution like marriage is first of all an established fact, whose arbitrary conventions are later legitimated by religious myths of participation in cosmic marriages and so forth.[86] But marriage as a given 'fact' is permeated through and through by rituals and taboos which only make sense within much larger narrative frameworks, including mythical elements. It may be a fact that is just taken for granted, but this taking for granted is possible because the fact itself includes an element of legitimation: it both depends on and helps to uphold the network of interlocking stories which societies recount and act out in reality.

Where ideology is associated with social consensus, as by Berger, rather than with asymmetries of social power, it actually proves impossible to discover any layer of social reality which is demonstrably obscured through later cultural justification. This is not to deny that sometimes the historical record will show that new *rationales* are given for old institutions, and the older *rationales* are suppressed or forgotten. But this usually marks a change in the social institution itself, and a concealing of the mode of the institution's previous rather than its present operation – as for example, when new, stronger claims were made for the power of the Papacy, and this coincided with an attempted extension of its jurisdiction. In this sort of case there is no real 'gap' between the reality of Papal power and the theory of Papal power; if one can speak of 'ideology' here, then the ideological component is not exposed by comparing cultural symbol or theory to social fact, but rather by pointing to the contingency of the seamless social-cultural complex – a contingency which is denied and evaded at the point where a real social and theoretical change pretends that it is no change at all.

It would seem, then, that what remains valid in Berger's account of ideology is the idea, not of obfuscation of social reality, but of 'alienation' of social reality, in that the humanly produced character of society must always be denied, and social arrangements must instead be ascribed to God or the gods, and accorded an eternal verity.

There is little doubt that many societies and many religions *do* suppress historicity in this manner, but one should draw back from Berger's view that religion, unlike sociology, is at best able only to half-escape this suppression.[87]

---

[86] Berger and Luckmann, *The Social Construction of Reality*, p. 107.
[87] Berger, *The Social Reality of Religion*, p. 95.

As he admits, Buddhism, Hinduism, Judaism and Christianity all contain, in different ways, protocols of caution with respect to the human conception of the transcendent, which tend to foreground also the purely human origins of institutions, like kingship, that are often taken to be sacred in character. In the case of the Old Testament, the ascription of the patterns and norms for laws, social arrangements and sacred buildings to God, never denies the human labour or historical genesis also involved, and never ascribes cultural inventions or social foundations to intermediary beings – lesser divinities or semi-divine heroes. In this case, however, Berger fails to see that it is not that acknowledgement of transcendence releases a 'secular' space of human autonomy, but rather that human origination is seen as *coincident* with divine, sacral origination.[88] Even where human origination is less clearly acknowledged, as in the Egyptian, Greek and Roman myths, which grant a great role to daemonic intermediaries, the reasons for this are not simply alienation of the human, but rather a conception of human genius as 'stolen' from the gods, whereas, for the Hebrews, Yahweh did not fear human rivalry. The Greek and Roman myths do not necessarily obscure the 'factual', rather they give an alternative ontological evaluation of the supplementation of nature by culture.

It is true that the pagan ascription of present cultural arrangements to direct divine or daemonic intervention tends to obliterate historical memory. Yet, as Nietzsche realized, this in itself expresses a cultural preference for 'forgetting', and for ascribing to the gods a certain beneficent trickery which constantly contrives a new oblivion. The price paid for this mythical attitude is historical ignorance, and yet the attitude itself is not demonstrably irrational or falsifiable. It is no more or less 'scientific' than the Biblical myth of a non-deceiving God who works through human wills, in advancing stages of revelation that all proceed from a single divine will. This myth denies the pagan mythical notion that each new stage is the victory of new gods, who obliterate the memory of the old. The modern 'historical' attitude, with its consuming passion for 'what really happened', is the heir of this particular mythical conviction that the transcendent is manifest through a non-deceiving *concursus* with human wills and a developing history that does not obliterate itself.

Berger's theory of ideology as alienation perpetuates this Biblical will to historical truth, which can indeed reveal how it is that many myths conceal history. However, Berger's historicism is limited by two points of non-reflection: first, he fails to realize that his commitment to the desirability of historical non-concealment itself perpetuates a Christian attitude which rejects the irrefutable pagan recognition of a beneficial truth *in* concealment and forgetting. Secondly, he fails to see fully that the Bible and Christianity were capable, long before sociology, of overcoming the alienation of historical origins, while remaining entirely within a religious grammar.

---

[88] Alexandre Ganoczy, *Homme Créateur, Dieu Créateur* (Paris: Editions de Cerf, 1979) pp. 124–7, 140–4.

Religions *may* conceal historical contingency and the role of human invention, but just as often this is true of modern secular systems of thought, which are unable to admit their own choice of values with respect to the conjunction of an empty freedom with an instrumentalist reason. Such an admission requires on the part of secular thought a nihilist courage, whereas, it is much *easier* for religious societies to own up to the contingency and singularity of their fundamental choices, for religions themselves acknowledge that these are not fully explicable, but wrapped up in mystery and the requirements of 'faith'. Just at the point of their greatest obscurity, where they most seem to invite a scientific suspicion, religions are more realistic about the inexplicable character of cultural existence than science normally dares to be.

2   Ideology and power: Bryan S. Turner

Peter Berger connects ideology with beliefs shared by an entire society. But a second approach to ideology regards it in terms of the self-legitimating beliefs of powerful groups within society, which disguise the arbitrariness of their own exercise of power. Although this view is most powerfully expressed outside the sociological tradition, by Marx, it can also be discovered in Weber, as has been seen, and it is a neo-Weberian approach with which we are here concerned. This approach is highly critical of the Parsonian endeavours so far criticized; however, I shall show that it does not escape my general strictures on the sociology of religion.

The best example is the work of Bryan S. Turner, although Turner conjoins his Weberian reading with elements from Marx and Engels, and dresses it up in a post-Nietzschean and Foucaultian language, which gives his writing more of the appearance than the substance of postmodernism. Turner is suspicious of most recent sociology of religion, such as has been discussed in this chapter so far: he rightly sees it as quasi-theological, and still confined by nineteenth-century perspectives.[89] He does, however, over-simplify when he says that the nineteenth century confronted the dilemma that religion, though necessary, was untrue.[90] It is more the case that both social thought and a perfectly sincere theology simultaneously tried to rethink the truth of religion in 'social' terms. Nor is it the case that Nietzsche proclaimed the 'non-necessity' of religion; rather, he proclaimed the inevitability of myths, and the need for a mythology *embodying* the nihilistic realization that we construct an always mythical truth.[91]

Turner, however, reduces Nietzsche and Foucault to Weber. His fundamental argument is that, in a certain historical phase, religion had a necessary function of control rather than integration, in terms of the restraint and reproduction of bodies, and the representation and registration of whole

[89] Bryan S. Turner, *Religion and Social Theory: A Materialist Perspective* (London: Heinemann, 1983) p. 3.
[90] Ibid., p. 38.
[91] See chapter 10 below.

populations, whereas now these functions are primarily carried out by secular, instrumental processes. These processes make little use of ascetic restraint, and concentrate on the 'scientific' control of reproduction through incentive and disincentive; likewise they make little use of ideological representation, but concentrate on the detailed classifications and *surveillance* of human populations. Religion is confined to ideological representation, but this is no longer a necessary task in a society that *does not require* an overall ideology: instead, representation becomes just the private concern of individual religious vision.[92]

This view of things remains thoroughly Weberian for two main reasons. First, Turner refuses Althusser's conception of ideology as 'material practice', in which there is no 'gap' between the exercise of social power and the justification of this power.[93] For Althusser, the most fundamental justifications are given at the level of the power-relations themselves, because there is never an exercise of naked power which does not for its very success employ a rhetoric which defines its mode of operation. Thus Marx demonstrated that the most mythical elements in capitalism were also its most factual elements, and that the units of its grammar were also the instruments of its coercion: namely money and capital which 'reify' the equivalences which we establish between objects exchanged.[94]

Turner, however, rejects the centrality of reification and fetishization in Marxism – arguing (on obscure grounds) that it no longer applies for 'monopoly capitalism'. He thereby rejects the element in Marxism which is most profitably critical of sociology's attempt to separate social facts from cultural ideas.[95] Instead, he insists that ideology is primarily a matter of 'belief', so that when he declares – admittedly following the line that leads from Althusser to Foucault – that the sociology of religion should concentrate on 'rituals and practices', not beliefs, he is suggesting that we somehow try to view these as pure material relations of power, without ideal formality. Given this highly metaphysical conception of 'matter' as a mysterious 'base', it is inevitable that Turner will see ideology as non-essential, and rituals and practices as gradually revealing an essential secular core of pure 'discipline' (a move always avoided by Michel Foucault). Turner is perhaps right to point to recent evidence which suggests that if religion is essentially an opiate for the masses then it worked much less well, even in the Middle Ages, than Marx and Engels supposed.[96] However, if it is recognized (following Althusser) that ideology is primarily present in structure and practice, not in secondary belief, then one can also pay far more attention to the fact that it is very

[92] Turner, *Religion and Social Theory*, pp. 5–10, 238–41.
[93] Ibid., pp. 138–41. Nicholas Abercrombie, *Class, Structure and Knowledge* (Oxford: Blackwell, 1980) pp. 174–5. Nicholas Abercrombie, Stephen Hill and Bryan S. Turner, *The Dominant Ideology Thesis* (London: Allen and Unwin, 1980).
[94] See chapter 7 below.
[95] Turner, *Religion and Social Theory*, p. 65ff.
[96] Ibid., pp. 63–86.

difficult for any oppositional movement to succeed, even against a not popu-larly-rooted religion, precisely because it can only employ the single public language of the dominant system of power.

Secondly, as has already been seen, Turner is Weberian because he makes secularization more or less inevitable, given his incorrect separation of the question of power from the question of belief and 'ideology'. The only serious question that remains for him with respect to religion is why, during a long historical period, did it exercise important functions of social discipline (if not for society as a whole, then at least for the dominant classes)? His answer here is not, as for Nietzsche and Weber, in terms of a cunning of historical reason which develops human self-control in an initially alien form. Instead, Turner introduces into his already eclectic analysis a would-be feminist adaptation of Marx and Engels. Weberian rationality is accorded the force of an always 'determinant' (though only in capitalist society specifically 'dominant') base, and linked to the immanence of a capitalist mode of production. Behind all the various phenomena of replacement of religions by secular discipline lies the single, fundamental fact of the separation of economic accumulation and ownership from familial relationships. In modern, monopoly capitalism, pri-vate ownership and family inheritance have ceased to be all-important, but in feudal society these things had, above all, to be guaranteed. The primary function of religion was precisely to secure for aristocratic males control over women and their sexuality. The Church insisted on legitimate sexual union and provided convents for unmarried females who would otherwise be a prey to their male relations, and might engender problematic illegitimate offspring.[97]

But this is an extraordinarily thin argument: as Turner himself intimates, the Church's regulations on divorce were often problematic for feudal rulers.[98] But, more seriously, Turner is surely quite wrong to refer the struc-tures of male control over women only to economic interests; to see the falsity of this, one can point out that men were interested not just in succession but precisely in (the symbolism of) *male* succession. Moreover, this filiative struc-ture of succession itself transcends the purely economic, because the interest in post-mortem survival, the passing-on of one's possessions, is more like a 'religious' than an economic impulse. It is not that the Catholic religion was 'functional' for economic inheritance, but more that at a certain point of fusion between Catholicism and ancient tribal survivals, inheritance is constructed as a basic grammar of social meaning.

For inheritance itself is to do with the survival of a name, of an honour, a mystery emblazoned on a field of arms, as well as with fields cultivated and tilled. If inheritance later ceases to be all-important, then this is not 'funda-mentally' an economic matter, but itself an aspect of a total change in social conception and practice, a new 'imagination' of human handing-over in terms

---

[97] Turner, *Religion and Social Theory*, pp. 108–33, 146–7.
[98] Ibid., pp. 146–7.

of abstract rights and complex title deeds. This is certainly not just the emergence of a more rational discourse, as Turner implies, interpreting in a like manner the separation of sovereignty from the being of the individual king.[99] For how much *greater* a fiction it is to think of a possession whose 'being owned' is indifferent to any actual possessor, or of a rulership which abstractly persists, in a now not even shadowy corporeal form, when the king lies dead, before his successor is crowned.

Turner integrates into Weberian sociology a Marxian base/superstructure dualism and makes this fit a sociological dualism of society and culture. But he rejects the elements in Marxism which question the latter dualism. As a result, he only goes half-way towards a post-sociological and postmodern treatment of cultural beliefs and values, which would consider their seamless integration into social practices and modes of power. This treatment goes beyond sociological and Marxist notions of 'ideology', because there is no question here of 'decoding' values in terms of their assistance and disguising of the exercise of power. On the contrary, the powers involved only operate *through* a certain scheme of valuation, and both the power and the values may be quite 'transparent': think, for example, of the increasingly open acceptance of naked competition and necessary inequity in recent capitalism. For such a conception, unlike notions of 'ideology', there need be no *contradiction* between belief and practice, however often one may discover local elements of ideological disguising of power and deception of the powerless. For it is always more basically the case that power and value are seamlessly one and transparent, because there is no belief without action and no action without belief. Given this situation, all one can do is question the arbitrariness of the entire complex and point out that things 'could be otherwise'.

If the analysis given in this chapter is correct, then sociology of religion ought to come to an end. Secular reason claims that there is a 'social' vantage point from which it can locate and survey various 'religious' phenomena. But it has turned out that assumptions about the nature of religion themselves help to define the perspective of this social vantage.

From a deconstructive angle, therefore, the priority of society over religion can always be inverted, and every secular positivism is revealed to be also a positivist theology. Given this insight, sociology could still continue, but it would have to redefine itself as a 'faith'. However, while there is a deconstructive moment in my analysis of positivism, it does not stop there. More fundamentally, I have offered a 'metacritique',[100] which does not wish to invert the respective positions of the 'social' and the 'religious', but rather to show that a certain hypostasizing and mutual positioning of the two, with a few variations (Durkheimian, Weberian, Parsonian), belong within a particular positivist 'grammar' which should not be simply turned upside down, but

---

[99] Ibid., pp. 178–98.
[100] See chapter 6 below.

rather opposed in the name of something else. In particular, the view that religion concerns the relation of the 'individual' to the 'social' can be opposed in the name of hierarchical societies (meaning a hierarchy of values, rather than of persons) for which both individuality and collectivity are subordinate to a substantive organization of roles, values and purposes. Here religion can be so fundamental that one cannot get behind it to either society or private experience.

But sociology is doomed simply to rediscover, everywhere, the specifically modern confinement and protection of 'the religious sphere'. The positivism which defines religion at, beyond, or across the boundaries of the 'social fact', is always subverted by a more radical positivism which recognizes the peculiarity and specificity of religious practice and logic, and, in consequence, the impossibility of any serious attempt at either scientific explanation or humanist interpretation. ·

Part III

Theology and Dialectics

6

For and Against Hegel

Introduction

The following chapter constitutes an important turning point in this book. It is 'for Hegel' in the sense that Hegel offered a critique (in his terms both 'rational' and 'Christian') of modern political theory, political economy, and Kantian philosophy which – as Gillian Rose has shown – can be used as a critique in advance of the sociological tradition.[1] This book seeks to perpetuate these critiques, and also to recommend the resuming of four Hegelian tasks. These are, first, a theological critique of Enlightenment; second, a historical narration of the interconnection between politics and religion; third, a self-critique of Christian historical practice; fourth, and most importantly, the transformation of the Greek philosophical *logos* through encounter with the theological *logos*, so that thought itself becomes inescapably Christian, and one is 'beyond secular reason'.

Mention of the last, most decisive task, requires a note of clarification. When I imply that we ought to 'redo' Hegel, I do not mean that we should seek once again to establish an 'encyclopaedia' of knowledge, in which all significant reality is included, and rationally demonstrated as necessary existence. If one takes this to be the centre of the Hegelian enterprise, then it is forever dead. However, it is a valid hermeneutic strategy to take instead the four tasks as outlined above, and then to argue that the Christian transformation of the philosophical *logos* is actually subverted and prevented by the encyclopaedic, totalizing ambitions. More precisely, it turns out that these ambitions are intimately linked with 'heterodox' and 'pagan' currents which have already been identified within secular social theory itself. This chapter is as much 'against' as 'for' Hegel because, it will be argued, he fails decisively just at the points where he promises most.

The main charge that will be brought against Hegel is that 'dialectics' is just a *new variant* of modern politics and political economy: Hegel's 'negative' thought has even less success than positivism in overcoming liberalism and the economic theory of heterogenesis. Hegel's logic *itself* is simply another

---

[1] Gillian Rose, *Hegel Contra Sociology* (London: Athlone, 1981).

'political economy', and so, inevitably, another 'theodicy'. However, dialectics discovers a new resource for both explicating the economic logic of heterogenesis, and linking this to transcendent destiny: the new resource is the 'heretical' and 'gnostic' idea about divine self-alienation transmitted to German tradition by Jacob Boeheme. It is above all this notion, the heart of 'dialectics', which ensures that Hegel can only qualify voluntarism by subordinating the personal to an impersonal and inexorable logical process. Because 'reason' (in the sense of something seeking self-percipient clarity and necessity founded in identity) and 'freedom' remain the two founding sites of Hegel's thought, converging towards a point of identity which absolutizes them both, he escapes neither from the Greek *logos*, nor from the Cartesian-Kantian philosophy of the subject, with its inextricable entanglement with liberalism. In this connection it will be suggested that Hegel's metaphysics assumes a totalizing aspect, not because it ignores Kant's strictures on the limits of human understanding, but rather because it does not go far enough in the questioning of Kant, and still accepts the idea of a sphere of 'pure reason', distinguished from the sphere of 'understanding'.

In chapter 1 of this book it was argued that modern political theory rested on three great denials; firstly, of 'Baroque *poesis*', or the idea that human making is not a merely instrumental and arbitrary matter, but itself a route which opens towards the transcendent; secondly, of the Christian doctrine of creation, in favour of a reversion to an antique mythology of rational action as the 'inhibitor of chaos'; thirdly, of Aristotelian ethics/politics, with its central notions of *praxis*, virtue and prudence. In the following three sections it will be shown, in turn, how Hegel begins by calling into question each of these denials, yet in each case ends up by reinforcing them. Indeed, the power of the 'negative', which is granted the initiative by dialectics, is nothing but the merely reactive force of these denials.

As we shall see in the following chapter, by embracing 'dialectics' Marx is implicated in these denials also, and utterly unable to mount a real critique of Hegel, which as a critique of dialectics itself would not be merely 'immanent' in character. In the final chapter of this sub-treatise on 'theology and dialectics' it will then become possible to show that 'political theology' is only half-right in seeking to form an alliance between Christianity and the thought of Hegel and Marx: beyond a certain point this alliance actually inhibits a historicizing analysis and prevents a Christian questioning of secular assumptions and institutions.

From Metacritique to Dialectics

1   The metacritical perspective

Charles Taylor and others have correctly pointed out that Hegel's thought is related not only to Kant and the post-Kantian turn towards idealism, but also to the 'metacritique' of Kant carried out by Hamann and Herder.[2] (There is a third important relation, to Scottish political economy, as we shall see.) Whereas Kant and his successors were concerned with the contribution which the thinking subject makes to its own thoughts in the internal sphere of consciousness, Hamann and Herder were concerned with the external, visible and audible modifications to matter made by human beings in 'art' (meaning all processes of 'making') and in language.[3] They both understood that there can be no conceivable 'thought', and so no subjective identity, outside these processes.

Their argument is that because we only think in language, and only grasp the world through language, it is impossible ever to disentangle the knowledge we have of ourselves and through ourselves from our knowledge of the world (or 'nature'), or vice versa. All we can say is that both nature and the human subject are 'expressed' in language, although this use of the term 'expression' should not be taken to mean that language can be decoded in terms of some content, natural or subjective, which is properly pre-linguistic. On the contrary, linguistic expression, like art, brings into being its own specific, new content; before language, humanity is simply contentless.

Despite this denial of priority to thought, Herder conceives language to be teleologically related to pre-linguistic, 'forceful' processes of nature, so that with the event of language, humanity arises as the true end of the natural world. It follows that access to this truth of both humanity and nature can only be an aesthetic one: as all knowledge occurs through the expression of reality in signs, it is never possible to compare the sign with the reality, and the fundamental function of language cannot be referential. Unless, in consequence, we trust our creative expressions, not as arbitrary, but rather as fulfilling a goal which is not merely our own, there can be no truth of any sort. The aesthetic decision for a particular linguistic content, which manifests a natural energy, is to be taken as also the instance of the manifestation of truth. One can properly speak here of a kind of 'aesthetic necessity' (which applies also for Herder to God, who in *creating* things makes them simultaneously a rational possibility).[4] A similar notion is mooted by Kant himself, in *The Critique of Judgement*, in terms of a transcendental 'aesthetic idea', which can yet only be recognized in a particular intuition or artistic product showing a merely 'indeterminate' conceptuality, provoking endlessly different thoughts.

[2] J. G. Hamann, 'Metacritique of the purism of reason'. J. G. Herder, 'Verstand und Erfahrung, Vernunft und Sprache, eine Metakritik der reinen Vernunft', in *Werke*, vol. 21 (Hildesheim: George Olms, 1967). Charles Taylor, *Hegel* (Cambridge: Cambridge University Press, 1975) pp. 3–50. The contribution of Jacobi was also crucial. For a further elaboration of the perspective offered here, see John Milbank, 'Knowledge: the theoretical critique of philosophy in Hamann and Jacobi', in, J. Milbank, C. Pickstock and G. Ward (eds.) *Radical Orthodoxy: A New Theology*. (London: Routledge, 1999) pp. 21–38.

[3] Taylor, *Hegel*. J. G. Herder, 'Essay on the origin of language'; in John H. Moran and Alexander Gode (eds.) *On the Origin of Language* (New York: Ungar, 1966) pp. 87ff, 107–33.

[4] J. G. Herder, *God, Some Conversations*, trans. F. H. Burkhardt (Indianapolis: Bobbs Merrill, 1940) p. 125.

However, Kant does not allow, like Herder, that 'proper' conceptual thought, 'of the understanding', is itself confined to mere aesthetic necessity.[5]

Hamann's and Herder's approach to art and language (and to some extent Kant's in *The Critique of Judgement*) preserves and extends the perspective of Mannerist poetics and Baroque rhetoric. Although this perspective is 'modern' and constructivist, it is really quite different from the attitude of transcendental idealism, although this distinction is very often lost sight of. Transcendental idealism, as a philosophy of the subject in the Cartesian tradition, thinks of the known object both as something 'beneath' the subject, and so as under the subject's control, like the instruments of technology, and also as 'within' the subject to the degree that it is fully known. This tradition, just like Cartesian philosophy, is profoundly *conservative* in the sense that it seeks to conceal the abyss opened to view by the post-Renaissance discovery that language creates rather than reflects meaning. The abyss is hidden by the attempt to establish a new pre-linguistic stability for meaning in the 'internal' domain of the 'subject'.[6]

Undoubtedly it was certain currents within a supposedly Augustinian tradition, which had always sought the road back to God through 'self-reflection', that suggested this reaction to the relativizing problematic opened up by the Renaissance humanist discovery of linguistic creativity. Yet paradoxically, the Cartesian raising of the subjective will 'above' language and the endless flux of human operations upon the world, meant that human creative operations came to be regarded in a manipulative or instrumentalist light. And thus it chances that the very 'Augustinian' *conservatism* of Cartesianism is yet seriously implicated in modern technologies, and voluntaristic approaches to social life. This situation is only modified, not truly overcome, by German idealism.

By contrast, the idea of 'aesthetic necessity' resists linguistic scepticism in an altogether different fashion. The road to transcendence is here not through an inward retreat, but rather stands both outside and before us, in the works and words which issue from us, determine what we are, and act back on us beyond the reach of our conscious intentions. The sum of these words and works comprises culture itself, and therefore the social order is in no way 'beneath' human subjects, and so fully within their control; neither can they step back from this social order to recover their identity. This is not, however, to say that the social order is a divinely revealed totality which is prior to the creative activities of human subjects, as for de Bonald, de Maistre and the positivist tradition. Instead, Herder has a different approach to the individual/society antinomy. As it is impossible to separate humanity and language,

---

[5] J. G. Herder, 'Ideas for a philosophy of the history of mankind'; in F. M. Barnard, *J. G. Herder on Social and Political Culture* (Cambridge: Cambridge University Press, 1969) pp. 259, 299–300. *God, Some Conversations*, pp. 123–5. Immanuel Kant, *Critique of Judgement*, trans. Werner S. Pluhar (Indianapolis: Hackett, 1987) pp. 82–4, 91–5, 128–43, 151ff, 182–3, 211–32.

[6] Henri Gouhier, *Les Premières Pensées de Descartes: Contribution à L'Histoire de L'Anti-Rénaissance* (Paris, 1979) pp. 29, 52.

he envisages the human creative process, or history, as simultaneously the divine revelation which is the bringing to completion of the natural order. Since language is revelation, it is natural that the central creative work of language should be the imagination of religion itself – and Herder is able to fit the centrality of the Christian revelation/religion within this scheme.[7]

In Hamann's and Herder's 'expressivism' (as earlier in Vico) one can locate something like a critique of secular modernity, which is yet itself modern, because it recognizes the creative power of language and tries to deal with this by reinterpreting revelation as our participation in the divine creative power of expression. However, this expressivist philosophy does not, like Hegel later on, regard secular enlightenment as a dialectically necessary phase of human becoming.[8] Rather it appeals, as it were, to a different, 'counter' modernity, a phantom Christian modernity which has never been. One may well describe this attitude, which still seeks a Christianization of the Renaissance, as a continuation of the Baroque.

And Hamann and Herder developed a critique of Kant's critical denial of transcendent metaphysics which was not a medievalizing reversion, but rather a post-Baroque 'metacritique'. 'Metacritique' does not imply a further critique founded on Kant's initial effort, but rather a *denial* of the possibility of Kant's critical endeavour, from a critical point of view that is a more genuine and secure one. This point of view is that of language. If it is true that we only think in language, then it is simply not possible to investigate our thinking instrument – to say what it can or cannot think in advance of its deployment. We can *only* know our thinking capacity to the extent that we have thoughts, use words, and this means to the extent that we assume we have some conception of what 'things' and objective realities are. Hence it is not possible to separate out within language the 'categories' – whether of 'reason', the 'understanding' or 'the imagination' – by which things are thought, from 'intuitions' or the empirical contents of thoughts themselves.

It is certainly true that in one sense this metacritique enmeshes us more deeply in physical finitude than even Kant would allow; but on the other hand, it also makes it less easy to draw the Kantian boundary between 'legitimated' knowledge of finitude, and illegitimate pretensions to knowledge of the infinite. For *no* expressive understanding of the finite world can really claim a legal 'title deed' such that one can see it as an instant of bringing a particular fact under the judgement of a stable and universal conceptual framework. And in that case, it becomes impossible to demonstrate that the 'understanding', or human discursive thought, is clearly limited to judgement of the finite and must not trespass beyond these bounds. As was said in the previous chapter, one no longer knows that the categories of, for example, causality, necessity and relation, belong essentially to the

---

[7] J. G. Herder, 'Yet another philosophy of history', in F. M. Barnard, *J. G. Herder on Social and Political Culture*, p. 218. 'Ideas for a philosophy of the history of mankind'. Ibid., p. 271.

[8] Herder, 'Yet another philosophy of history', p. 194.

framework of subjective grasp of reality – they are just part of the reality that we deal with and express, and therefore we are free to make 'eminent' or 'analogical' use of these categories in imagining the infinite and the relation of the infinite to the finite. Conversely, there is no reason to think that our construing of aspects of the world as purposefully ordered is any more 'subjective' than our construing of the world in terms of categories of 'mechanical' causality. Therefore speculative extrapolation from immanent teleology does not propel us – any more than extrapolation from mechanical causality – to a noumenal, supersensible world where 'spiritual' mind grasps purpose and spontaneous necessity as germane to its essence. For as was also noted in the last chapter, Kant is only able to delimit the understanding to the finite realm, because he posits a subject which stands above and *outside* the bounds of this realm, an 'apperceiving' subject which has the power of 'reason'.[9] Although, in the theoretical sphere, no *content* can be given to 'pure reason', it is at least able to grasp the 'antinomies', or the supposed point at which, in the infinite sphere which is *proper* to the human spirit, finite alternatives – like that between 'having absolute limits' and 'without end' – collapse. Reason is supposedly able to resolve the four antinomies – beginning/no beginning, freedom/causality, ultimate constituent parts/no such parts, necessary being/no necessary being – because, from its spiritual vantage-point, it grasps that spatial-temporal processes terminate in the underlying reality of the spirit, and that the antinomies are a sign (as they were for Plato) of the merely phenomenal, 'less real' character of temporality.

By contrast one should affirm, sceptically, that the antinomies destroy determinate knowledge of finitude, because concepts of freedom and causality and so forth *are* just part of the 'series' of phenomena, so ensuring, as Kant feared, that it is 'always too large or too small for understanding'.[10] Only aesthetic understanding then remains possible, and any 'transcending' of the antinomies becomes a pure act of faith, not a necessity of reason.

For Kant, while pure reason cannot give content to other *noumena* like itself, it can at least grasp that there *are* 'things in themselves' – including monadic quasi-subjects underlying empirical realities, other subjective minds, and finally God himself. In the sphere of ethics, or of 'practical reason', this purely formal knowledge of different free subjectivities is made to give rise to the actual content of legitimate activity. It is here, especially, that Kant shows just how Leibnizian he still really is, for while he rightly denies a rationalist, 'univocal' grasp of finite and infinite in the sphere of the understanding, by contrast we are able, in the sphere of reason, to 'determine' the supersensible in our practical willing, so grasping the essence of all spirit, finite or infinite,

---

[9] Immanuel Kant, *Critique of Pure Reason*, trans. Norman Kemp Smith (London: Macmillan, 1978) pp. 135–61, 168ff, 176–7, 300–01, 365–9, See chapter 5.

[10] Ibid., p. 466, and see pp. 384–485. Kant, *Critique of Judgement*, pp. 210–33, 265ff. Kant, *Critique of Practical Reason*, trans. T. K. Abbott (London: Longman, 1959). J. N. Findlay, *Kant and the Transcendental Object: A Hermeneutic Study* (Oxford: Oxford University Press, 1981).

as univocally 'freedom'. Only on *this* basis are we then permitted to posit the ultimate 'transcendental object' (God) as analogically the 'cause' of phenomenal nature.

If, however (to think further in the metacritical spirit of Hamann and Herder), there is no apperceiving subject standing above matter and language, then there is no vantage from which one can round upon the bounds of finitude and determine what is confined to the finite alone. And if, again, the normal, finite act of understanding is not a matter of bringing a particular under a general rule, then there is no clear division of spheres between 'reason' and 'the understanding'. Synthesis of a more than aggregate sort, the producing of new 'wholes', enters into our comprehension of the 'world out there', and this same comprehension is itself shot through with antinomy: for example the need to know boundaries, against the lack of unquestionable criteria for doing so. Language itself carries out more than empirical syntheses, which are nonetheless never purely *a priori*. And given the antinomous, intrinsically questionable character of these syntheses, one can never see any meaning as once and for all fixed and complete. The location of any meaning within a system of signs constantly subject to revision and further attempts at elucidation means (as Charles Taylor says) that for Herder there is always a 'background' of merely 'implicit' meaning which expression can never bring into total clarity, even though it may have *implications* for what it is that we appear to mean. From this background of the implicit, which constitutively conditions what we now mean and are going to mean, it is in principle impossible to exclude the pressure upon us of a transcendent and infinite reality. Indeed, the entertaining of a notion of 'aesthetic necessity' (as Kant himself partially explains in *The Critique of Judgement*) presupposes a transcendent meaningfulness which conditions our linguistic performance such as to render it 'true', although it can never itself be fully grasped in finite terms.

2   The myth of negation

In certain respects, Hegel retains the metacritical perspective. In the *Phenomenology* he repeats Hamann's and Herder's point that it is impossible to describe the thinking capacity of the mind while prescinding from any particular content for its thoughts.[11] For Hegel, human thought and subjectivity only evolve through cultural production, which involves an interaction of the subject with matter, and with other human beings. He also and accordingly thinks of religion as the very 'substance' of culture, as the set of values and practices which ultimately bind together a people, and which by token of this ultimacy is the point of their connection to the transcendent. The highest,

---

[11] Hegel, *Phenomenology of Spirit*, trans. A. V. Miller (Oxford: Oxford University Press, 1977) paras. 73–6.

'revealed' religion (Christianity) is for Hegel 'revealed' precisely because it is the religion that has become fully conscious of free human community as the essence of religion.[12] And Hegel rejects Kant's ban on constitutive metaphysics because, given the metacritical considerations, it is not possible to make universal statements about knowing (if, indeed, this is possible at all) in isolation from statements about universal being.

Yet at the same time, Hegel, in the wake of Schelling, fuses – and therefore *confuses* – metacritical reflection on the undeniable, external and 'surface' human constitution of culture and knowledge through art and language, with transcendental idealist reflection on the 'deep' internal and invisible constitution of the object of knowledge in a private realm of 'thought'. Instead of simply by-passing Kant through a metacritique of the very possibility of the transcendental endeavour, both Schelling and Hegel initially follow Fichte in trying to radicalize the Kantian approach. For Fichte, the finite ego, through its own self-willing, 'posits' its own existence, and from this act of self-positing can be deduced the forms taken by the categories of the understanding. Moreover, the mental instrument is responsible not only for the forms of knowledge, but even for its content, insofar as 'positing' enters into the shaping of particular objects of the understanding. Hence one can speak not merely, like Kant, of the 'empirical intuition' of such objects, but also of an 'intellectual intuition'.[13] In this way Fichte extends the Kantian model of practical reason – which arrives at content by a purely formal route – to theoretical reason also.

Schelling, the younger pioneer, concurred with Fichte about 'intellectual intuition', and Hegel later followed suit. But at the same time Schelling rebelled against Fichte's formalism and subjectivism. He argued that transcendental logic must be supplemented by a logic of nature, grounded in realistic apprehension. For Schelling, in consequence, 'intellectual intuition' still included the moment of Kantian 'empirical intuition', although this now implied a knowledge of *noumena*, not just of phenomena, for Fichte had already abandoned the notion of inaccessible 'things in themselves' behind natural objects. All knowing, for Schelling, involves a mediation between transcendental logic and the logic of nature, and he argues that such knowing is paradigmatically located in the work of art. Here he draws on Kant's third critique, and the latter's notions of aesthetic judgement as concerned with the mysterious 'adaptation' of logical categories to empirical intuition and the freely different forms which can be given to this adaptation by the imagination. But these particular forms, as I have said, do not, for Kant, have any bearing on knowledge, as they do for Schelling; for the latter (at this phase of his career) art is located beyond speculative philosophy at the point where

---

[12] G. W. F. Hegel, *Lectures on the Philosophy of Religion* (Berkeley: California University Press, 1985) vol. 3, pp. 218, 224ff.

[13] J. G. Fichte, *Science of Knowledge*, trans. Peter Heath and John Lachs (New York: Appleton Center, 1970) pp. 38–40.

nature and subject, determination and freedom, the constraining and the unconstrained come together and are revealed as identical.[14]

The distance from 'the metacritical perspective' must here be carefully noted. For Herder the subject is *realized* through *poesis* and language, and power and articulation are inseparable, but for Schelling (ultimately influenced by Jacob Boehme) the world has been sundered into two distinct spheres of subjectivity and objectivity which must be brought together again by art. Here the dialectical perspective already intrudes, and tends to override the metacritical. One may well object to Hegel's over-hasty dismissal of Schelling's raising of art above speculation, yet within the dialectical perspective the notion of 'aesthetic necessity' cannot really be retained. If art is but a moment in a process of the self-alienation of the same and its later cancellation, then *either* art is subordinate to logical necessity, or *else* what is essential in art is not its content, but the creative will which *enforces* a reconciliation, as it earlier enforced a separation. (Just as for Kant what ultimately matters in art is not its representation of the unity of nature and freedom, but its leading us towards the 'ethical' realm of pure, undetermined freedom.) Schelling's later philosophy then took this positivist, voluntarist direction of 'existential dialectics', whereas Hegel opted for the former, panlogicist programme.[15]

Hegel's logic is at once a transcendental logic or a logic of the possibility of knowledge, and a logic of nature or a logic of the possibility of reality, which can only be grasped after that reality has unfolded. Hegel accepts Fichte's 'positing', but qualifies this in terms of Schelling's notion of nature as really separate from, yet finally identical with, the subject. And Hegel adds that this identity is not only realized through culture and society, but can become conceptually transparent.[16]

From these assumptions, taken together, flow Hegel's three great philosophical errors, which condition all his ethical and political thought. First of all, Hegel retains the Cartesian subject. It is true that he considers that subjectivity and freedom are only truly realized through self-expression in matter and interaction with other people. However, at points during the development of the self, Hegel recognizes 'moments' when the subject thinks of itself as a pure, contentless self-identity – he mentions Roman stoicism, medieval Christianity and the Enlightenment.[17] Although these are indeed instances of illusion, the illusion is necessary, an essential phase of human development. This presupposes that while the separation of a 'spiritual'

[14] F. W. J. Schelling, *The Unconditional in Human Knowledge*, trans. Fritz Marti (Lewisburg: Bucknell University Press, 1980) p. 285. Robert F. Brown, *The Later Philosophy of Schelling* (Lewisburg: Bucknell University Press, 1976) pp. 101–2, 110–11.

[15] Robert F. Brown, *The Later Philosophy of Schelling*.

[16] Hegel, *Phenomenology*, 1–72. *The Difference between Fichte and Schelling's System of Philosophy*, trans. H. S. Harris and Walter Cerf (Albany: State University of New York Press, 1977) p. 170. Taylor, *Hegel*, pp. 3–50, 101ff.

[17] Hegel, *Phenomenology*, 178–229, 541–81.

sphere from the sphere of material cultural expression is 'contradictory', this contradiction is 'real', and belongs to the way things ultimately are. And 'real contradiction' in turn presupposes that mind or spirit is truly able to constitute a polar opposition to the objective sphere, whereas for a rigorously metacritical perspective any 'difference' between subject and object could only be a difference 'on the surface', or within one and the same medium (the 'surplus' of the subject over language is only real as the potential *for* language).

Moreover, the mode of resolution of the dialectic also shows that the Cartesian subject is still in place. The moment of objective self-expression gets retained in the final resolution in 'sublated' form, so that the subject remains 'for' and not just 'in' itself, but the resolution is a 'return' to self and an immediate, automatic restoration of negated self-identity.[18] Just like the Fichtean 'I', the Hegelian absolute subject can think all its thoughts, all its otherness, simply in thinking itself (like the Aristotelian first mover), with the Kantian and Fichtean addition that thinking itself means *thinking its own freedom*. In the end, self-thinking, the 'moral' thinking of freedom, is the certainty of being: *cogito ergo sum*.

Secondly, Hegel invents a 'myth of negation'. This is what makes his panlogicism unique. An earlier attempt to deduce being from possibility and to approximate to God's thought of the possibility of creation itself, that of Leibniz, conceived logic as a 'series', which unfolded by infinitesimal steps, such that every act of analysis of a 'single' thing revealed a slightly 'different' aspect of possibility. But Hegelian logic is in one aspect more *conservative* and more Aristotelian, in that it pivots more strictly round the principle of identity A:A. In consequence, difference cannot here result (as for neo-Platonism, stoicism and Leibniz) from analysis, or the unfolding of a series, but must imply contradiction, or denial of the ultimate identity.[19] This could only have been avoided if Hegel had stepped out of panlogicism and simply admitted 'other' identities: but this he was not prepared to do. As a result, difference cannot, for Hegel, result either from analysis or from simple 'positive' assertion: instead, the initiative lies with negation. And this coalesces nicely with the fiction of a polarity between subject and object; these are not, for Hegel, commensurable, but nor are they merely two different things to which one might add a third: on the contrary, they are comprehensive, totalizing *genera*. One can *only* relate them in terms of opposition, and only derive a separate object from an all-sufficient subject by means of a denial.

Because negation has the initiative, negation must always be 'determinate negation', which means that denial leads of itself to a new positive upshot. This becomes the primary instrument of Hegel's social and historical critique. It is, however, more difficult to see how 'negation' can govern a series, than to

[18] Hegel, *Phenomenology*, pp. 765–70. Hegel, *The Science of Logic*, trans. A. V. Miller, pp. 417, 431.
[19] Gilles Deleuze, *Différence et Répétition* (Paris: Presses Universitaires de France, 1968) pp. 66–77.

imagine how a series might be revealed by analysis. There are no 'inevitable' resolutions of historical tensions and conflicts. If one takes the case of the 'master/slave dialectic', then one can agree with Hegel that there is 'contradiction' here, in the sense that the master's power can be potentially challenged through the very context that holds that power in place: namely his subjecting of the slave to labour which permits the slave to rise to greater self-reflection than is possible for his overlord.[20] One can agree that here lie the seeds of likely change, but one *cannot* say that this situation of itself gives rise to what can be seen, in retrospect, as an inevitable 'next stage'. In Hegel the slave consciousness does not stop at the experience of labour, but goes on to grasp the inviolable possibility of thinking its own thoughts; this then gives rise to the 'stoic' phase of antiquity, when people seek consolation in resignation to, and withdrawal from, the external course of the world.[21] But this only appears as a 'determinate negation' if one imagines that from the extreme objective pole of submission to labour and loss of freedom there arises a denial which reaches back to the pure depths of internal subjectivity. By contrast one should say that stoicism was a positive response which *imagined* such a subjectivity, whereas a different imagination would have conceived instead a conjoining of labour to political power.

If one calls into question Hegelian logic and the principle of determinate negation, then one must also call into question the idea of 'immanent critique'. This is not clear to Hegelian commentators like Charles Taylor, who wish to affirm the logic of the *Phenomenology* as such a critique, but to deny the logic of the *Science of Logic* itself.[22] 'Immanent critique' suggests to Taylor both that one is doing justice to the Herderian background of implicit meaning, and that one avoids anchoring critique in an absolute, foundationalist starting point. Instead, one takes a value, usually 'freedom', as one finds it exemplified in one's given social world, and one locates the point at which the practice of freedom contradicts what it purports to promote: thereby critique is effected and a new era of freedom is opened to view. But such a procedure presupposes that there *is* a rational foundation – namely 'freedom' – even if it is inaccessible and can only be asymptotically approached. The value, freedom, is still for Hegel transcultural, because it is rooted, as for transcendental philosophy in general, in the ontology of the subject. Furthermore, 'critique' is supposed to proceed only as the unravelling of the contradictions, therefore as a closer and closer approach to the simple rational self-identity of freedom itself. But here it needs to be said that identifying the tensions in a situation – such as that of master and slave – is one thing, but it is quite another to give a moral critique of the situation: this presupposes that one contingently imagines a different situation which one takes as more realizing the true ends of humanity.

[20] Hegel, *Phenomenology*, 178–96.
[21] Ibid., p. 197–202.
[22] Taylor, *Hegel*, pp. 218, 347.

Taylor is right to argue that the *Phenomenology* can only be salvaged if one views it as hermeneutics, or as an exercise in historical interpretation. However, if one retains the notion of 'immanent critique', then hermeneutics is really subordinated to dialectics, or the identification of a necessary sequence in the coming-to-be of freedom. The *Phenomenology* is only the *Logic* in reverse form, commencing with the alienated finite subject, rather than the initial divine reality of Being which through diremption into finitude establishes itself as the subjective 'Notion'. For Hegel, the necessary stages of finite alienation, and the possibility of immanent critique, are given only because history is the self-becoming of the absolute.

'Dialectics', which depends upon the myth of negation, is therefore another mode of Cartesian conservatism. By its means, Hegel once more subordinates the contingencies of human making/speaking to the supposedly 'logical' articulation of a subjectivity which is secretly in command throughout.

The Realm of Indifference

Besides the retaining of the Cartesian subject and the myth of negation, Hegel's third mistake is to misconstrue infinitude. And here occurs the second respect (following the subordination of *poesis*) in which Hegel turns out after all to fall within the bounds of 'secular reason'. For in misconstruing infinity he ends up refusing also a fully Christian doctrine of creation in favour of a reversion to antique 'inhibition of chaos'. Supposedly, Hegel is trying to do justice to the transcendence of the creator God by escaping from a notion of the infinite which, by representing it as merely 'other' to the finite, thereby makes us think of it of it as something which might be 'in relation' to the finite, and so finitizes infinity itself. Yet Hegel himself (unlike for example the Plato of *Parmenides*, or Thomas Aquinas) places finite and infinite in a relation, namely of opposition sublated as identity. For Hegel, infinity is really nothing other than finitude itself taken as a present totality, as fully subsistent, and not dependent on anything else.[23] This conception accords with his almost Pascalian horror of the indefinite series, which he names the 'bad infinite'.

One can agree with Hegel that to think of the infinite in its non-dependence on finitude only as an unending series is to temporalize the infinite; but on the other hand, to conceive this infinite only in terms of 'presence', as Hegel does, is *also* to temporalize it. One has to remain content with making both contradictory predications – although this antinomous condition of the mere 'understanding' is exactly what Hegel claims to overcome.

Such an interpretation of Hegel's position will be resisted by those, like Emil Fackenheim, who have stressed that Hegel distinguishes, even at the

---

[23] Hegel, *Science of Logic*, pp. 138–9, 142–8, 151–4. *The Logic of Hegel* (from the Encyclopaedia of the Philosophical Sciences), trans. William Wallace (Oxford: Oxford University Press, 1892) paras. 92, 104.

level of speculative philosophy, between an 'immanent Trinity' (meaning here the infinite containment within God of the created world and human subjective response) and an 'economic trinity' (meaning God in his external action of creation and reconciliation).[24] When, however, Hegel discusses the immanent Trinity, he suggests that the 'pre-worldly' Trinity represents a relatively unrealized moment of divine being, a moment in which inner-relatedness is sketched out as a mere 'abstract' universality, and in which the generation of the *Logos* is a matter of 'play' (the immediate negation, yet 'preservation' of difference as identity) without the pain and seriousness of the incarnation and crucifixion which are necessary to full trinitarian realization.[25]

Hegel is not, however, 'unorthodox' in Christian terms (as is often claimed) for suggesting that in a certain sense the creation of the world was necessary for God; he is 'unorthodox' because he posits a prior 'moment' of relatively unrealized and merely abstract subjectivity in God. He is also 'heretical' because, in gnostic fashion, he conceives of creation as a negation which results in a self-alienation, and so as itself a 'fall', both for God and for humanity. This means that, unlike orthodox tradition, he makes evil a necessity for the development of finite subjectivity, for the emergence of virtue, and the final realization of love when finitude is 'sublated' and gathered back into infinite ideality.[26] Just as he still insists on certain inevitable 'moments' of Cartesian subjectivity, so he also sees a necessary beginning to self-conscious humanity in the merely self-seeking, self-preserving and 'evil' will.

It might be objected that I make it sound as if Hegel is either a pantheist, or an acosmic monist, for whom finitude is entirely identical with the absolute and infinite. In response, I would agree that he avoids both these positions, but he does so in a very peculiar way. The ultimate sublation of finitude does not for Hegel mean that the entire content of finitude is gathered back into the absolute, because there remains for him a realm of finitude that is purely arbitrary and contingent. Charles Taylor praises Hegel for this allowance for contingency,[27] but it seems to me, for reasons set out below, precisely the weakest aspect of his philosophy.

The key point here is that Hegel avoids, through his panlogicism, recognition of the fact that the most surprising contingency, the sheerest givenness, occurs at the macro, not the micro-level. Only *within* a contingent, given order, is it possible to recognize certain consistencies and determinacies. The panlogical presuppositions turn this metacritically apprehended situation on its head. For Hegel, it belongs to the condition of alienation, and of temporal finitude, that there is a sphere of the merely 'indifferent', whose main characteristics are that it is partially governed by chance, and that it is indefinite in

---

[24] Emile L. Fackenheim, *The Religious Dimension of Hegel's Thought* (Boston: Beacon Press, 1967) pp. 149–54.

[25] Hegel, *Lectures on the Philosophy of Religion*, vol. 3, pp. 195, 198–200, 275–6, 293–4.

[26] Ibid., pp. 296ff, 304–16; *Phenomenology*, 779, 780. On Hegel and Gnosticism see Cyril O'Regan, *The Heterodox Hegel* (New York: SUNY, 1994).

[27] Taylor, *Hegel*, pp. 316–20.

extent – a 'bad infinite'.[28] This bad infinite is *not* redeemed through sublation by the true infinite, and yet it is only within this sphere that the subjective spirit discovers its own self-expression. It follows that the basic problem of the Hegelian philosophy is to distinguish within the realm of finitude what is merely 'indifferent' from what is to be finally 'preserved' as an essential moment of the absolute spirit. But this distinction can only be carried out if it is really possible to arrange reality in a strictly hierarchical manner, such that each bringing together of opposites, of the two sides (spirit/nature) of the Hegelian pyramid of reality, is also an advance upwards towards the peak of the pyramid which gradually leaves behind a bottomless base diverging forever into the abyss of indefinite chance and fortune.

Each step upwards means that one has grasped absolutely, and once and for all, the law and the genus of a particular indefinite series, insofar as this is truly comprehensible. Both the *Phenomenology* and the *Logic* contain examples of why it is impossible for knowledge, or a self-sufficient and complete meaning, to find an absolute starting point.[29] For example, Hegel shows that it is impossible to think of 'quantity' without 'quality', and vice versa. But he seeks to extricate himself from this labyrinth of signification (rather like Kant 'resolving' the antinomies), by making such examples parts of a logical series moving not only 'forwards' by determinate negation, but also 'upwards' in such a fashion that the circular passages of the labyrinth can be constantly left behind as a merely earth-bound chaos. In consequence, Hegel is not content to say that 'quantity' and 'quality' can only be construed together; instead, he subordinates this inter-signification to a dialectic which begins in self-contained and merely ineffable quality, discovers itself through external quantitative relation, and finally returns to itself as 'measure', in a move which leaves behind the purely 'indifferent' aspects of the *quantum* – for example the arithmetic series, which Hegel (unlike Kant), regards as purely analytic.[30] Higher up the scale, 'genus' is a qualitative assessment which includes an element of sublated quantity because it supposes that, at a certain point, differences of degree have become differences in kind.

But as soon as one has noted that this point is *arbitrary*, and that there may be different, overlapping qualitative divisions made for different purposes and by different cultures, then it is not clear that quality can be raised hierarchically above quantity, nor that any contingent quantitative variant can ever be merely consigned to the indifferent – we never know just when it may not prove to make a decisive difference. (Hegel neglects the Leibnizian lesson that the quantitative is highly relevant to a genuine respect for the concrete and particular.)

These abstruse considerations of the Hegelian *Logic* are in fact (as we shall see in the following section) highly relevant to his treatment of social and

---

[28] Hegel, *Science of Logic*, pp. 104, 134–44. *The Logic of Hegel*, p. 104.
[29] Hegel, *Phenomenology*, 91–6.
[30] Hegel, *Science of Logic*, pp. 79–80, 185, 314ff, 327, 333.

political matters, where it turns out that the realm of the indifferent is the sphere of the practice of capitalism and the administration of punishment and discipline by the State. These practices are in themselves alien and irredeemable, yet they are necessary because the laws of the economy and of the State are themselves essential moments in the realization of the absolute idea. But what one should note here is that Hegel only distinguishes finite from infinite in a highly unchristian fashion, by placing a *certain level* of finite reality totally outside the reach of divine providence and divine goodness. As in the Machiavellian tradition, pagan chaos is here restored.

Whereas Christianity subscribes to a total, but unknowable providence, Hegel denies a complete providence, yet claims a full knowledge of providence in the limited extent of its workings. This latter aspect is the well-known *hubris* of his metaphysics. Yet this *hubris* cannot be ascribed to his insufficient attention to Kant's strictures on the limits of human understanding: instead, it results from his failure to overcome these strictures metacritically, and his *acceptance* of our confinement to a knowledge grounded in the transcendental structures of subjectivity and freedom. Hegel's claim is that, within the 'bounds' of our finite subjectivity, we can enjoy the 'absolute' knowledge of an infinite with which the finite subject is finally identical. This is *not* (as is so often claimed) the 'last' grand attempt to do traditional Greek/Christian metaphysics, because this is metaphysics accompanied by neither divine *illuminatio* nor Hamann's and Herder's revelation in language (the modern, 'Baroque' version of illumination). Instead, Hegel attempts to reason to the infinite from a finite 'starting point', and to such 'Gnosticism' appropriately adds a gnostic myth of a necessarily self-estranged and self-returning God who leaves behind him the scattered husks of the merely material and indifferent.

True and Counterfeit *Sittlichkeit*

In the previous two sections I have shown how Hegel partially succeeds, but finally fails, in questioning modern 'secular' assumptions with regard to *poesis* and the 'inhibition of chaos'. In the present section I shall show how the same verdict applies with regard to modern assumptions about *praxis*, or human moral action.

Praxis, in the old Aristotelian sense, referred to a dimension of action which was categorically 'ethical' because it could not be separated from a person's essential being or character (*ethos*); it meant a doing which was also a being. It also implied action directed towards a particular end (*telos*), but an end immanent within the very means used to achieve it, the practice of 'virtue'.

These two specifications imply that it is impossible to regard as essentially good the 'good will', or pure motivation, because until this defines itself in terms of external action, we will be unable to give any content to 'goodness'. At the same time, they also imply that external action can never be defined purely 'objectively', in terms of outcomes or consequences which prescind from both intentionality and the possession of virtuous character. This is because a human action is defined for us by the fact that it embodies some argument, reason or purpose, such that the 'end' which it realizes can only be construed in terms of its location within a whole complex set of cultural norms and expectations.[31]

Modern political theory, following Bodin, Grotius and Hobbes, abandoned this Aristotelian notion of *praxis*. Instead, morality became increasingly a matter of inner will and conscience, while external action came to be something that might be legitimately 'manipulated' by the State in a manner that by-passed subjective assent. No longer was politics thought of as rhetoric and persuasion: instead it became technology.[32] And no longer did the encouragement of specific virtues form part of the goal to be pursued by the community – once the very essence of 'politics'.

Hegel, however, reacted against this sundering apart of morality and politics, and reinvoked the 'customary' or *sittlich* morality of the *polis*. There are, in consequence, two aspects to his return to *praxis*: a critique of modern ethical theory, and a critique of modern political theory. In the first case, he dissents sharply from Kant's 'deontological' approach to ethics. For Hegel, it is a mistake to see the essence of goodness as lying in the possession of a 'good will', rather than the possession of certain achieved virtues, because supposedly perfect intentions become sterile, elusive, and collusive with the world's actual evil if they cannot be defined in terms of any actual practice of virtue.[33] The 'beautiful soul', who retains his purity of aim inwardly intact, is really the empty subject, and not the truly free subject, as Kant supposed. Likewise, it is not possible to deduce all genuinely moral actions from the single requirement that such action be what one could universally wish in a republic of disembodied free souls.[34] This attempt to deduce all moral norms from what is formally implied in the fact of our being a free subject (which Kant sees as logically including respect for other free subjects) will not really explain why (to provide Hegel with an example) societies encourage individuals to go on being honest even in circumstances where the effects of dishonesty may be seemingly harmless for freedom. One needs to refer here, not to a universal abstract reason, but to particular social and customary contexts which encourage the formation of certain virtues like those of honesty. Dependent on one's social role, and dependent also on the social occasion involved, will be the decision as to exactly what *kind* of virtue it is appropriate to exemplify in a particular instance. Aristotle called such fitting of the action

---

[31] See chapter 11 below.

[32] See chapter 1 above.

[33] G. W. F. Hegel, 'The spirit of Christianity and its fate'; in *On Christianity; Early Theological Writings*, trans. T. M. Knox (New York: Harper and Row, 1961) pp. 210–12, 235. *Hegel's Philosophy of Right*, trans. T. M. Knox (Oxford: Oxford University Press, 1952) paras. 124, 139.

[34] Ibid., pp. 135, 104–41. *Phenomenology*, 532–71. *Hegel's Philosophy of Mind*, trans. William Wallace (Oxford: Oxford University Press, 1984) paras. 506–12.

to role and circumstance the exercise of the all-governing virtue of *phronesis* (*prudentia* in Latin) and this aspect of *Sittlichkeit* is affirmed by Hegel in his own fashion.[35]

Hegel characterizes mere *Moralität* (Kantian, as opposed to customary ethics) as caught up in the bad infinite. For Kant, he points out, freedom, and therefore moral action, is only guaranteed insofar as one is *resisting* nature in the shape of one's own physical and sensual impulses, because nature, for Kant, is seamlessly governed by causal determination. Not only does this involve an antinomy, in that one is obeying the law of one's own will which is nonetheless against one's own nature, it also suggests that the good will can only be the infinite quest for a good will, as freedom depends upon a resistance to something which constrains it.[36]

Hegel detects this same subservience to the bad infinite in modern liberal politics. He denies that Rousseau has truly resurrected republican virtue, because his 'general will' is no more than the universal abstraction of all the individual particular wills, who merely will their own freedom of life and property.[37] As there exist always some restrictions on personal freedom, and always conceivable sources of danger to personal freedom, the general will is an essentially negative will, devoted to the removal of all actual and possible barriers to freedom. Quite rapidly, this merely negative liberalism will be transformed into political terror, as during the French revolution, with its *loi des suspects*. (Kant, notably, associated freedom with 'terrifying sublimity' and the enthusiasm which attaches – as in Islam – to the non-representable, yet unconvincingly tries to suggest that in the more intense negativity of moral freedom, terror and fanatical enthusiasm evaporate. He refuses to see liberal enlightenment as unleashing the arbitrary, and so as the purest form of terror.)[38]

Hegel makes similar observations about the political views of Fichte, tracing these to the transcendental philosophy of a self-positing ego operating against the background of an empirical reality without any determinable content of its own. In a political world where anything can be made of anything, the only common standard is protection of the finite ego, which, according to Fichte, must extend not only to the prohibition of deliberate crimes against person and property, but also to the numerous ways in which individuals may accidentally interfere with, and inhibit, the freedom of others. To prevent this happening, to ensure the smooth operation of the free market, and the maximum spread of available information and predictability of outcome, there must be a vast extension of the State 'police' (*polizei*) in the sense of 'surveillance'.[39] Hence Fichte's real positing is of a world of

---

[35] Hegel, *Philosophy of Right*, pp. 135, 142–57. *Philosophy of Mind*, pp. 513–16.
[36] Hegel, *Philosophy of Right*, p. 124.
[37] Ibid., p. 258.
[38] Ibid., *Phenomenology*, 582–95. Kant, *Critique of Judgement*, pp. 131–6.
[39] Ibid., p. 79. Hegel, *The Difference between Fichte and Schelling's System of Philosophy*, pp. 146–7. J. G. Fichte, *The Science of Rights*, trans. A. E. Kroeger (London: RKP, 1970) pp. 374–87.

identity cards, internal passports, overseers of overseers and proliferating bureaucracy. But this circumspection will never be satisfied, and in the course of its progress, protection of freedom will pass over into its gradual inhibition. (Hegel here anticipates Foucault's uncovering of *surveillance* as a key aspect of modern politics, but more clearly than Foucault he links this phenomenon to the protection of 'rights', and implies that such absolutism is merely the reverse face of liberalism.)[40]

Modern deontological ethics, and modern politics, are seen by Hegel as converging on the point of freedom as mere 'possession' – possession of the self, and of one's own property. Thus he regards Kant's theory of morals as giving a transcendental transcription of Rousseau's politics: the general will that the freedom of all shall be the freedom of each individual, becomes the categorical imperative. For Hegel this imperative demands only that one shall not act so as to violate the logical identity of private self-wills in their abstract freedom, and this substantive emptiness makes it a licence for anarchy and terror. Nevertheless, it is not the case that, for Hegel, Kant's theory of respect for the subject is merely *reducible* to bourgeois property relations – this would be a Marxian misreading of his position. On the contrary, Hegel distinguishes 'morality', which he thinks has characterized both Christendom and the Enlightenment, and which has been best grasped by Kant, from the Roman stoic consciousness which failed really to internalize the implications of self-possession.[41] In the Roman world, according to Hegel, the republic dissolved into the empire, where a 'democratic' impulse recognizing only one's own private rights confronted a law reduced to mere force and might. The stoic response was a resigned retreat from this realm into a private serenity of *apatheia*. Stoic consciousness did not rise to the grasp of abstract property right as respect for the will and integrity of the owning subject. On the contrary, the discovery of the subject as an end in himself, and as a *locus* of truth, is for Hegel a specifically *Christian* achievement, realized at first in the 'alien' form of *Moralität*, then finally in the form of a *Sittlichkeit* more genuine than any attained within the Athenian *polis*.

This relationship of Christianity both to the morality of subjective freedom, and to *die Sittlichkeit*, is the key crux of Hegel's ethical and political theory, and the one most relevant to this book. Here, especially, I am both for and against Hegel.

For Hegel, because he makes a profound attempt to identify the difference which Christianity has made to Western history, and does not, like sociology or Marxism, try to reduce the unique aspects of Christian social experience to some supposedly more 'basic' dimension of society. (Here a purer historicism can assist an ecclesially-centred theology.) The most extraordinary aspect to this attempt is that he attributes a great causal efficacy to the incarnation and crucifixion of Christ, and the early Church's experience of resurrection.

[40] Hegel, *Philosophy of Right*, p. 29.
[41] Ibid., p. 104.

The 'stoic consciousness' of the Roman Empire represents, for Hegel, an extreme moment of the sundering of spirit from nature on the eve of the decisive 'turning-point' of world history. However, he considers that this situation could not possibly have been overcome by mere inner striving of a Fichtean sort, just as 'inner piety' alone can never constitute true religion. This is because the *presupposition* for the positing of true substantive subjectivity which unites nature and spirit is the underlying real identity of these two, and of God with the finite world. But the 'stoic' subject is an abstractly infinite subject, which is incapable of real self-reflection and therefore of grasping its relation to the external and sensible.[42] As a result, the absolute idea itself – the unity of infinite and finite, spirit and nature – has to appear in the disguised form of 'sensible immediacy', as 'being for others': this is the only way in which consciousness at this stage can arrive at the notion of the subject 'in and for itself'. In this anticipation of the final state, the subject arrives at a true, fully realized freedom which is one and the same with natural necessity. What is strange about this conception (at least as presented in the *Lectures on the Philosophy of Religion*) is that the dialectic scarcely seems to be mediated through cultural forms at all. The Roman disintegration appears to be simply *interrupted* by the Incarnation – an extrusion of the affronted Idea into what Hegel stresses is a natural and sensory immediacy, *not* the mere cultural form of political representation.[43] One can see how the dialectical process would demand that the Idea appear as a concrete mythological image, but only with great strain can one see how this requires its appearance in the real historical life of an individual. The Incarnation is, indeed, a 'monstrous reality', and its 'necessity' in Hegelian terms is not fully apparent.

This is only one of the quirks within Hegel's insertion of the Gospel story into the centre of his dialectical metanarrative. The other main peculiarity resides in the fact that the incarnate *Logos* is, as it were, before its time and situated in the wrong place. There are elements of contingency here which both enrich Hegel's narrative and yet threaten to undermine it. If one stuck to the dialectical unfolding of human culture, one would expect that stoic resignation would simply evolve into the medieval 'unhappy consciousness', where the spirit is conscious of its separation both from nature, and from the God who is the object of its pious and moral aspirations, yet can do nothing to overcome this separation within the present life.

In the *Phenomenology*, Hegel does appear to suggest something like this. Here, stoicism passes over into a sceptical self-consciousness in which self is reduced to pure negativity, by doubting the sense-world and public ethical principles which it must continue apparently to affirm. This, in turn, becomes the 'unhappy consciousness', which sees itself as alienated from external nature, and an absolute which it locates in an infinite 'elsewhere'.[44] For this

---

[42] Ibid., pp. 34–104. *Lectures on the Philosophy of Religion*, vol. 3, pp. 210ff, 308ff.
[43] Ibid., pp. 110–14, 214–15, 313–16, 317.
[44] Hegel, *Phenomenology*, 204–30, 758–63.

medieval phase, the distance from the historical Christ merely seems to supplement and reinforce the alien character of the unchangeable God with whom unity is sought. Even though the idea of incarnation allows the insight that the 'unchangeable' is also 'individual', this idea has now become more sheerly mythological, because it is a matter of memory and 'representation': 'Christ' equals the idea of a Jesus who is always already absent, 'utterly remote' both in space and time. This is not the Jesus who is just 'present' as the initiative of an affronted absolute from the side of sensible nature.

The *Lectures*, however, mention clearly the initial concrete presence of Christ, who instils a definite, *sittlich* practice, and after his death gives rise to a community formed through a premature intimation of perfect 'reconciliation', of God in and for himself.[45] Here the Incarnation is premature, not simply in the sense that Christians seek an alien form of reconciliation in the memory of a dead saviour, but also in the sense that Jesus's *actual life* (or else the mode of representation of this life) is seen as anticipating the fully realized *Sittlichkeit* of modern times, though in a fashion that is peculiarly fated. His 'sensible immediacy' therefore transcends the alien presentation of salvation as 'elsewhere', and as consisting in an asocial ideal, directly confronting the individual. But the latter is all that dialectics would seem to require, and is all that the *Phenomenology* provides.

From the dialectical perspective of the *Phenomenology* one would expect Hegel to interpret Christianity as representing from the outset, in Christ's life and teachings, the turn of stoicism towards inward reflection – as, in fact, a proto-Kantianism. This is exactly how they are interpreted by sociology, by Durkheim, Weber and Troeltsch. But instead, the young Hegel had chosen to pit Jesus *against* Kant, and saw Jesus as the representative of a kind of hopeless, doomed, misplaced and premature *Sittlichkeit*.

This early rendering represents perhaps Hegel's most truly enduring contribution to theology. The Gospel is not 'beyond the law' in the sense that Jesus preached the internalization of the Law, or that what mattered was 'good intention'. On the contrary, the Gospel is beyond the Law, because every notion of the ethical as a standard 'over against' life and the human subject is here surpassed. As Hegel puts it, the command to 'love one's neighbour' does not place restrictions upon the subject, but on the object of morality.[46] It is not really a command at all, because instead of appealing to the 'ought' against murderous and covetous desire, Jesus appeals to the 'fact' of our natural ties to the neighbour in family, locality, and even among strangers whom we may chance to meet. This natural fact may lie concealed, but it can be brought to life as mutual reconciliation, and it is this bonding in love, this enjoyment, which really defeats and *overcomes* the will to hatred, jealousy and deceit. Hegel is profoundly true to the Gospel when he argues that Kant's endless progress towards the good will amounts to a denial of the

---

[45] Hegel, *Lectures on the Philosophy of Religion*, vol. 3, pp. 218, 317, 327, 329.
[46] Hegel, 'The spirit of Christianity and its fate', p. 210ff.

Christian belief that the Spirit overcomes evil altogether. He also understands better than Kant ideas of our 'need for grace', because this overcoming must first be *seen* in Christ and we only enter into perfection to the degree that we have really passed beyond a merely 'moral' striving.

In *The Spirit of Christianity and its Fate*, Hegel is therefore a great opponent of the confusion of Jesus's teachings with those of the Stoa. However, he also marks the distance between Jesus and antique *Sittlichkeit*. If reconciliation is the final goal, a shared mutuality, then specifically Christian virtue cannot be realized within the *polis*, where there are strict hierarchical distinctions, and some are the slaves of others, without any privileges of freedom. Reconciliation implies the equality of all and the freedom of all (although it transcends them both); but equality and freedom would lose their collective ground of justification if they were pursued merely for the sake of the just treatment of separate independent subjects.[47]

Freedom, nevertheless, is not merely a necessary condition for reconciliation, it is also a positive value to be pursued. This also marks Jesus's teachings out from the antique *Sittlichkeit*, just as the Christian conception of a creative God means a new combining of notions of ultimate truth with ones of ultimate subjectivity. If these are still important themes in the Enlightenment, however distorted they may have become, then this is only because they were already affirmed by Christianity; Hegel is surely right here. However, this is not to justify Kant and Fichte after all: for what belongs to the ultimate goal is a creative, expressive freedom, and this is to be *rightly* exercised in terms of its content as well as its means. In discovering the true content, which can be objectively acknowledged by all, mutual 'recognition' by subjects is continuously renewed. But where Hegel betrays this vision, as we have already intimated, is in claiming that there is a *logic* for the determination of the true content of freedom, whose determinacy can be retrospectively grasped.

For despite the brilliance of Hegel's analysis of Jesus's teachings, it also goes badly astray, in a manner that is connected with Hegel's dialectical distortion of *praxis* and promotion of a pseudo-*Sittlichkeit*.

Hegel is unable to accept the full contingency of Jesus's founding of a new sort of human community, despite the fact that he makes concessions in this direction, which create a problem of Christian prematurity for his metanarrative. Jesus, according to the young Hegel, could not realize his moral vision in social and political terms, because he promoted it within an uncongenial environment. The Jews had (supposedly) brought to an extreme pitch the sundering of God from nature, just as the Romans had completed the separation of nature and the individual.[48] As a result, even purely 'natural' institutions like marriage, the family and economic arrangements, were brought under the governance of a complex and artificial regime of legal regulations.

---

[47] Ibid., pp. 210ff, 215, 238–9, 287. *Philosophy of Right*, p. 124.
[48] Hegel, 'The spirit of Christianity and its fate', pp. 284–6.

Precisely at this point, in connection with his view of Judaism (significantly enough) one can see how Hegel wrongly naturalizes a whole range of cultural institutions; this error is of a piece with his subordination of expression to logic and gives an altogether naturalistic cast to his notions of life against law.

According to Hegel, as a result of this supposedly unsympathetic environment, the teachings of Jesus took a world-denying direction – or rather they advocated an 'impossible' world without private property rights and without punishment.[49] Being premature, Jesus's *sittlich* morality could only be exemplified within a small, cordoned-off community, lacking any grasp of social reality. After Jesus's death, the passing away of his immediate presence into mediated 'representation' of his figure, encouraged also a projection of the community into an 'other-worldly' sphere, so that Christians were now citizens in exile. Once Christianity has become, like art, a matter of 'representation', it can be thought of as the foreshadowing in 'pictorial' and so alien terms – representing the proper human goal as situated 'elsewhere' – of the universal *sittlich* future which is only fully grasped by speculative philosophy. This moment of representation clearly has its dialectical place in the phase of 'the unhappy consciousness'; however, according to the intrusive theme of Christian prematurity, such representation is only possible as the memory of an *actual*, anticipatory *praxis*, even though this was in some ways self-deluded. And it is even the case for Hegel that this anticipatory *praxis* is perpetuated within the early Church, for it is only with the 'infinite grief' of the loss of Jesus, the loss of this person of infinite significance, that the disciples of Jesus fully grasp the idea that all subjects can participate in this infinite significance. This phase Hegel sees as the beginning of the era of the Holy Spirit, which will only be truly fulfilled when mere memory, representation and aspiration are surpassed, and the Church becomes identical with the State, the political community.[50]

However, this fulfilment is not truly the realization of a *praxis*, but the outcome of a dialectic. The true Christian *Sittlichkeit* is only possible for Hegel in the circumstances of the modern sovereign State, and the developed capitalist economy. This, however, must be accounted, against Hegel, a pseudo-*Sittlichkeit*. For a confusion is already implicit in Hegel's teaching about the 'fate' of Christianity. He stresses that at the heart of reconciliation is forgiveness, and defines forgiveness as 'the cancellation of fate', meaning by this an escape from the endless succession of offence, followed by revenge or punishment leading to further offence and further revenge.[51] The latter is a 'fated' process, because an 'offence' is precisely – according to Hegel's *natural law* theory – the attempt to ignore some aspect of reality, which will inevitably reassert itself in the form of a reminder destructive to the perpetrator.[52] Both

---

[49] Hegel, 'The spirit of Christianity and its fate', pp. 227ff, 287–301.
[50] Hegel, *Lectures on the Philosophy of Religion*, vol. 3, pp. 339–47. *Phenomenology*, p. 763. G. W. F. Hegel, *The Philosophy of History*, trans. J. Sibree (New York: Dover, 1956) pp. 341–57.
[51] Hegel, 'The spirit of Christianity and its fate', p. 236.
[52] Hegel, *Philosophy of Right*, pp. 93–4.

revenge and its modification as punishment are natural reactions, which, however, can be surmounted and 'cancelled' in forgiveness. Yet the tragedy of Jesus, for Hegel, is that forgiveness and reconciliation can never be all-encompassing: in trying to escape fate, Jesus encounters the greatest fate of all, a tragedy which conditions the entire consequent course of human history.[53] Inevitably, the refused world of the natural family, revenge/punishment, private property and exchange-relations founded on personal need wreaks the most massive revenge, a revenge which makes the space of history *Anno Domini* a wounded space, albeit that the wound is (for Hegel's Gnosticism) a *pharmakon*, a poison/cure which heals itself.

This wound of history runs so deep that Christianity, which begins by questioning the stoic world, where the public sphere is governed only by abstract rights of ownership, finishes up by entrenching abstract right yet more deeply, because the alienation of all serious content to a supernatural sphere leaves the secular world as a mere field of formalized power-relationships. By exposing the distance of normal social practice from the sacrality of 'recognition', Jesus and the Church actually open the way to a more naked and dangerous secularity, where the manipulation of power becomes a more conscious procedure. In the phase of 'the unhappy consciousness' Hegel detects not only the beginnings of a duality of ineffective piety over-against unconstrained political power, but also mutual exploitation of their duality, so that the Church makes use of the science of power, while the State clothes its operations in elements of other-worldly mystification. The main fault of 'Enlightenment', for Hegel, is that it actually *exacerbates* these features of Christendom: in the enlightened period, the 'supreme being' is fully emptied of concrete ethical content, and this form of religion colludes with an autonomous/secular culture which is similarly lacking in collective moral commitment.[54]

As an interpretation of the actual course of Christian history, this remains powerful and important.[55] However, one needs to question Hegel's dialectical account of a *necessary* tragedy: the rejection of Jesus and his teachings was surely a contingent event – as one might put it, sin's refusal of the offer of salvation. For Hegel the rejection was only inevitable because he regards the family, punishment and absolute private property rights as *natural* realities which cannot be overridden. Thus while, at a certain level, one can transcend law, there cannot, for Hegel, be a society beyond law, a society where processes of forgiveness, contrition and expiation form of themselves a self-sustaining cultural process. Yet to deny that this is at least a *possibility*, is to deny that there can be complete salvation within the physical, bodily order. And this denial belongs intrinsically with Hegel's metaphysics, which posits a sphere of 'indifference', a realm which self-expression must enter, yet whose sheerly contingent elements can never be sublated by the Idea.

---

[53] Hegel, 'The spirit of Christianity and its fate', p. 286.
[54] Hegel, *Phenomenology*, 538–57. *Philosophy of Mind*, pp. 564–73.
[55] See chapter 10 below.

This can be seen most clearly with reference to punishment and economic exchange. Hegel, like Hobbes, traces the origins of human society to individual self-seeking, which eventually gives rise to laws which merely protect established power. Against this background, crime is partly 'rational', because it protests against an undeveloped notion of right and subjectivity.[56] And punishment at this level is virtually indistinguishable from 'revenge': the reassertion of the right of force. Crime and punishment, like revenge, belong to an endless 'fatal' process, because in the realm of force, which is a realm of sheer quantitative 'indifference', one action is only 'equivalent' to another, or 'compensation' for another, in a purely arbitrary sense. No-one is ever satisfied that justice has been done; there is always a balance to be rectified; the punishment can never fit the crime.[57] In exactly the same way, the 'equivalence' established between different goods in the economic market is an arbitrary ordering on a quantitative scale of the qualitatively different and essentially incomparable. For Hegel such economic transactions, ultimately grounded in superior physical force, are both rationally necessary and yet irrational in terms of their content.[58]

Punishment, property rights and norms of exchange only become rational, according to Hegel, when their general necessity is reflected upon. A person is not legitimately punished because he has done some specific, particular damage, but only because he has violated the law which embodies the rational idea that one should in general respect other people's persons and property, as a way of acknowledging the same freedom in them which one discovers in oneself. It is rational that one should 'restore' the violated idea of the law through punishment, although the particular content of punishment is ultimately arbitrary, and determined only by the 'understanding', not by 'reason'. But punishment is only an external sign: the real punishment is internal, because in violating the freedom of others, the offender has violated his own freedom, contradicted his own rationality, and therefore has already willed his own chastisement.[59] Hegel's conceptions here are really *no different* from those of Rousseau and Kant.

In the *Philosophy of Right*, Hegel refers to this level of legal rationality as 'the administration of justice'.[60] It includes also the upholding of economic contracts and exchange relationships. Here again, the content of agreement and the relative prices of goods are arbitrary, but it is objectively rational that they should be upheld. This position goes beyond the first phase of civil society – the 'stoic' one of abstract right – and corresponds to the Christian-Kantian recognition that freedom of person and property relates to the inner dignity of the individual. But both the first phase (where only contingency is visible) and the second, are retained as necessary moments of a 'present' civil society *even*

---

[56] Hegel, *Philosophy of Right*, pp. 34–104, 94.
[57] Ibid., pp. 101. *Philosophy of Mind*, pp. 529–31.
[58] Hegel, *Philosophy of Right*, pp. 199, 232–4. *Philosophy of Mind*, pp. 533–4.
[59] Ibid., pp. 90–103.
[60] Ibid., pp. 209–29.

after they are completed by the third phase of 'police and corporation' which subsumes civil society (the familial and economic realm) in the higher sphere of the political State.[61]

It is in this third stage that one is supposed to cross the boundary between *Moralität* and *Sittlichkeit*. Yet it is hard to see that one ever really arrives. The 'police' element concerns measures to secure person and property that are not merely negative, but positive and preventative. Yet right from the outset (as we saw) Hegel identified policing as a bad infinite and a mere consequence of deontological ethics. Now he can only say that there must be limits to *surveillance* and that this depends upon local custom and 'the spirit of the rest of the constitution'.[62] *This* custom and spirit however is not part of that universal *Sittlichkeit* which will be gathered up into the absolute – on the contrary, it is on a level with the necessary but ultimately discarded contingency of punishment and prices. The real *Sittlichkeit* supposedly intrudes in other ways.

First of all, it is none other than the *division of labour*, envisaged as something which accords each of us a particular role in an organic enterprise and exhibits the secret coordination of blind 'passions' by the concealed absolute.[63] Hegel has learned from the Scots the idea of a new, modern economic 'virtue' ('commerce' is the most potent instrument of culture),[64] but it is hard to see, in his case also, how this can be any more than a Machiavellian *virtù*. In the economic sphere, there are no representational anticipations of the final goal; on the contrary, the work of reason is performed by the blind passions who are its ministers. In retrospect, the bearers of those passions can rise to reason, and reflect on how their personal striving is really in the service of the collective purpose, and yet Hegel *defines* this collective purpose precisely in terms of the making to coincide of public and private interest: 'individuals...do not live as private persons for their own ends alone, but in the very act of willing these they will the universal in the light of the universal, and their activity is consciously aimed at none but the universal end'.[65]

This is really just like Rousseau, and Hegel tries to mark a difference merely by rejecting Rousseau's truly democratic and antique republican notions of direct participation. The *sittlich* element which Rousseau has neglected turns out to be nothing other than the rule-bound exercise of economic rivalry, which Montesquieu, Stewart and Smith had identified as a surrogate for former republican virtue.[66] But the division of labour, if it is governed by the heterogenesis of ends, as Hegel suggests, cannot embody civic virtue in the sense of a direct unity between the goals pursued by work and the goals

---

[61] Ibid., pp. 231–56.

[62] Ibid., p. 234.

[63] Ibid., pp. 198, 249, 260–1. G. W. F. Hegel, *Lectures on the Philosophy of World History: Introduction*, trans. H. B. Nisbet and Duncan Forbes (Cambridge: Cambridge University Press, 1975) pp. 77, 89.

[64] Ibid., p. 247.

[65] Ibid., p. 260.

[66] Marie-Joseph Königen, 'Hegel, Adam Smith et Diderot'; in Jacques d'Hondt (ed.) *Hegel et le Siècle des Lumières* (Paris: Presses Universitaires de France, 1974).

pursued by society as a whole. The goal of a society as a whole becomes merely the unity and freedom of a quasi-collective subject. And the division of labour is seen as an automatic process, emerging as part of the developing dialectic, which allows the freedom and power of the State to be solidly grounded and fully realized. Hegel contends that the division of labour provides a *sittlich* element because it introduces a differentiated content. But this differentiation is not a cultural matter, exhibiting moral selection; on the contrary, Hegel, as a political economist, sees it as part of a merely natural expansion of wealth.

Secondly, the *sittlich* intrudes as 'corporation'. This means that economic relations can be organically apprehended at a level beneath that of the State.[67] Sympathy and shared interest arise between those already engaged – through the 'blind' workings of the passions – in similar economic enterprises. Employers and employees will come together in corporate or guild groups to protect their own members and to ensure standards of production. The same welfare concern is continued at the State level, where, despite the fact that a part of the population must be 'sacrificed' to hard manual labour, the State tries to prevent over-accumulation of wealth through-counter-measures of progressive taxation, and makes provision for the destitute.[68] Yet all this *is* still Enlightenment 'sympathy' and 'benevolence', rather than ancient architectonic virtue: the corporations and the State do not enter into the question of *what* should be made and how, nor into the determination of fair prices (as in older medieval conceptions of corporation). Instead, like the police function, they merely extend the reflection of the 'administration of justice' on the formalizable aspects of contingent processes. Thus, for example, many originally *separate* boot-makers can unite round their emergent common interests.

It is, however, true that Hegel endows his corporations with many of the qualities of the medieval guilds, expecting them to qualify the 'barbarity' of civil society. One should salute his sensibility here, while realizing that the logic of his own position exposes this expectation as wishful thinking. For, given that the division of labour is involved in the 'indifference' of the understanding, there must be limits to the sympathy between employee and employer, and limits also to a common corporate interest which will preserve standards of quality in production and merchandise. These common interests only persist insofar as they reflect the interests of the whole economy and of the State: hence their intermediary function of providing a local context for participation will tend to collapse within a basically capitalist economy.

There is, therefore, no true *Sittlichkeit* in Hegel's ethical and political theory. It is undermined by negative dialectics, which turns out to be a blend of political economy and Kantian or Fichtean deontology, mediated by Boehme's gnostic Trinitarianism. The only *telos* for Hegel, as for Kant, is subjective freedom, because this is held to be the essence of rational, delib-

[67] Hegel, *Philosophy of Right*, pp. 250–6.
[68] Ibid., p. 245.

erative *Geist*, and Hegel remains, like Kant, committed to the modern natural law paradigm, because he believes that all moral norms can be deduced from the logical implications of human nature. Hence his political theory begins with the self-seeking individual and concludes with the quasi-subject of the State organism. The 'ideality' of the State, for Hegel, is ultimately the State's own power, cohesion and freedom, and he continues to affirm, in the Machiavellian mode, the irreplaceable role of war in maintaining internal solidarity or, as he puts it, its elevation of the mere accidentality of 'property and life' to 'the work of freedom'.[69]

Hegel is, therefore, still a liberal. It is true that he departs from Kant and Fichte at the point where he argues that the logical deduction from freedom includes the various determinate expressions of freedom that have historically arisen. But this turns out to mean that he believes both in the inevitability of violent acts of appropriation (like James Stewart) which inaugurate master/slave relationships, *and* in the naturalness of the division of labour (like Adam Smith). Just as for the eighteenth-century social theorists, the unfolding of the division of labour reveals for Hegel the essential *genera* under which things can be 'represented'. But Hegel adds to this that the revelation of *genera* allows one to escape from the infinite series of the sheerly arbitrary and contingent into a sphere of 'absolute' subjectivity. Hence boot-making might be grasped in a quasi-*sittlich* fashion as an essential part of the organic whole – but the variety of styles of boots and the proper price they should fetch remain a matter of indifference.

Hegel is here profoundly *un*-Aristotelian. Justice is for him something to do with upholding laws that can be ultimately connected with the freedom of person and property. But for Aristotle, justice could not be subordinated to freedom, because the ancient philosopher produced no straightforward hierarchy of the virtues, or scheme for deducing some virtues from others. This meant that justice was for him without *criteria*, save for those which are explications of our 'sense' of justice itself.[70] Justice only has its criteria in particular examples of justice, such as a fair price in a particular instance, or a particular punishment for a particular crime. If justice is only seen in such *exempla*, then one cannot divide an 'essential' element – that there is *some* punishment or *some* fixed price – from the inessential content of the punishment, or the terms of the exchange. It is precisely here that *phronesis* must be exercised, a 'lesbian rule' that depends upon a developed 'feel' in the truly virtuous person for what is just and unjust. Such *phronesis* finds after all no real place in Hegel's thought.

Like the 'economic' thinkers again, Hegel not only denies *phronesis*, he also subordinates ethics and justice to a *theodicy* which 'demonstrates' a benign heterogenesis of ends. It is this that really undergirds his political economy. But the theodicy has now been given a new 'Behmenist' twist.

---

[69] Ibid., p. 324.
[70] See chapter 11 below.

The operation of the passions is for Hegel essential to the emergence of human freedom,[71] and yet their blind domination of human history is also the fact of human fallenness. The central Christian story concerns 'God's passion', his undergoing and enduring of these passions in self-sundering from his own freedom, which is nonetheless the ground for its ultimate concrete realization. Hegel correctly recognizes an element of 'failure' in Jesus's mission – his offer of the kingdom is rejected, and so he dies – yet he wrongly denies the contingency of this failure, and refuses to see it as the rejection by the political-economic order of a completely new sort of social imagination. Instead, Jesus's failure is the result of his own blindness to fate, and is necessary because 'passion' must be both gone through and comprehended as estrangement, if concrete justice is finally to arise. (Indeed, concerning victims of the economic passions in general, there must, Hegel says, be no 'litany of lamentations'.)[72] Yet this 'blindness to fate' means simply that Hegel places limits on the possibilities of reconciliation and forgiveness, which he so well grasps as the heart of Christian morality. And he places these limits, *not* because of some sort of commendable social 'realism', but because of his ahistorical naturalism, and his rationalistic metaphysics.

Hegel, as we have seen, only supposes that Jesus rejects the world in the sense of 'social life', because he takes private property arrangements and arbitrary punishment as necessary constituents of any conceivable social existence. For this reason, although forgiveness can 'cancel' fate, by transporting us to the higher realm of subjectivity, it cannot obliterate the realm of fate altogether. Hegel understands that forgiveness involves more than individual 'good will', that it must extend to concrete reconciliation, yet he does not understand that reconciliation is possible precisely in terms of the specific details as to the sharing of goods and the making of reparations. Otherwise, 'reconciliation' would *remain* no more than formal respect for the freedom of others. If reconciliation is real, then it involves a self-sufficient *praxis*, which is not 'founded' elsewhere in the 'fated' workings of the passions, nor in the supposedly eternal truths of political economy.

Forgiveness is not dialectically related to an ultimately arbitrary law and punishment (Hegel's views here are a compound of Luther and Boehme); instead one should think of forgiveness as a different 'way of life' beyond the law, which radicalizes the stress of the *Jewish* law that no-one is constrained to belong to a particular social community, with its particular collective norms. As a 'way of life', forgiveness and reconciliation include elements of 'atonement' and 'penance' – the voluntary offering of signs and deeds which compensate for past faults and redress the balance. Where the particular content of punishment is not regarded as indifferent, it is much easier to pass over to the idea that *assent* to punishment and 'compensation' are the vital elements within punishment; at this point punishment itself passes

---

[71] Hegel, *Lectures on the Philosophy of World History*, pp. 71–7.
[72] Ibid., p. 91.

'beyond the law'.[73] One should say that, in Jesus's teachings, salvation is measured by the extension of forgiveness as an autonomous practice; but for Hegel's gnostic notions, salvation is the inevitable falling away into passion, and the return from this indifference back to a reconciliation that is really founded in the abstract kinship of one person's freedom to that of another.

Hegel only imagines that there is an indifferent world which cannot be wholly reconciled, because he thinks of punishment as the natural reflex of a neglected or thwarted aspect of reality. Thus he fails to identify punishment as a particular cultural language (however universally written and spoken) which is not a work of negation, but simply the positive piling of violence upon violence. In the latter case, punishment is never in essence self-punishment (as Hegel claims) but always a particular new social relation to the offender. The only way, therefore, to bring about reconciliation is to have a system of 'punishment' – of atoning suffering and compensation – to which all parties assent. And this means that reconciliation *is only possible at all* within the space of the indifferent, of the despised contingencies, despite the fact that the 'adjustments' involved in such exchanges can only ever be approximate, and lack criteria outside the agreement of the parties involved. In his notion of Jesus's appeal to 'life' against the law, Hegel only half-grasps Jesus's pragmatism: a full grasp would situate 'the kingdom' entirely within the realm of particular cultural practice, not in dialectical suspense between nature on the one hand, and the spiritual subject on the other.

There is no true *sittlich* in Hegel, and in this respect his moral philosophy succeeds less in overcoming 'secular reason' than that of Herder or Friedrich Schleiermacher. Both these thinkers give more satisfactory accounts than Hegel does of how one can supplement antique notions of virtue with Christian attention to personal freedom. Herder affirmed (rather like Irenaeus) a progress purely *within* the good, not from evil to good, and refused the economic idea of 'depravity' as 'a necessary condition for improvement and order'.[74] Schleiermacher stressed that freedom is a value insofar as it is connected with the *content* of individualizing expression, and that it is precisely *in* such expression (whether of particular persons or particular communities) that one has access to ideals of 'the Good'. Here history has truly the value of tradition and example, and the *narration* of ethical life, which is essential for ethical teaching, is not overtaken by an extractable logic.[75]

Such a philosophy of history, which is at one with a *sittlich* morality, was not achieved by Hegel; he preferred idealism, Boehme and political economy.

---

[73] See chapter 12 below.
[74] Herder, 'Yet another philosophy of history', p. 194.
[75] *Friedrich Schleiermacher, Grundlinien einer kritik der bisherigen Sittenlehre*, in Otto Braun and Johannes Bauer (eds.) *Werke*, Band I (Aalen: Scientia Verlag, 1968) paras. 8, 104, 108, 111–13. Herder, 'Yet another philosophy of history', pp. 187–8.

Yet Schleiermacher was not able to conceive a fully Christian *Sittlichkeit*, because religion for him (here his Kantian categorization overrides the Herderian elements) was concerned with 'piety' and 'feeling', not primarily with ethical actions.[76] Hegel in fact came nearer to such a conception. One can say that, trapped within his impossible meta-narrative of universal reason, lies concealed – its presence betrayed by 'prematurity' – the plain unfounded narrative of Christianity which is only 'universal' for those who situate themselves within it. The best way to 'retrieve' Hegel would be to try to see this narrative of Christian *Bildung* as itself 'foundational'.

In the final chapter of this book, we shall see the relevance of such a retrieval. Only in the context of the Christian narrative, not the dialectical metanarrative, should one take seriously the Hegelian view that it is the quest for the Absolute which provides the possibility of social and political critique.[77] This holds true for Hegel, because the quest for a more human world is the quest for a world where human aspiration and existing reality can be brought into a state of identity, and human aspirations are only viable if they correspond with the way things ultimately are. Yet this view can be affirmed all the more strongly if one denies that this correspondence is rationally demonstrable. If, on the contrary, it is only to be believed in by faith and searched for through practices, then it can be truly undergirded by belief in a transcendent, creative God. Thus despite the balance of the verdict turning 'against Hegel', I shall still uphold, against Marx, that theology, far from being mystification, is the only possible source for a political critique which claims to be grounded in 'truth'.

[76] F. D. E. Schleiermacher, *The Christian Faith* (Edinburgh: T. and T. Clark, 1928) pp. 3–5.

[77] Michael Theunissen, *Hegels Lehre von Absoluten Geist als Theologisch-Politischer Traktate* (Berlin: W. de Gruyter, 1970) pp. 77–100.

7

For and Against Marx

Introduction

In his critique of Hegel's political philosophy, Karl Marx makes a point which is close to my critical exposure of the 'realm of indifference' in the preceding chapter: the political freedom realized in the State, which Hegel champions, cannot be seriously distinguished from the mere economic freedom of 'civil society'.[1] Marx decisively breaks with Hegel, because he denies that civil society, or the realm of indifference, is a permanent, natural aspect of human community. Instead, he shows that the 'laws' of political economy are only (partially adequate) descriptions of the functioning of one particular economic arrangement, namely capitalism. Likewise, he shows that the absolute sovereign State, standing 'over against' society, is not a permanent necessity, but embodies certain assumptions that can be called into question.

Because he gives a critique of political economy and modern 'political science', both of which, as I have shown, help to define and construct 'secular' power and authority, it is possible to read Marx as a deconstructor of the secular. In this sense, the following chapter is 'for Marx', and will insist that certain elements of the Marxist critique of capitalism and the State need to be retained and re-elaborated. Yet at the same time, Marx altogether fails to realize the sheer contingency of the capitalist system as a whole, and to see that it can only be morally criticized and opposed in the name of another, equally contingent vision and practice. Instead, Marx retains the perspectives of liberalism in two distinct ways.

First of all, he gives a 'materialist' version of Hegel's dialectics, which still regards the capitalist economy as a *necessary* phase within the process of human becoming. Secondly, the utopian phase, which Marx envisages as inevitably supervening upon the collapse of capitalism, is conceived primarily in terms of the unleashing of human freedom and the unlimited possibility of human transformation of nature. This essentially liberal and secular goal is

---

[1] Karl Marx, 'Critique of Hegel's doctrine of the State', in *Early Writings*, trans. Rodney Livingstone and Gregor Benton (Harmondsworth: Penguin, 1984) pp. 58ff, 171.

no longer secured through market competition or state policing, but instead through the mysterious return of a lost harmony with nature, such that nature is clearly seen again as man's 'inorganic body', and the full development of human powers occurs spontaneously and without social 'antagonism', once certain cultural illusions – akin to religious illusions – have been overcome. Whereas Hegel envisages religion and the State – in the sense of a *sittlich* communal order – as a source of critique of civil society, Marx seeks for a critique in an impossible naturalism which deduces man's true cultural goal from his essence as 'species being'. Thus the true *theological* verdict on Marx – it will be argued – should be the following: on the one hand he promisingly calls into question the sundering of the sphere of 'making' from the sphere of 'values', and hence the separation of a 'technologically' conceived economics and politics from ethics, aesthetics and religion. On the other hand, the single realm of expression of human capacity, which embraces all these spheres, is conceived far too voluntaristically and naturalistically. Ultimately, modern natural law, and modern secular order are retained by Marx, but reworked as the myth of a natural process working towards an eventual harmony and equilibrium.

In the following three sections, these arguments will be unfolded in the following order: first, I shall indicate the mistaken assumptions involved in the Marxist shift from religion as source of critique, to religion as object of critique; secondly, I shall show that while Marx was able, in his own day, to penetrate uniquely the 'grammar' of capitalism, this grammar needs to be both elaborated, and separated from the view that capitalism is at once necessary and yet irrational. In the third place, and as a prelude to my critique of contemporary political theology, I shall argue that, while certain elements of Marx's analyses need to be assimilated, a more fundamental critique of capitalism is discovered in the traditions of Christian and republican socialism.

The Marxist Critique of Religion

The full complexity of the Marxist critique of religion has rarely been brought to light. To appreciate this, one must realize that it combines an 'antique materialist' element, a Feuerbachian materialist element, and an Hegelian dialectical element. According to the 'antique materialist' view, religion is culturally and historically 'later' and not original; it is the result of linguistic illusions, political mystification, and forgetting of human labour. According to the Feuerbachian view, religion possesses a genuine content, but has substituted an imaginary divine subject in place of 'man', its true subject. It is the third, Hegelian element which appropriately combines these two views together: the historically later illusion was a dialectically necessary illusion, and the epiphenomenon of socially mystifying processes. The Feuerbachian process of projection, alienation and return to the true human subject must be told as the narrative of human social, economic and political becoming.

By the time of the *German Ideology*, Marx had fully absorbed the Comtean picture of history as a journey from an initial, to a final, 'positive' state. In the 'pre-historical' human era, as Marx presents it in that work, there was no division of labour, and no separation between theory and practice. Thinking was the 'direct efflux' of 'material behaviour', and so there was no such thing as philosophy, and religion was totally 'natural', bound up with an expression of awe in the face of the physical environment with which human beings had constantly to grapple.[2] Just as for Comte, so for Marx, in primitive society 'science' is at one with the totality of relationships of man to man and man to nature, and this science is, itself, the only 'religion'. (The Tenth Thesis on Feuerbach indeed talks of 'the standpoint... of social humanity' replacing the individualistic, political economic standpoint of 'civil society'.)[3] Religion in a pejorative, reprehensible sense emerges only with the first division of labour. A priestly class foments the illusion that theoretical activity has its own *raison d'être* apart from *praxis*, and so philosophy is born, and imaginary theoretical objects – the 'gods' – are granted objective existence.[4]

Here Marx is giving his own version of ancient materialistic accounts of the birth of religion as the birth of illusion. Characteristically, these involved the interweaving of the themes of priestly trickery and of human self-delusion by its own linguistic inventions.[5] In primitive times, so these accounts ran, the original sensory reference of language was lost sight of, and metaphoric substitution necessary for the naming of real but unfamiliar objects was falsely extended to the catachretic imagining of unreal 'spiritual' objects – for example, the 'breath' of human life became a hypostasized 'soul'. But the objection to this materialistic critique, already voiced by Vico and Herder in the eighteenth century, is that metaphoric substitution is always already involved in every signifying procedure, insofar as every articulation of 'something' in terms of 'something else' necessary for there to be a 'meaning', involves more than the mere equivalence of a statement to a state of affairs.[6] Instead, meaning tries to *express*, and not merely to reflect, the tensions and transitions which constitute reality. For this reason, meaning is necessarily imprecise, incomplete and indeterminate. And this indeterminacy pinpoints the difference between nature and culture: every culture has its own metaphorical system and its own privileged metaphors which govern how it

---

[2] Karl Marx and Friedrich Engels, *The German Ideology* (Moscow: Progress Publishers, 1964) pp. 36–9, 42.

[3] Karl Marx, 'Thesis on Feuerbach', no. 10, in *Early Writings*, p. 423.

[4] Marx and Engels, *The German Ideology*, pp. 42–3.

[5] Jacques Derrida, 'Scribble (pouvoir/écrire)' and Patrick Tort, 'Transfigurations (Archéologie du Symbolique)', in Jacques Derrida and Patrick Tort (eds.), William Warburton, *Essai sur les Hiéroglyphes des Egyptiens* (Paris: Aubier Montaigne, 1977) pp. 4–15, 45–89.

[6] John Milbank, '*The Word Made Strange* (Oxford: Blackwell, 1977) pp 55–123.

understands what underlies the tensions of reality, or to what *telos* they are ultimately directed. Every culture must 'dispose' nature in a particular way, and in consequence there is no such thing as a purely 'natural' religion; nor will any 'natural' semantics indicate to us whether the forces of life or soul are material or more-than-material, always conjoined with matter as we know it, or sometimes separable from it, whether as 'spirit', or a less finitely-bound sort of body.

What is important to realize about the 'antique materialist' element in Marx's critique of religion, is that it stands or falls with his general view of the pre-historical beginning. The idea that original human meaning was natural, practical, and free of religious illusion, is questionable for the same reasons as the idea of a society before any division of labour, or a society geared only to positive purposes of work and personal relationship. Just as consciousness and language are never purely to do with communication – as Marx tends to imagine – but rather communication only arises in the course of the mutual elaboration of a 'mythical' expression of human interrelationships, so, also, specifically human labour occurs in the context of a particular (political) hierarchy of purposes which tends to engender emulation, rivalry, exchange of goods, and (usually) some degree of distribution of tasks.

While the 'antique materialist' critique of religion could be metacritically overthrown, it still possessed the merits of referring religion back to language and to social processes. The same thing cannot be said of Feuerbach's critique of religion, which exemplifies the contrast between the French outright rejection of Christianity and the German mode of 'retreat in due order' that attempts to salvage Christian dogmatic and ethical content in anthropological terms. Theologians often confuse Europe with Germany, so that they regard this gradual retreat as the main mode of European de-Christianization; the gradualness then takes on for them the appearance of an historical inevitability which theology must 'come to terms with'. But this disguises from view the earlier French Enlightenment return of a more *perennially renewed* clash between unbelief and belief.

It is, in fact, more helpful to view Feuerbach's work, not as a stage in a long story of retreat, but rather as another example of the nineteenth-century post-Enlightenment reaction *in favour* of religion, albeit in this case in the form of a search for a 'religion of humanity'. Earlier unbelievers had not necessarily wanted to deify man – to deify nature, rather, more commonly – but Feuerbach's goal was precisely to exhibit man as truly and in essence the subject of the divine predicates, the worthy object of worship.[7] His entire theory of 'projection' rests not – as for antique materialism – on the idea that religion generates through language a wholly illusory content, but rather on the idea that the content is displaced from its real site, man, to an imaginary site, God.

---

[7] Ludwig Feuerbach, *The Essence of Christianity*, trans. George Eliot (New York: Harper and Row, 1957) p. 31.

His critique of supernatural religion therefore depends upon a religious belief in 'man'.

The precariousness of this exercise is best shown by the fact that 'projection' is by no means a wholly negative category for Feuerbach. On the contrary, meaning is first of all found by us insofar as we posit it in the 'other', whether an object or a person.[8] The point at which we posit meaning is precisely the point of temporarily necessary religious illusion, for, at first, we imagine that attributes discovered in the other are placed there by a transcendent source to whom they pre-eminently belong. This moment is shown to be illusory, only because it is possible to receive back the qualities found in others as qualities known by us through their transcendental source in our own human ego. If Feuerbach had attended to Schelling's and Hegel's arguments against Fichte, his entire critique of Christianity would have broken down, because then he would have had to recognize that the moment of 'intuition' in objective, natural reality of truthful, aesthetic and moral qualities, is not reducible to the 'self-positing' of the Fichtean ego without a loss of real concrete content – the 'attributes' of God, which Feuerbach is trying to save for man.[9] If one thinks further than Hegel along these anti-Fichtean lines, then it is clear that all thought is projection-without-return, a process that we are not 'in charge of'. Reason may therefore plausibly subscribe to belief in a transcendent source which is itself the speculative object of our thinking/projecting.

Marx – at least in his early years – attempted to graft Feuerbachian 'warm' materialism onto Anglo-French 'cold' materialism. In ostensible opposition to Feuerbach, yet also in continuity with him, Marx wanted to surpass a merely contemplative materialism which could only comprehend the isolated individual of civil society, in favour of a grasp of 'sensuousness as practical activity'.[10] Here the whole, formerly spiritual content of ethics, religion, art and culture could be retained, but returned to its true sphere as a natural part of *praxis*. Marx assented to Feuerbach's notion that the alienated religious and theoretical riches were to be restored to man's real, practical existence. He also half-assented, in his earlier writings, to the view that the 'criticism of religion was the premise of all criticism', and that once the heavenly *oratio pro aris et focis* was discredited, then the 'profane existence of error' could be dealt with.[11] This appears to suggest that religious error is the *origo et fons* of all error.[12] Yet already in the *Contribution to a Critique of Hegel's Philosophy of Right* where the phrase appears, and in the *Theses on Feuerbach*, Marx takes Feuerbach to task for failing to trace religious error to its ground in the configurations of social power – for ignoring (despite Marx's *hubris* concerning 'the defect of all hitherto existing materialism') key elements in the 'antique

---

[8] Ibid., pp. 1–17.

[9] Gillian Rose, *Hegel Contra Sociology*, p. 210.

[10] Karl Marx, 'Theses on Feuerbach', no. 9, p. 423.

[11] Karl Marx, 'A contribution to the critique of Hegel's philosophy of right: Introduction', in *Early Writings*, p. 243.

[12] Ibid., p. 243ff. 'Economic and philosophical manuscripts', in *Early Writings*, p. 281.

materialist' tradition.[13] And later, in *The German Ideology*, and in *Das Kapital*, Marx is quite clear that the true critical method proceeds genetically, from the material base upwards, so that the critical goal is, quite literally, to demonstrate the inevitability of religious error as part of the history of *technology*, or of the history of human interactions with nature.[14] Post pre-historic history, which generates theoretical and religious illusion, is to be written from a positive and pre-historic vantage point, in order to show that while history appears to depart from nature, the very illusions of history are themselves the work of nature, such that in reality we have remained 'primitive' all along. The problems of such a critical proposal will be returned to shortly.

Had Marx's position altered by the time of *The German Ideology*? Not really, I would argue, because there remains a consistently ambiguous attitude on Marx's part to German philosophy, which he treats as an aspect of German cultural belatedness. Germany is behind, culturally and politically, yet in its efforts to catch up, it produces a sort of inverted image of western European progress.[15] Instead of the market taking the lead in economic development, the lead is taken by the State; instead of the liberal State preceding the articulation of liberal theoretical principles, in Germany political theory is far in advance of a lingering *ancien régime*. And yet, Marx implies, there is also a theoretical advantage in belatedness: German liberal defining-of-itself against German absolutism is more rigorous than Anglo-French liberalism, and more clearly reveals the imperfect liberalization of all western European states. Marx, of course, considers that he has himself brought to perfection the German critique of the State. And his own procedure is initially belated, because he starts with the State and not with what really maintains the State in being, the economy. Yet Marx perhaps saw an advantage here also: in focusing on the State, he grasped clearly the principle of abstractive alienation, namely that people treated the State as if it were a real entity apart from their own collective activity, standing 'over against them'.[16] The facts of alienation and reification are revealed more clearly at the superstructural level, although they are founded on an alienation and reification endemic to the capitalist economic base. In a parallel fashion, religion reveals these things more clearly still: for it is the 'general theory' of an alienated and inverted world, its 'encyclopaedic compendium ... its logic in a popular form'.[17]

There are then, for Marx, advantages in starting 'back to front'. In their analyses of religion, Hegel and the young Hegelians are considered to have pointed towards various phenomena – the practical character of human consciousness, the dialectic process of human society, the alienation of

---

[13] Marx, 'Thesis on Feuerbach', pp. 421–23.

[14] Marx and Engels, *The German Ideology*, pp. 37–42. *Capital: A Critique of Political Economy*, vol. 1, Part IV, ch. 15, trans. Samuel Moore and Edward Aveling (London: Lawrence and Wishart, 1983) p. 352.

[15] Marx, 'Critique of Hegel's philosophy of right', p. 246ff. *The German Ideology*, p. 29.

[16] Marx, 'Critique of Hegel's doctrine of the state'. 'Critique of Hegel's philosophy of right'.

[17] Ibid., p. 244.

human powers – ignored by the English and French materialists.[18] Religion is a secondary, superstructural phenomenon which must ultimately be explained by the genetic method, yet it also sums up, and exposes to the view of a suspicious gaze, the elusive logic of the economic base which evaded the sight of the political economists.

However, this can only be the case for Marx, because he *accepts* the Hegelian view which sees the State as embodying religious beliefs and practice, and thereby alone establishing itself. Marx tries to show, against Hegel, that the State in reality promotes merely the purposes of capitalism, but this involves him (because of this basic Hegelianism) in also arguing that it is the economic base which really operates 'like a religion'. Where Hegel reads historical society as the objective presence of God, Marx reads historical society as, right down to its economic *base*, the religious *illusion* of this presence. This is clearly indicated by all the coy and knowing metaphors comparing capitalist processes to Christian sacramental practices. It is the subversion and yet the acceptance of the Hegelian identification of state and civil society with religion, which allows Marx to combine a genetic, 'chronological' account of religion with a persisting humanist belief that the critique of religion is the key to critique as such.

However, before considering the central, 'transformed Hegelian' stress in Marx's critique of religion, it is important to be clear about an element in his thinking that remains merely Feuerbachian, and not Hegelian at all. This is the idea that religion is always and everywhere 'epiphenomenal', the projection of a projection. Marx historicizes Feuerbach to the extent that he refers religious projection to historical social processes (a move which Feuerbach himself half implies). But he fails to historicize Feuerbach to the extent that he sees religion as always occupying the same superstructural position in any possible human society. Marx says that religion *as religion* has no history, undergoes no development.[19]

By contrast, Hegel is much more historicist at this point: in certain societies, religion may stand close to the realm of 'art', in others to the area of ordinary social transactions. Marx not only denies, without reason, the possibility that religion may sometimes be the key determining cause at work, he also (more than Hegel) confines religion to 'belief', ignoring the fact of religious practice. This compounds the problem of why there should be, in Marx's view, a *separate* phenomenon of religion at all; if economic and political practices contain theoretical illusions (alienation, fetishization, reification) endemic to these practices, then why do they generate a further, 'epiphenomenal' layer of religious illusion? One could perhaps explain this in terms of religion as consolation, but Marx (unlike Nietzsche) does not really develop this theme,

[18] Karl Marx, 'The Holy Family, or critique of critical criticism', in Karl Marx and Friedrich Engels, *On Religion* (Moscow: Progress Publishers, 1975) pp. 53–61.

[19] Marx and Engels, *The German Ideology*, p. 38. 'Economic and philosophical manuscripts', p. 386. Rose, *Hegel Contra Sociology*, pp. 216–19.

and places much more stress on the *function* of religion in upholding systems of power, and operating as a 'dominant ideology'. The question here is, if, as Marx claims, the self-disguising of capitalism is so effective and complete, why does this need to be supplemented by religious illusion? Marx compares the commodity to a fetishistic sacred object and to an incarnate god, but cannot answer the question, why are capitalist commodities not actually *identified* with gods, or alternatively, why commodities *plus* gods?[20]

By presenting a Hegelian comparison of the economy at the level of the social relationships of production to religious belief and practice, Marx brings together antique and humanist materialism, yet renders his entire critique of religion somewhat precarious. To avoid the Hegelian historicist notion that religion – as 'the logic of a practice' – can be ultimately determinative, he faces a double task. First, he must confine religion always to an epiphenomenal, superstructural level. But secondly, he has to show that the 'quasi-religious' character of economic relations, which he compares to the operation of a semiotic system, is really governed by purely 'material' changes at the level of technology, and the development of 'forces of production' (which include the organization of human labour). Yet the entire story which Marx relates of the inevitable transformations at the level of the social relations of production, is still told, throughout *Das Kapital* and the *Grundrisse*, in entirely dialectical, and 'religious' terms. *Only* in telling this 'religious' story is Marx able to position and explain religion: one thus arrives at a similar paradox to that pointed out in the case of Durkheim. Let us see how this is the case.

In the first place, Marx accepts the Hegelian and Feuerbachian view that Christianity represents the highest development of religion as such: Christianity provides the key to the nature of all religion, although only after it has become self-critical.[21] Thus, the critique of religion is not, as for supposedly 'vulgar' materialism, a perennial possibility: on the contrary, it is precisely positioned on the historical agenda of the development of religion itself. In a similar fashion, says Marx (making an explicit comparison), capitalism provides the key to the nature of *every* economic system, although only after capitalism has come to be critically considered.[22] The two processes of determined development, religious and economic, run in precise parallel, culminating with Christianity as the most 'abstract' and contentless religion, and capitalism as the economy most regulated by the 'non-reality' of value. Of course, the economy is supposed to determine religion, but in fact the economy is presented as governed by the dialectical logic which Hegel ascribed to religion, and is only distinguished from 'religion' – an ideal, logical process – in terms of the precarious thesis of the priority of the (natural and uncoded) forces of production over the (conventional and coded) relations of production.

---

[20] Marx, *Capital*, vol. 1, pp. 76ff, 80. Bryan S. Turner, *Religion and Social Theory*, pp. 38–62.

[21] Karl Marx, *Grundrisse*, trans. Martin Nicolaus (London: Pelican, 1973) pp. 105–6.

[22] Ibid. *Capital*, vol, 1, pp. 31, 85.

In the second place, in order to go beyond the mere parallelism, Marx tries to show that the historical economic development has generated religious illusion, because it is *itself* governed by an illusion-generating logic. His analysis here is focused round the capitalist 'commodity', which is inherently 'mystical' and 'metaphysical', described by Marx as a 'social hieroglyph'.[23] This term recalls precisely the antique materialist notion (elaborated in the eighteenth century) that pictographic writing had originally an innocent, communicative purpose which was later forgotten, allowing a priestly class to appropriate hieroglyphs as mysterious symbols of divinity revealed to men by the gods themselves. The commodity is a hieroglyph, because it exists through the obliteration of its own genesis as a condition of its functioning; men forget that the 'value' embodied in the commodity expresses only the dispositions of power that persist within the human community. There is 'alienation' involved here, in the sense that human beings treat value and the commodity as if they possessed a sacramental efficacy, or a power in their own right. 'Reification' is also implied as the converse aspect of alienation: if human subjective powers are projected onto things, then human beings are represented as the mere objects of processes beyond their control. Finally, 'fetishization' is also involved, because the value of the commodity is not, for capitalism, its real 'use value', but rather its 'exchange value', which involves treating as equivalent the inherently non-equivalent and incomparable.[24]

In all three instances, the economic illusion exactly parallels the religious illusion: human beings imagine unreal, 'universal' entities, and ascribe to them a causality which is properly human. In fact, insofar as the religious illusion is grounded in the economic illusion, and furthermore, the latter illusion is itself not just *like* religious illusion, but actually a *variant* of it, Marx's critique of religion can only be valid if his account of economic processes is valid. The real religious projection happens within the economic projection – so much so that Marx assumes (by virtue of his almost 'occasion-alist' construal of Hegel's theology) that the 'God' of Judaism and Christianity stands for some causal power at work *within* the finite world, the power of the State, or of civil society. He never confronts at all the fact that 'God', for orthodox belief, indicates a purely transcendent, final causality, and for this reason must always remain partially unknown, only to be invoked as a cause when one is asking questions about the reason and purpose of Being as a whole.[25] For this reason, his criticism of political economy as a kind of religious belief, and of the capitalist economy as a kind of religious practice, only holds (and only functions further as a critique of Christianity) because he effectively *accepts* political economy's *own appropriation* of Christianity,

---

[23] Ibid., pp. 78–9.

[24] Ibid., pp. 48–87. Marx, 'Economic and philosophical manuscripts', pp. 324–34, 383–400.

[25] I recall Nicholas Lash making a point along these lines, at a lecture in the Cambridge Divinity School, circa 1979. See also Nicholas Lash, *A Matter of Hope; A Theologian's Reflections on the Thought of Karl Marx* (London: Darton, Longman and Todd, 1981).

which invokes God as heterogenesis, or as a cause required to fill a gap in finite explanation.

As to the account of the economic processes themselves, what Marx purports to provide is an account of how, in this area also, human beings have been subject to 'religious' illusion. But in actual fact this illusion is only 'exposed' within the framework of a humanist/positivist metanarrative which itself reflects a variant of religious immanentism.

One can discuss this metanarrative under the headings 'myth of origins' and 'myth of dialectical becoming'. In the first instance, Marx's critique of the 'hieroglyph' remains within the terms of antique materialism, which failed to perceive, as we saw earlier in the chapter, that *every* cultural reality is necessarily 'hieroglyphic' insofar as it deploys meanings which are always indeterminate and therefore escape its total control. Marx himself is actually close to recognizing this, because he knows that all specifically economic (as opposed to technological) categories fall within the realm of signs, and he knows, also, that the capitalist illusion is not an illusion in the sense of an appearance concealing an underlying reality (as commentators often wrongly suppose) but rather an illusion in the sense of a 'dramatic fiction' which human beings enact without recognizing its fictional character. This is clearly the case, because capital only has power over labour to the degree that the 'language of commodities' is generally accepted, and labour itself is fetishized as generalized, quantifiable labour time. There is only power *through* illusion, and all that really gets concealed is the unreal, imaginary character of value, the commodity and fetishized labour.[26]

However, Marx accepts too readily the notion of illusion, and fails to reflect that to be human, or to be a cultural being, is *necessarily* to inhabit a fiction. Merely to come to recognize the fictional character of capitalism need not lead one to denounce it as 'illusion', nor as the irrational seduction of humanity by its own signifying powers. To take the three key instances of fetishization, alienation and reification: it is true, in relation to fetishization, that to make different commodities and kinds of labour 'equivalent' in terms of abstract quantifiability cannot be rationally justified; it is true, also, that not all cultures operate this mode of equivalence, which is uniquely well adapted for calculation and predictability. However, *all* cultures operate, in their social relationships, some principle of equivalence, of 'equalizing the unequal' – this undergirds punishment and compensation as much as barter and gift-exchange – and *none* of these principles of equivalence can be rationally founded. In this sense, the capitalist 'economy' – or simultaneous disposition of forces and meanings-as-equivalences – is no more rational or irrational than any other economy.

As Jean Baudrillard has pointed out, Marx's critique of 'exchange-value' sustains an insupportable nominalism, because no specifically cultural use-

---

[26] Marx, *Capital*, vol. 1, pp. 43–87.

value really exists outside the various conventions of comparison and goal-orientated transformation which articulate things and capacities only in rela-tion to other things and capacities.[27] But Jean-François Lyotard is right to reject Baudrillard's celebration of primitive 'symbolic exchange' (where the things exchanged are seen as participating in each other, cannot be abstract-edly represented by money, and cannot be accumulated because they only have value in the 'gift' situation of exchange) as implicitly more 'natural' than capitalist exchange.[28] As he argues, from a 'rational' point of view symbolic exchange is just an alternative *dispositif*, and, moreover, one which may be just as inscribed by power, in the shape of rivalry in the exercise of patronage. Here accumulation is in fact not alien to the gift relationship, and the dimen-sions of time and production – in the sense of the construction and sustaining of an entire social process – are just as present in primitive as in capitalist society. Baudrillard is wrong, therefore, if he thinks one can give an alterna-tive demystification of capitalism, not in terms of use-value versus exchange-value, but in terms of exchange versus production. Capitalism does *not* suppress exchange by production, but makes both more abstract, quantifiable and, in principle, predictable.

If this abstract equivalence is not, as liberalism assumes, 'more rational' than traditional symbolism, it is nonetheless not 'less rational' – or rather, its irrationality cannot be demonstrated through the application of universal theoretical criteria (even if they are those of Kantian 'practical reason'), as the Frankfurt school and others have imagined.

In his talk of fetishization, therefore, Marx correctly identified an element in the logic of capitalism, and showed also that this logic is often concealed in the interests of power. He did not, however, succeed in demonstrating that this logic is inherently illusory, nor even that a wider recognition of this logic would cause it to lose its fascination and charm. Similar considerations apply to alienation and reification. 'Alienation' assumes that there are a set of needs and capacities proper and natural to human beings, which become distorted when these needs and capacities are defined by an illusory cultural logic, whose human invention is suppressed and forgotten. Yet, in fact, one element in Marx's conception of the human *proprium*, namely the unlim-ited development of all human and natural powers, is clearly derived from the capitalist projection of wealth accumulation as the ultimate goal, in con-trast to other societies which specify goals in terms of *what* is to be produced, and which *kinds* of human capacity are to be encouraged. To this degree, Baudrillard is right to argue that Marx sees production as the mirror in which human nature recognizes itself, without realizing that this is no neutral narcissistic reflection, but merely the distorting perspective of the glass called 'political economy'.[29]

[27] Jean Baudrillard *The Mirror of Production*, trans. Mark Poster (St Louis: Telos, 1975).
[28] J.-F. Lyotard, *Économie Libidinale* (Paris: Minuit, 1974) pp. 126–33.
[29] Baudrillard, *The Mirror of Production*.

Just as we have no access to purely 'natural' needs and capacities, so also it is true that there is no human property which is not something appropriated, not entirely in our possession at all. Right from the outset, we only have identity to the extent that we 'identify with' what is other to us, and therefore alien. And only *through* our submission to commodity production do we acquire the idea of ourselves as producing subjects, and so it is only through this submission that we possess this particular 'capacity'. Although capitalism is not natural, it is just as true that capitalism creates capitalist humanity as that capitalist humanity creates capitalism, and for this reason, the continued creation of capitalism is only possible if humanity is invented as an 'object' of a certain kind for capitalist processes. As with every culture, it is only on condition of being 'reified', or of permitting our consciousness to be structurally constituted by processes we have not originated, that we are also able to act as subjects, which means to allow our intentions to be embodied in alien 'things' which then can act back on us as 'quasi-subjects'.

The personification of things and the objectification of subjects expresses, therefore, the inescapable *pathos* of culture. This *pathos* would only become fallacious if subject and object were totally to change places, but this is as impossible as Marx's utopian notion of an innocent subject confronting an uncontaminated object. At no point in the capitalist process does 'alienation' necessarily mean a concealment of subjective freedom; even the conditions of appropriated labour under which the labourer is deprived of a part of the value of what he produces *can* come to be increasingly assented to by the labourer, who thereby makes a continual choice for the regularity, predictability and ease of commodity production, and the security, relaxation and leisure which the wage labourer may (in recent capitalism especially) come to enjoy. (Notice that I am *not* denying Marx's correct exposure of supposedly 'neutral' economic relations as embodying the 'political' exercise of power by some groups over others. What I *am* denying is the idea that capitalism necessarily and contradictorily produces a subject antagonistic to itself.)

The trio fetishization-alienation-reification therefore has its value merely to the degree that it identifies a particular mode of equivalence, of objectification and subjectification. In describing capitalism in these terms, Marx's account has the advantage of showing that 'religious' reasoning is not so remote from semiotic processes in general, so that while he takes religion and philosophy back into the practical sphere of making/doing (*praxis*) he is also able to demonstrate that all historical makings are not just 'technological', but governed by a thoroughly 'religious' logic. In this sense, Marx deconstructs the realm of the secular, but unfortunately he relocates the secular as the buried natural 'origin', which is to be regained at a higher level. His valid (but unrealized) insight is that religious logic is no more nor less strange than cultural logic in general; this allows one to go on to recognize that the 'critique of religion' is an impossible venture. But the invalid context for this insight is the notion of a general cultural estrangement from a 'natural' humanity, or species-being, which can consciously bring all natural capacities to fruition.[30] Hence the issue about the validity of Marx's critique of religion must be entirely transformed into the question of the validity of his critique of historical culture in general, and economic processes in particular.

As a 'myth of origins', this critique is a failure. But it is also a failure as a 'myth of dialectical becoming'. In his mature texts, Marx quite clearly insists that switches from one mode of production to another are in the last analysis determined by developments in the 'forces of production', of technological inventions and organization of the division of labour.[31] But there are also clear signs that he did not abandon his analysis of the social relations of production in terms of fetishization, alienation and reification.[32] Indeed, it is only this analysis which permits Marx to see the final stage beyond capitalism as qualitatively different from all that has gone before – a stage of non-antagonism and of 'unlimited production' – when human beings are simply 'at one' with their natural practical capacities, which include all their 'spiritual' and expressive strivings. There is no detectable tension between a 'positivist' and a 'humanist' Marx here: on the contrary, humanism and positivism become two sides of the same coin, because it is only in the final stage of freedom from illusion, and return to the objective and unproblematic, that all human capacities can be realized without contest, and without violent struggle. The scientific future is also the future of humanist freedom, even if Marx gradually institutes a clearer division between the collective industrial performance of 'necessary' work and the private enjoyment of a creative leisure.[33] Already, in *The Poverty of Philosophy*, he has little time for the 'craft idiocy' which thinks that each person in his work occupation ought to be able to enjoy some sort of creative fulfilment. Indeed, it is through the division of labour in the automatic workshop that 'the need for universality, the tendency towards an integrated development of the individual begins to be felt'.[34] *This* is Marx's humanism, and William Morris's celebration of craft was surely much more in the line of Proudhon, whom Marx is here attacking.

The qualitative distinction of history from both pre- and post-history, requires, therefore, Marx's account of the 'logic' of the relations of production. The 'dialectical' elements in this logic – namely the projections and displacements involved – are regarded by Marx as equivalent to the projections and displacements sanctioned by Hegelian idealism: to this extent, therefore, the tracing of the dialectical process is the tracing of an illusion, and, as Lucio Colletti points out, the end of this illusion, the utopian future, is unlike the Hegelian resolution of the dialectic in that it preserves subjects standing over

---

[30] Marx, 'Economic and philosophical manuscripts', pp. 327–30, 350–1, 386–91.
[31] Marx, *Capital*, vol. 1, p. 372, vol. 3, pp. 430, 772. *Grundrisse*, p. 495. G. A. Cohen, *Karl Marx's Theory of History: A Defence* (Oxford: Oxford University Press, 1978) pp. 134–72.
[32] Marx, *Grundrisse*, pp. 452–5, 705. *Capital*, vol. 3, pp. 823–8.
[33] Marx, *Grundrisse*, pp. 702–6. Marx and Engels, *German Ideology*, pp. 44–5.
[34] Karl Marx, *The Poverty of Philosophy* (Moscow: Progress, 1978) pp. 132–3. Marx and Engels, *German Ideology*, p. 67.

against objects, and does not so much resolve, as step outside dialectic tensions into a positivist relation to nature.[35]

Nevertheless, Colletti fails to note that there *is* an objectively real return from alienation, in the sense that all human powers are now fully under human control, and, likewise, the 'idealist illusions' of the historical logic of the relations of production were *necessary* moments of a dialectic which develops human powers from the innocence of pre-history, through the illusions which accompany the growth of productive forces, to the 'second innocence' of a humanity come to itself with the gain from historical processes it could never have deliberately willed. Despite Colletti, therefore, it makes perfect sense to call this 'historical dialectic' also a 'material dialectic', grounded in natural processes.

The problem with this material dialectic is easy to recognize. There is, simply, no necessary link between a particular development of the forces of production and a particular mode of production – only a complex set of affinities and interactions. Still less can one ever justify the idea that there is an inevitable link between the growth of technology and the necessity of linguistic illusion. Only his 'inversion' of Hegel's dialectic causes Marx to think this, but the movement from original self-presence, through estrangement back to self-presence, with the gain of explication, is no more credible in its materialist than in its idealist version. Exactly the same *mythos* is superimposed upon the historical data. So just as much as Hegel, Marx subscribes to a Behmenist version (with its Valentinian gnostic echoes) of the theodicy of political economy: history shows a record of suffering, but it is necessary suffering for the sake of the liberated future. Thus the Marxist critique of religion turns out to be only possible within a new variant of a gnostic, and so 'religious' metanarrative.[36]

To sum up my metacritique of Marxist critique:

1   Marx takes over from Feuerbach an account of projection which assumes that all human reality derives from a self-positing ego.
2   He cannot show why religion should occur as an epiphenomenon.
3   He exposes cultural processes as themselves 'religious', but can only contrast these with an imaginary, naturalistic norm, a new 'natural law' of humanity.
4   Historical religions, like Christianity, can only be shown to be illusory, if they are represented as departures from an impossible pre-cultural humanity, or else as necessary stages on the way to an impossible post-cultural humanity, where peace and freedom emerge 'spontaneously' with the mere negative abolition of what is holding them back.
5   Christianity is only criticized by 'situating' it within a metanarrative which has itself a quasi-religious and 'heterodox' character.

---

[35] Lucio Colletti, *Marxism and Hegel*, trans. Lawrence Garner (London: New Left Books, 1979) pp. 249–83. Marx, 'Economic and philosophical manuscripts', pp. 387, 392–5.

[36] Eric Voegelin, *Science, Politics and Gnosticism* (Chicago: Regnery, 1968).

The Marxist Critique of Capital

This metacritique breaks sharply with the dominant approaches to Marxism within Christian 'political theology' in recent years. In general, these fall into two categories: either an attempt is made to disentangle Marx's humanism from his scientism and determinism, or else Marxism is accepted as the science of socio-economic processes, though its wider metaphysical competence is denied.[37] In both cases, it is claimed that Marx has not conclusively shown that there could not be a 'non-alienating' form of religion, with the end of alienation in general. This approach fails, in the case of the 'scientific' preference, to ask how Marx's 'theodicy' is compatible with genuine Christianity, and it fails also in the case of the 'humanist' preference, to ask whether Marx's account of the human essence is either rationally justifiable, or compatible with the Christian account of human nature as consisting in its being ordered to the supernatural life of charity.

Where Marxism is endorsed by theology, either as humanism or as science, his critique of religion is accepted to the extent that it is agreed that Christianity is 'ideological' where it alienates essentially human powers, or provides a consolation which detracts from the presence of earthly unjustice. These positions are unexceptionable, because in both respects Marxism adds nothing to the self-critical capacity of Christianity, even if it acts as an important spur to its exercise. What is much more problematic is the general theological acceptance of *either* Marxist humanism or Marxist science, with the consequence that the Marxist account of capitalism is regarded as basically adequate, and not in need of any supplementation by critical considerations specifically informed by Christianity itself. In this section I shall show why the Marxist critique of capitalism is inadequate, and then in the final section of the chapter, how Christian socialism contains a greater depth of critique, which political theology needs to reinstate.

To some degree, as has already been suggested, Marxism really does assist a Christian critique of 'secular order'. This is because it shows that the presuppositions of liberal political theory and of political economy are culturally specific. Marxism penetrates to the level of the unconscious assumptions that are constantly reproduced by capitalism and which sustain it in being. This can be clearly seen in the case of the theory of value. Whereas Ricardo claimed that labour is 'naturally' the source of value, Marx showed that labour is a source of value within capitalism only because it is *constructed* as a source of value.[38] The diversity of particular, quantitatively different labour is treated as 'equivalent' in terms of the single quantitative measure

---

[37] Gustavo Gutierrez, *A Theology of Liberation* (London: SCM, 1983) p. 30. J. B. Metz, 'Political theology: a new paradigm of theology?', in Leroy S. Rourer (ed.), *Civil Religion and Political Theology* (Notre Dame, Ind.: Notre Dame University Press) pp. 141–53. Alfredo Fierro, *The Militant Gospel* (London: SCM, 1976) p. 236ff. Clodovis Boff, *Theology and Praxis: Epistemological Foundations*, trans. Robert R. Barr (Maryland, NY: Orbis) p. 55.

[38] Clarke, *Marx, Marginalism and Modern Sociology*, pp. 64–103.

of labour time.[39] In this way, Marx's 'labour theory of value', the centre-piece of his account of capitalism, is not a new empirical claim, like Ricardo's labour-value theory, but rather an unprecedented attempt to describe capitalism's 'conditions of possibility'. It achieves a partial exposure of 'secular order' to the degree that it pinpoints the arbitrariness of 'flattening out' qualities along a single quantitative scale, in order to permit a purely formal regulation of the economic realm, where substantive issues of justice need never arise.

Marx's theory of value breaks with the ideas of those Ricardian socialists who argued that, as labour is the source of value, all products 'naturally' belong to the individual labourer.[40] This conclusion does not follow if the labour measure of value is itself merely generated by capitalist exchange processes. However, in two respects Marx reveals himself as residually Ricardian and therefore as still bound by the assumptions of political economy.

The first respect relates to his comments on Aristotle, where Marx says that Aristotle was unable to see that labour was the measure of value, because of the restricted economic development in the Greece of that time.[41] This statement implies that, in some sense, labour was always 'really' the measure of value, although this has only been made explicit by capitalist practice. Here one can see how the dialectical vision actually distorts Marx's 'semiotic' analysis of capitalist power and meaning. For capitalism is not regarded by Marx merely as a particular historic conjuncture which has become so deeply sedimented as to appear unchangeable. On the contrary, it is regarded as a partial clarification of the purely economic, a revealing of true economic nature and a manifestation of its determining power, whereas previously this was concealed. In earlier, 'disguised' eras, the most important human relationships of power were familial or political in character, even though this fact was itself an aspect of a particular mode of production. Thus capitalism finally reveals the economic foundations of all societies, and helps us to interpret all societies, just as Feuerbachian Christianity interprets all religions, and the fully grown organism alone helps us to make full sense of an immature one.[42]

Given this residual teleology, it is not surprising to find that Marx remains a basically 'economic' thinker, rather than one who fully recognizes the historical particularity of the economic. Following Marx, Marxist anthropologists have persistently failed to acknowledge that in many primitive societies one cannot recognize a separate economic function at all: if acts of production and exchange are regarded as part of a religious ritual, as well as being necessary for the reproduction of a particular society, then only an unwarranted ethno-

---

[39] Marx, *Capital*, vol. 1, pp. 45–8.

[40] Clarke, *Marx, Marginalism and Modern Sociology*, p. 41ff.

[41] Marx, *Capital*, vol. 1, pp. 65–6. Cornelius Castoriadis, 'Value, equality, justice, politics: from Marx to Aristotle and from Aristotle to ourselves', in *Crossroads in the Labyrinth*, trans. Kate Soper and Martin H. Ryle (Brighton: Harvester, 1984) pp. 260–330.

[42] Marx, *Capital*, vol. 1, p. 65. *Grundrisse*, pp. 105–6.

centrism will see this as a case of category confusion, or ideological disguising of what is 'really' going on.

The second respect relates to the limitations of the labour theory of value. Marx recognized that the extraction of surplus value from surplus labour (labour performed over and above the requirements of the reproduction of the lives of the labourers) was not the sole determinant of prices, because market factors can also intervene. He consequently faced the problem of the 'conversion' of value into actual prices. Yet this entire problematic presupposes that value is engendered through production, not through exchange, and that it is always most fundamentally the costs of production which determines the rate of profit.[43] This giving the leading role to production suggests that Marx still envisaged his economics as the science of 'real' wealth, and could not fully recognize that the factors governing production will always be just as conventional as the logic of exchange. Inversely, he could not fully recognize that it is just as fundamental for capitalist logic to reproduce conditions of exchange and consumption as it is to reproduce the conditions of production; only in this wider sense are 'production' and 'reproduction' the key considerations.

Profits are not *only* generated from the extraction of surplus labour; they are also generated through monopolistic control of production, or through creation and manipulation of consumer preferences. Here, *also*, one can say, value is generated, because consumers are persuaded to accept that all products can be made 'equivalent' on a single quantitative scale, according to whether or not they are considered socially desirable. Jean-Joseph Goux argues that one can talk of 'surplus meaning', in parallel to 'surplus value', because over and above the consumption of a product which fully answers to its production, naturally 'terminates' the product and temporarily ends the desire to consume, there occurs the offering of a sign in the form of money, in which the desire remains and is conserved.[44]

This conception is extremely suggestive, but requires modification. The unique 'destiny' of a product is not 'naturally' to be consumed: this presumes the illusion of a pure 'use-value'. Instead one can say that its destiny may equally be to be made 'equivalent'. But in capitalist society this equivalence is not, as for Aristotle and Aquinas, the equivalence of 'justice', which presupposes some social consensus about the relative worth of different things *in advance* of particular market exchanges. (This is *not* to say that an attempt may sensibly be made fully to control market supply and demand. The ethical consensus that is coterminous with 'just' exchanges obviously cannot be imposed by the State. Being 'for' or 'against' the market should be a nonsense for socialism: what matters is *just exchange*.) Instead, the balance of supply and demand alone is here supposed to generate equivalence, but in practice this

---

[43] Marx and Engels, *German Ideology*, p. 47. Marx, *Grundrisse*, pp. 93–5. *Capital*, vol. 1, pp. 204–26.

[44] J.-J. Goux, 'Numismatiques', in *Freud, Marx: Economie et Symbolique* (Paris: Editions du Seuil, 1973) pp. 53–115.

means that those who are richer and more powerful will only exchange under conditions where they can extract some marginal advantage in the form of profit. Through monopoly, and the cultural stimulation of desire, a kind of 'surplus desire' – equivalent to surplus labour – is engendered, such that consumers not only pay the 'equivalent' of what they want, but in addition a premium for their so badly wanting it, a penal imposition on desire, despite the fact that desire is precisely what civil society expects from us.

If, therefore, one develops Marx's attempt to define the transcendental 'non-sense' from which capitalist sense arises, it can be seen that value has a dual generation in production and exchange. Marx failed to realize this, because he was still dominated by a metanarrative at once 'economic' and dialectical, which envisaged the human essence in terms of the production of wealth. To this extent he failed to describe fully the historical specificity of capitalism.

The Marxist metanarrative which tries to show that religion is temporarily necessary seeks to show the same thing in the case of capitalism also. Similarly, it tries to show that capitalism, like religion, is irrational, and destined to collapse under the weight of its own 'contradictions'. This is a singular mistake, because, as Lyotard argues, the extreme formalism of capital, its ability to define all the variety of human needs, labour and products as basically 'the same', make it inherently 'tautologous', and the least self-contradictory of social systems, in the sense that it is uniquely able to remain self-identical in the most various situations. As Lyotard suggests, it is a *dispositif de régulation de la conquête*, because its tautologous character means that it can always *precisely* measure what threats it is under, and so automatically make a corrective response.[45] If capitalism 'oversteps the mark' in its triumphal progress, then it knows about it immediately, in a way that a military or political process cannot, because the tactics of expansion – increase of wealth and profit – are precisely at one with the ultimate goal being sought.

A consequence of the 'tautologous' character of capitalism is that there are no productive purposes, defined in the capitalist manner, which one could ever see as being 'held back' by capitalist formations. Although there are inherent tensions within capitalism, like the conflict between the need to reduce labour costs, and the need to stimulate demand for products, there are, in theory, infinite possibilities of adaptation and adjustment by which a 'final crisis' could be endlessly postponed. Capitalism remains viable as long as certain asymmetries of wealth and power can be sustained, and the losers can be either coerced or seduced into quiescence. Much is made by recent 'liberation theologians' (following many others) of the contrast between functionalist sociology, which sees society as inherently 'organic' and Marxism which sees social processes as 'inherently conflictual'.[46] In fact, Marx himself emphasizes how social tensions can be functionally managed, and

---

[45] Lyotard, *Économie Libidinale*, pp. 187–8.
[46] Boff, *Theology and Praxis*, p. 57.

only believes that society is 'conflictual' because of his dialectical metanarrative, which makes these conflicts function 'in the long run'.[47] Moreover, there is no limit to the possibility of functionalization, and it is not even the case, as Marx claims, that the interests of workers are 'objectively' antagonistic to capital. For this presupposes that workers have an 'essential' identity as human beings which is not fully absorbed by their roles as workers, consumers and seduced admirers of capitalist wealth and glamour. Even if the ruses involved in the extraction of surplus labour and surplus desire were to become 'fully transparent', it is still perfectly possible that the majority could be persuaded to accept the fiction which rewards investors for nothing save precisely their willingness to seduce. Workers can be persuaded to adore this mechanism of seduction, for it is true that it alone guarantees the kind of society which capitalism delivers, with its further worship of all forms of empty, sublime equivalence. To acquiesce in the power of capital over labour is not, therefore, demonstrably 'irrational'. But for reasons belonging to a *different* desire, and a different fiction, one can still declare (as I would want to) that workers *should* construct themselves as subjects antagonistic to capital.

If capitalism is not inherently contradictory, then it is also not subject to a dialectical 'immanent critique'. For this would assume that there lurks within capitalism a seed of pure rationality, which grows, through contradiction, into the clear light of self-consciousness and self-consistency. However, opposition to capitalism does not emerge because it is discovered, for example, that capitalism does not deliver the freedom which it claims to deliver; on the contrary, capitalism delivers all too precisely freedom as defined within its own logic. Opposition to capitalism emerges only when a different mode of freedom is positively promoted, or the tempering of freedom with equality is recommended.

This point is often obscured from view by use of the concept of 'ideology'.[48] Ideology, in the Marxist sense, presupposes that there is a gap between real social pressures and their ideal representation. Sometimes this may, indeed, be the case, as where a politician makes it sound as if, in capitalist society, there is a real equality of choice for all. Encouraging such illusions may have a certain local importance for capitalist functioning, but there is no necessity for an all-embracing 'dominant ideology' standing apart from the assumptions built into economic and bureaucratic relationships themselves.[49] And these processes, as we have seen, are only 'mystifying' to the extent that they conceal *other* social possibilities from view, not in the sense that they disguise their own nature. Such ideological disguise, although a very common, and even a pervasive feature of capitalism, is not a necessary feature, and increasingly we will be faced with 'postmodern' apologies for capitalism which recognize its logic and yet embrace its unfounded values.

---

[47] Turner, *Religion and Social Theory*, pp. 38–62.
[48] Marx and Engels, *The German Ideology*, p. 29ff.
[49] Abercrombie et al., *The Dominant Ideology Thesis*.

They embrace capitalist logic because it is, precisely, a *secular* logic, which acknowledges no substantive norms, and which can absorb and overcome within its regulative rule every traditional constitutive system of cultural exchange. One can embrace, nihilistically, the necessity for this secular logic, without wanting to claim that it is 'natural', nor (as in the Marxist variant of political economy) that it will negate itself in the direction of some naturalistic utopian future. Nevertheless, the embracing of capitalism as formal, 'deterritorialized' regulation, does tend to suggest that this is the system which grasps 'arbitrariness' or 'difference' as the very essence of Being itself. Whereas Marxist 'theodicy' is prepared to justify a temporarily necessary violence, the postmodern embracing of capitalism becomes at once more clear-sighted about its nature, and more Machiavellian in its acceptance of a perpetual violence within the rules, that is sustained and re-created by the rules themselves.

The question of an 'alternative' to capitalism cannot therefore arise in the context of a purely rational or a dialectical critique. Capitalism can be opposed, but never exposed as irrational. Marx's scenarios for this event are quite unbelievable; in the version finally given in the *Grundrisse*, he suggests that a monopolistic and fully automated capitalism will pass from 'the appropriation of individual labour to appropriation of the general productive power of man, his understanding of nature and his mastery over it by virtue of his presence as a social body'.[50] At this point, it is supposed to become apparent that human power is being contradictorily turned against humanity itself, because a scientifically educated populace will realize the absurdity of subordinating the long-term interests of the many to the short-term interests of the few. However, in the first place, in the present age of monopoly and automation, what we seem to be witnessing is not what Marx predicted, but rather a new 'disorganized' capitalism, in which competition, new forms of work and a new extraction of surplus value re-establish themselves among sub-systems within monopolies.[51] Secondly, Marx did not demonstrate that a new system of oppression 'beyond capitalism', involving a continued direct compulsion of labour without mediation by the extraction of value, is an impossibility.

For technological education does not necessarily mean a technically more sophisticated level of education in general. And furthermore, the control of many human beings by a few through an enormous industrial machine is no more nor less 'rational' than the unlimited control over nature which this machine aims at, and which Marx endorses. This goal is the mere tautology of power, and therefore it cannot solve any of the problems of just distribution and exchange with which a socialist society would have to deal. Marx falsely imagines that the collective production of the industrial machine would be entirely uncontroversial, removing the need for government, and that the individual pursuit of freedom would provoke no further conflict. While it is true that the subordination of work and production to capitalist

---

[50] *Grundrisse*, p. 705.
[51] Scott Lash and John Urry, *The End of Organised Capitalism* (Cambridge: Polity, 1987).

exchange-processes prevents the emergence of a production not governed by the economic criteria of profit and 'saving time', it is wrong to imagine, as Marx did, that there are 'pure' criteria of production; what is produced, and the purposes of production, will in any society relate to codes of exchange of value that cannot be 'rationally' determined, although the codes need not be, as for capitalism, 'economic' ones.

There is, therefore, no benign rational power waiting to be unveiled after the mere negative removal of all the illusions which hold humanity in chains.[52] Hegel's critique of mere negativity as leading to terror must apply to Marx, as, likewise, his insistence that only a religiously informed 'State' can qualify market society: namely a society with definite ideas about what kinds of human virtue, which kinds of character-roles it wishes to promote. Such a *sittlich* conception must inevitably be grounded in some teleological belief that human beings are *supposed* to behave in certain ways rather than others. However, we saw that, in Hegel, political economy and dialectics already begins to undermine *Sittlichkeit*, and this is taken further by Marx, whose human norm is merely the Fichtean self-positing subject.[53]

Here one should not fall into the common trap of supposing that, because Hegel and Marx link values to what is historically emergent, they are really being true to the refusal of a fact/value dualism integral to a *sittlich* or customary ethics. For by asking about what *must* emerge and so be valued, they deduce values from the facts, rather than recognizing certain cultural facts – like, for example, the social existence of teachers or judges – as inherently involving certain evaluative and ideological descriptions. For Marx, the factual sequence of his metanarrative determines that the only real moral issue concerns the inhibition of the further development of the forces of production. But this factual sequence is not itself a moral one, in which means lead to ends in the course of a gradual growth in virtue. Instead, the supposed inevitability of the narrative makes the manipulation of means towards ends morally justifiable, a situation that would be impossible if the ends in view were truly 'moral facts', or 'states of character' which can only be freely developed, and never contrived. A *sittlich* ethics *recommends* certain narrative sequences, and sees these as fulfilling the objectively 'true' human ends, but it never deduces values from a supposedly inevitable history. This latter procedure, as found in Hegel and Marx, is just a new, dialectical variant of modern secular natural law.

Marxism, Christianity and Socialism

Given the impossibility of showing that capitalism is 'irrational' (that is to say, offends canons of rationality which cannot but be recognized by all thinking

---

[52] Taylor, *Hegel*, pp. 537–71.
[53] Marx, *Early Writings*, pp. 379–400. Rose, *Hegel Contra Sociology*, pp. 42, 53ff, 96, 210–12.

beings) or 'contradictory', only an ethical critique of capitalism remains viable. Moreover, this is likely to be also a religious critique, for the following two reasons. First, Marx himself realized that insofar as it was a culturally all-embracing system of signification, capitalism is somewhat like a religion. In consequence it can only be questioned or replaced by 'another religion', equally unfounded and not necessarily self-contradictory. Secondly, the 'religiosity' of capitalism is also, and pre-eminently, the paradoxical religiosity of the secular itself, which the preceding chapters have gradually disclosed. It is clear that the formal, regulative logic of capitalism can only be opposed by the constitutive logic of a metaphysical system which recommends certain social roles within a social narrative as objectively desirable.

In this sense only, all true opposition to capitalism is necessarily 'conservative'. But this is not to say that the alternative social formation proposed need be that of an organicist, socially-hierarchic society. A society directed towards *paideia*, the cultivation of certain virtues, may also be a society dedicated to economic and social equality, and to republican participation in political processes. In actual fact, perhaps the majority of nineteenth-century 'social-isms' tended to combine a 'conservative' concern for *paideia*, common public values and collective religiosity, with a 'modern' advocacy of equality and fraternity alongside liberal freedom. The very first unambiguously 'socialist' theory (in the sense of rejecting returns on unearned income to private individuals), that of Pierre Buchez, was an explicitly *Catholic* socialism, which conceived of the Church (thought of as an amalgam of voluntary associations), rather than the sovereign State, as the site of a new social order, a new post-political *Sittlichkeit*.[54]

By contrast, Marxism stands almost alone in the nineteenth century as a 'modernist', Enlightenment variant of socialism, which in the final vision of the *Grundrisse* envisages social cooperation in a purely utilitarian fashion, and subordinates this to the single value of a full realization of individual liberty. And in the course of time it has proved that the merely 'modernist' socialisms are unable to sustain their critique of capitalism, which is a much more self-consistent form of modernism than that which they themselves advocate. The central planning of Stalinism or Fabianism is shown to be far less flexible and adaptable than the market, which 'automatically' registers the chances and dangers of wealth expansion. For it is only the mechanisms of the market which permit regulation of a society where the one publicly recognized principle is 'freedom of choice'. Modernist, liberal socialists, who confine themselves to this principle, can advocate some correction of the unfairness involved in the gains and losses of one generation being handed on to the next, in the form of various state welfare and education benefits. Likewise they can advocate some measure of redistribution of income through progres-

[54] John Milbank, 'Were the Christian Socialists socialists?', in Jack Forstman and Joseph Pickle (eds.) *Papers of the Nineteenth Century Working Group*, AAR 1988 Annual Meeting, vol. 14, pp. 86–95.

sive taxation. However, in the much vaster area in which the decisions and preferences of individuals impinge upon the lives of other individuals, one can only restrict the triumph of mere abstract power (the possession and accumulation of more wealth) if there is some consensus about what ends to aim for, as Buchez and nearly all the first socialists insisted.

(If, for example, universal education is simply education into the possibility of free choice, then it is only, after all, an education in liberal capitalist values. Education especially reveals the concealed public dimension of political life which even liberalism cannot suppress: in deciding *what* to teach, what to pass on, any society expresses its view about what is really self-fulfilling, even if it is confined, as with liberalism, to saying that the only goal is self-fulfilment. In making this statement, it is also saying that the only goal is power, and the only means of government, a regulated, rule-governed economy of power.)

But unlike Marxist and Fabian socialism, which have proved unable to resist capitalist modernity, most nineteenth-century socialisms were 'postmodern', in the sense that they had absorbed some measure of a romantic, Counter-Enlightenment critique. They did not, like Marxism, locate socialism (or for Marx, 'communism') as the next stage in a narrative of emancipation, or the genesis of human autonomy. On the contrary, the enlightened goal of a self-regulation of the will, according to its own natural, finite desires and capacities, was seen as of one piece with the operation of political economy. The rejection of the latter could not, then, involve a 'dialectic of enlightenment', or an immanent critique of the present ideas of freedom. Two examples here, those of John Ruskin and Pierre-Joseph Proudhon, are particularly instructive.

Although Ruskin remained in some senses a 'Tory', and did not define himself as a socialist, nor always as an orthodox Christian, much of his critique of capitalism passed into Christian socialist thinking in England. Moreover, it can itself be regarded as 'Christian socialist' in so far as the critique is seen as possible in terms of the difference from capitalism presented by Christianity, especially in its past history – the first Christian communities, the monasteries, the medieval towns, and guild associations.[55] By contrast with their standard, capitalism appeared to Ruskin as a kind of apostasy, the most remarkable 'instance in history of a nation's establishing a systematic disobedience to the principles of its own religion'.[56] Here, capitalism is not regarded as a partial development of freedom, but instead as a contingent pseudo-progress, whose emergence was the shame of Christendom. For Ruskin, capitalism was supremely the practice of a false knowledge, which made self-interest moderate self-interest without the intervention of virtue, and secured public order without the architectonic of justice. The

[55] John Ruskin, *Unto this Last*, in *Sesame and Lilies; Unto this Last; The Political Economy of Art* (London: Cassell, 1907).

[56] Ruskin, *Unto this Last*, Essay II, 'The veins of wealth', p. 162.

triumph of political economy meant the promotion of certain quasi-virtues of busyness and frugality in place of true political *phronesis* and Christian charity. And the displacement of the ethical in the public sphere was held to be coterminous with the triumph of secularity. After the retreat of public religion, a vacuum was created, in which a merely 'economic' regime could 'manage' a society, even without moral or religious consensus.

Although this was a strictly moral critique of capitalism, one cannot say, with Marx, that this sort of socialism is blind to history. In the last analysis, what Marx meant when he accused other socialisms of being unhistorical was that they did not accept his own deduction to utopia from supposed laws of historical immanence. Ruskin never entertained any conception of this sort, but his moral critique precisely coincides with a historical vision which attempts to penetrate the level at which capitalism has inserted a completely different logic of human action, one which seeks to displace moral with 'amoral' regulation, or in Ruskin's words substitutes 'balances of expediency' for 'balances of justice'.[57] *This* level of historical change was *not* penetrated by Marx, precisely because he read back capitalist amorality as the supposed 'economic base', always finally determinative in every human society. By contrast, Ruskin realizes that the 'knowledge' embodied in political economy, far from being the ideological dress of underlying 'material' processes, is but the condensation and abridgement of the system of knowledge which capitalism itself consists of. This knowledge, for Ruskin, is actually the first historical instance of 'nescience' because it does not promote, directly, a maximum excellence, but instead advocates the deliberate exploitation of differences in knowledge and ability. Relative failure, weak ability, bad craftsmanship and stupidity have a definite function for capitalism in the reducing of production costs and the extension of wealth. This new mode of knowledge is also a new, amoral, 'moral economy' which (as we saw with Hume and Smith in chapter 2) made a sharp division between the private and consumerist sphere of 'natural' sympathies based on supposedly universal feeling, and the 'artificial' sympathies which arise in relation to the positive facts of property, possession and political power. The 'artificial' sympathies do not generate a genuine public virtue, but only a Machiavellian *virtù*, which exalts, in a new mode, a heroic, regulated discipline.

In contrast to the Scots (but in continuity with a Scottish tradition of reflection on wealth and virtue, turned critical of political economy with Thomas Carlyle), Ruskin desires an integration of wealth with genuine virtue. He notes that 'manly character' and 'production and exchange' are not easily reconciled.[58] Yet (one could add) this commonplace is specific to a classical legacy which subordinates the productive household to political relations in the city between property-owning males: economic production is ultimately subordinate to political virtue, yet production *itself* is not a virtuous activity.

---

[57] Ruskin, *Unto this Last*, Essay II, 'The veins of wealth', Essay I, 'The roots of honour', p. 112.
[58] Ibid., Essay IV, 'Ad valorem', p. 178.

By contrast, it is the post-Christian tendency to merge more perfectly the conceptions of *polis* and *oikos* – to make the household with its 'pastoral' oversight of material well-being the basic unit of government, and to include women, children and slaves as full members of the ultimate religio-political community – which permits us to demand that production and exchange discover within themselves immanent norms of virtue and *paideia*. (Like Proudhon and Mazzini, Ruskin looks to an apocalyptic fusing of the political and the domestic, and suggests that the domestic, 'economic' capacities of women make them the most suited for public, governmental tasks.)[59] The trouble is, Ruskin notes, that trade and manufacture have never been seen as included within a Socratic 'discipline of death'; it has not been recognized that there are here responsibilities for subordinates, and for the quality of products, which at the limit imply the same kind of sacrifice which we recognize as involved in soldiering, teaching or medicine.[60] Likewise, Ruskin wanted questions of the aesthetic quality of objects produced or exchanged to be coordinated with questions of ethical goals for social subjects. Economic value, he says, is properly 'the possession of the valuable by the valiant'.[61] A just exchange of goods and labour presupposes a match between the ethical capacities of persons, and the interpreted excellence of material objects. The virtuous deserve beautiful, truly useful artefacts; artefacts of fine quality deserve a good use. This concern for the cultivation of high aesthetic standards, correlated with a certain style of life, has no equivalent in Marx, whose interest in creativity extends only to subjective 'freedom of expression' and who can be contemptuous of 'craft idiocy'. Ruskin wanted to *abolish* 'the economic' as a realm of indifference to objective goodness, beauty or truth, whereas Marx merely wanted to fulfil it.

Still more clearly than Hegel, Ruskin divined that capitalism was the logical management of the death of excellence, or the belief that one can discover through art and practice the 'proper end' of things. The clear implication is that only in the invocation of transcendence can there be a critique of capitalist order, whose 'secularity' is its primary character. Moreover, Ruskin did not altogether fail to indicate how this concern to ethicize manufacture and exchange can go in an egalitarian direction. Although he stresses the all-importance of parental and pastoral roles, he wishes to remove them from their connection with wealth and privilege, and there is even a suggestion that the true character of these roles will only be secured if they are disseminated, and become as far as possible reciprocal in a kind of clerisy of all citizens.[62]

The real point of necessity for hierarchy in Ruskin is the transitive relationship of education, where an unavoidable non-reciprocity nonetheless works towards its own cancellation. Liberalism, by contrast, tends to disguise this

[59] Ruskin, 'Of Queen's gardens', in *Sesame ·and Lilies*, pp. 61–95. P.-J. Proudhon, *Selected Writings* (London: Macmillan, 1969) p. 92. See chapter 12 below.

[60] Ruskin, *Unto this Last*, Essay I 'The roots of honour', p. 125.

[61] Ibid., Essay IV, 'Ad valorem', p. 171.

[62] Ibid., Essay III, 'Qui judicatis terram', p. 150.

necessity, because it makes normative the spatial relationships between adult, autonomous subjects, a habit which received its *reductio ad absurdum* in William Godwin's vision of a world of finite immortality, without sexual passion, without birth, and without death.[63]

In this sense, because Christian socialism maintained a commitment to collective norms of justice which can only be handed down through time, it had a commitment to hierarchy. But it was *also* capable of realizing that an arbitrary hierarchy, of a non self-cancelling kind, is partially responsible for the formation of the modern machine of abstract power. For example, Charles Péguy later blames social hierarchies, and especially the ecclesial hierarchy, for a 'reversal' of the divine pedagogic *mystique*, such that right from the Church's very foundation the energies of the many were recruited to maintain the securities of the few.[64]

Likewise Ruskin does not merely celebrate the Middle Ages as a lost era of 'true craft'. Just as importantly, he invokes this period in a purely *allegorical* fashion, when he wishes to bestow 'kingly', 'queenly' and 'noble', rather than merely mercenary, attributes upon the sphere of work and trade.[65] There is a double profundity here: first, Ruskin grasps that if work and trade are to be transformed into 'virtuous' spheres of self-realization, then the only way for us to think this is in terms of an allegorical recuperation of past 'aristocractic' values. But secondly, the implication of this typological appeal to medieval kingship and warfare, rather than to medieval art, is that the latter was *not* adequately prized and promoted as a sphere of virtue. By not sufficiently integrating *poesis* with ethical *praxis*, both antiquity and the Middle Ages were themselves gradually nurturing the horrors of modernity. Ruskin 'gothicizes' in the obvious sense of favouring gothic ornamentation, but he also gothicizes in a 'gothick' sense of invoking the horrors perpetrated by lazy and absent aristocratic fathers, never fully true to their aristocratic role, which is to be virtuous. This 'gothick' plot is only to be finally resolved when aristocracy is democratized, and nurtured within the realm of labour.

Ruskin, therefore, was no mere medievalizing reactionary. Instead, he proposed something altogether new: a society where aesthetic perception of nature, and public standards of fine design, are seen as the vital keys to public virtue, together with the upholding of a sense of transcendence which goes along with a common sense of things 'in their proper place' and 'rightly finished'. (Is this not a materialist religiosity?)

The example of Ruskin shows how socialism was able *both* to appeal to the fragmentary justice of the past – the medieval towns, the guilds, the

[63] William Godwin, *Enquiry Concerning Political Justice and its Influence on Morals and Happiness* (Toronto, 1946) vol. 1, p. 86, vol. 2, pp. 520, 527–9.

[64] Charles Péguy, 'Clio I', in *Temporal and Eternal*, trans. Alexander Dru (London: Harvill, 1958) pp. 101–8.

[65] John Ruskin, 'Of Kings' treasuries', *Unto this Last*, in *Sesame and Lilies*, pp. 54–5, 150. *Time and Tide by Wear and Tyne* (London: G. and A. Allen, 1874) pp. 166–7. *Praeterita* (London: Rupert Hart-Davies 1949) pp. 5–6.

monasteries – *and* to connect present secular injustice with past social and ecclesial shortcomings.

In the case of Pierre-Joseph Proudhon, one is dealing, not, as in the case of Ruskin, with a relatively isolated (albeit later highly influential) prophet, but with a man who came to be the main representative of French 'republican socialism' – the tradition which Marx tried both to absorb, and to overcome. It is notable that nearly all the representatives of this tradition contain 'Counter-Enlightenment' elements in their thinking. One finds in their writings, characteristically, an attack on the idea that justice can be simply equated with the maximization of freedom, and an identification of religion with harmonious, fraternal agreement over against the inherent 'antagonism' of secular individualism.[66] Their initial appeal to the past was that of the 'enlightened' revolution itself – namely, to the classical republic. Yet this ideal was qualified in a more associationist, anarchist, pro-familial and pacific direction by reference to Christian tradition and to medieval exemplars.[67] The French-educated Christian socialist J. M. Ludlow recorded 'the way the idea – the *church* idea of universal brotherhood *haunts* these men [the Paris *ouvriers*] and links itself in their minds with the union of all trades connected with building'.[68]

One can say that, where Rousseau's 'civil religion' took on a more Christian cast, there, precisely, French 'socialism' was born. And neither the appeal back to the antique *polis*, nor the medieval guilds, is made out of 'nostalgia', but rather because it is *only* these contrasts which allow one to pinpoint the new and unprecedented factors in capitalist oppression. But the appeal had also another purpose. The republican socialists did not conceive socialism negatively as the removal of obstacles, nor as the unravelling of present contradictions, but rather *positively*, as a contingent piece of human imagination. In this positive socialism, the future possibility has to be composed out of the fragments of past justice. (Although most of the French socialists were not immune from many of the illusions of Comteanism, I am here deliberately indicating a respect in which there is an element in positivism superior to the dialectical tradition.)

No more than Christian socialism, therefore, was republican socialism a whig discourse about 'emancipation'. It is notable that Proudhon, unlike Marx, sharply rejected Feuerbach's humanism and the idea that 'man' is the new subject of a providential process.[69] In consequence, he also refused the idea of an 'essence' of human freedom which is to be liberated.

---

[66] P.-J.-B. Buchez, *Traité de Politique et de Science Sociale* (Paris: Amyot, 1866) tome I, pp. 55–68, tome II, pp. 69–89. *La Science de L'Histoire*, vol. 1 (Paris: Guillaumin, 1842) pp. 1–53. K. Steven Vincent, *Pierre-Joseph Proudhon and the Rise of French Republican Socialism* (Oxford: Oxford University Press, 1984) pp. 33–78, 127–65.

[67] Buchez, *Traité de Politique*, tome I, pp. 483–93. *La Science de L'Histoire*, tome I, pp. 88–90, 2, 82, 512–15. H.-R. Feugueray, *Essai sur Les Doctrines Politiques de St. Thomas d'Aquin* (Paris:) Chémerot, 1875) pp. 208–12, 220ff. Armand Cuvillier, *F.-J.-B. Buchez et les Origines du Socialisme Chrétien* (Paris: PUF, 1948).

[68] J. M. Ludlow, 'The working associations of Paris', *Tracts on Christian Socialism, no. 4* (London, 1851).

[69] Cited in Henri de Lubac, *The Un-Marxian Socialist*, trans. R. E. Scantlebury (London: Sheed and Ward, 1948) p. 160.

With reference to this idea, he declares that 'I did not take as a motto freedom, which is an indefinite and absorbing force which may be crushed but not conquered; above it I placed justice which judges, regulates and distributes.'[70] His appeal to the foundation of the ancient *polis* in friendship and reconciliation is more consistent than that of Hegel, because Proudhon realized that Hegelian dialectics subordinates the just balancing of the demands of different subjects to the self-becoming of subjective freedom, which is at once the will of the isolated individual and the will of the sovereign State (or the will of the revolutionary proletariat for Marx). He also saw that by insisting on the priority of material justice one can actually grasp freedom more radically than Hegel, as respect for specific and endlessly different choices. For such choices can only proliferate and flourish in *peace* where they are constantly coordinated with each other through a developing consensus about equivalence. (How, for example, given the desire to fulfil equally all people's rightful 'needs', does one equate inherently incomparable needs? And in the realm of free association, how can we ensure that people enjoy 'the same' amount of diverse luxury items – assuming an equally 'virtuous' capacity for their proper use – in view of necessarily finite time and resources?) While it is true that Proudhon actually places rather less emphasis on the New Testament values of fraternity and charity than other (more Catholic) republican socialists like Buchez (and this is undoubtedly a deficiency), one should see this in the context of his desire to distinguish the need for 'reciprocity' from the promotion of a spurious 'dependence' – for example through too great a removal of independent means of subsistence – which denies people the power of creative invention.

It was Proudhon's subtlety to realize that even the encouragement of creative diversity requires *also* the continued invention/intuition of norms of justice which makes equal the unequal. For this reason, he refused the principle of dialectical synthesis in favour of the idea of replacing an antagonistic tension between different options with a tension that is an 'equilibrium'. This philosophy of 'perpetual reconciliation' must, unlike dialectics, allude to a Platonic transcendent standard of unity and order which can be participated in, but never reflectively grasped by the human mind.[71] In contrast to Hegel and Marx, this 'Platonism' still permits history its open-ended indeterminacy. The republic *is*, where there is justice, although the republic is in history, and justice is not discovered prior to particular acts of adjudication.

Part of Marx's own critique of Proudhon rested on complete miscomprehension. He failed to realize that Proudhon rejected Feuerbach, and that he also rejected dialectics (in the sense of determinate negation) rather than simply misunderstanding it.[72] Marx assumed that with the removal of the

---

[70] Cited in Henri de Lubac, *The Un-Marxian Socialist*, trans. R. E. Scantlebury (London: Sheed and Ward, 1948) p. 160.

[71] Proudhon, *Selected Writings*, pp. 223–35. De Lubac, *The Un-Marxian Socialist*, pp. 151–65.

[72] Karl Marx, *The Poverty of Philosophy* (Moscow: Progress, 1978) p. 103ff.

last barriers to autonomous freedom and unlimited production, the perenni- ally-renewed question of just distribution would be rendered finally redun- dant, but Proudhon, in rejecting the dialectical notion of freedom as a kind of 'solvent', remained preoccupied with the issues of the detailed questions of justice in the future socialist republic: what *kinds* of property are allowable, under what conditions? By what *standards* do we exchange one thing for another? How can we outlaw profits in excess of just remuneration? How do we prevent money from assuming a power in its own right? How can we permit the meeting of demand with supply in the market and yet ensure that all market exchanges can be accepted as 'just'?

Marx was of course right to reject the tendency of Proudhon, and other socialists, to opt for simple *panaceas* to solve some of these questions – for example, the use of a sort of money that would directly represent labour time.[73] As Marx realized, such suggestions actually sustain the liberal as- sumptions peculiar to the logic of capitalism, a logic which Proudhon by no means truly escaped, and into which Marx had a unique depth of insight. Here Ruskin was much nearer than Proudhon to comprehending that just exchange and true equality are only possible where there is a continuously re-made agreement about cultural norms and values; no single economic mechanism can replace this complex requirement. But despite this, Marx was yet more culpable than Proudhon, in implying that the detailed business of trying to 'imagine' a socialist economy is not really necessary. One can sum up the contrast by saying that Proudhon failed to grasp that the formal equivalence, however reformed, of the modern economy, disguises a coercive relationship between capital and worker (and one can add, between capital and consumer). But Marx failed to see that any conceivable *culture* involves equivalence, which is necessarily 'metaphysical', yet can be constructed as an ethical language of just exchange. In rejecting equivalence and mere 'social- ism' (in favour of 'communism'), Marx invented an impossible naturalistic mysticism, at once anarchic, and technocratically totalitarian.

This chapter has shown that the real value of Marxism, from both a metacri- tical and a theological point of view, lies in his (incomplete) analysis of the logic of capitalism as a secular logic. But neither his account of history, nor his anthropology, are acceptable. The critique of secular reason is in other respects taken further by Christian and republican socialism than by Marx. And in demonstrating this, one demonstrates also that socialism is only really possible *as* such a critique. Yet it will now be shown that current 'political theology' proceeds upon completely opposite presuppositions.

[73] Marx, *Grundrisse*, pp. 15–16.

8

Founding the Supernatural:
Political and Liberation Theology in the
Context of Modern Catholic Thought

Introduction

In recent Catholic theology, the Hegelian and Marxist traditions have acquired an unprecedented degree of influence. To discover why this is so,
one must first examine an important shift that has occurred in modern
Catholic thought. Only in this context does it become apparent why many
Catholic theologians are so receptive to the dialectical tradition, and why
some should even aspire to found a theology upon Marxist presuppositions.

One's starting point should be the seemingly obscure claim made by the
most important of the Latin American 'liberation theologians' – Gustavo
Gutierrez, Juan Luis Segundo, Clodovis Boff – that the new theology of
grace espoused by the second Vatican Council is what has made liberation
theology possible: such, indeed, that liberation theology alone, is to be considered the authentic outworking of post-conciliar Catholic thought.[1] What is
alluded to here is the embracing by the council of what one can term the
'integralist revolution'. This means the view that in concrete, historical humanity there is no such thing as a state of 'pure nature': rather, every person
has always already been worked upon by divine grace, with the consequence
that one cannot analytically separate 'natural' and 'supernatural' contributions to this integral unity.

The liberation theologians contend, quite cogently, that the social and
political implications of this 'integralism' were not properly realized by the
council, although this was precisely because the council was rightly concerned to repudiate earlier 'integrist' politics. The 'integrist' viewpoint had
insisted upon a clerical and hierarchic dominance over all the affairs of
secular life, founded upon a 'totalizing' theology which presents a complete

---

[1] Gustavo Gutierrez, *A Theology of Liberation* (London: SCM, 1983) pp. 66–72. Juan Luis
Segundo, *The Liberation of Theology* (Maryknoll, NY: Orbis, 1975) pp. 141–2. Clodovis Boff,
Theology and Praxis: Epistemological Foundations, trans. Robert R. Barr (Maryknoll, NY: Orbis,
1987) pp. 92–6.

system, whose details cannot be questioned without compromising the whole. (This difference between 'integralism' and 'integrism' should be carefully noted.) The liberation theologians nonetheless argue that if the whole concrete life of humanity is always imbued with grace, then it is surely not possible to separate political and social concerns from the 'spiritual' concerns of salvation. Reacting against the hierarchic politics of the Catholic right, conciliar theologians like Yves Congar had insisted on the 'distinction of planes', or the idea that the Church should not ordinarily interfere in the secular sphere, which has its own proper autonomy under God, and is normally the concern of the laity alone. But such a model, argues Gutierrez, breaks down in the face of the experience of lay apostleship and 'base communities' in Latin America; where does the ecclesiastical end and the political begin, when the concern is to forge true 'Christian community' in the face of social anarchy and legalized terror?[2]

In this chapter I will contend that, up to this point in the argument, the liberation theologians are absolutely right. Beyond this point, however, I believe that they go profoundly wrong. The question at issue concerns the integralist revolution itself. Broadly speaking, there were two sources for this momentous change: a French source which derived from the *nouvelle théologie* and such thinkers as de Montcheuil and de Lubac, but more ultimately from Maurice Blondel; and a German source, meaning, primarily, the thought of Karl Rahner. Against many interpretations, and sometimes the protestations of these thinkers themselves, I shall contend that there is a drastic difference between the two versions of integralism: a difference that can be crudely indicated and misleadingly summarized by saying that whereas the French version 'supernaturalizes the natural', the German version 'naturalizes the supernatural'. The thrust of the latter version is in the direction of a mediating theology, a universal humanism, a *rapprochement* with the Enlightenment and an autonomous secular order. While these themes are not entirely absent from the French version, its main tendencies are in entirely different directions: for the *nouvelle théologie*, towards a recovery of a pre-modern sense of the Christianized person as the fully real person; for Blondel, towards a similar reinstatement, but in terms which stress action, not contemplation, as the mode of ingress for the concrete, supernatural life.

Without exception, the main proponents of 'political theology' in Germany, and 'liberation theology' in Latin America, accept the Rahnerian, not the French version of integralism. And it is this option in fundamental theology which ensures that their theology of the political realm remains trapped within the terms of 'secular reason', and its unwarranted foundationalist presuppositions. Marxism is embraced as a discourse which supposedly discloses the 'essence' of human being and a 'fundamental' level of human historical becoming. As has been seen in the last chapter, a Marxism of this kind can be critically dismantled, and therefore one should not accept the

[2] Gutierrez, *A Theology of Liberation*, pp. 66–72.

contention of political theology that basic Marxist conclusions are inviolable, simply in terms of a proper respect for the autonomy of secular social science.

It will be shown below that, despite the shift in political theology from an individualist to a social concern, the manner of dealing with the latter remains imbued with the transcendentalism of Rahner's account of grace. It is *this* perspective which makes it appear obvious that to take account of the social is to take account of a factor essentially 'outside' the Church and the basic concerns of theology. From the Rahnerian version of integralism to an embracing of Bonhoeffer's dialectical paradoxes of secularization[3] is an easy step: the social is an autonomous sphere which does not need to turn to theology for its self-understanding, and yet it is already a grace-imbued sphere, and therefore it is *upon* pre-theological sociology or Marxist social theory, that theology must be founded. In consequence, a theological critique of society becomes impossible. And therefore what we are offered is *anything but* a true theology of the political. Theological beliefs themselves, however much a formal orthodoxy may still be espoused, tend to become but a faint regulative gloss upon Kantian ethics and a somewhat eclectic, though basic-ally Marxist, social theory. The dialectical character of Marxism, which sees humanity as distilled out of a purely immanent outworking of 'contradiction', blends nicely with an essentially dialectical theology, which discovers God within the closed circle of his apparent absence, or in an abstract absolute freedom which patrols the boundary of this realm, where 'only the human' – that is to say, only the formal fact of human cultural construction – is permit-ted recognition.

Not without distress do I realize that some of my conclusions here coincide with those of reactionaries in the Vatican. But in no sense is it left-wing politics to which I wish to object; on the contrary, my fear is that, as the Marxist belief in the inevitability of socialism, or else a socialism arising merely from the lifting of restrictions on human freedom declines, so also does socialism itself atrophy. It should, in fact, be peculiarly the responsibility of Christian socialists at present to demonstrate how socialism is grounded in Christianity, because it is impossible for anyone to accept any longer that socialism is simply the inevitable creed of all sane, rational human beings. But this is *not* the main direction that has been pursued by the proponents of political and liberation theology; on the contrary, theirs has been simply another effort to reinterpret Christianity in terms of a dominant secular discourse of our day.

Once the dialogue with Marxism as an 'autonomous' science is ended, and we return to the more important matter of Christian socialism, then it can be seen that the French, not the Rahnerian version of integralism provides the basis for a true political theology: that is to say, a theological critique of society and politics. Only the French version truly abandons hierarchies and geog-raphies in theological anthropology, because it refuses even to 'formally

---

[3] Dietrich Bonhoeffer, *Letters and Papers from Prison* (Glasgow: Fontana, 1963) pp. 91–127.

distinguish' a realm of pure nature in concrete humanity. Nor, for this version, is the encounter with grace situated at the margins of every individual's knowing (as for Rahner), but rather in the confrontation with certain historical texts and images which have no permanent 'place' whatsoever, save that of their original occurrence as events and their protracted repetition through the force of ecclesial allegiance. No social theory can set limits to the capacity of these events to become 'fundamental' for human history, any more than it can in the case of any other events. The version of integralism which 'supernaturalizes the natural' is, therefore, also the more historicist in character, because it does not identify the supernatural as any permanent 'area' of human life. But neither does it locate 'nature', although it recognizes the always finitely mediated character of participation in the supernatural. Where the supernatural impinges as the cultural recurrence of an event, it is at once recognizable as 'different', and, at the same time, as limitlessly capable of transforming all other cultural phenomena. One can conclude that, in avoiding any hypostasization of human nature, in stressing the historical, by insisting that the later and superseding may assume priority over the earlier and apparently more 'basic', the French version of integralism points in a 'postmodern' direction which has more contemporary relevance than the view of Rahner.

The liberation theologians would still, however, be right to point out that thinkers like de Lubac and von Balthasar do not fully follow through the implications of their integralism, precisely to the degree that they fail to develop a social or a political theology. I shall argue that there are two dimensions to this failure: first, an unwillingness to confront the severe problem of possible Christian aversion to the existing secular order; second, a refusal to face up fully to the humanly constructed character of cultural reality. Here, an appeal back to Blondel's concept of action, of knowledge as invention, and of supernatural knowledge as mediated through human creative endeavour is vital. His 'supernatural pragmatism', which makes practice fundamental in the sense that thought and action are inseparably fused in the development of a tradition, is to be contrasted with the 'foundational *praxis*' of political and liberation theology, which appeals either to an impossible practice 'without theory', or else to a specifically 'political' practice, which is a practice outside Christian tradition. Whereas political theology remains the prisoner of the governing modern assumption that *poesis* marks out the sphere of the secular, Blondel's concept of a self-dispossessing action points the way to a postmodern social theology.

The rest of this chapter is divided into five further sections. In the second section I shall describe, successively, the three versions of integralism given by Blondel, de Lubac and Karl Rahner. The treatment of Blondel is somewhat extended, because I want to show that his version of integralism is also part of a new philosophy which goes beyond both positivism and dialectics so far as to anticipate a postmodern 'discourse about difference', which is the subject of Part Four of this book. Blondel's conception of a Christian version of such a discourse will prove important for my treatment of secular nihilism in the postmodern era.

In the third section, I trace the social implications of integralism as under-stood by the French tradition, and go on to contrast this with the Rahnerian approach of political and liberation theology, arguing that this disallows them any true 'social integralism' whatsoever. The fourth section shows that, in consequence, their conception of salvation is either individualist, or else reducible to a secular promotion of negative freedom. The fifth section shows that, as a further consequence, political and liberation theology embrace the metanarratives of Marxism and sociology, because they can no longer connect the invocation of transcendence with a concrete, narratable social content. The final section shows, similarly, that the foundational *praxis* appealed to by these theologies is not a genuinely historical and open category, but instead is a space *theoretically* marked out as secular political practice.

The Integralist Revolution in Modern Catholic Thought

1   Excursus *on Blondel*

At the centre of Maurice Blondel's *Action* of 1893 stands the argument that, without an acknowledgement of the supernatural, our account of reality is incomplete.[4] Indeed the demonstration that this is the case is the *only* proper concern of philosophy as a science. Philosophy is able to say nothing about the content of supernatural grace, precisely because grace is a divine gift over and above the given capacities of human reason. It is nonetheless able to affirm our need for grace, and the fact that in every human action it is either accepted or rejected (or rather, it is *always* implicitly accepted and sometimes, also, explicitly rejected).

The argument is made by developing a phenomenology of human action, which shows that the human will is 'never equal to itself', or never finds any satisfactory resting place in any of its natural intentions or actions.[5] Whereas Hegel's phenomenology passes through a similar succession of 'insufficien-cies' to arrive at a satisfactory finite synthesis in the form of the modern State, Blondel's phenomenology concludes negatively, with the paradox that the human will, from its most native desire, demands a completion that goes beyond its own resources. In its immanent impulses it requires the transcend-ent, which, though necessary to it, can only be superadded, freely given.

Superficially, Blondel's argument appears to resemble that of Karl Rahner in his *Spirit in the World* (1936).[6] Here, Rahner argued that, in every act of understanding, the intellect has a preconception (*vorgriff*) of the openness

---

[4] Maurice Blondel, *Action (1893): Essay on a Critique of Life and a Science of Practice*, trans. Oliva Blanchette (Indiana: Notre Dame University Press, 1984) p. 442.

[5] Ibid., pp. 363, 390, 391, 421, 425.

[6] Karl Rahner, *Spirit in the World*, trans. William Dyck (London: Sheed and Ward, 1968) pp. 440–2.

of Being itself, which alone permits a grasp of the contingency of the particular object understood. Blondel likewise claims that in every act of understanding, what is understood is not equal to the aspiration of the will. However,
Blondel, unlike Rahner, does not understand the transcending capacity of the
self only in terms of something permanently in excess of finite instances. On
the contrary, he also claims that the will cannot be equal to the product of its
own action. The significance of what we do, what we say, somehow permanently escapes us, such that our constant quest for new, more adequate, actions
is matched by an attempt to grasp, intellectually, the full import of what we
have already done: 'God acts in this action, and that is why the thought that
follows the act is richer by an infinity than that which precedes it.'[7]

Transposing Blondel's ideas into a not alien Kierkegaardian idiom, one
might say that the search for more adequate action is simultaneously an
attempt to *repeat* precisely, but in different circumstances, and so not *identically*, the things we have performed in the past.[8] Hence, for Blondel, vertical
self-transcendence is simultaneously a horizontal self-transcendence forward
in time, because our 'own' acts, which constitute our identity, are nonetheless
only actions insofar as they 'add' to us, go out from us, and even escape and
elude us. It follows that openness to Being and to grace, does not in Blondel,
as in Rahner, merely accompany in a general fashion each particular action,
but rather this openness constantly occurs *as* the particular action, as that
strange moment in which what we choose also 'occurs' to us.

For Blondel, there is no general, undetermined pre-apprehension of Being
that constitutes our openness to grace. Although philosophy is confined to
arguing for a need for an unspecified grace, this is because philosophy is
radically incompetent with relation to reality, and cannot really supply an
ontology. In the real, concrete situation of action, the supernatural has always
already offered itself in some specific form, and already been accepted, or else
implicitly accepted and explicitly rejected. Hence the 'negative dialectic' of
Blondel's *Action* resides only in the form of the philosophic argument, not, as
for Hegel, at the level of lived reality. If it resided at the level of lived reality,
then Blondel would, like Pascal, be simply calling on human beings to turn
towards the supernatural, and away from the world, in the face of a sceptical
demonstration of the latter's incapacity to satisfy. In fact, he is saying that
while *theoretically* (philosophically) there is nothing in any finite reality which
offers true meaning to human beings, yet in action itself – the unexhausted
will to act, and the unexhausted significance of the cultural products of action
– a true meaning is always in some measure encountered, although this is
only apprehensible by practical reasoning, the authentic reason which causes

---

[7] Blondel, *Action*, pp. 371, 314, 359, 361–3, 372, 373–88, 401. 'Letter on apologetics', in *Letter on
Apologetics and History and Dogma*, trans. Alexander Dru and Illtyd Trethowan (London: Harvill,
1964) pp. 180–1, 436.

[8] Søren Kierkegaard, *Repetition*, trans. Howard V. Hong and Edna H. Hong (Princeton NJ:
Princeton University Press, 1983).

something to happen. By the same token, Blondel is not, like Rahner, offering us an epistemology, because his philosophy does not claim to say where thought should begin, but merely points, impotently, to where thought is already begun, already has necessary premises which are beyond the reach of any critique.

Like Hegel, Blondel substitutes a phenomenology for an epistemology: instead of a Kantian account of the supposedly fixed conditions under which things appear to us, Blondel insists on the reality of successive, different appearances, which are the interactions which take place between humans and between human and other beings. There is no 'epistemological problem', since knowledge consists in the relation of beings and the mutual modifications that ensue. The event of knowledge *is* the reality of the thing, or rather its momentary reality, because there is no deeper reality of essences or substances underlying the 'series' of phenomenal appearances.[9] Blondel affirms that 'to be is to be perceived' (for, like Leibniz, he ascribes perceptive capacity to all material beings, but adds to this that the perceiver only *is* through his perceptions).[10] There is no possibility for theoretical reason to trace the origins of this finite world – which knows only relation, interdependence and transition – to some higher metaphysical realm. Likewise, the complexity of the real world permits no identification of essential fixed genres above the differences of species, nor any reduction of effects to causes, and so in neither case offers us any hierarchical clue to move us back towards a first cause. The question of Being, of the reality of the succession of phenomena, arises only in relation to the question of the meaning of *the whole series*: what is it that holds the monadic links of this chain together? This is not a question that can be answered theoretically, because to a speculative gaze there is only the interlinked chain and *never* any sufficient reason in the preceding links for the addition of a new link, or a new monadic synthesis.[11] Reality is a constant creative self-surpassing, and only a speculation at once theoretical and practical, the real concrete reason of action, can affirm the meaningful character of the series as a whole. This it does precisely at the point where it inserts into the series a new synthesis, which reinterprets and reaffirms the unity of what has gone before, and at the same time, in adding to the chain, is open to the infinity of what lies beyond past actions and happenings.[12] Just like Hegel, Blondel associates the metaphysical moment, the acknowledgement of an infinite ground for finite reality, not with an abstraction from finite qualities, but with a concrete act of expression whose power of interpreting the rest of finitude discloses to us the 'universal'.

But *unlike* Hegel, the next link in the chain, the proximate action, is not negatively implied by what has gone before. Blondel refuses the residual

[9] Blondel, *Action*, pp. 397–9, 414–16, 436, 441.
[10] Ibid., p. 416.
[11] Ibid., pp. 397, 401, 410, 413–14.
[12] Ibid., p. 400.

implication of dialectics with substance, in the form of the self-present subject, and precisely for *this* reason he invents the philosophy of the *surnaturel*. Each new synthesis in nature, in our action, although constrained by what has gone before, and although necessary to what comes after, is a pure *novum*, whose full causal explanation coincides with a description of itself as an effect.[13] Positive science which traces efficient causes can only account for already established relations, it cannot explain the new instance. Nor can dialectical science explain the effect as the outworking of a contradiction, because without ontology, without substance, there *are* no contradictions: one cannot imagine differences as contradictorily opposite expressions of some single more fundamental essence.

Differences or 'heterogeneous elements' (as Blondel puts it) do not jostle for the same space – there is only the space of heterogeneity itself, and hence there are no fundamental antinomies.[14] No longer need the differences of things be reducible to a source where these differences must be resolved into identity, if the logical law of non-contradiction is to be observed. For Blondel the law of non-contradiction has a merely existential origin in the exclusive occurrence of one thing rather than another: here alone what is different, what has not happened, is excluded by, and therefore, incompatible with what has happened.[15] Yet in a future synthesis previously 'opposed' differences may occur together simultaneously. They then become solidary moments of a new unity, because opposition is a relative matter, and heterogeneity is more fundamental than polarity. Whereas Hegel confines the cosmos to a Pythagorean pyramid – a base of indifferent analytic exclusion, a middle realm of necessarily-outworking polarity and contradiction, a summit of self-identical subjective unity – Blondel poses a truly Copernican and decentred universe of always dependent, yet endlessly new perspectives.

The crux in Blondel's philosophy (and, I contend, its least adequate feature) is therefore the confronting and the refusal of nihilism.[16] Can it be that reality is 'senseless', that things just come and go in a succession without reason? A succession that is *more* than reason? For Blondel, the succession is certainly more than theoretical reason, and yet action still coincides with reason in the fullest sense. He argues, without sufficient clarity (and in a way that exposes his residual mentalism), that the will cannot will 'nothing', that it must will purpose, entertain some meaning. But he does not reckon with the possibility that meanings might be purely temporary dispositions of body/language, successively opposed to each other in an agonistic struggle. Could not the final 'meaning' be violence, a Heraclitean struggle, where every action is a new assertion, and nothing further?

---

[13] Ibid., pp. 365, 381, 397, 425.
[14] Ibid., pp. 397, 425, 436–7, 440.
[15] Ibid., pp. 428–30.
[16] Ibid., pp. 330ff, 441.

Blondel does not sufficiently consider this as a possible alternative, and therefore hastens on to say that the logic of every action is precisely an affirmation of the meaningful character of that action, which 'means' precisely, its solidarity with the series of actions as a whole. An action is rational, a true 'event', because 'it works', and is a successful experiment which fits into reality and discloses a new reality. By 'experiment' Blondel does not mean the mere success of instrumental control: rather he implies the successful completion of an action, its endowment with a relative power of endurance. A statue which remains, which becomes significant, whose form imprints itself on people's minds, which can be recognized and repeated, is something which 'works', as much as a scientific law which enables one to repeat an experiment in identical fashion on many occasions and in abstraction from many differences regarded as inessential. The latter, for Blondel, represents but one mode of the way action 'works' and in fact it is not the most fundamental kind of working.[17] For the repeatable experiment still depends upon a particular contingent action, a unique synthesis, which gives no clue to ontology, and does not tell us how things really 'are' in general, but only how we have made things to be, and can continue to make things to be in the future.

But the criteria for true action, for successful 'experiment' in life and art, extend beyond mere singularity. The synthesis must be 'right', aesthetically appropriate, although each synthesis is ultimately its own norm. Following in a select line of Christian thinkers – Cusa, Vico, Hamann, Kierkegaard – Blondel utterly rejects the idea that action expresses a prior 'original' in thought, or that action is measured by a preceding *a priori* theoretical standard. On the contrary, the completed thought *is* the completed action, and, insofar as thought can be separated from action, then what we mean is a positively 'obscure thought', action in its character as force, as the vague groping towards a conclusion. Blondel sees thought/action as 'a procession, in the Alexandrian sense', a self-expression which can only be completed insofar as it 'goes out from us', and gains its completion in terms of external shapes and signs which we can never fully bring under our command.[18]

To act, therefore, or to think at all, may be to create, to assert oneself, but it is equally to lose oneself, to place what is most ours – much more so than any inviolable inwardness – at a total risk. It is also to restrict oneself, to select 'this', for us more essential course, rather than all the other possibilities. For both those reasons Blondel associates all action with self-immolation and sacrifice:[19] by acting/thinking we grope towards a synthesis which seems 'right' to us, and yet is not originally intended by us, but only 'occurs' to us out of the future plenitude of being, and has implications that we cannot

[17] Blondel, *Action*, pp. 90–1, 432, 439.
[18] Ibid., pp. 306, 313, 402.
[19] Ibid., pp. 366, 404.

contain. Every action, at the heart of its very intentionality, is inherently heterogeneous, becoming other to itself (though deepening, not betraying its author's purpose, if this was a good one, and it is received in a good spirit by other people). With this concept, Blondel overcomes the modern notion of the heterogenesis of ends, which, as we saw, depended on the illusion of a contrast between a subjective intention, of which the subject is fully in control, and the cumulative effect of this intention in its later, objective outworkings.[20]

Yet we still have not faced the central crux. According to Blondel, the logic of action, of every action, demands the supernatural. What does this really mean? Basically, two things: first, that in every action there is present an implicit faith that a new and 'correct' synthesis will be discovered, and that this self-grounded norm is somehow more than arbitrary. Its force of compulsion upon our will, its partial satisfaction of our will, shows that a power beyond the finite series is in profound agreement with us, and alone is able to bring our wills to self-agreement. (One could usefully compare Kant's transcendental account of the 'aesthetic idea'.) Inversely, the inner heterogeneity of every action, or its 'self-surpassing' character, disclosed by phenomenological analysis, provides Blondel with a new way of understanding the *concursus* of divine grace with human will. Every action is entirely our own, yet entirely transcends us.[21]

Secondly, the faith in 'true synthesis' implies that the meaning of all synthesis is 'mediation'. For the ground holding together the products of our action is not substance, but an intuited harmony, the combining together in infinite unity of disparate elements.[22] Likewise, successful action is sacrifice, our offering of ourselves to others, so that the action constitutes a 'bond' between us. In making a new synthesis, and in carrying out a new act of mediation, within what Blondel (like Nicholas of Cusa) calls the 'little world' of human cultural creation,[23] we also surmise or conjecture that the meaning of all the other monadic links in the chain – whose constitution our synthesis has to presuppose if it is to 'fit' – is also 'mediation'. Mediating action, then, is the key to the mysterious *vinculum substantiale* of Leibniz: only when *love* is affirmed do we have an ontology, and only when sin is acknowledged as the theoretical inhibition of action, or the abstract withholding of assent to the inevitable meaning of action, do we have any epistemological criterion for 'untruth', or theoretical as well as practical falsity. The discovery of mediation, and of the supernatural, brings us to 'the domain where the great peace of science reigns'.[24] (Notice that in linking science and peace, refusing negation, celebrating contingency, foregrounding sacrifice, Blondel retains many

[20] Ibid., pp. 306, 427, 432. See chapter 2 above.
[21] Ibid., pp. 373–89, 394–9.
[22] Ibid., pp. 414–16, 420.
[23] Ibid., p. 379.
[24] Ibid., p. 438, pp. 95, 405, 422, 441.

positivist themes, while transcending them and returning them to Augustinian roots.)

The task of philosophy, for Blondel, its truly *scientific* task, is to acknowledge its own inadequacy: for the least thought, as action, escapes it, in (implicitly) acknowledging the plenitude of supernatural super-addition, and the ever-renewed mediation of love. But although Blondel's philosophy is self-denying, it is also, *at* the philosophical level, unique. Like the ancient stoics, Blondel refuses transcendent hierarchy and a merely theoretic *episteme* which discovers permanent underlying causes; like them, he links truth to pragmatic effect, technological and rhetorical.[25] Yet, while abandoning the Aristotelian separation of *praxis* from *poesis* and *theoria*, he still affirms that action pursues an ethical/aesthetic quest for the *telos*. If the meaning of the series itself is love, then there is no 'underlying' series, as for the stoics. There are only the mediating links, and these themselves, taken altogether, must be mediated, or given by an infinitely plenitudinous power, if the ultimate 'meaning' is to be mediation, which is a principle at once of unity and of distinction. And yet again, this power, the goal we strive towards, embodies in itself nothing but an infinite series, an infinite mediation, so that it is at once and equally, total act and total potential: as the ultimate *vinculum*, it is also the infinitely complete yet infinitely never-ended exchange and process of love. Blondel maintains that even philosophy must affirm the generation of the Son from the Father in the Trinity, because love demands some inner distinction, some action and re-action in a processive outgoing, which maintains a passivity at the heart of action itself.[26]

Blondel is able to weld together the stoic approach to the cosmos, and to the unity of theory and practice, with the Aristotelian approach to ethical *praxis*, because he contends that all thought is participation in divine creative action, the force of origination, and, at the same time, that all creation is *kenosis*, a self-emptying mediation. Hence the finite series of reality seeks the *telos* of the Father's full self-realization in the *Logos*, and at the same time it is precisely this end which preserves simply the series, the endless interplay of creative mediation. Blondel seeks here to expound an ontology of supernatural charity, and he is quite explicit: 'Down to the last detail of the last imperceptible phenomenon, mediating action makes up the truth and the being of all that is. And it would be strange indeed to be able to explain anything apart from him without whom nothing has been made, without whom all that has been falls back into nothingness.'[27]

Yet Blondel does not merely wish to appeal to the God of creation: his philosophy marks out the place of the supernatural *tout court* – also as redemptive, and sanctifying. If what holds the monads and the chain in being is love, then the love expressed here must be perfect, the world must

---

[25] Blondel, *Action*, p. 263. See chapter 12 below.
[26] Maurice Blondel, *L'Être et Les Êtres* (Paris: Felix Alan, 1935) pp. 332–3.
[27] Ibid., p. 424, pp. 419–20, 432, 442.

offer itself back to the Father, on pain of ceasing to be the World. Blondel conjectures – against his own Scotistic leanings – that before the Fall, humanity might have collectively made this perfect return. But after the Fall, all human action is impaired by sin, and therefore if *God's* action is not to be denied and the world to collapse, there must somewhere be a perfect return still made, and a perfect counterweight to the imbalance of sin which upsets the whole equilibrium of action.

The logic of action itself, therefore, demands a divine-human mediator, and the quest of the human will to 'equalize' itself can now only be the attempt to be equal to the central revelation of the mediator, and to all the particular words and actions by which it is conveyed and repeated in the society of the Church.[28]

Human action, in consequence, requires a revelation, and it requires a dogmatic tradition. This tradition is not 'over against us' in the 'extrinsic' (to use Blondel's adaptation of a scholastic term) sense of mere revealed information, but only over against us in the precise sense that action itself is over against us – before, beyond and after us – for all that it is most intimate to us.[29] While stressing, with Maréchal and others, that doctrine is allied to mystical experience, Blondel adds that it is the product of an action, or 'the letter' which vivifies, the spirit *as* the letter and not the disembodied, unexpressed *élan* of human subjectivity taken alone.[30] He describes his philosophy of action as 'decentred', precisely because it neither refers reality to constant substances, nor to constant structures of the knowing subject, but rather (like Hamann's 'metacritique') locates the critical principle in the linguistic word or signifying image which interprets according to its own singularity, and can only be itself criticized by other, later words or signs.[31] Such a self-criticism of language underlies the development of a common tradition, and it is in tradition that Blondel locates the reality of action. But only in one particular tradition: in the community basing itself on the life of the one, true mediator.

It can therefore be seen that what matters in Blondel's thought is not negative dialectic at the level of philosophic theory, but rather the logic of positive assertion at the level of action: here, it is not merely that supernatural grace is shown to be *required*, but that it is shown to be always present. And *not* present in the transcendental conditions of action – present rather in the always particular self-supplementation of action, in the continuous eccentricities of a serial tradition, and present only insofar as all human traditions can refer themselves to a perfect act of mediation, which is accomplished in deeds which remain as signs and are repeated in 'literal practice'. Every human action – says Blondel, the philosopher – is prophetic of Christ, or secretly refers to him; this is no anonymity of grace in the general character of the human, as for Rahner. Rather, the anonymous reference is given in a precise,

---

[28] Ibid., pp. 264ff, 367–8, 420.
[29] Ibid., p. 425.
[30] Ibid., pp. 385–6.
[31] Ibid., p. 442.

historical, serial positioning in relation to the Incarnation – whether before, after or alongside.[32]

The claim of Blondel's philosophy not to trespass upon the content of grace, which must be always unprecedented in relation to human reason, surely collapses at the point where he affirms, as a philosopher, not just supernatural grace, but also the Incarnation, the need for atonement, and the Trinity.[33] Blondel feels that this still leaves something theological which philosophy cannot touch, because these doctrines would have a mere extrinsic, arbitrary force, were it not for the particular shape of Christic and ecclesiastical words and actions which encourage us to affirm them as divine, atoning and sanctifying. And yet he betrays a false order of priority here.

One ought to say that *only* because one first experiences the 'shape' of incarnation, of atonement, is one led to formulate the abstract notions of their occurrence; and only then does one construe reality in terms of the need for the perfect offering of love. Nothing outside the formal presuppositions of this content, which theology has adduced, is sufficient to persuade us of the need for salvation, or of charity as the ultimate *vinculum substantiale*. Some other religions, certain versions of metaphysics, are certainly rendered impossible by the logic of action: without the 'Platonic' priority of thought, without the Cartesian-Kantian subject, without causal explanation of effects, without the heterogenesis of ends, one can have *neither* antique metaphysics, *nor* modern rationalism and empiricism, with their concomitant secular social theories. But the logic of action alone cannot, as Blondel taught, decipher action as love. Only allegiance to a particular series of actions, or a particular tradition, does this. Blondel fails to reckon with the fact that, without this allegiance, action may appear to be nothing but violence and risk. The response of indifference to this or that (nihilism) or of a secret and tragic withholding of assent to the ceaseless additions our actions make (stoicism) – the two reactions which Blondel considers the very essence of sin – may appear to be the best resort of the sensitive person.

In short, Blondel dismisses too lightly the possibility of nihilism as an intellectual stance, and this is the question we shall have to confront in the final section of this book. One must go beyond Blondel to say that philosophy – which he begins to see as merely a therapeutic disabusing from illusion – cannot confirm the necessity of a determinate ontology as indicated by another sort of discourse. Blondel is right: the ontological question is only seriously posed and answered in practice, and only the practice of a tradition like Christianity can now assume all the traditional tasks of philosophy as metaphysics. But philosophy cannot mark out the site for a necessarily Christian ontology. It is theology, rather, and not philosophy, which explains things, which discovers reality as mediating action, which is alone certainty, alone science . . .

---

[32] Blondel, *Action*, pp. 367–8, 372, 441.
[33] Ibid., pp. 306, 367, 404, 422.

Yet, reunderstood as theology, Blondel's philosophy can mostly stand. It is, perhaps, the boldest exercise in Christian thought of modern times. More than any other Christian thinker, Blondel steadfastly refuses (at least in his original phase) either to return to unreconstructed medieval realism, or to embrace the modern philosophy which finds a point of stability in the subject: 'reverse realism' as Blondel dubs it.[34] Instead, he accepts the absolute historicism, the unrestricted perspectivism, which Cartesianism and transcendental philosophy attempted to keep at bay. Yet he also realizes the thoroughly traditional advantage that is thereby gained: no determination of fundamental categories of knowledge marks out any finite act of knowledge as merely finite, nor can one any longer define the 'transcendent' as what lies ineffably beyond – as the object of our mere aspiration – the well-defined circle of finitude. Instead of modern 'transcendence', which is but the projection of the restlessness of the human will, Blondel wishes to return to the medieval 'supernatural' (as embraced in that era by both theology and philosophy) which concerned the confrontation of our intellect with an infinite power of illumination outside itself. Here the sense of a 'beyond', and the awareness of moral and spiritual growth are inseparable.[35] Yet in Blondel's postmodern regaining of the supernatural, our receptivity does not reside primarily in the possibility of contemplation: instead, we are receptive at the point of our greatest activity, our own initiative.

More than Aristotle's *praxis* or Kantian practical reason, Blondel's action is focused on emanative *poesis*, and the key to his 'postmodernism' lies in his finding in what is made, the *factum*, the opening to transcendence, rather than the keeper of human autonomy. For Blondel, our thought depends entirely upon contingent, theoretically unjustifiable assumptions, and on equally unjustifiable additions to the received tradition, and yet it is precisely this historicist confinement of our thought which renders it *irreducible* to any immanent process, and always dependent upon its participation in a transcendent plenitude of realized action, of thought as word and deed. As mere thinkers, aiming to sum things up once-and-for-all, we are inclined to project God as ourselves, to make him in our own image. Yet as doers and makers, we *really do* 'invent' a God we cannot control, so that we are all, as Blondel says, *theotokoi*, giving birth to the divine image in our conjecturing practice. (Participation in the eternal generation of the *Logos* is, for Blondel, that to which *omnia intendunt assimilari Deo* properly applies.)[36]

Blondel, as it were, shifts the site of our humility from contemplation to action, and so overcomes both classical and modern forms of *hubris*. He succeeds in separating theological objectivism from philosophical realism, and thereby inaugurates a 'supernatural pragmatism', for which the reference

[34] Ibid., pp. 95, 413.

[35] Blondel, 'Letter on apologetics', pp. 175–9.

[36] Blondel, *Action*, p. 386. *L'Être et Les Êtres*, pp. 332–3. *Exigences Philosophiques du Christianisme* (Paris: PUF., 1950) pp. 217–73.

to an infinite, divine reality occurs through the effort 'outwards' from the subject and 'forwards' to the future, more perfect repetition of what is already given. But this occurs only through collective, cultural action; even Christ, says Blondel, is human by virtue of the humanity of the rest of us, which is to say that preceding human words created the possibility of Christ, although Christ recapitulated these words and infinitely surpassed their previous significance.[37]

Blondel, therefore, shows that if theology embraces a more thorough-going perspectivism, pragmatism and historicism, it can escape from the 'modern' illusions which claim that a purely finite, immanent science (including social science) can offer an ontology, or account of 'the way things really are'. And with the removal of the discourse of metaphysics from the competence of philosophy, the possibility of a 'supernaturalizing of the natural' is more drastically opened to view than ever before within the entire Christian era. Thus Blondel, more than anyone else, points us beyond secular reason.

2   Henri de Lubac and Hans Urs von Balthasar

Blondel offered a new existential account of the experience of grace. Nothing similar was provided by Henri de Lubac, who also, in an epoch dominated by a resurrected realism, failed to grapple with the stoic and pragmatist elements in Blondel's philosophy. However, de Lubac did usefully prescind from the negative dialectics of Blondel's philosophical account of grace, and instead attempted to retrieve a properly theological integralism, which he saw as betrayed by post-Tridentine scholastic orthodoxy.

De Lubac's original work on this subject, *Surnaturel*, of 1946, came under curial suspicion for supposed undermining of the gratuity of supernatural grace.[38] Some commentators have accordingly seen this work as tending, like Rahner, to 'naturalize the supernatural', whereas de Lubac's later book, *Le Mystère du Surnaturel*, is thought to 'supernaturalize the natural' in a way that appeases official misgivings.[39] But this is a false interpretation: De Lubac consistently 'supernaturalizes the natural', and, in his second work, he re-states his first thesis sometimes more strongly, albeit with contorted concessions to official suspicion.

De Lubac contrasts what he takes (over-simplistically) to be Blondel's emphasis on a discontinuity between human action and supernatural grace with a Patristic and scholastic stress on continuity.[40] For the traditional view,

[37] Blondel–Wehrte, *Correspondance* (Paris: Aubier, 1969) p. 99. Cited in René Virgoulay, *Blondel et le Modernisme* (Paris: Editions du Cerf, 1980) p. 417.

[38] Henri de Lubac, *Surnaturel* (Paris: Aubier, 1946). For a much more complex treatment of the *Surnaturel* debate and an account of differences between de Lubac and von Balthasar, see John Milbank, *The Suspended Middle: Henri de Lubac and the Debate on the Supernatural* (Grand Rapids, Ill: Eerdmans, 2005).

[39] Henri de Lubac, *The Mystery of the Supernatural*, trans. Rosemary Sheed (London: Geoffrey Chapman, 1967).

[40] Ibid., pp. 38, 243–6.

our mere desire to see God was a sign of a real presentiment of grace within us, not of a merely possible gift. More strongly than Blondel, de Lubac emphasizes the irreducible paradox of grace, whereby *ultimus finis creaturae rationalis facultatem natura ipsius excedit.*[41] He demonstrates that, for Augustine, Aquinas and Scotus, one can only specify human nature with reference to its supernatural end, and yet this end is in no way owing to human beings as a *debitum*.

The principle of Aristotelian metaphysics, whereby nothing external can prevent a creature reaching its natural end, here seems to be violated. But de Lubac points out that for the Fathers and the scholastics human nature was not simply identical with Aristotelian nature: they understood that something could become the most intimate 'property' of an *ens*, and yet be 'accidentally' imparted to it. Thus the real specific difference of the human being consists in his desire for God, even though this desire cannot 'require' its fulfilment, without betraying its own need, which is for a free satisfaction of this desire by the divine love. De Lubac repudiates any suggestion that this desire is something not fully specific, a mere 'velleity', or else some vague transcendental quest which never comes any nearer towards its goal.[42] (This conception he attributes to Maréchal.) And yet the givenness of grace is still to be distinguished from the givenness of creation: everything else is appointed to a relatively fixed natural end, but humanity alone is constituted such that its nature is to transcend itself towards a supernatural fruition. As for Blondel, this self-transcending is not accomplished merely abstractly and negatively: rather, it is accomplished in proper and exemplary fashion in Christ, who was joined to the *Logos* not by grace, but by nature. All other acts of self-transcending, or receptions of supernatural grace, are to be interpreted as anticipations of Christ, or else are known to be directly attributable to his influence.[43]

Hans Urs von Balthasar was therefore right to insist that de Lubac's version of integralism points to a stress on the historical, to the view that our humanity is only fully defined when it is referred to certain privileged historical events and images, which alone convey to us the style of our true destiny.[44] Whereas, for Karl Rahner, the implication of integralism was that we begin with something universal for each individual – his psychology, or rather the epistemic structure of his knowing – for Balthasar an opposite implication

[41] Ibid., p. 41.

[42] *Surnaturel*, p. 483.

[43] Henri du Lubac, *Catholicism: Christ and the Common Destiny of Man*, trans. Lancelot C. Sheppard (London: Barns and Oates, 1937) pp. 55–9.

[44] Hans Urs von Balthasar, *The Theology of Karl Barth*, trans. John Drury (New York: Holt, Rinehart, and Winston, 1971) pp. 239–41. *The Glory of the Lord: Theological Aesthetics*, vol. 1: *Seeing the Form*, trans. Erasmo Leiva-Merikakis (Edinburgh: T. and T. Clark, 1982). *Love Alone: The Way of Revelation* (London: Sheed and Ward, 1977). Rowan Williams, 'Balthasar and the analysis of faith', in John Riches (ed.) *The Analogy of Beauty* (Edinburgh: T. and T. Clark, 1986) pp. 11–34, 35–59. See also, for the non-duality of reason and revelation, John Montag, SJ, 'Revelation: the false legacy of Suarez', in, J. Milbank, C. Pickstock and G. Ward (eds.) *Radical Orthodoxy: A New Theology* (London: Routledge, 1999) pp. 38–64.

held true. Theology must stop 'moving from nature to its goal', and rather make sense of human nature in terms of 'divinely revealed' realities, which can only be construed according to their own inner logic. To remove any lingering ambiguities in de Lubac's view of things, Balthasar insisted much more strongly on the specific 'formed' character of the supernatural life; the 'difference' of grace is a visible, tangible difference, as conveyed through the unique shape of the Christic *forma*, repeated, replenished and completed in the various lives of the saints, and the organic unity of the body of Christ. To avoid the extrinsicism of mere assent to propositions about God's offer of grace, and to insist on the priority of grace in shaping our lives, one must develop a 'theological aesthetic' which identifies a truth and an ethical goal inseparable from a certain attractive appearance which has its own peculiar logic, indistinguishable from the order of its manifestation. This project is compatible with the earlier proposals of Blondel, although Balthasar failed to incorporate into his aesthetic Blondel's pragmatist, differential and 'postmodern' insights. (His ontology remained an uneasy mixture of pre-modern Thomist realism, Herderian expressivism and neo-Kantian personalism.)

3   *Karl Rahner*

Like Henri de Lubac, Karl Rahner appeared to reject the neo-scholastic, or 'two-tier' account of the relationship of grace to nature.[45] In this account, the Patristic and medieval notion of a *desiderium naturale visionis beatificae* had been lost sight of, and so the supernatural addition of grace was presented as 'extrinsically' related to a self-sufficient human nature already complete within itself. As this addition could not be connected with any intrinsic human need, grace became hypostasized as an 'entitative' transformation of our being, which had to be accepted by faith as a fact, and yet could not be experienced. In consequence, as de Lubac notes, neo-scholastic theology invented a kind of 'naturalized supernatural', such that there were two parallel systems of orientation to God: the one natural, and the other supernatural, with different verbal protocols, and yet essentially identical content.[46] Or else, and more ominously, a purely 'natural man' was discovered, a being that could be adequately described by philosophic ontology, or could discover in his own physical and rational make-up the 'natural law' for social and political life.

Karl Rahner appeared to refute these tendencies, and accepted that the concept of a 'pure nature' has tended to give a dark colouring to secularization. And yet he raised objections to de Lubac and Balthasar's version of integralism. Rahner argued that the notion of a pure nature should apply

[45] Karl Rahner, 'Concerning the relationship between nature and grace'; in *Theological Investigations*, trans. Cornelius Ernst. vol. 1 (London: Darton, Longman and Todd, 1961) pp. 297–317. 'Nature and grace'; in *Theological Investigations*, trans. Kevin Smith, vol. 4 (London: Darton, Longman and Todd, 1960) pp. 165–88.
[46] De Lubac, *The Mystery of the Supernatural*, p. 53.

not only to a possible humanity which has not, but might have been created, but also in a regulative fashion to the real human beings who actually exist. Without a 'formal distinction' of a merely natural humanity within the concrete human person, there must be a natural exigency for grace which betrays its gratuitous character. If the supernatural is also what is most intimate to us, as for de Lubac, then, Rahner claims, it is really naturalized. He also rejects the notion of the *summum as intimum* (or, one might say, in postmodern terms, the super-structure as the essential) as merely paradoxical, arguing that it cannot be 'proved' from positive theological sources (in fact *none* of the discourse about 'grace' could be so proved). Attempts to make sense of the paradox through the analogy of human love, which is 'required', yet can only be freely given, if it is to be love, do not apply because such love is not an actual ontological necessity.

To preserve the gratuity of grace, one requires the formal distinction of a 'pure nature'; how, then, is extrinsicism to be avoided? Here, Rahner invents the idea of 'a supernatural existential', an inner orientation to the beatific vision, which is given, along with the 'formal object' of this orientation, to every human being. This supernatural existential is something in addition to the *potentia obedientialis* of human nature to God, which is, in itself, more than a mere 'non-repugnance', but also an active longing for God present in the *vorgriff* of Being in general, that is given with every act of understanding. Although our natural self-transcendence and the supernatural existential are formally distinct, one cannot, in the concrete person, separate out what belongs to which, and so the *potentia obedientialis* is mixed up with 'trace elements' from the actual gift of grace. This entire conceptual apparatus is not, however, intended to pick out any existential realities, but simply to safeguard the gratuity of grace and yet avoid extrinsicism.

Rahner is not arguing directly with de Lubac, but rather with a view (probably closer to my own) which contends that there is no gratuity in addition to the gratuity of creation.[47] However, despite de Lubac's own contention, this view is scarcely distinguishable from his own, for all creation is grace-given and the constantly 'new' things bestowed on humanity[48] (whose specific creaturehood is defined *as* the exceeding of creaturehood) through history are not 'in addition' to God's single creating act. Rahner's conception of 'pure nature' is, in fact, clearly different from that of de Lubac.

This, however, is in part because he does not fully grasp the force of de Lubac's argument, and does not fully escape from neo-scholastic premises. The point, as de Lubac makes clear, is that God's gift of himself is not gratuitous in relation to a hypothetical nature, nor to an aspect of real human beings that could be 'merely natural', but rather remains gratuitous within itself, such that although the human person is only fulfilled through this gift, he must continue to enjoy it as a gift.[49] If the *mysterium* of *summum* as

---

[47] Rahner, 'Concerning the relationship between nature and grace', p. 304.
[48] De Lubac, *The Mystery of the Supernatural*, pp. 107–10.
[49] De Lubac, *Surnaturel*, pp. 492–7.

intimum does not apply, then the concrete human person who possesses a supernatural existential must either start to exact grace after it has been first given – because this is *now* part of his nature – or else the endlessly renewed supplies of grace will simply remain extrinsic to the person's essential needs. Another level of grace-given desire for grace (the supernatural existential) does absolutely nothing to reconcile gratuity with non-extrinsicism. Hence, it not surprisingly turns out that the contextual structure of the supernatural existential seems almost indistinguishable from that of the natural *vorgriff* of Being. In neither case does self-transcendence denote the encounter with a concrete, recognizable other. Rather, in both cases, the 'intrinsic' experimental side is reducible to a self-striving *conatus* away from finite limitations, while the infinite object sought for – *esse*, which the supernatural existential identifies as God – is still extrinsically separate as a 'formal object'. Our 'entitative raising', insofar as it is a meeting with God, still appears to be something externally and authoritatively confirmed by the arbitrary *fiat* of a positive revelation.

What Rahner effectively does is to rework the neo-scholastic scheme of two parallel supernatural systems, but in the terms of transcendental philosophy, which was *itself* initially indebted to the neo-scholastic invention of a merely natural transcendence. It is ironic that Rahner sincerely wishes to guard against what he perceives as the dangers of 'naturalism', in von Balthasar's position in particular. He wants to uphold, like von Balthasar, precisely the otherness, the unprecedented character of grace. Yet Rahner claims that this otherness is present in the *a priori* structure of every created human spirit. If this is the case, then how can we give it any content? How can we seriously distinguish the object of grace from the supernatural existential, or the supernatural existential as an *a priori* horizon from the mere *vorgriff* of Being? By preserving a pure nature in the concrete being, to save the gratuity of the supernatural, one lands up with extrinsicist doctrinal formulas confronting an account of human aspirations and human ethical norms which is throughly naturalized. In this case, the only remaining way to avoid extrinsicism is to understand Christian revelation and Christian teachings as just expounding, or making 'explicit', the universal availability of grace. The historical events, the human acts and images which can alone be the site of supernatural difference, are here reduced to mere signs of a perfect inward self-transcendence, always humanly available.

Karl Rahner fears to entrust the supernatural to the merely historical, to the succession of human actions and human images. Yet as the historical, the supernaturally given becomes also our nature, *all* of our nature. By contrast, when the paradox of grace is refused, then the gratuity of grace can only be safeguarded by once again effectively hypostasizing it through turning it into the ineffable goal of an endless aspiration. It follows that, by 'naturalizing the supernatural' one *denaturalizes* history, and so ignores actually constituted human nature altogether. As will be shown, the political and liberation theologians only embrace secular social science with enthusiasm because they refuse the truly non-extrinsicist historicism of Blondel, de Lubac and von Balthasar, and embrace Karl Rahner's ahistorical metaphysics of human subjectivity.

The Social Implications of Integralism

1 Blondel and Sturzo

Maurice Blondel understood *Catholicisme intégrale* to include a concern for social questions within the sphere of salvation.[50] But the two versions of integralism interpret the salvific import of the socio-political sphere in opposite ways, which precisely parallel their general differences with regard to the relations of nature and grace.

If integralism means 'the supernaturalizing of the natural', then, on a practical level, there can be no true justice without charity, and no true social order without transformation by the supernatural society which is the Church. On the theoretical level, secular theories of society can be, at best, tentative, and their conclusions remain subject to revision and correction by theology. Blondel upheld both positions, in opposition to the Catholic conservatives of his day, who maintained a strict separation between a Comtean positive science of society, and a theology which applied to 'spiritual' matters alone. In the ideology of Maurras and the *Action Française*, Blondel identified the dangerous political implications of extrinsicism: everyone, of all beliefs and none, can be bound together in a social and political order on the mere basis of agreement about natural 'facts'.[51] Upon analysis, this of course means that we are bound together simply in terms of *de facto* force and power. However, for the *intégristes* the Church lays claim to a privileged position in society because it is the repository of supernatural truth, of the secrets of salvation, and, in the Maurrasian programme, a mastery of positive power politics will best secure for it this position. In this programme, a formal theocracy, to which Blondel was utterly opposed, turns out to be the very reverse of a real, 'integral' transformation of society by grace, affecting all its beliefs, assumptions and practices.

From this indication, one can correctly infer that the integralist reaction against neo-scholasticism was not, initially (before the Second World War), far removed from the position of those who advocated a 'New Christendom'.[52] Like Maritain and his associates, Blondel totally rejected the model of medieval Christendom, where the ecclesiastical hierarchy had also wielded

---

[50] Virgoulay, *Blondel et le Modernisme*, p. 458–71.
[51] Ibid., pp. 466.
[52] Jacques Maritain, *Integral Humanism: Temporal and Spiritual Problems of a New Christendom*, trans. Joseph W. Evans (Indiana: Notre Dame University Press, 1973). For more on the cultural dimensions of the *surnaturel* debate, see Tracey Rowlands, *Culture and the Thomist Tradition after Vatican II* (London: Routledge, 2003).

political, coercive power. But like this group also, Blondel believed in the importance of the transformation of social and political structure by the working of lay Christian 'influence'. If there was a significant difference between the two approaches, then one would have to say that Blondel believed still more strongly in the idea of a specifically 'Christian society', because in his outlook there is less room than in Maritain for a permanent level of fixed natural law. Nevertheless, the whole purpose of Maritain's book, significantly entitled *Humanisme Intégrale*, was precisely to oppose the post-Renaissance emergence of a 'purely natural' humanity in the political sphere, a tendency which he rightly linked to the Molinist separation of human freedom from divine grace, and contrasted with Aquinas's view that even the political power, though 'natural', remains subordinate to supernatural judgement.[53]

If, however, one compares Maritain's text with a remarkable book, *The True Life: Sociology of the Supernatural*, by the Catholic Italian opponent of Mussolini, Luigi Sturzo, then one sees how a Blondelian position encourages a perspective at once more historicist, and more supernaturalizing, than that of Maritain.[54] Just as Blondel believed that philosophy must speak of the supernatural, so Sturzo believed that 'an integral sociology' must speak of the human community – ultimately and especially the Church – *as* supernatural. Unless, according to Sturzo, sociology proceeds in this fashion beyond secular reason, it fails to speak of human beings in the concrete, and fails to deal with their most fundamental aspect, which is precisely their relation to a transcendent, final cause. Despite many crudities and naïvetés in Sturzo's argument, he presents what is at bottom a cogent case. Sociology in the Durkheimian sense is not entertained: 'society' means only the bonds of relationship between individuals, which change and alter in time, so that sociology is, in fact, entirely coextensive with the field of history. The great 'law' of both society and history is the Blondelian 'trend to unification', or to new syntheses of relationship, but this is governed by no Comtean sequence, nor Hegelian dialectic of immanence. As these new unities are always different, there can be no general explanation of exactly what it is which unites human beings – in fact no 'sociology', in the usual sense, whatsoever.[55]

For there can only be sociology if an explanation is offered for the modes of human association, but this depends, for Sturzo, on the recognition of one particular mode of association as normative, and as the goal towards which all human societies are tending. And this normative character cannot be justified in natural terms, but must amount to the claim that here an objective human finality is encountered, and partially realized.[56] From this perspective,

[53] Jacques Maritain, *Integral Humanism*, pp. 18–21.

[54] Luigi Sturzo, *The True Life: Sociology of the Supernatural*, trans. Barbara Barclay Carter (London: Bles, 1947).

[55] Ibid., p. 8, 12–13, 19.

[56] Ibid., pp. 7–45.

that of the Church, one is able to read all human society as 'supernatural' or as groping towards the 'true life' of proper relation to God and to fellow human beings: here alone, one has a 'sociology'. Sturzo notes, following Blondel, that religion is not located primarily in theoretical speculation, but rather in 'action in common', or in social forms regarded as the most fundamental and the most 'binding': religious practices, and the ideas embodied in those practices. Echoing the Catholic traditionalists, he mentions that the frequent occurrence of ideas of 'expiation'[57] always exceed any theoretical justification that could have been given in advance of the invention of these ideas and practices themselves. History, as *action*, always goes beyond philosophy, but a sociology of the supernatural, which admits the principle of grace or of super-added finality, is able to interpret the meaning of the historical process without the need to transcend the bounds of mere narration. A philosophical or sociological attempt to comprehend history will always, like Hegel, take the produced object (Vico's *factum*, which Sturzo explicitly identifies with Blondel's product of action)[58] back into the rational subject, whereas Sturzo's historicist and supernaturalist sociology remains with the excess of the human product. If, for Sturzo, there is to be a social explanation, it must be in terms of our commitment to our own products, and the significance we accord to a particular tradition of acting. Thus, Sturzo succeeds in conceiving of 'historico-supernatural ends'.[59]

Like Blondel, Sturzo goes beyond Hegel in claiming that philosophy (and sociology) cannot simply subsume the historical transformation wrought by Christianity, but must efface itself before theology. However, just as Blondel was wrong when he said that philosophy can claim to recognize negatively the need for the supernatural, so Sturzo is wrong to talk of a 'sociology of the supernatural' rather than a 'theological sociology'. Sturzo's position is, in fact, the less coherent, because his sociology does not just negatively prepare a place for the supernatural, but discusses it insofar as it has been concretely infused into the historical process. Hence a residual positivism in Sturzo's thought: as for the traditionalists, revelation is a kind of undeniable fact, and the supernatural 'hypothesis' is alone capable of explaining social reality. But Sturzo's explanation is more properly a theological explanation, an attempt to read all historical and social reality through the practice of the Church. The claim to be able to do this is, I want to argue, really immanent within the Church's self-understanding as a truly universal society. So, in the final chapter of this book, I will resume Sturzo's endeavour, though under the guise of a 'social theology'.

2   De Lubac and Congar

When one turns from Blondel, and those influenced by him, to the later *nouvelle théologie*, which became influential in the post-war era, one discovers

---

[57] Ibid., pp. 179–81.
[58] Ibid., pp. 74–5, 181.
[59] Ibid., pp. 179–81.

a slight shift in emphasis with regard to the social dimension. While the social and historical character of salvation is strongly emphasized, there is a marked tendency to prescind from the political, and to insulate the Church from wider social processes.

This can most clearly be seen in the case of Henri de Lubac's *Catholicism: Christ and the Common Destiny of Man*, which is a seminal text in the development of modern Catholic ecclesiology and social concern. De Lubac here offers a fine account of how salvation is *inherently* social; it is not, for him, as so often for later political and liberation theology, that there is individual salvation *and also* a salvation of social structures. Rather, salvation means, as it did for Luigi Sturzo, reconciliation with one's fellow human beings, and reconciliation with God. Both mediations occur in the Church, so that the Church is not primarily the means of salvation, but rather the goal of salvation, because it is the community of the reconciled.[60] Furthermore, by insisting that salvation is incorporation into *ecclesia*, de Lubac makes salvation not only social, but also historical. The individual is always saved in a *particular manner*, according to his situation with regard to the Christian past, and in prospect of the Christian future.

By stressing the historical, as well as the social context of salvation, de Lubac is open to recognizing structural elements of emplotment, and does not confine salvation to the level of the I-thou encounter. He is not rendering a 'private' sphere immune from wider social processes. And yet he does appear finally to insulate ecclesial history from secular and political history in general. In the final chapter of *Catholicism*, entitled 'transcendence', de Lubac imperils his conclusions hitherto by asserting: 'There is in man an eternal element, a "germ of eternity", which always breathes the upper air, and which always, *hic et nunc*, evades the temporal society. The truth of his being transcends his being itself.'[61] When talking about the *Church* de Lubac is careful to avoid what I define as 'the sociological illusion' of making society and the individual spatially external to each other, and yet this care is forgotten when it comes to distinguishing the Church from secular concerns. Here, de Lubac rediscovers the evasive spark of purely psychic life, and makes the contrast of Church/secular society in terms of the contrast individual/social, despite the fact that the preceding chapters had argued that the Church is *also* a society. In this light, Marx's supposed 'dissolution of the human being into the social being' ought to be an entirely illusory spectre, yet, for de Lubac, this is what must be, above all, exorcized.[62] By invoking this spectre, de Lubac actually implies – like Weberian sociology – that there *is* a realm which is merely 'social' and which the individual might stand outside. Furthermore, this realm is an autonomous realm which the Church, as Church, should not interfere with, even in terms of advice, except at points

[60] De Lubac, *Catholicism*, pp. 8, 23, 51–4.
[61] Ibid., p. 202.
[62] Ibid., pp. 145–208.

where social actions impinge on the ethical and religious sphere, which now appears especially 'individual'. It does, however, have to be said that it was difficult for thinkers of this era to define a field of autonomy and free action for the *laity*, without also placing self-denying ordinances on the Church, which they still automatically identified with the clerical hierarchy.

This comment is especially pertinent to the work of the French Dominican, Yves Congar, who, more strongly than de Lubac, defines a 'distinction of planes' between ecclesial-clerical and lay-secular action, without regard for the incongruity between this dualism and the integralist revolution. (Congar takes over this formulation from Maritain, but tends not to stress sufficiently the 'integral information' of the temporal by the spiritual. At the same time, he too much preserves Maritain's belief in an autonomous, 'natural' order.) For Congar, the new life offered in Christ concerns 'the inward man' and cannot 'become very socialized', so that the New Christendom's 'persuasive influence' cannot, after all, extend very far.[63] Inversely, the Church occupies the protected time of a 'meta-history', whose inward events are essentially untouched by social processes. Yet although the secular is autonomous in its secularity, Congar agrees with Rahner that the secular can, in itself, be of intrinsic spiritual significance. He elaborates this notion in Christological terms, in calling for a revival of the Gelasian account of Church/State relations, according to which there are 'two powers' ruling this world, both owing their authority to Christ.[64] Arguing that the 'priesthood according to Melchizedek', in the Epistle to the Hebrews, is an essentially political priesthood, Congar proceeds to the exegetically unwarranted conclusion that Christ's priestly-political power is held in suspense till the eschaton, but meanwhile exercised by the State here on earth. In *Lay People in the Church*, the influential work in which this argument is made, Congar plays down what he himself brings out in his own more historical work, namely that for Gelasius there was a distinction between the *auctoritas* of the Church, and the mere executive *potestas* of the *imperium* – so that while Church members were subordinate to the secular arm in worldly affairs, nonetheless the *potestas* remained subject to the ultimate judgement of the *auctoritas*, as the body of Christ himself.[65]

Like some other Dominican writers, for example Marie-Dominique Chenu, Congar is anxious to avoid 'political Augustinianism', which reached its apogee in the Carolingian era, when *regnum* and *sacerdotium* became so coextensive that there was scarcely any longer any 'outside' to the Church.[66] However they do not avoid an ahistorical tendency to conflate both the earlier Patristic view that the empire was 'outside' the Church, and the later Thomist version of natural law, with a modern specification of secular autonomy. For

[63] Yves Congar, *Lay People in the Church*, trans. Donald Attwater (West-minster, MD: The Newman Press, 1965) pp. 80–1; Maritain, *Integral Humanism*, pp. 291–8.

[64] Ibid., pp. 82–91.

[65] Yves Congar, *L'Ecclésiologie du Haut Moyen-Age* (Paris: Editions du Cerf, 1968) pp. 249–59.

[66] M.-D. Chenu, *Is Theology a Science?* (London: Burns and Oates, 1959) p. 63. H.-X. Arquillière, *L'Augustinisme Politique* (Paris: Vrin, 1955).

Gelasius, and for St Augustine, the imperial order remained outside the Church because it was only partially redeemed. For Thomas Aquinas one can recognize the naturalness of the spheres of the family and of political life, yet both must now be pervaded by the law of charity. For modern thought, however, there is a closed circle of secular norms and practices. Compared to modernity, Augustine and Aquinas are in essential agreement: there can be no true fulfilment of natural justice and natural peace without reference to the Church and the workings of grace.

Congar's elaboration of the 'distinction of planes' model reveals, perhaps, some Dominican hesitation about integralism, and, at the same time, the post-war desire of the Church to draw back from sacral endorsement of right-wing regimes into an acknowledgement of the autonomous prerogatives of liberal democracy. However, he further entrenches an antinomy which we have already identified in de Lubac. On the one hand integral Catholicism is social in character: it has collectivist concerns. On the other hand, the only way in which one can unambiguously delineate what is secular and what is spiritual is in terms of a contrast between 'social' and 'individual' matters. In the Latin American context, this antinomy gets clearly exposed to view, because here the Church often provides the only social space in which political resistance (especially peaceful political resistance) can be pursued. Lay activity is here bound up with economic and political concerns, yet it remains also intra-ecclesial in character. Inversely, the pastoral outreach of the clergy quickly finds itself embroiled in the bitter details of political dispute. Hence the 'distinction of planes' was abandoned by the liberation theologians, in favour of a fuller outworking of integralism, which must include the political dimension.

3   Political theology after Rahner

But which *version* of integralism? In theory, political theology might have proceeded in the line of the supernaturalizing of the natural. This would have implied a strong emphasis on the Church itself as the ultimate location of the just society, and a general suspicion of all merely political associations which continue to rely upon coercion. Von Balthasar draws attention to the direction that such thinking would have to take: the 'political', he argues, cannot any longer be the primary context for Christian life, not because this life is asocial, but rather because the Gospel displaces or qualifies the political images for God with more intimate ones: God is parent and God is lover.[67] One might suggest that this *ought* to mean that the project of the Church is the establishment of a new, universal society, a new *civitas*, in which these intimate relationships are paradigmatic: a community in which we relate

---

[67] Hans Urs von Balthasar, 'Nine theses in Christian ethics', in *Readings in Moral Theology, no. 2: The Distinctiveness of Christian Ethics*, ed. Charles E. Curran and Richard A. McCormick, SJ (New York: Paulist Press, 1980) pp. 190–207.

primarily to the neighbour, and every neighbour is mother, brother, sister, spouse. What we require, therefore, is a new ecclesiology which would be also a post-political theology.

But political and liberation theology have not pursued this path. They have universally embraced the other, Rahnerian version of integralism. This is for two reasons: first of all, they associate any notion of a specifically Christian social programme with past Catholic attempts to find a 'middle way' between capitalism and socialism: attempts which usually drift in a rightwards direction. However, they do not sufficiently consider the ways in which Christianity has helped to give a specific content to socialism in terms of emphases on fraternity, on direct economic cooperation, on the professional association or guild which upholds common standards of work and production, and of suspicion of the sovereign State's desire to exterminate all 'intermediate associations' between itself and the individual. In the too-eager embrace of Marxism, these highly-relevant features of Christian socialist tradition tend to be lost sight of.

The second reason is that, in Germany, political theology developed as part of a continuing attempt to come to terms with secular modernity, and this emphasis was sustained by liberation theology for more clearly practical reasons. In Latin America, what had long been sought for was the elusive goal of 'development', although the liberation theologians hoped that industrial and economic progress could occur in that continent without the retreat from religious observance that had been its accompaniment in western Europe. However, this does not mean that they resisted secularization: on the contrary, they paid obeisance to an autonomous sphere of secular power/knowledge. Their conception of remaining ecclesial influence therefore appears to be one in which Church leaders exercise power and influence over essentially secular processes. David E. Mutchler has described how, since the 1960s, this has remained the consistent goal of Latin American churchmen, fearful of loss of religious allegiance, from right to left of the political spectrum.[68] Thus the imparting of great spiritual significance to an essentially secular and political educative programme of reading and writing, which may nonetheless be handled by the clergy who remain a considerable percentage of the clerical class, represents a typical aspect of the phenomenon of liberation theology.

Whatever the reasons for this fundamental theological option, the consequences are clear: integralism is embraced in such a fashion that it becomes identical with Bonhoeffer's dialectical paradoxes concerning a 'world come of age'. Gustavo Gutierrez is sufficiently aware of the other possible option to be able to say that this thesis appears incompatible with integralism; nonetheless, he proceeds to affirm their fundamental identity.[69]

---

[68] David E. Mutchler, *The Church as a Political Factor in Latin America* (New York: Praeger, 1971).

[69] Gutierrez, *A Theology of Liberation*, pp. 66–72.

For what precisely happens when an attempt is made to introduce a social dimension into the Rahnerian version? One of two things, or else both at once. Either the transcending impulse remains essentially individual in character, and merely provides motivation and creative energy for social and political action which retains its own immanent norms. Or else the social process itself is identified as the site of transcendence, of a process of 'liberation' which is gradually removing restrictions upon the human spirit. In the latter case, although the process is a purely human one, and although there are no human needs which cannot be immanently met, liberation can still be identified by theology as the anonymous site of divine saving action. In fact, Hugo Assmann, Segundo and Gutierrez all insist that the choice for salvation is *authentically* made in an anonymous fashion as a purely worldly and ethical decision to respect human freedom.[70] The *content* of salvation is therefore decided at the level of a Kantian principle of practical reason, and theology – including an apparently 'orthodox' Christology and Trinitarian doctrine – merely provides an elaborate regulative apparatus to secure this content and bestow upon it an infinite significance.

But whether transcendence is accomplished in the ethical (the 'liberating' social processes), or else in the epistemological (the surmounting of finitude by the individual knowing will), really makes little difference. In either case, the transcending impulse, which gives the conditions of possibility for theology, also safeguards the realm of the ethical from the impact of a theological critique. Ethics belongs to the world, and the world is a totality, self-sufficiently closed in upon itself. One deduces ethics from the mere formal fact of our freedom, our self-transcending capacity. Only in such a fashion is it possible to obtain ethics from reason *etsi Deus non daretur*, yet then declare that this ethics provides the content of salvation.

For political and liberation theology therefore, the ethical belongs to the social, but both remain essentially apart from the 'religious', which is either their anonymous secret, or else a categorically separate dimension of 'experience'. But the belief in a natural morality, essentially unaffected by religious belief, and shared in common with all humanity, goes along with a thoroughly unhistorical view of ethics, which can even survive the encounter with Marxism (for as we have seen, Marx preserves the idea of a universal imperative to maximize freedom as the real natural law of human existence). For these theologies, the single imperative to love others, which means to desire their liberation, is supposed to well automatically from the depths of the human heart. All other moral prescriptions must be judged according to 'situational' criteria, as to whether or not they maximize human love and freedom.[71] There is no sense here of the impossibility of giving any content to love, or the exercise of freedom, unless we articulate them in terms of a

---

[70] Gutierrez, *A Theology of Liberation*, p. 68. Segundo, *The Liberation of Theology*, pp. 42–3, 50, 71, 78, 83–5, 90, 105.
[71] Ibid., p. 172.

complex set of virtues, which means to appeal to a particular form of human social existence.

The Rahnerian ethics which are taken over by political and liberation theology rightly stress that moral imperatives do not proceed from the *fiat* of a revealed divine will, but are mediated by human reason, which itself participates in divine practical wisdom.[72] But Rahner and his followers fail to see that this participation proceeds historically: it is, for Christianity, restored by the incarnation of the *Logos*, whose peculiar practice upon earth provides us with the key to all human performance. The Rahnerian idea that Christian belief provides only 'motivations' for rational ethical behaviour, is by contrast, astonishingly shallow.

In the first place, as Vincent MacNamara has pointed out, many supposed motivations are really intentional 'reasons for' an action, which colour the mode of the action itself, since actions are always performed under some linguistic, or signifying specification.[73] In the second place, one should search for ethical distinctiveness, not just in generalized ethical recommendations, but in the whole, customary shape of behaviour within a particular society. In the third place, as Nietzsche undertook to show, we are the heirs of a Platonic-Christian 'transvaluation of values' so total as to be, for that very reason, visible only to the archaeologist of ideas. For it was Plato who first unequivocally identified 'the Good' with the highest being – that is to say, before him, nobody *was*, exactly, 'ethical' – and only Judaism and Christianity thoroughly extirpated the association of goodness with heroic strength. It is, ironically, the complacent Catholic moral philosopher who imagines that the term 'good' is somehow more finitely secure, less mythological than the term 'God'. Yet in reality the term 'good' condenses a narrative of absolute finality, and those who deny its essential connection with 'God' usually turn out not to believe in objective 'good ends' at all, but only in the 'right' of freedom, or the usefulness of whatever is useful.

And what is different about Christian ethics, and so implies a specific Christian social teaching, is precisely its supernaturalizing of 'the good', and its more absolute view of the priority and possibility of goodness. Thomas Aquinas explains that there is no *vera virtus* without *caritas*, the love of God (in a double sense of the genitive), just as there is no *vera scientia* without theology, the science of God (in a similarly double sense). We are to love our neighbours under the light of their being 'in God', and so we are called to infinite perfection by the self-replenishing, ceaselessly overflowing source of all goodness.[74] In the natural order, prudence (*phronesis*) is the form of the

---

[72] Joseph Fuchs, 'Is there a specifically Christian morality?', in Curran and McCormick (eds.), *Readings in Moral Theology, no. 2: The Distinctiveness of Christian Ethics* pp. 3–20. Vincent MacNamara, *Faith and Ethics: Recent Roman Catholicism* (Dublin and London: Gill and MacMillan, 1985) pp. 37–55.

[73] Ibid., p. 104ff.

[74] Aquinas, *ST* II II q.23 a7; q.25 a1.

virtues, yet in the real, historical, integral, supernatural order, even prudence is governed by charity.

Thus in the *secunda secundae*, the treatment of prudence is explicitly placed after that of the theological virtues. Prudence concerns moral tact, the giving of everything its due in the right place and at the right time, and charity must still be exercised with tact if it is to be a proper care. But charity also transcends the perspective of doing exact justice, of measuring up to the way things are. The supernatural perspective of charity reveals that from every finite position, within every social situation, an advance to perfection remains possible. This perspective does not simply negate the Aristotelian insight about 'moral luck', or the way in which our moral capacities are restricted by our social situation and fortune. For the perspective is only possible *as* a new social perspective, which is that of the Church. To be a part of the Church (insofar as it really *is* the Church) is to have the moral luck to belong to the society which overcomes moral luck. For the Church exists as a 'practice of perfection', as the working of charity, which ceaselessly tries to remove the obstacles in the way of people becoming perfect. Hence in place of the overriding Aristotelian concern to become the still-heroic 'magnanimous man' who distributes his stored largesse, Aquinas places the concern to promote charity as friendship, which is not only (as for Aristotle) an agreement in the good, and a goodwill towards the other, but also the intimate communication and mutuality which the Gospel has revealed as more ontologically ultimate.[75] In striving to bring everyone into this mutuality, we will to remove all difficulties in their path. So when Aquinas deals with the 'outward acts of charity', he actually elaborates an entirely *different*, ecclesial social practice which alone fulfils 'justice': what matters here is 'almsgiving' – the sufficient fulfilment of all the needs of the neighbour; 'fraternal correction', which is non-coercive, and yet an absolute stranger to any false indifference as to our neighbour's conduct; 'mercy', which is the only possible reaction to all actions falling short of the final end; and 'pity', which is grief for another's imperfection.[76]

Of course, Aquinas fails to realize the full 'political' implications of ecclesial practice. But the point is that the supernatural perspective of ever-advancing perfection does provide a different social vision. It suggests that there must be a progress to mutuality and equal sharing: that evil must be coped with, not simply by judicial punishment, but, more finally, by forgiveness and forbearance; it refuses to remain content with justice as a goal, but looks to joy and peace as the 'proper effects' of charity, to a community united in an equal but diverse participation in a limitless good – the power of creative sharing, which is always renewable.

The Rahnerian version of integralism by contrast, can only make the social the real site of salvation by a dialectical baptism of secular society. It has to annex Christian 'orthodoxy' to the practical rejection of Christian truth. And

---

[75] Aquinas, *ST* II II q.23 a 1; q.27a2, q.29a3.
[76] Aquinas, *ST* II II qq.28–33.

its assumption that there is a universally available social ethic ignores the historical genesis of morality. By contrast, the integralism which 'super-naturalizes the natural' is able to expound the difference of supernatural charity as the historical, though incomplete insertion of a different community, and a different ethical practice.

In the next section it will be shown that, by embracing the Rahnerian version, political and liberation theology is guilty, for all its protestations, of reducing the content of salvation to a quasi-Marxist concept of liberation.

Salvation or Liberation

1   *Social and individual*

Much of the controversy surrounding liberation theology has centred on the issue of whether it reduces the idea of salvation to that of social and political emancipation. The issues are normally posed within the terms of some such alternative as, is salvation a mechanism for the recruitment of individuals into heaven or is it the liberation of the human race from oppressive social structures, and the inauguration of the kingdom as a this-worldly utopia?

However, this manner of posing the question tends to be itself confined by the modern political and sociological assumption that there is an abstract opposition between individuals on the one hand and 'society' on the other. So that if one maintains that salvation is rooted in the capacity of the individual to transcend the given, then this is not necessarily to ignore 'the social dimension'. Rather, the realm of the 'spiritual', and of salvation, is regarded as a kind of remainder, as that which is irreducible to the admittedly formidable constraints of social reality. Within the same perspective, the transcending capacity of the human mind can be conceived as the very impetus that makes social transformation possible. We have seen that the Weberian attitudes of Troeltsch would tend to encourage this sort of approach. Here theology and sociology each have their own precisely defined subject matter. They can be seen as fruitfully entering into 'dialogue', but what is not seen is that they secretly and invalidly uphold each other's autonomy from within the internal structures of their own delusory epistemologies.

Inversely, if one stresses that the goal of salvation is social utopia, then this does not necessarily mean that one neglects 'the personal dimension'. This can still be upheld in two ways: first, one can construct a 'Durkheimian natural theology', in which one identifies religion primarily with the social, but also interprets it as having to do with securing the right balance between 'society' and the 'individual', such that the individual is permitted a proper, secular freedom.[77] Among those identifying salvation with social utopia, this

---

[77] Mary Douglas, *Natural Symbols: Explorations in Cosmology* (London: Barrie and Jenkins, 1973).

Durkheimian course is really only taken by Norman K. Gottwald, in a fashion we have already analysed.

On the whole, however, and perhaps surprisingly, the political and liberation theologians remain just as 'Weberian' as those who uphold a purely individual concept of salvation. While salvation is given *content* in social terms, the experience of salvation is treated in an entirely individualistic fashion, usually indebted to the theology of Rahner. Hence the question at issue with regard to liberation theology should *not* be, is salvation individual or collective? But rather, does liberation theology remain confined, in its treatment of salvation, by an abstract sociological opposition between the social and the individual?[78]

The answer here must be yes, and the consequences are transparent: political and liberation theology continues to think of salvation as belonging to a separate 'religious' category which concerns a particular dimension of individual *a priori* experience. In this respect, far from being guilty of reducing salvation to liberation, their fault is rather that they have an altogether asocial notion of salvation itself. However, salvation in this conception is to do with empty, formless epistemological transcendence: the Rahnerian *vorgriff* and the supernatural existential. If salvation is to be given content, liberation theology must look to the social realm, which it understands as being over–against the individual and religious. The social realm is thought to possess its own immanent ethical principles, which are those of an emergent 'humanity' and which cannot be qualified by theology. All that theology can do is to give these principles of liberation another name: 'salvation'. Theology is able to declare that natural, human ethics is approved of by God. It is able to do this because natural, human ethics has the goal of liberation – the setting free of the human capacity for transcendence, which is precisely the supposed source and foundation for our knowledge of God's existence. All revolves within this futile circle.

The process of liberation is conceived in fundamentally humanist-Marxist, rather than Weberian terms. However, the juxtaposition of society to the individual, which permits a realm of religious experience which never alters and which remains unaffected by social processes, is really 'sociological' rather than 'dialectical' in character.[79] Dialectics only comes into the picture (in a double fashion) at the point where the immanent emergence of human freedom, through the outworkings of contradictions, is identified with a divine salvific process. But Hegel never juxtaposed external, 'structural' factors to individual ones in the way that liberation theologians tend to do. Although they are right to treat with suspicion earlier 'personalist' doctrines, because these do tend to insulate an area of 'private' encounter from wider

---

[78] See Chapter 5 above. For further elaborations and partial modifications of my treatment here of liberation theology see Daniel M. Bell, jun., *Liberation at the End of History* (London: Routledge, 2001); D. Stephen Long, *Divine Economy* (London: Routledge, 2000).

[79] Segundo, *The Liberation of Theology*, p. 116. Clodovis Boff, *Theology and Praxis*, pp. 38, 44, 68, 120.

public processes, they fail to recognize that personalist thinkers like Emman-uel Mounier, far from being mere liberals, were in fact quite in line with Marxist-Hegelianism in seeking to transcend the abstract opposition of 'given' collective structure and 'free' individual action, in favour of grasping society as an open-ended historical continuum of mutual recognition and self-becoming through encounter with the other.[80]

Where personalism remained inadequate was in failing to locate all en-counters within a process of structuration. All personal relations embody an 'indirect' moment insofar as they are mediated by language, which is the *residuum* of previous social encounters. In this way, historical characters (persons) are only constituted through a plot, but, at the same time this plot-structure is nothing but the outcome of the totality of interactions between person and person, and person and nature. As we have seen from Ferguson and Blondel, every action is *in itself* heterogeneous, and so the plot can 'outrun' the character, surprising her with an unexpected (yet not un-deserved, nor objectively unintended) 'fate' or 'destiny' (to use Hegelian terminology). As lying before and after our actions, structuration escapes our control, yet every element of the plot remains retrievable: we can recog-nize the outcome as our proper fate, and so reincorporate and reshape it. Nothing is inviolably 'internal', or 'our own'; yet nothing is permanently 'outside us', nor fixed beyond human alteration.

This form of 'dramatic' or 'emplotted' personalism would help to press de Lubac and von Balthasar's perspectives in the direction of a social and political theology. It disallows both 'persons' outside the performance of social roles, and 'lawful' social processes surplus to the contingency of narrative plots.

If one adopted this view, one would be compelled to deal with Christianity as primarily a social phenomenon, although one would escape the inference that it is therefore primarily governed by 'general' sociological or material-historical norms. Political and liberation theology, however, engage in a characteristic sociological saving of religion, at the price – which Hegel pre-dicted – of a total emptying of its concrete practical content. When it comes to salvation as transcendental impulse, or private ethical option, they allude to an asocial, Cartesian subject, whose essential personhood is detached from role performance. When it comes to salvation as liberation, or as political process, then this is a matter of an innate natural tendency for human beings to 'remove barriers', proceeding through certain necessary historical stages. Both of these aspects will now be examined in turn.

2   *Salvation as private transcendence: liberation theology*

Among the liberation theologians, it is Clodovis Boff who most clearly articu-lates what they all, less consistently, maintain: namely, that salvation is a

---

[80] Emmanuel Mounier, *Be Not Afraid: Studies in Personalist Sociology*, trans. Cynthia Rowlands (London: Rockliff, 1951).

properly theological concept, belonging to a specifically theological discourse (or as Boff, after Althusser, has it, 'mode of theoretical production'). His account of grace is roughly that of Rahner: transcendence of beings to Being and to God is a universal feature of human ontology.[81] However, in a manner which is never clearly spelt out, Boff identifies the epistemological with the ethical moment. What he appears to suggest is that in the opening of love to the freedom of the other – the universal norm of practical reason – transcendence is especially present. Faith is the reflective consciousness of this situation, although it is a relatively inchoate, emotive sort of consciousness. Revelation and religion are the mere 'expressions' of this faith-consciousness, in particular socio-cultural forms. Such forms have no permanent significance in themselves, and are only accidentally related to what they express, because they can be entirely accounted for in terms of 'fundamental' social or material processes.[82]

Juan Luis Segundo takes a very similar view: the 'content' of faith remains entirely the same – *a priori* impulse of human self-transcendence – but for the faith to be historically effective, it must constantly dress itself in 'ideological' clothing which has a purely passing and functional significance.[83]

Clodovis Boff candidly explains that salvation is essentially 'ontological', rather than 'historical'; that the ecclesial content is essentially irrelevant to salvation; and that the Gospel can be detached from the institutions and traditions which accidentally carry it. The truth of salvation is, for Boff, totally immune to any possible socio-historical critique, and by that token, one must say, it is a truth that is also vacuous, and able to be associated with any content whatsoever (that Boff favours a Marxist content appears, in *theological* terms, to be quite accidental). Boff develops his own gloss on Aquinas's theological method, for the purpose of ensuring that salvation, as it is considered by 'first theology' (theology dealing with God, creation, redemption, the virtues, etc.), is a purely formal category of transcendence.

In Aquinas's mature texts, faith is implicit wisdom, because it already involves some cognitive content, some association of God with certain purposes and certain epiphanic events. And theology not only spells out, logically, the implications of faith, it is also explicit wisdom, because it remains imbued with the spirit of faith which is able to assent to what cannot be demonstrated.[84] Yet Boff, departing totally from the French Dominican writers, Congar and Chenu, whom he appears to admire, says that Aquinas should have kept a non-gnoseological faith, and a strictly 'scientific' theology, much more distinct.[85] For Boff, theology is a 'science', and strictly 'cognitive' in a sense that has really little to do with Aquinas. It is a science because, reflecting on the inchoate responses of faith seen as occurring in a Husserlian

---

[81] Boff, *Theology and Praxis*, pp. 92–6.
[82] Ibid., pp. 44–6, 48, 51–6, 120–1.
[83] Segundo, *The Liberation of Theology*, pp. 32, 74.
[84] Aquinas, *ST* I q. 1a 1, a5 ad 2; 96; 97; I–II q.57.a2; *CG* 2.4; *In Boeth de Trinitate* q.2 a2; q.3 a1.
[85] Boff, *Theology and Praxis*, pp. 115–16.

'life world', theology spells out with precision the conditions of possibility for human experience which faith merely intuits.[86]

For Aquinas, faith itself assents to a certain position with regard to this world – with respect to history, ethics, society – and theology is not *about faith*. Instead, it is a more conscious and reflective continuation of faith, and so is formally about God, and materially about everything else, insofar as it relates to God. But for Boff, faith is inscrutable – save in its ethical affirmation of the freedom of the other – and so theology which brings faith to understanding can only be an interpretation of a wordless experience; it cannot inherit from faith a cognitive relationship to God (which is, of course, far less determinate than any other cognition) – the very thing that, for Aquinas, renders theology 'a science'. Boff pursues, throughout his book *Theology and Praxis*, a supposedly pro-Thomist and anti-Augustinian polemic; yet ironically, by making theology be *about* faith, he tends precisely in the direction of medieval 'Augustinians' who separated theological 'wisdom' from science, because they believed that theology found an explicit finite subject matter in terms of 'the life of the soul'. While Boff rightly insists that theology only deals with finite things under the 'formality' of their relationship to God, he interprets this formality not as the Thomist participation of beings in Being itself, but rather as transcendent freedom, which is only an aspiration of finitude.

In reading Boff's book, one can easily be deceived by the complex theoretical apparatus which he erects in connection with his argument that 'first theology' elaborates its own specific content in terms of the category of salvation. Actually, all Boff is doing is renaming the categorical imperative as 'faith'. In common with all the liberation theologians, he makes ethics the mediating term between political commitment and theological interpretation.[87] As Marcel Xhaufflaire has remarked, this ethical mediation, in terms of a purely private moral imperative, stands in lieu of any social or political theory that can be *directly* validated by theology.[88] For nearly all the political and liberation theologians, theology baptizes a universal individualist ethic, the impulse 'of the heart' to love the neighbour. When one asks, but how is this love of the neighbour to be socially instantiated, then this is not seen as a form of the question what, precisely, *is* love? This is supposed to be obvious. Yet neither question can really be dealt with by liberation theology, because the 'social' supposedly transcends these discourses. Answers are only given in utilitarian terms, or in terms of a Marxist verdict on what is required at this stage of the historical process.

The decision for or against salvation is purportedly to be taken at an anonymous, ethical level: the purely categoric decision to love the neighbour leads inevitably to a willing of the necessary social means. Liberation theologians are fond of insisting that Jesus himself appears to demand an

[86] Ibid., pp. 18, 113–18.
[87] Ibid., pp. 49, 119–20.
[88] Marcel Xhaufflaire, *La Théologie Politique: Introduction à La Théologie Politique de J.-B. Metz*, tome I (Paris: Editions du Cerf, 1972) pp. 117–42.

anonymous response: the person who does charity recognizes Christ in the neighbour, and is his true follower.[89] However, for Christianity, love is a highly complex, learned practice, which Jesus spells out in fully exemplary fashion. It is only because charity is seen as fully defined by Christ's words and actions that one can speak of Christ as carrying out an irreplaceable restoration of human nature. If love were obvious, then the perfection of love would be primarily known though introspection, and not through a practical instantiation of love in a particular career. Indeed, if love were essentially a Kantian aspiration towards a perfectly 'disinterested' response, then it is unlikely (despite Kant's Christological affirmations in *Religion Within the Bounds of Reason Alone*) that we would recognize any finite career as perfectly fulfilling it. The drag away from self-interest is, for this perspective, an 'infinite task', because 'interestedness', the source of 'radical evil', remains bound up with our physical nature. Karl Rahner makes this clear: 'What is certain is that all nature which precedes liberty offers resistance to the total and free self-availability and self-disposability of the person.'[90] If everything before liberty is an *obstacle* – all that is given, mute, done, specifically compelling – then how could there be finite perfection? How can Christ be our criterion of love?

In fact, the liberation theologians only acknowledge in Christ a perfection of subjective *motivation*, a claim that is meaningless, because a motivation not tied to some specific objective intention to do this or that in certain circumstances cannot be morally assessed, least of all by the bearer of this motivation himself. It is true that Segundo believes that Jesus pursued precisely the right *praxis* for his time and circumstances, but this mode of perfection requires merely the right theoretical diagnosis within one's given situation.[91] By contrast, one can only claim Jesus's practice to be 'perfect' in a truly exemplary sense if one accepts that the spirit of that practice is bound up with its particular characteristic forms of action. Thus it is not that we are to exercise the same motivation of love within different historical circumstances which we interpret theoretically, but rather that we are to 'repeat' precisely what Jesus did in practice, but in different historical circumstances, which we interpret practically through subsuming them into our 'performance' of the original Christic text.[92] We cannot, it is true, deduce from this text precisely the right social arrangements for all time, but this is because, through our performance, Jesus consigns to us the fuller writing of the text, which he has only brought to an initial, though canonical closure. We realize through this 'writing' the spirit of the preceding words, but the spirit is only in the words, not in some prior ghost which the words embody. Therefore certain dominant, persistent features of Jesus's practice – such as his peaceableness – can

---

[89] Segundo, *The Liberation of Theology*, pp. 79–82.

[90] Karl Rahner, 'The theological concept of concupiscence', in *Theological Investigations* I, pp. 347–82.

[91] Segundo, *The Liberation of Theology*, pp. 33, 83, 118–21, 154–7, 166.

[92] Nicholas Lash, 'Performing the scriptures', in *Theology on the Way to Emmaus* (London: SCM, 1986) pp. 37–47.

certainly not be prescinded from, as though they did not define his intentions, but merely represented his strategy. Yet by and large, the liberation theologians attempt to reduce Jesus's peaceableness to the strategic level: arguing that violent struggle was not the path which love could conveniently take in Jesus's day, before industrialization and proletarianization made revolution a serious possibility. The objections one can make here are manifest; was not Israel herself the result of a successful peasant revolt according to Gottwald? Does not Jesus's commitment to non-violent persuasion as a precondition for the perfect society surpass the conceptions of later 'proletarian' revolutions?

3 Salvation as private transcendence: political theology

The mixture of deontological imperative to respect the freedom of the other with a consequentialist or situationist approach to the out-working of this duty reflects the point of juncture in liberation theology between the private-ethical and the public-scientific. The ethical, reduced to motivation, remains problematically empty of content, and the religious, reduced to regulation of the ethical, still more so. By comparison, German 'political theology' made more strenuous efforts to discover some absolutely distinct contribution that theology can make to social and political understanding. This occurred under the stimulus of the criticisms made of Johann Baptist Metz's initial work by Marcel Xhaufflaire, and other of his pupils. Xhaufflaire attacked Metz's reliance upon the Frankfurt school's 'dialectic of enlightenment', arguing that merely to appeal over against technocratic freedom-become-bondage to the Kantian will to preserve subjective autonomy, was still to remain captive to a modernist liberalism, whose only theme is choice.[93] If choice is our only value, then the single objective measure of choice in the public domain remains expansion of people's ability (individually and in consenting groups) to extend control over their own lives and over nature. Extension of autonomy will be likely to increase the instrumentalization of our relations to nature, and to each other, because only the market and the bureaucracy can mediate competing and incommensurable individual freedoms.

Both Xhaufflaire and Michael Theunissen accordingly argued that the mere removal of inhibitions on human freedom – or 'liberation' – could not be regarded as a sufficient principle of critique. Political theology needed to return from Marx to Hegel, who understood that true freedom was only obtainable in a *sittlich* community, where individual activities were substantially compatible in terms of common social goals.[94] Because a final *telos* is associated with an imagined *content* for the God who draws us forward, the imagination of God becomes here the immediate source of political criticism. I have shown, however, in chapter 6, that for this to be really true, one must, unlike Hegel, disassociate one's concept of God from that of 'immanent' social

---

[93] Xhaufflaire, *La Théologique Politique*, tome I.
[94] Theunissen, *Hegels Lehre von Absoluten Geist als Theologisch-Politischer Traktat*.

critique, and one must build *Sittlichkeit*, not on what negatively emerges, but on what is positively imagined by a particular, contingent community, such as the Church.

Xhaufflaire's and Theunissen's ideas moved, however, in the right direction. And they appear to be accepted by Metz in his later work. In *Faith in History*, Metz denied that Habermas's notion of an 'ideal speech situation', in which there are no coercive constraints on communication, represents a sufficient critical principle.[95] It is true, of course, that Habermas *does not* rule out – far from it – the possibility of substantive and pragmatic agreement (indeed, in a way, he leaves *too much* to a purely emotive 'community spirit' disconnected from a general rational discourse), but Metz's point is presumably that one should not hope to approach such agreement merely negatively, for this might imply that reason is somewhat indifferent to the form the substantive agreement actually takes. Rather, one needs positively to anticipate in thought the ideal community, and this means a constant endeavour to remember and recall its own past on the part of an institution – the Church – which exists precisely as such a lived anticipation.

Metz therefore proceeds to give an account of memory which owes a great deal to Walter Benjamin's *Theses on the Philosophy of History*. In Benjamin, the non-forgetting of the marginalized past (the 'counter-historical') extends not merely to the memory of the suffering innocent and excluded, but *also* to the recalling of 'happiness', that is to say to fragments of justice and true human life. From the restoration and synthesis of these fragments it is possible to form an image of redemption.[96] But in Metz the latter element is omitted: what is to be recalled are the suffering innocent, the past victims of all forms of human oppression.[97] This memorizing is supposed to provide a critical principle going beyond the liberal 'dialectic of enlightenment', because Christians are concerned, not just for the present and future living, but also for the past dead, whom they refuse to leave as dead. This may be all quite unexceptionable, but it does not truly compensate for the deficiencies of the original Frankfurt school model. There is no appeal here to Hegelian *Sittlichkeit*, or to a substantive anticipation of the future community. For such an appeal, what would matter would be the past saints and holy communities in their lives and the modes of their deaths: the provocations which they gave to injustice, and not their mere passive enduring of it. In particular, why should one remember Christ, beyond all others, if his provocation were not recognized as supremely great? The *memoria passionis* has its context in the memory also of Christ's deeds and words.

It is true that Metz sees not only the memory of the innocent dead, but also a sense of guilt and responsibility, as especially preserved by

---

[95] J.-B. Metz, *Faith in History and Society: Toward a Practical Fundamental Theology*, trans. David Smith (London: Burns and Oates, 1980) pp. 121, 233.

[96] Walter Benjamin, 'Theses on the Philosophy of History', in *Illuminations* (London: Fontana, 1970) pp. 255–66.

[97] Metz, *Faith in History and Society*, pp. 110–14, 121–4.

Christianity.[98] But he does not sufficiently note that the Church helps to *define* a practice of responsibility, and to discipline our guilt. Guilt and responsibility are seen as inherently religious impulses, and it is assumed that, by definition, collective institutions are impervious to these feelings, thereby implying that they are essentially 'private' in character. In any case, it seems that one is to be mainly guilty and responsible in relation to the issue of human autonomy and freedom, so it is not surprising that Metz still defines his enterprise as a retrieving of the Enlightenment. He is really trying to show that memory of the innocent dead, together with guilt and suffering, belong to the *universal rational foundations* of a sense of justice.

This is clearly recognized by Helmut Peukert, who, more logically, did not repudiate Habermas and Apel's critical criteria for the just society – the 'ideal speech situation' or, with slight differences, 'the perfect communication community' – but argued that they imply the will to include also the dead, and especially the past victims of injustice, in future perfected communication.[99] Peukert thought that he had here finally placed theology on firm 'foundations', in discovering the prior prepared site for religious understanding and practice which Christianity – with its doctrine of the resurrection of the dead – most perfectly fulfils. This is a new version of the Kantian idea that practical reason must 'postulate' God's existence, because only if there is a just God can the requirements of justice be perfectly fulfilled and justice be harmonized with nature in a realm beyond the present natural order.[100] But the problem with all variants of this argument is that, while the wish for such a harmonization proceeds clearly from the categorical imperative, one cannot see the imperative necessity to turn the wish into a postulation. For a respect for the free wills of others, treating others as ends not means, applies primarily to those others that we encounter in the present. The Kantian principle notably does *not* include an ethical concern to respect the past – one's parents, even though dead – and to transmit a certain heritage to one's children. It works, self-sufficiently, and with no debit of motivation, on the level of the present moment, and a concern with the past (or the future) can only be introduced by imagining 'an eternal present', a moment when all who have existed would be introduced into a situation where we could treat them as ends, not means.

Peukert's claim that theological postulation is implied by Habermas and Apel's criteria therefore fails. But, even if one were to entertain the postulate, he further fails in his attempt to provide a theological 'foundation'. Memory of the dead, and of innocent victims, only occurs in the context of a particular tradition for which the dead are not, primarily, anonymous 'victims', but persons identified by the culturally significant roles which they played. Only because their words and actions remain as traces and as effects, because their *personae* persist, do we still recall the bodies and the speaking voices.

---

[98] Ibid., pp. 56, 80, 123, 127.

[99] Helmut Peukert, *Science, Action and Fundamental Theology: Toward a Theology of Communicative Action*, trans. James Bohmann (Cambridge, Mass: MIT Press, 1986).

[100] Kant, *Critique of Practical Reason*, p. 218ff.

And religion is not founded upon burial. Instead, burial is usually an institution of religion, a mode of recording and memorializing lives already positioned within a sacral order. In the case of Christianity, we remember the members of the body of Christ; our 'religious' interest in them begins with their living participation in the community, and their representation of Christ, in a uniquely irreplaceable manner. Here it is in the living practice of the Church that salvation is first known about; it is not that a religious notion of salvation is invoked with relation to the dead in order to complete a non-religious ethical imperative. Were this the case, then salvation would once more have no concrete, ethical content.

The surprising conclusion of this section must be that, quite unlike the pioneers of a more integral, social, Catholicism, the political and liberation theologians try: (a) to identify *a priori* a particular 'site' for religion in the conditions of possibility of theoretical or practical reason, and (b) to understand the essentially 'religious' aspect of salvation as a fundamentally individual affair, which is only 'expressed' by the social institutions of the Church.

4   Salvation as political process

Political and liberation theology colludes with sociology's 'policing of the sublime' by splitting salvation into an ineffable, transcendental, 'religious' aspect (just dealt with), that is only *Christian* in an anonymous sense, and a social aspect that is purely secular, and only *religious* in an 'anonymous' sense. This social aspect will now be discussed.

Both these theologies accept – with unimportant reservations – the Cox-Gogarten view of secularization as something positive, and as always implied by Judeo-Christian religion, which is supposed to 'desacralize' the world. The earlier Metz, Boff and Gutierrez celebrated the gradual freeing of human action and knowledge from religious tutelage; hence physics has gradually replaced metaphysics, and ethical and political norms can now be deduced *etsi Deus non daretur*.[101] According to Gutierrez's classically 'enlightened' view (which commences with Spinoza), knowledge increases in mystical accordance with the release of human freedom: 'truth' lies in waiting for an unprejudiced, self-sufficient recognition. And what matters for the advance of truth is the negative casting off of the shackles of heteronomy. World history is essentially 'the progress of the awareness of freedom'.[102]

There are numerous things wrong with this account. In the first place, Jewish monotheism had no less sacramental a view of the world than polytheism – merely a different grammar or logic of the sacramental. We have

---

[101] J.-B. Metz, *Theology of the World*, trans. William Glen-Doepel (London: Burns and Oates, 1969) pp. 19–20, 29, 37–8. Gutierrez, *A Theology of Liberation*, p. 28ff. Boff, *Theology and Praxis*, p. 51.

[102] Gutierrez, *A Theology of Liberation*, p. 27. Stanley Hauerwas, 'Some theological reflections on Gutierrez's use of liberation as a theological concept', in *Modern Theology* 3.1 (1986) pp. 67–76.

already seen how a reading back of the post-Reformation desacralization of the cosmos belongs to 'the liberal-protestant metanarrative'. In the second place, we also saw, in the first two parts of the book, how the rise of modern 'scientific' explanation with regard to both nature and society could not be regarded as the displacement of divine, transcendent causes by immanent ones. Instead, what happened was that the old medieval hierarchy of primary (divine) and secondary (immanent) causes collapsed, and explanation was parcelled out between 'natural' causes operating in a manner 'testable' by human beings, because they could be experimentally manipulated, and 'transcendent' causes where a *direct* divine intervention, without intermediaries, was postulated – as in the case of Leibniz's pre-established harmony, Malebranche's occasional causality, Newton's 'active principles', Smith's 'hidden hand' and *even* (one should add, against Funkenstein) Kant's transcendental objects and supersensible free subjectivity.[103] So it was not that the Middle Ages overlooked finite, secondary causes, but rather that the modern age *invented* an incompatibility between finite and divine causes, and instead of initially proscribing the latter, made them operate on the same level with finite causes, though with a limited range of effect. In chapter 3 I showed how this 'division of responsibilities' even affects the founding assumptions of French sociology.

By still assuming incompatibility, Gutierrez remains the prisoner of the story that modernity tells about itself in order to conceal the archaeological level where this incompatibility is 'imagined'. The second thing wrong with the account he subscribes to is that the totalizing enclosure for the autonomy of finite knowledge and action can only be established by appealing to the formal regularities of instrumental control. As we saw, the laws which Grotius derived, *etsi Deus non daretur*, were attempts to ground ethics and political association on the stoic *conatus*, the natural effort of each individual creature at self-preservation. Only the formalities, dynamics and economies of power inscribe the closed circle of the secular. By contrast, within an ethics and politics appealing to substantive ends, the goal lies always beyond, always exceeds the present inscription of routine – it is always 'extra' to the abstract laws of sustainable equilibrium and therefore not derivable from them. One can speak, therefore, of this extra as superadded, supernatural: precisely as 'given by God'.

In the third place, Metz and Gutierrez take over from Cox and Gogarten the idea that the circle of instrumental enclosure is what is necessarily established by human creative action, or *poesis*. Ludwig Wittgenstein, in *Culture and Value*, drew attention to this all-pervasive assumption: 'It is very *remarkable*', he says, 'that we should be inclined to think of civilization – houses, trees, cars, etc. – as separating man from his origins, from what is lofty and eternal etc. Our civilized environment, along with its trees and plants, strikes us then as though it were cheaply wrapped in Cellophane and isolated from everything

---

[103] Funkenstein, *Theology and the Scientific Imagination*.

great, from God, as it were. That is a remarkable picture that intrudes upon us.'[104] The present book has consistently tried to exercise a 'therapy' precisely at this point, to show how, historically, this picture *has* intruded upon us. What has happened, as we have seen, is that secular autonomy, the 'enclosure' of reason, establishes itself at the point where *poesis* is publicly defined as *techne*: where the late-medieval/Renaissance discovery of human creative mediation (which could not be gone back upon) takes the direction of locating the essence of the human product as the measurable and quantifiable 'wrapping of the world in Cellophane'. What is refused here, or confined to a private 'artistic' domain, is the idea that the significant thing about the product is its peculiarly compelling aesthetic shape. This 'extra' can be seen as the mediation to us of the supernatural.

The fourth thing wrong with this account is the correlation of truth with negative freedom. Why should truth just 'show' itself to the person without assumptions? All our 'truths' are only 'assumptions', or takings up from previous linguistic arrangements. The naked truth apprehensible by freedom can only be the formal truth of the universal conditions for the extension of freedom (as 'choice') itself. The mere freedom to do and think as one pleases is fixed in a pre-established harmony with a merely instrumental reason. Thus already in Spinoza we discovered that the 'free' investigation of the Bible had to issue in the recognition that the Bible's rational meaning was a political one, relating to the formal logic of the exercise of absolute sovereign power.

And political and liberation theology continue to write a *Tractatus Theologico-Politicus*, which is precisely the hermeneutic 'capturing' of the text of the Bible by the State from the hands of a universal Church, that intrinsically threatened the modern concept of sovereignty. (Is this one aspect of the pedagogy of the oppressed?) For Gutierrez, secularization results in the total *politicization* of everything, meaning by this that a Weberian formality of power – bureaucratic, positive, instrumental rationality – dominates all human transactions in the modern age.[105] Like Weber himself, Gutierrez does not reject the 'iron cage', and Clodovis Boff urges acceptance of the inevitability of a Weberian 'ethics of responsibility', which means a Machiavellian ethics related to the preservation of sovereign power, and the balancing of forces within the modern State.[106] Theology itself is now to be 'political' (or, for Boff, all theology relating to the public realm must be 'of the political') because the 'political', and not the 'positive' or the 'existential', defines the modern framework, both of knowledge and of practice. This is, in itself, a wholly accurate observation, but only a thoroughly craven theology would imagine that its task is therefore to translate the Gospel message into 'political' terms. Here, Michel de Certeau's contention that to change one language for another is in itself to change the meaning-content must apply in its fullest

[104] Ludwig Wittgenstein, *Culture and Value*, trans. Peter Winch (Oxford: Blackwell, 1984) p. 50e.
[105] Gutierrez, *A Theology of Liberation*, p. 47. Boff, *Theology and Praxis*.
[106] Boff, *Theology and Praxis*, p. 279, n. 47.

force.[107] A 'political theology', in this sense, *could* only underwrite the modern understanding of politics, and declare to the credulous that the process of politicization is, after all, identical with what the Church has always meant by 'salvation'. Juan Luis Segundo would make it appear that he upholds 'a hermeneutic circle' between the indications of the Biblical text and the questions of the present, 'political' context, but in fact his circle is a purely political one, and his hermeneutics Spinozistic.[108] For he divorces the spirit of the Bible from its letter, by declaring that only the 'method' which the Bible teaches – its principles of 'deutero-learning' – remain of permanent relevance. And this method is none other, according to Segundo, than a political pedagogy which teaches us how to keep in dynamic balance the 'minority' interest in sustaining creative freedom, and the 'majority' interest in stability and permanent structure.[109]

By viewing modern secularization and politicization in a favourable, or, at least, resigned light, political and liberation theology sunder all their ties to previous Christian socialism. For even the Christian socialists who have most influenced the public affairs of our time, like R. H. Tawney, persistently connected the dominance of the 'free market', privately owned wealth, a bureaucratic politics, and an unrestrained centralized sovereignty with a secular age, where religion no longer supplied common values, common measures and standards.[110]

One might suggest that in this contrast lies the key to the inclusion of certain Marxist elements by political and liberation theology. The initial *theological* decision is not to embrace Marxism, but to embrace secularization, and the horizon of the political; later, a way is sought whereby one can still subscribe to socialist views, despite the fact that these can no longer be drawn from Christianity itself, but must be taken instead from the immanent principles of secularization and politics. Yet these processes manifestly favour only capitalism, instrumental freedom and bureaucracy.

Marxism here proves to be precisely that consoling doctrine which can appear to suggest that the aims of Christian ethics and of Christian socialism can be achieved, indeed *must be* achieved, through the apparently alien workings of secularization and politicization. The temporal dialectic which draws justice out of injustice, legitimates the theological dialectic which discovers salvation in human independence from God.

But as we have seen in the previous chapter, Marxism fails to overcome capitalism, because capitalism cannot be immanently criticized in terms of its own 'contradictions'. As a 'tautology', it is, rather, *inviolable*, and what Marxism offers is not the imagination of a *different* socialist future, but the

[107] Michel de Certeau, 'La rupture instauratrice où le christianisme dans la culture contemporaine', in *Esprit*, 6 (1971) pp. 1177–214. *Le Christianisme Éclaté* (Paris: Seuil, 1974).

[108] See chapter 1 above.

[109] Segundo, *The Liberation of Theology*, pp. 180, 280ff. *A Theology for Artisans of a New Humanity. vol. 5: Evaluation and Guilt* (Maryknoll, NY: Orbis, 1975).

[110] R. H. Tawney, *The Acquisitive Society* (Brighton: Harvester, 1982) pp. 176–91.

impossible dream of a spontaneous universal realization of freedom, arising naturally, with infinite abundance and therefore no conflict, once the final restrictions on autonomy have been at last swept away. Gutierrez appears to subscribe to this illusion, when he says that, by discovering the socio-economic determinants on the human, Marx makes possible our mastery of these conditions, and the final exercise of freedom.[111] The release of freedom alone is supposed to make socialism possible: but what is forgotten here, as we saw in the last chapter, is the priority of *justice* as far as socialism is concerned, and the continued need, even in a socialist society, 'to make equal the unequal', according to agreed-upon measures in all processes of exchange. Because there is never any immediately available plenitude, and because in a social existence we are continuously exchanging the incommensurable, freedom for all is only possible in a context of adjudication. Likewise, justice, which depends upon common, yet not theoretically prescribable standards, is only possible in the context of agreement about common goods and values. Hence the relevance, neglected by political and liberation theology, of the Church itself as a 'society of friends', the anticipation of a possible socialist community. (Of course this may be to say that liberation theology has not properly theorized the significance of the 'base communities' in Latin America itself.)

Justice, in history, remains a contingent possibility: it is not on the agenda for some appointed time, after necessary ages of alienation. But political and liberation theologies subordinate justice to a 'natural' freedom, which emerges partly through a straightforward process of enlightenment, the becoming-conscious of shackles and the casting of them asunder, and partly through the 'contradictory' process of dialectical becoming, in which each new stage forward before Utopia is at once a new stage in the release of freedom, and a more absolute degree of its tyrannical exercise.

We have already seen, in chapter 7, what is theoretically wrong with this, but what is troubling, theologically, is the embracing of an idea of a *necessary* passage through conflict and alienation, on the way from unfree nature to mature freedom. Segundo, in particular, affirms 'the impossibility of separating *good and evil*, virtue and vice, love and egotism. To separate these two elements in the constructive efforts of man would be equivalent to putting an end to the constructive effort itself in the whole of human existence – at least in terms of man's present existence.'[112] And the Canadian political theologian, Gregory Baum, declares that, while Christians are ethically obliged to side with those who are victims of oppressive social structures, these structures themselves are nonetheless to be thought of in objective, sociological terms, and not to be seen as the avoidable product of human injustice.[113] As we have

---

[111] Gutierrez, *A Theology of Liberation*, p. 30ff.

[112] Segundo, *A Theology for Artisans*, vol. 5, p. 147.

[113] Gregory Baum, *Religion and Alienation: A Theological Reading of Sociology* (New York: Paulist Press, 1975) pp. 193–227.

seen, this notion that social structures escape human responsibility, suggests in itself a very individualist notion of responsibility. In subscribing to a 'Marxist sociology', Baum takes over, unexamined, something much more fundamental: namely political economy's version of the heterogenesis of ends, according to which individual decisions are like windowless monads, having in their self-consciousness no connection with the long-term social upshot. In chapter 2, I tried to expose the fallacy involved here, and in the present chapter I have shown how Blondel overcomes this with his account of the human act as 'internally heterogeneous'. For while no-one deliberately planned capitalism, it is also true that we *never* discover precisely what we have done, what we really intend, except by contemplating our action in its first existence, as a new articulation within public discourse. A bad system is not just a heterogeneous upshot: it is also always already begun in its preparations, in all the complexly interwoven, apparently 'minor' social expressions of selfishness and self-delusion.

Baum's perspective would actually confine responsibility to a narrowly *private* realm, so his writings teach the opposite of what they superficially appear to teach. Public responsibility, for Baum, could only be Weberian, a resigned acceptance of the fatalities of power, though appearing in a dialectical disguise. Like all *political economists*, political and liberation theologians shift politics and economics from the site of ethics to the site of a theology of providence. For, in making the merely algebraic equation, liberation = salvation, they still celebrate a hidden working of divine design through purely immanent processes. What they really say is what they claim not to say: namely that Christians should say their prayers, be decent citizens, and otherwise just accept society as it is.

This should cause us to view in a different light the boast of political theology to have surpassed the perspective of 'Catholic social teaching'. Certainly the latter has been too much viewed within a modern natural law framework, detached from theological doctrine and the narratives of salvation. But political theology tends to leave behind ethics and political theory altogether, by locating its reflections in the space of a narrative of salvation that is really the story of an 'economic providence'. Gone is the narration of a humanly willed evil and the necessarily divine remedy; a story that purported to give the most *basic* account of history by privileging, through faith, a certain set of events. In its place stands a story of the evolution from a constrained natural finitude of a freedom which, through strenuous effort, overcomes this resistance and negatively asserts itself.[114]

In the next section, I shall argue that the claim of political and liberation theology that theology 'requires' secular social science always implies the displacing of the Christian metanarrative, essential for the constitution of faith, by new modern stories, which themselves arose partially as an attempt to situate and confine faith itself.

[114] Metz, *Faith in History and Society*, pp. 124–5.

Does Theology Require Social Science?

The division for political and liberation theology is therefore clear: insofar as salvation is 'religious', it is formal, transcendental and private; insofar as it is 'social', it is secular. What is occluded is the real practical and linguistic context for salvation, namely the *particular society* that is the Church. Such an occlusion could only have been prevented by adopting the 'French' version of integralism.

However, the political and liberation theologians are aware, as de Lubac, Congar and von Balthasar were not, that ecclesial history is not insulated from political and social history. Therefore, they realize that to uphold ecclesial (rather than political or private) practice as the site of salvation involves also subscribing to a particular theological interpretation of history and society (an enterprise which they take to be rendered impossible by the Enlightenment and its aftermath). For the Church was only constituted, historically, by a particular theoretical perspective upon history: a certain history, culminating at a certain point, and continued in the practice of the Church, interprets and 'locates' all other history. It 'reads' all other history as most fundamentally anticipation, or sinful refusal of, salvation. If one takes one's salvation from the Church, if one identifies oneself primarily as a member of the body of Christ, then inevitably one offers the most ultimate explanations of socio-historical processes in terms of the embracing or refusal of the specifically Christian virtues. Not to embrace such a metanarrative, or to ascribe to it a merely partial interpretative power, would undo the logic of incarnation. For why would we claim to recognize the divine *Logos* in a particular life, unless we had the sense that everything else was to be located *here*, despite the fact that this life is but one more life, itself situated along the historical *continuum*? Thus if the Enlightenment makes this sort of thing impossible, it also rules out salvation through the Church as traditionally understood.

One might say, the Church has only been causally effective in history because it believed itself to be in possession of certain keys to historical causality. It is therefore logical that Clodovis Boff, because he wishes to deny that theology could 'know' anything at the level of socio-historical causal processes, also presents a very minimal ecclesiology. For Boff, the entire historical process of salvation, including the life of Jesus, could be 'explained' in quite other terms – as a necessary part of the development of human forces of production, for example – and yet this would still leave the meaning of 'salvation' quite intact, whether as private transcendence, or as public liberation.

Political and liberation theology are right to this degree: if one wishes to have a strongly ecclesiological perspective – and to claim that salvation is *at once* both 'religious' and public – then one must also be committed to the thesis that salvation is tied to the ultimacy of a particular historical practice, which is ceaselessly *constituted* as a certain 'gaze' upon history and society. This gaze would have to regard itself as primary, if it were not to fall victim to total incoherence. Boff asks the question, could there be a theology of the political without mediation by the social sciences?[115] But the question is much more fundamentally, can there be *theology, tout court*, without mediation by the social sciences? Because only if the answer is yes (as I hold) can one go on upholding the fundamentally historical character of salvation: in other words, orthodoxy.

Theology is just another socio-historical gaze, just another perspective alongside other gazes, and faith, in its commitment to this gaze, constitutes a metanarrative: this is what I maintain, but political theology, and Boff in particular, denies. What is his basis for doing so? In the first place, he objects to the violation of the autonomy of the profane sphere; but this book has already demonstrated that this autonomy is a conventional construct, and a strategy of secular power. In the second place, he fears that if theology contemplates an 'unprepared text' it will fall a victim to mere social appearances. This is a legitimate fear, and I have recognized how Marxism can be of assistance to theology in exposing the disguised operation of semiotic conventions in the modern economy and the modern State; theology would, indeed, be foolish to forgo such aid. But what Marxism does is to give a better reading of the 'logic' and 'grammar' of capitalism; this reading is not complete, and is only 'scientific' in the sense that it pays better attention to the logic of certain relatively fixed structural processes. It does not, in the Bachelardian or Althusserian terms to which Boff subscribes, 'produce' out of its own theoretical resources a more adequate definition of the object of study – 'capitalism' – as though this object ('the social relations of production', 'the commodity' etc.) somehow emerges, in its 'essence', from the intentionality of the knowing subject, or some privileged, 'schematic' level of language.[116]

By contrast, the description of capitalism can never in fact be complete: there will always remain a scope for a fuller description in terms of capitalist motivations, the previous visions capitalism denies, the future visions it prevents and so forth. The theological 'gaze' upon capitalism would claim to say – in fully 'historical' terms – more precisely what it is that capitalism prefers, and what it refuses. And insofar as theology can entertain some of the suspicions raised by Marxism, then this is because, in the last analysis, they are suspicions theology itself raises: theology rebukes capitalism as abuse of language ·because capitalism suppresses other modes of metaphorical exchange, and the significance of the particular. Yet these suppressions are not *irrational* in the way that Marxism claims – we surpassed this viewpoint in the previous chapter. If theology rebukes 'fetishization', then this turns out to be precisely *for* theological reasons, not because theology cannot but be alert to the unmasking of ideology.

---

[115] Boff, *Theology and Praxis*, p. 20ff.
[116] Boff, *Theology and Praxis*, pp. 75, 176–8, 213, 247, 255, 268.

In the third place, Boff predictably compares the need for mediation by the social sciences with Thomas Aquinas's absorption of the Aristotelian *episteme* in the thirteenth century. But Aquinas never allowed that any other science was autonomous in relation to theology. Boff mentions that Thomas maintains that theology cannot deduce or establish the principles of human sciences like ethics, politics or rhetoric. This is, of course, true for Aquinas, because, according to our finite *modus significandi*, the principles of these sciences appear to be more self-evident and certain than those of theology, which are the principles of God's own knowledge, of infinite reason. Nonetheless, Aquinas also considers that because the principles of theology are *intrinsically* more certain, as belonging to the causal source of all that is, theology, participating as it does in ultimate 'wisdom', or knowledge *per causas*, can judge not only the principles, but also the conclusions of all other sciences.[117] The distinction between 'revealed' and 'natural' knowledge is really located by Aquinas in a much more fundamental framework of the participation of all human rationality in divine reason. (So *all* knowledge remotely implies faith in God for Aquinas.)[118] Revelation increases this participation through means that do not violate the normal workings of analogy and participation: the inner illumination of the mind is strengthened, new outer signs are provided in history.[119] In one sense, even *within* theological understanding, natural principles go on being 'more certain' for us than supernatural ones. But in another sense, the light of revelation strengthens our grasp of natural principles and of what is implied within them. Thus sacred rhetoric, supernatural charity, and the Church, do not simply leave rhetoric, ethics and politics unaffected; this would be altogether to deny integralism, and in implying the opposite, Boff reveals that, like all Rahnerian transcendentalists, he really makes such a denial. (Likewise, Boff does precisely what he claims to avoid, and ascribes to theology a specific finite subject-matter: namely spiritual transcendence.) Theology, for Aquinas, both has to make use of the techniques of human persuasion, human virtue and human community, and yet, in its own proper right, commands all these techniques in their ends and practices.[120]

So should one follow Aquinas's example and apply what he says to modern social science? No! For this would be to maintain Boff's level of perfectly wooden theoreticism: the point is not that scientific politics, political economy, sociology and dialectics are natural successors to rhetoric, ethics and 'politics'. But rather, as we have seen in earlier chapters, the point is that these modern discourses displaced rhetoric, ethics and politics, and this is precisely what should remain in contention. Belonging as they do to 'practical wisdom', rhetoric, ethics and politics are not totalizing discourses, for they inscribe no sphere of general legality which could not be significantly intruded upon by theology. By contrast, all the modern discourses force theology to stand

---

[117] Aquinas, *ST* I. II. q.57 a2 ad I; q7 a2 ad3, *In Boeth. De Trin* Q2.a3. resp.

[118] Aquinas, *In Boeth. De Trin* q.3. a1. resp.; *ST* I q1 a5 ad 2, a6.

[119] Aquinas, *In Boeth. De Trin* q.I a1, a2; q.6 a2.

[120] Aquinas, *ST* I–II q.7 aa2 ad 3.

transcendentally above human community, to extract a neo-Kantian 'meaning' or 'value' from the mediations of their own perspectives. Rhetoric, ethics and 'politics' are by contrast but the gazes of particular practices, subscribing to a general *topica* of probabilities and locations for human significance, but not to any fixed general categories which forever position and functionally characterize every social particular. Here theology, as the theory of a new practice, the Church, can position itself as a gaze at once above, but also alongside, (with or against) other, inherited human gazes.

Theology, then, does not *require* the mediation of social science, in Boff's sense that social science presents theology with the social object perfectly described and perfectly explained. Were this the case, then theology would only be left with the most vacuous of tasks: announcing the empty, algebraic equation liberation = salvation; or, all is as modern human beings, and especially social scientists, think it is, but what we have to announce is that God (as he cannot but) agrees with this analysis, and also 'values' this state of affairs. Theology is supposed to extract 'meaning', yet it is only permitted to extrapolate regulatively the significance already implied by the social scientific account. This is inevitable, because nothing remains as a surplus for 'meaning', once one has given a 'full' description and an account of causes. For to ascribe meaning is the same as giving a narrative account of antecedents, and a description in terms of final goal and purpose.

Inversely, though, to give a causal account of social reality which purports to provide some kind of ultimate depth of description is really to ascribe meaning in a manner that goes beyond any 'objective' justification. We have seen in Parts Two and Three of this book how sociology makes claims to generalize in terms of an illusory *a priori* construct called 'society', and Marxism makes claims to generalize and predict in terms of the illusory idea of an always 'fundamental' social level – namely the production of 'wealth'. At best, these social scientific theories are but narratives which seek to locate the ultimate meaning of human history by telling a story with certain emphases, and to insinuate that certain precedent conditions for events really constitute sufficient (efficient or formal) causes.

Theology itself purports to give an ultimate narrative, to provide some ultimate depth of description, because the situating of oneself within such a continuing narrative is what it means to belong to the Church, to be a Christian. However, the claim is made by faith, not a reason which seeks foundations. Surrendering this gaze to the various gazes of 'methodological atheism' would not prove to be any temporary submission.

From Foundational Praxis to Supernatural Pragmatics

For there to be salvation with a specifiable Christian content, there must be a directly theological discourse about the socio-historical: without this, theology occupies the pre-theologically-determined site of transcendentalist metaphysics. But just as there must be a gnoseologically primary Christian historical narrative, so also there must be a specifically Christian practice. To be involved in this practice is to entertain the narrative; to entertain the narrative seriously is to continue to enact it. This narratological perspective therefore clarifies that unity of theoretical and practical knowledge which Blondel strove to achieve. But the 'priority of praxis' of liberation theology has nothing to do with such a 'pragmatism': on the contrary, by rendering insignificant any specifically Christian practice, it makes the content of Christianity essentially theoretical, and prevents a unity of theory and practice altogether.

Gutierrez refers to theology as 'reflection on ecclesial practice',[121] and were this taken to mean that theology is a more abstract reflection on the given (and always already theorized) practice within which it situates itself, then this would be well and good. But in fact, Gutierrez and others seem too often to mean that there is some sort of 'spontaneous', pre-theorized practice to be found. Even Clodovis Boff, who is rightly critical of such a conception, still thinks of practically embodied meaning as fundamentally 'performative' in kind and therefore as belonging 'to the realm of the real', whereas theoretical discourse, like theology, is abstract and constative, belonging essentially to the noetic order.[122] This ignores the fact that performative action, of a conventional sort, is not truly originative, but is situated within a text, so that when a woman marries a man, she also invokes 'constatively' the institution of marriage, and all its past performances.[123] The participants of the marriage as much assume a theoretical framework for marriage as the reporter of the events in the local newspaper. Inversely, his report, which helps to establish the event publicly, is a continuation of its performance.

Unless one is aware of this mutual implication, it is very easy to slip into Boff's view that *praxis* is wholly performative, practical and 'ethical', whereas theology *introduces* into its reflections on practice its own theoretical framework, which is the outcome of a specifically *theoretical* labour (rather than something itself grounded in a particular performance). Talk about *God*, for Boff, in the sense proper to theology, seems to be something invented within this discourse. This is because he reduces theology to the discovery – or the internal 'production' – of an *a priori* transcendental horizon. For this reason, he is able to think of the fully 'Christian', universally valid notion of God, as constituting an 'epistemological break' with all previous discourse. As the bringing of everything under a certain transcendental perspective, theology is, in its own way, a precise 'science' – a 'well-ordered discourse', after the fashion of Condillac.

Against this, one must say that performance is really situated within a text; it is always also constative. One only imagines the contrary for Kantian

---

[121] Gutierrez, *A Theology of Liberation*, p. 14.

[122] Boff, *Theology and Praxis*, pp. 45–6, 48.

[123] Jacques Derrida, 'Signature event context'; in *Margins of Philosophy*, trans. Alan Bass (Brighton: Harvester, 1982) pp. 309–30.

reasons, because one thinks that there is some sort of 'transparent' performance located in a universal, 'natural' text. Thus, for Boff and the other liberation theologians, 'ecclesial practice' is only 'human' practice, ethical practice,
or political practice: precisely all three at once, and they never wonder at this
incongruity. As practice has become transparent, unproblematic performance,
it can also be seen as 'foundational', or that to which everything else should be
referred back. So as we have seen, salvation commences with an act of charity,
whose quality is immediately attested 'by the heart'; theology reflects upon
this action, and finally the pronouncements of theology must be judged by
whether or not they promote this action in the future. But this 'utilitarian test'
can only work because practical performance is 'universal', in terms of both
Kantian ethics and a historical dialectic which often justifies a compromising
of absolute imperatives.

Boff, admittedly, complicates this picture. Performance is supposedly its
own test and reference point, but theology adds its own, specifically *theoretic*
criteria for assessing the morality of *praxis*.[124] These criteria are hermeneutic-
ally derived from the Bible. And yet, as with Segundo, the 'otherness' of the
Bible is neutralized by a methodological injunction, which in this case declares that the Bible only 'clothes' for its own time a permanently available
attitude of 'faith'.[125] As we have seen, the content of faith is itself, first and
foremost, the Kantian moral imperative. So we are back where we started,
in an abstract evasion of history and language.

More fundamentally, for Boff, theology replaces the confusions and the
figurative language of the real, performative order with the clarity of the
concepts produced within the noetic order. In a curious amalgam of 'Thomist realism' with an Althusserian *a priorism*, Boff, like so many modern
Catholic thinkers, seeks to evade the historicist abyss by clinging to what
is really yet another mode of Cartesianism. An Aristotelian concept of the
difference between the order of the real and the order of knowing is applied
unthinkingly to the cultural sphere – whereas the specificity of this sphere
for us (as in everything for God) is precisely that here the order of logic
totally coincides with the order of reality.[126] This must be the case, if the
specificity of culture over against nature is found in human language (the
language that composes 'us') and it is here, in language, that theory and
practice are at root identical. This *prevents* any 'priority of *praxis*', any
founding in *praxis*, concepts whose meanings become clearest in Boff, who
more rigorously spells them out, thereby inadvertently exposing their total
lack of rigour.

Priority of *praxis* turns out, in Boff, to mean that there is a *theoretically*
knowable structure permanently undergirding the process of the production
of wealth which belongs to, and defines, 'the order of the real'. On the other

---

[124] Ibid., pp. 15–16, 202, 216.
[125] Ibid., pp. 44, 123–5, 139–43, 149–52.
[126] Ibid., pp. 45, 81–7, 288 n. 49.

hand, religion, in its most 'universal' aspect, is located in the noetic order which has a logic *quite apart from historical practice altogether*.

Against this foundational practice, one should set 'supernatural action', broadly as conceived by Blondel. Christian action is always 'textual', it always has theoretical presuppositions. On the other hand, theological theory is also a practice, in the merely historical sense. Since it *continues* the practice, it cannot, in any simple manner, be tested against the practice, not even against its own canonical texts. If it could be so tested, theology's place would be minimal: in fact it is prominent, precisely because of the problematic character of the practice – its uncertainty about its own presuppositions, and its exemplifica-tion of these presuppositions. Theology's 'rules' for the reading of the canon-ical texts, and their realization in practice, cannot then be referred at one end to efficacy of performance – whose character theology is precisely an effort to define – nor, at the other end, to mere preservation of the text from gross misconstrual.

There is no priority of *praxis*, but instead a single, seamless, theory/practice which has one privileged canonical moment, one canonical binding in words, and many lesser normative points of reference. This continuous action is open, through its creative surrender, to the supernatural. In the final chapter of the book I shall seek to explicate the narrative of Christian action as itself the primary account for theology of socio-historic processes, which therefore makes theology itself possible. Theology as 'metanarrative realism' will replace theology mediated by social science, just as supernatural prag-matism will replace foundational practice. But before then, in the penultimate three chapters, secular reason must be faced in its more virulent form, emer-ging clearly to view after the collapse of the modernist metanarratives of Marxism and sociology. Its final, postmodern form of nihilism.

Part IV

Theology and Difference

9

Science, Power and Reality

Introduction

In the previous two parts of this book, it has been shown that both sociology and Marxism rest on questionable assumptions. Only if one possesses a virtually religious faith in the truth of these assumptions can one derive from these traditions an 'explanation' of religion, or of substantial aspects of religion. Is social science, therefore, at an end? And with social science any possibility of subjecting religion to a valid critique?

Part Four addresses these questions, arguing initially (in the present chapter) that there can, in theory, be a science of human interactions that is simply part and parcel of natural science, not differing either in method, or in assumptions about the nature of the object being studied. However, it will also be contended that natural science itself possesses no privileged access to truth and cannot, purely on its own account, build up a realist ontology. Its 'truth' is merely that of instrumental control, and therefore, in the case of human interactions, is bounded by the peculiar fractiousness and innovative capacity of human behaviour. The only possibly universal truth that science can seriously entertain – namely the rule of contingency – becomes, in the case of the human sphere, something that must be constantly reckoned with in practice.

Here, the isolation of repeatable patterns, which is the hallmark of science, more obviously relates to the merely particular – to certain closed formal systems – and not to the general and universal. So, while some scientific 'explanation' of segments of human behaviour remains possible, though precarious, this is never explanation of the human as such, nor of human interaction as such.

On the contrary, human interaction in all its variety can only be narrated, and not explained/understood after the manner of natural science. It is supposed, by people who are still temperamentally Victorians, that historiography gathers particular evidence, which is then dealt with by social science in a more universal fashion. Yet something like the converse is the case: there can only be a 'science' of particular, relatively stable formal systems, whereas history is the royal discipline which contemplates the transitions of systems, and so alone approaches, although in a sceptical spirit, the questions of the human as such, human society as such.

Without the possibility of ascending to universal conclusions, it remains impossible for a science of society to determine the essence of religion, or to make any universal discoveries about religion. For society x, one might, indeed, persuasively argue that religion y was embraced by the ruling classes for its social usefulness. Yet however well a structural mechanism was here isolated and delineated, it would remain the case that this was a historical and not a social-scientific claim. To present it as the latter would be to pretend falsely that the isolated mechanism is regular because it is an instance of a universally operating tendency. Hence social science does not present theology with well-warranted conclusions that theology cannot possibly evade; above all, as we have seen, it fails to isolate any categorially 'social' factor in religious behaviour, because the category of the social, as an independent causal influence, is constructed either by hypostasizing the whole over against the parts (sociology), or regarding the production of 'material' wealth as the real driving force of history (Marxism).

Theology can evade all and every social scientific suspicion, and history is its ally: written history, which produces exceptions to the supposed universal rule; lived history, which permits us always to enact things otherwise. Ambitious social science – the positivist and dialectical traditions – belong, in the last analysis, to the project of enlightenment: the challenge to the particularist obscurantism of religion in the name of the humanly universal. But this challenge is at an end, for it is seen that it was itself made in terms of metaphysics, and as an expression of a religiosity. In the new era of postmodernity (which is yet in some ways but an exacerbation of modernity) the human has become subordinate to the infinitely many discourses which claim to constitute humanity, and universality can no longer pose as the identical, but can only be paradoxically invoked as the different.

However, the question will then be posed (in the following chapter) – is there a new, postmodern challenge to theology? The challenge of the thinking of difference? Such a challenge could no longer arise from social science, but rather from a metadiscourse, or a fundamental ontology which fixes its gaze on difference as the condition of possibility for thought and action. Heidegger, Derrida and Deleuze are the thinkers who present this challenge. It remains, nonetheless, a challenge of social theory, because the ontology of difference is inseparable from an absolute historicism, a philosophy which only thinks truth as the narrative of the constitution of strategies of power. Nietzsche, Deleuze, Lyotard and Foucault are the thinkers who complete the challenge in this fashion.

In the older, modern mode of suspicion, the problem was, 'isn't religion really x?' An x which is more basic, though concealed. Isn't it really a function of social control, really a means of discipline for production, really an aspect of the psyche's suppression of the unacceptable? But the new, postmodern mode of suspicion claims no ground upon which to decode the hidden truth underlying religion's spurious truth-claims. It cannot de-mythologize, nor question the content of belief over against a standard of truth. It can, however, relativize and question claims to universality. Its more insidious method reveals no secret behind the *mythos*, but merely points to other 'truths', and shows how these are suppressed or denied by a totalizing perspective. Yet the obvious implication of 'many truths', or rather 'many incommensurable truths', is that every truth is arbitrary, every truth is the will-to-power.

The second chapter of Part Four will accordingly trace the emergence of postmodern suspicion from Nietzsche through to the French neo-Nietzscheans. Particular stress will be laid on the fact that Nietzsche offers not so much a critique of religion in general, as rather of *Christianity* in particular, on the grounds that this religion, uniquely, dissimulates the will-to-power. Nietzsche appears, indeed, to burden Christianity and its 'slave morality' with the charge of untruth, and to account for the anomaly of asceticism and self-denial in terms of a cunning device whereby the will-to-power in the end fortifies itself, and redoubles its strength. Here he is not immune from dialectics, and from his own version of the narrative of pro-gress, as certain of the neo-Nietzscheans have correctly pointed out.

The final section of chapter 10 will pass from a consideration of Nietzsche and the neo-Nietzscheans to a brief discussion of the *nouveaux philosophes*, who have reacted against their influence. For these thinkers, Nietzsche may reveal the true possibility of suspicion, but this is at the price of showing that modern, critical thought was all along in league with arbitrary power and dominance, exposing it only in order to grant it ontological validity. If Nietzsche, Heidegger and Deleuze have only presented the truth of differ-ence, then this truth is nonetheless intolerable, because it is also the unleashed and unrestrained power of the twentieth century which built the concentra-tion camps, and the more subtle forms of bureaucratic oppression. For the *nouveaux philosophes*, one must reject Nietzsche also, as a 'thinker of mastery', yet this rejection can only take the form of a Manichean appeal to another, unknown world, not ruled by power. It is here correctly perceived that postmodern suspicion is more drastic, more all-encompassing than that of modernism, leaving no possible residue of secure, humanist meaning. It can, therefore, only be questioned at the level of its ontological assumptions. The *nouveaux philosophes*, however, in effect find the ontology of difference to be true, and yet not just; their questioning issues in a despairing refusal, a mode of gnosticism or, at best, a dualistic Platonism.

By comparison with the *nouveaux philosophes*, some Anglo-Saxon and Ger-man thinkers have been far more optimistic about the possibility of admitting irreducible difference, and the historical situatedness of all truth-claims, with-out lapsing into a perspectivism which denies absolute truth and value altogether. Chapter 11 discusses the viability of this more 'benign' form of postmodernism, concentrating particularly on Alasdair MacIntyre. MacIntyre also sees the need to question the 'malign' postmodernists at the ontological level, and argues for the renewed relevance of Plato and Aristotle's response to the relativism of the sophists (often positively invoked by Lyotard and others). Although I agree with MacIntyre that much from Plato and Aristotle must be retained – especially the belief in an objective Good which gives the true possibility of happiness, and is at one with Truth and Beauty – I also argue against him that a purely dialectical method of establishing these verities is inherently inadequate, and fails to rebut either sophism, or modern perspectivism. Although MacIntyre tries (like Hegel) to fuse dialectic with narrative, dialectics can be an attempt to disguise and conceal the mythic imperative: as such it is *already* 'enlightened', already a spurious claim to universality. In a similar fashion MacIntyre tries to demonstrate, from a detached point of view, that tradition-governed inquiry *in general* is rational, and makes objective progress, whereas the only possible response to nihilism is to affirm one's allegiance to a particular tradition, and derive an ontology from the implicit assumptions of its narrative forms.

In the final chapter of the book, this mode of response will be attempted. Claims for objective truth, goodness and happiness can only be made by identification with a particular form of life that is claimed to participate in them – and this identification cannot be dialectically tested. Christianity can be seen as representing such a form of life. However, Christianity is not, I shall contend, merely one more perspective. It is also *uniquely* different. Here I return to the fact that Nietzsche directed his historical critique particularly against Christianity. This turns out to be not just an aspect of an outmoded metanarrative; on the contrary, Nietzsche was objectively right to the extent that Christianity is unique in refusing ultimate reality to all conflictual phenomena. For this reason, I shall argue, it is the true 'opposite' of Nietzschean postmodernism, and also able to deny it in a more than merely despairing, Manichean fashion. By comparison, all other myths, or narrative traditions, affirm or barely conceal an original primordial violence, which a sacral order merely restrains. Even Plato and Aristotle were inhibited by such a mythical inheritance: in the end they could only think of goodness and happiness as occupying certain privileged sites of self-presence over against an irredeemably chaotic and conflictual cosmos. They isolated islands of peace, but peace was not seen as coterminous with Being. Only Christianity (and, to a lesser degree, Judaism and Islam) affirms such an ontology, and so fully evades an incipient nihilism. Yet this ontology is not dialectically established, but is rather implied in narratives about divine creation and redemption. By the same token, Christianity is quite unable to refute rationally the ontology of difference, or the thought of mastery. Nevertheless, it is uniquely able to reveal this doctrine of perspectivism as itself just another perspective: the perspective of a paganism made aware of its worship of violence by Christianity, and then nakedly espousing such worship.

It will be contended that the perspective of 'malign' postmodernism is the final, most perfect form of secular reason, in some ways reverting to and developing the neo-paganism of Machiavelli. Christianity reveals that nihilism sustains its ontology as another *mythos*. The only possible social critique 'beyond' nihilism will therefore have to be theological.

Thus, in the final chapter, I will elaborate, through a new reading of Augustine and Dionysius, the way in which the Christian transformation of Greek ontology was simultaneously the development of a social and historical critique, penetrating in advance beyond (from a Christian perspective) any possible secular reasoning about social reality, including its final form of nihilism. This critique, I shall contend, belongs to a narrative of social and historical reality which is *constitutive* of Christian theology – and so is, in a special, non-foundationalist sense, a 'metanarrative'.

Explanation, Understanding and Narration

In the postmodern era, as I have just indicated, social science ceases to be the main challenge for theology, and is replaced by absolute historicism and the ontology of difference. Here, however, a possible confusion might arise: this claim is not simply a new version of a sharp distinction between the natural and the human sciences, with the accompanying claim that the latter pursue goals of *verstehen*, or of understanding, while the former pursue goals of explanation.

The champions of *verstehen*, such as Paul Ricoeur, who have been very influential on theologians, have tried to stake out an inviolable 'human' sphere beyond the reach of scientific intrusion. It might, perhaps, be supposed that my own metacritique of social science is tending in the same direction. The remainder of this chapter will dispel any such impression. First of all, in the present section I shall show that understanding as well as explanation, humanism as well as science, is an aspect of modernist secular reason, which I am trying to isolate and refuse. In place of understanding/explanation, I shall put the single mode of narrative knowledge.

In the third section of this chapter, I shall ask what relation a narrated social knowledge has to natural science. And the reply will be that it stands in essential continuity with it, because natural scientific knowledge is also a mode of narration. However, the 'certainty' of both natural science and of a valid social science does not reside in their representation of reality, but in their homology with a power of repetition and ordered change that is nonetheless able to embrace and welcome a moment of unpredictability. Moreover, the implicit ontology of modern science suggests not uniformity at the level of 'ultimate reality' but rather randomness and difference. The question about the possibility of the extra-scientific then becomes not a question about the reality of human freedom, but of whether there can be a narrative that is not 'about' power, implying an ontology that does not legitimate the arbitrary. This will lead us into the last three chapters, which consider this new, postmodern issue.

The contrast between explanation and understanding was made in terms of specifically modernist assumptions. In the first place, both explanation and understanding were meant to establish exact and objective truth. In the second place, their division ultimately rested upon a Cartesian separation between a material sphere governed by efficient causality, and a spiritual domain of meaning and intention.

One can further clarify these assumptions by saying that they were positivist in character. Natural science was supposed to rely upon sense impressions which revealed indefeasible, isolated 'facts', whose regular modes of interconnection were further established by systematic observation and experiment, so establishing scientific 'laws'. The champions of *verstehen* did not question this account of natural science, but denied that this method could apply to the study of human, historical reality, which revealed no such fixed regularities. Instead, the 'scientific' aspect of humane studies was seen to reside in the decipherment of human texts, relics and monuments, where the aim is to translate these objective forms back into the process of their subjective, intentional constitution.[1] That operation was held to depend upon the assumption of an essential ontological identity between the object studied and the person studying; an identity not present in the case of natural science.

Before Wilhelm Dilthey, who was the most important exponent of this outlook, the theologian Schleiermacher had insisted that there is an objective element in interpretation, not just because of this ontological identity of knower and known, but also by virtue of the formal, grammatical structures of texts (or, one may say, of any human artefact assuming a conventional coded system).[2] However, the question arises as to whether there is anything in interpretation surplus to the formal analysis of structure, any level of 'meaning' over and above syntactic entanglements. A thinker in the 'hermeneutic' tradition of *verstehen*, Paul Ricoeur, while insisting that full justice must be done to the moment of formalist 'explanation' – the objective insistence of certain embodied norms of signification – nonetheless claims that when such analysis has been carried out, there remains a task of full interpretation or understanding to perform.[3] As with Schleiermarcher and Dilthey, this is still for Ricoeur a matter of re-animating an essentially dead text or artefact. The written text, in particular, exists for Ricoeur in a kind of lifeless suspension: it possesses a 'sense' but not full 'meaning', which only arises in the living context of speech, when self-conscious speakers are directly present not only to each other, but also, potentially, to the things about which they speak, so that mention often passes over into a simple 'showing'. The goal of interpretation, for Ricoeur, is to resurrect meaning from text, and restore it to this living context, which involves the presence to self of the reflective subject which makes speech and reference possible. An act of reading, therefore, is always completed in a moment of 'inner' self-understanding, and the

---

[1] See chapter 4 above.

[2] Manfred Frank, *Das individuelle Allgemeines: Textstrukturierung und interpretation nach Schleiermarcher* (Frankfurt: Suhrkamp, 1980).

[3] Paul Ricoeur, 'What is a text? Explanation and understanding', in *Paul Ricoeur: Hermeneutics and the Human Sciences*, trans. John B. Thompson (Cambridge: Cambridge University Press, 1981) pp. 145–64.

element of meaning in a text surplus to, and over and above explanation, turns out to be concerned with the universality of human subjectivity and inwardness.

It is clear that Ricoeur only continues to distinguish understanding from explanation, because he persists in a certain belief in a human spirit detachable from embodiment. Self-reflection, 'presence' to things and to other subjects, are thought of by him as 'external' to the inscriptions that one tries to decipher, whereas, in actuality, speech and self-reflection continue to inscribe in some medium, and they remain as bound by codes of signification as any book or portrait.

Conversely, the written text, for Ricoeur, possesses in itself only 'sense' and not 'reference'. This is because, for example, the characters in a work of fiction, including the character of the apostrophized author, possess 'reality' only in terms of the total articulation of the plot, where the conventional behaviour of one syntactic element towards another persuades us to treat a group of words as the words of a living agent. Even if a writer originally meant to refer to real people and events, the written text floats free of these circumstances, and the logic of the text can be treated quite independently of the accuracy of its reportage.

However, these conditions of the written text are also, as Ricoeur fails to realize, the conditions of cultural existence in general. In the first place, our identities are only sustained because of the regular ways we are treated by others, the consistent conventions observed in this treatment, and their significant infractions. As much as fictional characters, we only exist, as 'characters', in the framework of an emplotment.

Secondly, the floating free of circumstances, which characterizes written books, also marks indelibly all cultural activity: we get treated, not as we fantastically imagine 'we deserve', according to our own accounts of ourselves, and of the original circumstances in which we spoke and acted, but according to the multiple reading of our stories by others, and the way our actions appear in the light of later or quite alien sets of events.

Thirdly and finally, if we claim that someone or something is directly present, this does not transport us beyond mere sense to some mystical realm of ontological 'reference', but on the contrary, the conventions governing sense entitle us to say that the conditions for 'reality', as opposed to 'pretence', are here adequately fulfilled. For example: the king declaiming before me is not supported by a stage or framed by a screen; the preceding train of events that have brought me to France have in no way indicated that I am merely a part of a play, pageant, or tournament – where, for example are the spectators? – I conclude, sadly, that this *is* Agincourt, and this *is* King Henry V. Yet at another level, of course, the real Henry V is and can only be a player-king, part of a human fiction. The illusion of a surplus reference arises because we forget that usually, since primordial times, we have been deadly serious about our rituals, and only relatively recently has a wider and wider space of 'secondary' fiction opened up, where authors and actors reflectively distance themselves from the masks they wear. All that we now dub fiction, ought rather to be called 'fiction governed by the trope of irony'. And the contrast of 'serious' and 'ironic' fiction gives the truth of the unreflective contrast of 'reference' and 'sense'. (This is, of course, not to deny that our language operates with a conventional, grammatical distinction of sense from reference, distinguishing 'kingship' from 'this king' – although even here reference elaborates sense, and sense elaborates reference.)

Writing does not therefore suspend life, presence or reference, but through the trope of irony itself produces the 'ontological' gap between reference and sense. Without the characteristic hermeneutic contrasts of presence/absence, voice/inscription, distance from self/self-consciousness, there is no task of restoration or healing for understanding to perform, over and above the task of structural explanation. This does not, however, mean that reading is a purely objective, verifiable activity. In fact, Ricoeur accepts far too readily a structuralist account of formal mechanisms, so that he can represent the more uncertain interpretative element as beginning to escape from the text, from language, towards the *telos* of pure self-reference.[4] He does, indeed, talk of a textual intentionality which must be subjectively resumed, a movement of language itself, but what is questionable is to see this intentional element as something apart from the operations of syntactic forms. For, contrary to structuralist assumptions, it remains unwarranted to imagine that one can identify for every text, or for language in general, the fixed static formal patterns of *langage*, to which the particular innovative moves of *parole* – the unique use of language, in a particular instance – must be referred to uncover their true significance.[5] (This is the same illusion as an absolute grammatical distinction between sense and reference.) The isolation of such categoric universals – which is the linguistic development of Durkheim's teaching about 'social facts' – is finally an arbitrary operation, and is upset by an element of indeterminacy intrinsic to a structural formation in itself: where to place the emphasis, whether to see syntactic unit X as broader in scope, as 'containing' syntactic unit Y or vice versa? The issue of interpretation thus arises directly out of formal problems, not at a level which they do not anticipate. And to read is not, as for hermeneutics, to 'redeem' the text, to put an end to its alien distance, or to discover its essentially 'human' reference, but simply to add to the text, to answer its indeterminacies with a particular new, written emphasis which itself, far from ending puzzlement or estrangement, merely indicates new and promising uncertainties. If there is a question here as to what is the 'true meaning' of the text, then this can only mean what is the truly desirable *order* of the text?

This analysis of textuality suggests that one cannot set explanation and understanding over against each other. There only exist formal, structural means for the generation of sense, and therefore to understand is to encounter and reorganize a formal structure. It is always a matter of 'articulation', or of

---

[4] Ibid.
[5] Ferdinand de Saussure, *Course in General Linguistics*, trans. Roy Harris (London: Duckworth, 1983) pp. 99–189.

showing which element acts on which other and in what way. Therefore 'meaning' is not a precious pearl snatched from levels beneath the swirling flux of causal motion; on the contrary, to say 'meaning' is only to say 'movement' and 'causation'. On the other hand, explanation is scarcely an appropriate term for any theoretical proposal, as it implies that the prior and the original is the adequate source of what it engenders, or else that a 'lawful' regular process is truly more fundamental than the instances which embody it. The adequate explanation of a text, or indeed of anything whatsoever, means rather its representational repetition, a *narration* of text or thing which identifies causes as occasions taken serious notice of by later events. Thus, to say 'movement' and 'causation' is just to say 'meaning', because something becomes of causal significance only when connected with a later or subordinate event which presupposes it. As there is no pure, self-contained original cause that we are aware of, what we know first and last is simply a sequence, and the 'causal' relationship of a first element to a second is in fact necessary even to *define* the first element: who is the father but he who has a son, the chieftain but he who is obeyed, and so forth.

'Narrating', therefore, turns out to be a more basic category than either explanation or understanding: unlike either of these it does not assume punctiliar facts or discrete meanings. Neither is it concerned with universal laws, nor universal truths of the spirit. Yet it is not arbitrary in the sense that one can repeat a text in just any fashion, although one can indeed do so in any number of fashions. The text, if we are attentive, forms a loose and complex knot of resistance, but we do not first of all register this resistance and position it precisely (explanation), and then pass on to the more freewheeling tasks of the spirit. On the contrary, we register this resistance in any number of ways. We may place the pressure here or there, complicate the knot here, undo it a little there – yet, infuriatingly perhaps, we cannot undo the knot altogether (a 'final' deconstruction is endlessly postponed). Always we feel the resistance, although this is from elsewhere, and we cannot precisely place it, for it belongs, ultimately, to a whole wider network of resistances and counter-resistances, which we ourselves, by our intervention, are further adjusting and altering.

If reading texts means that we renarrate or repeat them, and if, as we have seen, textuality is the condition of all culture, then narration – of events, structures, institutions, tendencies as well as of lives – is the final mode of comprehension of human society. To understand or to explain a social phenomenon is simply to narrate it, although this remains an inherently questionable activity. In grasping this, we banish two metaphysical phantoms: first, the phantom of 'decisive causes' (retained by Ricoeur in his own theory of historiography) which lurk 'before' or 'behind' what actually happens, whereas a cause is only 'decisive' at the point where it has already *become* the event.[6] Secondly, the phantom of 'meanings', which hover like ectoplasm

[6] Veyne, *Writing History*, pp. 88–93. Paul Ricoeur, *Time and Narrative*, vol. 1, trans. K. McLaughlin and D. Pellauer (Chicago: Chicago University Press, 1984) pp. 175–226.

above the surface of material reality. Thus, a single operation, narration or (non-identical) repetition, replaces the two-fold sequence of an initial explanation, followed by a second act of understanding.

Again, Paul Ricoeur proves counter-exemplary. He can concede all he likes (for example) to Freud's Oedipal theory of desire, yet still claim that the explanation of the origins of desire does not exhaust the question of the meaning of desire, or of its possible finality.[7] In a sense this speculation is quite simply banal, but it re-echoes the old neo-Kantian quest after 'value' by invoking a possible significance surplus to causal requirements, finding its real fulfilment beyond society, and only able to modify our 'natural' desires in a certain measure. The meaning salvaged here is both secure and ineffable, leaving intact a fixed and constant explanatory structure. Just as Ricoeur's final site for interpretative recovery is private and asocial, so also he does not in the slightest question (and it would be against his strategic interests to do so) the modernist mode of suspicion: always and forever it is the Oedipal mechanism which first generates and shapes desire, as it might, for another 'dialogue', be always and forever the process of production which shapes consciousness, or instrumental reason which normatively governs society. This assumption means that he agrees with Freud that the 'secret' of our finite existence has been once and for all discovered. Any surplus of meaning for our reality over and above this cannot then really and truly find room within our finitude, but must represent a sublime exodus outside matter, outside society and outside the text. By contrast, the only postmodern strategy is that of Deleuze and Guattari: namely, to question the hermeneutic privilege accorded to Oedipal phenomena, and to ask whether they are, after all, universal.[8]

Because historical narration is the true mode of social knowledge, theology no longer has any need, like Ricoeur, to concede the foundationalist suspicion of Marx, Freud or sociology, and appropriate this as a supposed mode of the *via negativa*, or as a way of purifying the true subject matter of theology itself. For this is not really a path of denial leading to the always yet more unknown God, but a strategy preparatory to a phenomenological reduction which grasps in consciousness the *noemata* of 'religious' awareness. Instead, theology need only embrace as absolute its own narrative, which defines finitude in terms of its tension with the infinite source and *telos*. In place of (facing up to) the irremovable granite block of a suspicion which appears as the essence of finitude, it needs to take account of the multiple but 'unfounded' suspicions (some, indeed, unthinkable without the work of Marx, Durkheim and Freud) which can be raised about Christianity in all its localities: suspicions which are themselves, as Gadamer so rightly emphasizes, just acts of textual inter-

[7] Paul Ricoeur, *Freud and Philosophy: An Essay on Interpretation* (New Haven, Conn.: Yale University Press, 1977) pp. 494–553.
[8] Gilles Deleuze and Felix Guattari, *Anti Oedipus: Capitalism and Schizophrenia*, trans. Robert Hurley et al. (London: Athlone, 1983s). *A Thousand Plateaus: Capitalism and Schizophrenia*, trans. Brian Massumi (London: Athlone, 1988) pp. 26–39.

pretation, and not (as Habermas would have it) appeals to the influence of the forces and relations of production, somehow operating *in addition* to language or figurative coding. Such appeals imply that one has naturalized and universalized the realities of work and action.[9]

Dealing with suspicion now becomes a matter of complex narrative negotiations (retelling the ecclesial story so as to accept some external criticisms, now made into self-criticisms, and to rebut others) rather than of concessions made at one level to a source of critique which remains external to theology, but made to allow us better to man the impregnable spiritual citadel of 'religious meaning', poised precariously upon the granite outcrop of 'the secular'.

Narration, Science and the Extra-Scientific

All this, one might say, is very well, but even if (re)narration comprises both explanation and understanding, and negates their contrast, one is still left with the question of how narrative knowledge relates to the knowledge deemed 'scientific', in the sense of natural science as understood since the seventeenth century. Does not a new contrast of narrative/nomological knowledge supervene upon the displaced one of understanding/explanation?

This cannot be altogether denied, but nonetheless, the new contrast does not enshrine the Cartesian dualism of the old one. As the phrase 'natural history' suggests, natural science does not rid itself of narrative, and indeed, it is just as possible to tell a story in which the characters are atoms, plants, animals, or quasars, as one where they are human beings. Moreover, these stories are always necessarily – however disguised this may become – stories of our human interrelationships, and our social relationships to the natural world (Marx was right here). The gradual isolation of a more rigorous 'natural science', in contrast to a vaguer, more speculative 'natural philosophy', does not at all indicate success in prescinding from narrative and human relationship, to penetrate to an ontologically immutable level. On the contrary, right from the outset, with Bacon and Mersenne, the 'scientific revolution' claimed its specificity in the taking more seriously of the practical, effective and useful knowledge of artisans and medical practitioners.[10] Against a background of general philosophical scepticism, Mersenne could claim that technological or operational knowledge retained a certain 'truth' and reliability relating to human life and interests.[11] The new respect accorded to both 'machines'

[9] Hans-Georg Gadamer, 'Rhetoric, hermeneutics, and the critique of ideology: metacritical commentary on *Truth and Method*', in Kurt Mueller-Vollmera (ed.) *The Hermeneutics Reader* (Oxford: Blackwell, 1985) pp. 274–92.

[10] Webster, *The Great Instauration*. Paul Feyerabend, *Realism, Rationalism and Scientific Method: Philosophical Papers Vol. 1* (Cambridge: Cambridge University Press, 1981) p. 15ff.

[11] R. Lenoble, *Mersenne ou la Naissance du Mécanisme* (Paris: Vrin, 1943) esp. pp. 263–8.

and 'experiments' meant that nature was not to be known through observation alone, but more precisely at the point where she coincided with the achievement of some human purpose or regular procedure, which could be so specified as to become repeatable. The 'new science' was therefore, from the outset, preoccupied with narratives of the transformation of nature. However, these were no longer myths of magical action which could only be symbolically represented in ritual. Instead, they could be literally repeated under the proper conditions, artificially re-provided.

The positivist vision of scientific understanding, which usually undergirds accounts of 'explanation', tends to elide this narrative mediation of scientific knowledge. For it assumes, on the one hand, atomic items of sensory information, and, on the other hand, theoretical hypotheses embodying regular law-like connections, which can therefore be represented in an atemporal, synchronic idiom.[12] A more pragmatist account, however, which is in essential continuity with the thought of Bacon, Mersenne and others, assumes that we only apprehend nature as part of the narrative of our own lives, and that a more precise, disciplined, 'scientific' observation of nature involves applying some system of classification which relates to a more rarefied and deliberate specification of human purpose. In other words, we do not make experiments upon data; on the contrary, experimentation begins with the formulation of the data. In similar fashion, experiments do not simply test hypotheses, but a hypothesis is, as it were, the imagination of an experiment, or of a technology. Hence, the successful experiment only proves a theory in the sense that it proves the experiment. A certain narrative, a certain sequence of events, is a true one insofar as it has happened and goes on happening – but, however many times we light fires, drive cars or produce nuclear fission, we only know, with 'scientific' certainty, certain effects, not ultimate reasons, causes or natures.

This instrumentalist, or operationalist account of science does not, however, preclude a 'realist habit of mind' in the sense of speculation about the totality within which we are situated. Moreover, such speculation is not just a contemplative luxury (not even merely 'regulative') but will influence all our practice. It alters and delimits just what we try to do, just as thinking of the cosmos as a big machine spawned many actual, terrestrial machines. However, the specificity of modern science is linked to an *epoche* with regard to realism: the rule of objective, publicly undeniable knowledge is gained at the price of the foregoing, by science, of ontological ambitions. For all the attempts by Descartes, Kant, Whewell, Mill, Popper and Lakatos to 'found' science in an account of human knowing have always falsely pretended that we can unambiguously separate an observation language from a theoretical, explanatory language. Even if, like Lakatos, one says that the long-term

---

[12] Nikhil Bhattacharya, 'Knowledge *per caussas*: Vico's theory of natural science', in Giorgio Tagliacozzo (ed.) *Vico: Past and Present* (Atlantic Highlands, NJ: Humanities Press, 1981) pp. 182–98.

success of a research programme measures truth, this definitive 'success' still implies that other research programme have been once and for all defeated, and this can only mean falsified by a 'reality' apprehended apart from the theoretical conception.[13] Yet to claim that a theory can once and for all be falsified, is, of course, as Lakatos himself showed against Popper, no more tenable than the idea of a once and for all verification. Indeed, on a pragmatist view, verification has priority: if an idea is 'true' so long as it works, then science only makes positive progress when something is positively achieved. Yet by contrast to *mere* positivism, a pragmatist approach accepts that modern science has already theorized internally its peculiar specificity, simply by concentrating on experimental knowledge.

Narrative, therefore, is involved in scientific investigation in two ways: first, science has never done with, and continues to be fertilized by, 'pre-scientific', speculative natural histories. Secondly, scientific theories and experiments are themselves repeatable narratives.

However, there are two further involvements. In the third place, although a theory is itself a kind of imagined experiment, one can very often give different theoretical accounts of the same successful or unsuccessful experiment. This is because science involves not just the language of technology, but also written signs which represent the technology (the 'experiments'), and an experiment is never represented in isolation, but in relation to past scientific practice and to many looser speculations.[14] Theory can 'hover free' of a particular experiment, not because a theory embodies hypotheses conceived independently of the setting up of experiments (as for the positivism of the 'hypothetico-deductive' method) but because theory articulates, beyond the individual experiment, an always necessary surplus drive towards a bigger, general experiment on all reality, which can, of course, never be accomplished, without reproducing that reality. This widest level of theory also takes a narrative form, as natural history, and as the narration of the history of experimentation; showing how one experiment builds on another, how one negates another, how a previous theoretical account of a set of experiments can be replaced by another account, which also takes into consideration experimental results which appear to conflict with the first account.

Fourthly, some modes of science are interested in the absolute individuation of characters. A generally operating law can always be found again, but so too can a pattern which is never repeated elsewhere, like a fingerprint. Things are what they are, because of their absolute difference (two things similar in all respects must be in the same place, and so identical, as Leibniz realized) and where it is of human interest to recognize the individual – usually a human individual, in the context of social control, or the investigation of crime – then science shows how to repeat the story of finding this or

[13] Paul Feyerabend, *Against Method* (London: New Left Books, 1975) p. 181ff.
[14] Alasdair MacIntyre, 'Epistemological crises, dramatic narrative and the philosophy of science', in *The Monist* (October, 1977) pp. 453–72.

that character, with an absolute, indefeasible accuracy. Of course, this possibility contains an ideological danger: the regular motions of any given social system, subject to 'scientific' regulation, can encourage the delusion that there are permanent, universal regularities.

For insofar as we are entirely natural, material creatures, one can of course try to apply the procedures of the 'new science' to the *entire range* of 'human' existence; nothing is in principle excluded from its purview. What science tries to achieve here, as in the case of non-human nature, are narratives that can be repeated in *identical* fashion, either because one has found a principle for abstracting from the 'indifferent' variations from case to case, in the instance of 'the same story', which permits one to speak of 'a law of nature', or else because one has discovered a method for classifying along a continuum (in the tradition of Leibniz) absolute individual characteristics in genetic make-up, handwriting style and so forth, which allow one, in principle, always to 'find again' the suspect, like the police agent Javert infallibly catching up with Jean Valjean. Such *continua* can be artificial as well as natural: thus passports and credit card numbers, car numberplates and ISBN codes for books.

Is it harder to record or construct these narratives in the case of human interaction than in the case of the other physical processes? The answer here cannot be a straightforward one. Human processes are usually supposed to be less predictable: but can we count more, tomorrow, on the sun's rising yet again, than on English being still the dominant language of Great Britain? In the last analysis the sun is always, in every sense, further away from us; within the extent of our cosmic knowledge we could never rule out a bolt from an unknown blue that would tear the sun from its present course. This event would not upset all that we had known about the sun hitherto, in its relationship to us. But if we were all to wake up tomorrow speaking Urdu, this would entirely destroy our existing self-understanding. It could only be accounted for *in terms of* extra-human nature, some switching of our faculties entirely beyond our control or comprehension. But as long as we know them without such unprecedented interference, then we know *absolutely* that, if British people record the sun's demise tomorrow, they will still do so in English. And we do not know, with equal absoluteness, that the sun will rise again.

It seems, therefore, that predictions about human society are more secure than predictions about nature. It was something along these lines (rather than anything resembling Dilthey's notions) that Vico meant by saying that because we have *scientia* of what we make, our knowledge of the human world is better than that of the natural world. We know what ingredients 'we' have put in (in the very act of composing our own subjectivity), how they are arranged and so forth, at least for a certain range of practical use. One is not saying here that we know our own thoughts, or understand other people, in an intuitive way impossible in the case of magnets or stars, but rather that we can know both language and compasses employing magnetism better than magnetism itself, and all three better than the remote heavenly bodies.

The 'predictable' aspect of human society is also the most banal aspect, *and* the most contingent aspect – for, in the long run, we might gradually transform English into another language altogether. Yet this banality matters, because the limits to applying a scientific approach to social affairs are not theoretical, but practical: behaviour can be made systematically more regular, more predictable, and a scientifically comprehensible society would simply be a society for the time being under a totalitarian management.

However, this sort of thesis, which one tends to associate with the Frankfurt school, should not really be stated in quite such a bald fashion. In particular, not every predictable social process is 'bad', as the example of English in Britain so obviously shows. Therefore one cannot simply specify, as thinkers like Karl-Otto Apel tend to do, desirable social goals in terms of escaping from unconscious compulsions, which the strategies of suspicion serve to uncover, in favour of as wide a possible an extension of free, autonomous, self-conscious choice and collaboration.[15] Just as the ethical antithesis of true and false goal cannot be read as the Kantian 'moral' antithesis of autonomous and heteronomous, so, also, the antithesis unconscious-regular against conscious-variable carries no obvious ethical weight. The real question is that of the *quality* of the 'unconscious' processes; capitalism is not wrong because it has become compulsive and operates heteronomously, but because it is a system designed to operate without reference to principles of just distribution. For every new conscious decision, if it becomes effective, will persist into the future in a relatively unconscious way: far from signifying moral deterioration, this may mean the development of a desirable habit.

In a still more important way, the thesis is too bald. The twentieth century has, of course, revealed that societies can emerge which try to approximate to a state of 'total management', as it were 'making behaviourism to be true'. But what appears far more dangerous today is the threat of a more subtle totalitarianism, associated with the dominance of the free market and of liberal democracy. The goal of the capitalist market, formally considered, is not – like that of a Stalinist five-year plan – predictability, but rather, the stimulation of inventiveness and effort on the one hand, combined, on the other hand, with the *guaranteed* subordination of all this endeavour to a quantifiable measurement of its worth. This guarantee operates through a mechanism of supply and demand determined not by considerations of need, desire and justice, but the (abstract) desires of the owners of capital and of distributed income. As long as this subordination is maintained – then, let freedom and spontaneity reign! For without constant 'feedback', without leaving room for the creativity of subordinates, users and operators of processes, systems will not be, in the long run, so efficient and so well maintained.

As Lyotard has argued, there is a homonymity here between science, which helps to make capitalism profitable, and capitalism, which constantly invests

[15] Karl-Otto Apel, *Towards a Transformation of Philosophy*, trans. Glyn Adey and Davis Frisby (London: Routledge, 1980) pp. 46–77, 225–301.

in science.[16] Both the capitalistic and the scientific process shun merely closed systems; their shared concern with power means that they cannot rest content with existing modes of control, but must encourage a random inventiveness, which they can, according to the rules of their own language-games, always recruit to their own interest. This is because both science and capitalism make only one meaning publicly count: the meaning of power. All kinds of theories, products, interests – the origin of the universe, the question of human kinship with animals, love of the beautiful, humanitarian concern, faster transport – may provide power, in the end, with a greater repertoire, resourcefulness and flexibility.

It is in this context that one should understand what Deleuze and Guattari call the 'deterritorialization' and the 'decoding' carried out by capitalism.[17] The capitalist system is, in itself, indifferent to attachment to location and to the content of particular customs and traditions; it imparts no sacrality either to place or to hierarchical modes of rule. On the other hand, just as capitalism cannot dispense with producing 'use-values' or symbolic exchanges (in Baudrillardian terms), although it is itself only concerned with exchange value and abstract equivalence, so, also, a constant recycling of territorial and hierarchical attachments – rural nostalgia, the world-wide obsession with the British monarchy – proves a vital resource for continued production and profitability. However, Deleuze and Guattari are wrong to think that capitalism is constituted by prime sites of 'reterritorialization' – the sovereign individual, the State, the family – which could, in principle, be overcome if the process of deterritorialization were more rigorously carried through (as Marx thought that capitalism ultimately 'held back' production). On the contrary, absolute deterritorialization is the essence of *capitalism itself*, which may well dispense with state, family and individual, as we know them. But every deterritorializing strategy (as Deleuze and Guattari themselves affirm) will always and forever reterritorialize, in the sense that it can go on 'marketing' obliterated values in an ironical, cynical and sentimental spirit. For example, the bourgeois cult of the aristocratic country house in late modern England does not really spell a dangerous hankering after reactionary values, as the simplistic left-critique would have it. On the contrary, a pure preoccupation with the 'charm' of a past life, a creaming-off of the mere appearances of furniture, gardens, cuisine and so forth from an entire mode of life, is possible because certain aspects of aristocracy – the significance of birth, staying in one place, parental oversight, the obligations of honour – have been so contemptuously left behind.

Capitalism is, therefore, like science, because it is indifferent to anything but abstract power. It is also like science, because it does not merely override past attachments or theoretical prejudices. Instead, it keeps them in reserve,

---

[16] J.-F. Lyotard. *The Postmodern Condition: A Report on Knowledge*, trans. Geoff Bennington and Brian Massumi (Manchester: Manchester University Press, 1986).

[17] Deleuze and Guattari, *A Thousand Plateaus*, pp. 351–474.

all the way back to oriental despotism or Pythagoras, so that it can potentially recruit them to the interests of domination. The more subtle totalitarianism, which we already have, permits individual freedom, encourages the thought of the object of freedom as being the exercise of *personal* power, and so the better builds up both the energies and the assumptions which allow for a general extension of an efficient, all-powerful system. In this sense, we already have a society whose major processes can be comprehended by science, and quite often predicted, especially in probabilistic terms, although elements of unpredictability are also promoted by a 'scientific' social technology. This science is, as ever, a compound of the 'new science' of politics, together with political economy and the science of 'policing' and management. They 'apply', although they are in themselves mere descriptions of formal systems, simply because society has been made in their image, just as society, by inventing capitalism, helped at the same time to invent liberal politics and political economy.

But what is there then, besides abstract power, which would be the subject of non-scientific narratives alone? Is there, indeed, anything, or is this merely to long after the spiritualism of the *verstehen* tradition? Certainly, it is quite hopeless to go along (like so many contemporary theologians) with Habermas, and contrast 'emancipatory' interests with those of 'prediction and control'.[18] To say 'emancipate' is only to say maximize negative freedom of choice, and to say 'freedom' is to say arbitrary power – which, as we have seen, the subtle totality does not wish to promote only at the centre, but also at all the peripheries. If one goes beyond this Kantian contrast of causality with freedom, then the question, is there an interest besides that of prediction and control? becomes more difficult. In a sense, even ethical and aesthetic activities attempt to predict and control; they lay down tracks on which our life must run. Yet they appear to swerve away from concern with the identically repeatable – general principles are not for them iron laws, but rather a fount of inspiration, and subject to exceptions. The unique is sought, not along a continuum to be refound, but as an outstanding exception to be reproduced (the postcard of a Rembrandt, in contrast to a fingerprint in a police file). The unique is not therefore placed alongside proximate others, but itself provides a new context; it is selected as beautiful, which means as 'exemplary' (as Kant realized). *This* pattern is held to be preferable, this regularity or this exact repetition should apply almost universally . . . and yet not here, or there.

If such preferences are arbitrary, then indeed, only violence rules, and the aesthetic and ethical merely provide counterpoints in the scientific narrative which constantly 'recruits' to itself the stories whose point is their mere variation. If, however, the ethical and the aesthetic are ontologically objective realities, then there is an alternative to the narrative of arbitrary power, and something wider than science, which only records power, and whose truth ends with its passing. This alternative is the crux of this final section of the

---

[18] Jurgen Habermas, *Knowledge and Human Interests* (Boston: Beacon, 1971).

book. For only a metaphysics of objective goodness and beauty, not a mere epistemology of 'human' freedom (as for the Frankfurt school) can discover a realm other than that of science and technology.

The conclusion of this present section, however, must be that with the end of theoretical and practical modernism, one sees that the really valid social sciences are 'the new politics', 'political economy' and organization theory. They are sciences of power, and true only in the scope of their operations. They do not necessarily require any realist assumptions. By contrast, the positivist and dialectical traditions depended for their truth upon such assumptions. Both traditions hoped to explain and replace religion, both hoped to link science with the idea of a destiny for emergent humanity. In both cases, 'representing' the essential site of our humanity – productivity, freedom, the social whole, instrumental reason and charisma – was inextricably linked with telling a story about the necessary evolution, or evolution plus loss and regaining, of this essential humanity. The story was really a necessary rhetorical prop to offset the fact of the not always very obvious contemporary presence of the supposed human essence. Thus one can define, as Lyotard suggests, the modern period now perhaps passing away as 'the age of the metanarratives'.[19] (Though it must be noted here that I shall later on imply that 'a nihilist metanarrative', characteristic of postmodernity, was always latent within modernity itself.)

Contemporary proponents of 'realism' as opposed to pragmatism (like Roy Bhaskar, Russell Keat and John Urry) have endeavoured to rescue the Marxist and sociological traditions by expunging positivism from the inheritance. That they really fail to do so is perhaps indicated by the fact that their arguments for realism reduce to a continued recitation of the metanarratives. Rightly denying the empiricist view that one begins with isolated observations, and then proceeds to discover causal regularities, they nonetheless promote the metaphor of law-like process behind, underneath or before the phenomena.[20] This is odd, because if perception of tendencies, structures, dynamics and so forth enters into our very comprehension of the entities which they connect, then there is all the less reason to fall into this metaphorical trap. The 'tendencies' accompanying things are simply the tendencies that *are* those things, linked to certain relationships, and to their interactions with us, the actors and observers. By contrast, the celebration of a 'structure irreducible to, but present only in its effects', is a pure piece of metaphysics, out of place in this context.[21] The same thing should be said for 'society is not produced by thought, any more than is a magnetic field',[22] as can be seen if one translated this into 'societies are not composed of signs and figures, any

[19] Lyotard, *The Postmodern Condition*, pp. 34–7.

[20] Roy Bhaskar, *A Realist Theory of Science* (Brighton: Harvester, 1975); *The Possibility of Naturalism* (Brighton: Harvester, 1979) pp. 11–13. Russell Keat and John Urry, *Social Theory as Science* (London: RKP, 1975) pp. 27–30, 97.

[21] Bhaskar, *The Possibility of Naturalism*, p. 50.

[22] Ibid., p. 33.

more than are magnetic fields'. The 'beyond thought', or 'beyond language' turns out to be either Durkheim's social fact, so that one gets the statement, 'in social life only relations endure',[23] or else to be Marx's social relations of production, where 'real relations' are supposed to give rise to more secondary 'phenomenal forms'.[24] Although the supposed structures and forces are seen as extending unimaginably 'beyond' given society, they are only, of course, known as present in that society, and can only be hypostatically isolated by a false abstraction from its surface features.

It is the *story* of the 'enduring' of these things beneath the passing show of everything else which creates the illusion of a 'real' realm of social objectivity, recognizable outside the determinations of a theory.

The demise of scientific realism and the end of the metanarratives therefore belong together. The 'challenge' of social science turns out not to be the challenge of a knowledge that mirrors, but of a knowledge that is arbitrary power. Let us now, therefore, pass to the postmodern implications of absolute historicism, and the question, is there anything *but* such insolent abstraction? Is violence the master of us all?

[23] Ibid., p. 52.
[24] Ibid., p. 89.

10
Ontological Violence or the Postmodern Problematic

Introduction

For the secular postmodernists, Nietzsche became the only true master of suspicion: the thinker of a 'baseless suspicion' which rests, unlike the suspicion of Marx, Freud and sociology, on no foundationalist presuppositions. In the present chapter, I am concerned with what is common to the outlook of the major Nietzscheans, and I deliberately treat the writings of Nietzsche, Heidegger, Deleuze, Lyotard, Foucault and Derrida as elaborations of a single nihilistic philosophy, paying relatively less attention to their divergences of opinion.

This single philosophy will be regarded as having two necessary aspects: on the one hand, a historicist 'genealogy', on the other hand an 'ontology of difference', the two being interconnected in a fashion somewhat analogous to the relation between Hegel's *Phenomenology* and Hegel's *Logic*. Primary texts of genealogy are: Nietzsche's *Genealogy of Morals* and *The Will to Power*; Foucault's *Discipline and Punish* and *The History of Sexuality*; Deleuze and Guattari's *Capitalism and Schizophrenia*; Lyotard's *The Postmodern Condition*. Primary texts of differential ontology are: Heidegger's *Being and Time*, with the later works; Deleuze's *Différence et Répétition* and the *Logique du Sens*; Derrida's *Of Grammatology* and 'Violence and Metaphysics'; Lyotard's *The Differend*.

Postmodernism, as represented by these texts, articulates itself as, first, an absolute historicism, second as an ontology of difference, and third as ethical nihilism. The task of this chapter is to show how its historicist or genealogical aspect raises the spectre of a human world inevitably dominated by violence, without being able to make this fearful ghost more solid in historicist terms alone. To supplement this deficiency, it must ground violence in a new transcendental philosophy, or fundamental ontology. This knowledge alone it presents as more than perspectival, more than equivocal, more than mythical. But the question arises: can such a claim be really sustained without lapsing back into a metaphysics supposedly forsworn? It will be argued that differential ontology is but one more *mythos*, and that the postmodern realization that discourses of truth are so many incommensurable language games does not ineluctably impose upon us the conclusion that the ultimate, over-arching game is the play of force, fate and chance.

The impossibility of exceeding a merely mythical status for nihilism – as 'neo-paganism', or whatever – constitutes one aspect of 'The Postmodern Problematic'. The second aspect concerns the implications of the new *mythos*: its anti-humanist thrust demonstrates that Kantian liberalism is merely the 'great delayer' (to use George Grant's phrase). For once it has been conceded, as by Kant, that ethics is to be grounded in the fact of the will and of human freedom, then quite quickly it is realized that freedom is not an ahistorical fact about an essential human subject, but is constantly distilled from the complex strategies of power within which subjects are interpellated as unequal, mutually dependent persons. The protection of an equality of freedom therefore collapses into the promotion of the inequality of power. And it is here that a problem arises. If freedom effaces itself in favour of arbitrary power, then how can one ever talk of there being more or less freedom in one society rather than another? Every society will exhibit both freedom and unfreedom, and a post-humanist, genealogical discourse must confine itself to the deconstruction of regimes of power, and not present this task as also a 'philosophy of history with a practical intent', or an emancipatory potential.

Yet all the recent French neo-Nietzscheans, if not Nietzsche and Heidegger, are loath to renounce the emancipatory claim, and are therefore doomed to smuggle back into their philosophies an ahistorical Kantian subject who is the bearer of freedom. For it is *this* subject which remains the only possible subject of a discourse of emancipation. In consequence, every new disguised, or semi-overt version of a Kantian practical reason put forwards by Foucault, Deleuze or Lyotard always succumbs to reapplication of the Nietzschean reduction of liberty to power. The neo-Nietzscheans cannot, in consequence, wriggle out of the implication that, while nihilism may be 'the Truth', it is at the same time the truth whose practical expression must be fascism. One's only resort at this juncture, other than mystical despair, is to return to the demonstration that nihilism, as an ontology, is also no more than a *mythos*. To counter it, one cannot resuscitate liberal humanism, but one can try to put forward an alternative *mythos*, equally unfounded, but nonetheless embodying an 'ontology of peace', which conceives differences as analogically related, rather than equivocally at variance.

This strategy, of course, necessitates also a different genealogy, one which sees in history not just arbitrary transitions, but constant contingent shifts either towards or away from what is projected as the true human *telos*, a true concrete representation of the analogical blending of difference.

The present chapter, then, will show first, that a nihilistic genealogy requires an ontology of violence; second, that this ontology is only a mythology; third, that it is an entirely malign mythology. Running through all these demonstrations a fourth thematic will emerge: this mythology is the best, the least self-deluded, self-description of the secular, which fails only at the point where it will not admit that it has shown the secular to be but another 'religion'. This religion is not quite accurately described as 'neo-paganism', because it is an embracing of those elements of sacred violence in paganism which Christianity both exposed and refused, and of which paganism, in its innocence, was only half-aware. The secular *episteme* is a post-Christian paganism, something in the last analysis only to be defined, negatively, as a refusal of Christianity and the invention of an 'Anti-Christianity'.

Genealogy

Postmodernism is, first and foremost, an absolute historicism which overcomes 'the Kantian delay'. Before Kant, as Foucault well explains, the classical era still understood finite limitation in terms of its relationship to the infinite.[1] Our knowledge of the infinite was considered to be imperfect, but, by the same token, our knowledge of the finite to be limited also. Yet, at the same time, a metaphysics, or a representation of the permanent circumstances of the relation of finite to infinite, was still considered possible. After Kant, the possibility of this metaphysics is denied, supposedly on 'critical' grounds, but in fact on the basis of a new and equally 'metaphysical' dogmatism which redefines finitude in terms of certain closed positive conditions, such as temporality, closed spatiality and mechanical causality.

In addition, it was claimed by Kant that every rational person can have knowledge of the essence of the finite subject as sublime freedom standing precisely at the point of direct 'presence' of the ineffable to the cognizable, and can apprehend the practical laws deducible from this essence. In Kant's wake, these claims to 'represent', not the finite/infinite relation, but finitude itself and the 'bounds' of finitude in the finite subject, become the basis for new philosophies of history making no reference to transcendence, or claiming that transcendence is only knowable via immanence. For these 'metanarratives' (to use Lyotard's term) history is essentially the history of certain stable properties which define finitude – such as production, labour, society or instrumental reason – and its rational direction is towards revealing more clearly the essence of finitude: freeing humanity as 'the producing animal', or arriving at Durkheim's 'fully social' society.

Nietzschean genealogy is a more absolute historicism because it refuses to tell these Kantian and Hegelian (or sociological and Marxist) stories about a constant human subject. Instead, it is only interested in disinterring the thresholds of emergence for many different fictions of subjectivity in the course of human history. With the denial of the Kantian representation of finitude, the classical problematic of the finite/infinite relation, placing freedom and causality in a *single* series, returns to view in postmodernity.

---

[1] Foucault, *The Order of Things*, pp. 312–18.

However, the nihilists claim to handle this in terms of 'infinite difference', or by redefining a critical knowledge of the finite as the historical tracing of the possibly infinite series of self-transgressions on the part of humanity. Equally, however, it is thought that a redefined critical discourse must itself productively transgress the received versions of human existence. Like nineteenth-century or modern thought, postmodern nihilism is still concerned with the emergence of knowledge through time, but knowledge is now diversified, and infinity is reinvoked as an anarchic dimension. The problem, to which we will return in the next section, is whether this reading of the infinite as the anarchic does not in fact reinstate a classical eighteenth-century claim (made paradigmatically by Leibniz) to be able to 'analyse' – not on the basis of faith, but of natural reason – the permanent ahistorical conditions of the finite/ infinite relationship.

Nietzsche's *Genealogy of Morals* is subtitled 'an attack', and he means, of course, an attack upon Christianity, and the illusion of eternal moral values. But the relation between title and subtitle indicates the key ambiguity of all genealogical method. On the one hand, it is dedicated to reducing the apparently same and persistent to its process of origination (*not* to 'preceding' origins). On the other hand, this task is not undertaken disinterestedly, out of motives of curiosity, but rather the concern is to undermine some present constellation of power by exploding the 'eternal verities' which it claims to promote, and exhibiting the 'base' origins of its apparently noble pretensions. The question that arises is whether the narrated genealogy is in consequence but one possible interpretation, a story told with a bias intended to unsettle the incumbent heirs? But neither Nietzsche nor Foucault understand genealogy in this fashion. When they suggest that there are no facts, only interpretations, they are not thinking of genealogical history, but of the relationship of any human culture to its inheritance. Cultures exist as interpretations, but the arbitrary displacement of one interpretation by another can still be objectively narrated. It is true that this does not happen once and for all. Genealogy is an endless task, because every discourse and practice always presupposes more than it can be fully aware of. The limitations of each individual genealogist will be defined by the particular concern he has to unmask this or that form of domination of which, in the circumstances of his particular era, he becomes aware.[2]

The claim, then, is that genealogical accounts are objective, but that at the same time they stand in an intimate relationship to the question of justice. As Foucault points out, the earlier Nietzsche related 'scientific history' to the exposure of unjust social structures. The later Nietzsche, on the other hand,

<hr/>

[2] Guy Lardreau and Christian Jambet, *L'Ange: Pour un Cynégétique du Semblant* (Paris: Grasset, 1976) pp. 40–2. Friedrich Nietzsche, *The Will to Power*, trans. W. Kaufmann and R. J. Hollingdale (London: Weidenfeld and Nicolson, 1967) paras. 218, 481. Michel Foucault, 'What is enlightenment?' and 'Nietzsche, genealogy and history', in Paul Rabinow (ed.) *The Foucault Reader* (Harmondsworth: Penguin, 1984) pp. 32–50, 76–97; 'Questions of method: An interview with Michel Foucault', in *Ideology and Consciousness*, no. 8, Spring 1989.

came to regard every regime of power as necessarily unjust, yet now believed still more strongly in the liberating role of history, which exposes this fact of injustice.[3] By revealing the injustice, the arbitrariness, of every power-constellation, history leads us gradually to the realization that this state of affairs proper to 'life' is not to be condemned, but rather celebrated. Hence, genealogy is not an interpretation, but a new 'joyfully' nihilistic form of positivism which explains every cultural meaning-complex as a particular strategy or ruse of power. No universals are ascribed to human society save one: that it is always a field of warfare. And yet this universal history of military manoeuvres is also to be regarded as in some sense liberating, as assisting the emergence of an *übermensch*, or a post-humanist human creature.[4]

Is this convincing? Can genealogy really sustain itself as more than an interpretation, a more or less likely story? I shall suggest that it cannot. Let us look at the stories which Nietzsche and Foucault seek to tell.

The key to the deconstruction of these stories is simply this: how can the understanding of the *event as such*, of every event, as a moment of combat, justify itself in merely historicist, genealogical terms? Supposedly, the genealogist is quite neutral with respect to the different sorts of value promoted by different historical cultures: he should be equally suspicious of them all. Yet in fact, if the transcendental event, every possible event, is a military ploy of assertive difference over against 'the other', then cultures closer to realizing this truth will come to be celebrated as more 'natural', more spontaneous cultures. Hence Nietzsche celebrates a Homeric nobility delighting in war, trials of strength, spectacles of cruelty, strategies of deception.[5] Unless it is clear that this really is a more 'natural' form of life, then the general thesis must fall into doubt, and Nietzsche's genealogy will appear as itself but another perspective: an account of the rise of Christianity, written from the point of view of the paganism which it displaced.

And, of course, this cannot possibly be made clear. Nietzsche does not even claim that universal human warfare is the upshot of a utilitarian necessity of the struggle to grow stronger and survive, but rather that it is a concomitant of the pure creative will to difference, to self-assertion.[6] This preference for originality, even at the cost of danger, is purely (as Nietzsche admits) a matter of taste, and Nietzsche is not able to demonstrate that such a taste is more primordially lodged in human existence than the despised desires for security, consolation, mutuality, pleasure and contentment. It follows that only in terms of Nietzsche's own unfounded hierarchy of values is the primitive noble who tramples upon or patronizes the weak free from blame. Let me explicate.

---

[3] Foucault, 'Nietzsche, genealogy and history'.
[4] Michel Foucault, 'Truth and power', in *The Foucault Reader*, pp. 51–75.
[5] Friedrich Nietzsche, *The Genealogy of Morals*, trans. Francis Golffing, Essay One (New York: Doubleday Anchor, 1956).
[6] Ibid., Sections I–II.

Nietzsche argues that the weak fail to realize that they are dealing, not with a deliberating will, but with a natural force: an activity which is no more culpable than the eagle swooping down upon its prey.[7] In the moment of their invention of a new 'slave morality', the weak falsely imagine a subjective doer standing behind the deed, an impossible noble who would be capable of refraining from his noble nature. The implication here is that the weak are already 'Platonists', that they already imagine that the strong noble possesses essentially their own set of supposedly abiding values. In response to these values he should ascetically restrain his baser, aggressive impulses. However, Nietzsche is quite wrong to suppose that the notion of a 'moral interval', of a possible doing or refraining, arises only through the metonymic displacement which substitutes a subject behind the action for the subject which is the action. For within the latter subject there is *already* an interval, which is one of necessary *metaphoric* tension: not only is his action akin to that of the eagle – or the lion, dog or whatever – it *consists*, precisely, in a totemic identification with the eagle's swooping flight. The behaviour of the strong man is never spontaneous, it is always imitative of a cultural paradigm of strength, and he never exercises a natural power, or the power of a man which is 'like' that of the eagle, but always an invented, simulated power, which is that of the man-becoming-eagle. Moreover, the strong man is *already* an ascetic, for he is already organizing his natural energies towards the achievement of this single goal.

Given the dedication of the strong to a narrative which invents their strength, it is possible for the weak to refuse the necessity of this strength by telling a different story, posing different roles for human beings to inhabit. This might, indeed, be a questionable, metaphysical story about a disembodied, characterless soul always free to choose, but it could also be a story which simply changed the metaphors: which, for example, proposed a humanity becoming sheep-like, pastoral.

Not unlike positivist sociology, Nietzsche declares to be universal a certain condition of primitive humanity: in this case a society which celebrates the *agon* or playful, competitive struggle. However, Nietzsche's picture of paganism is also overdone. One can certainly characterize Homeric morality as not clearly distinguishing between 'good' and 'success', between demonstrations of strength and the achievement of what we should think of as 'moral' goals.[8] Yet this is not to say that it did not possess codes governing what constituted a fair display of strength. Such codes insisted that magnanimity, protection of dependents and hospitality to strangers were the *duty* of the strong, rather than merely one possible manifestation of their power. A heroic society characteristically ranks different degrees of achievement, has scales of value, and requires certain specific performances from different social strata. Yet these emphases find very little place in Nietzsche's account: what one gets

---

[7] Ibid., XIII.
[8] See chapter 11 below.

instead is a description of how compromises were reached between the many heroes, the 'strong' patriarchal heads of families.[9] This produced, according to Nietzsche, a highly 'economic' culture, dominated by processes of bargaining, exchanges and the finding of equivalents. In this development, which is none other than the emergence of the city and the political state, all the fictions which we mistake for the universally human are formed: logic, which pretends that the unequal is equal so that it can be practically managed; moral guilt and conscience, which are but the gradual internalization of a demand objectively made upon us by a creditor; punishment, which becomes a reduced equivalent for an original act of spontaneous vengeance, or else sadistic anger on the part of an outraged noble caste.[10] The economic activities from which logic, morality and punishment take their birth, are, according to Nietzsche, strictly agonistic in character. Every fixing of an equivalent – so much money for this product, so much punishment for this crime – is but the asymmetrical triumph of some power over another. This is because, for Nietzsche's nominalism, no objective equivalents can be found to mediate between the radically diverse; there can, therefore, be no just prices, nor appropriate punishments.

But, in that case, Nietzsche is still a *political economist*, and he tells us as much when he defines man as 'an assaying animal'.[11] By contrast, primitive heroic societies themselves believe in hierarchies of values and the objective equivalence of different objects.[12] If Nietzsche denies the reality of these beliefs, then he does not really offer us a deconstruction of heroic societies, nor an exposure of the naked power 'behind' the claims to meaning and value. Instead, what he does is scarcely more than what political economy, sociology and dialectics had already done – namely to claim that an 'economic' mode of behaviour has always been the secret truth of every society hitherto, a truth now at last openly admitted, and more fully practised. It is not very difficult to see that primitive societies always, in fact, accompany and reinforce their hierarchies of value with violence, nor that they sometimes conceal the practice of this violence. However, to say, with Nietzsche, that violence is the substance of what is going on, requires not just pointing out the violence, but also a denial of the objectivity of the values. But the question of their objectivity evades the scope of a discourse of universal reason, which is what Nietzsche's version of 'nihilism' remains.

A discourse of universal reason, and, moreover, a new positivism. Positivism narrates the emergence of scientific truth, whereas nihilism narrates the nihilistic destiny of science, namely, the necessity for the discipline of truth-finding to admit that there are no truths, and therefore no objective goods. Yet, in one respect, the story has not changed: like positivism, nihilism

---

[9] Nietzsche, *The Genealogy of Morals*, Essay One, VIII, Essay Two, VIII, IX.
[10] Ibid., Essay One, VIII, IX, Essay Two, IX.
[11] Ibid., Essay Two, VIII.
[12] Tcherkezoff, *Dual Classification Reconsidered*.

discovers a certain universal primitive religion of an immanentist character, which involves sacrifices, games and wars, a religion resigned to 'the circulation of blood'. Like positivism too, it does not simply privilege and universalize the standpoint of the primitive, it also claims to understand the primitives better than they understood themselves. Thus Nietzsche, first of all, celebrates primitive nobility, but secondly, makes agonistic struggles, understood 'economically', the real defining characteristic of their existence.

Positivist, also, is his general approach towards religion. All forms of supernatural religion are declared irrational and traced up to metaphysical mistakes in the reading of nature and society: Nietzsche sees the metonymic invention of the soul as the starting point for the elaboration of all transcendent entities and the idea of a continuing dependence on immortal ancestors as the origin of a positive valuation for *self*-sacrifice, as the constant repayment of a debt.[13] Yet, at the same time, a more naturalistic religion is celebrated, and aligned with the discourse of nihilism itself (just as Durkheim aligned primitive religion with sociology). The future 'overman' able to impose his will in the form of a new law can transform mere *amor fati* into a mystical wish for an exact repetition and eternal recurrence of all that is different, all who have been strong enough to sacrifice and to offer themselves to be sacrificed.[14]

The nihilist treatment of religion is, however, only complete when, like other positivist discourses, it has been able to explain Christianity as the transition from the primitive half-concealment of power, to the modern liberation of power. Why should this become a necessary task? To understand this one must return to the earlier point, that nihilism conceives some cultures as nearer to realizing the truth of nihilism than others. One might suppose that it would rather wish to see every culture as equally a manifestation of the will-to-power – either 'openly', or by means of ruse and subterfuge. However, the fact of ruse, and the possibility, which nihilism itself represents, of exposing ruse, are things which themselves render this strategy problematic. A 'naked' manifestation of the will-to-power, either by a culture or a philosophy must, in fact, claim interpretative priority over a disguised manifestation, otherwise the transcendental status of the will-to-power would be open to question. For this reason Klossowski and Lyotard are surely wrong to claim, against Nietzsche and Deleuze, that the preference for active, noble virtues against reactive, slave virtues can be dropped, as both, equally, manifest the will-to-power.[15] If one is still arguing for a liberated morality, or a 'transvaluation' based upon a knowledge of the will-to-power, then the reactive strategy can only attain to moral equality with the active one when it comes

---

[13] Nietzsche, *The Will· to Power*, pp. 226, 487. *The Genealogy of Morals*, Essay One, XIII, Essay Two, XVI, XIX.

[14] Friedrich Nietzsche, *Thus Spake Zarathustra*, trans. R. J. Hollingdale (London: Penguin, 1989) pp. 97–9, 159–63, 217, 219. René Girard, 'Le meurtre fondateur dans la pensée de Nietzsche', in Paul Dumouchel (ed.) *Violence et Verité: Autour de René Girard* (Paris: Grasset, 1985) pp. 603–13. I am indebted to discussions with Philip Goodchild on this point.

[15] J.-F. Lyotard, *Économie Libidinale*.

to self-consciousness of its own hidden stratagem, and thereby, of course, abandons it in self-contempt.

The logic of Nietzsche's 'active' nihilism would, therefore, seem to require that one define as 'bad conscience' any denial of the will-to-power as manifest in the reactive virtues of the weak. But, at the same time, there are problems, not recognized by Deleuze, in keeping 'bad conscience' totally distinct from the 'unhappy consciousness' of the dialecticians.[16] If power can be manifest, non-occulted, for some persons and cultures – at least at some moments of awareness – then why is it not always naked, why is it sometimes concealed? The answer of course, is that through trickery it becomes all the more power-ful, all the more effectively itself. Only with the ruses of the priestly caste, says Nietzsche, 'has the human mind grown both profound and evil'.[17] But what does one say when the wielders of arbitrary power are themselves fully deceived, when they claim not to be wielding arbitrary power, and, espe-cially, when they turn power against power in an ascetic denial of their own energies? Here again, power must be thought (unlike everything else in nihilist philosophy) to have its own 'sufficient reasons', such that the only possible explanation for the self-suppression of power is that thereby, in the long-term, power is all the more effectively stored up and recruited. It seems then that, after all, bad conscience is only a kind of unhappy consciousness, not just contingently 'wrong', but also fated and necessary as the temporary self-alienation of power from power, which finally returns power to power.

Above all, nihilism must discover a sufficient reason for Christianity. This is because Christianity, as Nietzsche so brilliantly diagnosed, is the total inver-sion of any heroic identity of virtue with strength, achievement or conquest. It celebrates dependency and claims to refuse violence. It defines the arbitrary will which sets itself up in pride, and casts other things down in an act of destruction, as the very essence of evil. Heroism, as solely the celebration of one's own achievement, ceases to count as a virtue at all. Nietzsche, therefore, presents Christian ethics as the exact opposite and denial of all hitherto prevailing human norms.[18] This claim is extravagant, and disguises the fact that it is rather that nihilism inverts Christianity; yet, nonetheless, it is true that by devaluing the heroic, Christianity marks an epochal shift.

However we assess Nietzsche's claim here, the important point is that he has established, within his own philosophy, an absolute opposition. And oppositions, of course, pertain to dialectics. Unsurprisingly, Nietzsche se-cretly succumbs to the seductions of the Hegelian story: if every denial of power is a ruse of power, then the absolute denial of power must be the final ruse of absolute power. The extremity of Christian asceticism stores up in

---

[16] Gilles Deleuze, *Nietzsche and Philosophy*, trans. Hugh Tomlinson (London: Athlone, 1983) pp. 79–82, 148–51.

[17] Nietzsche, *Genealogy of Morals*, Essay One, VI.

[18] Nietzsche, *Genealogy of Morals*; *Daybreak: Thoughts on the Prejudices of Morality*, Book I (Cambridge: Cambridge University Press, 1982) p. 71. *The Will to Power*, pp. 184, 186, 204, 1122.

human beings a capacity for self-will which prepares the way for the coming of Zarathustra, and the time of the *übermensch*, when constant transvaluation will be the only surviving norm.[19]

Because he has defined Christianity as negation, Nietzsche is forced to follow Hegel in putting the crucifixion, and a related, but additional 'death of God', at the centre of his thought. The 'spectacle of an animal taking up arms against itself' was 'one of the most unexpected throws of the Heraclitean child', and like any spectacle of cruelty it needed a 'divine audience'. It is through this event that 'man' is most seen as a 'bridge', 'a great promise'.[20] Rather like Hegel too, Nietzsche makes a separation between Jesus and the later Church, in ascribing to Jesus a kind of Buddhist 'indifference' to faults and failings, which is doomed to ineffectuality, like Jesus's teaching of forgiveness in *The Spirit of Christianity and its Fate*.

There is, then, also a dialectical element in Nietzsche's positivist narrative. And as we saw in chapter 4, Nietzsche transmitted this element to Weber, who also accords world-historical roles to asceticism in general, and Christianity in particular. Another version of the same story is given by Foucault, who is caught on the hooks of similar dilemmas about power being always present, and yet more present in some epochs than in others.

Foucault is concerned to show that knowledge and self-identity are always the effects of particular regimes and strategic interplays of power. Yet at the same time he traces the growth in the modern Western world of a 'carceral' or 'disciplinary' society in which power operates 'more continuously', not through forbidding or repressing our desires, but by a positive construction, organization and tabulation of them, along with every other aspect of our behaviour. In one sense this is only, for Foucault, 'another form' of power, yet, in a different sense, it is also a 'more power-like' power. In the Middle Ages, he notes, kings were expected not only to be powerful, but also to be virtuous, and public, ritualized punishment was effective because it was taken as a symbolic enactment of divine justice. In the modern era, by contrast, or the period considered by Comte to be 'metaphysical' rather than 'theological', it is imagined that law and politics are a matter of contract and of a balance of forces amongst free sovereign individuals. Only in the case of a 'continuous' technocratic positive power (already emergent even in the 'liberal', early modern era), which operates through the organization of populations, through 'listening' to what people have to confess and a 'survey' of every aspect of their lives, does power truly understand itself to be unlimited either by absolute divine standards or else by the free human subject. The 'gaze' of the State is now that of science, and power is the only possible object of a fully scientific knowledge.[21]

---

[19] Nietzsche, *Genealogy of Morals*, Essay Three, XIII, XXVIII.
[20] Ibid., Essay Two, XVI.
[21] Michel Foucault, *Discipline and Punish: The Birth of the Prison*, trans. Alan Sheridan (Harmondsworth: Penguin, 1977). *The History of Sexuality: An Introduction*, trans. Robert Hurley (Harmondsworth: Penguin, 1978). Gillian Rose, *The Dialectic of Nihilism* (Oxford: Blackwell, 1984) p. 200.

Like Nietzsche, therefore, Foucault has to conclude that power was the real substance of medieval natural law and early modern natural right. But, in addition, he has effectively to believe that later modern power is a more self-conscious and less trammelled form of power: his thought must collude with what it 'exposes'. Again, as for Nietzsche, Christianity appears to be the ultimate enemy, as the concealer of power and the promoter of the soul and 'inwardness'. But still more emphatically for Foucault, Christianity is also the great 'bridge' which gives historical access to the late modern, disciplinary society. Foucault points (with great cogency) to the development in medieval Christianity of a confessional practice, a mode of dealing with the populace positively rather than negatively, by getting them to 'confess' their desires, and at the same time encouraging them to think about these desires according to a strictly formalized institutional code.[22] The general Christian 'forbidding' of desire helps to encourage a later reversal which identifies (as with Rousseau and Freud) a buried realm of natural desire, either beneficent or, at least, requiring some outlet for the sake of health. But this reversal within a continuity permits a still more 'positive' form of power to be wielded by the modern priests, psychoanalysts and others, who encourage us to 'express' our desires, again persuading us to think about our most inner secrets according to highly public formulae.[23]

There is here, of course, a truly critical aspect to Foucault's thought, which permits him to grasp the hidden continuities linking Christian 'repression' of sexuality (actually, constitution of what it prohibited through its prohibitions) with modern 'liberation' of sexuality (a continued, but now more openly positive constitution). And it must be stressed that he did not, of course, view with favour the disciplinary society to which Christianity has given rise. Yet, at the same time, by more fully recognizing the inescapability of power, this society must for Foucault be in some sense 'truer' than previous societies. In addition, the apparent sequence of suppression-of-desire/liberation-of-desire not only produces the illusion of a natural desire, it also helps to foment a genuine creative desire, which Foucault hopes will finally be able to flourish in all its diversity. This optimism again adds to the positivist story a dialectical flourish.

So far we have seen that, while genealogy claims to be merely the narration of differences, and so neither sociology nor Marxist-Hegelianism, it does, in fact, experience more difficulty in making this distinction than at first appears. Because active nihilism proclaims an ahistorical and transcendental identity of reason with power, it always finishes up by telling, after all, a positivist story about the evolution of power/knowledge. And since, furthermore, it is bound to recognize in Christianity a precise opposite of nihilism – a creed which rigorously excludes all violence from its picture of the original,

---

[22] Michel Foucault, *The Use of Pleasure: History of Sexuality*, vol. 2, trans. Robert Hurley (Harmondsworth: Penguin, 1985) pp. 5–30. 'Technologies of the self', in Luther H. Martin et al. (eds.) *Technologies of the Self* (London: Tavistock, 1988) pp. 16–49.

[23] Foucault, *The History of Sexuality: An Introduction*, pp. 81–131.

intended and final state of the cosmos – Christianity has to be dealt with dialectically, and is thereby accorded a pivotal role.

Nietzsche had already identified an active 'celebratory' nihilism as the inversion of Christianity, and the question really is: on what basis can he see this as more than an interpretative inversion, more than an *ad hoc* suspicion which arises when one shows how one might subvert a received dominant narrative? In the *City of God*, Augustine already adopted the 'counter-historical' strategy of retracing the story of the pagan virtues. The main gist of his great book (as will be argued in the final chapter) is that these virtues were hopelessly contaminated by a celebration of violence. What else, one might ask from the Christian point of view, is the *Genealogy of Morals* but a kind of *jeu d'esprit*, a writing of the *City of God* back-to-front from a neo-pagan point of view which adopts the brilliant rhetorical strategy of granting one enormous *concessio* – namely the fundamental truth of Augustine's claim about pagan virtue. It is this contention which I want gradually to elaborate and endorse, in the remainder of this book.

What should be said, for the moment, is that Nietzsche and Foucault's reading of Christianity has to be objectively correct, if the nihilist genealogy is to be defended as more than just an interpretation. But, in fact, it is highly questionable, as a few remarks should serve to indicate. I shall take first the question of *ressentiment*, and then the question of asceticism.

Nietzsche conceives of the 'natural' human state as one of the active flow of a ceaselessly inventive power (not so much the deliberate willing of the subject as, rather, an impersonal force of willing which brings the subject into being).[24] By contrast, the perverse, merely reactive condition of the Christian subject defines itself, negatively, as a refusal of this natural strength. Clearly, however, this is not how Christianity understands itself: for Christian self-understanding, the primary receptivity of 'weakness' is in relation not to the strong, but to God, the source of all charity. And this receptivity is a paradoxical, active reception, because the lover of God is authenticated by the love which she actively transmits to her neighbour. But then one may ask, why should the natural, active, creative will not be understood, as it is understood by Christianity, as essentially the charitable will, the will whose exercise of power is not a will to dominate, or to condescend, but rather to endorse, raise up, increase the capacity of, the human other. The problem, of course, from the Nietzschean point of view, is that an exercise of love involves, at least in some of its phases, an increase in influence and dependency, making it the most subtle instrument of coercion. An element of 'disinterestedness', of true concern for the welfare of the other, can only qualify and legitimate this exercise of power, if there really are objective human goals which can be acceptably understood as desirable for others as well as for ourselves. The Christian understanding of the positive and non-reactive act as an act of charity therefore problematically presupposes objective goals of

---

[24] Nietzsche, *The Will to Power*, pp. 266. Deleuze, *Nietzsche and Philosophy*, pp. 79–82, 270.

value, and especially the goal of charity itself as selfless interest in the welfare of, and 'non-possessive desire' for, the other.

On the other hand, the Nietzschean understanding of the positive act as the will-to-power is equally problematic. As Gilles Deleuze stressed, the will-to-power negates nothing, and is not entailed by any dialectic of negation, but is rather a pure affirmation of difference.[25] However, no action ever remains safely within the sphere of the doer, but always already emanates beyond the doer, affecting those others by whom he is surrounded. It is at this point that, for a Nietzschean philosophy, difference is defined as oppositional difference, a difference which enters the existing common cultural space to compete, displace or expel. Yet if the objective effect of affirmative difference is aggression and enmity, then even if the noble will is 'without malice', even if, like the bird of prey, it has no conception of its victim, then there is a transcendental assumption of a negative relation persisting between all differences.

Now, quite clearly we do not live in a world where differences just lie benignly alongside each other, without mutual interference, but, rather, every difference is in itself an 'overlap', a disturbance within some area of common space. Yet does one need to interpret every disturbance, every event, as an event of war? Only, I would argue, if one has transcendentally understood all differences as negatively related, if – in other words, one has allowed a dialectical element to intrude into one's differential philosophy. If one makes no such presupposition, then it would be possible to understand the act of affirmative difference, in its passing over to the other, as an invitation to the other to embrace this difference because of its objective desirability. At the same time, it would have to be admitted that the reception of this difference by the other itself effects a further displacement, a further differentiation. The 'commonness' which now embraces them both is not the commonplace of the given neutral terrain, nor of the act in its initial conception, but instead of the new differential relationship. The question of the possibility of living together in mutual agreement, and the question of whether there can be a charitable act, therefore turn out to be conjointly the question of whether there can be an 'analogy' or a 'common measure' between differences which does not reduce differences to mere instances of a common essence or genus. In other words a likeness that only maintains itself through the differences, and not despite nor in addition to them.

To argue that the natural act might be the Christian (supernatural) charitable act, and not the will-to-power, is therefore to argue that such an 'analogical relation' is as possible a transcendental conception as the positing of an *a priori* warfare. And what is more, the former conception permits a *purer* 'positivism', a purer philosophy of difference, still less contaminated by dialectics. For *a priori* warfare not only supposes an ineradicable presence of the negative, it also supposes its dominance, as giving the only possible meaning-in-common. In the public theatre, differences arise only to fall;

---

[25] Deleuze, *Nietzsche and Philosophy*.

each new difference has a limitless ambition to obliterate all others, and therefore to cancel out difference itself. Although the postmodern subject is supposed to disintegrate schizophrenically, if every simulated personality wears military dress, it must, after all, aspire to the dominance and solipsism of the Cartesian ego. The soul sundered from the body is only an epiphenomenon of the militant body, of Hobbesian and Spinozan *conatus*.

The reading of Christianity as *ressentiment* can, therefore, be questioned by a simple switching of the transcendental codes. By contrast, the reading of Platonism and Christianity as uniquely perverse asceticisms can be questioned partly on the grounds of the logic of description, partly on the grounds of history, as I shall now show.

The 'heroic' ideals, celebrated by Nietzsche, because they are not truly a spontaneous expression of nature, must logically have involved a certain ascetic disciplining to model the self in a noble, military image. Moreover, in the heroic ideal lies the seed of the idea that is celebrated by Nietzsche and Foucault, namely that self-control, consisting in adherence to a certain 'aesthetic' model of the self, is the only virtue to be recommended. It is Nietzsche and Foucault, not Christian tradition, who see ascetic self-discipline – a 'care of the self', as Foucault puts it – as an end in itself, and who elevate the cultivation of a singular individuality over self-forgetting, or the dissolution of the subject.[26] This renders suspect their whole criticism of Platonism/ Christianity for perversely turning power back against the wielder of power, thereby inventing an 'inner space' of self-goading and self-torture – the sphere of 'guilt' and 'conscience'. For it is much more likely that the self-referentiality of the heroic ideal is itself the parent of 'the myth of interiority', and, indeed, what one discovers historically is that in later antiquity, once goals of public, political virtue have come to be despaired of, the stoic, cynic and Epicurean Sages (Foucault's declared heroes) teach a mere individual morality of resignation, self-control and self-consistency.[27] The freedom of the stoic sage, in particular, is a newly invented 'inner' freedom over and above the fated network of causation.

Foucault draws attention to the fact that Roman stoic 'examinations of conscience' never reveal a 'depth' of inner life, as exhibited later in the *Confessions* of St Augustine, and argues that the displacement of ethical concern into an inner private realm, concerned mainly with motivation, arrived only with Christianity and its new determination of the subject as a desiring subject. However, this is muddled thinking: an internality which can only aspire to control and resignation is, of course, an empty internality, and the austerity of the goal is, in fact, a measure of the purity of the retreat to an inner sanctum. By contrast, an internality crossed by desire can open itself to reveal a rich drama of aspiration, illusion, frustration and achievement. But

[26] Michel Foucault, 'Truth, power, self', in *Technologies of the Self*, pp. 9–15; 'On the genealogy of ethics: an overview of work in progress', in *The Foucault Reader*, pp. 340–72.

[27] Foucault, 'Technologies of the self' and 'On the genealogy of ethics'.

this is precisely because an internality crossed by desire is an impure intern-ality. The depth that can be reported does not really arise from diving expeditions into the soul, but, on the contrary, from an indefinite hermeneutic endeavour which constantly delivers new judgements upon one's external attitudes and emotions. The pernicious effect of the rhetoric of depth (which Foucault and Deleuze, like Wittgenstein, so rightly expose) is indeed to encour-age us to ask 'but is my motivation *really* pure' and to seek out an insincerity more 'real' than our apparent good faith. Yet such self-questioning, in its more valid form, may really be an attention to the ambiguities of our surface construction of motivation, and a stimulus to dissatisfaction with such con-structs. The original Christian suspicion of a perpetual inadequacy in all our desiring is generated not by the trope of depth beyond depth, but rather by the trope of a height beyond height, of an object of desire which is infinite, and with which our willing can never be commensurate. Unlike the stoic inward-ness, which does indeed concern pure 'attitude', Christian inwardness is opened up by a revisability that accompanies all external modes of expres-sion. Thus, the 'depth' revealed in Augustine's *Confessions* is the effect of his reflections on past actions, of the realization that they might have been different, that they can be totally re-read in the context of the more general story of the Church, and that he can transform himself in the future.

Foucault fails to see that the Christian shift, which he notes, from the self-forming or self-controlling self to the desiring self, is not really compatible with the emergence of a purely 'inner' space. Rather, such a space was manufactured, as Hegel realized, by the apolitical pessimism of the late Roman empire and the convergence of Roman law on the idea of an absolute, unrestricted ownership.

Foucault is, of course, aware that desire necessarily implies a radical orien-tation to the other, but instead of interpreting this as a structuring of the self in terms of goal and aspiration, he takes it as implying a pure heterogeneity, a handing of the self over to the spiritual director or to God. What he ignores here is that total obedience, in the former case, assumes a prior agreement that the director is further advanced towards the goal that the postulant wishes to arrive at, so that self-realization (given this understanding of the self), not self-negation, is here presupposed. Likewise, in the latter case, the dissolution of one's present self-coherence is risked in the belief that only a life dynamically orientated to the infinite will allow an adequate 'positioning' of the self.

In consequence, certain questions arise about Foucault's understanding of Christianity as preparing the way for a 'disciplinary' society. The monastic relation of director to novice, marked by the disciplining of desire, required a constant and particular shepherding of the one by the other. Sometimes, in the early Church, this form of intimate guidance was extended by the 'holy man' to lay Christians also. But Foucault does not really reckon with the gap between this, and the later, late-medieval regulation of populations according to a tightly normalized systematization of 'inner' attitudes and motivations, along with a regular system of penitential exercise. In the latter case a much more formalized and impersonal system is combined with an increased shift to 'self-discipline', by cowing people into a permanent state of suspicion about their 'real' motivations. The later system of confessional practice (emerging from the tenth to the twelfth centuries) was not precisely akin to earlier monastic spiritual direction, and nor was it like earlier practices of public confession. In the earlier time, open confession to a bishop, rather than private confession to God, had not been concerned with the subtle shiftings of desire at all, but rather the violation of certain quite specific norms, and the committing of obviously public crimes. Penitence was normally undertaken once in a lifetime, and it permanently transferred the penitent to a semi-religious state of life. Thus the new legalistic regulation of everyday sins and the inner life emerged within the Church as a great anomaly, and was much protested at. *Pace* Nietzsche and Foucault, one should note that it first arose in Britain, in a still *heroic* society accustomed to the usages of *wergeld*, which conceptualized offences in terms of debt and obligation. (Note here that there is *some* truth in Nietzsche's 'economic' view of heroic society; I shall try to clarify this issue in chapter 12.)[28] The appeal of a more 'continuous' confession was the possibility of a constant cancelling out of sins in terms of a strict equivalence of offence and penance. If desire gets interwoven into this scheme, it tends to mean the virtual elimination of the dynamic and ambiguous aspect of desire, and its reduction to mere punctiliar event.

While, therefore, Foucault may be right to discover in the new confessional practice, fully fledged by the twelfth century, the first form of a disciplinary society, wielding its rule over its members by knowledge and surveillance, one cannot necessarily see such an outcome as latent in Christianity from the start. It is true that Christianity doubly reinforced the Platonic notion of a 'pastoral' rule, a governance that may not wish always to coerce its subjects, but can never leave them alone, because it expresses an ultimate concern for their total well-being and happiness. Yet the later formalization and bureaucratization of the Church's rule seems to represent a retreat from the flexibilities of an immediate pastoral oversight of each and every one. The new rule 'by classification' appears like a dangerous simulacrum (false by virtue of its content, not its imitative secondariness) of the original endeavour, a disguised admission of failure. Foucault *blames* this development on the imposition of a common goal, yet something like the opposite is true: formal, disciplinary, and later legal control was more and more resorted to in a period when the unity of the Church became harder to uphold, and the principle of substantive consensus was abandoned.[29] Likewise, in the same period, the failure of originally charitable schemes for every community to deal with the problems of leprosy and prostitution quickly passed into schemes for segregating, confining and disciplining lepers and

[28] Cyrille Vogel, *Le Pécheur et la Pénitence au Moyen Age* (Paris: Editions du Cerf, 1969) pp. 15–36, 202.
[29] Peter Brown, 'The rise and function of the holy man in late antiquity' and 'Society and the supernatural: a mediaeval change', in *Society and the Holy in Late Antiquity* (London: Faber, 1982).

prostitutes.[30] It is, again, the simulacrum of charity that is to blame, so revealing to us the supreme danger of the failure of charity. The entire modern world which commences in the twelfth century (so that one can venture to say, it is not that there are medieval *and* modern disciplinary atrocities, but rather that they all form one continuous series) is a kind of false copy of the Platonic/Christian shepherding ideal.

Not just the 'success', but also the failure of Christianity, is therefore written into the 'carceral society'. The process reaches its ideological consummation with the voluntarist perversion of theology traced in the first chapter. At the same time, Foucault may also ignore a heroic and pagan root of the social world he has so brilliantly identified.

The subject totally preoccupied with the management of its own desiring energies, with their suppression, or else their liberation, is the subject engendered by disciplinary practices. But this subject is less the Christian, desiring subject, than it is the more purely ascetic subject, who, as we have seen, is a child of the hero. If pure power without goals defines the disciplinary society, as Foucault sometimes admits, then it takes part of its lineage from a heroic asceticism, the mere pursuit of strength and persistence, whether public or private. Undoubtedly, Christianity was a medium of transmission for stoic and other ideals of asceticism in late antiquity. Yet sometimes this resulted in a manifest perversion of the Christian ethical substance, as can be shown, for example, in the case of teaching on marriage.

St Paul, in line with the Hebrew scriptures, had stressed that the sacredness of marriage consists in its mutuality, but, under stoic influence, procreation became the only good of marriage until (with some exceptions) the twentieth century. The confessional manuals in this area, which focus never on mutuality, but always on one's attitudes to the fulfilling of duties and the legal satisfaction of one's spouse's physical desires, seem to reflect pagan downgrading of the marital relationship, and obsessive preoccupation with male 'control' of sexuality, rather than the Biblical outlook.[31] To a certain extent, the Christian 'desiring' subject is also a prototypically 'female' subject, and Christian virginity becomes a matter of female 'integrity' as much as male 'virtuosity'. In addition, as Foucault himself declares, sex becomes more typically a passive experience, a desire one is 'subject' to, rather than a desire one might, in certain controlled circumstances, be in command of.[32] Unfortunately, the spiritual re-evaluation of passive desire, and the redefinition of the typical sexual subject as 'female', rarely came together in the West to deliver a new positive assessment of bodily desire as both vulnerable and good. But for all

[30] Walter Ullmann, 'Public welfare and social legislation in the early mediaeval councils', in *The Church and Law in the Earlier Middle Ages* (London: Variorum, 1975) pp. 1–39. R. I. Moore, *The Formation of a Persecuting Society: Power and Deviance in Western Europe 950–1250* (Oxford: Blackwell, 1987).

[31] Jean-Louis Flandrin, *Le Sexe et L'Occident* (Paris: Seuil, 1981) pp. 10, 101–9, 127–9, 135ff, 157, 279, 280ff.

[32] Foucault, 'On the genealogy of ethics', pp. 346–7.

that, *pace* Foucault, a sexually 'other-regarding' ethic is logically implied by Christianity, and if this was held back, it was held back by a pagan and especially stoic residue.

Because Christianity is the precise opposite of nihilism, the nihilist genealogists are forced to narrate Christianity as the operation of the ultimate ruse of power, the final 'training' of humanity which produces a modern military (Nietzsche) or carceral (Foucault) society, and yet also prepares the transgression of this society by the *übermensch* or the 'aesthetic individual'. However, I have shown that the interpretation of Christianity as *ressentiment*, and of its historical role as primarily the promotion of asceticism, are both, at least, highly questionable. This has an important consequence: if nihilism cannot 'position' Christianity in its genealogy, in a way that amounts to more than interpretation, then it emphatically cannot – as we already suspected – justify historically its reading of every event as an event of warfare. The possibility of a different counter-history (the counter-history given by Augustine) which reads war as an absolute intrusion, an ontological anomaly, remains still intact.

In that case, it is clear that an *a priori*, transcendental discourse which secures ontological violence, is a necessary supplement for every nihilist genealogy. So next we must ask, what are the bases for the claims of differential ontology to expose and displace all traditional metaphysics and 'onto-theology'?

Ontology

1   *Theology and the critique of metaphysics*

Nietzsche interpreted Western philosophy or metaphysics – that is to say the attempt to give a 'total' classification of being, and to ground the temporal and shifting in 'truth', the permanent and unchanging – as the child of the Socratic invention, before Christianity, of a 'moral' good.[33] Socrates and Plato distinguished the attainment of moral virtue from mere strength or excellent achievement in general, by associating it with the vision of a permanent, abiding idea of the Good, immune to the stray chances and fortunes affecting our everyday actions. From this invention of a new moral regime, characterized by Nietzsche as asceticism and as a perverse, reactive achievement, arose the whole supportive edifice of metaphysics: a discourse that 'theoretically' secures a self-identical, transcendent reality undergirding 'propositions' concerning an objective 'truth'. The critique of this Greek *logos* – and that is to say of the entire Western philosophic, cultural and scientific tradition – has been carried forwards by Martin Heidegger, and in his wake by Jacques Derrida, Gilles Deleuze and Jean-François Lyotard among many others.

[33] Nietzsche, *The Will to Power*, p. 5.

There have already been many theological responses to this critique of metaphysics. These can be said to fall into three groups. First, a response which aligns itself with the secular humanist attempt to confine critical reason to the Kantian level, to hold onto the notion of a 'reality' with which propositions made in discourse can be compared and so confirmed or disconfirmed, and to defend the integrity of the noumenal subject as a *locus* for certain constant, universal predilections and dispositions.[34] This response assumes, broadly, that it is in the interests of a discourse claiming the objective existence of 'God' to defend realism in general, and of a discourse centred on 'persons' to resist the disintegration of the human subject. But the specific alliance of this stand with empiricist and Kantian attitudes that are part and parcel of the modernist attempt to give a positive 'once for all' representation of finitude, and its minimal connection with the 'realisms' of the Middle Ages, are usually glossed over.

The second response, as exemplified by the writings of Mark C. Taylor and John D. Caputo, fully embraces the postmodern critique of metaphysics and consequently seeks to 'de-Platonize' Christianity.[35] Characteristically, the theological content in these endeavours turns out to be small: the transcendental rule of anarchic difference can be renamed God or the death of God, Dionysiac celebration can be declared to include a contemplative mystical moment – and very little has really been added, nothing is essentially altered.

The third response, as articulated especially well by Joseph O'Leary (in the wake of several French Catholic thinkers), also embraces the critique, but refuses the identification of theology with a nihilist ontology. Instead, the Greek experience of Being and the Christian experience of God are declared to be phenomenologically diverse and incomparable.[36] The difficulty here is that, first, an appeal is made to a pre-linguistic level of subjective encounter with phenomenal reality, which is wholly ruled out by the postmodern critique of metaphysics itself.[37] Second, if the experience of God is really and truly an experience *of God*, then the question of God's being, as of any other named reality, cannot help but arise for *reflective* discourse, which is inescapably Greek (Derrida himself affirms this view in his essay, 'Violence and metaphysics').[38] But if God is not Being itself, then for ontology he can only be a being, and this produces an idolatrous and unsatisfactory result for theology. To refuse these questions altogether suggests – for us to whom the

---

[34] Rahner, *Spirit in the World*. Bernard Lonergan, *Insight, A Study of Human Understanding* (London: Longman, 1957). David Tracy, *The Analogical Imagination: Christian Theology and the Culture of Pluralism* (London: SCM, 1981).

[35] Mark C. Taylor, *Erring: A Post-Modern Atheology* (Chicago: Chicago University Press, 1987). John D. Caputo, *Radical Hermeneutics: Repetition, Deconstruction and the Hermeneutic Project* (Bloomington & Indianapolis: Indiana University Press, 1987).

[36] Joseph O'Leary, *Questioning Back: The Overcoming of Metaphysics in Christian Tradition* (Minneapolis: Winston, 1985).

[37] O'Leary, *Questioning Back*, p. 29.

[38] Jacques Derrida, 'Violence and metaphysics: an essay on the thought of Emmanuel Levinas', in *Writing and Difference*, trans. Alan Bass (London: RKP, 1978) pp. 79–154.

Greek questioning of Being has happened irrevocably – either an impossible schizophrenia of *logos* and *mythos*, or else a faith-content reduced to a set of fideistic assertions beyond all logical discussion or development, even within their own terms.

None of these three courses will be pursued in what follows. Instead, I assume that a theological response has to be much more complex and discriminating in character. The possibility of a more selective attitude to the postmodern critique is opened out by the initially questionable character of Nietzsche's virtual identification of Platonism with Christianity, and the consequent Heideggerian equation of metaphysics with onto-theology. What these identifications ignore, as I shall argue more fully in the final two chapters, are the radical changes undergone by ontology at the hands of the neo-Platonists and the Church Fathers: in particular Augustine, and Dionysius the Areopagite. The neo-Platonic/Christian infinitization of the absolute, the Christian equation of goodness, truth and beauty with Being itself, combined with the introduction of the relational, productive and responsive element into the Godhead, all give rise to an ontological scenario which is no longer *exactly* Greek, because no longer inside the horizons projected by the Greek *mythos*, within which the Greek *logos* had to remain confined. For this new ontological scenario, the notions of presence, of substance, the priority of idea over copy and cause over effect, of a subject with a rational essence, and of Being as 'mirrored' by this rational essence are, I contend, no longer fundamental. Of course, this was not realized all at once, and is still, today, not fully realized. Nevertheless, one can trace the sporadic modification of all these notions by a series of Christian thinkers. (One should cite at least Augustine, Eriugena, Thomas Aquinas, Nicholas of Cusa, Leibniz, Berkeley, Vico, Hamann, Kierkegaard and Blondel.)

However, other notions, equally rejected as 'metaphysical' by the nihilist critique, remain primary for a Christian theological ontology: these are those of transcendence, participation, analogy, hierarchy, teleology (these last two in modified forms) and the absolute reality of 'the Good' in roughly the Platonic sense. The strategy, therefore, which the theologian should adopt, is that of showing that the critique of presence, substance, the idea, the subject, causality, thought-before-expression, and realist representation do not necessarily entail the critique of transcendence, participation, analogy, hierarchy, teleology and the Platonic Good, reinterpreted by Christianity as identical with Being. This strategy, far from just denying the nihilist critique, or leaving it altogether intact, points out an unexpected fissure traversing its blank face of refusal. The fissure is opened up precisely at the point where the nihilist critique passes over into a differential ontology, with its presupposition of transcendental violence. By exposing the critical non-necessity of the reading of reality as conflictual, and the hopelessly metaphysical nature of even *this* ontology, an alternative possibility of reading reality as of itself peaceful is gradually opened to view, and the notions of transcendence, participation, analogy, hierarchy, teleology and the Platonic Good will be shown to belong inextricably to this reading. It can be denied that they involve foundationalist assumptions, and claimed that they are only refused by nihilism as part of its option for original violence, its preference for, or resignation to, an imagined cosmic terror.

The character of my theological critique of nihilist ontology will be, therefore, quite distinctive: not an attempt to repristinate realism, because I deny that postmodern anti-realism is a threat to theological objectivism (see chapter 8, on Blondel). Nor, certainly, an embracing of the devil to call him God in the manner of Mark C. Taylor; but, rather, a bifurcation, which partially affirms the postmodern reduction of substance to transition, and yet questions the transcendental reading of transition as conflict.

Whereas the first kind of theological response accepts the terms of secular modernism, and the second the more naked secularism of postmodernism, my response seeks a theological critique of secular reason, and tries to move beyond this into a 'countermodern' articulation of a specifically Christian onto-logic.

2   *Heidegger and the fall of Being*

To grasp fully the true character of nihilist, or differential ontology, one must relate it, as has already been indicated, to the emergence of a more absolute historicism. This conjunction is already apparent in the work of Martin Heidegger.

Heidegger contended, against his teacher, Edmund Husserl, that the understanding of phenomenal 'things in themselves' could not be confined to the level of epistemology, bracketing off all ontological issues. The possibilities of our knowing are none other than the possibilities of our existence, which means the possibilities inscribed in our temporality, mortality and historicity. Thus, transcendental philosophy is converted into a fundamental ontology, an account of the being of *Dasein*, or of human existence. *Dasein* is characterized by 'thrownness', its 'being there', without choice, in a particular time and place; by its having death as its 'most extreme possibility', a fact which grounds its historicity; by its being not merely 'present at hand' like a 'thing', but receptively open to the actuality of past human existences which persist as 'possibilities' available to be 'repeated' – albeit in an inevitably different fashion – in a projected future.[39]

According to Heidegger, an 'authentic' human existence takes account of the existential (*existentiell*) circumstances of the life of *Dasein*. It takes responsibility for its own mortal life and exhibits a 'care' for the distinctive possibilities which have been handed down to it. However, although these circumstances, and this responsible attitude, are implicit at the *existentiell* level of lived existence, they are also constantly obscured at this level, and

[39] Martin Heidegger, *Being and Time*, trans. John Macquarrie and Edward Robinson (Oxford: Blackwell, 1978) esp. pp. 329–31.

require to be expounded by the 'existential analytic'.[40] Otherwise, human beings remain lost in the 'forgetfulness of Being' which characterizes human historical existence as such, and Western culture and metaphysics in particular. Normally, we do not live authentically, but become forgetful of our thrownness, our mortality and our dependence upon a contingent tradition. We lapse into an 'everydayness' which is absorbed, in both a trivial, gossipy and a scientific-technological fashion, in the merely instrumental and manipulative arrangements that pertain between things and people. Fascinated by our limited abilities to control things and people that are immediately present to our grasp, we neglect our constant suspension between the absent past and the absent future and the constant happening of presence which remains beyond our ability to comprehend or control.[41] Heidegger shows that our ignoring of our mortality and temporality is at one with our forgetting of 'the ontological difference', the difference between beings on the one hand – which 'are' in particular, relatively understandable and controllable ways – and Being itself on the other: the fact of their being, of their constantly happening in time.

Now the ontological difference has been, of course, traditionally the preoccupation of metaphysics and of theology. Yet Heidegger wishes to 'overcome' metaphysics in a new fashion, not belittling or reducing the value of this preoccupation, as so many previous critiques of metaphysics had done, but rather by showing that, from the outset, the metaphysical manner of treating the difference actually obscures it, and is complicit in the forgetfulness of the average 'ontical' attitude. Again, temporality and historicity are the key to understanding how Heidegger can make this double movement. On the one hand the bodily, interactive and temporally foreclosed character of our understanding, together with our dependency on a historically derived set of linguistic categories, actually rules out the Kantian distinction between a possible knowledge of mere appearances and a real but impossible knowledge of Being. On the other hand, the radical identification of Being with temporality refuses, unlike Kant (who in the *Critique of Practical Reason* still expounds a metaphysic of transcendence), the traditional metaphysical equation of a plenitudinous being with an atemporal reality. Being is in no sense 'something' other than beings, and Heidegger accuses traditional metaphysics and theology of evading the primordial fact of Being's occurrence, its 'opening' in time, by inventing a transcendent, hypostasized Being, which is really just a projection of the idea of a particular being understood in an ontical, 'present to hand' fashion.[42] This then permits a theoretical speculation about the relationship between manipulable objects 'presented' before us.

To understand what is really going on here, it is vital that one grasps that Heidegger now expects the facts of our embodiment, mortality, temporality,

---

[40] Ibid., pp. 359–64.
[41] Ibid., pp. 315–19.
[42] Ibid., p. 73.

historicity and linguisticality to perform all the critical work of expunging metaphysics and onto-theology. If they *cannot* do this work, then the entire post-Kantian enterprise is thrown into disarray, because the same facts also unsettle the Kantian critical achievement, which gave clear grounds for distinguishing between possible finite knowledge and illegitimate speculation about divine causality, participation in the Godhead and the eminent attribution of finitely known characteristics to God. For Kant, as for modernism in general, there is something positive in the finite that we can take our stand upon: the bringing of empirical intuitions under *a priori* categorical schematization, and the legal implications of our possession of free will. For Heidegger, by contrast, there is nothing positive whatsoever: to face up to the circumstances of finitude means to confront radical contingency and indeterminacy, and an *infinite* possibility of things being other than they are. The most radical thing about our finitude is the fact of its sheer givenness, so that the only place on which knowledge can take an ultimate stand is at the point of the irreducible questionableness of the relation of beings to Being. Heidegger's contention is that we should remain with this questionableness, and not seek in any way to reduce the mystery of the ontological difference. Only in this fashion can our knowledge remain within critical bounds. However, it is to be doubted whether this is really possible: the necessity for commitment to some historical tradition, to some mode of linguistic ordering, suggests rather that we must always see our preferred finite stance, which otherwise would be sheerly arbitrary, as a particularly privileged key to Being itself. A 'metacritical' perspective, as Hamann and Herder realized, makes a constitutive and not merely regulative metaphysics an inescapable aspect of our historical destiny. We *have* to say 'how things are in general', to be able to say anything at all.

Heidegger, of course, is well aware of this, but tries to distinguish the *necessary* transgressions of pure questionableness, the *necessary* metaphysics that occur as particular cultures, from his own transcendental determination of the true character of this questionableness. One might, however, suspect that thereby Heidegger does not really succeed in grounding understanding on the mere inescapable formalities of the Being/beings relationship, but instead, gives an *answer* to the question of Being which is as arbitrary, and as metaphysical, as any other cultural or philosophical reply. And one might further suggest that *all* modes of posing the question already provide some sort of answer, and therefore are themselves 'transgressive', constitutively metaphysical, and not just transcendental in character.

For *Being and Time*, it is relative easy to confirm this suspicion. For there, Heidegger conceives the hermeneutic endeavour which constitutes human being in time as also an interpretation of the ontological difference. The interpreting subject which transcends given being projects the horizon of 'the meaning of Being' forward upon beings, and conjectures that the character of *Dasein* is fundamentally that of care and resoluteness, both in relation to the autonomous character of one's own decisions, and the handing on of what has come down to us.[43] There exists no logical or empirical proof of this conjecture, which can only be 'proved' through our living out of the attitude of care for Being. Heidegger later came to realize, however, that this hermeneutic of Being contained a residue of Kantian epistemology and humanistic metaphysics. Although the event of Being and our interpretation of this event belong together in a hermeneutic circle, the less than tautologous character of this circle still opens up an interval of representation between our interpretation on the epistemological side, and Being on the ontological side. In some sense it is possible to 'check' the authenticity of our attitudes, whereas if the happening of Being in the event of human linguistic response to the world enjoyed a true, metacritical priority, this should not be possible. Nor should one be able to speak of a 'projection' of a horizon of the meaning of Being upon beings, because this still smacks too much of an epistemological division between the *a priori* categories of understanding on the one hand and an empirical content on the other, grounded in a spiritual 'transcendence' of the world by a still Cartesian subject. Without this subject, there is no way in which the fundamental character of any particular attitude of *Dasein*, even that of 'anticipatory resoluteness', can be guaranteed, or taken as a clue to the meaning of Being itself.

In the later Heidegger, therefore, the hermeneutic circle is deserted, in favour of talk of a primordial 'belonging together' of Being with the event of human language.[44] No longer, also, is the prospect of death seen as the only context in which temporality and the repetition of past possibilities can be recovered. Instead, Heidegger pursues the near-impossible task of occupying the vantage point of the repetition of Being itself, its endless happening as the 'difference' of the various historical epochs, the various cultural orderings.[45] And the final elimination of any residual idea of a human 'essence', or human 'transcendence', which once for all reflects the 'truth' of Being itself (though not of the idea of *Dasein* as the site of an opening upon Being), points to a shift of attention from an always absent and unknown Being to the constant 'fall' of Being into an ontic condition. The question is no longer about Being, nor even about the ontological difference, but about what lets Being be *in* this difference, about the *sache* that always is different.

However, while the attempt to secure the essence of *Dasein* and to regard *Dasein's* 'care' as the unique site of the opening of Being is now abandoned, the determination of Being as difference engages in a yet more direct fashion with the question of the meaning of Being. As both Jacques Derrida and Gilles Deleuze later say (in a more emphatic fashion), 'difference' has now become the sole 'transcendental' in both a Kantian and a scholastic sense. In the first

[43] Ibid., pp. 278, 361, 435–8.

[44] Martin Heidegger, *On the Way to Language,* trans. Peter Hertz (New York: Harper & Row, 1971) p. 51; *Discourse on Thinking,* trans. Hans Freund and John Anderson (New York: Harper & Row, 1966) pp. 64–7; *Lettre sur L'Humanisme,* German text with French translation by Roger Munier (Paris: Aubier, 1964) pp. 164–7. John D. Caputo, *Radical Hermeneutics,* pp. 95–106.

[45] Martin Heidegger, *Der Satz vom Grund* (Pfulligen: Neske, 1965) p. 154.

case one assumes *a priori* that a radical heterogeneity, incompatibility, non-hierarchy and arbitrariness pertain amongst every knowable thing, and in the second case one affirms that every thing really is constituted by such a radical heterogeneity. But if this is the case, then the *sache*, the constant temporal mediation of the ontological difference, must itself be characterized by a rupture, an entirely arbitrary break with the unanimity of Being. A unanimity which of course only 'is' through this series of 'breaks'.

Such an idea of an inescapable rupture had been, in fact, already articulated in *Being and Time*. There it is declared that, in ontology, 'any springing from is a degeneration' and it is explained that the concealment of being or the lapse into 'everydayness' is a quite inevitable process.[46]

Ontical presence is, for Heidegger, *constituted* through its concealment of Being as such. There is therefore a kind of primordial violence at work here, which can only be countered by a mode of interpretation which is itself a 'doing violence' (*gewaltsamkeit*), and which follows the opposite course from the 'falling tendency' of Being and of customary understanding.[47] In *Being and Time* there is an emphasis on the negating of forgetfulness, of recovering a primordial experience of Being itself; this stress never quite disappears in the later works, but it is more and more insisted that Being only *is* in the event of its own self-occlusion and the arbitrary series of differential breaks which constitute the battles of history, the replacement of one cultural regime by another.

The idea of an inescapable ontological 'fall' (*zug*) is, consequently, the transcendental support for Heidegger's nihilist version of historicism, and the very heart of his philosophy. Yet it is a thoroughly questionable notion. Heidegger is, of course, right to insist that the ontological difference can never be held up for our inspection: if beings are entirely *constituted* by their relationship to Being, then this is not a relationship we can survey, and Being remains forever absent, forever concealed behind its presentation in the temporal series of beings. However, to give this concealment the overtones of dissimulation, of violence, of a necessary suppression, is an entirely different matter. One might want rather to say that as much as a being is a particular existence and not Being itself, it yet exhibits in its sheer contingency the inescapable mystery of Being. Precisely because Being and beings are not on the same level, nor related within any common arena, the difference of a being from Being in no way necessarily obliterates or conceals Being itself, any more than Being necessarily reduces to temporal sequence, which can rather be regarded as every bit as 'ontic' as instantaneous presence. It would then follow that to live in forgetfulness of Being is to live in a culture which discounts religion, and seeks purely immanent explanations; it would not mean, as for Heidegger, to fall prey to a fated ontological destiny.

---

[46] Heidegger, *Being and Time*, p. 383. *On Time and Being*, trans. Joan Stambaugh (New York: Harper & Row, 1972) pp. 29–30.

[47] Heidegger, *Being and Time*, p. 359.

This seems to be a *possible* way of interpreting the ontological difference; but Heidegger has to believe that his own way is more 'fundamental', because he wishes to show that ontological difference is properly dealt with by philosophy alone, and cannot belong to the terrain of the theological imagination. Yet to do this he actually borrows themes from ontology-as-transformed-by-theology (notably from Augustine, Pascal and Kierkegaard), and translates language about God (and the Being of theology) into his own language about Being. In particular, he takes over (without full acknowledgement) Kierkegaard's thematic of 'anxiety', or of the 'fear and trembling' which characterizes our relationship to an unknown and sublime infinitude. He connects this, following Kierkegaard himself, with Augustine's teaching about original sin, and the ineradicable sense of human guilt.[48]

For Augustine, all evil was a matter of privation, of not being what we ought to be, and only in this ethical context does the idea of 'non-being' acquire any real significance. Heidegger's phenomenology of *Dasein*, however, is supposed to show that there is a 'guilt' more fundamental than moral guilt, and a 'fall' more basic than that resulting from a willed rebellion against God. He argues that if guilt and conscience are regarded in a moral context, then something is 'nihilistically' declared to be 'lacking' in our present existence.[49] Present existence is regarded as the 'basis' for a fuller being, for *bonum*, and yet it possesses a 'nullity' in comparison with that for which it is the basis. However, at the level of its being, argues Heidegger, there can be no lack in *Dasein*: it fully is, as *Dasein*, and is not more or less. If, therefore, *Dasein* does not fundamentally owe something which is lacking to it, then its ineliminable sense of 'guilt' must be there before its indebtedness. Guilt, or the feeling of anxiety and dread, does not relate to a divine 'ought' over against us, but rather to the 'uncanniness' which characterizes our situation within Being.[50] Our present existence is a basis for something else, not because it is lacking, but because it might be otherwise: so, therefore, it is a 'nullity of itself'. (This is Heidegger's *own* nihilism.) Every being which has inevitably lapsed into 'presence' precludes, through its arbitrary and groundless insistence on some preferences and some values, the sublime perspective of infinite difference which is the (non) point of view of Being itself. Hence in the structure of thrownness, as in that of projection, there lies essentially a nullity, and it is impossible to cancel guilt by doing the right thing, impossible to make an adequate response to the sublime in 'ethical' terms, as Kant supposed. Instead, we must simply 'be guilty authentically' (an idea which the Lutheran tradition had unfortunately paved the way for).

Heidegger sees his account of guilt as giving a more fundamental ontology than that of Augustine, because the notions of *bonum* and *privatio* arise from 'the ontology of the present at hand'.[51] For Augustine, something which

[48] Ibid., pp. 326–34.
[49] Ibid., p. 330.
[50] Ibid., pp. 335–7.
[51] Ibid., p. 332.

should be present is not present, something which derives from an infinite fullness of presence. However, what was lacking for Augustine was not a static state, but rather a rightly-directed *desire*, an ever-more-true orientation of our thoughts towards an infinite plenitude of love.[52] This no more precludes the perspective of *Dasein* as temporal becoming than Heidegger's account; the difference arises rather from the fact that Augustine admits a hierarchy of values and a teleological ordering into his view of our becoming. Only because Heidegger has flattened everything out, and still (like any positivist or neo-Kantian) turns historical differences into so many value-neutral facts, does he see the ontological 'not', the reverse copula, as indicating transcendental violence, a fundamental rift sundering ourselves from ourselves and ourselves from others.

By contrast, one could construe this 'not' as *either* the mere reflex of positivity (a cow is not a sheep, etc.) *or* the contingent, willed absence of what is necessary for our natural/supernatural completion. Augustine's *privatio* and Heidegger's 'radical nullity' tell different stories about Being, but neither would be able to show, in neutral terms, that it embodied a more basic, a more rational ontology – although only the Augustinian ontology affirms an ultimate 'reason' for beings. In trying to discuss the ontological difference in non-metaphysical, and non-theological terms, Heidegger seems only to have succeeded in inventing his own religion. Indeed, in the notion of an ontological rather than a (pre)historical fall, there are many echoes of Valentinian gnosis, with its idea of primal disaster within the divine *pleroma*, or of Jacob Boehme, with his ideas of evil as arising within the workings of desire in the Trinity itself.[53] Just as for the Valentinians, Boehme and the Kabbalists, salvation was the salvation of God himself from his involvement in temporality, so, likewise, for Heidegger, man is the predestined 'shepherd of Being'. The vital difference is simply this: Heideggerian nihilism tends to indicate remorselessly the *aporia* of Behmenism and drive it to its logical conclusion. If the 'fall' is original, and pertains to the first principle, then salvation can only be the endless repetition of falling, the 'eternal return' of what is both revealed and violently occluded.

3   Nihilism and univocity

The conversion of Gnosticism into nihilism is already firmly in place in Heidegger, and in this respect Derrida and Deleuze merely add refinements. Nevertheless, they much more rigorously refuse any suggestion of a nostalgia for a more authentic and original presence of Being, and insist that the *sache* is

[52] See chapter 12 below.
[53] Hans Jonas, *The Gnostic Religion* (Boston: Beacon, 1958) pp. 64, 320–40, 174–205. Jacob Boehme, *The Signature of all Things* (London: James Clarke, 1969) pp. 13–22. Cyril O'Regan, *Gnostic Apocalypse: Jacob Boehme's Haunted Narrative* (New York: SUNY, 2002). David Walsh, *The Mysticism of Innerworldly Fulfilment: A Study of Jacob Boehme* (Gainesville, Fl.: Florida UP, 1983).

transcendental difference. In particular, they both suggest, as Gillian Rose emphasized, that not Heidegger, but Duns Scotus, was the first inventor of a fundamental ontology, and that Heidegger is pursuing an essentially Scotist line of thought.[54] This has considerable implications for a theological critique of nihilism, as I shall try to show.

Duns Scotus, unlike Thomas Aquinas, already distinguished metaphysics as a philosophical science concerning Being, from theology as a science concerning God.[55] Being, he argued, could be either finite or infinite, and possessed the same simple meaning of existence when applied to either. 'Exists', in the sentence God 'exists', has therefore the same fundamental meaning (at a logical and ultimately a metaphysical level) as in the sentence, 'this woman exists'. The same thing applies to the usage of transcendental terms convertible with Being; for example, 'God is good' means that he is good in the same *sense* that we are said to be good, however much more of the quality of goodness he may be thought to possess. Scotus wants to find a place, in theology, for an analogical attribution of words like 'good' to God in an eminent sense, but his metaphysics appears to restrict the scope of eminence to a mere greater quantity, or else an unknown exercise of a quality whose sense and definition is fully understood by us (since the degree of 'greater' is here infinite).[56] And just as being or goodness are attributed in the same sense to both infinite and finite, so they are attributed in the same sense to finite genera, species and individuals.

Aquinas, by contrast, had interpreted Aristotle's denial that Being is differentiated amongst beings in the way that a genus is differentiated by its species, or a species by individuals, to mean that the relationship between genus and genus or generically different species is of an analogical character.[57] Being cannot be regarded as a genus, because there is here no single common essence like 'animal' which can be further specified as 'two-legged', 'four-legged' and so forth. Generic determination does not *qualify* being, but simply exemplifies it, diversely. It follows that one cannot compare genera in the way that one compares species: by saying that man and dog share animality but diverge as two or four legged. On the contrary, genera are different, and yet in some sense alike and comparable in respect of their very differences: the 'goods' of a stone, a plant, an animal and a man are all diverse, yet also similar in terms of qualities of resistance, persistence and growth. But Duns Scotus, while agreeing with Aristotle and Aquinas that Being is not a genus (because he confined genera to the divisions of finitude),

[54] Gilles Deleuze, *Différence et Répétition* (Paris: PUF, 1972) pp. 52–8, 91; *Logique du Sens* (Paris: Editions du Minuit, 1989) pp. 208–11. Jacques Derrida, *Writing and Difference*, trans. Alan Bass (London: RKP, 1978) p. 319, n. 84. Gillian Rose, *Dialectic of Nihilism*, pp. 104–7.

[55] Duns Scotus, *Ordinatio* I d.3, d.8. Olivier Boulnois, *Être et représentation* (Paris: PUF, 1999), pp. 223–7.

[56] David Burrell, *Analogy and Philosophical Language* (New Haven, Conn.: Yale University Press, 1973) pp. 95–119.

[57] Aquinas, ST I. Q. 13 a5 ad I.

nonetheless considered that it was distributed in a univocal fashion, having precisely the same meaning for every genus: in the aspect of Being, things 'are' in the same way. The divergences of genera, therefore, like the divergences of infinite and finite, become sheer, absolute differences. As Deleuze argues, the reverse side of the univocity of Being is the philosophy of pure heterogeneity.

Scotus, therefore, invented a separation between ontology and theology, which depends upon our having a fixed and stable – almost, one is tempted to say, an *a priori* – sense of the meaning of 'Being', 'goodness' and so forth. Deleuze and Derrida, in the wake of Heidegger, give Scotist univocity a nihilist twist by denying the hierarchy of genera, species and individuated *res*. There are no stable genera, but only complex mixtures, overlappings and transformations. Hence the absolute diversity of genera becomes the absolute diversity of every *ens* as such (a move of course itself anticipated by Scotist *haecceitas*). But the reverse side of this diversity remains the univocity of being: only 'Being', declares Derrida, has a literal and not a metaphorical sense.[58] Likewise, for Deleuze, every differential happening is also the eternal return of the same, the repetition of a self-identical existence, while difference is not fundamentally a matter of irreducible relation, but rather of the 'original' and continuous variation of a primordial 'unity'.[59]

The question to be posed is this: is the nihilist philosophy of the simultaneous occurrence of univocity and equivocity more demonstrably 'fundamental' than the Catholic philosophy of analogical difference? The matter is open to doubt: for nihilism must here perpetrate a form of transcendental philosophy in which Being, as 'the same' (yet entirely undetermined), performs the categorical-regulative function of organizing phenomena, though now at an ontological as well as an epistemological level. This transcendental univocity, being entirely empty of content, and indeed the medium of a sheerly differentiated content, cannot possibly appear in itself to our awareness, but can only be assumed and exemplified in the phenomena which it organizes. Yet if Being remains in itself unknowable, always absent and concealed, then how do we justify the characterization of Being as univocity? The transcendental arrangement cannot be separated from a particular way of organizing images and words that is favoured by nihilism: simultaneous univocity (of Being) and equivocity (of beings) provides a workable code, which could even become a guide for practice – but nothing grounds a preference for this coding.

An analogical code remains equally viable; although Deleuze insists that analogy is complicit with identity, presence and substance.[60] It must be conceded that the traditional presentation of analogy did not altogether

---

[58] Jacques Derrida, *Violence and Metaphysics*, pp. 81, 143–4.
[59] Deleuze, *Différence et Répétition*, pp. 37–9, 382–8; *Pure Immanence: Essays on a Life*, trans. Anne Boyman (New York: Zone, 2001). Alain Badiou, *Deleuze: The Clamor of Being*, trans. Louise Burchill (Minneapolis: Minnesota UP, 2000).
[60] Deleuze, *Différence et Répétition*, pp. 45–52.

avoid this: if analogical predication applies mainly at the level of *genera*, and across the categories of substance and accident, in such a fashion that the substantial is the 'basic' meaning, to which the accidental is referred, then this suggests a hierarchical convergence towards a literal 'sameness' of being, which is the presence of God.[61] The mysterious analogical unity of like and unlike (whereby beings are, *in the same respect*, like and unlike, not like as Being and unlike as beings) here seems to be invoked merely to cope with difficulties at the margins of our classificatory schemes, and to uphold a unity at the top of the hierarchy, where it threatens to shatter apart. But while this is correct, analogy does not imply 'identity', but identity and difference at once, and this radical sense can be liberated if one relativizes the genera/species/individuals hierarchy in the face of a more fundamental equality in created being, and recognizes, *with* the nihilists, the primacy of mixtures, *continua*, overlaps and disjunctions, all subject in principle to limitless transformation. If the Aristotelian categories are subordinated, then the way is open to seeing analogy as all-pervasive, as governing every unity and diversity of the organized world – Aquinas already opened the way to this. In the case of the analogy of beings to Being, such a mode of analogy would be divorced from *pros hen* predication, insofar as this gives priority to substance, because God would be less the subject of the 'proper', literal application of the analogical quality, than rather the infinite realization of this quality in all the diversity and unity of its actual/possible instances. Meanwhile, in the case of analogy amongst finite beings, every temporal ontological arrangement would have to be grasped in aesthetic terms: x and y may be different, yet they belong together in their difference in a specific 'exemplary' ordering, and this 'belonging together' means a certain sort of convergence, a certain commonality. (Such a belonging together is only a 'kind of' likeness; in the notion of analogy, the meaning of alike is itself analogically stretched almost to breaking point, just like the meaning of 'part' in Platonic 'participation'.) Unlike genera and species, these contingent unities are not fixed once and for all: if they persist (either in nature or in culture), then this is not the result of an Aristotelian hierarchy of gradual differentiation reaching down from the abstract to the concrete, but by virtue of a 'Platonic' hierarchy, which accords to some particular cultural arrangement the privilege of an 'ideal' status, and a generative productiveness in marking out the scope for new combinations and disposals.

If analogy is seen as entering into all unities, relations and disjunctures, then it is rendered dynamic: the likenesses 'discovered' are also constructed likenesses (whether by natural or cultural processes) which can be refashioned and re-shaped. And if certain things and qualities are 'like God', then it must also be true that the analogizing capacity *itself* is 'like God'. A certain transcendentalism (as compared with medieval philosophy) does indeed

---

[61] Aquinas, ST I. q. 13 a10 resp. See John Milbank and Catherine Pickstock, *Truth in Aquinas* (London: Routledge, 2001) pp. 46–8.

seem unavoidable here. The analogical code is chosen in preference to the univocal code, and an analogizing process appears to organize *schematically* the empirical content. However, no attempt need be made (by Christian faith) to claim that this transcendentalism is any more than the effect of a linguistic code. And furthermore, for the analogical code, the analogizing process does not stand in a precisely 'categorical' relationship to the analogized content. On the contrary, between the infinite capacity for analogizing and the particular analogies there is a constant exchange of predicates, as there is not between the univocal process and the differential instance, in nihilist philosophy. For whereas the univocal process is absolutely indifferent to each particular difference, the analogical process is a constant discrimination of preferences and erection of hierarchies. Hence the character of these preferences, and the order of these hierarchies, is attributed to the analogizing process itself: it *is* the very ladder which it erects. What this implies in practice is adherence to a particular tradition. Only such adherence permits a meta-critical philosophy to remain *not* strictly transcendental, in the sense of a dualism of scheme and content, without exchange of predicates. Nihilism, by contrast, which refuses adherence to a particular tradition, produces a metacritique which unavoidably lapses back into a transcendentalism, into mere 'critique'.

When I talk about 'the analogizing process', I am trying to give a Catholic theological equivalent to Heidegger's temporalizing of Being. This process is our participation in divine Being, now understood as a participation also in the divine creativity which reveals itself as ever-new through time.[62] But there is no glorification of mere originality here: a series of discriminations are irreversibly made within this process, and without these preferences it would collapse back into nihilism and univocity. By exactly the same token, the analogical code also requires an exchange of predicates between finite and infinite – meaning the plenitudinous, divine infinite, and not just the infinite of possible temporality. A double argument is required to see the possibility of this aspect of the code: first of all, one shows that such an exchange of predicates between infinite temporal process and finite instances cannot be critically ruled out. Secondly, one must show the same thing for the projection of an infinite beyond the infinity of time.

The first argument is simple, and has already been given: infinity does not appear, yet has to be presupposed, and if we are to have norms and values – to say what ultimately counts 'for always' – then it has to be 'conjectured about' (to echo the terminology of Nicholas of Cusa). This necessary conjecture must, however, remain always ungrounded, or otherwise one lapses into the 'critical' illusion of transcendentalism. To speak of a univocal Being indifferent to the differences of being is a conjecture, and to speak of an analogical Being which shows hierarchical preference amidst the differences of being is also a conjecture. As to what we should conjecture,

---

[62] See chapter 12 below.

nothing helps us decide apart from the subjectively recognized lure of analogical participation itself.

The second argument is more difficult. If, for the analogical coding, the temporal infinite is not indifferent to the differences, and a hierarchy of differentiation *is* this infinite process itself, then that which we see as desirable, that which we choose to construct as sign or image, must 'already belong' to infinitude as non-identical repetition. The last phrase indicates that what we do or make is not prescribed by a preceding idea; on the contrary, we have to discover the content of the infinite through labour, and creative effort. But if we are talking about genuine innovations, genuine additions, rather than changes emerging inevitably from an immanent, perhaps dialectical process, and yet we wish *also* to claim that certain *preferred* additions are deemed essential to our conception of the true direction of this process, than one has to posit a plenitudinous supra-temporal infinite which has 'already realized' in an eminent fashion every desirable effect. Otherwise, *either* everything truly desirable will be precontained in the process, as in an *a priori* idea, and the priority of language and cultural invention will be obfuscated, *or* we shall not truly be able to maintain the notion that certain human products are more desirable than others. Thus a historicism upon which one superimposes an analogical, rather than a univocal coding, requires the positing of transcendence.

By these sorts of arguments one can begin to expose the element of sheer preference in the fundamental ontologies of Heidegger, Derrida and Deleuze. Notice here that I am not, like Emmanuel Levinas, claiming that ontology as such is complicit with violence. If one follows this path, then one still tends to read the historical time of cultural exchange which is 'Being' as inevitably violent, and to long for an impossibly pure encounter of mutually exterior subjects without mediation across a common domain, which is always doomed to infect and coerce the genuinely responding will. By contrast, I am suggesting the possibility of a *different* ontology, which denies that mediation is necessarily violent. Such an ontology alone can support an alternative, peacable, historical practice.

4   *Positive or negative difference?*

The contestable idea of the univocity of being is only one aspect of a coding which upholds difference as violence. A second important aspect concerns the conception of the movement of Being within time, and especially of its movement as linguistic, signifying Being, which gives rise to 'humanity'.

A contrast can be made here between Derrida and Deleuze. In Derrida's case it can be argued that differential violence is upheld by a failure fully to overcome dialectics. In the case of Deleuze, his non-dialectical, 'positive' version of difference seems only to issue in nihilism because of lingering Kantian assumptions and sheer cultural bias.

Derrida's critique of metaphysics is centred around an assault on the notion of a 'meaning' that can be separated from the play of signs and referred to the original 'presence' of a thing or a thought.[63] Signs do not denote pre-existing realities, but are caught up in a chain of connotations that can be infinitely extended. Hence the transcendental premise of all language is a logic of 'supplementation' and of 'deferral'. If the primary unit of language is the sign, then we never possess an original uncontaminated meaning, for that which we signify is only known by reference to something else: a sign, image, or metaphor for the absent signified. This is the 'supplement at the origin'. Similarly, we can clarify our first use of a signifier by adding further signifiers, moving further away from the original in an endless process of 'deferral'. This appears to be a mode of scepticism only if one remains stuck in the illusion that there can be meaning and presence: in fact, there is only the play of dissemination, and this extends to ontological reality itself. Being, like language, consists only of traces, effects of absent causes which are clarified merely through the appearance of further traces. It is not supreme substance, but a road without origin and without end: 'immotivation of the trace has always *become*', and in this immotivation, in which 'the completely other' is 'announced as such', there is contained 'all *history*, which metaphysics has defined as being present, starting from the occulted movement of the trace'.[64] Thus Derrida implies that motion and signification are essentially at one (in a somewhat Spinozistic and Bergsonian fashion).

The continuity of material motion with language is best exemplified by writing, and especially pictographic writing.[65] Pictographs are the instituting of the trace, the transcendental possibility of signification, and not mere ciphers for spoken words, whose immediate presence encourages the illusion that they express a prior fullness of thought in the speaking subject. Whereas the absence of the speaker from the written text is for Emmanuel Levinas a mark of fallenness, and the alienation of language, for Derrida it reminds us of the true condition of all language, spoken or written.[66] Words always already float free of their first contents – otherwise they could not signify at all.

Despite this transcendentally anarchic condition of language as writing, we cannot simply dispense with the illusion of presence. Just as, for Heidegger, beings only happens in the fall of Being, so also, for Derrida, supplementation and deferral only operate by constantly throwing up this delusory appearance. Every closed or relatively closed system of conventional signification, found in all our cultural practices, has to occlude the play of dissemination and conjure the illusion of stable entities and persons to which language merely 'refers'. Grammatology as a transcendental philosophy must therefore be accompanied by a ceaseless 'deconstruction' of every 'textual' (i.e. cultural)

[63] Jacques Derrida, *Of Grammatology*, trans. Gayatri Chakravorty Spivak (Baltimore: John Hopkins, 1982) pp. 3–73, 313–16.

[64] Ibid., p. 47.

[65] Ibid., p. 269ff.

[66] Emmanuel Levinas, *Totality and Infinity: An Essay on Exteriority*, trans. A. Lingis (Pittsburgh: Duquesne University Press, 1979) pp. 73, 226–32. Derrida, 'Violence and metaphysics'; 'Différance', in *Margins of Philosophy*, trans. Alan Bass (Brighton: Harvester, 1982) pp. 3–27.

formation, which exposes the concealed mode of its construction of an apparent presence. Deconstruction is, in effect, Derrida's equivalent of genealogy, and can be applied to political and cultural formations as much as to philosophic and literary works, although Derrida has mostly concentrated on the latter.[67] Despite many divergences, Derrida, as much as Foucault, means to focus on 'practices' that are at once material and linguistic in character. Yet like Foucault also, he transcendentally determines the character of practice ('writing') as concealed violence.

For Derrida, this violence is inscribed at the point where the supplement, bearing the illusion of presence, dissembles the origin which it signifies: an origin which only *is* through this dissembling. He is fond of referring to Babylonian, Egyptian and Greek myths which portray gods of writing as the ministers of a supreme god, indispensable for the transmission of the divine commands, yet also as the betrayers and subverters of the divine plans.[68] These myths are supposed themselves to betray the fact that communication is primordially and unavoidably ruse and trickery. Is this conclusion the achievement of a more rigorous critique of metaphysics, or does it reflect just one more mythical encoding?

There are reasons for taking the latter view. In the first place, Derrida's philosophy upholds a rigorous separation between the level of ontological anarchy ('writing'), where systems of meaning and reference can be ceaselessly made and unmade, and the level of conventional signifying systems.[69] The first level constitutes a kind of active *a priori*, rather like the supracategorial Fichtean ego. The second level constitutes a kind of empirical content, which is wholly constituted by the very *a priori* which it disguises and betrays. But does one need to assent to this dualism, any more than to earlier idealist dualisms, like that between synthetic reason and analytic understanding? Systems shift and modify, they allow feedback from particular usages. For Derrida, every such modification is a kind of partial deconstruction, and substitution of a new illusory construct. But this assumes, once again, that transcendental 'dissemination' is entirely indifferent to every empirical content. If, instead, one permitted the notion of a 'tradition', then the modifications need not be ruptures, but can be thought to function to disclose a more fundamental (though partially absent) 'identity' of the received traditional wisdom. Here one assumes a coding that permits an exchange of predicates between scheme and content. As long as one persists in the belief of the truth of one's particular tradition, there is no way in which this coding can be shown as more arbitrary than the nihilist assumption that there is one true universal *a priori*, independent of all particular languages – namely, conflictual difference or *différance*, (as Derrida writes, to indicate deferral).

---

[67] Jacques Derrida, *Positions*, trans. Alan Bass (London: Athlone, 1987) pp. 49–50, 89.

[68] Jacques Derrida, 'Plato's pharmacy', in *Dissemination*, trans. Barbara Johnson (London: Athlone, 1981) pp. 65–171. *Of Grammatology*, p. 313.

[69] Ibid., pp. 27–73. *Positions*, pp. 56–8, 105.

The dualism in Derrida between dissemination and particular signifying systems is only upheld by the assumption that the relationship between the two levels is one of rupture and dissembling. And here one has to insist that it is not that the myth of Thoth concerning the supreme god and the treacherous scribe anticipates the positive truth of grammatology, but rather that grammatology just repeats (identically) the myth of Thoth. For why should supplementation and deferral imply subversion? If rightly one insists upon an ineradicable dimension of absence, then violence, as a universal, transcendental determinant of the absence/presence relationship, can never appear to view. If it *does* appear to view, then one has lapsed back into a philosophy of presence. For if it is to remain unseen, it must also remain essentially unknown; signs can only *conjecture* about the absence/presence relationship. A possible alternative conjecture would be that the image conveys the original which is only constituted through this imaging, in an entirely peaceful, self-giving fashion. This is as valid as the conjecture articulated in the myth of Thoth. Furthermore, it could be argued that the Christian doctrine of the Trinity (as Hegel failed to perceive) *is* precisely such a conjecture: the Son who is always given with the Father is the supplement at the origin; the Spirit who is always given with the Father and the Son is the infinite necessity of deferral.

Here one should note that Hans-Georg Gadamer, with his aesthetics of original emanation, or of a model which cannot exist apart from a series of copies, provides a version of supplementation, without Derrida's implications of violent rupture, that has been rather overlooked. Moreover, Gadamer specifically connects the emergence of such an aesthetic, and the discovery of the necessity of language for thought, with the historical influence of Trinitarian and Christological doctrine.[70] And Derrida himself takes over from Kierkegaard a view deriving from that philosopher's attempts to give a 'non-Platonic' ontology to Christian faith. For this view, sameness does not belong to an original which is 'recollected', or 'repeated', but arises *out of* non-identical repetition itself,[71] just as divine 'essence' only *is* through filial imaging. But Kierkegaard's conception of non-identical repetition belongs specifically to the religio-ethical aspect of life, to *Sittlichkeit*, to mundane variety in continuity like marriage, which is exactly adverse to the thought of betrayal.[72]

The idea that in supplementation there is necessarily and always treachery appears, in one way, actually to *draw back* from the full implication of supplementarity. For if the supplement constitutes the origin, and deferral is required by supplementation, then any suggestion of a rift, or arbitrary

---

[70] Hans-Georg Gadamer, *Truth and Method*, trans. Wilhelm Glen-Doepel (London: Steed & Ward, 1975) pp. 366–449.

[71] Jacques Derrida, *Speech and Phenomena*, trans. David Allison (Evanston: Northwestern University Press, 1973) p. 68; 'The theater of cruelty', in *Writing and Difference*, p. 248. Caputo, *Radical Hermeneutics*, pp. 11–36, 120–53.

[72] Søren Kierkegaard, *Repetition*.

discontinuity, appears almost to qualify these affirmations. Might it not be that difference as violence conserves some sediment of the Husserlian duality of being and meaning? For Derrida, Being is always necessarily supplemented by meaning, or 'sense', and yet the sense-bearing sign always betrays the being which it is, and is therefore arbitrarily related to Being, like Husserlian meaning and neo-Kantian evaluation or validation. Hence the Derridean trace is a (faint) trace of a real presence after all – namely the fact/value distinction.[73]

However, this Husserlian element is conveyed by Derrida in terms of a Hegelian dialectic which never reaches synthetic completion – and this is fair enough, because Hegelian alienation involves a necessary moment of separation of fact from value. Every signifying supplement is, for Derrida, a negation and alienation of Being, and the negation of negation, which ushers in a further dissemination, is achieved by deconstruction. But both negations are highly questionable: the first for reasons already explained in the chapter on Hegel, and the second because it suggests that every semiotic artefact is inherently contradictory. Not only is its construction arbitrary, but in its inevitable concealing of this construction the artefact must occlude it in a negative fashion, so that what it appears to say is the opposite of what it *must also say*, according to the mode of its own constitution. In a highly 'psycho-analytic' formulation, close to Lacan's Hegelianized Freudianism, Derrida declares that 'desire of presence carries in itself the destiny of its own non-satisfaction. Difference produces what it forbids, makes possible the very thing that it makes impossible.'[74]

Now it is true that every assertion implies an excluded, and so 'opposite' possibility. But only an intrusive, 'psychoanalytic' belief in the universality of the suppressive mechanism, and the tie of desire to impossibility of fulfilment, gives to this exclusion the force of a secret affirmation. One can suggest, instead, that no such link of a deconstructive, yet necessary *logos* holds opposites together, because opposites are not naturally 'real' poles, but the accidental *effect* of whatever is conventionally coded as the same. Having isolated a globe, one gets north and south, but they do not magically constitute the globe (in our understanding) by the power of mutual resistance. And they are joined, not by negation, but by their connection along the continuum of the global surface.

To stress negativity, and 'exact' opposition, as with deconstruction, is therefore to remain within the same, plus the dominance of a dyadic logic, and to exclude from view the infinite variety of possibly different readings, which are positively affirmed and 'added to' the text, rather than negatively implied by it. For this reason a sheerly 'wild' deconstruction – which Derrida sometimes points towards, beyond dialectics – which exhibits just the arbitrariness of the text's architecture and the infinite number of perspectives

---

[73] Jacques Derrida, *Edmund Husserl's Origin of Geometry: An Introduction*, trans. John P. Leavey jun. (New York/Brighton: Nicholas Hays/Harvester, 1978) pp. 151–3.

[74] Derrida, *Of Grammatology*, p. 143; 'From restricted to general economy: for a Hegelianism without reserve', in *Writing and Difference*, pp. 251–300.

upon it, makes more sense than a 'scientific' deconstruction which seeks to trace its concealed fault line. The latter is discoverable only in the trivial, dialectical sense that 'is' suggests 'is not'. To say whether a text in a more serious sense belies its surface meaning is by contrast a matter of fine judgement, of debatable interpretation, and where one should place the emphasis.

Derrida contends, against Hegel, that the process of negation continues indefinitely, and that synthesis is always postponed – in this sense only, a residue of positive difference always escapes a negation of the negation.[75] The trouble with Derrida, therefore, is that he is still a dialectician. And as he is only deconstructing or inverting Hegel, he thereby remains (as he well knew) also within 'the same' of Hegelianism.

Like Heidegger, Derrida sees Hegel's achievement as the consummation of metaphysics.[76] This belief is itself metaphysical, in the most pejorative sense. For first, it has only been the aim of post-seventeenth-century metaphysics to deduce all reality from a single principle, and, secondly, Hegelian logic is imbued with an idiosyncratic *mythos* of inevitable fall and return through alienation. If one claims that in some objective manner, Hegel's is the final, most complete version of metaphysical ambition, then one's critique of metaphysics must inevitably fall under the Hegelian shadow. Thus, both Heidegger and Derrida fully retain Hegel's Gnosticism, which from the Christian viewpoint is the most questionable part of his enterprise. Rather like Sophia herself in the gnostic pleroma, they know that they must attempt to know the unknowable, and yet that this attempt will meet with the inevitable rebuff of violent expulsion.[77] Unlike Valentinus, they draw the clear conclusion: if violence is the result of the search for knowledge, then violence is what there is to be known.

In the case of Gilles Deleuze's version of differential philosophy (which Foucault almost regarded as the ontological complement to his own genealogy),[78] one cannot so easily attribute ontological violence to the persistence of dialectical negation. Following Bergson (and we might recognize some kinship with Blondel), in a more purely Gallic line of thought, Deleuze sees negation as but a secondary effect of continuous variation, and as doing no positive work. He subordinates opposition to the pure externality of difference, and insists that difference escapes every dialectic, as it escapes also the mere differentiation of a genus which is bound within a philosophy of substance, or of the identical. Deleuze therefore limits the scope of a logic of identity, not in favour of a *coniunctio oppositorum*, but in favour of a kind of transcendental empiricism, or an assertion that ultimate univocal reality is always, endlessly, 'other' to itself. In accordance with this positive version of difference, Deleuze does not, like Derrida, think of an indeterminate 'absence'

---

[75] Derrida, 'The theater of cruelty', p. 248; *Positions*, pp. 43–4, 101.

[76] Derrida, *Of Grammatology*, p. 71.

[77] Jonas, *The Gnostic Religion*, pp. 174–205.

[78] Michel Foucault, 'Theatrum philosophicum', in *Language, Counter-Memory, Practice* (Oxford: Blackwell, 1977) pp. 164–96.

as 'negatively' and mystically conjured up by the work of the signifier, but instead insists that every new signified arrives by force of its own positivity, and its solid, 'diagrammatic' (though still encoded) character.[79]

Deleuze is, nonetheless, well aware that differences jostle and overlap within a common space. Yet because of his univocal coding he is only able to perceive this intermingling as agonistic conflict. It must here be asked whether this agonism does not in fact compromise the purity of his assertoric logic and Gallic positivism? Granted that the negative performs no positive work, an element of resistance and refusal must still, for Deleuze, be grafted onto every differentiated thing. Every *res* or 'intensity' expresses in partial fashion the general process of self-differentiation. This permits it to 'compose' ever-new and surprising bonds of unity with other *res*. Yet this peaceful solidarity reaches its limit at the point where the very existence of separate, mutually-related entities depends upon the always necessarily-occurring *suppression* of pure virtual self-differentiation – which can never 'be' as such. But why should such a transcendental circumstance hold?

Here it is important to realize that Deleuze's 'Kantianism' is more marked than Derrida's. For Deleuze, Kant provides some of the first inklings of radical difference. In particular, Kant suggested (without providing a full transcendental analysis of this circumstance) an ineradicable difference between concept and intuition, which arises within the very necessity of their belonging together. Deleuze wishes to go beyond Kant (in at once a 'Leibnizian' and a 'neo-Kantian' direction) by conceiving this difference as something which is external, something one must constantly, empirically 'notice' in one's pragmatic interactions with the world, and yet as a difference belonging to the very 'idea' of empirical realities as they occur – just as for Leibniz the absolute uniqueness of each individual thing is entailed by the logic of reality, and is not something open to confirmation or disconfirmation.[80]

Nonetheless, the simultaneously empirical and logical difference between concept and intuition is reworked by Deleuze as the belonging together in distinction of being and meaning, in a way highly parallel to Derrida's conception of the trace. For Deleuze (in an interpretation of ancient stoic philosophy) there are deep things or bodies which 'exist', and are related in a lawful manner which apparently exhibits causality, and there are also *simulacra*, 'intensities', or 'incorporeals', which 'insist' on the surface of life. This sphere of 'insistence' includes both the series of natural 'effects' or 'events' which 'express' embodiment, and the series of meanings that 'happen' in language. An event is a transition, but it only 'occurs' or persists, because it already detaches itself from body and temporal causality in terms of its infinite 'tensional' character: the stoic *tonos*. If we identify a moving cart, then this is already an *ideal* cart, a cart that could be bigger or smaller, whose movement could be slower and faster, and whose actual movement

---

[79] Deleuze and Guattari, *A Thousand Plateaus*, pp. 75–149.
[80] Deleuze, *Différence et Répétition*, pp. 39–40.

is infinitely divisible. The cart's happening – its standing out from the monotonous continuum – is *already* the happening of a meaning which steps outside the series in which it arises, and in our meaningful articulation of 'cart', the cart continues to 'happen'. This is why Zeno said, 'When I say cart, a cart passes through my mouth.' Words do not, therefore, first of all, denote a pictured reality. Words first happen in continuity with reality.

As Deleuze sees it, every event is like a wound, an entirely ideal gap which only exists in relation to a certain conventional organization of a surface; every event is also like death, which only fully happens after it has already ceased to happen. The realm of these incorporeal events, or of 'Platonic ideas on the surface', is in fact one and the same with Plato's region of shadows. This is a chaotic realm in which every sheerly different happening at the same time exemplifies exactly the same univocal sense: the sense of nonsense, or the joker without meaning who sorts and resorts the pack of meaning and deals out their differences.[81]

Incorporeals are, it is true, only 'effects' of bodies, and there is a level of 'double articulation' (always of intuition with concept) which links a particular bodily ordering with a particular 'regime of signs' (as, for example, in Foucault, the 'power' of the ordering of bodies in prisons is inseparable from the 'knowledge' of legal and punitive theory)[82] according to a diagrammatic or figural, rather than merely semiotic coding. (A non-semiotic coding means the – natural or cultural – 'conventionalities' of spatial or temporal distribution, which ensure that there is no pure *continuum*: for example, time is always measured by certain conventional 'intervals'.) Nevertheless, the incorporeal level of 'expression' through signs takes the lead, by virtue of its indeterminacy, in constantly reworking or 'deterritorializing' diagrammatic singularities (which have already escaped the generic determinations of universal 'strata') and so must disclose to us transcendental difference (or 'the plane of consistency') which ceaselessly engenders the 'abstract machines', or bodily/incorporeal composites. (For example, every temporal 'interval' like a date – 26 August 1989 – has a nominal, incorporeal reality which ensures that this 'figure' operates also as a sign: of particular events, perhaps of a particular epoch.) Just as, for Derrida, the supplement is prior to the origin, so also, for Deleuze, the surface is prior to the depths (which are not really depths, but rather sedimented regularities of bodily becoming). And, as for Derrida, a radical indeterminacy results: both series (of 'surface' and of 'depth') are permanently incomplete, because precisely 'placing' an event, or defining a meaning, is a function (as Saussure recognized) of relation to a total, completed, differential system, which, however (as post-structuralism realizes), never arrives. The series of meanings must suppose a signified reality which is always deficient, while this deficiency in the signified series of events

---

[81] Deleuze, *Logique du Sens*, pp. 13–22, 122–33, 175–80, 208–12.
[82] Michel Foucault, *Discipline and Punish: The Birth of the Prison*, trans. Alan Sheridan (Harmondsworth: Penguin, 1977) pp. 29, 177.

constantly compensates by expressing itself 'excessively' in the signifier, which is *never* justified and always 'problematic'.[83] Thus, for Deleuze, unlike Kant, there is a problematic 'exchange' between the series of categories (or 'senses') and the series of intuitions (or 'references'), which prevents the category/intuition difference from providing determinate knowledge, and instead ensures that it reinforces the indefinite character of both series. It follows that the two series are only co-ordinated by a non-coordination. The 'diagonal' which correlates horizontal, temporal signifying expression with vertical, spatial 'content' tends to escape the hold of both in a nomadic 'line of flight'. However, pure escape into pure variation would sink into a 'black hole'. If any nomadic resistance is to remain actual in its composition of wider and wider forces, it must still partially affirm the arbitrary tyranny of the signifying and corporeal series. Thus it never escapes from violence.

That the deficient depth can only 'become' through the excessive surface, like the lacking origin through the supplement, is a critically valid conclusion. However, the arbitrariness and 'nomadic' warfare involved in deterritorialization, the refusal of even an 'aesthetic' self-justification for the excessive signifier, suggests that Being is still divided, in neo-Kantian fashion, from meaning or value. This occurs precisely at the point where the manifestation of depth through the surface alone is also a disjunctive violence. Such violence is therefore the last residue of a scheme/content dualism – even, in the last analysis, of a Cartesian duality of spirit and extension.

And how are we to think of this disjunctive violence, other than as a kind of negation of negation? The elimination of dialectics, or of the attribution to negativity of a certain positive influence, can only be achieved (although it does not *have* to be rationally desired) when not only the negative, but also the conflictual, is denied any real ontological purchase. As I shall show in the final chapter, Augustine's understanding of *privatio boni* included just such a denial, and it is Augustine who truly points the way beyond dialectics, in an Hegelian sense of the term.

Ethics

In the Spinozistic idiom which Deleuze, in particular, favoured, the last section might just as well have been itself entitled 'ethics', for while the ontology of difference does not prescribe particular evaluations, it also teaches the needlessness of regret, and the necessity for resignation to the whole process, where all is equally necessary and equally arbitrary; where everything depends on everything else, and this dependence is enacted through constant struggle and counter-resistance. Nothing in this section need be

[83] Deleuze and Guattari, *A Thousand Plateaus*, pp. 39–149, 310–51, 501–17. Deleuze, *Logique du Sens*, pp. 63–7. See also Catherine Pickstock, 'Quasi una sonata: 'Music, postmodernism and theology', in Jeremy Begbie (ed.) *Theology through Music* (Cambridge: CUP, 2005).

added to an ontology that is already an ethics, but we must be clear what it means to enact such an ontology. For the nihilists this enacting is inescapable; for the present interpretation it is only the performance of a code. However, are the nihilists clear-sighted, even when it comes to the inseparability of being and enactment? Aside from Nietzsche, this is scarcely the case.

The rigorous implication of post-humanism is this: freedom is only a reality as arbitrary power. The Rousseauian-Kantian egalitarian extension of freedom has been transformed into the asymmetrical extension of power – the promotion of the strongest, the most enduring, the most all-pervasive. In civil society this is manifest as the growing postmodern dominance of market systems (which may, nonetheless, take a 'governmental' form) over both political and bureaucratic structures which concentrated on the formal equality of free subjects. In a more market-orientated society, this formality can be much more rapidly translated into the possession of actual resources of wealth, believability and rhetorical power. It would seem, apparently, in the 'post-Fordist' age, as if power is being more distributed, being made more accountable to informational feedback and so forth.[84] In fact, the new spaces of permitted creativity, segmentation and indeterminism are only differences which secure yet more strongly the dominance of the same, the univocal: the same basic car, house, restricted language, conformist behaviour, conjoined with the same individualistic narcissism. Instead of various real skills and social roles, which required a particular education to master, all social and technical procedures are becoming increasingly flattened-out, so that easy transitions and adjustments can be constantly made. The new flexibility of persons and things, the new dominance of trivial, day-to-day 'innovation', spells the end of resistance by subjects who believed that they possessed an inviolable death, and the beginning of an endless interpellation of subjectivities through a more effective, apparently more yielding kind of power.

Deleuze, Lyotard, Derrida and Foucault all sought to present a version of Nietzsche's philosophy which allows for some sort of critique of this neo-capitalism. For them all, however, this remained, despite everything, an *emancipatory* critique, or a critique predicated on the possibility of a further release of freedom. Yet this is to remain harnessed to a deception, namely, to the idea that one can still step back from Nietzsche to Kant. Nietzsche himself entertained no such illusions, and taught that, in future, for those unable to sustain the rigours of artistic self-determination, the best that could be hoped for was the discipline of a State organized for war.[85] Of course, he did not envisage the reality of recent capitalism, of a discipline operating surreptitiously, disguising itself as 'pleasure', of a war that is constant and invisible, of all against all, and all against created nature. But the ontology of difference should logically embrace this reality – and, indeed, it half does so, yet still tries to claim for itself a continuing critical reserve.

---

[84] Scott Lash and John Urry, *The End of Organized Capitalism* (Cambridge: Polity, 1987).
[85] Nietzsche, *Will to Power*, pp. 126–7.

Jacques Derrida insisted that deconstruction has emancipatory potential, because it protests against the contradictions inscribed in every fixed social structure.[86] Yet given, for Derrida, the *necessity* of presence, this implied a tiresome, red-guard politics of ceaseless negativity. Worse, given the same necessity, how is one to decide when to abide in illusion, and when to dismantle it? Either course is in a sense hopeless, and nothing can really guide our decision as to *when* is the appropriate moment for one or the other. The decision must itself be arbitrary, and persuasion to either course a strategy of deception. In which case, it would appear, only a fascistic politics remains viable.

Much closer to such an insight was Michel Foucault. For Foucault, it was the need to wield power which would betray every possible revolution.[87] A more effective oppositional politics should operate at the level of micro-strategies; yet here, also, there is little real room for optimism. For Foucault was the first to realize that a more dispersed, more indeterminate and more differentiated power was also a more effective, more total power. Against this, he at times invoked the 'power of bodies', yet he knew that as soon as such power enters into discourse (and it has always already done so), it has also entered into the conventionality of culture, which is a purer reinvention of the 'naked' force that we borrow from nature. In the face of this dilemma, his later philosophy sought unconvincingly to reintroduce an autonomous subject, able to 'shape itself' and exercise a stoic self-discipline in an Epicurean self-isolation from the political arena.[88]

Neither Deleuze nor Lyotard, by comparison, sought out this mode of retreat; nor did they subscribe to Derrida's mere negativity. Instead, they advocated an embracing of the 'neo-capitalist' *agon* in all its positivity and counter-positivity. Yet they hoped that by pushing the logic of capital still further, it could be tilted over into something else, truly liberating (which was also, for Deleuze, 'The Absolute'), a measured deterritorialization which constantly outstrips every temporary but necessary location of the reterritorialization of capitalism on abstract capital itself. As Bernard Henri-Lévy remarked, this homoeopathic hope is but a residue of Marxism rather than its denial, but Deleuze and Lyotard became much vaguer than Marx about the actual point of transition.[89] The 'beyond capital', for Deleuze, would be the process of a controlled line of flight that never entirely abandons sedimented terrain.[90] However, I have already contended, in the previous chapter, that 'reterritorialization' must infinitely keep pace with the latter process. For outside particular cultural commitments, territorial representations of what

---

[86] Derrida, *Positions*, p. 62ff.

[87] Foucault, 'Politics and ethics: an interview', in *The Foucault Reader*, pp. 373–80; *Power/ Knowledge*, pp. 78–146.

[88] Foucault, 'Technologies of the self'.

[89] Bernard Henri-Lévy, *Barbarism with a Human Face*, trans., George Holoch (New York: Harper & Row, 1979) pp. 8–9.

[90] Deleuze and Guattari, *A Thousand Plateaus*, pp. 472–3.

is 'desirable' – however illusory we may deem them – there is, in fact, no desire, and therefore no great creative force of desire (or 'innocent' power, *puissance*) to be 'set free' in the fashion that Deleuze envisaged. For every time that desire renews itself, to invent creatively a new object, it is reborn with that object, with that posited value, with the mythical distance of its unattainability. Deleuze's own ontology recognizes that the univocal or the deterritorialized happens, without surplus, *as* temporary territorial difference, and so he ought to have seen that it cannot be 'more closely approached' by an apparently greater degree of deterritorialization in any given era – since, *to the degree* that escape is achieved, it must also be without actual positive effect. As the abstract equivalence of such territories, capitalism already *is* the absolute balance of constant escape and resettlement.

Lyotard, by contrast, was a little more sceptical about a (still Rousseauian) natural desire that is, in itself, innocent and benign. Yet no more can be said in favour of his own politics of 'libidinal intensities'. Not mere deconstructive negativity, nor the inviolable subject, nor yet the unleashing of an objectless desire was advocated by Lyotard, but rather the multiplication and speeding up of the infinitely many and overlapping language-games promoted within late capitalism. Access to these games, he argued, should be made more egalitarian: and this is the sole remaining redoubt for socialist aspiration.

So far, it is Lyotard who made the most sustained attempt to articulate the ethics of an agonistic politics.[91] What emerged was a strange blend of primitivism, sophism, Aristotelianism and Kantianism, which best of all illustrates the contradictions inherent in trying to distil a residue of modernist freedom, after it has been already dissolved into the fluid of postmodern power.

The 'pagan' elements (as he calls them) in Lyotard, represent his attempt to do justice to power, and to difference. The Jewish philosopher, Emmanuel Levinas, is right, he argues, to say that our fundamental moral situation is not one of autonomy, but of heteronomy, or obedience to the voice of the other. Unlike Yahweh, however, in paganism even the gods emerge as a response to an alien voice. For the 'mythical' consciousness which Lyotard seeks to reinstate in a more adamantly pluralistic form, there are many gods and many heroes, subject to the imperatives of many stories, but in such a fashion that the original hero in his historical circumstantiality is forgotten about: he survives, in his real, continuing heroism, only as a name. Yet in contrast to this persistence of the self-identical myth (which is like Deleuze's univocity), Lyotard also insists on the variants we supply to the story, and the absolute non-prescribability of moral decision, as supposedly stressed by both the sophists and by Aristotle. In his account of the latter's ethics he disingenuously elides the element of formation of character, of maintaining an analogical consistency from one moral decision to the next. By emphasizing the isolation

---

[91] J.-F. Lyotard and J.-L. Thébaud, *Just Gaming*, trans. Wlad Godzich (Manchester: Manchester University Press, 1985). J.-F. Lyotard, *The Differend: Phrases in Dispute*, trans. Georges Van Den Abbeele (Manchester: Manchester University Press, 1988).

of the moment of action, the way is clear to convert heterogeneity and non-prescribability into a new, nihilistic formulation of the categorical imperative: 'act always so that the maxim of your will may (almost) not be erected into a principle of universal legislation'.[92]

Yet this inversion of the categorical imperative enshrines the impossible tension between power and freedom. On the one hand, like Kant, Lyotard wants simply to guarantee freedom; on the other hand, he realizes that this can only be secured as real positive difference, not confined to an unreal 'private' space. To admit freedom, we must also admit the power of the other over against us, our insertion in the story of the other, who is both narrator and narrated, the hero that we must in turn become. Since, in mythical discourse, roles are always handed down and taken over, there is for Lyotard a permanent occultation of the speaking subject, and the 'inauguration' of a narrative can only be ascribed to the work of a god. To exercise freedom therefore, we must submit to the arbitrariness of myth, and find ourselves within its uncontrollable power. Lyotard wishes, nonetheless, to blend with this 'paganism' a liberal affirmation (which is discursive and not narrational) of the rights of all to participate, of all to engage in the agonistic combats which the myths narrate, repeat and supplement through new hybridizations, new incorporations of alien stories into the mythical corpus.

But the problem here is insurmountable. The narratives we have heard and appropriated already fatally determine our strength and weakness, our cunning or our frailty. These commencements are inimical to any neutral start which seeks to reinvoke the social contract. By the same token, how can we discriminate, as Lyotard desires, between legitimate competition, and illegitimate terror, which denies the rights of others to participate? For the rules of the many language-games or *mythoi* are in no way fixed; instead, the resourceful appropriator of the name of the hero is the one who speaks more loudly this same name through new ruses, new trickeries which both command the game and allow it to absorb other games within its sway. Lyotard may proclaim: let an infinite diversity of language-games rule! but he cannot pass this off as liberal pluralism, because nothing in his philosophy in principle renders illegitimate the infinite expansion of one language-game at the expense of others, nor the capture and manipulation of many language-games by a single power.

This implication is, however, obfuscated by Lyotard, for reasons that have to do, once again, with a residual Kantianism. Whereas, with Deleuze and Derrida, I showed that fact/value and scheme/content dualisms remain faintly transcribed in the thesis of transcendental violence, in the case of Lyotard the same thesis is muted in a liberal direction which connects agonistic struggle to the Kantian division of the discourses on truth, goodness and beauty.[93] Equating the separate scopes of the Kantian faculties to 'language

---

[92] Lyotard and Thébaud, *Just Gaming*, p. 94.
[93] Lyotard, *The Differend*.

games', which are, however, infinite in number, Lyotard implies that there are distinct grammatical spheres governed by their own formal rules, and that these spheres, although agonistically competing, need not violate each other's formal integrity – just as for Kant, cognitive and practical discourses should be kept distinct. Although every addition of a new linguistic phrase is, from a transcendental viewpoint, a purely arbitrary attempt to 'present' the never exhaustibly presentable assumptions of a preceding phrase, the only really serious differences – the 'differends' – occur not within, but *between* genres of discourse. The problem of politics for Lyotard is, as Plato saw, the same as the problem of philosophy, or of ethics and ontology: how to 'distribute' the various genres of discourse, do justice at the point where 'differends' arise.

In two ways, however, this dilutes the dilemmas of difference. First of all, the mere formal conventions of a language game do not always adjudicate (as Lyotard knows) as to the content of what is to be said – what the next phrase is to be. Hence, surely, equally serious differends arise *within* genres of discourse. Secondly, genres of discourse are not tidily distinct, and therefore within genres there are also, paradoxically, transgressions of genres. Lyotard really knows this also, as, for example, when he points out that the Kantian language game of 'practical reason' secretly involves a theoretical conception of how it is possible for a community of free spirits to operate.[94] To obtain a purer genre of the discourse of practical reason, Lyotard adopts the new version of the categorical imperative already cited. As regards our attitudes to others this implies (following Levinas) that we respect their freedom, not as a universal legislating power, but in its heteronomous specificity. And yet, as Lyotard points out in discussing Levinas, as soon as we 'obey' the other, appropriate his words, we bring his freedom under *theoretical* scrutiny.[95] A 'pure' genre of practical reason would be utterly ineffable. Hence the Kantian denial of the interdependency of the discourses of truth, goodness and beauty can only be preserved in a nihilistic guise as the view that these discourses (and the infinity of different genres in general) necessarily and yet always without justification impinge upon each other, phrase by phrase.

If this is the case, then one cannot try to smuggle back the benignity of Kantian liberalism, as Lyotard desires: no natural, 'philosophical' ethics, ontology or politics can appeal to a justice which demands that every discourse be allowed to be true to its own formality. Between nihilistic univocity and Catholic analogy (which includes the 'convertibility' of truth, beauty and goodness) there is no longer any third liberal path. (In *The Differend* Lyotard sounds ironically like his great opponent, Habermas.) This applies particularly to Lyotard's desperate attempt, in *The Differend*, to reinstate some form of Marxism: capitalism, he claims, represents the unwarranted dominance of the economic language game of the exchange of represented time, over the

[94] Lyotard, *The Differend*, p. 125.
[95] Ibid., p. 114.

language game of work and production.[96] This seems to ignore the arguments of Baudrillard which we encountered in chapter 7: there is no 'pure' genre of production, because production is always of a particular kind, determined by 'values' which arise through human exchanges. And the 'economic' language game is articulated at a complex intersection with the game of 'conquering nature' – here capitalism itself backs unlimited production as part of the very meaning of 'wealth'. Of course it also *holds back* production, in the sense of a production defined by other priorities of value, but every system of reasons for production would imply, also, reasons for not-producing, and therefore 'hold back' production and work of some kind or another. Postmodern thought disallows the rational demonstration that there is some reality or realm of reality – here a persecuted genre of discourse – which awaits recognition and demands emancipation (yet Lyotard speaks of a 'signal' made by nature, and of heterogeneity as 'providentially' willed as a kind of *telos* of non-teleology).[97] And as we saw in chapter 7, socialism must therefore now seek grounds other than those of enlightenment.

Lyotard, like his fellow post-structuralists, fails to come up with any convincing reasons as to why the ontology of difference is detachable from fascism, or a politics of the mythical celebration of power. It is this failure on the part of all the philosophers of difference which gave rise in Paris, in the late 1970s, to the reaction of Guy Lardreau and Christian Jambet's crucial work, *L'Ange*, which articulated a kind of Manichean-gnostic Marxism. This in turn influenced the more neo-liberal group dubbed the *nouveaux philosophes*.[98] Both sets of thinkers did not, first of all, challenge the analysis of political culture as dominated by power: indeed, they sought to accentuate this, but they denied that from the nettle, power, can ever be plucked the flower, hope. If Nietzsche completed the Western quest for truth and discovered that the untruth of truth is power, then this power-reality must be refused, and the Platonic quest must be taken up again, yet this time as a wager of faith that there is 'another world', not dominated by power. This 'other reality' was sometimes seen as announced by Plato himself, sometimes by the Christian gnostics, or else in the somewhat kindred, but more Christian philosophies of Maurice Clavel, Louis Marin and René Girard, as once, and once only, present in the life and power-refusing death of Jesus Christ.[99]

Importantly, both the 'angelists' and the *nouveaux philosophes* at times tried to resist the temptation, apparent in the later Foucault, to creep back into humanism. We may hanker after the liberal subject as a bulwark against

[96] Ibid., pp. 171–81.
[97] Ibid., pp. 135, 181.
[98] Henri-Lévy, *Barbarism with a Human Face*. Lardreau and Jambet, *L'Ange; Le Monde* (Paris: Grasset, 1978). André Glucksmann, *The Master Thinkers*, trans. Brian Pearce (Brighton: Harvester, 1980).
[99] Maurice Clavel, *Deux Siècles avec Lucifer* (Paris: Seuil, 1978) pp. 21, 29–90. Louis Marin, 'Discourse of power, power of discourse: Pascalian notes', in Alan Montefiore (ed.) *Philosophy in France Today* (Cambridge: Cambridge University Press, 1983) pp. 155–75. René Girard, *Of Things Hidden Since the Foundation of the World* (London: Athlone, 1987).

fascism, but fascism will always be able to announce, truly, the illusory universality of this subject. As Lyotard already realized, fascism cannot be *refuted*, precisely because it takes its stand on myth, and not, like Marxism, on a controvertible meta-narrative, making claims which require, on its own terms, to be substantiated, and yet cannot be.[100] The best we can theoretically do in the face of fascism is to point out its mythical form. But the *nouveaux philosophes* went further: because fascism, as Nietzsche and his follows have shown, is the true character of all politics, it follows that *all* politics assumes a merely mythical guise. It is not, as for Hobbes or Foucault, that the essence of all politics is power, but rather, as for de Maistre, de Bonald and Carl Schmitt, that all politics invents power by proclaiming a religion which channels the mythical power of a fictive God or gods ('fictive' does not here necessarily mean 'untrue'). If power after all dominates, then this is not because of its material reality, but because of the arbitrariness of all mythical inventions. The perfect form of politics, as of religion, argued Bernard Henri-Lévy, in the wake of Carl Schmitt and the Catholic positivist tradition, is monotheism, because this posits a single, absolute source of power.[101] On the other hand, it is also religion, and religion alone, that places a check upon political power, because it posits a source of power over and above political sovereignty, and invents 'the soul' as a place of direct contact with this power.[102] At this point (the weakest in their argument) the *nouveaux philosophes* themselves still sought to bring Kantian freedom back into play but in a way that fully accorded with *Religion within the Bounds of Reason Alone*: the idea of the subject and of human rights depends *wholly* on a religious narrative. There is no possible conceptual or intuitive access to a pure subject over and above the domain of power, yet the invoking of such a sublimity can make some small practical difference between naked totalitarianism and a liberalism that is, nonetheless, in essence totalitarian.[103]

There is much in this line of thought that is of great value, and which the rest of this book will seek to pursue. In particular, the 'angelists' and the *nouveaux philosophes* realized that one can only oppose Nietzsche and his followers by invoking a counter-mythology and a counter-ontology, not by trying to reinstate a humanism founded upon 'universal reason', nor by seeking a level of narrated 'reality' beneath the play of *simulacra*. Yet at the same time they were still too close to acceptance of a Nietzschean genealogy and ontology, so that they had to place what is 'beyond power' in another world, which is to us purely ineffable. The crucial question here would be: why, if power is only an idea, a fiction (albeit a fiction in whose trammels we seem inextricably caught), cannot there be an alternative invention of a social and linguistic process that is not the dominance of arbitrary power (that is to say, of power in the sense of violence)? Obviously, such a concept is itself

---

[100] Lyotard, *The Differend*, pp. 156–8.

[101] Henri-Lévy, *Barbarism with a Human Face*, pp. 9, 12–17, 131–5, 148. Hermann Schwengel, *Der Kleine Leviathan* (Frankfurt-am-Main: Athenaum, 1988) pp. 55–87.

[102] Ibid., pp. 115, 135, 190, 195. Clavel, *Deux Siècles chez Lucifer*, pp. 289–92, 327–8.

[103] Henri-Lévy, *Barbarism with a Human Face*, p. 142ff.

intensely problematic, but it is prematurely ruled out by Henri-Lévy and others, because of the account which they give of *desire*.

Rightly rejecting the Deleuzian notion of an original primitive desire which ceaselessly invents its own objects, they insist, after Lacan, that desire is the by-product of our 'imagining' a grasp of unattainable goals presented to us by the cultural 'symbolic order'.[104] Every politics, every *mythos*, keeps us in the thralls of arbitrary power, because it holds out to us the goal of possession of what can never be possessed; in this space the empirical, political subject – the *subjected* – is always inscribed. The goal, therefore, for Guy Lardreau, is not, as for Christianity, to change the *object* of desire, to make 'God' our master, but rather to discover some form of 'not desiring'.

However, this pessimism about desire excludes, and does not refute, the possibility of a non-possessive desire. If the subject emerges in her desire for the other, who is both present and withheld in her surplus as a signifier, then this desire, if it is truly desire for the other (which means inevitably, desire *of* the other's desires), seeks at once a cancellation and a preservation of distance; an encounter constituted through the depth of past and future, rather than their violent appropriation. We can, indeed, desire only *simulacra* (and *simulacra* of the other's *simulacra*), but what if the mark of a non-possessive desire was precisely the refusal of the illusion of stepping behind the mirror to find more than a dream-world concealed there? Between the notion of a solipsistic, inventive desire on the one hand, and an always doomed and self-deceptive desire on the other, lies the possibility of a desire not betrayed by process and difference. For this desire, the endless 'dissatisfaction' that remains, even in the realization of desire, is not really the 'lack' of frustration which is still mastered by power, but the surplus delight of fulfilment, which only knows its consummation in holding the other (including the endless chain of others) at a distance, a distance that consists solely in the other's unlimited self-giving – an element not alien to her desire itself. Of course, in this desire, also, a power is exercised, the power of influence by the other (all the others) which the lover cannot control, working through a constant *invention* of desirable objects so as to ensure, as Deleuze claims, that desire is not finally of a Lacanian 'nothing'. But the question once again should be, is this influence necessarily arbitrary, or can it rather mediate the analogical bonds which bind us together in an objective aesthetic order? That infinite order of deferral and referral which is, itself, what is truly desirable? One should refuse *both* Deleuze's universalism of an innocent, heterogeneously perverse desire, *and* Lardreau's universalism of a generally poisoned desire.

Against the *nouveaux philosophes*, therefore, one should ask: are we condemned to Manicheanism, to the negative invocation of a sublimity which can only make the difference of an increasingly imperceptible delay to the slide of liberalism into quasi-fascism? For the emptiness of the sublime, of the sovereign will, is endlessly re-recruited by a rhetorical, Machiavellian strategy of

[104] Ibid., p. 16. Lardreau and Jambet, *L'Ange*, pp. 17–42, 213–24.

power. Or can we take again Augustine's step beyond the Manichees, can we conceive an alternative that is a real social practice, a transmission of desire that is (despite the overlays of power) still faintly traceable as a pure persuasion without violence? 'To conceive' means of course to experience, to discover, for we cannot know in the abstract that there is such a desire.

Only, therefore, if we can reinvoke, like Augustine, another city, another history, another mode of being, can we discover for ourselves a social space that is not the space of the *pagus* crossed with the *dominium* of an arbitrary, voluntarist God. In the final chapter, I shall start to delineate such a programme. But the Christian counter-history and counter-ontology perpetuates, breaks with, and fulfils a counter-history and counter-ontology already in part imagined by Plato and Aristotle. However imperfect the Greek contribution, it is yet part of what remains, despite everything, a single *Western* history of 'ethics': the imagination of 'the good' as an alternative to power. To oppose all secular reason, all secular social theory, we must make two returns: in the last analysis to the *Civitas Dei*, but in the first place to the 'aristocratic' republic of Plato and Aristotle.

11

Difference of Virtue, Virtue of Difference

Introduction

Just as, in the realm of contemporary architecture, alongside the trend to postmodernism, there exists also a not always easily distinguishable revival of neo-classicism, so also in the realm of social theory, nihilistic postmodernism is challenged by a more 'benign' postmodernism, which shares some of its themes, and yet also advocates some form of return to the perspectives of antique political philosophy. This advocacy of the antique is best represented today by Alasdair MacIntyre, although he is in part the heir of earlier writers like Jacques Maritain, Eric Voegelin and Leo Strauss. For MacIntyre, as for the present book, the validity of modern social theory – of liberal politics, political economy, sociology and Hegelianism-Marxism – is strictly confined to their homology with modern political practice, a practice that can be called into question.

Like the present book again, MacIntyre understands postmodern nihilism as occupying a special position between modern social theory and practice on the one hand, and a revived classicism on the other. Once secular reason has exposed its own efforts to ground itself in the universal, then its advocacy of a polity and an ontology which is confined to the (non)regulation of conflict through conflict emerges clearly to view. From now on, the secular means the nihilistic, and this practical and theoretical orientation cannot be seriously opposed by a repristination of enlightened reason, but only by a recovery of what secular reason initially refused, namely a social order grounded on *virtue*.

For a polity based on virtue, the goal of authority is not simply an effective peace and order, nor the representation of majority will, nor the liberty and equality of individuals, but rather the education of individuals into certain practices and states of character, regarded as objectively desirable goals for human beings as such. The possibility of such a politics depends upon the acceptance of the view that there is a 'right', and in this sense a 'natural' way for human beings to be, although this cannot be discovered from an empirical survey of our pre-cultural constitution. The latter approach, which appeals to the 'subordinate', is typical of modern natural law theory and the search for foundations. Instead, for a pre-modern perspective, the 'natural' mode for human existence is only discovered through aspiration to what transcends even humanity (Plato), or else, via social practice, to the fuller realization of the ends implicit in that practice (Aristotle). In both cases, the education of citizens (*paideia*), which is the differentiating mark of a politics of virtue, assumes that humans stand at the apex of a natural order, and that there is an objectively right way to be human, grounded beyond and above humanity, and not simply beneath or within it. In this sense, pre-modern social theory in the Platonic, Aristotelian and even stoic mould was not 'secular', and did not accord such a notion any validity. But without virtue, and after the collapse of modern natural law, which tried to find a cultural norm in a constant 'subordinate' element (self-preservation, the urge to freedom, production, etc.), what remains is the irreducible *difference* of opinion and aspiration, or the arbitrariness of impulse and invention. Inevitably, for MacIntyre, the ruling of such a denial of rule can only be capitalistic and bureaucratic: hence the futility of Marxism, which accepts all the assumptions of secular reason.

With none of the above do I essentially disagree, and the following chapter could be read as a temeritous attempt to radicalize the thought of MacIntyre, whose work I consider to merit the consideration already accorded to Weber, Durkheim, Marx and Nietzsche. Despite this, however, some of its space will be taken up by disagreements with him; disagreements which have something to do with the fact that I approach social theory finally as a theologian, while he approaches it as a philosopher. The key point at issue here is the role that must be accorded to Christianity and to Christian theology. For MacIntyre, it is true, the latter has come to matter more and more, but it remains the case that he opposes to the philosophy and practice of difference not, primarily, Christian thought and practice, but the antique understanding of virtue, with the accompaniments of Socratic dialectics, and the general link of reason to tradition. Of course, for MacIntyre, one must subscribe to some *particular* tradition, some *particular* code of virtue, and here he identifies himself as 'an Augustinian Christian'. But, all the same, the *arguments* put forward against nihilism and a philosophy of difference are made in the name of virtue, dialectics and the *notion* of tradition in general.

Against MacIntyre, I simply do not believe that there *are* any arguments against nihilism of this general kind. This statement should immediately cause readers to anticipate two things. First of all, in contrast to most critiques of MacIntyre, I do not find him to be *sufficiently* relativistic or historicist. Secondly, I do not hitch the cause of virtue to the cause of dialectics in the way that MacIntyre does (much more in *Whose Justice? Which Rationality?* than in the earlier *After Virtue*). Indeed, part of the project of this chapter could be described as 'the detachment of virtue from dialectics'. There is for me no method, no mode of argument that charts us smoothly past the Scylla of foundationalism and the Charybdis of difference. Nor do I find it possible to defend the notion of 'traditioned reason' in general, outside my attachment to a tradition which grounds this idea in the belief in the historical guidance of the Holy Spirit. The primacy given to teaching and tradition in the neo-Platonic and then Christian understanding of the *logos*, pushes the practice of virtue much closer to a rhetorical than a dialectical habit of mind – to a *logos* giving pride of place to opinion (*doxa*), testimony (*marturia*) and persuasion (*pistis*). This new linking of rhetoric to the cause of transcendence – already happening in Cicero and the Alexandrian schools – is passed over by MacIntyre, who associates rhetoric exclusively with loss of transcendence, loss of virtue and emergent individualism.[1]

Of course, MacIntyre recognizes, with Socrates, that the initial assumptions of dialectics – the customary virtues and opinions we subscribe to – are rhetorically mediated. However, he also believes that the dialectical questioning of the starting points establishes them more securely in their relationship to reality, if they constantly withstand sceptical interrogation.[2] Thus, perfectly contingent starting points progressively but negatively struggle free of the historical chrysalis and float upwards to universality. This 'securing' of virtue, I shall argue, is a new mode of foundationalism. Likewise I shall reject MacIntyre's dialectical rendering of the modification of tradition, and the abandonment of one tradition for another. This is particularly apparent in his account of the grafting of the Christian onto the Greek inheritance; Augustine's and Aquinas's ethical thought is validated primarily because they give better answers than the Greeks to Greek problems, according to Greek criteria. Such a perspective may not, however, do justice to the fact that the Fathers and the scholastics understood the beliefs grounding their ethics as matters of persuasion, or of faith. These positions of faith could not be dialectically inferred or called into question but were, rather, 'rhetorically' instilled. MacIntyre, of course, would not seek to deny this, for his position is not that Christian faith can be arrived at dialectically, but rather that, once accepted, it gives better answers to problems always found dialectically problematic. This does, however, imply an apologetic: there are strong grounds in a reason pressing towards universality for 'Greeks' to accept Christianity. A tension arises here, between MacIntyre's philosophic perspective upon Christianity on the one hand, which concedes the rhetorical, persuasive character of its fundamental texts, practices and credal beliefs, but then treats these only from the point of view of testing their validity by a universal method (dialectics), and, on the other hand, a theological perspective (whether that of Augustine or Aquinas, or Barth) which speaks in modes beyond the point where dialectics leaves off, namely, in terms of the imaginative explication of texts, practices and beliefs.

The dominance of the philosophic perspective in MacIntyre will not really allow him to enter as far into the task of explicating the *differentia* of Christian ethics as he would like. What he concentrates on in Augustine

---

[1] Alasdair MacIntyre, *Whose Justice? Which Rationality?* (London: Duckworth, 1988) pp. 55–6.
[2] Ibid., p. 71ff.

and Aquinas is what can be dealt with philosophically: for example, Augustine's discovery of the will as an element 'lacking' in ancient psychology, but obviously seen by MacIntyre, from a 'universal' perspective, as a valuable addition to the ethics of virtue. Aquinas's major achievement, for MacIntyre, is to have shown this, by integrating an account of will and intention into Aristotelian ethics, without surrendering their basic intellectualist orientation. Comparatively less attention is paid by MacIntyre to the theological validation of a different set of virtues from those favoured by the Greeks; these differences are indeed noted, but the real, measurable 'progress' has been made in terms of the general conception of the structure of an ethics of virtue and its accompanying psychology. The tradition-specific *content* that one pours into this container cannot easily come under discussion by MacIntyre because it does not fall within the purview of philosophy as he understands it. Thus at the *philosophic* level, an air of non-commitment hovers over MacIntyre's work, an implication even of the inevitable *liberalism* of philosophy itself.

If one focuses, like MacIntyre, on a general mode of procedure – dialectics – then it will be found that the more one is able to argue in favour of the objective good, in favour of justice, and of *paideia*, the less one can give any content to these things. Specific content seems to be a matter of rhetoric, of unmediable difference after all; hence MacIntyre suggests at the end of *Whose Justice? Which Rationality?* that his arguments could be developed in an Aristotelian, an Augustinian, a Thomist, or even a Humean fashion, for these are all 'traditioned' discourses, over against foundationalist versions of liberalism on the one hand, and nihilism on the other.[3] Can the appeal back to Plato and Aristotle then really rescue us from liberalism and secular reason? In retrospect, one may discover that the slide towards a merely vacuous universalism is inherent in 'metaphysics' (post-Platonic discourse) from the outset. Like MacIntyre, Plato tried to secure a remedy for plural difference, but like MacIntyre also, was unable fully to find a way of simultaneously pointing to the universally valid and objective and to the customary particulars which instantiate it.

I will argue that a virtue yoked to dialectics, and even to the Aristotelian account of practical reason, finds it impossible to do this. A solution is only really possible in terms of a tradition like Christianity, which starkly links particular to universal by conceiving its relationship to transcendence in a rhetorical fashion. In this respect, Christianity offers a social alternative to *either* the civic mode of sophistry and 'democratic' politics on the one hand, *or* dialectics and 'aristocratic' politics on the other.

However, the reader will notice that I speak of a 'solution', and this implies that I do not altogether mean to repudiate MacIntyre's apologetic manner of connecting antiquity to Christendom. Indeed, in a highly MacIntyrean way,

---

[3] Ibid., p. 401.

I will argue that one can retrospectively narrate Plato's and Aristotle's writings as a groping towards the linking of universal with particular, as also the individual with the whole, the family with the city, contemplation with practice – all achieved more satisfactorily by Christianity. This 'more satisfactorily' is objective in the sense that I identify a series of antinomies in Plato and Aristotle's accounts of virtue, the city and the individual soul, which they can never satisfactorily resolve within the terms of their inherited *mythos*, but which *are* resolved within the terms of the Christian *mythos*.

Despite this dialectical mode of procedure, I want to insist against MacIntyre that at this level of 'objective' reasoning one is only talking about the inner consistency of a discourse/practice, and that insofar as Christianity is able to render a discourse/practice more consistent, this *in no sense* necessarily suggests a new adequacy of discourse to 'reality'. Likewise, the greater coherence in the Christian account of virtue, the city and soul, does not imply, as I think it might for MacIntyre, that simply by antiquity's own criteria it should abandon its own *mythos* and embrace Christianity. This is where I see much narrower limits to dialectics than MacIntyre does: it is, for me, *never* sufficiently clear that the inherited criteria or rationality within a particular tradition will dictate the embracing of a new tradition (that, surely, is pure Hegelianism). No sufficient reason is here available, because the collapse, rather than the mere modification of a tradition, implies that what was once held together is now split asunder: in the present case, after the intervention of Christianity, antique *mythos* on the one hand, and the philosophy and politics of virtue on the other. If virtue is chosen, then one may well choose also Christianity, as the new conserver of virtue. But it remains open to one still to embrace instead the *mythos*, which now admits only an etiolated version of virtue. One could argue that stoic philosophy followed the latter path: in highly sophisticated conceptual terms it returned (in some measure), against the academics and peripatetics, to pre-Socratic perspectives with their greater closeness to fundamental pagan myths. And virtue in their philosophy got reduced to either resignation to the fate of one's place within the whole, or to private self-control, omitting, in either case, the civic sphere, which was the original space for the very meaningfulness of virtue. Not implausibly one can understand stoicism as a predecessor of both modernist liberalism and postmodernist nihilism; in the latter case, especially, we have seen how a pagan *mythos* can be more and more reaffirmed after the collapse of both virtue and Platonic reason.

MacIntyre, of course, wants to *argue* against this stoic-liberal-nihilist tendency, which is 'secular reason'. But my case is rather that it is only a *mythos*, and therefore cannot be refuted, but only out-narrated, if we can *persuade* people – for reasons of 'literary taste' – that Christianity offers a much better story. This all sounds much less serious than what MacIntyre has to offer, but I must still press my case. MacIntyre opposes to difference virtue upheld by dialectics, yet his deployment of dialectics will be shown still to belong to a foundationalist mode of metaphysics. Against difference, by contrast, I do not bring forward dialectics, *nor even* virtue in general, but rather Christian virtue in particular, which means that I can claim to be the more serious advocate of the conjunction of the universally objective with a particular social option. I cannot, like MacIntyre, recommend virtue in general, because, for me, Plato and Aristotle's account of the virtues founders on certain antinomies they lack the resources to resolve. In fact, within the terms of the antique *mythos*, their attempt to oppose virtue to difference fails, and their versions of virtue are always deconstructible to difference after all – this is especially shown to be the case in Plato's *Sophist*. Their ideas are only now redeemable *typologically*, as anticipations of the Christian *Civitas Dei*, although they still help to constitute the true city, just as Christ is partly *made up* of the Old Testament 'allegories' which foreshadow him, and which he recapitulated. But in this true city, I shall argue, in this and the final chapter, one has a variant of virtue that is *not* deconstructible to difference, but that also embraces an analogically understood difference (just as the alternative *mythos*, the stoic option, includes also an etiolated version of virtue). So to accept Christianity's 'resolutions' of the antinomies which afflicted antique virtue, one has also to accept a *non-dialectical* adjustment of the very notion of virtue, as an effect of Christian *mythos*. The new Christian 'non-heroic' virtue (almost a contradiction in terms) is also a virtue that less refuses difference.

The 'reconciliation of virtue with difference' (or of classicism with post-modernism – and again, one might compare architectural instances of this) suggests, of course, a kind of Hegelian synthesis of virtue and freedom, and the parallel is a deliberate one – although my synthesis is not dialectical and does not resume the other in identity nor abandon a residue of contingent otherness to indifference. The reconciliation is possible because Christianity, as I shall show, more emphatically construes virtue as that which aims towards, and is possible within, a fundamental condition of peace. If the *polis* can adjudicate to all their roles, and assign a virtuous way of life, then justice must be possible. And a justice that is living together in agreement, rather than mere mutual toleration, implies a real peace that is more than just suspended warfare. However, it will be shown that Plato and Aristotle found it finally impossible, because of the gravitational pull of Greek *mythos*, to imagine a civic or an ontological peace that was more than suspended warfare. This then marks the limits of their attempts to overcome sophistic 'liberalism', difference, or even secularity. It is, in fact, the source of all the antinomies regarding their conception of virtue. The more radical imagination of peace within the Christian *mythos*, and the separation of this imagination from any dialectical foundation, makes its version of virtue immune from deconstruction, which can *only happen* within the terms of 'philosophy', or of Greek metaphysics. Derrida and Deleuze only half realize this, because they do not grasp the new singularity of Christian theology.

Unlike MacIntyre, therefore, I do not oppose to nihilism the mere formality of a practice of virtue of some kind. Instead, I argue that the *content* of

Christian virtue – its promotion of charity, forgiveness, patience, etc. – which explicates the Christian *mythos*, actually reorganizes this formality, and thereby alone renders it capable of standing as an alternative to nihilism. In a way, the virtue that is charity is *not* virtue in the antique sense, because the very formality of *arete* and *virtus* is itself permeated by the content of preferred virtues, which are mainly of a heroic kind, and therefore ultimately related to victory in some sort of conflict. Is virtue that is in *no sense* fundamentally a victory, still virtue at all? The point is arguable, and it is not possible to keep separate the levels of form and content of virtue in the manner implied by MacIntyre. The issue of heroic versus non-heroic virtue cuts through this contrast. Moreover, if non-heroic virtue *alone* coherently divides 'ethical' virtue from the virtue of mere achievement (as I contend), then the most important historical watershed is not that which divides the times before and after virtue. Much more crucial, as Nietzsche and now René Girard surmise, is the fuller *invention* of virtue by Christianity, in the midst of a history manifestly or secretly dominated by warfare, heroism and difference. The peace/war thematic, which always accompanies antique reflections on virtue and justice, turns out to be just as fundamental as both these themes, and the key to their further explication.

In the following two sections, I try to foreground this thematic. In the first section, I show how it is involved in 'the opposing of virtue to difference' by the Greek poets and post-Socratic philosophers. After describing how they seek to transcend the inherently conflictual vision associated with sophistic relativism, I shall show that a parallel impulse motivates MacIntyre in the contemporary cultural situation. In the second section, I show how the peace/war thematic is the key to the deconstruction of an ethics of virtue which remains only at the antique level. In conclusion, I shall begin to indicate the new Christian imagination of peace, which is 'the reconciliation of virtue with difference'.

Virtue Against Difference

1   *The arrow and the circle*

In antiquity, the notions of virtue and peace were intrinsically, and yet problematically, linked. *Arete*, or virtue, was an excellence displayed in a noble, rule-bound conflict, the *agon*, whose issue was *hesuchia*, an honourable peace. This virtue was goal-directed, towards peace, though by means of war, and therefore might be well represented under the sign of an arrow. The goal itself, however, naturally loses both the element of directedness, and the element of combat: peace is circular, like a ritual dance, or else the laurel crown adorning the brow of the victor. If the circle is secured and defended by the arrows of the heroes, then within the circle itself, heroism must be severely constrained.

This ambiguous relationship between peace and virtue is dealt with mytho-logically by Hesiod, in *Works and Days*.[4] Originally there was a Golden Age, when the spontaneous fruitfulness of the earth secured conviviality, and skills of cunning and combat were not required. The divine-kingly rule of justice embraced the fertile earth without military interruption. But in the third, Bronze Age, titans rebelled against the gods, and ungovernable cyclopean warriors ravaged the earth. Regrettably, military methods had then to be resorted to if peace itself was to be restored. So the titans and the cyclops were driven back, and after the Bronze Age came the age of the heroes, of a mitigated conflict subject to rules, leading to a regained peace. In the succeed-ing Iron Age, which is our own, a regulated violence is also to be used against the earth, in the shape of the technical skills that are the gift of the titan, Prometheus. Far better even than heroism in warfare is a channelling of *eris* (strife) into economic competition, which sustains an abundant agriculture. Writing in an extra-civic, rural context, Hesiod celebrates agricultural labour and the rule of justice, but does not yet accord to the heroes that semi-divine status which they will acquire in the *polis*.[5]

The *polis* was originally an armed camp, a temporary settlement of war-riors, and continued to be marked by its origins. The original role of outsiders, of military nomads, in its constitution, is reflected in Plato's proposal in *The Republic* that guardians and auxiliaries – or political and military classes – be brought in from elsewhere to refound the city in an ideal form.[6] But while the military appear much more continuously necessary to the civic Plato than to the rural Hesiod, he is also alert to the ambiguity of the military character. To be serviceable, they must concentrate on being 'spirited': the exercise of strength must be their primary concern.[7] But this very training in autonomy, provided by the city for its own service, is also, unintentionally, a training in independence from the city; hence the guardians and auxiliaries are always a source of potential internal disruption. For this reason, stern measures must be taken to ensure that they will act like faithful guide-dogs, friendly to their masters, and savage only to strangers.[8] These measures are primarily educa-tive: torn away from their mothers at birth, the guardians must be made to believe that they are the offspring of the sacred earth of the city itself. Only the force of this myth will counteract a nomadic tendency, which might be supplemented by devotion to a mobile mother and family.[9] Likewise, their military training (and the guardians as well as the auxiliaries still retain something of a military type) must be accompanied by a philosophic

---

[4] Hesiod, *Works and Days*, pp. 10–40, 90–334.

[5] J.-P. Vernant, 'Le mythe Hésiodique des races', in *Mythe et Pensée chez lez Grecs*, vol. I (Paris: Maspero, 1978) pp. 13–80.

[6] Plato, *Republic*, 415d.

[7] Ibid., 440a5–440e7.

[8] Ibid., 375–6, 416, a–b.

[9] Ibid., 414d–15d.

education which breaks with the mainly bellicose stories of the poets, by stressing the goodness of God, and his unchanging character.

Divine goodness, for Plato, is clearly cut off from mere heroic excellence, for it is not an achievement, but an abiding state. It cannot, therefore, be primarily linked with 'the goods of effectiveness' (to use MacIntyre's term) or of mere pragmatic success. Instead, its connection must be rather with some assessment of the upshot, *the hesuchia* – of the circle rather than the arrow. Only the philosopher, and not the man of action, really encounters this divine good, which remains in a fashion ineffable, but when mediated to human beings takes the form of justice (*dike*), meaning the proper distribution of roles and rewards within the bounds of the city. The justice secured in the city constitutes a more reliable sort of peace: not a mere suspension of hostilities, but a peace founded upon agreement and organic harmony, when each person sticks to his allotted task.[10]

Already, at the end of the *Oresteia*, Aeschylus understood the *polis* as a new kind of asylum: as an end to the eternal process of vengeance within and between families, bestowed by a justice proceeding from an authority higher than the familial. Like Hesiod's benign *eris*, and Plato's propertyless guardians, the furies are for Aeschylus locked up, restrained, and yet, in a more measured form, unleashed, by the power of justice which adds punishments to its judgements which are 'eternal', and therefore without further fateful consequences.[11] In Plato the logic of the *polis* as 'the end of conflict' gets further spelled out: the actions of political authority transcend the mere reactions of a violated familial power, which are themselves nothing but further violations. Instead, the absoluteness, the 'goodness', 'truth', and 'justice' of these actions presupposes that they reflect an eternal order.

What justice secures, for Plato, is peace, rather than a regulated conflict; and what education secures is the 'musical' ability to play, which is yet more important than the heroic ability to fight. War is for the sake of peace, and not vice versa, and it is even excellence in the arts of peace which guarantees the strength necessary for war: 'we should live and pass life in the playing of games – *certain* games, that is, sacrifice, song and dance, with the ability to gain heaven's grace and to repel and vanquish an enemy when we have to fight him.'[12] Justice secures a circular repetition of harmony, and therefore is primarily 'brought down from heaven' and architectonically imposed, even if for the later Plato this must happen more approximately and according to an ever-vigilant renewal.

The new peace and justice of the *polis* is not, therefore, dictated by the immanence of conflictual striving, but supervenes upon this striving, putting an end to it, by determining what is truly excellent within warfare, and what is also virtuous as play, festival and conviviality beyond it. This new,

---

[10] Ibid., 433a–b.
[11] Aeschylus, *The Eumenides*, pp. 752–1047.
[12] Plato, *Laws*, 803d–e.

post-heroic virtue, as supervening and more stable, can only be conceived as a participation in an eternal goodness. The problem of participation in the idea of the Good does not then stand alone: it *is* also the problem of whether there can be moral goodness at all, and this problem is in turn identical with the problem of justice and peace, or of whether there can be an harmonious human order. How, within the *polis*, can one assign to their respective tasks and places many different activities, many different desires, many different social formations? Are these things (the civic 'many') in any way comparable, or hierarchically orderable to a single good, the good of the *polis* as such? If the answer is no (as it is for Lyotard and the nihilists), then only an 'effective' peace is possible, a 'secular' peace of temporarily suspended violence or regulated competition. This is how Plato understands the operation of 'democracy', which does not aim to nurture any character save heroic devotion to the *polis*, and which he believes is perpetually liable to be taken over by tyranny, or the dominance of a single power. In the absence of virtue, democracy remains for Plato the 'best state', which we are mostly doomed to put up with, yet it is not a real *polis*, not the real game of human beings, but a mere 'masque of centaurs'.[13] The *polis* can only become a musical, worshipping realm, when it is in the hands of those acquainted with the true 'art of government', which means those who understand how what is different can be combined, because they have a vision of their common, superordinate origin.[14]

This idea of the participation of all goods in a single, transcendent Good is therefore identical with the metaphysical invention of ethical good and justice (as Nietzsche realized). It does *not* imply (*pace* Martha Nussbaum and others) the denial of difference, nor the measurement of all goods as different quantities of a single substance.[15] This is clearly indicated by Plato in the *Phaedrus*, where the beholding of justice, 'the veritable knowledge of being, which veritably is', coincides with the circulation of contemplative souls with the gods in the heavenly revolution, and every soul is found in the company of his/her appropriate tutelary deity.[16] Our differences, affinities and inclinations are themselves grounded in the realm of forms, and justice, or the idea of the Good, is itself the harmonic blending of these differences: a blending which, in the preceding chapter, I chose to describe as 'analogical'. As the *Parmenides* clearly reveals, the form of the Good is essentially the *source* of diverse goodness, not simply 'like' the many goods in the sense of being their totality or the fullness of the common stuff from which they are composed.[17] It is however, in its absoluteness as source, problematically *incomparable* with finite goods. This is why, from *Parmenides* onwards, Plato talks

---

[13] Plato, *Statesman*, 303a–d.
[14] Ibid., 307d–11c.
[15] Martha C. Nussbaum, *The Fragility of Goodness* (Cambridge: Cambridge University Press, 1986) p. 108ff.
[16] Plato, *Phaedrus*, 247–8a.
[17] Ibid., 133a–5c.

less of a 'vertical' participation of goods in the Good, and more of a 'horizon-tal' participation among the goods themselves, and also among the eternal forms. There must still be an eternal standard, if there is to be justice, but now the discovery of this standard is more to be approached by determining what properly combines with what, and what mixtures are impossible within the finite order.[18]

The later Plato is therefore beginning to regard questions of peace, partici-pation and justice as immanent as well as transcendent in their scope. Aris-totle, by contrast, ceases to see these issues as *divine* matters at all, but as strictly confined to the human realm. Justice cannot be in question for the first mover, who is single and self-contained, nor for the heavenly realms, where Aristotle does not discover the same place for difference as Plato.[19] Certainly Aristotle is more concerned than his teacher for diversity within unity in the *polis*, but he has ceased to regard difference as a *transcendent* reality; this is strictly homologous with his attitude to justice. And because justice is less *theoretical* for Aristotle, it has shifted slightly from the realm of the circle to the realm of the arrow. It is achieved in the midst of a continuing internal conflict of reason with the passions, and a ceaseless civic rivalry for honours – not in the post-conflictual Dionysiac dance, where (one might say) Plato conceives *the city itself* as engaging in a kind of collective *theoria*. Still more than for Plato, *theoria* is, for Aristotle, an individual, extra-civic matter, now actually disconnected from questions of justice.[20] The concomitant effect of this is to drive justice and virtue back towards the traditional sphere of virtue as *metis*, or skilful cunning exercised in the context of a conflict. Of course, Aristotle reinvents this cunning – *phronesis* – so that it takes on a more 'moral' tinge, and is now to do with goods of excellence that are not mere 'goods of effectiveness'. Nevertheless, as I shall later argue, Aristotle's ethics is more agonistic than Plato's, and this ought to affect our assessment of the two thinkers.

Despite this agonism, and the separation of justice from *theoria* and the-ology, Aristotle still subscribes to the Platonic view that there is a single, practical or political good for human beings, and that this means the exercise of virtue according to one's role within the *polis*. Hence Aristotle also is concerned with a substantive justice which assigns to things their proper place: the order of the *polis* is a natural, eternally appointed order, even though it does not relate to the character of divinity. In part, this justice is permanently distributed in the arrangement of a social hierarchy. But within this bound there are no further rules for making commensurable what is inherently diverse and incommensurable. It is when one is faced with a particular case, when one sees what justice would be *here*, or *there*, that one actually grasps justice at all, and for this reason justice and law fall under

[18] Plato, *Sophist*, 249d–e.
[19] Aristotle, *Metaphysics*, 1072a18–1075a10. Leo Strauss, *The City and Man* (Chicago: Rand McNally, 1964) p. 21.
[20] Aristotle, *Nicomachean Ethics*, 1177a5–1179a25.

the sway of *phronesis*, of practical reason, which deals only with particulars and probabilities.[21]

Like Plato, therefore, Aristotle links the possibility of an objective virtue with that of a truly just *polis*, which can form its citizens' characters and assign to them particular tasks and objectives. For both thinkers, this is identical with what one might call 'the problematic of harmony', or the peaceful coordination of difference. Neither seeks to resolve this problem by inventing a reductive calculus; rather, they *both* resort to metaphysics. Plato declares that there is a higher unity of, or amidst differences, on a transcendent plane. Aristotle declares that in groping toward an immanent *telos* for this life, our practical reason can constantly discover in the particulars an approximation to just and peaceful harmonizations.

2   The revival of an ethics of virtue

In a way, the whole of academic and peripatetic thought is about this problematic: they are both 'civic philosophies' concerned to undergird a true 'aristocratic' polity based on virtue, which implies a substantive peace and an objective justice. Earlier philosophy was perceived by Socrates as specifically anti-civic: either, like Parmenides, it celebrated the identity of everything, and so downgraded civic life to illusion, or else, like Heraclitus, it celebrated the ultimacy of flux, diversity and conflict, a nomadic military order, which could only envisage the *polis* as a temporary encampment of natural forces.[22] The city can only become a subject of philosophical discussion, or even be related to ultimate realities, when an *intermediary* realm between the one and the many is granted ontological reality. This realm is not one of chaotic diversity, but a multiplicity ordered, though not cancelled out, by unity. Dialectics is supposed to be the art which shows how the many is ordered – which combinations are possible, and which not.[23] Hence the problem of logic, in Plato, is one and the same with the problem of justice, just as the possibility of philosophy is related to the possibility of the true polity.

These reflections are vital when one comes to consider why Plato and Aristotle's ethical and political ideas are the subject of a revival, as best represented by the writings of MacIntyre. For there is a perceived correspondence between their social-intellectual situation and our own. We find ourselves in the midst of a debased democratic politics, frequently tending to tyranny, and at the same time struggling for responses to 'non-civic' philosophies which instil an uncompromising relativism. For MacIntyre, it is especially significant that one can interpret Socratic thought – our 'philosophy' – as commencing in a response to philosophies which either collapsed all

---

[21] Aristotle, *Nicomachean Ethics*, 1140a1–630, 1145a10.

[22] Aristotle, *Metaphysics*, 987b1–5.

[23] Plato, *Statesman*, 283c–284c. *Sophist*, 249d–255d. Paul Ricoeur, *Être, Essence et Substance chez Platon et Aristote* (Strasbourg: CDS, 1957).

differences, or rendered them arbitrary and conflictual.[24] For already, in antiquity, the relativist problem intruded: not so much with respect to general cultural, linguistic and historical differences, as more specifically in reference to the conventionality of human laws. Plato notes that for many thinkers human inventions, especially laws, are shadowy things compared with natural realities like air and fire: he argues, instead, that they are equally natural, because derived from mind, which is itself nearer to ultimate being than physical entities.[25]

MacIntyre's return to Plato and Aristotle belongs, therefore, in the context of a contemporary response to the problem of relativism. Plato's and Aristotle's solutions to this problem acquire a new appeal once it it seen that modern rationalist/empiricist attempts to ground ethics in universal 'natural' facts about human nature – desire for pleasure, avoidance of pain, natural sympathy or the freedom of human will – are untenable. Moreover, by adopting Platonic or Aristotelian solutions, one can argue that modern relativism is itself but the reflex of the falsely dogmatic claims of foundationalism. This claim does, however, sit uneasily with the recognition that relativism had already appeared in antiquity as a practical problem and an initial stimulus to thought, rather than as a mere consequence of the collapse of universalizing claims. And, in fact, in post-Renaissance times also, a relativistic scepticism often precedes a later dogmatic rationalism. Nevertheless, the idea that the antique tradition provides an alternative to foundationalism, and so prevents also a sceptical backlash, is crucial to MacIntyre's position.

By refusing foundationalism in ethics, one refuses mainly the attempt to define the goodness of an ethical action in terms of some more fundamental, 'non-moral' good which can be non-controversially recognized by everyone – such as a state of emotional happiness, instinctual sympathy or the preservation of human freedom. The former two approaches subordinate action to consequences (problematically assuming a uniform calculus for their assessment) while the latter subordinates it to the will behind the act: if the will, and not the act, is the thing to be primarily characterized as good, then it can only be the freedom of the will itself that is unqualifiedly good, because any more diverse and precise recognition of goodness – for example 'it is good to be generous' – involves a primary reference to an action, not to a will, motivation or intention. If neither the subordination of action to consequence nor to willed motivation really succeeds in giving us a universal ethics that can direct our behaviour, then one is left with the genuinely wide scope of *sittlich*, customary morality, which does not just provide procedures for taking isolated 'ethical decisions', but prescribes a variegated list of virtues appropriate to different social roles. Hence virtuous action does not instantiate a pure motivation, making it 'legally correct' (as for Kant), and nor does it seek to promote maximally beneficial consequences (as for the utilitarian tradition),

[24] MacIntyre, *Whose Justice?*, pp. 78, 392.
[25] Plato, *Laws*, 889a–90d.

but is itself at once a 'habit' to be acquired, and a goal to be aimed at. This goal, unlike the punctuality of either will or consequence, has a certain 'density of texture', for a 'good' action is one performed skilfully, with precision and nuance, out of the depth of a long practice. Ethics becomes a kind of artistry applied to one's own actions.

However, since such an ethics is not a species of expressive emotivism, which would not be able to sustain the notion of the action as the primarily good thing, this account assumes a social setting like that of the *polis*, which in its *paideia* prescribes for its members genuine 'practices' (MacIntyre's term). That is to say, sets of actions desirable in themselves and leading only to their own increase, or to the promotion of yet more important actions with which they are in intentional, and not merely instrumental continuity. The question of the possible arbitrariness of this 'unfounded' promotion of certain virtues does not really arise at the individual level, because for the individual within a world embodying *Sittlichkeit* (like that of the *polis*) virtues are 'facts' about his world, and not evaluations applied to it – for example, one would not be able to describe 'factually' what a judge or a teacher was, without reference to what constitutes excellence in these professions. And such an absence of a fact/value distinction can be philosophically supported by the reflection that all our 'factual' descriptions are mediated by cultural codings, which simply *are* the world as it presents itself to us, not something coming 'between' us and the world. There is then no reason to think that our evaluative codings, both ethical or aesthetic, are more subjective than all our other codings in daily use.

This, however, only shifts the problem of relativism to the level of a culture as a whole. The individual may move in an apparently solid, factual *ethos*, but there are in space and time many such worlds, which differ and often conflict in terms of what they deem to be valuable. The curious, although highly interesting paradox of MacIntyre's ethical philosophy, is that the same appeal back to an ethics of virtue invokes at once a metaphysical, and at the same time a historicist dimension. What saves the *sittlich* ethic from scepticism is the belief, entertained in different ways by both Plato and Aristotle, that the society of the *polis* known to them – especially if it were to take an improved form – reflects in its order a 'proper' and natural ideal for humanity. Yet what is one to do when one is faced with many different societies, all making similar claims? MacIntyre rightly insists that one can only have a true ethic of virtue, rather than an etiolated modern *Moralität*, if one situates oneself within a tradition, and initially accepts its standards upon its own authority. As he puts it, one must place oneself within a 'narrative', or the accepted and ever-to-be-repeated 'plot formation' of a particular society.

However, this insight into the relativity of one's starting point – that one begins by embracing a *mythos*, not a proposition – was not fully available to Plato or Aristotle. For while MacIntyre may have repudiated the Enlightenment, he has certainly not gone back on *Renaissance* historicism, or the insight that we make our own cultural world through the invention of language and other signifying systems. He is not, however, content to leave the matter at the point of saying that one might embrace by 'faith' a particular ethos because of its persuasive power of attraction, while at the same time maintaining the universal rightness for humanity of this way of life. Instead, MacIntyre is still interested in a mode of dialectical validation for narrative preference. Consequently, his modern historicism must more and more be forced within the confines of a quasi-Hegelian dialectics, a confinement which actually denies its radical character, along with the affirmation of the priority of *mythos*.

In the next section, I shall show how MacIntyre, by subordinating narrative to dialectics, implicitly confines himself within the antinomies of the antique ethics of virtue which dissolve it into difference, and ensure that it cannot, after all, provide a metaphysical grounding for the possibility of human peace. In the first sub-section, I will argue that MacIntyre's realism conflicts with his historicism, and in the second, that he actually downplays the potentially more relativizing, rhetorical aspects in Aristotle. This means that MacIntyre is more firmly bound within Aristotle's ethical categories than Aristotle himself, by making them more emphatically a matter of universal reason and natural law. In the next two sub-sections I shall attempt a deconstruction of these categories, suggesting that within their terms alone the break with a 'heroic' ethics and mere 'goods of effectiveness' is only precariously and even incoherently achieved. In the final sub-sections, I shall trace this incoherence back to the limits posed by Greek *mythos* itself, which generates three 'antinomies of antique reason'.

Difference Against Virtue

1   Narrative, relativism and dialectics

The fact that MacIntyre is unwilling to push cultural situatedness to the limit can easily be concealed by his defence of a strong thesis of incommensurability. Arguing against Davidson, Putnam and others, MacIntyre claims that in certain cases, the signifying terms of one cultural outlook simply cannot be translated into the signifying terms of another, without betrayal and distortion.[26]

Davidson's and Putnam's contentions against this position run roughly as follows. Our sense of something 'real', in any particular instance, depends upon our ability to connect this up with all the other elements of what we take to be meaningful. If we are unable to make any such connections whatsoever, then the upshot will not be a recognition of 'incommensurability', but rather pure incomprehension. It is *possible* that this incomprehension may imply that we are up against an alternative *schema* of understanding, incommensurable with our own, but given the holistic, infinitely ramifying and interlocking

[26] MacIntyre, *Whose Justice?*, pp. 326–403.

character of linguistic meaning which alone provides us with a 'reality', we would never be able to recognize, or encounter such an alternative *schema*. This means that there is actually no justification for talking about 'schemes' of knowledge at all, as if there were different linguistic universes standing as 'third things' between knowing subjects, on the one hand, and a reality 'in itself' on the other. Where we are faced with incomprehension of another language or culture, then the presumption must be, not of an entirely alien 'world view', but rather that we have not yet discovered our own linguistic equivalents for those strange signs. Because we have *simultaneously* to find these equivalents, and ascribe beliefs to the alien culture, in a situation of first encounter (or of 'radical interpretation'), one can never in fact ascribe beliefs, however 'alien', without finding some verbal equivalents, and so, in some fashion, connecting up these beliefs to what we already 'know'. Cultural differences, therefore, cannot be totally incomparable, nor ever escape the scope of our usual processes of assessment and valuation (however complex and problematic these may be).[27]

MacIntyre, as Stephen Fowl (partly following Jeffrey Stout) has pointed out, does not really offer very complete counter-arguments to this position.[28] However, one can see that in general he wants to pose against it the idea that one can only really 'learn' another culture if one becomes fluent in its language and signifying practices, to the point where one has the 'poetic' ability only available to the insider to make an original move in the use of a language, and yet still make a claim for the 'rightness' of this move in terms comprehensible by that culture. The problem here, of course, as Fowl rightly says, is that it suggests that one can only understand a view by actively embracing it, only know Greek religion, for example, though initiation into the cult of Demeter. A second problem, which Stout and Fowl also indicate, is that one cannot talk about 'incommensurable' options unless there is *some* common subject matter in question; otherwise one just has different microcosms lying peacefully alongside each other, like an inkpot and a radish. Stephen Fowl argues on these bases that a radical incommensurability of meaning is neither defensible nor necessary for MacIntyre's relativistic claims, which are really more to do with incommensurability of truth. One can comprehend two different meanings, two different solutions, and yet still have no means of deciding between them.

There can be no hesitation with respect to the second problem. There must be *some* background of assumed agreement for a radical disagreement even to be possible – and MacIntyre would presumably assent to this. However, in the case of the first problem, MacIntyre is surely right to deny that an outsider's knowledge is just equivalent to that of the insider: the difference

---

[27] Donald Davidson, 'Radical interpretation' and 'On the very idea of a conceptual scheme', in *Inquiries into Truth and Interpretation* (Oxford: Oxford University Press, 1984) pp. 125–41, 183–99.

[28] Jeffrey Stout, *Ethics after Babel* (Boston: Beacon, 1988) pp. 82–105, 191–219. Stephen Fowl, 'Could Horace talk with the Hebrews? Translatability and moral disagreement in MacIntyre and Stout' (unpublished).

is small, but vital. For the outsider can know all the rules, even the rules for modifying the rules, and in many circumstances will be able to predict the behaviour of the cultural aliens. However, he will be unlikely to have the ability for 'poetic' innovation, nor to be able to predict this, precisely because the sense of a continuity-in-difference involves an imprescribable judgement which necessitates a belief that the tradition in question is 'going somewhere', pressing towards a *telos* that it can never adequately express in words. The outsider, being by definition a non-believer in this immanent/transcendent directionality, will only be able to make innovations which he finds 'attractive' in a playful spirit, but is bound to see these as essentially arbitrary departures, not further specifications of an elusive *telos*. At this limit one can say that the difference between a committed, insider perspective, and an uncommitted, outsider one, does amount to a difference of description as to what is going on. For the insider, without belief, the understanding of the outsider can only be partial. So any claim to full understanding on the part of the outsider *must* negate the alien tradition's own self-understanding.

In discussions between insider and outsider there is always, therefore, a hovering, if usually postponed disagreement, even about meaning. Stout and Fowl would be correct, however, to insist that these discussions are endlessly possible, and that this possibility implies that one can *entertain* culturally alien meanings, understand them at least up to a point, yet without embracing them. The expression 'to entertain' seems usefully to suggest that one holds the notion somehow in theatrical brackets, on a stage aside from one's usual ruminations. This suggestion, nonetheless, propels us beyond the terms of the discussion hitherto. For the trouble is that both sides of this argument still assume a united mental subject. Yet in point of fact, we are not wholly united individuals occupying a single 'holistic' world; instead we find it quite possible to hold inside our heads several subjectivities, even if some of these are merely 'entertained'. Thus, if I am bilingual, I can almost become American in the USA, and I may be haunted by the disturbing sense that my emergent 'American' character is in some ways in radical discontinuity with my British one. Davidson is wrong: the alternatives are not between finding English equivalents for American, and an incomprehension implying either ineffable otherness or else a failure of linguistic skill. Something else happens: I simply become American *as well as* British, or more American for a time, before reverting. As Paul Feyerabend pointed out against Putnam, translation is not the vital crux of the problem of relativism, because to negotiate 'the Other' one can bypass the moment of translation altogether – were this not so, infants would never learn their native tongue.[29]

So, for an alien tongue to be comprehensible to us, need not mean that we have found some linguistic equivalents, merely that we have begun to be ourselves alien to our former selves through the process of the encounter. Moreover, Davidson and Richard Rorty fail to grasp the full implications of

---

[29] Paul Feyerabend, *Farewell to Reason* (London: NLB, 1987) pp. 265–72.

their own insight that language is not a 'third' medium between the subject and the world.[30] If the world of organized figures and signs is simply the always temporary and yet endlessly connected world in which we move, constantly unifying and dissolving, then 'holism' of language does not really possess any single unity, for this notion would be the shadow of the idea that language is 'correct' in its reflection of stable external 'objects', or else in its 'expression' of the unified will of subjects. The absence of any *schema* separable from content does not imply one world, but an infinity of different worlds, discontinuous as well as continuous. This is why pragmatism, as Deleuze realized, cannot recognize only a single, pragmatic standard, but must pass immediately over into a philosophy of difference.[31] Without representation or expression, the standard of language and action is 'what works'. But everything works. To be anything at all, a thing (*pragma*) must work, and this cannot supply us with a criterion of choice. Let us certainly choose something that works – 'a machine'. But machines offer endless diversities of pleasure, and these pleasures jostle and compete within finite space and time.

A coherence theory of truth, such as variously espoused by Davidson, Putnam and Rorty, does not therefore provide a barrier against scepticism and radical incommensurability. This could only be the case if there were one, single coherence, the shadow of a stable given world, or a united, sheerly 'spiritual' subject. The pragmatist strategy of substituting talk of actions and practices for talk of 'meanings' does not thereby refer us to a single unambiguous standard of comprehension. On the contrary, it is at the most practical, the most 'material' level that radical differences arise; in the same physical space one can build a cathedral or a nuclear power station, but there is no 'commensurability' between the desire to build the one or the other, and the difference in the organization of their structures, their configurations and symbolic evocations, is as great as that between the jargon of nuclear technology and the language of prayer. Both these languages have to be mastered on their own terms; there can be no question of an even partially adequate 'translation', but the same truth applies to the logic of the cathedral and the logic of the nuclear power station. Both structures 'work'. They remain in place and organize flowings in and out of human beings, materials and signs, but there is no neutral standard of measurement between their different modes of working, and no way of neutrally resolving the conflict that might arise over the use of this particular, limited physical space.

Within our culture there are cathedrals and nuclear power stations, theologies and technologies, arts, sciences and so forth. In consequence, incommensurability is always already present. Besides endless overlaps, like the ground and the building materials common to both structures, there are also endless

---

[30] Richard Rorty, 'The contingency of language', in *London Review of Books*, 17 April 1976, pp. 3–6.
[31] Deleuze and Guattari, *A Thousand Plateaus*, p. 146.

disjunctures, endless things not truly comparable, though often in competition, because they have internal properties peculiar to their own size, position, speed, inclusion of other things – just as a triangle or a square is a unique world in itself, whose laws arise from its own construction and are not deducible from other geometric figures. Every stabilization, every removal from a series, every drawing of a circle, in effect constitutes an incomparable 'singularity', which, were it not in some ways incommensurable with other things, would not 'stand out', would not be repeatable or memorable, would not, in fact 'occur'. Even the 'parts of a whole' are only recognizably parts, because they are detachable as 'elements', or as worlds in themselves which could belong to another whole, or become themselves a context for inclusion. The problem of incommensurability, of establishing orders of priority amidst these disjunctures (between different arts, between arts, games, science, technology and warfare, and *within* an art, a game, a science itself) is therefore a problem *internal* to every culture, as Plato's *Republic* already recognizes.

If follows that there is no such thing as the encounter between one culture 'as a whole', and another culture 'as a whole'. Rather, existing discontinuities can be added to, or else existing consistencies can be modified. In the latter case, the finding of equivalences in translation does not just leave the host language unaffected, as if the apparently alien, in order to be understood, must be 'accommodated' within the single world of pragmatically explicated meaning. Instead, it makes a difference to the host language, effecting a lesser or a greater alteration to its stable shapes, its characteristic patterns of utterance.

If these arguments are accepted, then MacIntyre is right to insist, against Davidson, on the reality of incommensurability of meaning. This kind of incommensurability *is* important for any serious relativism, including that of MacIntyre, because relativism *assumes* the priority of meaning over truth. There are only undecidable questions of truth because truth is relative to a 'perspective', or a particular preferred syntax or figuration for construing reality. But if all meanings could be expressed in the 'same' language, then this 'sameness' would only have application if it implied common standards of assessment, and the possibility of a neutral adjudication. A single language of meaning, as Davidson assumes, suggests that we can at least hope to resolve our disagreements through continued conversation and practice. MacIntyre's quarrel with Davidson *is* crucial for the upholding of radical difference.

However, I have defended MacIntyre in terms he might not much like. That is to say, I have argued for incommensurability on 'linguistic idealist' grounds, whereas MacIntyre – curiously enough – wishes to charge idealism with an incapacity to recognize cultural difference.[32] Only philosophic realism, he contends, which does not confuse its own present outlook with the way things really are, will be open to other ways of looking at things.

---

[32] MacIntyre, *Whose Justice?*, p. 169.

No doubt this sounds seductive for the many 'critical realist' theologians of our times, but it assumes, first, that different cultural discourses are approximations to the same external (even if not independently specifiable) reality, and, second, that our openness to the recognition of cultural difference keeps pace with our acknowledgement of new dimensions of 'reality'. In this way, MacIntyre totally subordinates the telling and acting out of different stories to the dialectical process of question and answer which gradually opens up for us the real. His own, imperfectly developed arguments for incommensurability of meaning are not intended to deny the priority of truth over meaning, nor the ultimate 'sameness' of truth. Instead, they are supposed to guarantee the irreplaceable position of 'traditions' and of historical narratives within the dialectical process.

MacIntyre claims that his outlook is at once historicist and dialectical, yet denies that this is Hegelian.[33] However, all that he seems to mean by this denial is that the historical process will not issue in a self-perspicuous moment of total illumination. Otherwise, the attempt to comprehend decisive narrative shifts in dialectical terms sounds thoroughly Hegelian. As a 'realist', however, MacIntyre is not open to the Hegelian insight that the object of knowledge itself undergoes modification in the course of being known. What one is left with, instead, is a curious overmapping of the historical gap between present and past epoch upon the epistemological gap between knower and known. As MacIntyre puts it, 'the original and most elementary version of the correspondence theory of truth is when it is applied retrospectively as a correspondence theory of falsity.'[34] In other words, the idea of a possible gulf between belief and reality is opened up at the point where one recognizes a discrepancy between older beliefs, and the world as one now understands it. This initial recognition may challenge a culture to produce an explanation, in terms of its current beliefs, of how the earlier beliefs arose, and of why such mistakes could be made. Aristotle, one may note, already understood a *philosophical* history of philosophy to be of this kind: he systematically explains earlier Greek ontologies as stumbling dialectic steps towards his own position.[35] This narrative can indeed be considered an integral part of Aristotle's metaphysics, because it shows how earlier positions collapsed in the face of objections, and how Aristotle's own position can still comprehend why the previous explanations were put forward. (For this reason, MacIntyre understands Aristotle to be, in this instance, *already* historicist.) Nevertheless, this story is only the story of the emergence of a discourse which transcends story, which indeed *puts an end* in ancient Greece (at least for a time) to the cultural primacy of *mythos*. For the new discourse involves the dialectical testing of an assertion through comparison with a present, stable and therefore non-narratable reality. All the dialectical questions and successful

---

[33] MacIntyre, *Whose Justice?*, p. 360.
[34] Ibid., p. 356.
[35] Aristotle, *Metaphysics*, 983a24–993a10.

rebuttals can be, must be, reiterated in the present era; therefore they belong to no specific time and place. But MacIntyre implies that the story of the times and places was more than accidental to the comprehension of the emergent 'superior' philosophical position. He makes Hegelian-sounding noises and yet suggests that his own historicism is already contained within the role of the dialectical process in Plato and Aristotle. But just for this reason, MacIntyre's historicism cannot really be a true historicism at all, as I shall now show.

In the curious 'overmapping' already referred to, MacIntyre suggests that the narrated gap between past and present is more than accidentally necessary to the perception of the gap between opinion and being. It is clear, however, that he cannot really mean this, and that *mythos* is no more constitutive of *theoria* for MacIntyre than it was for Aristotle. This latter situation would only pertain if *either* the narration of earlier theoretical positions from the vantage point of later ones charted the evolution of an internally necessary logical process, as for Hegel, *or* one was retracing the simple complexification of a story, in which a first narrative thread had been subsumed by a later one. In this second case, the development is also strictly internal, but there is no question of the later narrative emphasis exhibiting a manifestly broader context or scope than the earlier one. It is simply that what was once the whole of the plot is now but a part of a larger one, while fully retaining its latent, 'elemental' power to encompass in itself the themes by which it is temporarily swamped; as, for example, a family can once again suck politics back within its dynastic sway, or the selling of State secrets can become the sub-plot of a sexual intrigue. For MacIntyre, however, the superiority and broader scope of the later theoretical development can be, in certain circumstances, irreversibly apparent. But no *narrative* could ever make this apparent, because every lived story can always be re-enacted backwards, can undo its upshot by later practice. Therefore, the superiority is not constituted by narration, and this really contributes nothing to the theoretical triumph; instead, one narrates the story of how some positions have irrevocably succumbed to dialectical falsification. Sometimes MacIntyre describes such falsification, in a distinctly post-seventeenth century, and indeed, Popperian-sounding 'scientific' mode, as also experimental falsification. But the essence of this latter kind of falsification is the exact repeatability of experiment, and therefore an *escape* from the narrative contingencies of place and time.

For MacIntyre, therefore, dialectics – the questioning of an assumed position (or of nature) through question and answer – has priority over narrative; it is not fused in a perfect balance with historicity. Is this, however, necessarily wrong? There is, certainly, an important scope for dialectics in the uncovering of incoherencies in positions hitherto received. As stated in the introduction to this chapter, I myself will later engage in such an exercise with respect to the relation of peace to ontology in antique philosophy. However, this procedure cannot really cope with the entire range of intellectual development within and across traditions. Most rival positions cannot be easily adjudicated in terms of their coherence and withstanding of critique alone. Positions alter and modify, not just in response to criticism, but quite gratuitously, as an explication or an extension of their reach of application. The 'poetic' ability to innovate, which MacIntyre discusses, yet ultimately ignores, is responsible for many decisive shifts in sensibility when an older outlook suddenly appears 'worn out', though it has certainly never been refuted. The most crucial case, however, is that where one tradition is abandoned for another.

Here MacIntyre wants to say that such a switch can be legitimated according to the criteria of the older tradition itself; in other words, it becomes apparent that in the light of the newer tradition the earlier one is incoherent and can explain less of what it seeks to explain than the newer one.[36] However, if the criteria are still in full force, and if, as MacIntyre says, all criteria are tradition-specific, then how can we really talk of a rational switch in tradition? If a tradition has *really* collapsed, then this must mean that its criteria – which are part of its very woof and warp – have split asunder. Only what is now a mere isolated *aspect* of the older tradition (and therefore treacherous to its integrity) can acknowledge the newer one, else the whole of the older one would still be in full force. Hence there is a *questionableness* about every switch of tradition, which escapes dialectical adjudication. What triumphs is simply the persuasive power of a new narrative, which gives an important position to some themes and characters in the old plot, while abandoning others that were once equally important.

It is similarly impossible to adjudicate the claim to 'explain more'. Every tradition constitutes for itself a penumbra of what appears vague or obscure, but this is positioned in relation to its sense of what can be clearly known: for example, the Middle Ages defined the ultimate springs of motion in the universe as lying within the power/knowledge of God and therefore as outside human comprehension. This penumbra may recede or shift just a little within bounds that do not fundamentally overthrow the tradition: thus the recognition of 'secondary causes' can be seen as quite compatible with agnosticism concerning the operation of divine causality. However, when one tradition embraces another as 'explaining more', this does not just mean that new light has been shed on the hitherto incomprehensible. On the contrary, it means that the veil of the penumbra is rent, and with it the whole distribution of possible knowledge that belonged to a particular paradigm. A Galileo can claim to give the 'elemental' laws of motion of the universe, because he now claims that God operates by means of mathematical and mechanical formulae fully surveyable by us also. If it is true that the Galilean and then Newtonian understandings of motion were more 'successful' than earlier views, then this was not because they 'explained more' – no independent scale of measurement exists – but because they proved to provide models more easily buildable, repeatable and operable in human practice. MacIntyre often takes scientific development as his paradigm for the emergence of a 'manifestly' more comprehensive theory, yet in this case greater comprehensiveness

---

[36] MacIntyre, *Whose Justice?*, pp. 164–82, 356–60.

always means just greater operational success; a state of affairs always in principle subject to reversal, if an earlier, abandoned yet not incoherent theory should suddenly be built into mechanic patterns of interaction with the environment, allowing a yet greater control over this same interaction. And of course, reversions are much more likely in areas where control and pre-dictability are not the only criteria of pragmatic value.

MacIntyre's stress on a diversity of reasons, corresponding to a diversity of traditions, needs, therefore, to be radicalized. The encounter of these diverse reasons cannot be contained and mediated by dialectical conversation alone: at the limits of disagreement it will take the form of a clash of rhetorics, of voices addressing diverse assemblies. And decisive shifts within traditions, or from one tradition to another, have to be interpreted as essentially 'rhetorical victories'. In a rhetorical perspective, narrative really does cease to be a mere appendage, because here the story of the development of a tradition – for example, in the case of Christianity, a story of preachings, reflections, visions, speculations, journeyings, miracles, martyrdoms, vocations, marriages, icons painted and liturgies sung, as well as of intrigues, sins and warfare – really *is* the argument for the tradition (a perilous argument indeed, which may not prove persuasive at all), and not just the story of arguments concerning a certain X (for example the nature of human virtue) lying outside the story.

2   Dialectics and rhetoric in Aristotle

It is important to note, at this point in the argument, that the place which MacIntyre accords to dialectics may not, in fact, be fully consistent with Aristotle's account of practical reason, which is what he primarily wishes to defend.

For Plato, virtue was a matter of contemplative knowledge of the Good, and therefore a proper subject for dialectical reasoning. MacIntyre sees more continuity between Plato and Aristotle in this respect than most commenta-tors, and argues that Plato's *Republic* posits an *arche-telos* for human, political behaviour, without specifying its content, and that, Aristotle then attempts to provide that content.[37] Hence MacIntyre suggests that, for Aristotle, *theoretical* reason still posits the goals of human action, but that specification of these goals is constantly modified through the deliberations of *phronesis* or *practical* reason (already accorded an important place in Plato) about how these ends are to be realized.

However, Aristotle never speaks of a theoretical contemplation of 'the Good' as an ideal source of notions of justice, only of the eternal motions of the heavenly bodies and the first mover which are supremely 'good' in their degree of self-sufficiency and self-propulsion. Theoretical knowledge, *epis-teme*, is about the stable and the universal, and only extends to the sublunary world to the degree that one can identify stable channels for the flux of life:

[37] Ibid., pp. 88–102.

the constitution of form and matter, the hierarchical gradation of genera and species. This hierarchical order of Being is 'good' insofar as it forms an organic whole, with the relatively 'aimless' lives of temporal creatures being directed to the service of the eternal bodies, just as slaves in a household serve free men. The comparison of the *cosmos* to the *oikos*, rather than to the *polis*, shows that for Aristotle the cosmic good does not resemble the issues of justice that constantly arise in the dealings of free citizens.[38] These issues, less prescribable by reference to a pre-established social order, are given more metaphysical ultimacy by Plato, precisely because he posits an idea of the Good *beyond* any order of Being, which *theoria* can ascend to and relate to questions of justice.

Accordingly, the opening sections of the *Nicomachean Ethics* belong to *episteme* to the degree that they concern the position of human beings in the order of Being, and through the use of dialectical interrogation establish that human beings are creatures who seek to realize their true end in a state of happiness.[39] However, when it comes to asking if there is a single goal which provides true happiness, it is much less clear that the reasoning remains purely theoretical. The dialectical arguments now have to make strong use of examples: as in, particular men have particular functions, so should not the human race have a function also?[40] Now examples, Aristotle makes clear elsewhere, are especially resorted to in rhetoric, whose mode of dialectical reasoning is imperfect; they offer a kind of approximation to induction (*epagoge*) which ideally does not have recourse to comparison with something outside the field being dealt with, but from within this field alone infers the general case, or the most primary cause.[41] Aristotle can only make out a *probable* argument, making use of examples, for a single human end, and he can only make a rhetorical, persuasive appeal to human beings to recognize the political life as the realization of that end. (By contrast, dialectics is merely 'likely' reasoning as compared with *episteme*, simply because it proceeds by negation towards a clarification and does not offer a positive demonstration – this procedure depends finally on assumed definition and the law of identity, not on analogical illustration.)[42] The appeal is made not to our theoretical faculty, but rather to our natural appetite and sense of practical wisdom.

Access to the practical *arche-telos*, in its initially indeterminate, diffuse character, is provided not through dialectical induction (as MacIntyre suggests) but through natural energies and drives towards happiness in the form of courageous strength, pleasure, riches, honour, fluency of speech, spiritedness and friendship.[43] Then comes the question of whether these things can be integrated together, such that one's life pursues a single, although complex

[38] Aristotle, *Metaphysics*, 1075a10–24.
[39] Aristotle, *Ethics*, 1094a1–1103a10.
[40] Ibid., 1097a15–1098a20.
[41] Aristotle, *Rhetoric*, I i.
[42] Aristotle, *Topics*, 1.1 100a–b. *Posterior Analytics*, 71a1–71b20. *Ethics*, 1139618–36.
[43] Aristotle, *Ethics*, 1104a30–1105b2.

goal. Here the most that a general, quasi-epistemic reflection can offer is the rhetorical appeal to examples, and the likelihood that the political life, which uniquely attempts such an integration – implying also an integration of the domestic, technical, economic, literary and military spheres – provides the natural single end for humankind. However, such rhetorical induction will not give the content of integration, nor the principles of political organization. This is only provided through the operation of *phronesis*, or practical wisdom, which does not concern itself with ends, but with deliberation concerning the means to realize the desired ends.[44] In this respect, it is quite unique among the virtues, because all the rest of them, like courage, temperance, truthfulness, liberality and friendliness, have a 'practical' character which arises naturally from appetites directed towards fulfilling the ends that appetites imply. When such appetites are exercised in a 'moderate' fashion – for example, when our desire for honour does not lead to excessive ambition – then one can speak of the natural or accidental possession of a single virtue, not necessarily implying the presence of other virtues, and without any role being played by *phronesis*.[45]

Phronesis however, although the very heart of ethical *praxis*, is not itself 'practical' but 'intellectual' in character.[46] This is because it interrupts the spontaneous flow of the appetites with a reflection which seeks to ensure that they are exercised with the right measure – that the appropriate amount of words are spoken on the right occasion, that generosity remains within sensible bounds, that courage does not become foolhardiness, and so forth. But finding the *true* mean, as opposed to an 'accidental' temperance, cannot be done for each appetite taken singly. On the contrary, it is a matter of giving each inclination its 'due', and so of that internal justice within the soul already spoken of by Plato. Hence in the case of true, praiseworthy, and not merely 'accidental' virtue, it is impossible to possess one virtue without also possessing all the others.[47] It is true that Aristotle envisages situations where there can be a clash of duties, but these situations of 'moral ill-luck' are characteristically engineered by tyrants, and the point of them is that they tend to take us outside the possibility of morality altogether.[48]

Phronesis, like rhetorical induction, is a kind of 'quasi-theory' because it seeks a relative constancy, a balance amidst what is inherently subject to change. However, it is not *episteme*, nor even simply a practical dialectics, because to achieve this balance it has to concern itself with the 'last particular', with minute factual differences observed by the adjacent faculty of *sunesis*, and with the question of what precisely is to be done in a given circumstance. This is a question of justice, of giving everything its due, which is yet not fully

---

[44] Ibid., 112a18–1113a12, 1141b25–1142b12.
[45] Ibid., 1105a12–20.
[46] Ibid., 1140a24–610.
[47] Ibid., 1144, 633–1145a11.
[48] Ibid., 1109b30–1110b8.

answerable in terms of any preceding set of criteria.[49] Discovering the means towards the end – and every end, short of the final good which is true happiness, can also be a means – apparently has a deductive form, that of 'the practical syllogism' (as the Middle Ages put it) which states that if X is the final goal, Y is conducive to X, and my present situation Z permits me to perform Y, then I should perform Y, this performance being itself the conclusion of a practical argument, as MacIntyre rightly insists. However, if, as MacIntyre also insists, the process of deliberation, or the identification of appropriate means, is not a matter of straightforward deduction from the end, but rather a process where a determination of means helps to specify the end more clearly, then the practical syllogism cannot be so easily assimilated to the theoretical, dialectical syllogism as he desires.[50]

The dialectical syllogism is not simply concerned with establishing that Y is a case of X, but assumes some sort of fixed table of hierarchical subordinations to which it refers – like Aristotle's table of genera and species or else a looser categorization expressed in a topical 'commonplace'. The active reasoning moment here is emphatically the third movement of logical deduction. However, the practical syllogism is equally concerned with both moments of identification, Y with X and Z with Y, and both are inherently problematic, such that the reasoning is as much concerned with *making* these identifications as with assuming them. In the case of the first identification, X with Y, an appeal is made never to a fixed table, but always to a stock of *topoi*, of 'commonplaces', which are at once the rough categorical arrangements which opinion accords to the changing world and 'springs' or 'sources' for new arguments. Hence the first identification, making appeal to this rough categoric arrangement, has characteristically the form of a maxim – for example, 'the political life is good for man', or 'those who sacrifice themselves for the city win great honour'. In the case of the second identification, Z with Y, however, beyond dialectics one has to fashion a new maxim for oneself, as it were, exactly attuned to one's situation. Here the topics, the general truths, have to become generative sources for new insights, arising to meet new occasions. Therefore, it can be argued that the practical syllogism approximates to the 'enthymematic' form of the *rhetorical* syllogism, of which Aristotle says, somewhat mysteriously, that it 'lacks' certain stages (probably meaning that the making of the identification is here *itself* the key rational moment) and also that a maxim can stand either as its premise, or as its conclusion.[51]

It can be argued, therefore, that Aristotle's understanding of both induction to the ends, and deduction from them, in the sphere of ethical *praxis*, is a rhetorical one, and that this detaches the practical sphere more firmly from *theoria*, and so from the theological, than MacIntyre allows. There is, in

---

[49] Aristotle, *Ethics*, 1142a25–29, 1142, 633–1143a18.
[50] MacIntyre, *Whose Justice?*, pp. 124–45.
[51] Aristotle, *Rhetoric*, 1357 i 5.

Aristotle, no 'dialectical' give and take occurring between a theoretical projection of ends and a practical specification of means. Instead, final ends in the sublunary sphere are initially indicated by the direction of our appetites, and theory can only have a probable intimation, on analogical grounds, of a single, united end. But real knowledge of this end, and its constitution, is provided (paradoxically) by a purely practical wisdom which concerns itself directly with means alone. Strangely enough, the relatively theoretical component in the sphere of ethics is not, as MacIntyre supposes, that which concerns itself directly with final ends, but rather practical wisdom *itself*, insofar as its intellectuality (applied to the balancing of the passions) contrasts with the other virtues. Something is happening here which, we shall shortly see, is a key to deconstructing Aristotle. At the heart of his ethics the apparent dominance of final causality, the end/means axis, is in fact subverted by formal causality and a form/matter axis, which still has the basic Platonic concern with imposing a fixed order on the unruly: the finding of the mean amidst the appetites or passions.

The important consequence of stressing the rhetorical component in Aristotle, and the disconnection of *praxis* from *theoria*, is that it makes it much harder to read him as providing a permanently valid support for any kind of theory of natural law. Aristotle does not really connect the ethical with what is eternally valid, and MacIntyre has to try and argue away his statement to the effect that even natural laws are subject to change, because they are, precisely, laws of *physis*, which is the changeable.[52] There is a sense here in which Aristotle's thought finds a place for what he could never have envisaged, namely, a situation where it is no longer 'persuasive' to argue that political life is our final practical end, because the organization of the Greek *polis* no longer seems the clear fulfilment of rightly regulated human desire. The life of the *polis* simply *is* Aristotle's argument for our relatively fixed place in nature, and where appeal to the *polis* breaks down, so also does any purely Aristotelian argument for a law of nature.

MacIntyre, at times, seems close to assenting to this statement, and insists that an ethics of virtue makes sense only within a community practising a *paideia*. However, because he intrudes into Aristotle a truly theoretical moment concerning our reasoning about ends or the final good for humankind, he makes it appear easy to assume some sort of permanent, natural, universal validity for the general *framework* of Aristotle's terminology of ends, virtues, praxis, *phronesis*, the mean and so forth, even if the *content* of virtue must change within an altogether different practice of *paideia*. Without this framework, according to MacIntyre, we are condemned to intellectual scepticism about human behaviour, which is a mere irrational reflex of an unsustainable foundationalism. The framework belongs to the very immanence of reason, to the characterization of genuine 'traditioned reason' as such. Therefore it can be dialectically modified, but not fundamentally denied. Similarly, even the

---

[52] Aristotle, *Ethics*, 1134b29–30. MacIntyre, *Whose Justice?*, p. 121.

changing content of the virtues can perhaps be the subject of dialectical adjudication, although MacIntyre is not so clear about this (as I have already noted). Certainly he stresses that Augustine and Aquinas later see moral virtue as possible *in any social circumstance*, and therefore as more a matter of 'a law of nature' rather than a law of the *polis* (which is natural only 'at one remove').[53] MacIntyre appears himself to go along with this minimization of 'moral luck' (although he recognizes that the moral imperative may disallow many modern social roles that are normally seen as perfectly respectable: that of the financier for example) and therefore seems, at least at this point in his argument, to edge discussion of the virtues towards the control of *theoria*, and a universal natural law.

Whatever the case here, MacIntyre does not recognize the possibility that even the framework of Aristotle's ethics is historically specific and historically relativizable. This is because he believes that this framework is theoretically knowable, as a constant object, whereas for Aristotle this framework is itself rhetorically locked within the bounds of the *polis*, along with the virtues it commends.

3   *Calling Aristotle into question: contemplation, doing, making*

I have shown that compared with MacIntyre, Aristotle more recognizes the place of rhetoric in human practice. However, this very recognition suggests that Aristotle's own account of a sphere of *praxis* and of practical wisdom can be seen as bound within a particular rhetoric that can be called into question.

Obviously, there are features of Aristotle's substantive account of the virtues that few would want to subscribe to today. Slaves, women, children, artisans, the relatively poor, the ugly, the misshapen, are all, according to him, debarred from full happiness, and the exercise of complete virtue. His ideal of the virtuous person, the 'magnanimous man', is still in part heroic, and decidedly aristocratic.[54] Although this person must only seek honours as rewards for a true exercise of virtue, he is still primarily motivated by this seeking for public acclaim. Hence magnanimity is the crown of the virtues in parallel to the way virtues receive honour as their prize. Not only does the magnanimous man seek to be liberal, he seeks to outshine others in liberality, which implies a competition for limited economic resources. He prefers to be a benefactor rather than receive benefit, and if this sounds possibly 'Christian', one must note that he also remembers his giving rather than his receiving, and is encouraged to be 'haughty' to those above him in station, but to 'hold back' to those below.[55] This jealousy of munificence shows that Aristotle's ideal of virtue is not perfectly separable from a heroic pursuit of

[53] Aristotle, *Ethics*, pp. 146–63, 183–208.
[54] Aristotle, *Ethics*, 1099a32–b5, 1122a18–1125a15.
[55] Ibid., 1124b14–1125a1.

honour. Excellence is still in some measure 'effectiveness', which can emerge only from engagement in an *agon*.

But it then becomes difficult to separate content from form: if the highest virtue is still permeated by heroic honour, then will this not be true of Aristotle's very *idea* of virtue, of what ethics actually is? This suspicion is confirmed by the fact that what qualifies virtue to be real, rather than merely accidental virtue, is not intention of the end (as it was for Plato and will be again for Aquinas) but rather the prudential ordering of 'the mean' in the exercise of the natural appetites. What is to the fore here is self-control, a disposition which gives each passion its due and no more, and ensures that all remains under the governance of reason. But intellectuality is not for Aristotle, as for Plato, a realm illuminated by justice, so that to say that the ethical means a rational control of the passions is *already* to start to refer the ethical to a standard outside the ethical; already to anticipate, albeit discreetly, the much later voice of the Enlightenment, which loudly proclaims such a reference. However faintly, Aristotle already begins to think 'secular reason', and unsurprisingly, as we should by now have realized, this is also conjoined with a relative archaism as compared with Plato (i.e. a 'greater paganism'), a reinvocation of *metis* or *phronesis*, as the ability to adapt cunningly to circumstances and so retain the upper hand.[56] Of course *phronesis* is now confined to 'moral' tricks, and yet, at the limits of the bounds of the soul, what we are talking about is simply a self-government that retains stability and minimizes disturbances, while at the bounds of the city what we are talking about is ensuring that others depend on us, rather than vice versa.

This deconstruction of virtue back into honour tends to cast doubt on MacIntyre's claim that one can separate (in the case of Aristotle, specifically) the general notion of an 'aristocratic' republic – meaning a republic where the virtuous rule by direct participation, and virtue is spread as widely as possible – from our usual notion of aristocracy, meaning privilege of birth, wealth and education. If virtue is still heroic honour, then virtue as such is linked to a competition for scarce resources, albeit *not* a modern, naked, economic competition, but a competition in the exercise of excellence and patronage, and for the educative and political means to do so. (Even MacIntyre himself suggests that excellence should be *rewarded*, rather than merely provided with the resources necessary for its exercise – an idea that is certainly not socialist, and perhaps not fully Christian either.)[57] Aristotle's exclusion of virtue from the domestic sphere, from women, from artisans, from the poor, is therefore not so much a register of an inadequate vision of 'virtue', which could nonetheless be expanded to include these categories, as a register of his whole understanding of the term. If the idea of virtue is to be

---

[56] Marcel Détienne and Jean-Pierre Vernant, *Cunning Intelligence in Greek Culture and Society*, trans. Janet Lloyd (Brighton: Harvester, 1978) pp. 313–18.

[57] MacIntyre, *Whose Justice?*, p. 105.

retrieved by Christians, or by socialists, then its formality as well as its content has to undergo a revision more radical than MacIntyre envisages.

Aristotle's partial return to a heroic perspective in his account of the virtues belongs together with his detachment of *theoria* from the good-as-justice and his repristination of *metis*. These things, in turn, are aspects of a wider redistribution of knowledge and practice which is itself contingent and questionable. Here it is highly important to qualify the usual celebrations of Aristotle's metaphysical figure over-against that of Plato. In Plato's figure, one finds, at the apex, contemplation of eternal truths, but only under the light of the Good which disciplines our desires and causes us to see truly. All practice is a kind of artistic imitation of this vision, a *mimesis* that is necessary, and yet highly precarious: copies falsify, and we must especially beware mere copies of copies.[58] Both knowing and being good are a matter of 'sight', and the realm of action, of contingency, time and change is subordinated to this stable vision. In Aristotle, by contrast, the contemplation of eternal verities is one thing, and ethical goodness quite another. The latter is accessible through *praxis*, governed by practical wisdom. In a further important division, *praxis* or doing is distinguished from *poesis* or making; the latter is also not concerned with the ethically good, but with the humanly useful and beautiful.[59]

Usually, Aristotle gets praised for his linking of virtue with uncertainty, change and approximation, and his insistence that the human good can only be known through practice. How foolish to think that there is THE GOOD, when there is only a good way to be a fish or a carpenter. But the point is that there is no obvious human function as such, and therefore no obvious human good – to say that one knows this good via a practice that *remains in the soul* (see below) makes no more sense (or nonsense) than saying that the human good resides peculiarly in a relation to a supra-human GOOD, which one primarily 'sees', rather than enacts. The advantage of Plato's figure is that he still regards the question about what we should desire as inseparable from the question about whether there is something we can properly know. Likewise, he does not divide 'ethical' from 'artistic' activity, but rather sees both as proceeding from our determinations of the truth in the light of the Good. By comparison, Aristotle has already forgotten (a fateful forgetfulness) that ontology is intimately tied to ethics, because only the recognition of a fixed sun of the Good allows us to see that there are fixed objects of truth and beauty – in other words, an order of things that absolutely are, and cannot not be. Likewise, a real loss is sustained through the disconnection of *praxis* from imitation of the forms. Plato allowed for the role of *phronesis*, or of a wisdom tied to circumstance, but *phronesis* in tandem with contemplation suggests that every particular decision about justice really can accrue to one's sense of permanently abiding justice. Without the idea of participation, a response 'appropriate to the circumstances' threatens to become something that must

[58] Plato, *Republic*, 502d–521e, 595a–602e.
[59] Aristotle, *Ethics*, 1139b18–1140b31.

die with these circumstances, something *dictated* by the circumstances, rather than a good which the circumstances gave us occasion to realize, so revealing a new facet of the Good itself. Finally, it is a loss to think that neither the contemplator or the maker is directly concerned with ethical goodness. Again, this loss was epochal, because the 'cold' theoretical gaze was later extended in the West to nature, and making became more and more emancipated as an autonomous realm of 'technology'. One reason why John Ruskin was a major thinker was that he sought to restore questions of virtue both to *theoria*, our looking at nature, and to the practice of the artisan – in a way that did not subordinate either our looking at nature, or our imaginative construction, to an initial 'timeless' vision, but instead worked towards the latter by means of the first two.

The example of Ruskin leads us to the crucial point. Aristotle's tripartite scheme – theory, doing, making – conceals from view a third possibility, namely, a 'reversed Platonism' which would preserve Plato's integration of the True, the Good and the Beautiful, and yet ground theory in making, the original in the copy, the cause in the effect, and stable beauty in the music of transition – although it remains the case that true making 'sees', the copy originates, the effect causes, and process punctuates. Such a reversal is, indeed, partially implied by Plato himself and is further encouraged by the Trinitarian reworking of neo-Platonic emanation – which makes emanation integral to infinite perfection – by the Church Fathers. In Augustine's version of creaturely participation in the Trinity, ideas stored in the memory are only fully realized and perfected in the expressive, 'emanative' moment of intellectual recollection and reordering of past time, under the further and unexhausted prompting of desire. Thus, for this reversal (which Augustine by no means perfects), the divine ideas are participated in by the productions of space and time in their aspect of ideal repeatability and elemental latency of suggestion. And the Platonic flux of phenomena is still permitted to be a flux, whereas Aristotle tried to channel flux through a relatively stable order. For nihilism the flux is all there is, but for Christian Trinitarianism the 'ideal passages' of time are 'complicated' within an infinite unity which is itself 'ideal' only insofar as it is a productive emanation, a 'Word' which has the power of surplus suggestion in a third, 'Spiritual' moment. Participation is not now an imitative relation of making to vision, but rather is the endless visionary construction of the (infinitely) perfect work, and the contemplative response to this artifice.

Aristotle's metaphysical figure has tended to prevent a clear perception of this possibility, partially elaborated, beyond Augustine, by Nicholas of Cusa and Maurice Blondel. Instead, he provides us with a separation of making and doing, to supplement an initial separation of theory and practice. The second separation is vitally necessary once the first is made, because otherwise there will be no space for the ethical good to inhabit, apart from the realm of technical luck and skill. The science of ethics would then possess no subject matter. However, this second separation, of *praxis* and *poesis* is questionable, as I shall now argue.

Praxis opens up already, long before Augustine or Descartes, an interiority, or a realm of the *psyche* that is really much more secure than in Plato, where one could hardly catch the soul still, in the midst of its upward and downwards ecstasies. For *praxis*, unlike *poesis*, does not 'aim at an end other than itself', but merely at 'doing well'. Whereas *poesis* is not concerned with the mode of doing (one might say, with the 'arrow' of activity) but only with the shape of the completed production (one might say, the 'circle' of the result), *praxis* draws a circle around the arrow of activity itself, ensuring that the excellence that truly belongs to a person does not pass beyond his control. As the scholastics will say, *poesis* (making) is transitive, *praxis* (doing) intransitive.

Although the *phronesis* which governs *praxis* must constantly respond to civic events, this response is never an exit, but a move to conserve in the flux the equilibrium of the self; in this sense, it already presses towards the stoic *conatus* and is situated half-way between externally related *poesis* and the ideal self-movement, or action without change, of *theoria*. And yet the strange thing is that this self-contained activity is accorded by Aristotle a greater civic scope than *poesis*: it concerns the whole of life, and is 'what is conducive to the good life generally'.[60] Yet must not the highest *praxis*, the educative and legal life of the *polis*, include a transitive element? Aristotle cannot see that it is external power relations which construct our interiority, but instead gives priority to the self-government of the soul. Educative and rhetorical transmission is therefore not, for Aristotle, itself a 'moral' moment, but the mediation between one internal moral 'action' of the teacher or law-giver, and another of the pupil or the citizen. By contrast, because Plato saw the internal organization of the soul as 'poetic', he *was* able to see artistic, rhetorical and educative activity as – albeit in a secondary fashion – itself a moral moment. Hence craftsmen, in their working, were to attend to the eternal forms of truth, just like the guardians in their civil artistry.[61]

The contrast between *praxis* and *poesis* is in part specified by that between the intransitive and the transitive, but also by a different relationship between skill and chance. In one respect *poesis* is *closer* to *theoria* than to *praxis*, because the Greeks, as Jean-Pierre Vernant insists, did not think of the products of art and technology as things 'made up' by us, and so as specifiable only via the making-activity itself (except, perhaps, in the case of law, which was the first subject of scepticism), but rather as natural realities whose forms were always available to an initial theoretical awareness.[62] Hence the artist or the technician characteristically tries to impose a 'form' in his mind upon a 'matter' external to his mind, and art (*techne*) in Aristotle's words is 'a productive state that is truly reasoned'.[63] What matters here is control, and, according to

[60] Aristotle, *Ethics*, 1140a24–30.
[61] Aristotle, *Politics*, 1260a33–41. Plato, *Republic*, 595a–597d; *Laws*, 9656. Strauss, *The City and the Man*, pp. 24–8.
[62] J.-P. Vernant, 'Remarques sur les formes et les limites de la pensée technique chez les grecs', in *Mythe et Pensée chez les Grecs*, vol. 2, pp. 44–64.
[63] Aristotle, *Ethics*, 1140a1–23.

Aristotle, mistakes in art do not carry a moral culpability, so that a mistake is rated higher if it is a voluntary one, whereas in the case of prudential reasoning, the opposite applies.[64] However, once the form is embarked upon the sea of matter, it enters into a realm of chance, which can affect its material embodiment: thus 'art has a love for chance and chance for art'.[65] Art is a kind of game played out between stable forms which are 'above' the soul, and unpredictable matter which lies in front of it.

Phronesis, on the other hand, knows no such degree of stability, and yet eschews also such a frank engagement with the fleeting: it more purely belongs within the soul itself. Although it is exercised only as a response to contingencies, it tries to *limit* the risks posed by the contingencies. Martha Nussbaum is mostly wrong to see Aristotle as celebrating risky moral activity in a situation where the very possibility of moral action is precarious. On the contrary, ethics itself, for Aristotle, unlike *techne*, is a strategy for minimizing risk within our temporal and finite life. Here the haven of fixed forms is not available – but at least we can remain on board the ship of the soul.

Yet can we? This is the question which one must pose against the *praxis/poesis* distinction. The idea of the soul as an internal realm, which for Aristotle can potentially 'include' all forms by 'actualizing' them in their complete detachment from matter (this is what he takes 'intelligence' to be)[66] tends to uphold the notion of an action that 'remains with us', that indeed 'is' ourselves. (Aquinas later crucially modified this final self-referentiality by inserting the notion of the *verbum*, an inner emanative intentional orientation to the exterior.) One can be so impressed by the Aristotelian recognition that we *are* our actions, rather than a contentless will hidden behind them, that one fails to see the questionability of the idea of 'our' actions, actions without exit, which we possess. As Nietzsche and Foucault realized, the idea of the soul does not really precede notions of guilt and imputation: it is rather those notions which engender the idea of a soul. Thus one should begin with the realization that *every* action is an outgoing and a displacement, every action is 'poetic', a loss as well as a gain, a self-exposure as well as a self-imposition. The distinction of 'actions' from 'makings' arises only according to social and linguistic convention, whereby *certain* makings are more strongly attributed to a person than others, and so are thought to 'remain' with her, and thereby to 'characterize' her. This convention is, in fact, what gives a person a 'character' at all. Hence certain things we are allowed to do 'any old how', and our clumsiness is forgotten, not held against us, or else laughed off: we can walk down the road (in our society) with any gait, although more will be expected from debutantes.

---

64 Ibid., 1140b20–30.
65 Ibid., 1140a20.
66 Aristotle, *De Anima*, 429a29–430a25.

Yet even in the case of debutantes we are talking more about 'style' and 'manners' rather than morals (again, *only* in our society); this is a semi-aesthetic practice that is still seen as half-external, rather than as a matter betraying our fundamental 'attitudes'. Aristotle himself notes that some artistic practices like lyre-playing or dancing are relatively intransitive, in that here the doing is itself the end.[67] But the aim of these activities is still excellence in an external 'product', even if this is transitory; both music and dance begin as prior known 'forms', and in either case a deliberate mistake would presumably count higher than a chance one. The reversal of this rule only occurs when we are talking about actions entirely inseparable from 'who a person is'. But what are these actions? What makes them internal? *Every* action, even our thoughts, because they are expressed in language, proceeds outwards, away from ourselves hitherto, and back into a public domain, as 'a gift' that is in principle appropriable by others. Thus only by *convention* are some makings thought to be 'doings': only by a particular coding. This coding determines first, that in this area of life there can be no 'indifferent' series of makings that are just steps towards the goal – like the mess in an artist's workshop, or his sexual dalliance with his model – instead, everything 'counts', like the way you make every stroke in zen painting. Secondly, *these* particular makings are going to be remembered and linked together as a series composing 'who you are', unlike other makings which are closed off as punctiliar instances, and deemed independent of you altogether. One should note here that all the 'life and works' arguments – does his depraved conduct affect his art? does his depraved art reflect his character? – are undecidable, precisely because it is not seen that the two contrasting points of view are simply selecting different codes: one refuses to ascribe artistic products as actions to the artist, the other decides to do so.

The point here is not that one kind of coding is necessarily right and another wrong: *all* cultures will code a difference between doing and making, although these codes will widely vary, and our culture is arguably vastly *overcoded*, so that ethical action has become more and more elusive and 'internal', and most 'continuous' makings – manners, style of behaviour – as well as everyday 'products' like buildings and furniture, are thought to fall outside moral criteria altogether. However, what is theoretically significant is that the distinction between doing and making must itself be made 'poetically', by deciding which external actions count, which do not, and which belong within an ironic circle of fictional 'pretence'. One's sense therefore, that certain makings are properly the subject of ethical judgement, only emerges from a broader *aesthetic* sense of the place of these makings within the whole of human life. At the extreme limit of its possibility ethics is only a sub-sphere of aesthetics, governed by criteria of good taste. The 'ethical' only arises, as a local sphere, because certain continuous aesthetic performances are regarded as highly desirable for all, or at least for people in certain roles.

[67] Aristotle, *Eudemian Ethics*, 1219a12ff.

A *certain* sequence of makings, a *certain* pattern of speech, is deemed to 'be' a person, to constitute his or her character, which is as much a fictional product, subject to aesthetic analysis, as a character in a novel.

Against Aristotle, therefore, one should revive the Platonic insight that both 'looking' and 'making' are of primary relevance to ethics, although in a 'reversed Platonism' the stress should be placed upon making. 'Doing' is a matter of the codes of attribution which *poesis* itself constructs; it does not stand for a permanently distinguished sphere of internal activity, governed by a particular kind of knowledge. Art and prudence (*techne* and *phronesis*) are at root interfused, because all our actions 'emanate', and no action is a mere response to circumstances, but itself modifies those circumstances, however infinitesimally, and helps to constitute the circumstances and norms that will be delivered over to the future. This is where Derrida is in some measure right to point out that *both* the Socratic tradition *and* the sophistic-rhetorical tradition tended to ignore the primacy of 'writing'.[68] For they opposed the fixity of what is written, or otherwise permanently secured in memory, to the flexibility of a sense of eternal justice (Plato) or else of a response to circumstances (the sophists and Aristotle). Here action rather than making is seen as primary, because one adjusts 'one's own' conduct to contingencies. Yet it is writing, and what is 'poetically' recorded, which continuously moulds the very bounds of convention within which circumstances can arise. In writing, our action and meanings 'escape' from us and become sedimented, having unpredictable effects. This is the unavoidable condition of all human action. Although we can sometimes claim that our real intentions have been betrayed, this is a matter of assessing continuities and discontinuities of signification and of teleological direction, not of securing a neat division between 'our own' actions and their 'consequences'. Every action begins to be a consequence. In aiming for a goal, it also emanates.

Against Aristotle, one can conclude that there is no universal, special sphere of 'action', and therefore no distinct subject called 'ethics'. Questions of 'the moral' rather intrude everywhere – wherever there is a question of an imperative gap between a present state, and the condition of truly desirable beauty. To hang on to 'action' as a special 'ethical' sphere is still to cling to certain notions of internality. Hence many current proponents of an 'ethics of virtue' began by insisting on 'the agent's perspective', to distinguish intentionally informed action (although not a Cartesian intention positioned

---

[68] Jacques Derrida, 'Plato's pharmacy', in *Dissemination*, trans. Barbara Johnson (London: Athlone, 1981) pp. 65–156. This assessment, however, is but partially true. Catherine Pickstock is also right to point out that, for Plato, the sophists operate a kind of 'written' *mathesis* of abstract power, while Socratic orality *is* linked to temporality, not, as for Derrida, to 'presence', and moreover in a manner that does more justice than Derrida to *embodiment*. Pickstock also indicates that oral *poesis* includes the 'written' moment that establishes cultural bounds. See Catherine Pickstock, *After Writing: On the Liturgical Consummation of Philosophy* (Oxford: Blackwell, 1999).

'before' the action) from mere natural causation, which can be fully comprehended from 'outside'. However, they have quickly realized that post-Witt-
gensteinian considerations force one to see that if an intention is situated
within an action, then it is also constituted through language, and so is in
principle as comprehensible to an outside observer as to the agent herself.[69]
Switching, therefore, to the social plane, they then try to save 'the agent's
perspective' as an internality belonging to human cultural forms, and especially to narrative emplotment, which presupposes goals, plus successful or
thwarted projects. However, stories do not need to have *human* characters,
and in fact (as Aristotle is near to grasping) narrative is simply the mode in
which the entirety of reality presents itself to us: without the story of the tree,
there is no distinguishable, abiding tree. For nothing is first known to us as a
mere indistinguishable continuum, nor as a sequence of efficient cause and
effect. Instead, relatively stable entities and isolatable sequences – facts and
motions – always present themselves (as Deleuze argues) to us already as
'meanings' or as 'incorporeal' elements ('Platonic ideas on the surface'),
which we can detach from their particular occurrence and think of as larger
or smaller, faster or slower, occurring elsewhere and as capable of turning
into something else, indeed as 'ordering' a transition. This is how we recognize a seed; but we recognize everything only as a seed, or as constituted by
what it will or might become. Hence in a certain sense our apprehension of
everything is teleological and narratological: only reflectively and with great
effort (taking, precisely, millennia) can we come up with the notion of a pure
continuum, or a causality distinguished from intention. But, as Deleuze has
contended, one is still left with the circumstance that the continuum 'gives
rise' to (and indeed only 'happens' through) these effects of meaning, and it
is only *as* meaning (or as semiotic articulation) that one encounters energies
and forces for change at work.[70] It is *not at all* that our teleological reading of
trees is anthropomorphic; for it is equally true that our teleological, or
intentional reading of our own actions is dendromorphic.

Thus I am suggesting, against MacIntyre, that what makes an action is *not*
the presence of a 'human' or a 'cultural' motive or 'internal' reason: all this is
really still Cartesian and Kantian. What matters is the objective surface presence of a teleological ordering where intention of a goal shows up in visible
structure. And likewise, the real division here is not between natural causality
and cultural action, but rather between staying at the phenomenological level
of 'apparent' meanings or phenomena, on the one hand, and 'reducing' these
to a mere seamless, directionless continuum on the other hand. Of course one
can still see phenomenal drag of effect upon cause as infinitely wild and
interminable, rather than properly teleological. This is Deleuze's path,
which a Catholic ontology must clearly refuse.

---

[69] Stanley Hauerwas, *Character and the Christian Life*, (San Antonio: Trinity University Press,
1985) pp. xiii–xxxiii.
[70] Gilles Deleuze, *Logique du Sens*, pp. 41–50, 115–22.

But on either the stoic-nihilist, or the Aristotelian-neo-Platonic-Catholic reading, narrative is our primary mode of inhabiting the world, and it characterizes the way the world happens to us; not, primarily, the cultural world which humans make. There is, therefore, no special 'human' sphere of narrative action, and no sphere of 'ethics' which uniquely characterizes human life, even if human life is systematically more 'open' and 'intense'. Instead, the question about what the whole of nature should look like, even of how it would like to appear, impresses itself through all our apprehensions.

4   *Calling Aristotle into question: charity and prudence*

So far, I have been trying to deconstruct Aristotle from within, but a second way of calling him into question is to contrast the structure of his ethics with that of Thomas Aquinas. My case here is that MacIntyre underestimates the way in which a different content for virtue in Aquinas also entails a revision of the very formality of virtue as such.

Again, one can begin at the level of content, and note that whereas Aristotle's civic ideal is that of the 'magnanimous man', Aquinas's ecclesial ideal is that of 'the person of charity' (the switch to gender neutrality here being historically appropriate). Unlike the magnanimous man, the person of charity does not build up a fund of resources and then economically dispense them: instead, her very mode of being is a giving, and this constant outgoing paradoxically recruits again her strength. A kind of giving can be exercised even in negative situations of poverty and weakness, and the charitable person is first and foremost the *recipient* of charity from God, and so charity begins and ends in gratitude, which the magnanimous man prefers to keep within bounds. As friendship with God, and with fellow humans, charity always involves mutuality: Aristotle himself had made this point about friendship, but he did not, like Aquinas, place friendship quite at the apex of civic achievement. Friends, for Aristotle, share a common love of the good, but this good is ultimately that fine economy of honour which is magnanimity. If friendship becomes the actual summit of virtue, then this suggests that virtue itself is a relational, rather than a self-contained, internal matter. And, indeed, Aquinas says that charity and friendship are not just the sharing of a good otherwise available, but rather that mutual benevolence is itself *fundatur super aliqua communicatione*. In other words, a transitive giving of something to someone else is constitutive of friendship, and therefore the thing most ultimately characteristic of virtue.[71] This note of 'communication' (meaning not essentially communication of information, nor even of subjectivity, but a kind of 'bestowal', where the act of bestowing is itself the content of what is bestowed) is absent in Aristotle; it marks the idea that goodness is fundamentally a gift or an emanation, which Aquinas has learned from the theologians Dionysius and Augustine, and not from 'the philosopher'. This conception

---

[71] Aquinas, *ST* II.II. q.23a1.

makes of the *telos* no longer an action remaining in the mover, but rather a surplus overflow – a kind of endlessly self-cancelling end.

However, the contrast does not stop at the point of a differing content for virtue. The entire Aristotelian conceptual framework is also disturbed. For magnanimity was just a particular moral virtue, it was not what made virtue really and not accidentally virtuous: this was rather *phronesis or prudentia* – not a moral virtue at all, but an intellectual one. Charity, by contrast, is not merely the highest ethical ideal: it is also what makes virtue virtuous, the very 'form of the virtues' according to Aquinas.[72] In the supernatural ordering, to which everything, *in concreto*, must refer (else there will not even be any true natural virtue, since lack of grace perturbs also nature), everything is topsy-turvy and back-to-front. Friendship no longer assists and accompanies, but *is* itself the end; moreover, this ever-renewed and ceaselessly-excessive outgoing regulates even prudence, which is supposed to inhibit excess and keep everything in balance. Of course, Aristotle had said that from the point of view of excellence the mean is itself an extreme,[73] but by this he meant a precise maximum of intellectual virtue, not that extreme which is a limitless proceeding to infinity of a particular moral virtue. The conception of charity is the totally un-Aristotelian conception of a kind of 'appetite' that can be – indeed, inherently must be – 'excessive', and can never be 'too much'. A subtle displacement is going on here, of the primacy of the concept of 'the mean'.

The primacy of the mean belongs with the idea of a soul that is ideally self-contained, and a city without external relations – both conditions guaranteeing peace, and a more perfect peace in the case of the soul. For 'balance' can only be primary within fixed bounds, whereas a constant outgoing and overflow will ceaselessly upset every possible equilibrium. The necessity of charity, even for proper prudence, tends to imply that while patience, bravery etc. have to 'hit the mark', there is always room for more patience, more bravery etc., and that charity as communication has a power, unknown to Aristotle, to *initiate* the extension of these things. Moreover, a gradual approach to *perfection*, a perfect suffusion by charity, will mean that we no longer possess even impulses that are excessive or deficient. For charity does not, like prudence, really 'form' a passionate material that wells up from below; rather it produces its own material, shaping it according to its precise needs for every occasion, and in this precision also engenders an 'excess' that is by no means culpable. For Aquinas, following Augustine, culpable 'excess' and 'deficiency' are therefore pure negations, whereas for Plato and Aristotle they are real, permanent places lurking in the soul, just as the city is surrounded by barbaric wastes.

This is most strongly suggested by a passage in Plato's *Statesman* where he claims that the 'additional postulate' necessary to define a statesman, namely 'excess and deficiency are measurable not only in relational terms but also in

---

[72] Aquinas, ST II.II. q.8a1, q.23a7.
[73] Aristotle, *Ethics*, 1107a1–5.

respect of attainment of a norm or due measure' is parallel to 'the additional postulate' required to defend dialectical reasoning in *The Sophist*, which runs: 'What is not X, nonetheless exists'.[74] The first postulate implies that there can only be an art of statesmanship, or of the administration of objective justice, rather than the mere balancing out of conflicting forces, if there is a real measure, and not just a relative more or less. This in turn means that there is an absolute 'too little' and 'too much' which is permanently negative, and not just negative in relation to some arbitrary position on a scale. The second postulate, from *The Sophist*, is similarly concerned to defend absoluteness, here not of justice but of truth: the argument is that the negative in the denial of a false statement, the 'not X' must nonetheless have some reality even as 'not being', if negation is to be possible, and the distinction of truth and falsity upheld. Although dialectics primarily concerns truth, it is also said here to be an art of 'purification' which casts out the bad, and leaves a deposit of the good.[75] The comparison of the two postulates in the *Statesman* and the *Sophist* therefore seems to suggest that 'excess' and 'deficiency' are both absolutely negative and yet 'real', having some ontological situation like 'not X'. This would fit with Aristotle's view that prudence both holds back an excessive action, like vulgarity (*apeirokalia*) and eschews a deficient one like pettiness (*mikroprepeia*), holding to the mean of magnificence (*megaloprepeia*), just as in the city one ostracizes the excessively strong, and expels as a scapegoat (*pharmakos*) the excessively weak.[76] It is true that, unlike Plato, Aristotle did not think that 'non-being' in some strange sense exists, and did not regard matter as evil. However, he still accorded to matter an ontologically original fount of negative 'potential', falling short of full rationality and comprehensibility. This accords with his view of the passions as pre-given outside rationality, as 'neutral' with respect to practical reason, and as permanently tending of themselves to be either deficient or excessive. Excessive or deficient passions positively intrude in the wrong places, just as, for Aristotle, a theoretical mistake combines things which should not be combined (albeit that this misplacement now happens, in contrast to Plato, only in the internal space of the knowing soul).

But where evil is understood (as for Catholic faith) as pure privation, or as not having any ontological purchase, then the negative will always be just the lack of some positive virtue, an insufficient quantity of virtue, rather than a domain which surrounds virtue, like the terrain round the city, so relating to it either as too little or too much warlikeness. In Aristotle, virtue is almost *squeezed out* between prudence and the appetites, defined in terms of their proper equation, whereas only in Christianity, after virtue has become charity, which is a virtue uniquely productive of virtue, does virtue also become truly self-measuring. Christianity, therefore, achieves at a new level

[74] Plato, *Statesman*, 283c–84c.
[75] Plato, *Sophist*, 224d, 237e–238a, 256e–257b.
[76] Aristotle, *Ethics*, 1107a28–1108b9. *Politics*, 1284a, 1–1284b2.

the Platonic desire to refer everything else to the Good, rather than vice versa. *Only* Christianity, once it has arrived, really appears ethical at all . . .

Aquinas, of course, accepts a great deal of Aristotle's organization of the field of knowledge – for example, the tripartite division, *theoria, praxis, poesis.* Yet at the supernatural level this division starts to come unstuck. Charity, one could suggest, has to include both *praxis* and *poesis*, just as it is already, for Aquinas, a part of *theoria*. The latter perspective makes virtue not only inherently relational, but also insists again, like Plato, that it is a relationship to the transcendent. Aquinas articulates this by saying that virtues not only have an appetite or inclination to the end, but also intellectually *intend* the end – so permitting moral virtue *itself*, and not just prudence, to have a view of finality. For when finality lies 'beyond', it is impossible for it to be provided only by a prudence which balances out what is to hand.[77] Aristotle's 'secularizing' moves are therefore reversed. Yet there is also an *Aristotelian gain* here, over against certain modes of Christian Platonism: the relationship to the divine itself is practical and rhetorical as well as theoretical, and God has to first 'teach' us, just as ethics must first be learnt from the virtuous. However, the abandonment of heroic virtue for virtue as charity involves a disturbance of the entire Aristotelian conceptual equipment: of the tripartite division, of the duality of *praxis* and *poesis*, of the governing role of prudence, and of the idea of virtue as a mean.

5   *Antinomies of antique reason*

As we have just seen, in the Christian understanding, virtue remains *virtus*, power and virtuality, but this now means a power that constantly generates its own field of operation, which is no longer something to be formed, dominated or inhibited, but instead to be liberated as a new power and a new freedom. Here it must be said that while MacIntyre is absolutely right to contest the Enlightenment referral of ethical action to the criteria of consequence and abstract freedom, one should also recognize the specifically *post-Christian* character of these reductions. For example, 'benevolence' which looks to maximize consequences is clearly a secularization of charity. That is to say, for the Christian understanding, the ethical action itself *embodies* the passage to consequence, and in this passage seeks a *telos* which is the further promotion of creative freedom – not, indeed for anything, but for precisely what charity will unpredictably require, according to its own higher prudence. By contrast, for the antique understanding, virtue remained essentially a heroic power to restrict a preceding violence, to organize formally a material field, and to rein in forces around a stable, non-ecstatic centre.

As Hegel realized, that which still appears valid, from a Christian perspective, in antique virtue, is precisely its *sittlich* character, the tying of morality to *ethos* and of moral obligation to specific roles within a particular social order.

---

[77] Aquinas, *ST* I–II, 9.1, 12.4. 20.2. Stanley Hauerwas, *Character and the Christian Life* pp. 65–7.

This means, however, that, in one sense, the question of justice (*dikaiosune*) has precisely the same scope as the question of virtue itself. There can only be an objective virtue if there is objective justice, or the possibility of a fair distribution of roles and goods within the *polis*. But in turn, objective justice implies that there can be a harmonious 'mixture' of human beings, a genuine peace of consensus, which is more than an uneasy peace of contract, or agreement to differ. As we shall see in the next chapter, Augustine charged the Romans with having no real virtue, because they knew no real peace – either at the level of practice, *or* at the level of mythological and ontological conception. My analysis in the present chapter is an attempt to extend this charge against the whole of antiquity and, like Augustine, I am arguing that where virtue is conceived even in residually heroic terms (as by Aristotle) it will tend to reduce to a matter of self-control, whether of the soul, or of the city. Since the relationship of self-control is not one between subject and subject, is not essentially concerned with either communicative bestowing or with freedom, it therefore in its own way tends also (like the Enlightenment reductions *to* freedom and consequence) to reduce the ethical act to something else – in this case a relationship of control of 'form' over subordinate 'material forces'. Hence the word *arete* (virtue) is always the standard of a victory, and while conquest puts an end to war, it requires a preceding war, and only ends war by war. It appears, of course, that the Greeks believed that a stable peace depends upon justice, yet their aspiration to a justice that is more than victory is, in fact, precarious.

Because virtue presupposes justice, and justice involves a real peace, *the ontological priority of peace to conflict* (peace is what is most real, most secure, most guarantees human life) is an issue of *yet more importance* than that of virtue. Peace is not a virtue, notes Aquinas – and he does not talk about a particular virtue of peaceableness – because peace is the final end, the *principium* that is being itself.[78] Considerations concerning ontology, peace and conflict (the prime concern already of the pre-Socratics) have therefore, as Augustine realized, a power to unsettle one's whole conception of virtue, or of what morality is at all. And the main consideration here is that antiquity failed really to arrive at the ontological priority of peace to conflict and therefore failed – from a Christian point of view, and *even* from that of certain aspects of the aspirations of Plato and Aristotle – to break with a heroic conception of virtue, and arrive at a genuinely ethical 'good'.

I will briefly try to indicate this double failure by outlining three antinomies of antique reason.

i.   **Polis or oikos** Both Plato and Aristotle believed that a full exercise of virtue was impossible within the domestic sphere. One may try to say (in parallel to what MacIntyre says about their views on slavery) that this simply

---

[78] Aquinas, *ST* II.II. q.29a4.

means that they had failed to see that the limited lives led by women, domestic servants and artisans were the result of a cultural convention, rather than a 'fact of nature'. (Rather different issues are raised by the denial of full happiness and virtue to children.) However, virtue means participation in the *polis*, and the *polis* itself, as I shall show below, was partly constituted as a machine for minimizing the *oikos*, or as a kind of cultural bypass operation to disassociate continuity and succession from wombs and domestic nurture. Hence a virtue (like Christian virtue) that can also be possessed by women, and be exercised as much in the home as in the forum (and also as much by the immature as the mature) cannot be 'virtue' in the same 'political' sense at all: it must be an entirely transvalued virtue.

Antique reason found difficulty in conceiving a virtue that could be seamlessly exercised between *oikos* and *polis*. For while, synchronically, political justice was placed above family loyalty, from a diachronic perspective the political community depended upon biological succession and upon domestic organization for economic activity and the initial rearing of children. The *oikos* possessed a priority in time; this made it necessary to take a detour and consider the maternal function of women.

This antinomy is least apparent in Hesiod, who writes from a rural perspective, warding off the political-military combination of the *polis*, in favour of a political-agricultural combination which has an 'oriental' complexion, and perhaps Hebraic resonances. However, even in Hesiod, as in the Genesis narrative of the Bible, there is a connection of women with the onset of decline from a primeval state of perfection. In Hesiod's case, the diminution of piety in the second, Silver Age, is conjoined with an over-dependence of emollient sons upon their mothers.[79] Nevertheless, as in Genesis again, there is no suggestion as yet of a *continuous* autochthony (birth of males from the earth) in the Golden Age. Later, this evasion of the female will assume a positive complexion, but in Hesiod autochthony (here birth from ash trees) is located in the third, Bronze Age, the time of hubristic, totally individualistic, cyclopean warriors.[80]

In Aeschylus, by comparison, a more civic perspective dictates a reworking of myth. The earliest era, the mythical period of respect for elders, hospitality to strangers, peace and justice, has become something of essentially *contested* value. Those who defend the primacy of the *oikos*, and of the rights of wives and mothers, daughters and sons, by virtue of their position in the *oikos* (Clytemnestra in *Agamemnon*, Antigone in *Seven Against Thebes* and Sophocles's *Antigone*) see the primal rupture as being the overriding of family law, and indeed, the commentary of the chorus in the *Eumenides* seems to side with them, insofar as it identifies the rule of the *polis* with the displacing of older by younger gods, and expresses foreboding at the implications of this for the

---

[79] Hesiod, *Works and Days*, pp. 125–36.
[80] Ibid., pp. 142–55.

fertility of earth and womb.[81] On the other hand, those who defend the primacy of the public sphere, like Agamemnon, and the right of fathers over mothers as the point of intersection of royal with domestic rule, like his daughter Electra, interpret the primal rupture which unleashes the Furies as an abrogation of this kingly/paternal authority.[82] In *Seven Against Thebes*, the male sphere of royal power gets further abstracted from familial mediation and the protection of chthonic powers, through the invention of a rival antiquity based on place rather than lineage. Eteocles, the spokesman for this new *mythos*, invokes the new Olympian gods, whereas his opponents fight under the protection of titans. He connects the new authority of civic justice with the ancient springing of warriors from seed sown in their native soil. Primary loyalty is not to mother or father but to 'this dear earth, your mother and your nurse',[83] an appeal to which Eteocles may be driven because both he and his brother Polyneices stand under the curse of their own father Oedipus.

Indeed, one might well suggest that the successions of murderous relations between father and son from Uranus to Cronos to Zeus in Hesiod's theogony, render troubling a primary appeal to familial loyalty, which now seems to imply an endless chain of revenge, where one can never really be in the right. Must one be revenged upon one's husband for killing one's daughter, upon one's mother for killing one's father, and so forth? Olympian justice, 'God', is a new star that rises above fate, and claims to restrict its operation, just as the *polis* pardons Orestes, and chains up the furies at the end of the *Oresteia*. Yet this means, of course, that from the point of view of the *oikos*, and of ancient justice which is vengeance, the justice of the *polis* is nothing more than the arbitrariness of its starting point, and its fixing of a *status quo*. Why should Orestes' fate be lifted? And why should Eteocles' brother Polyneices, who died in conflict with him, go unburied? Eteocles' claim alone to receive civic burial rests simply upon his initial claiming of sole political inheritance from Oedipus, just as Romulus cast out Remus in the founding of Rome. Hence *Antigone* is *not* a drama about the eternal conflict between public and private duty, but rather about the moment of the establishing of a particular public sphere as a *status quo* whose guarantee of peace and order overrides former loyalties, and whose invention of justice as fixed in a geographical place obscures its foundations in just one more act of vengeance. Creon is a true *political* founder of the *polis* because he sides, arbitrarily, with the victory of one half of a family over another. Antigone, however, truly foreshadows a different social solution that is *not* the *polis*, although for her this can only be a community with the dead. Favouring neither one brother nor the other, and refusing to allow the terrain of the *polis* to tilt the balance, she detaches herself both from the vengeful past and from the political 'justice' of the future. The

---

[81] Aeschylus, *Eumenides*, pp. 780–822.
[82] Aeschylus, *The Choephori*, pp. 120–50.
[83] Aeschylus, *Seven Against Thebes*, pp. 12–24.

polis cannot 'give equal honour to good and bad' and yet 'who knows? In the country of the dead that may be the law.'[84]

Behind the contestation of the Golden Age, the divergent female/familial, male/political interpretations, it is possible to speculate that there lies a dim memory of a period when the connection between sexual intercourse and the bearing of children was not comprehended. In this situation, natural succession would be perceived as being that of children from mothers. The only possible male succession would not be from natural father to natural son, but rather in terms of the taking over by one man from another of a certain terrain, certain weapons, certain symbols of rule. Without postulating this biological ignorance in the background, Giambattista Vico, in the eighteenth century, in his interpretation of Greek and Roman mythology, already suggested that the *authochthones* were connected with the idea of birth from the graves of fathers; that these graves marked the boundaries of a terrain to be possessed; and that possession was achieved by repeating the father's acts of violence against outsiders and defending the *terminus* which was considered to have a magical power of the dead to ward people off. Becoming a son, Vico realized, was a cultural affair of appropriating a 'name', which was first of all inscribed in the terrain, the grave, and the terminus (later, says Vico, a 'term' of language).[85] This picture gains in plausibility if one adds the probability of biological ignorance, which also makes it more likely that many of the violent acts of appropriation would be seizures from living fathers. Therefore, one can conjecture that the fear and awe attached to ancient places marked by graves would form a rival pole of continuity to biological inheritance; but as space is inherently badly adapted to mediate continuities in time, a continuity always marked by *dis*continuity and violent rupture. Even after the onset of biological knowledge, the ancient linking of male power to place would tend to half-sanction the displacement of fathers by sons, the suspicion of sons by fathers. For where place matters most, the son, by taking over the 'name' of the father, *becomes* the father, obliterates the memory of his life, so that he is forever only a marker, only the power stored in the grave.

This speculation is only useful insofar as it helps to fill out what otherwise appears to be the incomplete logical reasoning of the myths of autochthony, and to show how place, the political, the male, and violence are implicitly-linked within it. These linkages do not, however, imply that female succession is entirely associated with peace: quite to the contrary, Aeschylus connects respect for the sanctity of the family with an endless succession of vengeance which only comes to rest in the sacred *topos* of the *polis*. This may mean that Martha Nussbaum is wrong to think that the Greeks primarily connected women with the fixed, the growing, and the plant-like.[86] Certainly feminine

---

[84] Sophocles, *Antigone*, pp. 520–30.
[85] Giambattista Vico, *The New Science* (Scienza Nuova Terza) paras. 485–7, 529–31, 549–51.
[86] Nussbaum, *The Fragility of Goodness*, p. 400ff.

imagery was applied to the first two, but the idea of fixed womb, the feminine mother earth, was part of a male-political *mythos* set in contrast to the actual 'wandering wombs' of real females, which were the very principle and possibility of a succession without place, an externally hysteric, nomadic existence upon the face of the earth. And the nomads were the war-bands, living by vengeance and counter-vengeance, raid and counter-raid. This state of a constantly resumed warfare that extends or retreats, but defends no terrain – therefore is somewhat 'incalculable', intuitive, and outside the *logos* – is inherently female. Hence, perhaps, the Amazons: female warriors outside the *polis* as opposed to male warriors sprung from a female soil.

At the end of the *Seven Against Thebes*, Aeschylus, or a later redactor, makes the chorus split: half to follow Polyneices, and the 'female', nomadic cause, which sees that 'what a state upholds as just changes with the changing of time', and half to follow Eteocles and the male cause of place where '*polis* and justice speak with one voice'.[87] At the end of the *Oresteia*, however, the balance is definitely tilted to the *polis*: earth triumphs over blood, the role of rhetoric over physical force, and war is to be made only 'at the stranger's gate' (whereas for families, the enemies were *never* strangers). In Plato, the balance gets tilted still further, because the Golden Age is no longer contested, but is now emphatically 'male'. Hence, in *The Republic*, the noble warrior class are to come to regard themselves as 'plants' sprung directly from the terrain of the land, and in the *Statesman* he locates universal autochthony in the earliest times.[88] Plato evinces how important he considers it to be to attach military forces to a place (curbing their inherently nomadic tendencies) but this cannot be achieved via the *oikos*. Instead, it makes desirable the extremest possible bypass of the *oikos*, and the usurpation of as many female, domestic functions by the male state as possible.[89] The myth of autochthony which the guardian-sare to learn may appear quite ludicrously untrue, but at a philosophical level it is perhaps an echo of Parmenidean views about the unreality of change and becoming. Essential birth, for Plato, is of the soul into the body, and the myth gives this philosophical view a political correlate: it is also the *republic* which suppresses both birth and time. Hence the philosophic myth of the cave is matched by the *counter-historical* myth in the *Statesman*, which contrasts a golden age of autochthony without wives or children, of direct rule of men by tutelary deities without recourse to law, with a subsequent 'catastrophic' period, when the real guardians retire, autochthony gives way to female birth, and humans are given over to vengeance and to wandering, like the deserted planet itself.[90] The domestic house, the cave, is the negative point of convergence for both the philosophic and political myths. It is this domain that might be changed for another, this domain which

---

[87] Aeschylus, *Seven Against Thebes*, pp. 1053–78.
[88] Plato, *Republic*, 414d–e. *Statesman*, 2696. Nicole Loraux, *Les Enfants d'Athéna: Idées Athéniennes sur la Citoyenneté et la Division des Sexes* (Paris: 1981).
[89] Plato, *Republic*, 415d–417b, 457a–468a.
[90] Plato, *Statesman*, 269b–276e.

shelters 'effeminate' artisans who do not contemplate things in the light of day, this domain which operates as a *camera obscura*, distracting us with the flickering images of real, abiding things.[91] Hence the Greek duality of theory and practice, which Plato strove, but failed to overcome entirely, is *also* the duality of *polis* and *oikos*.

Despite this Platonic antipathy to the *oikos*, it is Plato who wishes to make the *polis* a real *oikos* as far as possible: an imitation of the lost, divine, 'pastoral' rule. (Just as it is Plato, not Aristotle, who seeks to overcome the duality of theory and practice.) It is in this cause that the real *oikos* is to be diminished, or bypassed.[92] With the establishment of a single *oikos* connected by place not blood, there need be no more feuds, and inter-familial rivalries. Aristotle, by contrast, who allows far more autonomy to the *oikos*, also thereby places more things outside the realm of civic management in a site of domestic subordination of female non-citizens, slaves and children to adult male citizens (whereas Plato's female guardians enjoy cultural if not natural equality). He is therefore also more resigned to the presence of relatively unregulated conflict within the city gates. But neither Plato, nor Aristotle, being still entrapped by a *mythos* tracing two lines of succession, could really conceive of an extension of public peace and justice into the domestic sphere, without also violating its integrity. The *oikos* continued to signal possibly unlimited vengeance, which could be contained to the degree that the *polis* distributed rewards and punishments, ending the sequence of vengeance only through 'containment', or intervention from a higher plane. The thought of a domestic, tribal rule that would be peaceful without alien civic law did not occur to them. Such a thought is rather contained in the Bible, in the ideas of the protection of guilty ones (like Cain), the periodic reversions of property distribution to relatively equal portions among family units, expulsion from the community of the non-cooperating offender (instead of confinement), and of forgiveness and cancelling out of debts. Such practices do not, in principle, require supplementation by a law founded on place. Instead, they tend towards a pure diachrony without violence, and at the same time a synchrony which is the seamless inter-meshing of domestic places, instead of the dark huts of the peasants, artisans and traders huddling up to the outer face of the city walls.

In the case of the later, Christian dispensation, the contrast becomes still more acute. Where neither women, slaves, nor children were citizens, then the relationship of *oikos* to *polis* was *external*, and mediated by the father. But where, on the other hand, women, slaves and children (though still subordinate) are equally members of an *ecclesia*, then the relationship of every part of the *oikos* to the public realm is a much more direct one. As for Plato, so for Augustine, and other Christian thinkers: the public ecclesial (and even ecclesio-political) rule becomes pastoral, immediate and direct (ideally without

[91] Plato, *Republic*, 514a–517a.
[92] Ibid., 449a–457e.

law, as in Plato's myth of the tutelary deities) and therefore 'economic' in character. Inversely, the domestic – child care, economic activity, artisanal production, medical care – becomes 'political', a matter of real significance for law, education, religion, and government[93] (although this has only been spasmodically realized in Christian history).

One might, indeed, suggest that law, education, religion and politics, without child nurture, medicine, economic activity and art, are conceived in an inherently unreal and abstract fashion. The *polis* was, in reality, a male abstraction of 'ideas' away from their accompanying 'bodies'. A violent abstraction, which reinterpreted Hesiod's pastoral fields as metaphorical fields for the nurture of heroic warriors, whose stance towards 'other fields' was ultimately just as ungoverned and interminable as the wandering violence it sought to overcome.

By contrast, I shall suggest in the next chapter, the Christian *polis* that is also a household, containing only a ramifying network of households (although monasteries and the 'Christian State' have a potentially over-abstractive character) is no longer exactly a *polis*, just as Christian virtue is no longer exactly virtue.

ii.   Polis or psyche   Plato makes the right ordering of the *polis* dependent upon the right ordering of the *psyche*; and the same idea is still discernible in Aristotle. He erects in *The Republic* a strict parallel between the parts of the soul and the parts of a city: the soul is composed of desire, 'spirit' and reason, while the city is made up of economic, military and political classes.[94] In either case, the tripartite division corresponds to that distinction of three functions – ruling, fighting, sowing and reaping – which is an important structuring principle of Greek mythology (and which Georges Dumézil thought underlay all Indo-European mythology). However, one can argue, following Leo Strauss, that this parallelism breaks down, and turns into an alternative soul *or* city, parallel to the alternative of a life of *theoria*, or a life of practice.[95]

The main problem arises because the city has, in fact, no collective soul. Although, perhaps, the 'music' of politics is a kind of a collective contemplation (as I earlier suggested), this is not an idea which Plato can coherently elaborate, because, for him, contemplation only arises in the individual *psyche*. The unity of the city, although celebrated, can only be seen as a 'material' unity, and this may be, as Strauss suggests, why Plato does not clearly speak of an 'idea' of the city, and why he requires *historical* myths concerning the periodic genesis and retreat of earthly justice.[96] The sanctity of space, of the maternal womb of the *polis*, fits uneasily into Plato's ontology, for it is a constant element, and yet something only persisting, or reappearing in *time*,

---

[93] See chapter 12 below.
[94] Plato, *Republic*, 427e–444e.
[95] Strauss, *The City and Man*, pp. 50–139.
[96] Ibid.

not eternity. It is highly significant that such a rogue being, neither eternal stasis, nor temporal becoming, later finds a place in Plato's cosmology: in the Timaeus he talks of the cosmos being bounded by infinite possibility, which is a 'third nature' or mother substance (*chora*), of which we have a 'dream-like sense'.[97] Thus the receptacle of what changes and differs also abides, and the elusive totality of the *polis* would appear to have the same kind of stability.

But this somewhat negative, contentless stability, is obviously quite different from the stability of the soul, which is secured only in its upward flight towards the fixed content of the eternal ideas. It is *supposed* to be the case in *The Republic* that the virtuous should rule over the military and economic classes, just as reason should govern spiritedness and desire. However, perfect justice abides in the *idea* of justice and is achieved, outside the *polis*, in contemplation. Thus the philosopher does not finally need the city in order to realize justice, which he experiences in his own soul, and the soul's flight to the eternal. He will have to be *cajoled*, if he is to take part in politics.[98] And what is the practical, as opposed to the theoretical content of the political? It is the economic and the military elements which, by definition, because of their material birth in the womb of the *polis*, permanently escape the complete jurisdiction of reason and justice. Every time that justice 'descends', whether within the soul or within the city, it is therefore also in some measure lost, and indeed, given the total heterogeneity of economic desire together with military energy (whose search for power in the realm of becoming is indifferent to the logic of same and difference) from the mathematical calm of philosophic reason, it becomes difficult to grasp any degree of isomorphy *whatsoever*, permitting the necessary mediation. Here again, it can be seen just why the 'problem of participation' is a *political* problem, and in addition, what makes it so *acutely* problematic.

Despite Plato and Aristotle's promotion of justice and reason over against a mere *de facto* exercise of power, they never envisage that dialectics alone might be sufficient. On the contrary, reason has to add power to its truth, even though power is absolutely external to truth. Thus the military and economic powers always have to be coerced, which means a division of these powers, which are intrinsically coercive in themselves, in order to rule them. While reason aims to rule through reason not force, it finds that it must, after all, supplement itself with a rule of force over force. This is not just a matter of timeless 'political realism', but rather arises from an entirely mythical belief that both in 'the soul' and in 'the city' (themselves mythical entities) there reside permanent powers 'outside reason' escaping the full reach of intelligibility. In consequence, they must be disciplined by reason, yet *cannot* be disciplined by reason – for outside the mathematics of reason there will be no real isomorphy – and can *only* be disciplined by other powers, or by a division against themselves. Justice makes a regulated use of the power of the

---

[97] Plato, *Timaeus*, 49aff.
[98] Plato, *Republic*, 519d–521b.

furies trapped in the *agora*, but it requires, and cannot really command, an 'economic' fury that arises outside itself.

To invoke justice, the common good, or the city as a whole, means, on one available option, to 'ascend' to the soul, yet this involves a paradoxical retreat to the individual. In Plato it proves difficult to connect justice itself to the practical, while in Aristotle, justice belongs only to the practical-political, but is disconnected from *theoria*. Contemplation, however, continues to be the more ultimate goal for the individual, and even within the practical domain, it is only the 'more individuated', the more self-controlling magnanimous man, able to command and not just suffer his social relationships, who is truly virtuous. Virtue remains in Aristotle an essentially individual goal, and basic public justice, the distribution of roles and property (as opposed to secondary, corrective justice), is organized towards the nurture of a minority who will direct themselves and others.

For a second option, to invoke the 'city as a whole' would mean to 'descend', but this would imply not the collapse of *polis* into *psyche* (as in the first option) but putting the analogy altogether at risk. For if the unity of the *polis* consists only in its internal social interactions, then one has merely spirit matching spirit, desire matching desire, in a self-regulating *agon*. Alternatively, if one thinks of the unity of the *polis* as its solidarity against external forces, then again (as Strauss says) the analogy breaks down, because the relations of city to city, are not, like those of soul with soul, ideally governed by the rule of reason, but only by the logic of trade and warfare.[99] The 'same' which is the identity of a place to be defended, of one's native soil – a pure contingency – is scarcely commensurable with 'the same', which is the universal self-identity of the eternal ideas. Yet Plato insinuates a bizarre isomorphy here: the guardian rulers are guardians both of justice and of the city. In the first respect they are 'philosophers', and in the second they are 'watchdogs'. But dogs are 'philosophical beasts', because in distinguishing between owner and stranger, friend and foe, they perform the philosophic operation of distinguishing the familiar from the unfamiliar.[100] This comparison is at once nonsense, and at the same time the nonsensical point on which Platonic sense is founded (yet also breaks down). Nonsense, because the friend/foe distinction is contingent and material, whereas the eternal/becoming distinction is universal and makes 'reason' possible. Indispensable nonsense, because the second distinction entails the necessity of the first: poised between a permanent reason, and a permanent realm of unreason, one must live also in unreason, also under the rule of warfare. Therefore, the Platonic *logos* – dialectical truth itself – is *not* the *logos* that proclaims love for the enemy. Rather it still 'makes war at the stranger's gate' and the peaceful dispositions of virtue, of justice, only go on *inside* the city (precariously) and (less precariously) inside the soul. All *externalities* start to be governed – wholly or partly – by

---

[99] Strauss, *The City and Man*, pp. 50–139.
[100] Plato, *Republic*, 376a–c.

the extra-virtuous. And the internal, the perfectly self-acting (the 'contempla-tive') would not appear to be a region requiring virtue, in the sense of justice, as Aristotle indeed concluded. In antique reason therefore, virtue threatens to disappear, or to flicker momentarily within the uncertain middle region labelled 'participation'. (Nevertheless, beyond *The Republic*, Plato in the *Phaedo* and the *Phaedrus* qualified the unreason of the lower passionate realms by speaking of a 'higher *eros*' crucial for the recognition of the good itself. It is also arguable that in the *de Anima* Aristotle makes the same modification in other terms.)

What was lacking for it was both a notion of the interpersonal, and of the collectively corporeal as not 'debased'. Where the predominant figure is of the organization of an interior, then one is confined to ideas of the subordination of below to above, or of resistance to all that threatens self-sufficiency. One can think in terms of the soul as the discipline of reason over ever-recalcitrant forces inside us, or of the *polis* as material solidarity against an enemy, but not of external relations and outgoings as the very substance of thought and virtue. Such a perspective is much more provided by the Johannine idea that we are 'in one another'. Here 'participatory mixture', both within God, and for ourselves, is *prior* to the question of what is 'proper' and self-identical. But this is not a mere spiritual mixing, and the contemplative dimension does not arise first in the gaze of soul on soul, or isolated soul upon the eternal. At the heart of 'communion' lies the material exchange of sacramental elements, and this allows the figure of 'body' to become, for St Paul, that which primarily mediates the divine to us. Thus contemplation becomes something first and foremost exercised by the body which is the Church, which can itself assume a quasi-personal, Mariological character, as that which simultan-eously looks at, and generates the *Logos*.

By contrast, the Socratic *logos* rendered organism a merely material, de-based figure, and could not conceive of the interpersonal. Its duality of the 'merely' organic and the psychic individual actually foreshadows secular reason more than MacIntyre is prepared to admit. First of all, the vision of international relations is already 'Hobbesian'. Secondly, the Platonic under-standing of justice (still present in Aristotle) as 'each minding his own busi-ness' does to a degree anticipate a Machiavellian political economy, because what matters for the more 'spirited' and 'desiring' members of society is simply that they play their necessary but supplementary role in a 'blind' fashion, except when they work as artists. They do not and cannot have any personal 'onlook' upon the ideals of justice themselves. (This restriction is nonetheless mitigated in *The Laws*, where ritual processes mediate the ideal to all levels of society.) From the pagan to the modern there runs a hidden continuity, and Platonic-Aristotelian virtue is but a semi-abortive attempt to think against the dominant currents of the Western tradition (perhaps of Indo-European reason also). Neither the *polis* nor the *psyche* really flow above these currents, whereas Christianity, as we shall see, truly implies a different current, which does not attempt to stay the exterior and the outgoing, as if these were inevitably alien and irrational. This Christian *polis* will be *not exactly* the *polis*, and the Christian soul a constant exodus.

iii.   Gods or giants The third antinomy lies between ascribing ultimate reality either, on the one hand, to unity, self-identical being or the ideas, or, on the other to 'matter', becoming and difference. As I shall show, inability to resolve this antinomy in antiquity undermines the conceptual space in which 'virtue' is located. Virtue is, in fact, threatened by difference, and Plato himself arrives at this insight, only to retreat from it. Aristotle, by contrast, does not face up to the problem.

The crucial text here is Plato's *Sophist*. As a 'civic' philosophy, Platonism situates itself between the one and the many, recognizing reality both in forms and in matter. In 'the battle between the gods and the giants' it refuses to take sides, but is 'like a child begging for both'.[101] Dialectics itself is the art of having both, because predication occurs in a region between absolute identity and absolute variation, permitting certain combinations which show the influence of the one upon the many, and disallowing others which are contradictory, or illusory, and are a pure effect of 'the realm of unlikeness'. Without this art, either all is really identical and at peace, or all is chaotically different, arbitrary and conflictual. In either case, civic justice is an irrelevancy.

Yet besides opposing the Parmenidean One, the parricidal stranger of *The Sophist* suggests that it is also necessary to oppose the view of 'Father Parmenides' that 'never shall this be proved, that things that are, are not'.[102] The 'is' of an ascription of falsity, as in 'X is Y, is false' (implying that X is different from Y) assumes that an 'is not' is. Otherwise, if falsity does not in some sense exist, the distinction of true and false will have no ontological foundation. A falsity, for Plato, is essentially a *simulacrum*, a fleeting appearance which is real for a moment and yet hides the ultimate reality which remains the same, and therefore true. However, Parmenides' principle was itself part of the guarantee of truth as identity, and to call it into question involved a highly precarious defence of dialectics. In *The Sophist*, Plato identifies what one might call 'five meta-forms': being, rest, movement, same and difference, and discusses how they participate in each other. All participate in being, because, for example, rest is not movement, yet both 'are', so being must be a third thing in which they both share. Likewise, they all participate in the same, because they are identical with themselves. However, in addition they all participate in difference (*thateron*) because even the same is different from difference, and being is different from motion, as motion is not the whole of being. Yet this already suggests that difference has as great, although a *different* scope, as does being itself, and

---

[101] Plato, *Sophist*, 246a–c, 249d.
[102] Ibid., 237a, 241d.

even a larger scope, because difference is also participated in by the realm of *non-being*, which opens up in the ascription of falsity.

Because of its involvement in questioning the Parmenidean principle of identity, *thateron* 'strikes a discordant note – defying the philosophical muse'.[103] Yet despite this, it threatens actually to define the *arche* and displace 'the Good' of the Republic as the *epekeina tes ousias*, that which is beyond being.[104] Whereas, in the *Timaeus*, this 'discordant note' is assigned a mythical position as the receptive womb of becoming, in *The Sophist* its logical position among the forms themselves survives, along with its claim to be the 'super form'. But clearly, this claim threatens to undo Platonism altogether, and to situate both 'being' and 'becoming' within something like a 'super-becoming' which organizes even the possibility of a distinction between truth and untruth. And because Plato has hitched the cause of the Good to the cause of the True (despite aspiring to the opposite) this means that difference threatens to relativize the Good, justice and virtue themselves.

Plato's resort to a distinction between proper and improper mixtures does not seem to help very much here. One is not supposed to mix movement with rest, and yet the acknowledgement of the reality of falsity indicates that movement really can give rise to effects of rest, perhaps even 'is', at a certain level, a kind of rest, and so forth. If one insists, rather, that a thing cannot be both at rest and in movement in precisely the same respect, then one is just affirming the purity of difference at the level of the forms. As *Parmenides* points out, the forms, with their self-identity, seem to be necessary to support predication. Yet because ideas only relate to other commensurable ideas and participation is for us inscrutable, it is also true (one could infer) that predication is an irrelevancy for the realm of becoming. Here no combinations can really be outlawed, and the problem is compounded in the ethical sphere, where one cannot easily adjudicate correct mixtures in terms of the principle of identity. It becomes imperative for the cause of objective justice to distinguish permanent social types, and fixed compatibilities and incompatibilities, although these can only be arbitrary. Aristotle applies this procedure both to nature and to society. Abandoning participation as too ineffable, he instead tries to organize the manifold upon a hierarchical scale of species and genera in the case of nature (so occluding the problem of overlaps between *genera*, the *inevitability* of metabasis, the impossibility of saying what makes a 'specific difference' and the arbitrariness of every classification) and assumes a fairly rigid scheme of distributive justice between social classes in the case of the better sort of *polis*. In addition, Aristotle interprets the horizontal process of natural growth as itself a vertical ascent to the *arche*, in the case of the human soul. This combination is achieved by the reinvention of the soul as a space of

---

[103] Plato, *Sophist*, 259e.

[104] Jacques Rolland de Renéville, *L'Un-Multiple et l'Attribution chez Platon et les Sophistes* (Paris: Vrin, 1962) p. 195ff.

self-contained, self-activating activity. In place of the problematic ecstatic relation of soul to forms, Aristotle puts instead a smooth, immanent process tending to self-actualization. This, of course, occurs under the stimulus of the first mover, but given that motion for Aristotle is normally via the 'contact' of form with matter, and the first mover is by definition cut off from matter and remains entirely within himself, it is hard not to see the immanent motion of the soul as a kind of 'impulse from below', although matter is not supposed to be self-actuating (this is one reason why one requires the neo-Platonic idea of 'emanation').[105] Hence Aristotle's response to the late-Platonic dilemma of relating the changing to the transcendent *already* includes a kind of 'turn to the subject' (which is why 'the transcendental Thomists' are able to elide the neo-Platonic elements from Aquinas, re-Aristotelianize him, and then link him up with Kant) and the beginnings of an ethical 'individualism'. The positing of a permanent chaotic, material realm of violent conflict, means that it is finally hard to account for this realm without either retreating to a dualist metaphysics, or else making an arbitrary, violent difference itself the ultimate principle.

In antiquity, therefore, the giants are always threatening to trample upon virtue. It is of no use to protest that the Platonic ontologizing of logic is absurd and that the 'is' of the ascription of falsity simply belongs to a meta-language, because Plato's arguments about ontology are what support our inherited 'logical' ideas that truth and the self-identical are the things that are spiritually and socially important.

It is true that Aristotle was able to go beyond Plato to perceive the transcendental status of Being, its inclusion of both form and matter, and in consequence could de-ontologize notions of falsity, and ascriptions of non-being. However, the antinomy between gods and giants resurfaces in Aristotle in another fashion which, according to Edward Booth, Aristotle quite explicitly recognizes and foregrounds.[106] 'Substance' is no longer to be ascribed to detached forms, but primarily to the essential binding principle in the particular form/matter composite. This is the prime object of knowledge, and yet scientific knowledge (*episteme*) cannot be of particulars, but only of universal categories which always remain the same. Otherwise, there will be no clearly definable identities, and no dialectical reasoning able to define impossible mixtures and 'contradictory' predications. As for Plato, but in a different fashion, there is still for Aristotle an ontological interval between the being or 'actuality' of true understanding, and a positively real sphere that falls short of this; an ontological contrast necessary to generate the idea of 'truth'. In Aristotle, this sphere outside understanding is the material instantiation of substance, and the *aporia* of his ontology consists in the fact that substance is only knowable when brought under the universal, non-material categories of genera and species. Matter *itself* can never, as for Plato, be

---

[105] J.-M. LeBlond, *Logique et Méthode chez Aristote* (Paris: Vrin, 1937).

[106] Edward Booth, OP, *Aristotelian Aporetic Ontology in Islamic and Christian Thinkers* (Cambridge: Cambridge University Press, 1983) pp. 1–35. Aristotle, *Metaphysics*, 1003a5–15, 1027a9–1041b33. I am grateful to the late Gillian Rose for drawing my attention to this matter.

'mistaken', and yet its distance from the full actualization of reason shows up in the capacity of the human soul to put things in the 'wrong' combinations and to be overtaken by 'delusory' passion. Although Aristotle's bringing of matter under transcendental Being points the way for a Christian thinker like Dionysius to free the notion of difference from Platonic negativity (the 'is not') and ontologization of negation, he is, in a way, further than Plato from seeing that difference in its positivity can exceed every system of classified identities. He could only have arrived at this 'nominalism' by making the individual fully the subject of science, and qualifying hylomorphic dualism in favour of a view which, under the perspective of creation *ex nihilo*, regards matter as a kind of projected shadow of the forms or structures themselves. In contrast with such a 'nominalism' (although I would want to argue, like Berkeley, that every 'particular' is also in *itself* a universal, not definable, like an Aristotelian *genus*, but open and productive like a Platonic idea, which is also ineffably singular),[107] Aristotle's dialectics and Aristotle's 'truth' lie exposed, like Plato's, as less than an ultimate key to how things are. For the ontologically primary individual substance (although it is always already situated in a relational web) possesses a knowable difference of truth in being which exceeds that between an epistemologically true and an epistemologically false statement, and can upset the identities which found true predication and non-contradiction.

One cannot, therefore, oppose antiquity with better logic, but only with a different *mythos* which liberates difference both from heavenly suppression and gigantic violence and negativity. This is later supplied by Christianity, and some of the implications for ontology were elaborated, as we shall see, by Augustine and Dionysius. According to these thinkers evil, or untruth, is not a *simulacrum*, not a bad copy of a real thing, nor even a 'mistaken' combination, but rather a 'pure negation' of what it is itself supposed to be. A pure negation is not a contradiction, nor a denial of identity, which suggests a real act of gigantic violence, but simply a *lack*, and therefore defined in relation to *desire*, not to logic (and this fulfils the Platonic dependency of the True on the Good). Once evil and falsity are no longer seen as permanent forces over against the Good, True and Beautiful, but as the omissions and displacements of a false desire, then there 'are' no more illusions, and there is no longer any need for 'truth' in the pagan Platonic (that is to say 'usual') sense.

The Christian *mythos*, as I shall show in the next chapter, is able to rescue virtue from deconstruction into violent, agonistic difference. This is what Derrida and Deleuze both fail to see. Instead, despite the latter's protestations, they simply opt for a deconstructed or (merely) reversed Platonism, which is still, after all, the *logos* of the Greeks. The Derridean deconstruction, or the Deleuzian reversal, of Platonism, both depend upon a dualism mediated by conflict that is already encoded by Platonism itself. This deeper 'identity' of Platonism they do not question, but merely reproduce as transcendental

---

[107] Aristotle, *Metaphysics*, 1040a5–10.

violence. They correctly identify, following Plato's lead in *The Sophist*, a hidden dominance of difference as ruse and arbitrariness at the centre of Greek thought, but then proceed, as 'Greeks', to celebrate and ontologize this version of difference, rather than inquiring into its historical-semiotic conditions of possibility. For the Greek *logos*, as the *Sophist* shows, was, by a secret and yet unnecessary *fiat*, a *logos* of monstrosities, able to itself 'distribute' the temporary regimes of good distinguished from evil, beauty from ugliness. But Christianity is *not* located between the real one and the real many, and therefore is not subject to either deconstruction or reversal. As much as Deleuze, Christianity places in the *arche* (the Trinity) a multiple which is not set dialectically over against the one, but itself manifests unity. But unlike Deleuze, it is not still confined by the gigantic side of ancient myth, and shares no taste for monstrosity. His multiple is still secretly over against a banished unity, or only diversely singular in its solitary arbitrariness (like the volantarist God), whereas the Christian multiple, the infinite flow of excessive charitable difference, is, in a much more genuine sense, simultaneously Unity, and simultaneously Beauty. This Unity and Beauty now, more than ever, alone secure anything that can be called either 'virtue' or 'truth'. But not exactly virtue, not exactly truth. And not exactly the soul, not exactly the household, not exactly the city – this is the city we must finally explore.

12

The Other City:
Theology as a Social Science

Introduction

The foregoing eleven chapters of criticism were but preludes to an assertion: of theology as itself a social science, and the queen of the sciences for the inhabitants of the *altera civitas*, on pilgrimage through this temporary world.

Theology has frequently sought to borrow from elsewhere a fundamental account of society or history, and then to see what theological insights will cohere with it. But it has been shown that no such fundamental account, in the sense of something neutral, rational and universal, is really available. It is theology itself that will have to provide its own account of the final causes at work in human history, on the basis of its own particular, and historically specific faith.

This is not, however, to propose a Tridentine deduction of Christian social teaching from Christian doctrine. On the contrary, there can only be a distinguishable Christian social theory because there is also a distinguishable Christian mode of action, a definite practice. The theory explicates this practice, which arose in certain precise historical circumstances, and exists only as a particular historical development. The theory, therefore, is first and foremost an *ecclesiology*, and only an account of other human societies to the extent that the Church defines itself, in its practice, as in continuity and discontinuity with these societies. As the Church is *already*, necessarily, by virtue of its institution, a 'reading' of other human societies, it becomes possible to consider ecclesiology as also a 'sociology'. But it should be noted that this possibility only becomes available if ecclesiology is rigorously concerned with the actual genesis of real historical churches, not simply with the imagination of an ecclesial ideal.

Talk of 'a Christian sociology' or of 'theology as a social science' is not, therefore, as silly as talk of 'Christian mathematics' (I suspend judgement here) precisely because there can be no sociology in the sense of a universal 'rational' account of the 'social' character of all societies, and Christian sociology is distinctive simply because it explicates, and adopts the vantage point of, a distinct society, the Church. But the claim here is not that theology, conceived in a broadly traditional fashion, can now add to its competence certain new, 'social' pronouncements. On the contrary, the claim is that *all* theology has to reconceive itself as a kind of 'Christian sociology': that is to say, as the explication of a socio-linguistic practice, or as the constant re-narration of this practice as it has historically developed. The task of such a theology is not apologetic, nor even simply argument. Rather it is to tell again the Christian *mythos*, pronounce again the Christian *logos*, and call again for Christian *praxis* in a manner that restores their freshness and originality. It must articulate Christian difference in such a fashion as to make it strange.

In an important sense, indeed, such a theology takes up again the Hegelian tasks discussed in chapter 4. For it refuses to treat reason and morality as ahistorical universals, but instead asks, like Hegel, how has Christianity affected human reason and human practice? Abandoning all neo-scholastic attempts to graft faith onto a universal base of reason, it instead turns to the Church Fathers, and indeed goes beyond them, in seeking to elaborate a Christian *logos*, or a reason that bears the marks of the incarnation and pentecost. At the same time, it seeks to define a Christian *Sittlichkeit*, a moral practice embedded in the historical emergence of a new and unique community. Both tasks, indeed, are in turn situated in the re-narration of Christian emergence, a story which only constitutes itself as a story by re-narrating previous stories, both of past history, and of the relation of creation to Godhead.

Therefore to think a Christian theology, and at the same time to think theology as a social science, one must first of all sketch out a 'counter-history' of ecclesial origination, which tells the story of all history from the point of view of this emergence. Secondly, one must describe the 'counter-ethics', or the different practice, which emerges. It is here that the qualification of 'counter' will especially be justified, because it will be emphasized that Christian ethics differs from both pre-Christian and post-Christian ethics, and differs in such a fashion that, by comparison, certain continuities between the antique and the modern are exhibited to view. Christianity starts to appear – even 'objectively' – as not just different, but as *the* difference from all other cultural systems, which it exposes as threatened by incipient nihilism. However, it is only at the ontological level, where theology articulates (always provisionally) the framework of reference implicit in Christian story and action, that this 'total' difference is fully clarified, along with its ineradicable ties to non-provable belief. The articulation of a 'counter-ontology' is therefore the third necessary task.

In the fourth place, however, the 'counter-history' has to be taken up again, but this time under the aspect of ecclesial self-critique. Theology cannot shun the task of reflecting on 'the fate of the counter-kingdom', or on how, for the most part, the Church failed to bring about salvation, but instead ushered in the modern secular – at first liberal, and finally nihilistic – world. In a brief final *coda*, which reflects upon the route taken from the first Christian centuries to the early modern 'invention of the secular', we are brought, in a deliberately 'secular cycle', back to this book's starting point.

Counter-History

1   *Metanarrative realism*

A postmodern (or 'post-liberal') theology, as George Lindbeck has rightly argued, must reject two forms of 'foundationalism'. First, it has to refuse the idea that faith is grounded in a series of propositions about 'objects' available to our rational gaze: God, eternity, the soul, or incarnate divinity, 'proven' by miraculous events and fulfilments of prophecies.[1] Secondly, it has to refuse equally the idea that Christian beliefs are somehow 'expressions' of experiences entirely preceding those beliefs.

For how, one may ask (elaborating Lindbeck), could we ever know that such expressions were appropriate? And how can one speak of an experience, a kind of 'event', if this is not either semiotically or imagistically linked to other events, and therefore in principle already publicly available, and positioned in terms of certain pre-existing codes, whether of signs, visual figures, or sound sequences? The experience that 'searches for expression' should rather be understood as the intimation of, or the already-begun commencement of, a new figurative, musical or linguistic articulation. And the inviolability and subjectivity of such an experience belongs not in interior ineffability, but rather on the surface, as a visible or audible modification to the public stock of sounds, words and images. The subjective, therefore, is conserved not in Cartesian or Kantian interiority, but rather in a Spinozan or Leibnizian structural positionality, which makes it at once 'more objective', and at the same time less universal, and more confined to a perspective. In consequence, the realm of feelings, affections, aspirations and experiences can no longer pose as a new site of universality, a firm 'base' in which to locate the religious, and on which to build a theology.

Instead, a postmodern theology has to understand that both the objects of Christian faith – insofar as they are imaged and articulated – and the modes of Christian experience, are derived from a particular cultural practice which projects objects and positions subjects in a conjoint operation, relating the one set to the other. If anything refers to reality here, then it must be, as Lindbeck says, the *entire practice*, with all its signs, images and actions, and not just a set of propositions taken in isolation.[2] However, a rigorous understanding of the implications of this thesis will show that more importance must be given to propositions, and so to ontology, than Lindbeck appears to allow.

---

[1] George Lindbeck, *The Nature of Doctrine: Religion and Theology in a Postliberal Age* (London: SPCK, 1984).

[2] Ibid., pp. 65–8.

In the first place, as D. Z. Phillips has pointed out against Lindbeck, even this version of reference cannot be neutrally conceived, as in the sentence 'the whole of Christian practice refers to the absolute'.[3] What *kind* of absolute? one would want to ask here. In fact, questions of reference to the absolute only arise because the practice *internally* defines itself as 'a response to the absolute' (though in its own, particular terms) and indeed only constitutes itself as a practice insofar as it imagines, in a hesitating and provisional fashion, the shape of 'the absolute' to which its own practice is a response. This means that it must also have always already imagined, albeit in a 'mythical' form, the relationship pertaining between 'the absolute' and the practice, which makes this response possible. Hence, while every dimension of religious practice, including the articulation of a theology, is fundamentally 'performative', it is also the case that no performance could be staged without the assumption (itself projected by a performance) of a historical and mythical scene within which that performance is set. A 'propositional' level, grounded not simply on intellectual 'vision', but simultaneously in creative imagination, is therefore implicit even within a religious practice confined to worship and the recitation of stories. It is when interpretative doubts set in about the permanent 'setting' assumed for the human drama, that a theoretical, doctrinal, level tends to 'take off' from the level of narrative. Once the 'setting' has been seen as questionable, this moment cannot really be revoked.

In the second place, since doctrine arises out of interpretative undecidability, doctrinal issues cannot be settled simply by recourse to a more exact reading of preceding practices and narratives. Were this the case, then the answer to 'heresies' would be but to repeat the narratives in a louder tone, in the vain hope that the setting they assumed would become transparent. But in fact, doctrine represents a kind of 'speculative moment' that cannot be reduced to the heuristic protection of narrative (in the sense of merely safeguarding what is properly implicit in the narrative) because it relates to the synchronic, paradigmatic instance of ultimate 'setting' which *every* syntagmatic sequence has to assume, and yet cannot adequately represent.

Consider, for example, the doctrine of the Incarnation. At the 'first order' level of narrative and practice, Christians regard Christ as 'their judge': they try to gauge every aspect of their lives by a standard embodied in the stories about his life. Furthermore, they consider these stories to be a kind of climax, situated paradoxically in the middle of history, for all other stories, so that all history before Christ can be narrated as anticipating his story, and all history since as situated within it, such that everything which subsequently happens is nothing but the acceptance or the rejection of Christ. This, then, is to treat Christ as measuring all reality, in the same way that God's generated wisdom, his Word, is taken to do. The doctrine of the Incarnation therefore asserts that an identification of Jesus with the *Logos* is implicit in Christian practice, and

[3] D. Z. Phillips, 'Lindbeck's audience', in *Modern Theology*, vol. 4, no. 2, January 1988, pp. 133–54.

the doctrine itself helps to secure and promote an already existing Christo-centrism. And yet it does more than articulate the implicit: it also emphatic-ally pronounces with regard to doubts that narrative and practice do not clearly resolve. Does Christ's measuring of all time hitherto allow us to deny the possibility of a still further revelation? Such a possibility has been entertained in Christian history, notably by the Joachites. And is God's 'ultimate' word, expressed in Christ, nevertheless merely an expression of his declared will, rather than indissociable from his very being and identical with deity itself? The former possibility seems to have underlain Arius's rejection of the Trinity, and so of the Incarnation.[4] Disconcerting as it may appear, one has to recognize in the doctrinal affirmation of the Incarnation a radically inventive moment, which asserts the 'finality' of God's appearance in a life involving suffering and violent death, and claims also that in a certain sense God 'has to' be like this, and has not just 'incidentally' chosen this path. Significantly, these implications open out further questions about whether the God so finally revealed can at some later stage intervene with a 'coercive' force: questions which Christianity has never collectively resolved, and where, again, the narratives do not simply impose an answer, because one is faced with questions about whether metaphors of coercive action by God in the book of Revelation – which concerns Christ's eschatological action – are to be taken literally, and so forth.

If there is, in the doctrine of the Incarnation, a radically 'inventive' moment (an ungrounded addition of new presentational 'phrases', in Lyotard's terms), then what can possibly justify this? In part, it is justified by the redoubled force which it gives to existing Christian practice, defined by its attempt to place itself under the judgement of Christ. But even in this respect the doctrine seems 'excessive', for reasons I have just indicated. The only possible additional justification must come from the inherent attractiveness of the picture of God thence provided: no other picture, save of incarnation in a joyful and suffering life in time, gives quite such an acute notion of divine love, and involvement in our destiny. To speak of 'a' joyful and suffering life, relatively to abstract from the concrete life of Jesus, is, in the speculative moment – which is not for me, as for Hegel, the final moment – unavoidable. Thus the *idea* of a God-become-incarnate, since it is in some measure 'exces-sive' in relation to the stories about Jesus, inevitably tends at times to remove these stories from our attention, and this process has clearly already begun in the New Testament, and even in the Gospels themselves. In fact, one should say that it had 'always already' begun, because the dazzling effect of Jesus upon his followers caused them to use divine metaphors with regard to him, which both 'reflected' Jesus (and in a real sense *were* the presence of Jesus) and also, in a certain, not really-to-be-regretted fashion, obscured him in favour of an 'idea'. In fact, the 'idea', which becomes the idea of the Incarnation, quickly

---

[4] Rowan Williams, *Arius* (London: Darton, Longman and Todd, 1987) pp. 95–117.

works itself *back* into the first-order level of mythical narrative and devotion: think of the Christian poetry laden with conceits about the infinite in the finite, or the pathos in devotion to the dying God on the cross. When I say 'idea', I am not therefore thinking of something alien to the level of popular piety.

And I also want to claim that this 'idea' is an inseparable part of historical Christianity, and that such speculations are unavoidable, though they remain ungrounded, except in the pleasing character of the conceits to which they give rise. Nevertheless, there is more than a danger that a contemplation of the paradigmatic 'setting' for the Christian drama – the sublime Baroque scenery – will totally efface the syntagmatic, narrative dimension. Properly understood, the speculative idea does *not* encourage this, but rather (as Hegel half understood) of its own nature demands a return to the concrete, narrative level: if Jesus really is the Word of God, then it is not the mere 'extrinsic' knowledge of this which will save us, but rather a precise attention to his many words and deeds and all their historical results. The idea helps to confirm *that* God is love, the narrative alone instructs about *what* love is.

For this reason George Lindbeck and Hans Frei have been quite right to call us back to narrative as being that alone which can 'identify' God for us. But more attention must be paid to the structural complexity of narrative, and especially the way it has to assume a never fully representable synchronic setting, which means that it always in a fashion anticipates the speculative task of ontology and theology. Narratives only identify God because they simultaneously invent the unpresentable 'idea' of God. And it is precisely because this invention is hesitating and uncertain that problems also accrue around the identification. Such narratives are difficult, hard to read, and one cannot abstract, as Lindbeck tries to do, a few simple rules about how to interpret them (as, for example, one of Lindbeck's rules which prescribes 'Christocentricity'), rules invariant throughout Christian history and sup- posedly more basic than actually formulated doctrines which translate these rules into the intellectual language of a particular time and place. The very necessity for 'rules' marks the highly problematic character of the attachment of the 'identification' of God to 'the idea of God'. Precisely what force is one to give to the narrative, and to what degree does it represent the Godhead? 'Rules' are, in effect, speculative interpretations of the implicit assumptions of the narrative, and the articulation of these assumptions will necessarily en- gage with the conceptual resources available at a particular historical time, which then become an inescapable part of the Christian inheritance, not a mere husk to be easily discarded, as Lindbeck implies. In this way doctrines, although they are 'second order' reflections on narrative and practice, and do not 'refer' on their own, but only in conjunction with their 'regulation' of first order discourse, nonetheless do contain an inescapably 'surplus', prop- ositional element which contributes, in a distinct moment, to the overall 'imagination of reference'.

All this bears crucially on George Lindbeck's attempt to develop a kind of 'metanarrative realism'.[5] As has been said, if anything 'refers' for Lindbeck, it is the entire Christian performance. Correct performance, however, is for Lindbeck defined in advance by the exemplary narratives of Jesus. These stories are not situated within the world: instead, for the Christian, the world is situated within these stories. They define for us what reality is, and they function as a 'metanarrative', not in the sense of a story based on, or unfolding foundational reason (Lyotard's sense) but in the sense of a story privileged by faith, and seen as the key to the interpretation and regulation of all other stories. However, Lindbeck's ignoring of the structural complexity of narrative means that his account of metanarrative realism becomes dangerously ahistorical. Because he fails to see the tension in any narrative between the assumption of a paradigmatic setting, and the unfolding of a syntagmatic development, he proceeds to graft the paradigmatic function inappropriately onto the narrative structures as such. Thus Christians are seen as living within certain fixed narratives which function as *schemas*, which can organize endlessly different cultural contents.[6] These 'hypostasized' narratives are not seen as belonging within the sequence of history itself, but instead as atemporal categories for Christian understanding. Christianity possesses in them a permanent, essentially unproblematic code, which can be described and operated as well by an 'outsider' as by an 'insider'.[7] Although they 'organize' our lives within different cultural situations, these situations are just regarded as neutrally empirical from the perspective of the narratives. Hence Christianity can readily be translated into many different conceptual schemes and (presumably) social situations. There is no real possibility here for Christianity to exert a critical influence on its cultural receptacles, nor for these in turn to criticize Christianity. This possibility is occluded by Lindbeck, not because he is a postmodern relativist, but rather because he has artificially insulated the Christian narrative from its historical genesis. A narrative that is falsely presented as a paradigm is seen as over and done with, and easy to interpret. Hence, for Lindbeck, apparent divergences among Christians can often be exposed as mere over-estimations of the importance of conceptual articulation in different cultural settings.[8] He thereby converts metanarrative realism into a new narratological foundationalism and fails to arrive at a postmodern theology.

To have a genuine metanarrative realism, one would have to pay attention to the play between the paradigmatic and the syntagmatic. Here the narrative itself is always already internally torn between 'staying in the place' of its assumed frame of reference, or breaking out of this frame to project a new one through the temporal course of events. In the case of the Biblical narratives,

---

[5] This phrase was first used by Ken Surin in relation to one of my own articles, but I think it can be usefully applied also to Lindbeck's perspective.

[6] Lindbeck, *The Nature of Doctrine*, pp. 67, 82–4.

[7] Ibid., pp. 101–2.

[8] Ibid., pp. 81–3, 96.

where the projected frame of reference is the relation of the supernatural to the natural, the paradigmatic is sketched in vaguely, and gets constantly revised in response to syntagmatic unfolding. These features are actually accentuated in the course of the formulation of Christian doctrine. Yet by substituting narrative for doctrine in the articulation of the paradigmatic setting for Christian life, Lindbeck ensures that we get something *more* rigid, and less open to revision. The doctrinal 'idea' – which is inherently vague, general, approximate, negative – is an inherently more cautious, less determinate way to handle 'setting', within which stories, both 'mythical' and historical, can unfold.

But if, as with Lindbeck, on the one side, paradigm-become-narrative loses its provisional character, then, on the other side, narrative-become-paradigm loses its temporal, historical character. Whereas the idea allows the narrative to flow, Lindbeck's narrative-paradigm is insulated, in a mystifying fashion, from its narrative genesis and later narrative consequences.

For we do not relate to the story of Christ by schematically applying its categories to the empirical content of whatever we encounter. Instead, we interpret this narrative in a response which inserts us in a narrative relation to the 'original' story. First and foremost, the Church stands in a narrative relationship to Jesus and the Gospels, within a story that subsumes both. This must be the case, because no *historical* story is ever 'over and done with'.[9] Furthermore, the New Testament itself does not preach any denial of historicity, nor any disappearance of our own personalities into the monistic truth of Christ. Quite to the contrary, Jesus's mission is seen as inseparable from his preaching of the Kingdom, and inauguration of a new sort of community, the Church. Salvation is available for us after Christ, because we can be incorporated into the community which he founded, and the response of this community to Christ is made possible by the response to the divine Son of the divine Spirit, from whom it receives the love that flows between Son and Father. The association of the Church with the response of the Spirit which arises 'after' the Son, and yet is fully divine, shows that the new community belongs from the beginning within the new narrative manifestation of God. Hence the metanarrative is *not* just the story of Jesus, it is the continuing story of the Church, already realized in a finally exemplary way by Christ, yet still to be realized universally, in harmony with Christ, and yet *differently*, by all generations of Christians.

The metanarrative, therefore, is the genesis of the Church, outside which context one could only have an ahistorical, gnostic Christ. But once one has said this, one then has to face up to the real implication of a narrative that is at one and the same time a recounting of a 'real history', and yet has also an interpretative, regulative function with respect to all other history. The real implication is this: one simply cannot exhibit in what its 'meta' character

---

[9] Kenneth Surin, 'The weight of weakness: intratextuality and discipleship', in *The Turnings of Darkness and Light* (Cambridge: Cambridge University Press 1989) pp. 201–21.

consists, without *already* carrying out this interpretation, this regulation, to the widest possible extent. One has to pass from Lindbeck's 'Kantian' narrative epistemology of scheme and content to a 'Hegelian' metanarrative which is 'a philosophy of history', though based on faith, not reason. For the Christo-logical-ecclesial narrative *arises*, in the first place, not simply as an 'identifica-tion' of the divine, but also as a 'reading' and a critique-through-practice of all historical human community up to that point. Initially, it defines itself as both in continuity and discontinuity with the community of Israel; later on it defines itself as in still greater discontinuity with the 'political' societies of the antique world. This account of history and critique of human society is in no sense an appendage to Christianity – on the contrary, it belongs to its very essence. For first of all, its break with Judaism arises from Christianity's denial that the Jewish law is the final key to true human community and salvation. And secondly, Christianity's universalist claim that incorporation into the Church is indispensable for salvation assumes that other religions and social groupings, however virtuous-seeming, were, in their own terms alone, finally on the path of damnation.

In this fashion a gigantic claim to be able to read, criticize, say what is going on in other human societies, is absolutely integral to the nature of the Chris-tian Church, which itself claims to exhibit the exemplary form of human community. For theology to surrender this claim, to allow that other dis-courses – 'the social sciences' for example – carry out yet more fundamental readings, would therefore amount to a denial of theological truth. The *logic* of Christianity involves the claim that the 'interruption' of history by Christ and his bride, the Church, is the most fundamental of events, interpreting all other events. And it is *most especially* a social event, able to interpret other social formations, because it compares them with its own new social practice.

A genuine 'metanarrative realism' does full justice to the internal tension within narrative. In particular, the temporality of the syntagmatic dimension is not betrayed, because the metanarrative ceases, as we have just seen, to be *only* a privileged set of events, but rather becomes the whole story of human history which is still being enacted and interpreted in the light of those events. This ensures that the 'redescription' of Christianity advocated by Lindbeck and the Yale school will now have a fully social and political dimension. But if history is to return, so also is ontology, which has been shamefully neglected by a theology too permeated by analytic philosophy (at its most mind-numbingly obscure and tedious). The paradigmatic dimension of narrative shows that an ontological questioning is 'always already begun'. Therefore, having first tried to narrate Christian difference in its historical emergence, we shall then have to continue the doctrinal-ontological effort to interpret that difference of setting which the narrative has always presupposed.

It is, in fact, at the point where the metanarrative requires a speculative ontology to support its meta-status, that Christian counter-history is revealed as also a 'Christian sociology'. The privileging of the synchronic which soci-ology involves is unjustifiable in terms of a purely immanent 'science', or else in terms of a 'Malebranchian' alienation of 'the social' from human causation (as we saw in Part Two). However, a near priority of the synchronic over the diachronic is *unavoidable* in terms of the need of any normative narrative (and no society or historiography can avoid this normative dimension) to represent the infinite/finite ratio, or 'the way things are' as the ultimate 'setting' for history, even though this representation must be constantly re-made and cannot be made once and for all. In the dimension of metaphysics and theology therefore, sociology, which I earlier banished, makes a *return* (as Luigi Sturzo already suggested). But in its proper function as 'speculative' discourse it does not usurp the historical, in the way it did as 'scientific' discourse.

But before articulating this sociological/ontological speculation about 'setting', I must first try to give substantive content to the Christian counter-history, and then the Christian counter-ethics.

2   The two cities

In my view, a true Christian metanarrative realism must attempt to retrieve and elaborate the account of history given by Augustine in the *Civitas Dei*. For one can only stick fast by the principle of 'intratextuality' – the idea that theology is an explication of the developing and rationally unfounded Christian cultural code – if one seeks for one's fundamental principles of *critique* within the Christian 'text', and not in some universal, and so foundationalist, principle of 'suspicion'. A re-reading of the *Civitas Dei* will allow us to realize that political theology can take its critique, both of secular society and of the Church, directly out of the developing Biblical tradition, without recourse to any entirely alien supplementation. (Nevertheless, this development only occurs through the new disclosures of latent content arising through contact with new external settings.) For within Augustine's text we discover the *original* possibility of critique that marks the Western tradition, of which later Enlightenment versions are, in certain respects, abridgements and foundationalist parodies. Friedrich Nietzsche quite correctly diagnosed that both liberalism and socialism are not truly universal rational ethical codes, but rather new variants of the Christian *mythos*, which is a sheer contingency, a particular invention within historical time.

Nonetheless, Nietzsche was also forced to recognize that there was something uniquely 'perverse' about Christianity, and that its peculiar mode of difference, the celebration of weakness (as Nietzsche inadequately described it) showed up by contrast a *common* element in all other cultures, namely, a heroic ethical code celebrating strength and attainment. In this way, therefore, as I have already noted, *The Genealogy of Morals* is a kind of *Civitas Dei* written back to front. And this observation should help us to see that, from a postmodern perspective, Augustine's philosophy of history appears more viable than that of either Hegel or Marx. These two provide 'gnostic' versions of Augustine's critical Christianity by giving us a story in which antagonism is inevitably brought to an end by a necessary dialectical passage through conflict. Augustine, on the other hand, puts peaceful reconciliation in no dialectical relationship with conflict, but rather does something prodigiously more historicist, in that he isolates the codes which support the universal sway of antagonism, and contrasts them with the code of a peaceful mode of existence, which has historically arisen as 'something else', an *altera civitas*, having no logical or causal connection with the city of violence.

In part, though, it must be conceded that what Augustine achieves is a kind of immanent critique, or deconstruction of antique political society (which I endeavoured to extend in the last section of the last chapter). He tries to show that, by its own standards, its virtue is not virtue, its community not community, its justice not justice. Here I shall demonstrate that this deconstruction is possible for the same reasons that Plato in *The Sophist* could broach the deconstruction of antique philosophy: namely, the inherent *dualism* of reason and disorder within the antique *mythos*, which was gradually abandoned in late antiquity (not just by Christianity, but also by stoicism and neo-Platonism). There is consequently a profoundly sceptical moment in Augustine's analysis, and those commentators who see him as opening up the 'liberal', or even nihilistic possibility of a regulation of power by power are, to a degree, quite correct.[10] However, what the same commentators – falsely attributing to Augustine an entirely privatized and spiritual notion of religion – often fail to realize, is that the more important critical element in the *Civitas Dei* arises beyond this point: in a demonstration of how the nihilistic competition of power with power is itself entrapped within a certain *mythos*, a certain coded practice. But this more decisive critique, going beyond Plato, is only opened out through a contrast between pagan religion and practice with Christian religion and practice, in which the former is regarded as a distorted and distant echo of the latter. The non-antagonistic, peaceful mode of life of the city of God is grounded in a particular, historical and 'mythical' narrative, and in an ontology which explicates the beliefs implicit in this narrative. It is in fact the ontological priority of peace over conflict (which is arguably the key theme of his entire thought) that is the principle undergirding Augustine's critique. However, this principle is firmly anchored in a narrative, a practice, and a dogmatic faith, not in an abstracted universal reason.

Thus Augustine's contrast between ontological antagonism and ontological peace is grounded in the contrasting historical narratives of the two cities. The *Civitas terrena* is marked by sin, which means, for Augustine, the denial of God and others in favour of self-love and self-assertion; an enjoyment of arbitrary, and therefore violent power over others – the *libido dominandi*.[11] To show that pagan political communities were fundamentally sinful, Augustine consequently had to argue that their structures of *dominium* – of self-

---

[10] R. A. Markus, *Saeculum: History and Society in the Theology of St Augustine* (Cambridge: Cambridge University Press, 1970) p. 177ff.

[11] Augustine, *Civitas Dei*, XIV, 15, 28, XV, 7.

command, economic property ownership, and political rule – were not truly subordinated to the ends of justice and virtue, but rather pursued *dominium* as an end in itself. In making this argument, he draws a contrast between a certain kind of limited, apparent peace, consequent upon the victory of a dominant force over other forces, and a real peace, which is a state of harmonious agreement, based upon a common love, and a realization of justice for all.[12] The peace of Rome, he claims, is only an apparent one, because it is but an arbitrary limitation of a preceding state of anarchic conflict. To prove this, he points first to the unjustifiability of Rome's sway over other peoples, secondly to the injustice of an idea of ownership which allows the owner to 'do as he likes' with what he owns, and thirdly to the consistently inhuman treatment of the *plebs* by the Roman aristocracy.[13] However, he also, and still more importantly, shows that the Romans only had the vaguest intimations of a justice and peace that were *not* fundamentally the exercise of *dominium*. Hence (as I shall further elaborate in the next section) Augustine contends that the Roman notion of virtue itself reduced to the pursuit of glory and pre-eminence that is involved in an attainment of self-control and victory over one's passions. The Romans, like all pagans, think that there can only *be* virtue where there is something to be defeated, and virtue therefore consists for them, not only in the attainment and pursuit of a goal desirable in itself, but also in a 'conquest' of less desirable forces, which is always an exercise of strength *supplementary to*, although supporting, a 'right desire'.[14]

While Augustine notes that the philosophers sometimes had intimations of an idea of goodness going beyond such assumptions, he also realizes that they could not fully escape them, because they were so deeply inscribed at the level of myth and ritual.[15] Only changes at *this* level can really alter public belief and practice, and make a genuinely non-polytheistic ontology possible. In the story which Rome tells about its own foundations, the principle of a prior violence 'stayed' and limited by a single violent hand is firmly enshrined.[16] Romulus, the founder, is the murderer of his brother and rival Remus; he is also the enslaver of the *clienteles* to whom he offered protection against foreign enemies. In battle, Romulus invoked the staying hand of Jupiter, who then received the title *stator*. The supreme God, therefore, like the founding hero, arises merely as the limiter of a preceding disorder. (Before Augustine, Origen had already noted that pagan emperors derived their authority from a god who was not only a 'stayer' of prior violence, but also a *usurper* of the preceding order of father Cronos.)[17] Mythical beginnings of legal order are therefore traced back to the arbitrary limitation of violence by

---

[12] Augustine, *CD* XIV, 1; XV, 4; XIX, 19, 20, 27.
[13] Augustine, *CD* II, 18, 20; III, 10, 15; V, 12.
[14] Augustine, *CD* XIV, 9; XIX, 4, 10, 27.
[15] Augustine, *CD* II, 22; III, 13; V, 12; IX, 6–23.
[16] Augustine, *CD* III, 6, 13, 14; XV, 5, 6.
[17] Origen, *Contra Celsum*, VIII, 68.

violence, to victory over rivals, and to the usurpation of fathers by sons. And, according to Augustine, the Romans continued to 'live out' the *mythos*: within the city gates the goddess most celebrated was *Bellona*, the virtues most crowned with glory were military ones. The statue of the goddess *Quies*, by contrast, stood outside the gates, as if to indicate that peace was a benefit brought through war by Rome to others. But if virtue and peace result through war, argues Augustine, the real goddess celebrated by Romans is 'foreign injustice'[18] – a 'preceding' anarchy and arbitrary domination must always be newly sought out if the founding story is to be again re-enacted.

However, this Roman world has been interrupted by another beginning, and another continuity. Instead of Jove, the stayer of a preceding battle, Christians worship the one true God who originates all finite reality in an act of peaceful donation, willing a new fellowship with himself and amongst the beings he has created. In 'the heavenly city', beyond the possibility of alteration, the angels and saints abide in such a fellowship; their virtue is not the virtue of resistance and domination, but simply of remaining in a state of self-forgetting conviviality.[19] Here there is nothing but 'the vision of peace', a condition that originally pertained also for the temporal creation, before the sinful assertion of pride and domination introduced a pervasive presence of conflict leading to death in both society and nature. But God and the heavenly Jerusalem – our 'true mother' – reach down in compassion for the salvation of the world. Salvation from sin must mean 'liberation' from cosmic, political, economic and psychic *dominium*, and therefore from all structures belonging to the *saeculum*, or temporal interval between the Fall and the final return of Christ. This salvation takes the form of a different inauguration of a different kind of community. Whereas the *civitas terrena* inherits its power from the conqueror of a fraternal rival, the 'city of God on pilgrimage through this world' founds itself not in a succession of power, but upon the memory of the murdered brother, Abel slain by Cain.[20] The city of God is in fact a paradox, 'a nomad city' (one might say) for it does not have a site, or walls or gates. It is not, like Rome, an *asylum* constituted by the 'protection' offered by a dominating class to the dominated, in the face of an external enemy. This form of refuge is, in fact, but a dim archetype of the real refuge provided by the Church, which is the forgiveness of sins.[21] Instead of a peace 'achieved' through the abandonment of the losers, the subordination of potential rivals and resistance to enemies, the Church provides a genuine peace by its memory of all the victims, its equal concern for all its citizens and its self-exposed offering of reconciliation to enemies. The peace within the city walls opposing the 'chaos' without, is, in fact, no peace at all compared with a peace coterminous with all Being whatsoever.

---

18 Augustine, *CD* IV, 15.
19 Augustine, *CD* XIV, 17; XIX, 10, 13, 27.
20 Augustine, *CD* XV, 2.
21 Augustine, *CD* I, 35; V, 12.

Space is revolutionized: it can no longer be defended, and even the barbarians can only respect the sanctuary of the Basilica.[22]

3   *Violence and atonement (the work of René Girard)*

Augustine's critique of pagan religion concerns also its many gods and the ritual relations of the city to these gods. A diversity of gods, governing different areas of cultural life, implies that these areas may be fundamentally in conflict, and that they require their own consecrating deities precisely because their distinctness is at bottom a matter of the self-assertion of power. Thus Augustine says that the diverse pagan virtues were 'commanded by demons' (the gods being really malign demons) and consequently 'relate only to themselves'.[23] The honour due to the diverse gods is fundamentally a matter of satisfying their lust, greed and power, and therefore what they demand is *sacrifice*. They desire to subtract something from us, and delight most of all to be spectators at festivals of violence, the gladiatorial combats in the stadium at the heart of the city.[24] By contrast, the unified God of Christianity is utterly removed from any idea of rivalry or self-assertion, and does not demand any sacrifice save that of the offering of love.[25] Just as the act of creation takes away nothing from God, so also our self-giving involves no real self-loss, but is rather a new reception of being which consists fundamentally in orientation to the Other. Whereas, within Rome, there are many sacrifices to many, sometimes rival gods, no sacrifices, properly speaking, occur within the Church, but rather, the Church community is *itself* the real sacrifice to God, because its bonds of community are constituted by mutual self-offering.[26]

Recently, the French cultural critic, René Girard, has, in effect, revived a two cities philosophy of history, precisely in connection with the phenomenon of sacrifice. Any attempt to renew an Augustinian perspective must clearly now take an account of his work, of which I will, therefore, offer a brief consideration.

Before Girard turned his attention to the Bible, and elaborated his new vindication of Christianity, he had already devised a new theory of religion, which owed much to Freud, Frazer and Durkheim.[27] For this theory, all cultural behaviour is dominated by the phenomenon of 'mimetic rivalry', exemplified in the tendency of imitation to pass into an attempt to outstrip its model. For Girard, we desire through imitation, we desire what others desire, and this is often complicated by a desire *for* others, for those whom we

---

[22] Augustine, *CD* I, 7, 35.
[23] Augustine, *CD* XIX, 25.
[24] Augustine, *CD* III, 14.
[25] Augustine, *CD* X, 5, 6.
[26] Augustine, *CD* X, 5.
[27] René Girard, *Violence and the Sacred* (Baltimore, MD: John Hopkins University Press, 1978). See also John Milbank, 'Stories of sacrifice', in *Modern Theology*, vol. 12, no. 1 (Jan 1996) pp. 27–56.

are also trying to displace.[28] Conflicts, therefore, are usually between 'doubles', and primitive peoples show logic in their horror of close similarities, whose danger is reflected in stories of competing twins, like Romulus and Remus.[29] But the will to difference is *also* malign, and antagonistic, because it is a desire to distinguish oneself from the similar rival in some respect or other. Conflict differentiates, although it is rooted in similarity.

As soon as one has culture, or a system of coded marks and signs, then one also has mimetic rivalry, endlessly self-duplicating conflicts of 'brother' with 'brother'. To put an end to this anarchic condition, societies fix upon a single 'rival' of the collectivity, and expel him as an enemy.[30] The solidarity which results, allows the community to believe that it has got rid of a 'poison', while at the same time the path traversed by the scapegoat appears curative, and the victim himself may get endowed with a certain 'sacral' aura. This mystification of the socially beneficial effects of scapegoating constitutes the precise point of birth of religion, whose real function is to legitimate and conceal acts of founding violence. By the same token, religions are machines for the forgetting of history and the substitution of mythology. In the course of time, scapegoatings and human sacrifices are usually commuted to the use of animals or to mere ritual gestures. However, these commutations themselves conceal from view the real violent basis of society, and the fact that its most important social practices continue to be marked by mimetic rivalry, and collective attempts to control this.

These conclusions, are, for Girard, those of a rigorous social science, which has at last managed to decipher religion and so unlock the secrets of human culture as a whole. However, these scientific conclusion are, he now considers, anticipated by the texts of the Old and New Testaments.[31] The Bible, he claims, is unique, because it gradually exposes and rejects 'the sacred', as understood by all other cultures. Whereas they mystify the expulsion of victims, the Bible, from Abel onwards, takes the part of these victims, and protests at the arbitrariness of their treatment. The Hebrews define themselves *as* the rejected, the community of an Exodus. For a long time such expulsions are still considered in some degree sacrally efficacious, even where the victim's part is taken, but finally, in the New Testament, all violence, and all sacralization of violence, is totally eschewed. Jesus reveals that even Jewish law and society is founded upon exclusion and expulsion. In response, Jesus is himself excluded and finally done to death, but his own identification with victims exhibited no desire to become himself a sacral victim. Rather, Jesus came to expose the secret of social violence hidden 'since the foundation of the world', and to preach 'the Kingdom' as the possibility of a life refusing mimetic rivalry, and, in consequence, violence. The Gospels do not, according

[28] René Girard, *Violence and the Sacred* (Baltimore, MD: John Hopkins University Press, 1978). René Girard, *Things Hidden Since the Foundation of the World*, trans. Stephen Bann and Michael Metteer (London: Athlone, 1987) pp. 3–48, 326–51.

[29] Ibid., pp. 3–48, 105–26, 299–305.

[30] Ibid., pp. 3–48, 126–38.

[31] Ibid., pp. 141–280.

to Girard, in any way imply that Jesus was a sacrificial victim, and this idea is only introduced by the Epistle to the Hebrews. (More recently, however, Girard has cogently argued that even this text resists a 'sacrificial' thesis in the received sense.) Most 'orthodox' views of the atonement, by making Jesus himself the universal scapegoat, represent a monstrous self-misprision on the part of Christianity, although other aspects of Christological orthodoxy can be vindicated, when Jesus's preaching is properly understood. (Again, Girard has later plausibly argued that orthodox views of the atonement are in fact non-sacrificial.) For if the victimage mechanism is culturally all-pervasive, then it could only be grasped, and exposed within culture, by one standing also outside culture. Only, therefore, by God incarnate. ·

Now much of this analysis is profoundly perceptive, and manifestly in accord with the Augustinian perspective which I am advocating. Nevertheless, there are two major criticisms to be made of this metanarrative: the first concerns Girard's theory of religion, the second, his Christology.

With regard to religion, Girard stands fully within the positivist tradition. It is religion that first of all secures 'society'; feelings of social solidarity are linked with arbitrary sacrifice; religion can be 'explained' in social terms; social science replaces philosophy and is itself identical with true religion, in this case Christianity, slightly reinterpreted.[32] The criticisms which I have already made of this tradition can, therefore, all be applied to Girard. But more particularly, Girard is guilty, like Lévi-Strauss, of projecting a modern, liberal grid onto traditional, 'hierarchical' societies. This is shown by his attitude to desire: desire, he assumes, is never for the *objectively* desirable, but only for what others deem to be desirable. Thus the 'original' cultural situation is one of competing equals, and differences are generated from dualistic oppositions arising out of rivalry. However, a society of equals is not a more 'natural' society, and would rather require a particular cultural coding. Equally possible would be a primordial hierarchical society, in which certain positions and values were regarded as objectively more important and desirable than others. In such a society, rivalry would appear to be a secondary phenomenon in comparison with the given objects of rivalry and desire, and this appearance could only be rationally denied if one assumed the arbitrariness of all desire. But such an assumption is clearly rooted in modern, liberal culture. It follows that Girard's entire attempt to 'explain' religion also privileges this same liberal culture, because in the case of a traditional, hierarchical society it would not be feasible to show that religion was a later, secondary phenomenon, invented to cope with recurrent cultural crises. Here expulsions and sacrifices (which Girard too easily tends to conflate) would not found order, but would be components of an already given order, mechanisms by which a hierarchy sustained itself. In fact, by positing a real pre-religious phase of unlimited and anarchic conflict, Girard himself falls victim to a component of the pagan *mythos* as diagnosed by Augustine. For it is the claim of the legality of the *civitas*

---

[32] Serge Tcherzekoff, *Dual Classification Reconsidered.*

terrena to have suppressed an anarchy that is necessarily ontologically prior. Augustine concedes that this may have been historically the case, but denies any necessity to sinful confusion. And one should go further than Augustine to suggest that every legality has always claimed validity by virtue of its keeping at bay an essentially imaginary chaos. What came 'first' was not anarchy, but this legal, coercive and itself 'anarchic' assertion, meeting always a partial resistance from nomadic forces outside its city gates.

With regard to Christology, Girard's arguments fail also to convince fully. He is undoubtedly right to lay stress upon Jesus's refusal of violence, but he allows little place for the concrete 'form' taken by Jesus's non-violent practice.[33] In fact, given Girard's identification of culture with a mimetic desire, and apparent denial of the possibility of an objective desire or a benign *eros*, it is difficult to see what 'the Kingdom' could really amount to, other than the negative gesture of refusal of desire, along with all cultural difference. Girard does not, in fact, really present us with a theology of two cities, but instead with a story of one city, and its final rejection by a unique individual. This means that while his metanarrative does, indeed, have politically critical implications, these are too undiscriminating, because every culture is automatically sacrificial and 'bad'. At the same time, criticism cannot really be used to promote an alternative practice taking a collective, political form.

These defects are not present in a theology which contrasts two different cultural practices. However, for this to be possible, one must refrain from offering a scientific, explanatory account of the violently sacrificial character of most human cultures. As Wittgenstein intimated, in his remarks on Frazer, their speaking of a common, sacrificial language must simply be accepted as a surd coincidence.[34] If any discipline can elucidate this coincidence further, it is theology, which deciphers it as the dominance of original sin, the refusal of the true God. But this is not really an explanation (sin, in particular cannot be explained) but only a conceptual redescription, which arises from the contrast with Christianity as a 'counter-sacrificial' practice.

Girard, however, does not really seem to think in terms of a positive, alternative practice, but only a negative refusal. This actually has implications for his claims about the uniqueness of Christ. Given that the Hebrews had already arrived at a 'partial' rejection of sacrifice, why should they not have arrived at a total one, out of entirely human resources, if all that Jesus really seems to offer is a denial of culture, and not the imagination of something beyond culture, which would indeed be humanly problematic? It might be protested here that it is not possible for us to isolate, even negatively, the ultimate cultural 'conditions' of our being, for every statement outlining such conditions will itself make assumptions (assume a 'setting') which can in turn be elaborated, so making cultural exposure an infinite task. But Girard clearly does not accept

---

[33] Raymond Schwäger. *Der Wunderbare Tausch: Zur Geschichte und Deutung der Erlosungslehre* (Munich: Kosel, 1986) pp. 273–312.

[34] Ludwig Wittgenstein, *Remarks on Frazer's Golden Bough*, trans. A. C. Miles (Retford: Brynmill, 1979) p. 3.

this valid insight, because he thinks we can scientifically 'test' Jesus's exposure of our ultimate cultural assumptions. Indeed, he seems to have previously himself made the same exposure, without the benefit of divinity.

If we do accept the insight, then it becomes clear that there is no way of proving the finality of Jesus's diagnosis. If, on the other hand, we could so prove it, then it would not seem to follow that Jesus is God incarnate. What is especially noticeable here is that Girard presents his own form of *cur Deus Homo* which is structurally very similar to the arguments of St Anselm. Anselm argued (in essence) that only God himself, free from the blindness of sin, could fully 'suffer' sin, and so make an offering to God, or a return of love fully commensurate with the ontological gulf caused by sin, and therefore able to cancel it out. Girard argues that only God, outside the system of cultural violence, whose inescapable codes blind us to other possibilities, can really and truly refuse such violence.[35] The former argument is not in essence a 'sacrificial' one, however much Anselm may appear to have allowed sacrificial elements to accrue to it. But the trouble with *both* Anselm's *and* Girard's arguments is that, however formally appealing they may be, and however much as ideal 'conceits' they may help us to a profounder imagination of God, they tend to become dangerously 'extrinsicist' in character, and unrelated to experience and practice, if they are totally separated from their regulative function with regard to the narrative level. For similar problems arise here as those earlier mentioned with respect to the Incarnation: if Jesus suffered perfectly, or if he alone really refused a dominating violence, then how do we *know* this, how does it 'come through to us'? A real perfection of character cannot be something locked away in an inviolable interiority, else there would be no reason to talk about it. Instead, the attribution of 'a final perfection' (in addition to its invention of a compelling conceit which itself works its way back into the discourse of devotion) must be meant to call our attention to, and to reinforce, a discovery in the 'shape' of Jesus's life and death, of the type of an exemplary practice which we can imitate and which can form the context for our lives lived in common, so that we can call ourselves 'the body of Christ'.

Anselm's 'idea' of atonement, and Girard's 'idea' of Jesus's divinity, both, in fact, only make sense if they remind us that Jesus is significant *as* the way, the kingdom, *autobasileia*. One can rescue Girard's argument for Jesus's finality and divinity if one links it with the idea that the exemplary narratives of Jesus show us the 'shape', and the concrete possibility, of a non-violent practice. Similarly, Anselm's argument is justifiable if one adds that the atonement itself, insofar as we are able to assimilate it, is only the continuation of the proclamation of the Kingdom. Raymond Schwäger, who accepted Girard's argument, failed in some degree to grasp this point, arguing that Jesus's death was in no sense *necessary*, but only occurred contingently, because of the rejection of God's offering, through Jesus, of the message of the Kingdom. For Schwäger it was only *in* the killing of Jesus that sin becomes

---

[35] Girard, *Things Hidden*, pp. 224–62.

absolute or fully 'original', a total blindness to the presence of God.[36] While, however, this does important justice (following Balthasar) to the historically neglected 'dramatic' or narrative level of Christology, it also fails to see that the 'speculative' treatment of the finite/infinite setting *cannot* be collapsed into a narratological form, precisely because it attempts to conceive the relationship of time to what is beyond time. And from a speculative perspective it seems fair to say that *every* sin is absolute sin, the rejection of God, and therefore that, while from a temporal point of view the acceptance of Jesus's message of the Kingdom is a real possibility, from a speculative, would-be infinite point of view (which we of course only 'imagine') it is not. Sin was always already 'original' – the refusal of the presence of God – even if it is finally exposed and defined upon the cross.

Schwäger does, indeed, suggest that an acceptance of Jesus's message was practically speaking impossible, but he ascribes this to the social mechanisms of mimetic violence and mutual limiting of freedom. This 'translation' of the notion of original sin is in part reasonable, yet on its own it should imply that the event of Christ – the Kingdom – is a purely human work, as the event of suffering and so of 'realizing' these structures. Instead, Schwäger, like Girard, wants to argue that the all-dominance of these mechanisms makes a 'supernatural', extra-social intervention necessary, in the shape of 'incarnation'. Yet as we have seen, this *deus ex machina* element is redundant, if Jesus's practice is only atoning by his exposure of the logic of *mimesis*. By contrast, a more 'speculative' understanding of original sin can be correlated with the notion of a concrete way of being that we have lost sight of (rather than the mere 'idea' of non-rivalry, which could be realized without 'incarnation'), a way that nonetheless occurs again in Christ. Here Jesus's divinity relates to the demonstration of the possibility of non-violence in a particular pattern of existence, not to the intrusion of extra-human enabling capacities. Speculatively, Jesus is divine, because whereas the self-punishment of sin does not overcome sin's constitutive blindness, forgiving practice is an entirely new beginning, whose infinite generosity is 'adequate' to God, and which inaugurates, *ex nihilo*, a series in no ontological continuity with sin and its own self-antidotes.

After Jesus's death our redemption becomes possible, for two reasons. First, we speculatively grasp that sin is negation, arbitrary violence, the refusal of pure love itself, and this speculation is an *indispensable* and yet independent moment of faith. But secondly, the speculation is only occasioned by the horrifying and sublime compulsion of Jesus's death, whose concrete circumstance makes us feel that here we really 'see' sin, and at the same time the essence of human goodness. Knowing the shape of sin, and the shape of its refusal, we can at last be radically changed. However, the Anselmian speculation, that only God incarnate could define and so endure sin, precisely ensures that we can be drawn back to the Cross as the very consummation

---

[36] Schwäger, *Der Wunderbare Tausch*, pp. 290–5, 304–12. See also pp. 161–92.

of the preaching of the Kingdom. Finally the Kingdom means (speculatively) and illustrates (practically) bearing the burdens of others, even of our accusers. Thus it is Jesus's end, as well as his life, that we are to imitate. Mutual forgiveness and bearing of each other's burdens becomes the *modus vivendi* of the Church: an 'atoning' way of life. It is highly significant that from Paul, through Origen to Augustine, the early Christians seem to have thought in terms of a 'continuing' atonement. Paul talks of 'filling up what is lacking in the sufferings of Christ', Origen of the *logos* 'suffering to the end of time', Augustine of the Church, the whole body of Christ, as the *complete* sacrifice to God which is yet identical with Christ's own offering.[37] Hence to the Anselmian speculation one needs to add: only God incarnate could first make an adequate return of God's glory to God, but the point of the incarnation was also to communicate to human beings both the spiritual power and the Christic idiom of an adequate return, so that this could be made universally. For until there is a universal return, then surely God must continue to suffer the 'contradiction' of a loss of his glory, an alienation of his participated being. (Jews are right to see in many versions of Christology a denial of eschatological suspense.)

It is this question of 'idiom' which Girard really ignores. Do we not need to know the idiom of peaceable behaviour if we are to be able to distinguish it from the coercive? For only a shallow notion of violence would imagine that it is always empirically evident. Violence must be deemed to occur wherever we are 'forced' without true reason to do something, even when we may appear to do it willingly, for very often we are 'manipulated'. If, indeed, there are no objective standards of truth and goodness, as nihilism claims, then every act of persuasion is in fact an act of violence. Yet, on the other hand, Christianity does not claim that the Good and the True are self-evident to merely objective reason, or dialectical argument. On the contrary, it from the first qualified philosophy by rhetoric in contending that the Good and the True are those things of which we 'have a persuasion', *pistis*, or 'faith'.[38] We need the stories of Jesus for salvation, rather than just a speculative notion of the Good, because only the attraction exercised by a particular set of words and images causes us to acknowledge the Good and to have an idea of the ultimate *telos*. *Testimony* is here offered to the Good, in a witnessing that also participates in it. This commitment to a rhetorical as well as a dialectical path to the Good opens out the following implication: only persuasion of the truth can be non-violent, but truth is only available through persuasion. Therefore truth, and non-violence, have to be recognized simultaneously in that by which we are persuaded. Without attachment to a particular persuasion – which we can never *prove* to be either true, or non-violent – we would have no real means to discriminate peace and truth from their opposites.

[37] Colossians I:24, 2. Corinthians I:3–12. Augustine *CD* X, 6; XIX, 23. Henri de Lubac, *Catholicism: Christ and the Common Destiny of Man*, pp. 253–8.

[38] James L. Kinneavy, *Greek Rhetorical Origins of Greek Faith: An Inquiry* (Oxford: Oxford University Press, 1987).

An abstract attachment to non-violence is therefore not enough – we need to practice this as a skill, and to learn its idiom. The idiom is built up in the Bible, and reaches its consummation in Jesus and the emergence of the Church. By drawing our attention to sacrifice, Girard helps us to articulate part of this idiom – and indeed his contribution has been one of epochal decisiveness. However, it is given a more social form if one contrasts (like Ballanche, as we saw in chapter 3) a way of life based on the victimization of others with one where we choose voluntarily to bear each others burdens.[39] For further elaboration of the idiom we must turn back from Girard to Augustine, who by placing the Church, and not Christ alone, at the centre of his metanarrative, pays far more attention to the concrete shape of a non-antagonistic social practice.

Counter-Ethics

1   *Ecclesiology*

Does Christian ethics possess a distinctive shape? There are those who would deny this altogether, but among those who would return a positive answer to the question, there is a drastic division between the opinion that Christianity is essentially in continuity with an antique understanding of ethics, while modifying, decisively, the content of virtue, and the view that modern liberal, and especially Kantian, ethics is essentially the child of Christianity. The whole topic is in addition complicated by the phenomenon of stoicism, which quite clearly both influenced early Christian attitudes, and also anticipated certain characteristics of modernity. Is there a real proximity between Christianity and stoicism, or has the frequent perception of such proximity been a pernicious error?

In general, my sympathies lie with the first position, which affirms a continuity with antiquity and a distance from stoicism. However, as I suggested in the previous chapter, this continuity is over-estimated if one does not realize that Christianity implies a critique not only of the prescriptions but also of the formal categories of antique ethics: of *arete, phronesis, telos*, 'the mean' and so forth. When this is recognized, I shall argue, then certain limited comparisons with stoicism appear more valid, while at the same time the clearly post-Christian and even vestigially Christian aspects of Enlightenment ethics – particularly the ideals of liberty, equality, fraternity and progress – can be more exactly specified. However, I shall also contend that, from a Christian perspective, certain continuities between the antique and the modern, and between the academic-peripatetic and the stoic appear to view. My case is that one needs to emphasize more strongly the interruptive character of Christianity, and therefore its difference from *both*

[39] See chapter 3 above.

modernity *and* antiquity. (This therefore implies a refusal of *both* liberalism *and* conservatism.)

Protagonists of both theses concerning Christian ethical identity would agree that the context for a new *ethos* was a new kind of community, the *ecclesia*. Those, however, who understand Christianity as the cradle of liberalism tend to see the Church as a turning away from the idea that final human significance is to be found in the social life of the *polis*, and the fulfilling of social tasks which will be remembered and celebrated by future generations. Members of the Church, it is pointed out, on the whole remained within their existing political communities, and must therefore have regarded the Church as simply a spiritual association of souls. The Protestant view of the Church, which understands it as an association of individual believers who possess, outside the social context, their own direct relationship to God, articulates more fully what was always latent within Christian self-understanding.

The fallacy present in this 'liberal protestant metanarrative' has already been commented upon.[40] How does one show that a particular development discloses an essence? But in any case, this view seriously underestimates the social aspects of the early Church. Although Christians remained within existing political communities, whole households became Christian and the household itself – including women, children and slaves as well as adult free males – came to be regarded as a primary context for *paideia*, a 'laboratory of the spirit', in a fashion virtually unknown to antiquity.[41] In addition, the 'household' became a metaphor for the Church itself, indicating that association between its members, and mutual support, was a vital aspect of its life. Moreover, the pre-Constantinian Church frequently advocated some measure of refusal of secular offices involving either warfare or coercive judicial measures, and writers like Origen and Gregory Nazianzus contrast a 'rule' exercised 'without power' within the Church, with the 'rule' exercised within the pagan world.[42] If submission to pagan political authority was, nonetheless, earnestly advocated, then this was because a coercive order ensuring a certain rough justice (but no longer defence of race or territory) was seen as God's will for the limitation and discipline of sin in the interval before the final *eschaton*. However, it is abundantly clear from the writings of Ambrose, Augustine and others, that the gradual conversion of Roman citizens and of Roman rulers was expected to have implications for the character of political governance, and indeed (in a manner they found inherently problematic to define) to bring this rule also within the scope of the ecclesial rule. At the same time, the gradual confusion of boundaries between *imperium* and *ecclesia* led to fears that the distinctive character of the ecclesial rule was being lost, and so encouraged the monastic movement: precisely the setting up of relatively self-sufficient Christian societies.

[40] See chapters 4 and 5 above.

[41] Augustine, *CD* XIX, 17. Rowan Williams, 'Politics and the soul: a reading of the City of God', in *Milltown Studies*, no. 19/20, 1987, pp. 55–72, 64.

[42] Gerhard B. Ladner, *The Idea of Reform* (London: Harper and Row, 1967) p. 113ff.

Augustine, in particular, has been interpreted as foreshadowing Protest-antism and liberalism. It is contended that he invents an individualistic understanding of both Church and State, because, on the one hand, he interprets the State as merely a compromise between individual wills for the satisfaction of material conveniences, and, on the other, he understands the true Church, the *Civitas Dei*, as the collection of elect true believers, known only to God.[43] This contention is, however, almost totally erroneous. To take, first of all, Augustine's views on 'the State' (the term is anachronistic). Notoriously, Augustine calls into question Scipio's definition (which he says is recorded by Cicero, in a part of that author's *De Republica* now lost) of the commonwealth, the *res publica*, as an association united by a 'common sense of right and a community of interest'.[44] Instead, he proposes as an alternative that a *res publica* or a *populus* is 'the association of a multitude of rational beings united by a common agreement on the common objects of their love'.[45] The new definition is broader, as it can include communities not bound together by agreement on what is just, and on what goals should be pursued. Augustine is often interpreted as thereby abandoning the antique ideal of the political community as an educative one, and as making claims to an equit-able distribution of possessions and rewards. But in fact, as Rowan Williams has argued, Augustine does *not* simply abandon Scipio's definition, and the new one is offered in a partially ironic spirit: *Rome* cannot count as a commu-nity according to Scipio's standards, but quite clearly it managed to stay together somehow or other.[46] Worldly justice and government as *paideia* are not thereby abandoned as desirable objectives. On the contrary, Augustine explicitly claims that they are truly realized in the city of God: fully in heaven, but also partially here on earth.

The new definition, however, is more than ironic in that it indicates that the *direction of desire* is the key factor in determining whether or not a community will be truly just and united. For antique thought, on the whole, desire was split between an inherently 'proper' desire under control of right reason, and the excessive desires of disordered passions. This picture was, however, already qualified by the Platonic notion that only a true *eros* discerns the Good, in whose light alone truth itself appears to view. But Augustine accen-tuates this perspective by suggesting that reason itself can be perversely subordinate to a wilful desire for a less than truly desirable object. Hence there opens up a new perception of a possible radical perversity for both human beings and societies. While all human association is in some measure 'good' (insofar as it 'is' at all), it yet remains the case that the most predom-inant governing purpose of an association is not automatically justice or communality. Its most consistent desire can be for a false goal, which means a goal *denying* its own being, and its own social nature. Thus while August-

---

[43] Markus, *Saeculum*, pp. 164–71.
[44] Augustine, *CD* II, 21; XIX, 21–4.
[45] Augustine, *CD* XIX, 24.
[46] Williams, 'Politics and the Soul', pp. 59–60.

ine's new definition is, if anything, still *less* individualist than the old one – because it suggests, in an almost 'Durkheimian' fashion, that societies require some collective 'object of worship' to bind them together – nevertheless, when he explains what it is that the Romans collectively desire, this turns out to be precisely the pursuit of individual *dominium*, honour and glory.

The Roman commonwealth, therefore, is actually condemned by Augustine for its *individualism*, and for not really fulfilling the goals of antique politics. It is important to realize that Augustine associates this individualism with the heroic basis of all antique ethics and politics, and I shall elaborate this point in the next section. Nevertheless, it is also clear that Augustine recognizes an individualizing degeneration in Rome's more recent history, and condemns the 'incipient liberalism' as found, for example, in Cicero's view that the object of a commonwealth is that each may 'enjoy his own'. Augustine sums up such a view in the following derogatory fashion: 'No-one should be brought to trial except for an offence, or threat of offence, against another's property, house or person; but anyone should be free to do as he likes about his own, or with others, if they consent.'[47]

It is clear, then, that Augustine does not endorse, indeed utterly condemns, every tendency towards a view of personhood as 'self-ownership', and of ownership itself as unrestricted freedom within one's own domain. The Roman stoics approached towards a resignation to such views because they considered that, in the period after a cyclical fall away from the *ekpyrosis*, or cosmic conflagration, when all is melded together in unity (and a perfect state of tension, *eutonos*, is reached), the private and excessive passions devoted only to *oikeiosis or conatus* – the preservation of one's self and the close associates one 'sympathizes' with – must inevitably dominate. The stoic sage, who regards himself as primarily a citizen of the *cosmopolis*, not of any particular human community, can only express this membership by his resignation to the cyclical process and inward anticipation of the perfect peace, *homonoia*, achieved in the *eutonos* at the periodic cosmic destruction.[48] Augustine, by contrast, believes that the universal community has a particular, visible expression, and therefore that the realm of absolute *dominium* can progressively recede in time. It remains, nonetheless, the case, that Augustine has his own, though more mitigated form of resignation: as long as time persists, there will be some sin, and therefore a need for its regulation through worldly *dominium* and the worldly peace, which takes the form of a bare 'compromise' between competing wills. There can be no doubt that Augustine here contributes to the invention of liberalism, though in a negative manner, by insisting that in the economy of things there remains a place for a kind of political rule which is not really justice, indeed whose presumption

[47] Augustine, *CD* II, 20.
[48] G. B. Kerford, 'The origin of evil in stoic thought', in *Bulletin of the John Rylands University Library of Manchester*, vol. 60, no. 2, Spring 1978, pp. 482–94. William L. Davidson, *The Stoic Creed* (Edinburgh: T. and T. Clark, 1907) pp. 51–3.

is of the essence of sin.[49] To the problems which this mode of resignation bequeaths us, I shall return in sub-section 4.

In the second place, Augustine does not have an individualistic conception of the Church. The life of the saints is inherently social, because it is the opposite of a life of sin, which is the life of self-love. Through his new definition of a *populus* and his denial that the political, coercive community truly realizes a *res publica*, Augustine allows us to see many forms of 'the social' beyond the political, and also implies that the political is necessarily *imperfectly* social, because it contains elements of compulsion and of mere compromise. True society implies consensus, agreement in desire and harmony amongst its members, and this is exactly (as Augustine reiterates again and again) what the Church begins to provide, and that in which salvation, the restoration of being, consists.

Certain commentators, notably R. A. Markus, attempt to play down Augustine's explicit identification of the visible, institutional Church with the 'city of God on pilgrimage through this world'. Markus argues that Augustine progressively drew away from the general tendency of African Christianity to define clearly a visible and separate Christian community, in favour of a purely eschatological separation by God of the elect from all ages.[50] However, while Augustine is certainly at pains to stress that many true members of the city of God lie outside the bounds of the institutional Church, just as many of the baptized are not true members at all, this does not mean that he regards institutional adherence as a secondary and incidental matter. This is not, for example, how one should interpret Augustine's opposition to the re-baptism of returning Donatists, or his insistence, against the Donatists, that sacramental acts involving the participation of *traditores* (those guilty of handing over, under compulsion, sacred texts to the imperial authorities) were not thereby contaminated or invalid. Both these oppositions in fact show that Augustine attached greater weight than the Donatists to the public, symbolic aspect of Catholic truth, and was critical of both their attempt to base a community entirely on an 'inward' purity of intention, and of any construal of the Catholic community in similar terms. His typological apologetic for accepting Donatist baptism – that some true children of Israel were born from the slave-wife Hagar, not the free wife, Sarah – shows also an insistence on the Church as a historical community bound together by a historical transmission of signs, whose dissemination will necessarily be muddled, imperfectly coordinated with 'true belief', and not fully subject to prediction or control.[51] Hence the suspicion in Augustine of drawing over-tight boundaries around orthodoxy (or perhaps, 'orthopraxis') implies not at all that true belief is inscrutably locked within interiority, but something more like the very opposite. In their over-concern for purity of attitude, and for association only with the pure, the

---

[49] Augustine, *CD* XIX, 5, 9, 13.
[50] Markus, *Saeculum* pp. 170–1. Augustine, *CD* XV, 1.
[51] Augustine, *On Baptism: Against the Donatists*, I, 15, 23–16.25, VI, 5.7.

Donatists are thought by Augustine not merely to underrate the objective validity of the sacraments, but also the importance of visible unity to which it is inseparably tied. The Donatists are 'heretical' simply because they have cut themselves off from the main body of Christians who share the same basic beliefs and practices.[52] They fail to see that the unity and inter-communion of Christians is not just a desirable appendage of Christian practice, but is itself at the heart of the actuality of redemption. The Church itself, as the realized heavenly city, is the *telos* of the salvific process.

And as a *civitas*, the Church is, for Augustine, itself a 'political' reality. However, as a city measured more by endurance through time than by extension through space, it also has a strongly 'tribal' aspect to it, which the pagan *polis* or *civitas* tended to negate. What matters is not the cultivation of excellence in the heroic present, which cyclically appears and disappears, but rather the ever-renewed transmission of the signs of love and the bringing to birth of new members from the womb of baptism. (Mother Church is mediated by real female generation, unlike the 'mother earth' of the *polis*.) All recipients of divine love and grace are, by this favour, and not by any heroic excellence, full members of the community, which therefore has equal concern for the women, children and slaves in its midst. (This is not, of course, as yet a demand for equality of status.) The antique 'antinomy of *polis* and *oikos*' discussed in the last chapter is overcome, because every household is now a little republic (a *Lebensgesellschaft*, or 'unlimited society', in Leibniz's phrase, concerned with every aspect of the human good, as it was not, in antiquity) and the republic itself is a household, including women, children and slaves as well as adult males. The conception of the *polis* as also an *oikos* does not involve for Augustine and Christianity, as for Plato, collective possession of wives and collective child-rearing, because it is not now thought necessary to snatch women and children away from domestic 'care' into the military and judicial ethos of the city, if they are to receive an education in true virtue. And the new Catholic notion of rule by 'reconciliation' combines, beyond the ancient Greek outlook, a 'female' stress on direct relation (freed of the need for vengeance) with a 'male' stress on general principle (freed of the reactive character of previous legality).

The overcoming of the antinomy between *oikos* and *polis* is fully achieved by Augustine and not by Plato, because Augustine allows both household and city to stand, yet conceives a kind of micro/macrocosmic relationship between the two. And the same pattern, he believes, should be repeated on a world scale: in the world there should be, not a single *imperium*, but rather many cities, just as there are many households within a city.[53] But both instances can be seen as repetitions on a larger scale of the relationship that pertains between the individual and the community. As for Plato and Aristotle, the soul is a sphere of 'government' for Augustine, but much more

---

[52] Ibid., I 44.86–45.88, V 7–7.
[53] Augustine, *CD* IV, 15.

easily than the Greek thinkers he is able (following St Paul) to conceive of the community as an 'individual', or as a body governed by Christ, the head. This difference is further marked by the fact that whereas, for Plato, as we saw, there is not really an 'idea' of the city, for Augustine the city is, first and foremost, a heavenly reality. Thus for Augustine, in contrast to Plato (and Aristotle), the achievement of a true state of inward self-government does not tend to convey one ecstatically outside the sphere of community, making one essentially 'indifferent' to it, but on the contrary, propels one further *into* relationships both with God and the saints in heaven and on earth. The man truly in charge of his soul may indeed be finally indifferent to the fate of the *civitas terrena*, and thereby fit to rule it (just as only the indifferent wise man was fit to rule for Plato) but he is not similarly indifferent to the fate of the celestial city on pilgrimage, insofar as the true 'rule' of charity is being enacted, and not simply a *usus* being made of earthly things.

This contrast with Plato appears to view, if anything, still more clearly in the sixth-century writings of Dionysius the Areopagite, where (in new indebtedness to the pagan Proclus, yet in improved consistency with the Gospels) the more ultimate goal of hierarchic initiation is not contemplation of God, but a 'co-working' with God (now more emphatically conceived as inwardly self-exceeding) when one starts oneself to transmit the power of divine charity and the light of divine knowledge to those initiates within the churches who have not yet risen so far in the scale. Both Dionysius and Augustine overcome the second antique antinomy, between *polis* and *psyche*, because they conceive the goal of the soul as itself a social goal. Indeed, for Augustine, our vision of God will only be complete after the universal resurrection, when 'we shall then see the physical bodies of the new heaven and the new earth in such a fashion as to observe God in utter clarity and distinctness, seeing him present everywhere and governing the whole material scheme of things by means of the bodies we shall then inhabit and the bodies we shall see wherever we turn our eyes'.[54]

In each of the two instances: *oikos/polis* and *polis/psyche*, there is, therefore, for Christianity, a kind of micro/macrocosmic relationship. However, that is not quite all: this internal correspondence is only possible because the soul, household and city from the outset place their 'internal' organization in an entirely external (in other words, public, visible) continuity with other souls, household, cities, according to the laws of the city and of the *cosmos*. (Augustine explicitly says that the *paterfamilias* must arrange his household according to the laws of the city.)[55] Souls, households and cities can only be 'internally' right insofar as this apparently 'internal' order is really part of an entirely 'external' sequence within which it must be correctly placed. This way of putting things is directly implied by Augustine's *De Musica*, where the soul is

[54] Augustine, *CD* XXII, 29. Dionysius, *The Celestial Hierarchy*, 165A–165C. *The Divine Names*, 889D–893A.

[55] Augustine, *CD* XIX, 16.

defined as a 'number' that must be correctly positioned in a series. For this text, it only has an internality surplus to its position in the series, in the sense that every number (like the stoic 'incorporeal') has an infinite capacity to self-expand through division or multiplication, just as every musical note or poetic syllable can be infinitely divided or prolonged.[56] Internality, therefore, is here simply the power of freedom commensurate with the series, and alone able to alter and revise the series. Such freedom, however, is only fully and properly exercised when it opts for harmony, for the beautiful form of the series, however infinitely various; otherwise, freedom will be inhibited by disharmony, the resistance of other freedoms, and will not be perfect freedom. In this sense, the freedom of each is the freedom of the whole (infinite) series: 'In the heavenly city then, there will be freedom of will. It will be one and the same freedom in all, and indivisible in the separate individuals.'[57] (One can see how Rousseau and Marx later both continue and parody this maxim.) Not only, therefore, is there a structural parallel between the 'whole' and the unit; in addition, the 'whole' is in some sense present within the unit, because the unit *exists* in a position fully defined by the unfoldings of an infinite sequence. In this way Augustine overcomes the third antique antinomy between *polis* and *cosmos*, or between the law of the gods and the anarchy of the giants.

The part echoes the (infinite, so 'non-total') whole because it defines itself within the whole, but it also includes the whole (not 'already' as for Leibniz, but according to its final, eschatological position) because the whole is only a series, and is thereby itself entirely effaced in favour of the *differentia* of the parts, where each particular difference is defined by its interactive relation to all the other differences. The goal of the *ecclesia*, the city of God, is not collective glory, as if the city were itself a hero, any more than it is the production of heroic individuals. Instead, it really has no *telos* properly speaking, but continuously *is* the differential sequence which has the goal beyond goal of generating new relationships, which themselves situate and define 'persons'. Like the stoics, Augustine in *De Musica* conceives of finite being as a tensionally expanding 'numerical' series in which 'time spans' have a causal priority over 'space spans' (these numbers are physical/spiritual, and so Augustine is here beyond hylomorphism). Yet unlike the stoics, Augustine does not present a dualism between a periodic time of perfectly realized 'tautness' over against intervals of 'slackness'. In this stoic conception, individual persons, or 'rational numbers', can only relate themselves to the whole – and to an ultimate harmony which includes the necessity of periodic 'slackness', and of defects in the parts – by withdrawing from surface relations and attaining an 'internal' reflection of the

---

[56] Augustine, *De Musica*, 7(19), 17(58). See Catherine Pickstock, 'Music: soul, city and cosmos after Augustine', in J. Milbank, C. Pickstock and G. Ward (eds.) *Radical Orthodoxy: A New Theology* (London: Routledge, 1999) pp. 243–78.

[57] Augustine, *CD* XXII, 30. For an account of the denial that Augustine is proto-Cartesian (appealing much to Rowan Williams and Lewis Ayres amongst others) see Michael Hanby, *Augustine and Modernity* (London: Routledge, 2003).

whole within their own soul. Augustine's dualism, by contrast, is a dualism of two different temporal 'series'.[58] One series is a kind of 'anti-development', the second represents a true melodic progression. In this dualism, the individual searching for peace and harmony does not make a direct internal identification with the whole, but rather must remain on the surface, and situate himself within a progression that contains no fated imperfections, but is, in its tendency to God, itself perfectly harmonious.

The stoic ontology is grandfather to the political tendency of modernity to cut out all 'middle associations' and erect a direct relationship between a 'sovereign' state and a 'private' individual, sovereign within his own sphere of ownership – as well as to a 'new-age' spirituality focused only on self and cosmos. Augustine's Christian ontology, however, stands directly opposed to such developments. For it implies both that the part belongs to the whole, and that each part transcends any imaginable whole, because the whole is only a finite series which continues indefinitely towards an infinite and unfathomable God. This series is *nothing but* a sequence of mediations between individuals, households and cities. The 'whole' is Christ, the mediator, and he articulates his body and conveys this mediation as an endless series of new mediations which interpellates human 'persons'. Otto von Gierke correctly recognized such a social ontology as precariously present during the Middle Ages, and realized also that it stood over against what he called 'antique-modern' thought.[59] Whereas Rome was already developing the notion of an unrestricted *imperium* cut off from the realm of private law, and ideas of unrestricted private property ownership and market exchange, Christianity, for a time, interrupted this tendency. More than is usually recognized, Christianity implies a unique and distinctive structural logic for human society. And this is what ecclesiology is really all about.

2   Against 'Church and State'

All 'political' theory, in the antique sense, is relocated by Christianity as thought about the Church. The difficulty, for Patristic and medieval thought, was how and whether to conceive of a political structure in addition to that of the Church. In Augustine, there is, disconcertingly, nothing recognizable as a 'theory of Church and State', no delineation of their respective natural spheres of operation.[60] The *civitas terrena* is not regarded by him as a 'state' in the modern sense of a sphere of sovereignty, preoccupied with the business of government. Instead this *civitas*, as Augustine finds it in the present, is the vestigial remains of an entire pagan mode of practice, stretching back to Babylon.[61] There is no set of positive objectives that are its own peculiar business, and the city of God makes a *usus* of exactly the same range of finite goods, although for different ends, with 'a different faith, a different hope, a

[58] Augustine, *CD* XIV, I, XV, 1–2.
[59] Otto von Gierke, *Political Theories of the Middle Age*, trans. F.W. Maitland (Cambridge: Cambridge University Press, 1987).
[60] Williams, 'Politics and the soul', pp. 57–8.
[61] Augustine, *CD* XVI, 4.

different love'.[62] For the ends sought by the *civitas terrena* are not merely limited, finite goods, they are those finite goods regarded without 'referral' to the infinite good, and, in consequence, they are unconditionally *bad* ends. The realm of the merely practical, cut off from the ecclesial, is quite simply a realm of sin. In fact the only thing that *can* place it outside the Church, or the true commonwealth, is the use of a coercive force that is inherently arbitrary or excessive, in the sense that it goes beyond the 'disciplinary' purposes envisaged by love, and involves some elements of *dominium*, self-assertion, and the love of power over others for its own sake. Certain phrasings in the *Civitas Dei* show that Augustine regards the institution of slavery after the Fall, and the institution of political power, as virtually one and the same event.[63]

Political rule, for Augustine, is only 'natural' in a twofold manner. First of all, the intellectually and morally inferior should naturally be guided by their superiors, just as women should be guided by men.[64] In this sense there would have been 'government' even before the Fall; very similar affirmations were made by the stoic Seneca about the Golden Age, when there was no political coercion.[65] Secondly, coercive political rule, like slavery, is 'natural' for the period after the Fall, because providentially ordained by God to curb human sin. Nonetheless, this is a curbing of sin by sin, and, in a way by more serious sin, because more self-deluded in its pride and claims to self-sufficiency. It is here that Augustine's social thought is most problematic.

For the Church is to make *usus* of the peace of this world – of slavery, 'excessive' coercion, and compromise between competing economic interests.[66] It must never derive these things from its own rule and order, and yet should try to make them work towards the ultimate purpose, the true heavenly peace. Within the space of this ambiguity alone, the earthly city must continue to have a separate identity. Quite clearly, though, there would, for Augustine, be no point in laying down 'Christian' norms for an area which was intrinsically sinful. Instead, his nearest approach to political recommendation comes in the form of a 'mirror for princes'. Here Augustine lays down what qualities will characterize a ruler who also happens to be, *as an individual* a member of the Christian Church: he will rule with justice and humility, will be slow to punish and ready to pardon, and so forth.[67] Insofar as is possible, the Christian ruler will make a *usus* of the earthly peace, by subordinating it to the ecclesial purposes of charity and of a 'loving discipline' (the problem here, to which I shall return, is how can such a proper use not simply *negate* the earthly peace altogether?). The 'Christian emperor', therefore, is a just ruler

---

[62] Augustine, *CD* XVIII, 54.
[63] Augustine, *CD* XIX, 15.
[64] Augustine, *CD* XIX, 14, 15.
[65] Seneca, *Epistulae*, XC, 5.
[66] Augustine, *CD* XIX, 14, 20.
[67] Augustine, *CD* V, 24.

exactly to the extent that he treats his political function as an inner-ecclesial one, or as an exercise of pastoral care.[68]

Although attempts have been made, it is in fact really impossible fully to assimilate this conception of Augustine with Catholic accounts, since Aquinas, of the relation of the Church to politics. The problem here is not, as it is usually taken to be, that Aquinas revives, from Aristotle, the idea that we are naturally a 'political animal'. As a Christian (despite R. A. Markus's claims)[69] Aquinas could not possibly recognize a coercive politics before the Fall, and hence his conception of prelapsarian government was not really all that far distanced from that of Seneca and Augustine, although Aquinas had a much stronger (and nor altogether Aristotelian) sense of politics as the artificial, consensual erection of convenient frameworks for human life. This element could easily be welded with Augustine's scheme. But what is more alien is the idea of a permanent political sphere concerned with positive goals of finite well-being, and clearly distinguished as a 'natural' institution, from the Church as a 'supernatural' one. It is true that Aquinas, like Augustine, does not recognize any real justice that is not informed by charity, and that he has, in consequence, moved not very far down the road which allows a sphere of secular autonomy; nevertheless, he has moved a little, and thereby created the possibility of a theoretical dualism of nature and supernature in the social sphere – even if this is to mis-read his thought. By beginning to see social, economic and administrative life as essentially natural, and part of a political sphere separate from the Church, Aquinas opens the way to regarding the Church as an organization specializing in what goes on inside men's souls; his affirmation, for example (possibly inconsistent with his own affirmations of the 'consequences of charity') that the new law of the Gospel adds no new 'external precepts', seems to tend dangerously in this direction.[70]

Once the political is seen as a permanent natural sphere, pursuing positive finite ends, then, inevitably, firm lines of division arise between what is 'secular' and what is 'spiritual'. Tending gardens, building bridges, sowing crops, caring for children, cannot be seen as 'ecclesial' activities, precisely because these activities are now enclosed within a sphere dubbed 'political'. They become subject to the totalizing operations of a central sovereign power, which is concerned to contain them within this sphere, by subordinating them all to general, finite objectives which can only be of a formal kind, concerned with the 'balance of interests'. A desirably parochial existence of small local groups, constant adjacent mediations, plural membership of many different, inter-involved and overlapping corporations is bound to be eroded. One ceases to see social, spatial and temporal life as itself the continuum which shades off into infinity, despite the attempts (noted by Gierke) of later thinkers like Nicholas of Cusa and Leibniz to articulate more fully, and to

---

[68] Williams, 'Politics and the soul', p. 65.

[69] R. A. Markus, 'Augustine and the Aristotelian revolution'; appendix to *Saeculum*, pp. 211–30.

[70] Aquinas, *ST* II, I, 108 a 2.

promote, such a social ontology.[71] Instead, Aquinas's small commencement of a nature/supernature duality itself paradoxically gives encouragement to those proto-Cartesian elements in Avicennian thought which he so rightly tried to modify: in particular the tendency to see the finite/infinite relation as something 'inwardly' encountered. The individual not situated on the ecclesial continuum is either a 'subject' whose spiritually valued freedom is situated outside society, or else a mere part of a totalizing whole. (This duality between the 'one' individual and the 'one' social whole is something which the non-Trinitarian monotheism of Islam has often fallen prey to.) Moreover, a Church more narrowly defined as a cure of souls is also a Church granting more power to the regular clergy over both monastics and laity. And a Church which understands itself as having a particular sphere of interest will mimic the procedures of political sovereignty, and invent a kind of bureaucratic management of believers.

Better, then, that the bounds between Church and State be extremely hazy, so that a 'social' existence of many complex and interlocking powers may emerge, and forestall either a sovereign state, or a statically hierarchical Church. Significantly enough, the first Christian socialists in France, the group round Pierre Buchez, who were arguably the first *proper* socialists *tout court*, recognized precisely this point, and deliberately rejected a neo-Thomist account of politics in favour of a much more Patristic vision.[72] They considered that Augustine had discovered a 'social' realm (which, nonetheless, under the influence of St Simon, they understood in too positivist a fashion) and that 'socialism' would restore and extend it, through a proliferation of self-managing, egalitarian and cooperative groups. Like medieval guilds, these groups were also to be religious associations, 'orders' within the Church, although by no means subordinate to clerical control. Their attitude contrasts sharply with the prevalent blanket disapproval of 'political Augustinianism' within contemporary liberation theology – although it would seem plausible to speculate that 'base communities' where the lines between Church and world, spiritual and secular are blurred, and relative independence and mutual nurture within small groups is pursued, might just conceivably be the nearest thing to its contemporary exemplification.

3   The critique of virtue

Aquinas's inauguration of a natural duality of Church and State has important implications (already pointed out by Buchez's friend H. R. Feugeuray) for his treatment of ethics.[73] While again it is true that he acknowledges no

---

[71] Gierke, *Political Theories*, p. 23. G.W. Leibniz, *Political Writings*, ed. Patrick Riley (Cambridge: Cambridge University Press, 1988) esp. pp. 79–80.

[72] P.-J.-B. Buchez, *Traité de Politique et de Science Sociale* (Paris: Amyot, 1866) tome I, p. 23ff, tome II, p. 64. *La Science de l'Histoire* (Paris: Guillamin, 1842) tome I, pp. 512–15. H. R. Feugeuray, *Essai sur les Doctrines de St Thomas d'Aquin* (Paris: Chémerot, 1857) pp. 212–37.

[73] Ibid.

genuinely true virtue that is merely natural, and that his account of the supernatural virtues radically modifies the form and content of Aristotelian ethics (as I showed in my discussion of charity and prudence in the last chapter), it is nonetheless the case that Aquinas accepts Aristotle's account of politics and ethics as basically 'correct', if one deals, in the abstract, with the natural aspects of human existence. Because he speaks, even in the abstract, of a natural and a supernatural virtue, he is less able than Augustine, to think instead a true single virtue, now transformed by Christianity, through a critique of its antique form.

Such a thoroughgoing 'critique of virtue' is only possible where antique political institutions are not seen, ahistorically, as embodying the permanent form of a natural sphere of politics, but merely as contingent social formations which may be destined to disappear. It is possible for Augustine, precisely because he sees the Church community as able to realize the political object-ives of justice and virtue which the *polis* could not arrive at. His new ideas about justice and virtue assume the existence of this new form of society, ontologically characterized, as we have seen, by:

1   micro/macro cosmic isomorphism;
2   the non-subordination of either part to whole or whole to part;
3   the presence of the whole in every part; and
4   positioning within an indefinite shifting sequence rather than a fixed totality.

Exactly why does Augustine deny the existence of true justice and virtue in pagan society? The main reason he gives is that the pagans failed to offer the worship, *latria*, in justice owed to the true God.[74] This, however, does not mean that Augustine's real criticism lies solely at the level of religious practice. On the contrary, Augustine believes that the form taken by true worship of the true God is (as Rowan Williams stresses) first of all the subordination of the passing to the abiding (God and immortal souls). This subordination exposes all desire to make worldly *dominium* an ultimate end to be idolatry and the prime source of injustice. It is therefore the *lack* of 'otherworldliness' that promotes social inequity. In the second place it is the offering of mutual forgiveness in the community; at one point he associates absence of the practice of forgiveness ('true sacrifice') with the absence of monotheism.[75] In addition, thought of God the Father seems for Augustine to have been quite inseparable from the thought of heaven, our Mother, or the eternal community of all unfallen and redeemed creatures enjoying the vision of the infinite Trinity. Thus, when he says that the pagans failed to 'refer' all earthly *usus* to the peace of the one true God, he adjoins to this a failure of referral to the peace of the heavenly community. Without 'mutual forgiveness' and social peace, says Augustine,

---

[74] Augustine, *CD* XIX, 21.
[75] Augustine, *CD* XVIII, 54.

'no-one will be able to see God'.[76] The pagans were for Augustine unjust, because they did not give priority to peace and forgiveness.[77]

Augustine acknowledges that the pagans tried to ensure that the soul ordered the body. But the true principle of this ordering, he argues, was lacking, because they ignored a third level beyond the soul, which places the soul itself in order. This is the dimension of God/heaven/peace. But the way in which the pagans thought the soul ordered the body is not comparable to the way in which Augustine thought the third level ordered the soul. The soul violently constrains the body and represses the passions, but in the third dimension the soul realizes its true desire, and enters into reciprocal relationships of affirmation with other souls.[78] In right relation to this level, not just the soul, but rather now the whole person, the soul-body continuum, just *is* as it should be, affirmed in its correct external positioning, which still involves hierarchical subordination, yet no longer coercive suppression. After all, according to Augustine's *musical* ontology, both soul and body are different intensities of the same 'numerical' stuff – both emerging, not from matter, but from nothing.[79] Augustine's doctrine is that nothing that properly is, by nature, resists other natures, and therefore one must pass beyond suppression of passion towards the rectification of desire, and a peaceful order that is a pure consensus.

Justice that is content with less than absolute social consensus and harmony is therefore less than justice, not because justice is only founded in conventional agreement, but because one has faith in an infinite justice, in the idea that there is a temporally 'proper' (even if changing) position for everything, without any chaotic remainder. But the pagans, Augustine implies, were resigned to inherently unruly social elements, which had to be disciplined somehow or other. Similarly, they were resigned to the existence of unruly and inherently dangerous psychic elements which had to be eternally held at bay. Public virtue, in consequence, was for them at base military virtue, the securing of inner dominance of one class over another, and outer security against enemies, both in the interests of the 'whole' over the parts. If the city encourages virtue in individuals this is, nonetheless, fundamentally private virtue, for it is the glorious out-stripping of rivals in the defence of the city, related to an achievement of inward control of the passions and vices.[80]

Augustine here rightly detects a fundamental individualism at work in the heroic ideals of antiquity, an individualism both of public *imperium* and private *dominium*. This is necessarily present, because whole and part are turn and turn about subordinated to each other, and the part/whole ratio is given predominance over the *relational* sequence which endlessly threatens to

---

[76] Augustine, *CD* XV, 6. Augustine, *CD* XIX, 24, 25, 26, 27.

[77] Augustine, *CD* XIX, 23, 27.

[78] Augustine, *CD* XIX, 14.

[79] Augustine, *De Musica*, 17(57). *De Trinitate*, 12.12, 8. *Epistulae*, 137.3, 11. Hubertus R. Drobner, *Person-Exegese und Christologie bei Augustinus* (Leiden: Brill, 1986) pp. 114–26.

[80] Augustine, *CD* V, 18, 19, 20; XIV, 9; XIX, 4.

break out of any totality. And between the whole and the part, as between soul and body, there persists a kind of fundamental discontinuity, as between two different *media*, which means that subordination of the one by the other can only be forceful, and not a matter of continuity in a series, or isomorphic echo. By contrast, the Christian social ontology, linked to the neo-Platonic idea of an emanative procession of all reality from a single divine source, abolishes this duality which supports the idea of an ineradicable ontological violence.

Antique ethics, therefore, were not really, for Augustine, 'ethical', because not finally about the realization of community as itself the final goal. They failed to arrive at a relational perspective and therefore, when deconstructed, can be seen as celebrating the greater strength shown by the *polis* or the *soul* in its control of its members or its body. From the viewpoint of antiquity, it must appear that, in heaven, where there is only harmony and tranquillity, there is no scope for virtue at all, whereas for Augustine, after St Paul, it is only here that virtue, and the full range of human powers, will be properly displayed. All the antique virtues are for him ambiguously virtuous, because each is necessitated by an absence of charity and peace.[81] In all of them there lurks an element of 'excessive' compulsion, or an arbitrary ordering of what can only be properly ordered if it responds with a true desire. By contrast, in heaven, in a sense, only charity remains, because this concerns a gratuitously received exchange, and not the necessary inhibition of something threatening.[82] This is not to say that other virtues altogether disappear; it is just that they are no longer in any sense 'in addition' to charity. Charity indeed is *not* for Augustine a matter of mere generous intention: on the contrary, it involves that exact appropriateness of reciprocal action necessary to produce a 'beautiful' order, and, in this sense, charity is the very consummation of both justice and prudence.

How does it help though (one might protest) to imagine a state of total peace, when we are locked in a world of deep-seated conflict which it would be folly to deny or evade? It helps, because it allows us to unthink the necessity of violence, and exposes the manner in which the assumption of an inhibition of an always prior violence helps to preserve violence in motion. But it helps more, because it indicates that there is a way to act in a violent world which assumes the ontological priority of non-violence, and this way is called 'forgiveness of sins'.

Augustine asserts that, for us, the approach to divine perfection cannot be by any achieved excellence of virtue, but only through forgiveness.[83] This does not, I think, imply a Protestant resignation to sinfulness. Instead, the assertion belongs with the social character of his thought: given the persistence of the sin of others (as well as our own sinfulness, which we cannot all at once overcome, but remains alien to our better desires) there is only one way to respond to them

---

[81] Augustine, *CD* XIX, 27.
[82] Ibid.
[83] Ibid. For the theology of forgiveness see further, John Milbank, *Being Reconciled* (London: Routledge, 2003).

which would not itself be sinful and domineering, and that is to anticipate heaven, and act as if their sin was not there (or rather acting with a 'higher realism' which releases what is positive and so alone real in their actions from negative distortion) by offering reconciliation. Augustine's real and astounding point is this: virtue cannot properly operate (in any degree) except when collectively possessed, when all are virtuous and to the extent that all concur in the sequence of their differences; hence the actual, 'possessed', realized virtues which we lay claim to, *least of all* resemble true, heavenly virtues. On the contrary, the only thing really like heavenly virtue is our constant attempt to compensate for, substitute for, even short-cut this total absence of virtue, by not taking offence, assuming the guilt of others, doing what they should have done, beyond the bounds of any given 'responsibility'. Paradoxically, it is only in this exchange and sharing that any truly actual virtue is really present. Thus Augustine contrasts Cain's name, 'possession', with Seth's name 'resurrection'.[84] Only the bodies which we have in common arise.

4   *Christianity, Aristotelianism, stoicism*

Is the main goal for Christian ethics the achievement of a certain state of individual character, according to the role which society prescribes for us? The primacy given by Augustine to forgiveness, suggests not. Virtue in this sense is just vice for Augustine, unless 'referred' through forgiveness and the search for consensus to the absolute social harmony of heaven. In a way, one could argue that this means that Augustine gives priority to the stoic *officium*, duty, over the idea of virtue. (It is arguable that here, also, he is true to St Paul.) I do not at all mean to imply by this claim that, like Kant, he attributes moral goodness more to the motivating will than to action, nor that he elevates adherence to moral law over moral judgements of the charitable disposition in a particular instance, nor that he regards absolute obligation, like Kant, as more basic than non-identically repeatable 'example' (which for Kant is 'aesthetic', not 'ethical'). Priority to *officium* over virtue does not here mean attention to the 'inward' rather than to the 'outward' and particular, but rather a *yet more* outward and particular perspective than that provided by Aristotle. Let me explain.

Aristotle is primarily concerned with the judgement of character, so that for him the adjective 'good' is most properly attributed to the whole course of a single life. Goodness 'accumulates' in the form of habit, and a really good action has to be performed out of a certain 'depth' of habit. By practice, and an increasing exercise of skill, one can improve in the performance of virtue, as gradually one's prudence leads one delicately to balance the display of one's emotions and passions. Now this dimension of habit and skill should certainly not be denied or subordinated (as it is by Kant), because it is true that one only acquires slowly an aptitude for good actions. However, Aristotle's

[84] Augustine, *CD* XV, 17.

account also contains the implication that goodness itself, as a quality, increases as it 'sediments' in the character, so that it *is* primarily a matter of 'character' – something that we 'have' to the degree that we possess prudence, or an ability to discipline our emotions in response to circumstance. But goodness is surely *not* something that we store up 'within' in this fashion, and Aristotle is nearer the mark when he says that assessing a person's virtue is a matter of running through the narrative of his actions (a view echoed by Cicero).[85] However, what makes these actions right or wrong is not their contribution to an accumulation of 'character', but rather their appropriateness or inappropriateness within an entirely public, external and 'impersonal' (yet always *particular*) sequence that belongs to no-one in particular. The ethical sequence is in disjunctive discontinuity with the biological sequence of growth and decay, because ethical actions only *occur* as actions 'ideally' narratable as what anyone should have done in the circumstances (which *include* being such and such a social character) and as exemplary actions which are 'repeatable' by analogy. In the biological series there is perhaps a dualism of process and goal, but in the ethical series every instance has an equal place in the series, and precisely insofar as it is good, harmonizes with all other goods. In separating ethics from biology the stoics recognized more than Aristotle the cultural, historical character of ethical time. This is why *officium*, or duty, is proclaimed by them to be a more basic category than virtue: good action *is* only a matter of the series of punctiliar decisions, although there are an infinite, and infinitely divisible number of micro-decisions, and no decision stands alone. Decision will, of course, as a matter of fact, always emerge from the sedimentation of character, but it will always be *judged* by the surface criterion of 'duty' – in the sense of what ought to be done, specifically here and now, with reference both to past convention, particular circumstances and tendency of outcome (what is 'opportune', according to Cicero).[86]

For this reason, the stoics affirmed, against the peripatetics, that 'the good is not constituted by addition'. Because goodness primarily qualifies an action, and actions are entirely momentary and 'particular', public and external, one cannot talk about more or less good as one would about more or less of quantity. Good either is or is not, according to whether an action is 'appropriate', that is to say, possesses the qualities of *honestas* and *decorum*. These categories are the stoic equivalents for *phronesis* (the latter word being applied by them rather to wisdom as a whole). But whereas *phronesis* concerns a certain inner compromise of reason with states of feeling, *honestas* and *decorum* refer to a *tonos* within the individual who is composed of a single material stuff which both 'thinks' and 'feels': a *tonos* which is correct when in decorous harmony and balance in relation to its 'extended' environment.[87] *Honestas* and

[85] Cicero, *De Officiis*, I, 20.
[86] Cicero, *De Finibus*, III, 14, 45–8.
[87] Cicero, *De Officiis*, 1, 4, 15, 28, 35. Kerford, *The Origin of Evil*. E. Vernon Arnold, *Roman Stoicism* (Cambridge: Cambridge University Press, 1911) p. 196.

decorum, therefore, approximate the ethical condition much more to an aesthetic one, and make of the instance of ethical decision a matter of *theoria* as well as *praxis*: the vision of the good dawns upon the soul in a sudden instance, according to the stoics.[88] This instance is a moment of *conversion*, of revelatory insight, which one cannot really progress towards, no more than a person just beneath the surface of the sea is any more able to breathe than a person sunk in the depths.[89] No doubt, by emphasizing this 'all or nothing' aspect, the stoics began to downplay the importance of habit. However, an acknowledgement of 'conversion', and of a discontinuous leap which can break the force of habit, is required to solve the *aporia* of Aristotelian ethics whereby virtue must be always first possessed if it is to be enacted, and is therefore first acquired through education, its primordial origin being attributed to the 'action of a god', *by-passing* (unlike Christian grace) our human free will. Conversion – and continuous re-conversion – is, of course, a central notion for Christian ethics, because only by admitting it can one conceive of the idea that inherited tradition might be fundamentally perverse, and unable without radical renewal any longer to guide us.

Although the stoic notion of the 'true' ethical wisdom of the sage points in the direction of Cartesian inwardness, and an unmediated relation of the individual to total process, its conception of the everyday duty of 'all' possesses elements that qualify Aristotelian inwardness in its over-emphasis on character. The primacy of *officium* insists more strongly on the social, impersonal (and interpersonal) character of ethics: what matters is that duty be done, according to *decorum*, by whomsoever, given an *utterly* particular 'position'. This goes along with the idea that the Good is 'absolutely' right, without any question of degree, because defined by the decorous position of an action within a series and not by the 'more or less' of prudential administration of the passions. In both respects, there is an anticipation of Augustine, and it is likely that Augustine, like St Paul, is in some measure indebted to stoicism. In the first place, what lies beyond 'virtue', in the sense of virtue of character as self-control, is for Augustine the realization of a public peace. In the second place, the stoic idea of the good as *proprietas*, (or 'right position') anticipates in some measure the Christian notion of an absolute harmony based on right desire, no longer even potentially threatened by warring passionate elements.

To substantiate this second point, it is worth examining Augustine's treatment of the passions in the *Civitas Dei*. Quite clearly, he rejects the stoic ideal of *apatheia*: one cannot, he says, consider a man perfectly happy and in a state of peace if he suffers a serious physical disability.[90] Here Augustine, committed as a Christian to the perfect restoration of all being, sides with 'peripatetic materialism' against the stoics, who erect a dualism between physical and

---

[88] Cicero, *De Finibus*, III, 14.
[89] Ibid., 14, 48ff.
[90] Augustine, *CD* XIX, 4.

moral good. Likewise, Augustine expresses horror at the stoic ideal of unfeeling in the face of tragedies in time which are to be regarded as things 'indifferent'. In certain circumstances, Augustine contends, the good man *should* feel, horror, anger, pity and so forth; what matters is not the having or not having of strong feelings, but whether or not they are occasioned by right desire, which alone will indicate what it is appropriate to feel.[91] In this life, for example, a certain feeling of fear for our own and others salvation is right and proper, while emotions of love will endure, and even be infinitely magnified, in the life to come. Augustine explicitly says that here the peripatetics were nearer to the truth than the stoics.[92]

However, there is a more interesting point to be noted. In remarks about two of these passages in the *Civitas Dei* (CD XIV, 7 and 9) Aquinas endorses Augustine's point of view, and adds some discussion about why the peripatetics allowed that passions could be good, while the stoics denied it.[93] He rightly says that at the heart of the issue lies the fact that stoic materialism did not distinguish between sense and intellect, nor between passions of the soul and movements of the will. A passion, therefore, was not something for the stoics arising outside the movement of intellect, but was simply a state of mental (also material) imbalance: 'a movement that exceeds the limits of reason'. From a peripatetic perspective, however, passions are fundamentally physical rather than mental: for example, anger is 'a kindling of blood about the heart'. They are, in consequence, basically natural, and of themselves neither good nor evil – only their direction by the will, in accordance with the reason, makes them one or the other, although a *lack* of direction by will and reason renders a passion both defective and more purely passionate in character.[94] Now clearly, Aquinas believes he is making precisely the same point as Augustine here. But is he? Although Augustine in general is more 'idealistic' and 'spiritualistic' than Aquinas (and there are aspects in Aquinas's account of the soul that are preferable to that of Augustine) he also has, in a way, a 'richer' concept of the soul, related to his (stoically and neo-Platonically influenced) idea that time and place, which lie extensionally without the soul, can come to be intentionally within it. Indeed, there is a kind of latent *materialism* here that is more thoroughgoing than Aquinas's hylomorphism. Thus (I think one can say) the passions are rather more 'inside' the soul for Augustine than for Aquinas, as would tend to be implied by his use of the Roman stoic term *perturbationes animae* rather than the Greek-derived *passiones*.[95] This would suggest that, like the stoics, Augustine *also* does not make any absolute distinction between passions of the soul and movements of the will, and that he does not regard the passions as in themselves neutral. Whereas, for Aquinas, they are primarily physical forces,

---

[91] Augustine, *CD* IX, 4–F; XIV, 6, 7, 8, 9.
[92] Augustine, *CD* IX, 4.
[93] Aquinas, *ST* II.I. q. 24. aa1, 2.
[94] Aquinas, *ST* II.I. q.22 a2 ad3 aa1–d; q.24 a1.
[95] Augustine, *CD* XIV, 9.

for Augustine they are *fundamentally* movements of desire; hence he defines them as 'all essentially acts of will', and continues, 'for what is desire or joy, but an act of will in agreement with what we wish for?' Likewise a 'rightly directed will is love in a good sense'.[96] 'Act of will' does not therefore imply, as it would for Aquinas, a formal operation on a matter, or the direction of passion by reason-informed will, but instead a *dilectio* that is itself both an emotion and a will, and is right or wrong according to its own tendency to a goal, not in relation to an *external* ordering by reason. (At times, however, Aquinas sounds more like Augustine, especially when deploying Aristotle's *De Anima*, which more stresses the role of the sensations and passions in reasoning than do other Aristotelian texts.) This desire is itself the soul at work and therefore reason at work – for, unlike Aquinas, Augustine does not regard intellect as just a particular 'power' of the soul (though it may be possible to harmonize their views at this point).[97] In Aquinas's view, passions belong more to the 'appetitive' part of the soul, and are subordinate to a higher 'apprehensive' part.[98] But for Augustine all apprehension occurs through appetition (although he speaks of the 'turbulent passions of the lower part of the soul' which are disordered in fallen creatures, desire, which involves passion, is central to the higher aspect).

For Augustine, therefore, in keeping with the general 'supernaturalism' of his thought, there are no neutral, natural passions. And while, unlike the stoics, he thinks there can be 'good passions', he echoes the stoic view about all passion being 'excessive' in relation to reason, in that he sees bad passion as wrongly directed desire, rather than as an 'uncontrolled' *natural* element. Animosities, he says, are clearly concerned with *animus*; quarrelsome enmity, jealousy and envy are faults of the mind, not of the body, and when St Paul speaks of these as 'works of the flesh', he is clearly just employing a synecdoche.[99] It is the whole desiring person who sins or does right, and the measure of right desire is not the rule of reason over body, but the external relation of person to person in the community of peace, under God.

5   *Charity and* Sittlichkeit

The foregoing considerations begin to suggest why we need to place Christian ethics at a distance both from stoic *and* from Aristotelian ethics. But the social implications of this need to be indicated also.

Stoicism aspired towards a universal ethic, based on reason, transcending all political boundaries, and also towards a universal and ontological peace. However, it was unable to conceive of any new, non-political *practice*, and so the realization of peace had to remain 'inward', and its political transcription

---

[96] Augustine, *CD* XIV 6, 7.
[97] Anton C. Pégis, *St Thomas and the Problem of the Soul in the Thirteenth Century* (Toronto: Toronto University Press, 1934).
[98] Aquinas, *ST* 21.q.22 a3.
[99] Augustine, *CD* XIV, 2.

could only take the form of a respect for the free space of others, and a formal acknowledgement of equality. This incipient 'liberalism' broke with the *sittlich* form of antique ethics, where roles were prescribed by the community, and a collective, concrete agreement was sought after.

But Christianity is *neither* antique, nor stoic-modern. Unlike stoicism, it did take the form of a new, non-political social practice. *Sittlichkeit*, as Hegel half-realized, is here not left behind, but rather reinforced, because the *ecclesia* seeks a more absolute consensus than that demanded by the *polis*, and ethical conduct, after St Paul, is to be related to one's role within the body of Christ. However, virtue is now placed in a new and positive relation to difference, and, like stoicism, Christianity starts to validate liberty and equality. For if forgiveness alone, a gratuitous self-offering beyond the demands of the law, reflects virtue, then this is because virtue itself as charity is originally the gratuitous, creative positing of difference, and the offering to others of a space of freedom, which is existence. As an infinite serial emanation, charity does not lay down a *fixed*, as opposed to an educative hierarchy, and every 'position' it establishes is of equal importance, and of equal necessity to all the other positions, even if there remain inequalities of ability and necessary inequalities of function. As stoicism had already begun to see, the absolute uniqueness of every individual, which follows from its necessarily unique position in a series (so that nothing can be exactly repeated), makes difference ontologically ultimate and worthy of the highest valuation. Thus, although this was not all at once seen as a positive feature, Christianity from the start considered that it could be adequately repeated in very diverse cultural settings, involving very different sets of cultural roles. Unlike the antique ethics of the city, the ethics of the *ecclesia* is able to accord only a *qualified* value to particular historical formations. It is even able to recognize an advance *in* the Good (not just from evil to good) in the replacement of one formation by another, so that there is a Christian foreshadowing of Enlightenment progress (including technical progress, mentioned by Augustine)[100] as well as of liberty and equality.

But at the same time, the Christian insistence on fraternity as fulfilled only through harmonious consensus, makes Enlightenment versions of fraternity, as of liberty, equality and progress appear merely parodic (though this does not disallow altogether a secular stressing of things Christianity *ought* to have emphasized). Although 'the goal beyond goal' (the non-telos) of charity, is the creation of difference, and in consequence, liberty and equality, it aims also in this creation to reproduce itself as love and friendship. It follows that charity has to be a *tradition*, that innovations must locate themselves in the tradition, be accepted within the tradition, even though such a tradition must also be radically open-ended. Christianity is therefore (in aspiration and faintly traceable actuality) something like the 'peaceful transmission of difference', or 'differences in a continuous harmony'.

[100] Augustine, *CD* XII, 24.

This sounds formalistic, but one nonetheless *cannot* present this as a mere abstract humanist ideal. This is what Hans-Georg Gadamer tries to do, with his concept of a 'horizon' of developing tradition, developing infinitely new interpretations of an original canonical text, which yet are 'true' to the original, and are indeed necessary to manifest its truth. This would be splendid as theology, because Gadamer seeks to articulate (like the present book, but unlike Derrida) an original, necessary and ongoing supplementation which is yet not violent and subversive in relation to the original.[101] However, it is precarious as philosophy, because nothing 'justifies' such a peaceful transmission, such a nomadic *Sittlichkeit*. That it exists, cannot be presented as a universal transcendental claim about how transmission works, but only as a claim of faith and experience that that is how *this* particular tradition works, and that this is the clue to how things really are. And in fact, Gadamer's transcendental hermeneutics presents itself (a very long way from Heidegger) as a secularization of the aesthetics implicit in the Christian doctrines of the Trinity and incarnation: the Father is only present through his image, the presentations, and representations of Christ through time. It is certainly true that Christianity claims to have discovered the true 'music', which differentiates itself without dissonance, but *only* this music, heard in this fashion, encourages and supports the ontological speculation about differentiation and imaging in general.

The distinctiveness of Christianity, and its point of contrast with both antiquity and modernity, lies in its 'reconciliation of virtue with difference', or of *Sittlichkeit* with freedom. Only because it allows difference does it truly realize *Sittlichkeit*, whereas the antique closure against difference meant that it really promoted a heroic freedom which was only for the few. The reconciliation, however, is not achieved, as Hegel wrongly supposed, by an exposition of the formalities of freedom, or (like Gadamer) of interpretation, but rather (if at all) on the side of the particular unfolding *sittlich* order itself.

6   *Christianity and coercion*

One could say that Christianity denies ontological necessity to sovereign rule and absolute ownership. And that it seeks to recover the concealed text of an original peaceful creation beneath the palimpsest of the negative distortion of *dominium*, through the superimposition of a third redemptive template, which corrects these distortions by means of forgiveness and atonement.

This is all very well, but what of the persistence of the second text, and the way the Church compromises with it and continues itself to write it? This is the problem that Christianity can scarcely claim to have resolved. For Augustine, as we have seen, as for the early Church in general, the division coercion/non-coercion was the important criterion in separating the political from

---

[101] Gadamer, *Truth and Method*, pp. 345–448. I am indebted to an unpublished paper by Paul Morris on the Christian character of Gadamer's thought.

the ecclesial. It is true that Augustine increasingly saw the necessity for the Church as well as the *imperium* to use coercive methods, and that he distinguishes the two not in terms of pure presence or absence of coercion, but according to the purpose that coercion has in mind. However, the purpose of ecclesial coercion is peace, and this can only in the long-term be attained by non-coercive persuasion, because the free consent of will is necessary to this goal. Augustine admits, correctly in my view, the need for some measures of coercion, in some circumstances, because freedom of the will in itself is not the goal, and sometimes people can be temporarily blind and will only be prevented from permanent self-damage when they are forced into some course of action, or prevented from another. Such coercive action remains in itself dangerous, as it risks promoting resentment, but this risk is offset by the possibility that the recipient can later come to understand and retrospectively consent to the means taken. Such action may not be 'peaceable', yet can still be 'redeemed' by retrospective acceptance, and so contribute to the final goal of peace.

The coercion used by the earthly city does not, however, have the true final peace in view, but only the peace of compromise between wills, which contains in consequence a sheerly arbitrary element within itself, an element of power exercised by some over others, which is then bound to be enjoyed by the powerful for the pure sake of this exercise. A 'balance' of such power can secure a kind of peace, but it is not subordinate to a pastoral concern for developing a true desire: 'In this life the wrong of evil possessions is endured, and among them certain laws are established which are called civil laws, not because they bring men to make a good use of their wealth, but because those who made a bad use of it become thereby less injurious.'[102] The coercion exercised in the earthly city is, therefore, as I earlier said, in some ways 'excessive' as far as Augustine is concerned, although this excess is necessary. Hence when writing to Marcellinus concerning the judicial treatment of Donatists, Augustine requests that as his task is *pro ecclesia utilitate* he will only use the methods resorted to by school-masters, parents and bishops: for example, securing confessions only by beating with rods, not with the torture of fire. It is, in fact, more important here to *investigate* than to punish; once the truth of the offence is known, then the main thing is to restore the offender to spiritual health.[103] Likewise, writing to Emeritus, Augustine says that the Church asks from the *imperium* not persecution, but only protection. But he somewhat disingenously adds that, knowing the danger of schism, emperors will also issue 'such decrees as their zeal and office demand'.[104] This is the 'excessive' element, outside the scope of the Church's wisdom.

There does, however, appear to be an ambiguity. The Church is to make *usus* of the earthly peace: Donatists threatened with worldly deprivations are encouraged back within the Catholic fold. Such measures are eventually

[102] Augustine, Epist., 302.
[103] Ibid., 133.
[104] Ibid., 87.

given pastoral justification by Augustine, and compared with the operation of God's educative justice. But in that case, is it not the *Church* itself that carries out such measures, albeit through the agency of the *imperium*, because they have here *ceased* to be 'excessive'?

There is a further ambiguity, also. The Christian emperor must try, as far as possible, to exercise a pastoral rule; only so can he rule justly, truly rule at all: *imperant enim qui consulant*, declares Augustine, in Book Nineteen of the *City of God*.[105] It follows that the good ruler must reduce the scope of the political, precisely insofar as he is a good ruler. As Rowan Williams argues, for Augustine a war in defence of the state – or one might add, any form of excessive coercion – is paradoxically justified only when what is being defended is fundamentally unjust.[106] Williams goes on to say that this suggests virtually unsolvable dilemmas, certainly not subject to any general theoretical ruling, about when it is right to go on defending the indefensible, and when this has become pointless because the indefensible *dominium* is so dangerous, in itself, to the true ends of human life.

The implication of this must be that insofar as *imperium* lies outside *ecclesia*, it is an essentially *tragic* reality, involved in a disciplining of sin, which constantly threatens to be (even, in fact, *always is*) itself nearer to the essence of sin as the self-exclusion of pride from the love of God. But the great danger of 'political Augustinianism' as H.-X. Arquillière and others have pointed out (though not quite in these terms) is that this precariously upheld tragic distinction of 'State' from Church will simply disappear.[107] Augustine himself implies that the Christian emperor will make the empire recede into the Church, and later Western rulers, in particular Charlemagne, read the *City of God* in just this light, and saw themselves as exercising a particular pastoral office (the relation of the Eastern emperors to the Church was a totally different one – they made *the Church* a 'department of state'). Augustine also, as in his attitude to the coercion of the Donatists, opens up almost unlimited possibilities for interpreting most coercion as 'pastoral' coercion. So that later, a ruler like Charlemagne comes to see himself, without incongruity, as a kind of bishop with a sword, and his court theologians no longer talk, like Pope Gelasius, of two powers, imperial *potestas* and ecclesial *auctoritas* within one *mundus*, but of *potestas* and *auctoritas* within the single *ecclesia*. While the positive influence of political Augustinianism in this guise was immense, infusing a new concern for 'welfare' into Western political institutions from the outset, it also helped to sow the seeds for a new sacralization of a sovereign, coercive, and legally defined authority. (Later 'Latin Averroist' tendencies towards a 'physicalization' of power were, however, far more to blame for this.)[108]

---

[105] Augustine, *CD* XIX, 14.
[106] Williams, 'Politics and the soul', p. 66.
[107] H.-X. Arquillière, *L'Augustinisme Politique* (Paris: J. Vrin, 1955) p. 55ff.
[108] Ibid., p. 40. See also Henri de Lubac, 'L'autorité de L'Église en matière temporelle', in *Théologies d'ocasion* (Paris: Aubier, 1984) pp. 217–40 and John Milbank, 'Politique Théologie', in J.-Y. Lacoste (ed.) *Dictionnaire Critique de Théologie* (Paris: PUF, 1998).

Yet Augustine's own real mistake was in the realm of ontology. The revolutionary aspect of his social thought was to deny any ontological purchase to *dominium*, or power for its own sake: absolute *imperium*, absolute property rights, market exchange purely for profit, are all seen by him a sinful and violent, which means as privations of Being. But his account of a legitimate, non-sinful, 'pedagogic' coercion partially violates this ontology, insofar as it makes some punishment positive, and ascribes it to the action of divine will. This is inconsistent, because in any act of coercion, however mild and benignly motivated, there is still present a moment of 'pure' violence, externally and arbitrarily related to the end one has in mind, just as the schoolmaster's beating with canes has no intrinsic connection with the lesson he seeks to teach. What matters is not the particular form of pain, but the arbitrary association of pain with a particular lesson; Augustine was one of the first fully to appreciate that memory can be strongest when compounded of the traces of suffering. Thus although a punishment may be subordinate to essentially suasive purposes which are at variance with worldly *dominium*, he fails to see that the duration of punishment has to be an interval of such *dominium*, for the lesson *immediately* and intrinsically taught here must be the power of one over another, and it is always possible that the victim will learn *only* this lesson, and build up a resentment which prevents him from seeing what the punishment was really trying to point out. Punishment is always a tragic risk.[109]

Because punishment must, by definition, inflict some harm, however temporary, it has an inherently negative, privative relationship to Being, and cannot therefore, by Augustine's own lights, escape the taint of sin. It therefore becomes problematic to talk about 'God punishing', and this idea was, indeed, denied in the ninth century by John Scotus Eriugena (a thinker greatly indebted to Dionysius), who used Augustine's own ontology of evil to defeat his later affirmations of a double predestination.[110] Eriugena declares that God neither foresees nor forewills punishment, any more than he foresees or forewills human sin. God is not in time, and he only knows sin as it happens, in terms of its negative effects. He does not will to punish sin, because punishment is not an act of a real nature upon another nature, and God always remains within his nature. Punishment is ontologically 'self-inflicted', the only punishment is the deleterious effect of sin itself upon nature, and the torment of knowing reality only in terms of one's estrangement from it.

Interestingly enough, the social context of Eriugena's reflections on predestination was the Frankish kingdom in the years after Charlemagne, when the attempt to impose a pastoral order through political rule had somewhat

---

[109] John Milbank, 'An essay against secular order', in *Journal of Religious Ethics*, December 1987, pp. 199–224.

[110] H. D. Liebeschutz, 'Western Christian thought from Boethius to Anselm', in A. H. Armstrong (ed.) *The Cambridge History of Later Greek and Early Mediaeval Philosophy* (Cambridge: Cambridge University Press, 1967) pp. 565–86.

broken down.[111] Eriugena's sponsor, Bishop Hincmar of Reims, was seeking to substitute a more voluntary ethical discipline through purely pastoral resources, and he needed a theology which would deny, against Gottschalk, the idea that certain people are foreordained for sin and punishment. Perhaps, also, the climate of imperial collapse was favourable to a theology which strongly played down the importance of externally inflicted punishment. (Ironically, Gottschalk was himself brutally imprisoned by Hincmar – a fact which well exposes the tragic dimensions of this theme.) It may, therefore, be possible to read Eriugena's improvement of Augustine's ontology of evil as also a critical modification of 'political Augustinianism'.

This is the more plausible as Eriugena, with his Irish background of oriental Christian learning, looks back to the tradition of Origen. Whereas Augustine appears relatively resigned to the temporal inevitability of a sphere of *imperium* and *dominium*, Origen seems to have envisaged a gradual recession of these things, culminating in an apocalyptic time when the *Logos*, acting like the stoic eschatological fire, will 'finally have overcome the rational nature' and a perfect consensus and peace will be arrived at.[112]

Thus, while Augustine certainly understands that salvation *means* the recession of *dominium* (of the political, of 'secular order'), he does compromise this theme by his inadequate ontology of punishment. One needs to add to Augustine that *all* punishment, like the political itself, is a tragic risk, and that Christianity should seek to reduce the sphere of its operation.

For every time we punish, or utter a judgement against someone held in our power, we deny that person's freedom and spiritual equality: she does not have equal rights to speak about or act against *our* sins.[113] This stance of judgement and punishment is *never* occupied by God, because he pronounces no sentences that we do not pronounce against ourselves, and permits us to judge him and condemn him to death here on earth, although he is also beyond the reach of all possible condemnation. The trial and punishment of Jesus itself condemns, in some measure, all other trials and punishment, and all forms of alien discipline. It is here not enough to say, in a Hegelian fashion, like Walter Moberly, that external punishment is a symbolic language which can be internally appropriated as the real, 'self-punishment'.[114] For however tragically necessary this may be at times, it still preserves an alien moment which is not just 'sign', but also corporeal and psychic pain. The Hegelian idea that the alien moment, though tragic, can have a positive function, is actually foreshadowed in Augustine's sanguine approach to disciplinary measures, an approach perhaps encouraged by the tendency to see *usus* in terms of the more functional and convenient employment of bodies and signs, for the sake of an inward 'fruition' in the soul.[115] (This tendency is more marked in the

---

[111] Ibid.

[112] Origen, *Contra Celsum*, VIII, 72.

[113] Pierre Emmanuel, 'Avec Ballanche dans la ville des expiations', in *L'Homme est Intérieur* (Paris: Le Seuil, 1962) pp. 206–25.

[114] Walter Moberly, *The Ethics of Punishment* (London: Faber and Faber, 1968).

[115] Drobner, *Person-Exegese und Christologie*, pp. 114–26.

period before the *Civitas Dei*, by which time, under Christological influence, and perhaps also reinvoking his 'musical' ontology, he is thinking more in terms of 'persons' than of souls and bodies. In the *Civitas Dei*, where 'fruition' evidently includes a social dimension, it is much clearer that *nothing* is merely used, but, being used rightly, is also enjoyed.)

The only finally tolerable, and non-sinful punishment, for Christians, must be the self-punishment inherent in sin. When a person commits an evil act, he cuts himself off from social peace, and this nearly always means that he is visited with social anger. But the aim should be to reduce this anger to a calm fury against the sin, and to offer the sinner nothing but goodwill, so bringing him to the point of realizing that his isolation is self-imposed. This instance of real punishment is also the instance of its immediate cancellation. However, in a line of symbolic economy quite different to that of Moberly, the practice of forgiveness involves also a practice of restitution and of 'compensatory offering'. Wrongs must be put right, either by rectification and restoration, or, where this is not possible, by other acts and signs which sufficiently show that we now will again a harmony with our fellow human beings.

The Church, while recognizing the tragic necessity of 'alien', external punishment, should also seek to be an *asylum*, a house of refuge from its operations, a social space where a different, forgiving and restitutionary practice is pursued. This practice should also be 'atoning', in that we acknowledge that an individual's sin is never his alone, that its endurance harms us all, and therefore its cancellation is also the responsibility of all. Here we *do* echo God, not in punishing, but in suffering, for the duration of the *saeculum*, the consequences of sin, beyond considerations of desert and non-desert.

Likewise, the Church should be a space (a space whose boundaries are properly ill-defined) where truly just economic exchanges occur, in the sense that equivalences of value are established between product and product, service and service, just as a sense emerges of 'equivalent' restitution for moral fault. Both equivalences can only arise within a *sittlich* society of friends, sharing remote common goals, where each new product and social role as it emerges is nonetheless given its 'position' and relative weight in the community. By extending the space of just exchange, it can be hoped that the space of arbitrary exchange, motivated by the search for maximum profit, and dominated by manipulation, pretence and absence of any standards of quality, can be made to recede, even if it cannot ever, within fallen human time, altogether disappear. Although such an attempt must continue to involve certain elements of central organization of the distribution of basic necessities and the supply of finance, the idea of a totally 'planned economy' is actually inimical to it, because this imposes an external central authority and inhibits the free development of personal creativity and developing community preference.

The Church, in order to be the Church, must seek to extend the sphere of socially aesthetic harmony – 'within' the State where this is possible, but of a state committed by its very nature only to the formal goals of *dominium*, little is to be hoped. A measure of resignation to the necessity of this *dominium* can also not be avoided. But with, and beyond Augustine, we should recognize the tragic character of this resignation: violence as such delivers no dialectical benefits, of itself it encourages only further violence, and it can only be 'beneficial' when the good motives of those resorting to it are recognized and recuperated by a defaulter coming to his senses. The positive content of benefit flows only in the quite different series of purely positive acts, including, decisively for us, the active enduring of unmerited suffering – a series that knows of its *own* impulses only conviviality, and seeks to escape, forever, the mesmerizing lures of tragic *aporia*.

Counter-Ontology

Christian belief belongs to Christian practice, and it sustains its affirmations about God and creation only by repeating and enacting a metanarrative about how God speaks in the world in order to redeem it. In elaborating the metanarrative of a counter-historical interruption of history, one elaborates also a distinctive practice, a counter-ethics, embodying a social ontology, an account of duty and virtue, and an ineffable element of aesthetic 'idiom', which cannot be fully dealt with in the style of theoretical theology. However, the developing idiom is also an allegorical representation of an idea, a speculation, which practice itself both promotes and presupposes as 'setting'. In the speculation, social ontology (which is really a description of, and prescription for, the Church) is grounded in a general ontology (concerning the ratio of finite and infinite) and a 'counter-ontology' is articulated.

This counter-ontology speculatively confirms three major components of the counter-ethics: first, the practice of charity and forgiveness as involving the priority of a gratuitous creative giving of existence, and so of difference. Secondly, the reconciliation of difference with virtue, fulfilling true virtue only through this reconciliation. Thirdly, the treatment of peace as a primary reality and the denial of an always preceding violence. Let us take each in turn.

1   *Difference and creation*

According to the Christian speculation, the absolute is no longer just 'limit', no longer finite, as it was for antique philosophy. What was chaos, *apeiron*, the unlimited and infinite, is now God himself.[116] God is the infinite series of differences, and what he knows is the infinity of differences: as Maximus the Confessor said, God is 'the distinction of the different'. And as the reality which includes and encompasses in his *comprehensio* every difference, God is

---

[116] Dominique Dubarle, 'Essai sur L'ontologie théologale de St Augustin', in *Récherches Augustiniennes*, 16 (1981), p. 212ff.

also the God who differentiates. This means that while, as Dionysius the Areopagite realized, God is superabundant Being, and not a Plotinian unity beyond Being and difference, he is also nevertheless, as Dionysius also saw, a power within Being which is more than Being, an internally creative power.[117] As infinite power which is unimpeded, nothing in God can be unrealized, so that it would appear that God is *actus purus*, yet it must be equally the case that no actualization of every 'limit', even an infinite one, exhausts God's power, for this would render it merely finite after all. (For Dionysius God actually exceeds the infinite/finite contrast.) The pre-Thomist intimation in Dionysius of a kind of surplus to actuality in God is therefore correct, but one needs to state clearly that no priority can be given to either pure *actus* or pure *virtus*. Infinite realized act and infinite unrealized power mysteriously coincide in God, and it must be this that supports the circular 'life', that is more than *stasis*, of the Trinity.[118] Yet 'power-act' plays out through, and is constituted by, the Trinitarian relations: it is not that the Father is power and the Son act, for this would depersonalize their relation and make it *not* a real surface relation at all (this is why the Father-Son relation is not *just* a signified-signifier one, implying an 'absence' of the Father, but also an 'adjacent', figurative relation). A relation, even a relation constituting its own poles, can only be a relation between act and act, although it is the play of potential which introduces relation as a moving and dynamic element.

This movement, as Dionysius explains, is from unity to difference, constituting a relation in which unity *is* through its power of generating difference, and difference *is* through its comprehension by unity.[119] But one may legitimately wonder here whether difference that is generated in an emanation which constitutes (as Augustine explains) a 'pure relation', where the two poles only are through their relating, might appear to be locked within this relation, which would then appear just as closed off, and as monistic as an isolated 'substance'. Likewise, the differences which are unified through the Paternal origin can appear to be enclosed within a totality, and *denied* as differences, in the sense of an infinite series of 'escaping' differences. This is why (speculatively speaking), within the Godhead, there is held by Christianity to arise after the 'first difference' which is the Son, also the 'second difference' of the Holy Spirit, constituted as an equally pure relation to the Father, but 'through' the Son. The Spirit *is* this relation of the one and the many, this *ratio* of charity, but the relational character of this ratio is now truly affirmed, because the Son, and the differences contained within the Son, has now become a moment of *mediation* between Father and Spirit. The differences can be 'received' or 'interpreted' in an instance of reception which is *not*

---

[117] Dionysius the Areopagite, *The Divine Names*, 588B, 542D–593A, 817C–817D, 821B, 825A, 892B, 912D–913B.

[118] Nicholas of Cusa, 'On actualised possibility' (*De Possest*), in Jasper Hopkins, *A Concise Introduction to the Philosophy of Nicholas of Cusa* (Minnesota: University of Minnesota Press, 1978) pp. 93, 121.

[119] Dionysius the Areopagite, *The Divine Names*, 649B, 649C.

the Father, and which is beyond the perfect relation of Father and Son (though purely constituted as the 'gift' of this relation). Therefore difference, after first constituting unity (the Son causing 'backwards' the Father) becomes a *response* to unity that is more than unity, which unity itself cannot predict – since mediation exceeds unity just as it exceeds difference. The 'between' is now absolute. The harmony of the Trinity is therefore not the harmony of a finished totality but a 'musical' harmony of infinity. Just as an infinite God must be power-act, so likewise the doctrine of the Trinity discovers the infinite God to include a radically 'external' relationality. Thus God can only speak to us simultaneously as the Word incarnate, and as the indefinite spiritual response, in time, which is the Church.[120]

This God who differentiates is not one who 'causes' anything, nor a God whose knowledge precedes his action. As Eriugena already affirmed, 'making', in the sense of a spontaneous development (unlike causality) is, for Christianity, a transcendental reality located in the infinite, and God acts and knows because he internally 'makes' or 'creates'. Likewise he knows and acts upon things in time insofar as he creates them, and there is no question of 'before' and 'after' here.[121]

The created world of time participates in the God who differentiates; indeed it *is* this differentiation insofar as it is finitely 'explicated', rather than infinitely 'complicated'. Just as God (as Augustine already affirms in *De Trinitate*) is not a 'substance', because he is nothing fundamental underlying anything else, so also there are no absolute self-standing substances in creation, no underlying matters not existent through form and no discrete and inviolable 'things'. One can only think of the elements of creation as inherently interconnected 'qualities' which combine and re-combine in all sorts of ways (Basil, Gregory of Nyssa) and as 'seeds' or 'monads' (Eriugena) or numerical, sometimes 'seminal' ratios (Augustine) which participate in the divine creative power/act, and themselves continuously propagate *ex nihilo*, in the sense of continuously re-providing their own 'matter' which is the condition for their mutual externality (as Eriugena affirms) through time.[122] There are no 'things' (as Augustine sees in *De Musica*) but only tensional *ratios* which in their 'intense' state, do not pre-contain all that they later unfold, but have an 'incorporeal' power for expansion. Creation is therefore not a finished product in space, but is continuously generated *ex nihilo* in time. To sustain this process, the monads, seeds or ratios also self-generate, but in this they do not 'assist' God, who supplies all power and all being, but rather participate in God. For if God is an internally creative power-act, then he can only be

[120] John Milbank, 'The second difference', in *The Word Made Strange: Theology, Language, Culture* (Oxford: Blackwell, 1997) pp. 171–94. On the ontology of 'the between' (*metaxu*) see William Desmond, *Being and the Between* (New York: SUNY, 1995).

[121] John Scotus Eriugena, *Periphyseon: On the Division of Nature*, trans. M. L. Uhlfelder (Indianapolis: Bobbs Merrill, 1976) pp. 185–8.

[122] Basil, 'The Hexaemeron', in *Nicene and Post Nicene Fathers*, vol. VIII (Oxford: James Parker, 1898) p. 63. *De Trinitate*, VII, 5–10. Ladner, *The Idea of Reform*, pp. 310ff, 399ff.

participated in by creatures who do not embody an infinite coincidence of act and power, but a finite oscillation between the two, yet are themselves thereby radically creative and differentiating. (In this sense everything created 'lives' and even 'thinks' such that humanity intensifies the deepest impulsions of the cosmos.)

As against this ontology (intimated by Eriugena) Aquinas denied participation in creation by creatures for two reasons. First, under Aristotelian influence, he thought of making as merely a modification of existing forms, not as the inauguration of radically new 'types' of thing. Secondly, he supposed that co-creation implied an 'assistance' to God in the act of creation, whereas of course, for Christianity only God is commensurate with the bringing about of Being from nothing, in the absolute sense of positing existence at all, impossible for creatures.[123] However, he only came to this latter conclusion because he did not conceive God as internally creative, or as power-act, and therefore failed to see that a creature is *not* primarily something which is, but primarily something which is creative. A creature *is* a creature by mediating the power to create, even if it does not hold this power absolutely of itself, any more than it holds being of itself. Forces *do* cause rocks to be, seeds *do* cause creatures to be, human beings *do* cause houses, bridges, novels to be. (For where are these in nature? A novel does not *exist* simply as a particular set of marks on thin pieces of wood.) It is only the infinity of Being, plus the actuality of being over-against nothing as such, and a new being without precursors, that creatures do not make. Yet in creating things, creatures do not assist God, for *all* this power/act of a finite creation is created by God.

Eriugena's ontology, based on God as internally 'creator' (even though this ineffably coincides with an 'uncreating') and then on different degrees of participation in creation, is therefore more profoundly Christian than that of Aquinas.[124] However, he did not fully realize that his 'pragmatist' notion of God's knowledge denied the traditional paradigm of art, whereby art is first causally in the mind of the maker before it is in the work of art, and he did not extend his 'pragmatist' view fully to human knowledge. Here he seems to anticipate a subjective idealist idea of an 'internal' creative operation of mind upon received sensation, but does not arrive at the notion that the mind only *has* ideas in what it imagines or makes, and so in the contingent products of culture. As has been mentioned, this notion was first broached by Nicholas of Cusa (though in development of a Proclean line of thought), and it is vital to realize that contingent 'making' should naturally be conceived by Christianity as the site of our participation in divine understanding – for the latter is also a 'making',

---

[123] Aquinas, *ST* I.Q.45 a5. Richard Sorabji, *Time, Creation and the Continuum* (London: Duckworth, 1983) pp. 290–4, 302–5. However, as O.-T. Venard, OP, has pointed out, Aquinas at least once sees the inner emanation of the human *Verbum Mentis* as analogous to divine creation as an act not involving change: *ST* I q.45 a3 ad4. The Scotist univocity of being later allowed a notion of human creation of being in all too literal a sense. It was *this* and not the ideas of Cusa which encouraged Promethean hubris, although Ficino is also to blame in this respect.

[124] Eriugena, *Periphyseon*, pp. 17, 189–98, 228.

combined with the 'reception' of what is made by the Holy Spirit (in which we participate as the exchange of created gifts). The great failure of modern Christian ontology is not to see that secular reason makes the unwarranted assumption that 'the made' lies beneath the portals of the sacred, such that a humanly made world is regarded as arbitrary and as cutting us off from eternity.

The task of human creative differentiation is to be charitable, and to give in 'art' (all human action) endlessly new allegorical depictions of charity. Through this charity, 'God' is both imaginatively projected by us and known, though with a negative reserve which allows that our initiative, precisely *as* an initiative, is a response, and a radical dependency. Theological realism amounts to this. But it does not seem to me that it at all supports or requires philosophical realism: God, as the Pagan Iamblichus already realized, is not something in any way seen, that we could 'refer' to. And as for the finite world, creation *ex nihilo* radically *rules out* all representational realism in its regard – as the Cappadocians, Maximus and Augustine all realized. There are no things, no ultimate substances, only shifting relations and generations in time which only *exist* in their constitution of ideal, logical patterns. Knowledge itself is not 'something else' in relation to Being, a 'reflection' of Being, but only a particularly complex form of relation, another happening, and a pragmatic intervention amongst finite happenings. One should read again what Augustine says about memory: knowledge, he maintains, is not of space 'seen', but always of time remembered. All that we ever know is a memory, because the present has always already passed by.[125] This is *not* a thesis about the essentially subjective reality of time, but rather a thesis (which seems to show some kinship, perhaps accidental, with stoic ideas) about the event itself. This can be inferred from the fact that, in *De Musica*, Augustine does not confine the 'intense' phase of the time-span, as exemplified in memory, only to mind, but sees it as the generating power present in everything. Also from the fact that he is interested in the moment of the *passage* of an event from external time into memory.[126]

If time were only a pure flow, then one would have only a seamless continuum; not only would nothing be known about, nothing would actually *happen*. For an event to 'occur' at all, it must pass into an intensional, or what the stoics called an 'incorporeal' condition: a state of affairs, or a connection, must *remain* although it has in fact also already passed away. Hence, for example, the window of a house simply does not 'occur' except as an idea, as a particular 'section' out of a really *moving continuum*, which because it is 'frozen', we can then immediately conceive as larger or smaller, or even as not surrounded by bricks, like the grin that remains after the Cheshire cat has vanished in *Alice in Wonderland* (to use Deleuze's example).[127] Events already take an ideal form, already happen as knowledge, and although they seem

---

[125] Augustine, *Confessions*, XI (240–31).
[126] Augustine, *De Musica*, 17 (57).
[127] Gilles Deleuze, *Logique du Sens* (Paris: Editions du Minuit, 1969) p. 274.

to float 'above' the continuum, they also reveal to us the 'seed' power of expansion and contraction which moves the *continuum*. Body always is, with and through the incorporeal, as fact always is, with and through value, and the Father with and through the Son; the Spirit being akin to our mental prolongation of events. This would be a way of reworking Augustine's Trinitarian analogy: the finite bodily 'stuff' of memory has always already passed into the 'intense' incorporeal state of something judged, or uttered in the *verbum mentis* (a phrase which implies an idea that 'emanates' from memory, which continues to 'occur' as an idea). This in turn can be judged in its relative significance or as situated in such and such a new juxtaposition according to the 'spiritual' promptings of our will and desire.[128]

If we think seriously about time and creation, and follow in the tradition of Augustine, we shall conclude that knowledge is not a representation of things, but is a relation to events, and an action upon events. Our judgement of the 'truth' of events, according to Augustine in the *Confessions*, is essentially an aesthetic matter.[129] We recognize beauty or not, and the measure of truth is likeness to the form of the divine beauty of which our soul has some recollection. Augustine is basically right: truth, for Christianity, is not correspondence, but rather *participation* of the beautiful in the beauty of God. However, beyond Augustine one should re-conceive the mind's kinship to beauty as the capacity of a particularly strong 'intensity' to become the fulcrum for events, and to shape events in an 'honest' and 'decorous' fashion.

2   Difference and harmony

Thinking an infinite differentiation that is also a harmony: this is what grounds the reconciliation of difference with virtue. For antiquity, as was mentioned, that which is without limit, the *apeiron*, was a chaotic element. For Plato, dialectics leads us to the conclusion that reality consists both of what is, self-identical and rational, *and* of that which is not, the non self-identical and therefore irrational. Being, it then appears, is a hopelessly infected area, for the only discourse which can include both the same and the different (the non-self-identical) is itself a discourse of difference, which is not dialectics, not a discourse of reason. In a somewhat similar fashion, Aristotle's epistemic discourse on Being, which identifies a real knowledge of substance with knowledge of the universal, is problematically infected by his occasional placing of substance primarily in the concrete material particular, which, as particular, is ineffable and unknowable.

To save Greek reason, therefore (which I do not altogether wish to do), one must derive it from a now inconceivable, unknown unity, which lies beyond Being and beyond the infections of difference. This is the move of neo-Platonism. For this philosophy, especially in Plotinus, Being participates in Unity and

---

[128] Augustine, *De Musica*, 7 (19). *Confessions*, XI (24).
[129] Ibid., VII, 10, 17.

yet participation appears threatened by the absolute gulf fixed between pure unity, and a unity only thinkable in relation to difference.[130] The precarious solution to this problem was to make all reality 'emanate' from unity in a series of degrees of unified purity, and to make even the 'nether limit' of unlikeness something projected by this chain of emanations. However, the reassuring presence of the ladder cannot really disguise the gulf which opens to view at its top, nor the break which now threatens between a mystical discourse on unity, and a dialectical reasoning about being which requires, and yet is subverted by, the emanative becoming-different of the same.

For this reason, as Anton C. Pegis long ago pointed out, there is a hidden continuity between Plotinian neo-Platonism (mediated by Avicenna) and the late scholastic voluntarists: the latter, in the light of the doctrine of creation, became suspicious of all doctrines of essences and universals which imply some presence of 'necessity' within the ontological order – failing to realize that a certain 'convenient' reflection of eternal divine order does not compromise created contingency, which is the utter dependency of finite being as such.[131] Being comes to be seen as an essentially revisable, shifting diversity. The only way that the voluntarists could characterize God in contrast to this was to emphasize his unity, and absolute simplicity; these become the properties of a sheerly inscrutable will, of whom no finite qualities can be eminently predicated.

As was seen in chapter 1, voluntarist theology is one of the two important sources of 'secular reason'. The other is a revived 'paganism', deriving mainly from Machiavelli. However, the comparison of Plotinian neo-Platonism with voluntarism reveals the logic of a fusion between these two different currents, a fusion perfectly realized not in liberalism, but in nihilism: the only transcendental self-identical reality is the recurrence of an empty will, or force, which always returns as the arbitrarily and unpredictably different.

In opposition to this antique-modern 'secular reason' should be set, not a revived Platonism or Aristotelianism, including their Christianized versions (viz. MacIntyre) which secular reason can easily deconstruct, but rather the Christian critique and transformation of neo-Platonism (although a vital Aristotelian influence is necessarily involved here). Building on the neo-Platonic recognition of the One as itself 'without limits', beyond the sphere of division and contrast which involves dialectical negation, both Augustine and Dionysius (in their Trinitarian theologies) went further by situating the infinite emanation of difference within the Godhead itself, and in this fashion yet further overcame the 'third antinomy' of antique reason, between the 'gods' of truth and the 'giants' of difference. Unity, in this Christian outlook, ceases to be anything hypostatically real in contrast to difference, and becomes instead only the 'subjective' apprehension of a harmony displayed

---

[130] Rowan Williams, *Arius*, pp. 181–232.

[131] Anton C. Pégis, 'The dilemma of Being and Unity', in Robert E. Brennan (ed.) *Essays in Thomism* (Freeport, NY: Books for Libraries Press, 1972) pp. 149–84. See further Conor Cunningham, *Genealogy of Nihilism* (London: Routledge, 2002).

in the order of the differences, a desire at work in their midst, although 'proceeding' beyond this towards an ever-renewed 'confirmation' of difference in the active circulation of works as gifts. (This is in God the place of the Holy Spirit.) For Dionysius, unity has become both a dynamic happening and a complex relation. It is, in fact, transcendental peace which 'overflows in a surplus of its peaceful fecundity', 'preserving [all things] in their distinctness yet linking them together'.[132] This entirely reinvents the idea of order. Order is now more purely an aesthetic relation of the different, and no longer primarily self-identity or resemblance. Nor is order something essentially synchronic, within which a serial development must be situated; on the contrary, the infinity of God, his never exhausted 'surplus', means that the context for development is always open to revision *by* the development. The unity, harmony and beauty of the emanation of difference cannot, in consequence, be anticipated in advance, even for God himself. As Eriugena realized, God's knowledge is not 'before' but *in* the infinity of generation, and this knowledge can only be ordered, only be, in some sense, as Dionysius says, 'limited', if it is the infinite happening of the new in harmony with what 'precedes' it.[133] In this fashion, Dionysius embraces (unlike Aristotle) the transcendental difference of the *Parmenides* and the *Sophist*, yet conjoins it with transcendental peace in a fashion inconceivable for antiquity, which identified peace with finitude and rational 'containment'.

In aesthetic terms, there is something 'Baroque' here, in contradistinction to both the antique-classical and the modern secular avant-garde. In the perspective of infinitude, ornamentation overtakes what it embellishes; every detail (as Deleuze points out) is a 'fold' within an overall design, but the design itself is but a continuous unfolding, which reaches out ecstatically beyond its frame towards its supporting structure.[134] Structural supports are consequently overrun by the designs they are supposed to contain, and massive architectural edifices appear merely 'suspended' from above, by aery, celestial scenes. This hierarchy is not an antique, natural order, but nor is it a postmodern 'plateau' where all is 'indifferent'. 'Baroque' hierarchy, as already described by Dionysius, is instead the appearance of the divine self-realization in finitude, and therefore as a vertical sequence up which each individual can contemplatively and actively rise. At its summit lies not a static completion, but a full participation in the suspension downwards of hierarchies (the aiding of others by charity) and a greater participation in the suspension forwards of the thearchy, God's infinite self-realization.[135] Here the analogy switches from architecture to music, which resounds within the earthly building. In Baroque music, the individual lines become increasingly

---

[132] Dionysius, *The Divine Names*, 949c, 952B, 912D–913B.

[133] Ibid., 980c. For a fine elaboration of my thesis here that Christianity infinitizes beauty, see David Bentley Hart, *The Beauty of the Infinite* (Grand Rapids, Ill: Eerdmans, 2003).

[134] Gilles Deleuze, *Le Pli: Leibniz et le Baroque* (Paris: Éditions de Minuit, 1988).

[135] Dionysius, *The Divine Names*, 696a, 980b. *The Ecclesial Hierarchy*, 376b. *The Celestial Hierarchy*, 165a–168a.

distinct and individually ornamented; there is an increasing 'delay' of resolutions, and an increasing generation of new developments out of temporary
resolutions. The possibility of consonance is stretched to its limits, and yet the
path of dissonance is constantly re-integrated within an unexpected harmony.
To say (with Deleuze) that an ultimacy of dissonance and atonality are here
'held back' or 'not arrived at', would be a mistake of the same order as
claiming that nihilism is evidently true in its disclosure of the impossibility
of truth.[136] Instead, one should say, it is always possible to place dissonance
back in Baroque 'suspense'; at every turn of a phrase, new, unexpected beauty
on the 'diagonal' between horizontal melody and vertical harmony may still
arrive. Between the nihilistic promotion of dissonance, of differences that
clash or only accord through conflict, and the Baroque risk (later taken further
by Berlioz, Messiaen and Gubaidulina) of a harmony stretched to the limits –
the openness to musical grace – there remains an undecidability.

Where, however, Christian theology helps to invent this nihilism, as in the
case of a voluntarism blind to the possibility of an aesthetic account of
analogy, then it betrays itself. For the Trinitarian God does not possess the
unity of a bare simplicity, a naked will, nor does he stand in an indifferent
relationship to what he creates. God's love for what he creates implies that the
creation is generated within a harmonious order intrinsic to God's own being.
And only by means of this conception, this admission of some analogous
exchange of predicates between God and finitude, can one conceive of an
absolute that is *itself* difference, inclusive of all difference, unlike nihilism,
which can only posit a transcendental univocity.[137] The way was opened to
such an exchange of predicates by both Augustine and Dionysius, who broke
with neo-Platonism by ascribing all Being, and in consequence difference, to
God himself. And yet they could only do this, because, in effect, they had
already made the 'post-philosophical' move of separating difference from
dialectics (even if this is latent in Plato himself). The Platonic, Aristotelian
and neo-Platonic problematics were entirely founded on the idea that difference is distinguished from sameness through the medium of denial and of
non-Being. Augustine and Dionysius, by contrast, in effect redefine Being as
itself that which is different. But, in consequence, God, or the first principle,
can no longer be arrived at by dialectics, by the discipline of 'truth', or by the
careful distinguishing of that which remains self-identical. A knowledge that
is rather the infinite maximal tensional harmony of difference has to be something persuasively communicated, something constituting the positive reality
of the finite world, and also something continuously *added to* this world, rather
than uncovered within it. Hence the relationship of God to the world becomes,
after Christianity, a more rhetorical one, and *ceases to be anything to do with
'truth'*, or, in other words with the relation of reality to appearance. Creation is

---

[136] Deleuze, *Le Pli*, pp. 164–89. And see Catherine Pickstock, 'Quasi una sonata: music,
postmodernism and theology', in Jeremy Begbie (ed.) *Theology through Music* (Cambridge:
CUP, 2005).
[137] See chapter 10 above.

not an appearance, a mixture of truth and untruth, related to God by a minus sign, nor yet an Aristotelian hierarchy of identities, but is rather the serial occurrence of differential reality in time, and related to God by a mysterious plus sign which construes *methexis* as also *kenosis*: God who is 'all' being nonetheless 'gives' a finite being which he is not. Negation, here, as Dominique Dubarle has noted, is reduced to the purely heuristic functioning of a zero sign, in the speculative expression: 'creation out of nothing'.[138]

The God who is, who includes difference, and yet is unified, is not a God sifted out as abstract 'truth', but a God who speaks in the harmonious happening of Being. As Dubarle argues, this is affirmed by Augustine in the *Confessions*, where the God of Moses who defines himself as the God who is (*est*), the 'ontological' God, is also (as the verbal form indicates) the God who announces himself; while, inversely, the historical God who declares 'I am the God of Abraham, Isaac and Jacob' is also the ontological God, the God of what positively *occurs*[139] (not a God attained through any final relinquishing or denial). Narrative and ontology reinforce each other in an ontology of difference, because God must be known *both* as the 'speaking' of created difference, *and* as an inexhaustible plenitude of otherness. This ontological background, or 'setting', finally steps into the foreground when the heir of Abraham, Isaac and Jacob himself announces 'I am before the creation of the world'. Then the positive given event becomes itself inexhaustible, itself the setting of past and future lives.

The reconciliation of virtue with difference implies a harmonic pattern in the happening of difference, a 'tradition' whose norms are only seen in the course of its unfolding. But a tradition (is Christianity the *only* tradition in this sense?) automatically *consists* in the imagination of a reality in which traditioned processes themselves participate. The thought of God as infinite Being, as difference in harmony, is this speculative imagining. And such a speculation tends to subsume all philosophy, just as the Christian counter-ethics tends to subsume all politics.

3   *Peace and privation*

If, for Christianity, 'philosophy' is finished and surpassed, then there can be no more 'truth and falsity'. Because no positive non-being is posited, as by Platonism, and no pure material potency, as in Aristotelianism, nothing that is, can be in any sense wrong. There can be no more illusions, and no unmaskings: instead, there are *deficiencies*. To be 'wrong' is now to do evil, and to do evil is rather not to do the good, for something 'to be lacking'. Neither ignorance nor sin make 'mistakes'; instead, they somehow do not do enough.

---

[138] Dubarle, 'Essai sur l'ontologie', pp. 248–9.
[139] Ibid., p. 203ff.

What can this mean? Not that all creatures sin because they can never have done enough (though Augustine sometimes lets this neo-Platonic relic intrude, and so opens the way to theodicy).[140] Rather, that there is a way of acting which inhibits the flow, which prevents the infinitely more being done in the future. This is the failure to 'refer' our desire to God, to make good *usus* of things. A well-made deed should be like a picture which admits the sublime within the scope of its beauty: the perspective upon a distant landscape, the shaft of light from an upper window. But at the same time, the sublime must not just intrude upon the beautiful, nor hover, emptily (as for Kant, who reduces ethics to the upholding of freedom)[141] upon its margins, but allow its perspective to infuse the entire scene, to decompose the scene, so that we are invited to enter into it as an opening to what lies beyond it. And this opening must entrance us, we must be seduced; hence the beautiful form taken by the opening of the sublime gulf ought to make the gulf appear attractive, must seem to manifest, be suspended by, the gulf itself. It is not just that the infinite calls out to our freedom to affirm its own incomprehensibility, but also that the infinite is opened out along a particular path, and *within* the scene we become a free, but concretely desiring subject. (The aesthetic reconciliation of the sublime with the beautiful is the same task as the ethical reconciliation of difference with virtue.) To 'refer' things to the infinite is to arrange them in their proper place in a sequence, and hence 'privation' implies not just inhibition of the flow, but also a false, ugly, misdirection of the flow. Although evil is negative, it can be 'seen' in an ugly misarrangement. All the same, nothing is positively wrong here, for every scene can be adjusted by rearrangement, omission and re-contextualization. Indeed, finding the right perspective on the infinite is a matter (to adapt Augustine) of being open to the risks of new and unexpected beauty.

Thus Augustine affirms, against antiquity, that for true happiness and virtue one must not only possess the goal (which for antiquity would have been enough) but also envisage the right 'way' to the goal, which remains with the goal in the sense that one must continue to possess it with the right desire. Although goal and way are ultimately identical, such that to love *God* must be to love him rightly, for us the one does not guarantee the other: they must be grasped in separate moments. To be virtuous one must both 'refer' all to the infinite goal *and* find the right path, the right perspective and sequence for desire – the path constantly laid out, redrawn, re-traced, by Jesus and the Church (all genuine Christian community) in history. This double requirement supplements the goal with the way, and reconceives the goal as itself *still* the way, thus collapsing together the 'circle' and the 'arrow', and preserving the moment of the arrow, which antiquity tended to negate and leave

---

[140] Augustine, *Confessions*, VII, 13.
[141] John Milbank, 'A critique of the theology of right', in *The Word Made Strange* pp. 7–36; 'Sublimity: the modern transcendent', in Regina Schwartz (ed.) *Transcendence* (London: Routledge, 2004) pp. 211–35.

behind. It is this supplementation which is summed up in Augustine's Christian re-definition of virtue as 'rightly ordered love'.[142]

In contrast to the true goal, and the true desire, stand the spurious goal and false desire. Both are entirely privative: insofar as they 'are', they are good, and there is no nature or essence of evil. But as both Augustine and Dionysius emphasize, an evil which is purely privative is also an evil whose *only* essence must be 'violence': the denial of Being both as infinite plenitude and as harmonious ordering of difference, or as peace.[143] Whereas, for both these thinkers, peace is essential for existence (so that peace becomes a transcendental attribute of Being), violence is an unnecessary intrusion. Thus Christianity, uniquely, does not allow violence any real ontological purchase, but relates it instead to a free subject who asserts a will that is truly independent of God and of others, and thereby a will to the inhibition and distortion of reality (so that, in a sense, the Cartesian subject only exists as the sinful subject). I do not think that there is any way of *demonstrating* this ontological priority of peace, although one can argue for the *conceivability* of a purely 'positive' Being without the 'non-Being' of violence. But it follows as an explication of the doctrine of creation.

If nothing is evil insofar as it exists, then it is only evil in terms of its failure to be related to God, to infinite peace, and to other finite realities with which it should be connected to form a pattern of true desire. Evil becomes the denial of the hope for, and the present reality of, community. Yet this has implications also for how Augustine begins to think (and we should think further) of the reality of the Good, or the reality of what is. For what makes something to be good, what makes it to be, is not any essence which it possesses (indeed self-possession *is* privation) but its existing (without any reserved 'surplus' of individuality, which is but a false freedom) entirely in particular patterns of desire, which remain open to, and whose beauty constitutes a path to, the unknown infinite. What is 'free' here, what gets adjusted, is not contentless wills, but relationships or exchanges of gifts. When we change we alter others, and the changes of others alter ourselves. Salvation is only in common: it is only the peace of the *altera civitas*.

The Fate of the Counter-Kingdom

However, if this is salvation, then we are forced to admit that it can only have been present intermittently during the Christian centuries. My onslaught, in this book, against secular reason, has not at all been in the name of a past epoch of Christian dominance. On the contrary, while it is possible to recover the narrative and ontological shape of the Christian 'interruption' of history (and to suggest that this has been resumed by Christian socialism), one should also recognize that this interruption appears to have

---

[142] Augustine, CD XV, 23. *De Moribus Ecclesiae*, 3(4), pp. 302–32.
[143] *The Divine Names*, 949C–953A.

tragically failed, and that it is the course of this failure itself which has generated secular reason. Once there was no secular...but the invention of the secular began at least in the eleventh century.

Two points should be noted here. First of all, Christianity has helped to unleash a more 'naked' violence. During the Middle Ages, the attempts of people to rule directly over people in small communities, without recourse to an elaborate formal mechanism of law, gradually failed. The Church did not succeed in displacing politics, and as a result, politics returned, yet in a virulent form unknown to antiquity. For once purely sacramental and charitable bonds alone had failed to uphold community, then the aid of new legal forms had to be sought: forms thoroughly desacralized through the impact of Christianity itself. Hence the later Middle Ages engendered a newly rationalistic and formalized approach to law, from the twelfth century onwards. Law now dealt in 'pure' possession and control, in the regulation and balancing of power. Hence, too, the theorists of papal absolutism pressed further than antiquity towards a doctrine of unlimited sovereignty, progress was made towards a liberal conception of property rights, and relationships between 'corporate' bodies came to be conceived on a contractualist basis.[144] In this way the scope of the *civitas terrena* was tragically extended by the Church itself.

Secondly, although politics returned, the State itself assumed the form of a perverted Church, an anti-Church. It is here that theologians can learn much from Michael Foucault in the construction of a 'theology of Church history'. For the Church's non-legal, 'pastoral' rule worked through knowledge, through the exact understanding of communities, and the attempt to regulate time and activity into a pattern that would discipline human desires. Gradually however, *ordo* became almost a goal in itself, and pastoral rule, concentrating on the minute regulation of bodies in time and space, fused with the return of formal legality (this process being much encouraged by the failure to see all punishment as negative and in some sense sinful). 'Mystical bodies', like monastic communities, become more and more subject to fixed, legally enforceable codes of regulation.[145] Concomitantly, a firmer distinction arose in the twelfth century between 'healthy', well-regulated individual and collective bodies, and those 'outside' these bodies – lepers, primitive villagers, prostitutes, homosexuals, charismatic preachers – who became increasingly liable to persecution.[146] Gradually *ordo* got separated off from both true *usus* and ultimate *frui*, and pastoral rule became, within the secular State, a rule

[144] Peter Brown, 'Society and the supernatural: a mediaeval change', in *Society and the Holy in Late Antiquity*; Gierke, *Political Theories of the Middle Age*.

[145] Rowan Williams, 'Three styles of monastic reform', in Benedicta Ward (ed.) *The Influence of St Bernard* (Oxford: SLG Press, 1976) pp. 23–40. G.C. Coulton, 'The interpretation of visitation documents', in *English Historical Review*, XXIX, 1914, pp. 16–40.

[146] R. I. Moore, *The Formation of a Persecuting Society* (Oxford: Blackwell, 1987). The concluding section of this book is perhaps all too abrupt. It should be supplemented by a reading of the 'Transition' section of Catherine Pickstock's *After Writing: On the Liturgical Consummation of Philosophy* (Oxford: Blackwell, 1998) pp. 121–67.

through the classification of populations in terms of medical, psychological, economic and educational canons of 'normality'. Such rule is a kind of mimicry of ecclesial peace, because it can be based upon a consensus, yet the basis of this consensus is not agreement about either 'the goal' or 'the way', but merely a deferral to 'expert' opinion. And expertise is only expertise about power.

From these considerations we can see that attempts to do a relative calculus of evils inflicted by the medieval Church versus evils inflicted by secular modernity are naive: the worst oppressions of the Middle Ages *were* the result of a commenced invention of the secular, and the still worse modern oppressions remain in the same 'Gothick' sequence.

In the midst of history, the judgement of God has already happened. And either the Church enacts the vision of paradisal community which this judgement opens out, or else it promotes a hellish society beyond any terrors known to antiquity: *corruptio optimi pessima*. For the Christian interruption of history 'decoded' antique virtue, yet thereby helped to unleash first liberalism, then positivism and dialectics and finally nihilism. Insofar as the Church has failed, and has even become a hellish anti-Church, it has confined Christianity, like everything else, within the cycle of the ceaseless exhaustion and return of violence.

Yet as we are situated on the far side of the Cross – the event of the judgement of God – no return to law, to the antique compromise of inhibition of violence, remains possible. Both nihilism and Christianity decode the inconsistencies of this position. And the Catholic vision of ontological peace now provides the only alternative to a nihilistic outlook. Even today, in the midst of the self-torturing circle of secular reason, there can open to view again a series with which it is in no ontological continuity: the emanation of harmonious difference, the exodus of new generations, the diagonal of ascent, the path of peaceful flight...

Index of Names